Americans as Proconsuls

*Papers and Proceedings
of a Conference held in
the Leonard Carmichael Auditorium
at the National Museum of
American History of the
Smithsonian Institution,
Washington, D.C.
May 20–21, 1977*

Edited by Robert Wolfe

Americans as Proconsuls

United States Military Government
in Germany and Japan, 1944–1952

Southern Illinois University Press

Carbondale and Edwardsville

Library of Congress Cataloging in Publication Data
Main entry under title:

Americans as proconsuls.

"Papers and proceedings of a conference held in the
Leonard Carmichael Auditorium at the National Museum of
American History of the Smithsonian Institution,
Washington, D.C., May 20–21, 1977"—P. ii.
  Includes bibliographical references.
  1. Germany—History—Allied occupation, 1945–   —
Congresses. 2. Japan—History—Allied occupation, 1945–
1952—Congresses. 3. World War, 1939–1945—Occupied
territories—Congresses. 4. Military government—
Germany. 5. Military government—Japan. I. Wolfe,
Robert, 1921–
DD257.A68   1984   940.53'38   83–4764
ISBN 0–8093–1115–1

Edited by Stephen W. Smith

Production supervised by Kathleen Giencke

87 86 85 84   4 3 2 1

Contents

Illustrations
ix

Foreword / *Forrest C. Pogue*
xi

Introduction: A Minor Keynote / *Robert Wolfe*
xv

First Session: Presuppositions, Prejudices, and Planning

Introduction / *Hugh Borton*
1

1. American Wartime Planning for Occupied Japan:
The Role of the Experts / *Marlene J. Mayo*
3

2. Improvising Stability and Change in
Postwar Germany / *Earl F. Ziemke*
52

Discussion
67

Second Session: The Realities of Implementation

Introduction / *Willard A. Fletcher*
75

3. The MacArthur Shogunate in Allied Guise / *Ralph Braibanti*
77

4. Governing the American Zone of Germany / *John Gimbel*
92

5. Proconsul of a People, by Another People,
for Both Peoples / *Lucius D. Clay*
103

6. From Military Government to Self-Government /
John J. McCloy
114

Discussion
124

**Third Session: Reparations, Economic Reform,
and Reconstruction**

Introduction / *Jacques J. Reinstein*
135

7. From Deconcentration to Reverse Course
in Japan / *Eleanor M. Hadley*
138

8. From Morgenthau Plan to Marshall Plan / *John H. Backer*
155

Discussion
166

**Fourth Session: Purging the Body Politic—Help
or Hindrance to Reorientation and Rehabilitation?**

Introduction / *Eli E. Nobleman*
179

9. United States Military Courts in Germany: Setting an
Example and Learning Lessons / *Eli E. Nobleman*
181

10. The Purge in Occupied Japan / *Hans H. Baerwald*
188

11. Denazification in Germany: A Policy
Analysis / *Elmer Plischke*
198

12. War Crimes Trials and Clemency in Germany
and Japan / *John Mendelsohn*
226

Fifth Session: Reeducation for Democracy

Introduction / *Carl G. Anthon*
261

13. Civil Censorship and Media Control in Early
Occupied Japan: From Minimum to Stringent
Surveillance / *Marlene J. Mayo*
263

14. Comparing American Reform Efforts in Germany:
Mass Media and the School System / *Harold Hurwitz*
321

Combined Discussion
342

**Sixth Session: Source Materials for the History
of American Military Government**

Introduction / *Mabel E. Deutrich*
351

15. State Department Records in the National Archives
Relating to the Occupations of Germany and
Japan / *Milton O. Gustafson*
354

16. United States Military Records in the National Archives
Relating to the Occupations of Germany and
Japan / *James J. Hastings*
361

17. Resources of Presidential Libraries for the History of
Post–World War II American Military Government
in Germany and Japan / *Benedict K. Zobrist*
370

Discussion
376

**Seventh Session: Impact of the Proconsular Experience
on American Foreign Policy, National Security,
and Civil Affairs Doctrine**

Introduction / *John D. Montgomery*
385

18. Impact of the Proconsular Experience on American
Foreign Policy: An Engaged View / *Jacob D. Beam*
387

19. Impact of the Proconsular Experience on American
Foreign Policy: A Reflective View / *James W. Riddleberger*
392

20. Impact of the Proconsular Experience on Civil Affairs
Organization and Doctrine / *William R. Swarm*
398

21. The Occupation as Perceived by the Public, Scholars,
and Policy Makers / *Edward N. Peterson*
416

Discussion
425

Summary: Artificial Revolution Revisited—From Success
to Excess / *John D. Montgomery*
437

Notes
447

Biographical Notes
535

Conference Participants
544

Archival Sources
SCAP / 550
OMGUS / 551
HICOG / 554
PRO / 556

Illustrations

(following page 230)

1. Brigadier General Cornelius W. Wickersham and staff, August 1943
2. *Shogun* and *Tenno,* September 27, 1945
3. General Douglas MacArthur leaves his headquarters, Christmas Day, 1945
4. Captain Ralph Braibanti, 1946
5. Lieutenant John D. Montgomery at Hiroshima, January 1946
6. Hugh Borton, 1946
7. Eleanor M. Hadley in Tokyo, 1947
8. Assistant Secretary of War John J. McCloy with General Douglas MacArthur and Lieutenant General Robert L. Eichelberger, November 6, 1945
9. United States High Commissioner for Germany John J. McCloy, June 26, 1952
10. John J. McCloy and James W. Riddleberger returning on May 15, 1950, from a foreign ministers' meeting
11. Telegram received in the Department of State on July 3, 1949, from James W. Riddleberger
12. United States and Soviet delegations at an Allied Control Council meeting, Berlin, February 11, 1948
13. General Clay addresses the *Länderrat,* January 8, 1947
14. Entrance to United States Military Government Headquarters in Berlin-Zehlendorf during the occupation
15. Publication Control officers Robert Wolfe and Conrad M. Mueller, Heidelberg, March 19, 1946
16. Memorandum by Robert Wolfe, December 2, 1946
17. Military Government poster announcing court sentences, August 17, 1945
18. Lieutenant Eli E. Nobleman, Bavaria, October 8, 1945
19. Lieutenant John H. Backer, somewhere in Europe, 1945
20. Jacques J. Reinstein, State Department, 1949–50
21. John Gimbel, stationed in Friedberg, Hesse, in early 1946
22. Lieutenant (jg.) Elmer Plischke, July 1945
23. Allied Military Government *Fragebogen*

24. Colonel William R. Swarm, Major General William F. Marquat, and Richard M. Scammon, Fort Lee, Virginia, May 5, 1955

25. Colonel William R. Swarm greeting Major General J. Strom Thurmond, Fort Gordon, Georgia, October 13, 1961

26. German and American members of the OMGUS microfilming project and families, 1977

27. Speakers and program staff during the "Americans as Proconsuls" conference, May 20, 1977

28. Speakers during the "Americans as Proconsuls" conference, May 20, 1977

29. John J. McCloy during a pause in the "Americans as Proconsuls" conference of May 20–21, 1977

Foreword

Forrest C. Pogue

The symposium "Americans as Proconsuls" held in the Leonard Carmichael Auditorium of the National Museum of History and Technology (now the National Museum of American History), Smithsonian Institution, May 20–21, 1977, was the happy culmination of a collaboration by several archives and organizations to study the American occupations of Germany and Japan after World War II. The symposium capped earlier efforts by the Dwight D. Eisenhower Institute for Historical Research, of which I am the head, to collaborate with the Douglas MacArthur Memorial at Norfolk and the George C. Marshall Research Library at Lexington, Virginia, in discussions of problems of this phase of the war's aftermath.

The Eisenhower Institute had been activated by the Smithsonian Institution in July 1974 to carry out an earlier congressional resolution establishing a center that would encourage the study of the problems of war and peace. Early that fall Captain Robert H. Alexander, United States Navy, ret., director, MacArthur Memorial, asked what the Eisenhower Institute could do to help acquaint scholars with the research possibilities of his collection. Shortly thereafter I discussed with former Ambassador Fred L. Hadsel, my successor as director of the Marshall Library, a possible conference at Lexington to make scholars more aware of research resources in his library. It seemed to me that here we had an opportunity for several organizations working together to stimulate study of an important phase of World War II.

A steering committee was set up, and by early 1975 plans were under way for the holding of three different conferences in 1976 and 1977 on various phases of military occupation. It was arranged that universities and colleges in the Norfolk and Lexington areas be invited to help plan a conference at Norfolk on the occupation of Japan and one at Lexington on the occupation of Germany. These would be followed by a larger conference on military occupation in Germany and Japan at the Museum of History and Technology in 1977. Each organization would be responsible for developing its own program but the steering committee would endeavor to lend some unity to the undertaking.

At the first meeting, at the MacArthur Memorial in 1975, specialists on the Far East, former members of the American occupation forces in Japan, and Japanese representatives gave their versions of the MacArthur era in Japan. Their papers were published by the MacArthur Memorial in *The Occupation of Japan: Proceedings of a Seminar on the Occupation of Japan and Its Legacy to the Postwar World* (no editor, no date). This was followed April 23–24, 1976, by a larger conference at the Marshall Library in which a number of scholars and diplomats outlined the problems of German occupation. These papers in turn were published by the Marshall Library in *U.S. Occupation in Europe after World War II* (Edited by Hans A. Schmitt; Lawrence: Regents Press of Kansas, 1978).

Before the holding of this symposium at the Smithsonian Institution, several developments had greatly broadened the scope of the cooperative effort. The originally hoped-for conference in Washington in 1976 was postponed because of various programs scheduled for the bicentennial year and, in particular, because of the holding in the Museum of History and Technology of a conference of the International Commission of Military History, in which the United States Commission, members of the Office of the Chief of Military History, and the Eisenhower Institute cooperated. This effort helped to establish a pattern for this broadened conference in 1977.

Prior to my selection as director of the Eisenhower Institute, when I was serving as chairman of the American Committee on the History of the Second World War, I had asked on behalf of that committee if we could cosponsor with the National Archives a conference on documents of the 1939–45 conflict. James B. Rhoads, archivist of the United States, agreed and a highly successful conference was held at the Archives building in 1971. This was followed by other conferences on topics relating to the documentary holdings of the National Archives. In 1968, a conference on captured German documents had been sponsored by the Archives with Robert Wolfe, head of its Modern Military Headquarters Branch, as director. He also edited the proceedings of that conference.

While the conferences on military occupation were being developed, Arthur L. Funk, now chairman of the American Committee on

the History of the Second World War, and Donald S. Detwiler, secretary of the same organization, approached officials at the National
Archives about another jointly sponsored conference on some diplomatic or military topic not yet covered. Since the National Archives was already preparing a conference on a different topic, a
decision was made to arrange a conference that would complete the
program already begun with the MacArthur and Marshall libraries
and that would also bring in other organizations. The American
Committee on the History of the Second World War was invited by
the Eisenhower Institute to cosponsor a symposium on military occupation in Germany and Japan with the assistance of the Marshall
and MacArthur libraries, the United States Commission on Military
History, and the Center of Military History. As a member of the
executive committee on the American Committee on the Second
World War, Robert Wolfe was empowered to work with me in developing a program for a symposium in the spring of 1977; it was also
understood that he would edit the final proceedings. He took the
lead in preparing the program, drawing on experiences gained as an
army officer in the occupation forces in Germany after World War II.
His extensive experience with captured German records and with
military records of World War II also contributed to his knowledge
and skill.

The Museum of History and Technology bore the expenses of the
symposium. Funds to publish the proceedings were not immediately
forthcoming but through a generous anonymous gift from a private
foundation, and the assumption of the remaining costs by the
Southern Illinois University Press, this volume has been compiled.

In the coordination of planning, invitations to participants, special arrangements for the conference, and various activities connected with editing, I wish to express my deep appreciation to my
coworkers at the Eisenhower Institute, James S. Hutchins and Mrs.
Barbara Lane, and my especial thanks for the firm backing by the
director of the Museum of History and Technology, Brooke Hindle,
and his deputy, Silvio A. Bedini. We enjoyed full cooperation from
the various affiliated and cosponsoring organizations and by many
members of the Smithsonian Institution staff. The present director,
Roger G. Kennedy, and his deputy, Douglas E. Evelyn, have given
great support to publication of this volume.

Personally, I have derived great pleasure from the cooperative effort that developed between the Eisenhower Institute and the Marshall and MacArthur libraries and the wider collaboration that
made the 1977 conference a success. I have been pleased to see that
the MacArthur Library has continued to hold annual conferences on

topics associated with the Far East. The Marshall Library has held a number of conferences dealing with various topics of international security.

All of us owe a special debt to the outstanding scholars and leaders who took part in the 1977 conference. Robert Wolfe will speak in greater detail about their contributions, but I wish to express thanks to John J. McCloy, who added a warm personal note to our proceedings. General Lucius D. Clay was prevented by bad health from taking part in the conference but we have been permitted by his family to make use of portions of interviews conducted by Robert Wolfe and George K. Romoser on behalf of the Conference Group on German Politics on problems of the German occupation. Ambassador James W. Riddleberger, who was unable to take part in the conference, has filled by oral and written comments certain gaps in our record.

I cannot say enough about the outstanding work of Robert Wolfe and the kindness of the National Archives in permitting him to take a leading role in this undertaking. It has been a pleasure to work with him. I prize the contacts I have had with him and members of the various libraries and organizations that helped make this symposium a success.

The proceedings reflect the type of historical assessments and research which the Eisenhower Institute was founded to encourage. I consider the entire effort a fine example of scholarly cooperation and I hope that its stimulating effect will continue to be felt for years to come.

Introduction

A Minor Keynote

Robert Wolfe

This is by way of an outline, a preview of coming attractions, and a subtle reminder to our speakers of the themes—not, of course, the interpretations—they agreed to cover in our conference sessions and papers. It is not a keynote speech—well, perhaps we can call it a "minor keynote."

Historians have long been aware of the "thirty-years after" syndrome, when nostalgia for the remembered or imagined glories of youth seeks to reconjure the experiences and the feelings of that heyday, particularly when it was part of a significant and historic enterprise. I, like many of you, have now reached the age of nostalgia, and the constructive educational experience of my youth, my growing-up catalyst, was three and one-half years in the United States military government of Germany, rather than the preceding destructive experience of combat infantry service in two theaters of war. I encountered a society reduced closer to a state of nature than any the natural law political theorists had ever known, although not imagined, and had a small part in trying to put it together again.

Now this great constructive educational experience, the pride of my youth, is under attack by revisionists, and worse still, has been eroded in my own mind by subsequent sad experience. As a member of the historical fraternity, and as custodian of some of the official documentary sources, however, I was not reduced to aimless reminiscence nor to my own biased reconstruction. I could offer the records to the experts, ask them the questions, and thanks to the Eisenhower Institute and the American Committee on the History of the Second World War, assemble them in one place and one time to confer and debate, all recorded for posterity—to say nothing of my own nostalgic needs.

My questions to the experts necessarily derive largely from my personal experiences in Germany, but there is reason to believe that comparison and contrast of our German and Japanese occupation experiences will tell us something not only about our impact on postwar German and Japanese history, but particularly on our own. John D. Montgomery, chairman and commentator of the final session of this conference, which deals with that impact on Americans, already conceived and wrote about that idea more than twenty years ago. It is our deliberate purpose to emphasize our own role in the two occupations, as part of our own history, rather than as part of German or Japanese history. For that reason, we are featuring an all-American cast, although we had originally thought of staging a session entitled "To See Ourselves as Others See Us," with Japanese and German students of the occupations on the stage.

While apologizing for burdening you with personal reminiscences, may I suggest, however masked by scholarly apparatus, however indirectly derived through oral history, memoirs, private papers, or official records, the imperfectly recorded and remembered experiences of the actors therein are the source of all written history. And somewhere amidst all of this scholarly analysis of the significant events of these occupations, we must, if necessary by reminiscence, invoke the spirit and evoke the feel and flavor of those extraordinary times. Historians should be annalists as well as analysts.

Some of my colleagues on the program committee were concerned that our conference title, "Americans as Proconsuls," had an invidious flavor, but they accepted it as intended to convey a promise of honest self-examination rather than self-glorification. At any rate, the word "proconsul" has the imprimatur of John J. McCloy. To ward off being appointed civilian military governor of Germany in 1945, he recommended Lucius D. Clay for the job, which McCloy later described as "the nearest thing to a Roman proconsulship the modern world afforded." When he eventually succeeded Clay in 1949, the reduced powers of the military governor no longer warranted the appellation "proconsul." As for the Allied military governor of Japan, I cannot imagine anyone finding the term "proconsul" too overblown for Douglas MacArthur.

To be sure, not only Germany and Japan, the ringleaders among our conquered enemies, were ruled by proconsuls, Allied or quadripartite. But, as we became concerned that we might overtax your seats, if not your minds, in this two-day marathon we inadvertently evolved, we grasped for some rationale to hold the program to manageable proportions. Applying the disputed terminological distinction between civil affairs in friendly and liberated territory, and military government of conquered and occupied enemy territory, we have eliminated from our ken North Africa, Western Europe, and the Pacific island groups. We could also eliminate Italy because it became a cobelligerent; Austria because it was declared liberated; and Formosa and Korea because they were certainly liberated, after a fashion and for a time. All but the two major enemy powers of the Second World War have thus been pared from our program by this after-the-fact rationale. I suggest, however, that civil affairs in the narrow or broad sense would be a worthwhile subject for another full-scale conference, perhaps elongated chronologically to cover United States armed forces civil affairs plans and operations earlier and later than 1944 to 1952.

Our next and first substantive session is entitled "Presuppositions, Prejudices, and Planning." During the Second World War Americans recalled the origins of the First World War and its aftermath, German noncompliance with the Treaty of Versailles and Hitler's exploitation of the stab-in-the-back myth; some even remembered back to Bismarck, that wily instigator of three aggressions. (We forgot that for several preceding centuries it was the French who were the perennial disturbers of the peace, and the Germans often their victims.) Twice in this century—five times in the past hundred years, went the argument, those heel-clicking automatons, the Prussians, had invaded and seized other peoples' territory. Roosevelt remembered Wilson's failure to win the peace. Truman, Stimson, and Marshall had all fought "les Boches," the "Huns," in France. American civilian and military leaders of World War II were determined not to make the same mistake twice in one lifetime. (Ironically, they could not be aware of Hitler's reverse reading of the lesson: Allied atrocity propaganda in World War I— Belgian nuns, and all that—was unfair because it was untrue. But the Kaiser's real sin was not having been as ruthless as necessary. Hitler would not make that mistake.)

And the image of the Japanese, our erstwhile ally of World War I? That image was no better than that of the Nazis, after "Remember Pearl Harbor," that "day of infamy," to say nothing of the Bataan "death march." Then we also remembered farther back to the *Panay,* and even way back to the "Yellow Peril." It was enough to frighten us into moving Japanese-Americans away from our imperiled West Coast!

With such underlying distrust of the character of the ruthless Germans and sneaky Japanese, to say nothing of the evil incarnate of their leaders, Hitler and Himmler, Hirohito and Tojo, the requirement of unconditional surrender was inevitable. This meant not just a "cordon sanitaire," but (in Cordell Hull's words) it made unlimited and extended occupations inevitable, involving a complete takeover of central and even local government, and the removal of, and retribution against, the leaders.

It is not surprising then, given Roosevelt's emotional bias against Germans, augmented by Morgenthau's understandable influence in the same direction, that he unthinkingly made the probably counterproductive announcement on "unconditional surrender," envisaging a dismembered Germany reduced to a pastoral existence. I am relying on Marlene J. Mayo and Hugh Borton to enlighten my ignorant assumption that our postwar plans for Japan did not go beyond that ineffable early wartime song hit, "we're going to have to slap, the dirty little Jap, right in his own backyard!"

At the Marshall Library conference of April 1976, I suggested that Roosevelt's political instincts served him better when, in an attempt to keep his options open, he tried to defer concrete planning for postwar occupation and territorial arrangements. At least, the unexpected timing and conditions of the war's end in Europe and Japan would not have found us following through on occupation policies and plans that did not comport with reality. In spite of Roosevelt's reluctance, however, military government planning went forward for at least the initial phase, and in true New Deal fashion he left ample room for intra-American disputes paralleling the inter-Allied differences which were paralyzing decision at a higher level. The result was *ad hoc,* but specific, planning for military and technical purposes, while political and economic plans merely reflected the conviction of our wartime propaganda that all Japanese were sneaky and all Germans were Nazis, a conviction hardened by the disclosures of the unbelievable conditions in concentration and POW camps overrun in the last weeks of the war.

In Germany, in particular, the presumptions were far from the reality, the war having ended not in the bang of a Redoubt *Götterdämmerung,* but in the whimper of a bunker suicide amidst wholesale surrender. Despite the initial distrust and hatred felt by most of us who served in Germany during the spring of 1945, despite the "hard line" inherent in JCS 1067 whatever the Potsdam modifications, improvisation became the rule, and with it *ad hoc* softening of policy. Headquarters in Frankfurt and Berlin eventually approved *faits accomplis.* Whether the State Department planners in Washington ever got the word, we were not given to know. But then, as I learned from listening to an all-star cast at the Marshall Library symposium in April 1976, the high-level lucubrations, conflicting views, and eventual compromises seldom got through to us in the field either.

Given this gap between policy and reality, and the resulting improvisation and contradictions in both, Earl F. Ziemke's paper necessarily carries the story of planning for Germany until mid-1946, which means that he occupies some of John Gimbel's territory—by agreement, of course. It is interesting for me, and I hope for you, to compare and contrast how the transition between planning and implementation for Japan is dealt with successively by Marlene J. Mayo and Ralph Braibanti.

General Lucius D. Clay, United States military governor in Germany through most of the occupation, was unable to accept our invitation to speak on the theme, "Proconsul of a People, by Another People, for Both Peoples," but through the kind permission of the McCloy Fund and the Conference Group on German Politics, we include here under that title excerpts from a July 1977 interview of General Clay by George K. Romoser (of the latter organization) and me. John J. McCloy, former assistant secretary of war and former United States military governor and high commissioner for Germany, describes the problems of planning for, and the difficulty of passage from, military government to self-government.

A major current debate revolves around whether economic and ideological self-interest dictated our decisions in Germany and Japan, rather than our concern for the reorientation and well-being of those peoples. Under the experienced guidance of Jacques J. Reinstein, the session entitled "Reparations, Economic Reform, and Reconstruction," puts into sharper focus the economic aspects of the occupations. The following two sessions deal with the negative and positive aspects of ideological reorientation. In both occupied countries, the pattern appears to move from an initial hard line toward a later soft line. This has been construed as a twentieth-century "diplomatic revolution," a reversal of wartime alliances under the impetus of cold war, with Communist or capitalist cold-warriors being blamed for its initiation by nationalist and revisionist historians, respectively.

These polarized interpretations discount the influence on the evolution from hard to soft line by the ebbing of wartime bitterness and collective judgments of wartime propaganda, and by the human sympathy that derives from common experiences and personal involvement. But it is well that they recall to nostalgic old hands that our motives were not entirely pure, that considerable self-interest and much cupidity, consciously or unconsciously, masqueraded as paternalism, if not altruism. When the occupation budgets had to be presented to Congress and the American public, however, the economic and ideological self-interest had to be unmasked and stressed, and the putative altruism downplayed.

Again, there is inevitably considerable overlap in the discussion of SCAP political implementation by Ralph Braibanti, and of SCAP economic policy by Eleanor M. Hadley. The same is true in the handling of those two functions of OMGUS by John Gimbel and John H. Backer. But such topical overlap, like the geographical comparison and contrast, may also disclose enlightening differences in interpretation.

In March, 1975, the conference Group on German Politics sponsored, in the National Archives theater, a conference on "The Nuernberg War Crime Trials as History, Law, and Morality." In the context of our session on "Purging the Body Politic," denazification and the purge were in numbers of accused, and in the impact on the military governments, much more important but much less conspicuous than war crimes trials. But, as it turned out, these political purges had their own built-in clemency in the onset of the cold war and the transfer of responsibilities from the occupiers to the occupied, as Hans H. Baerwald and Elmer Plischke demonstrate. Clemency for war criminals provoked much vocal opposition, but the trend from hard to soft line was in the same pattern, although the timing and level seem to have been different in Japan and Germany. John Mendelsohn, in comparing and contrasting clemency in Germany and Japan, provides our only "tricontinental" paper.

Political purge and the punishment of war criminals dealt only with alleged or past crimes during the Third Reich. Preservation of law and order in the American zone fell to our military government police and courts, as replacements for the deposed SS and Gestapo-tainted German police and courts. The uniquely qualified Eli E. Nobleman examines two significant aspects of that subject: the problem of operating military courts for a population whose own legal system had ended in travesty and tragedy, and the effect of that experience on the participating American lawyers. We trust that Hans H. Baerwald and others in the audience can tell us something of the Japanese side of that story. Carl G. Anthon analyzes both the negative and positive aspects of societal reorientation in Japan and Germany, before Marlene J. Mayo and Harold Hurwitz do so for each country, respectively.

It is not so farfetched to ask whether overt and moralistic meddling in other peoples' affairs, deposing undesirables and installing desirable leaders, results in the habit and justification for their covert support or removal, even by assassination. And what we can do to others, we may also have to do to our own people, if our national security is threatened. To a reluctant realist, it seems to come down to the horrible dilemma of a cynical Hobbesian or a deluded Lockean view of human society.

In moving from Hobbes to Locke, from the stick of purge and punishment to the carrot of reorientation, we move from the negative: demilitarization, decartelization, denazification, and purge (thank God nobody ever thought of deshintoization!) to the positive: reorientation (or did they say "reoccidentation" in Japan?), reeducation, rehabilitation. The last word may give us a clue. The only way short of extermination to avoid the permanent unlimited occupations that Cordell Hull feared, was to attempt reorientation of the general population, especially the young, in the same way that short of capital punishment or life imprisonment, rehabilitation of the criminal seems to many to be the only solution.

Whether one believes rehabilitation will work with the bulk of Americans who run afoul of the law may be influenced by individual temperament. Whether one believes reorientation worked in Japan or Germany, may depend on whether one believes most Japanese or Germans needed it, or it may depend on whether one thinks the military is capable of reeducating anyone for democracy, or whether Americans are capable of giving the right kind of reeducation.

Did we "Americanize" as well as, or instead of, democratize? Is Americanization only synonymous with mass production, for which neither conquered enemy needed our postwar teaching? But mass production requires mass consumption, and mass consumption requires catering to mass tastes, the horrors as well as the benefits of which we and our German and Japanese protégés have been experiencing more and more in the last quarter century. Whatever we call it, did it result in more harm to the alien, exquisite culture of Japan, than to the kindred German culture? Is the latter more Americanized than Western Europe? Than European or non-European places where American troops never set foot? Can Americanization come without democratization, or without troops—merely through Coca Cola or Pepsi Cola?

You may be beginning to suspect that I have lost some of my confidence in the civilizing mission of my youth: the conversion of unregenerate Nazis to democratic NATO allies. I do think that most of those who ever needed it are by and large converted; but I suspect that Hitler, Himmler, and Goebbels—and Josef Stalin—had more to do with it than "me and Lucius Clay." In terms of personal freedom and security, the Third Reich was an easy act to follow, even for a military occupation, while thousands of Germans participated in a straw poll of their relative opinions of life in the United States and Soviet zones by "voting with their feet."

Actually, my own full-blown smugness was punctured perhaps earlier than many other military government "old hands." But I did neglect one early, on-the-job, opportunity for real critical appraisal, deeper than superficial griping about our performance as military governors of Germany. I have in mind, in particular, the wife of a Heidelberg professor of philosophy of whom I saw a great deal because I was courting her niece. Separated by a quarter of a century in age, by a wide ocean in birthplace and upbringing, and by the chasm of contrast between the German experience of 1900 to 1945 and the American from 1920 to 1945, we logged-in many hours of intense debate on the legality, morality, and practicality of what I and my OMGUS colleagues were doing in the American zone of Germany. I stood my ground, unconvinced; she stood hers, unintimidated. Only in retrospect did I realize what a fine, unconscious compliment she had paid to the American military government— and to me. For fearless though she was, she would not have ventured her views with impunity in some other occupied zones of Germany, let alone during the years when the Nazis occupied her German fatherland.

It was not the aunt, but the niece, who shook my complacency without even trying. She appeared to have experienced an instant reorientation to democracy, for which I credited my arrogant lectures on the superior wisdom of the American electorate, which would never have fallen for the Nazi siren song. My efforts at personal reeducation were not as instantaneous. It took more than three years to persuade this "indigenous person" that marriage to me would make her part of the American elite, but I was delayed by the several months' handicap of the nonfraternization decree. Having demonstrated her morality, health, and political reliability by passing successive muster of a United States Army chaplain, an Army medico, and a public safety officer, I took my stateless war bride—this country still was not admitting Germans—to the land of promise and plenty in late October 1948, just in time for the windup days of the unedifying election campaign of that year. As we watched this exemplar of American democracy on the new-fangled instrument of truth and enlightenment known as television, my credibility sustained an irrecoverable loss. My recently reeducated German war bride murmured something about "familiar types," and assumed a "this is where I came in" expression. After the loss of that early marital encounter, I was never able to reassert my military governor's claim to a "right to rule," even before the era of Joe McCarthy, Vietnam, and Watergate gave the lie to my naïve pride in the superiority of the American national character and democratic system. Fortunately, my wife is well bred, and also capable of seeing fundamental differences, so she has not drawn my attention to possible parallels between FBI and Gestapo, between CIA and Reich Security Main Office.

But for all my belated comeuppance, I am not yet ready to accept the charge implied by John D. Montgomery's application of Rousseau's phrase that our conquered enemies were "forced to be free." Rousseau meant the voluntary, total submersion of the individual will to the general will, of the citizen to the majority will. This gives the appearances of sanction to absolute authority, which may be democracy but is not liberty. Rousseau's theory fits totalitarianism of right or left more than it fits democracy. Those who object to "forcing people to be free" through the means of purge and reorientation are in much the same quandary as civil libertarians who, in the name of freedom of speech, defend the freedom of those who advocate suppression of that freedom.

For me, Montesquieu is the safer guide, when he defines liberty in societies directed by law as "the ability to do what one ought to desire, and not being forced to do what one ought not to desire"; more concretely, as "not being compelled to do the things to which the law does not oblige one, nor forced to abstain from things which the law permits." Perhaps the most important thing we can learn from our attempts to reorient others is how to reorient this society and this government back toward the original spirit of our own laws.

Researchers should derive incomparable advice from our panel of experts on the chief research sources in this country for the history of American military government in Germany and Japan. But, permit me to preface this with two comments of my own about the sources. A dozen years ago, as a guest of the Federal Republic visiting the Federal German Archives, I was asked if the indispensable OMGUS records could be opened to German scholars writing about the beginnings of the Federal Republic. Regretting that it would take some time, I promised my German colleagues that when conditions permitted, I would use to that purpose whatever influence I had with my government and my institution. I am proud to have been the instigator and the negotiator of the German-American joint venture in describing and copying the OMGUS records. James J. Hastings describes that project and similar arrangements with the Japanese in detail. I am only sorry that the agreement could not incorporate an earlier provision for reciprocal copying of records of the German substructure under United States military government, such as those of the Conference of Minister Presidents, the *Länderrat,* and the Bi-Zonal Council.

Also worth noting is that one of the prime postwar uses of captured and seized German and Japanese records was for military government purposes, including the prosecution of political purges and war crimes trials. Mention is scarcely needed here that the serendipitous fallout of funds and manpower from military government use of those records, as from military intelligence and foreign relations use, considerably augmented the captured records collections in the National Archives and the Library of Congress.

Our closing session represents the harvest of the preceding conference sessions. There have been, there should be, we hope there will be, other such conferences—on civil affairs, on individual occupied countries, on specific aspects. But this conference was intended as a look at ourselves, in self-congratulation and in self-criticism, and the title of the final panel, "Impact of the Proconsular Experience on American Foreign Policy, National Security, and Civil Affairs Doctrine," indicates (in the current vernacular) "where it's at." With Jacob D. Beam, William R. Swarm, and Edward N. Peterson as engaged and assertive experts on one or more of the three topics, with a thoughtful postconference comment by Ambassador James W. Riddleberger, with the father of the concept of comparative analysis of military government, John D. Montgomery, refereeing the debate and summing up, and with the audience given ample chance to contest the conclusions, the result was an offer no one could afford to refuse.

Since I cannot properly reserve a closing word for myself, I steal the liberty of having it now. Most people learn from their mistakes, but taking success for granted, they leave the reasons unexamined. Our ostensible success in bringing unparalleled prosperity with political democracy to defeated totalitarian societies, made us self-righteous and self-assured. I suggest that it was not our failures, but our unexamined and misunderstood successes that did us in later—in Korea, in Vietnam, and almost in Watergate. Our belated recognition thereof has caused us to assume a low profile; we must take care that we do not end up prone or supine.

Why did we appear to succeed? Misperceiving the real reasons for the unparalleled prosperity and successful democracy soon flourishing in Germany and Japan, we assumed that it was the result of our occupation policies. So we tried larger dosages of the same at other places and other times, and became outraged and frustrated when they accomplished no cure-all. But our medicine *had* helped in

Germany and Japan to stimulate antigens already present in both bodies politic. Having suffered the worst possible consequences of aggressive totalitarian leadership, and in imminent threat of an alien totalitarianism from the other ideological extreme, the majority of the Japanese and German peoples fled into our arms, accepting our tutelage for lack of a real alternative. They were forced to be free, but not by us. Democracy was an easy choice, with its promise of eventual, built-in civil rights.

Democracy was eventually accompanied by widespread and continued prosperity which confirmed the wisdom of that choice. That this enforced democracy worked, however, was less the result of American military government's pedagogical skills and example, than the fact it took place in industrialized countries, with literate, skilled, and disciplined populations. Democracy, like Marx's socialism, cannot be imposed where economic and social conditions are not ripe; unlike Marxist socialism, democracy cannot be permanently imposed against the will of the majority of the people. Democracy requires ripe conditions *and* a willing people, both incipient in Germany and Japan in 1945.

Our readers may benefit from a brief explanation of the planning for this conference and the editing of its proceedings. In selecting our speakers, the program committee sought, where available, persons who had participated in planning or implementation of the postwar occupations of Germany and Japan. But to avoid mere reminiscence, we chose only such "old hands" who had in their subsequent years continued to reflect and write on their occupation experience, either in the scholarship of academe or in the practicing sphere of government. Where desirable, we supported this cadre with younger scholars of demonstrated expertise in the subject. We also invited the same mix of occupation "old hands" and younger experts to sit in our participating audience. Without them, we would not have obtained the caliber of questions and comment from the floor which produced the high quality of discussion worth printing with the formal papers.

As is the custom after scholarly conferences, speakers were given an opportunity to edit formal papers before publication; furthermore, the regrettably long interim between presentation and publication has required some updating. The discussions published in this volume are, with minor exceptions, faithful to the verbatim transcripts of the sound recordings of the conference proceedings. These transcripts may be read, and the recordings heard, at either the National Archives or the Eisenhower Institute of the Smithsonian Institution. They have been edited here only to delete asides of merely momentary import, and to assure that the reader will understand the intent and context of the remarks made by participants.

Acknowledgements are due to those who participated in the planning, the conduct, or the editing of the conference proceedings: my colleagues on the program committee, Forrest C. Pogue and Donald S. Detwiler, and Arthur L. Funk, chairman of the American Committee on the History of the Second World War; Johanna M. Wagner, Petronilla Hawes, Cynthia Jackson, George Wagner, William H. Cunliffe, John E. Taylor, and John Mendelsohn of the National Archives Modern Military Headquarters Branch, and the archivist of the United States who authorized their and my contributions, as well as those of the National Archives and Records Service staff who participated in the panel on Sources; James S. Hutchins and Barbara Lane of the Eisenhower Institute, who handled most of the conference arrangements; Stephen W. Smith, Kenney Withers, James D. Simmons, John DeBacher, Kathy Giencke, Dan Gunter, and Gordon Lester-Massman of the staff of the Southern Illinois University Press who patiently converted a somewhat spotty manuscript into print; my wife, who has lived with the distractions of this conference through preparation, performance, and publication, and who permitted the references in this introduction to her contribution to my reeducation on the subject of military government. For me, she also exemplifies, as a German employee of United States Information Services Branch in Heidelberg from 1945 through 1948, the contribution of the "occupied" peoples to the success of the occupations, collectively as important as those of the German and Japanese leaders noted by Willard A. Fletcher and Carl G. Anthon during these proceedings.

So to our task, to tell the rest of the world, admirers and critics alike, especially our own skeptical progeny, not only the way we were, but how that led to the way we are.

First Session

Presuppositions, Prejudices, and Planning

Introduction by Hugh Borton

The development of policy and the whole formation of military government for both Germany and Japan were similar. For example, there was established back in 1941 under the leadership of Leo Pasvolski, formerly of the Brookings Institution, and a very close associate of Cordell Hull, an advisory, postwar policy committee which was chaired by Cordell Hull. In order to feed into this committee, Pasvolski got the consent of the secretary of state to form the Division of Special Research. Its members included President Isaiah Bowman of Johns Hopkins University (whom we used to dub "Prophet Isaiah"), Hamilton Fish Armstrong, and others. The Division of Special Research began as early as 1942 to feed papers into this committee. Professor Philip Moseley of Columbia University was one of the first people appointed to do this work.

A similar group in the early years worked on postwar German policy just as the rest of us were working on postwar Japanese policy. There was a similarity, too, in the fact that the Civil Affairs Division in the War Department had been established, and General Cornelius Wickersham had been able to persuade the War Department, over a good deal of objection, that a school of military government should be founded at the University of Virginia. I can assure you that a person such as Hardy Dillard of that university's law school, who was in charge of the whole instruction program of the school of military government, was far from a *Gauleiter* in the attitude that he and other staff members of the school took toward training the future civil affairs and military government officers. Most of their time was spent on strictly military matters but, as the war progressed, they learned they would have to know more about

such nitty-gritty as taking care of displaced persons, and that their
training was far too theoretical.

You may be interested to know that each class received twelve
hours' instruction over the three or four week period—twelve hours
instruction or twelve hours of lectures—on Germany, Italy, and
Japan. How can you train a military civil affairs officer in twelve
lectures for what he is going to get into when he goes to a defeated
Germany, or a defeated Italy, or a defeated Japan? We tried to do
something, but already in Charlottesville the trainees felt that they
were overeducated. My hat is certainly off to them wherever they
went for the job that they were able to do.

There were in Special Research competently trained people working on German policy and on Italian policy. The great difference in
the German group from those of us in the Japan group was really
the result of the influence of Henry Morgenthau. As soon as he won
the ear of President Roosevelt on his pastoralization policy for Germany, most of the people that were working on German policy in the
State Department resigned because they realized that all of their
work was for naught. Also, in April of 1945, a month after Secretary
of the Treasury Morgenthau had forced Roosevelt to create an Interim Policy Committee on Germany (IPCOG), all German policy
papers went into IPCOG. So this meant that the State-War-Navy
Coordinating Committee (SWNCC) concentrated almost entirely on
Japan and Korea. After the early part of 1945, the two were different so that, in a sense, this is why you hear nothing more about the
hard work, and the training, and the policy papers on the German
side of the State Department because they were simply ignored and
began to collect dust.

Chapter 1

American Wartime Planning
for Occupied Japan

The Role of the Experts

Marlene J. Mayo

American wartime planning for the occupation and reform of defeated Japan was part of a large and grandiose effort to reshape the
postwar world and advance the security and interests of the United
States as a global power.[1] While the armed services and the home
front concentrated on the immediate task of fighting and winning
the war, the government's postwar planners postulated ultimate
victory and formulated peace aims. Planning for occupied Japan,
like that for Germany, developed over several years and involved
many individuals and committees throughout the wartime bureaucracy; indeed it was very much influenced, particularly at higher
policy levels, by prior decisions for Germany. But unlike that for
Germany it remained primarily American in conceptualization and
implementation. Planners at all levels, from research to high policy,
were constantly bedeviled by the question of what was special about
Japan's case and what was general to the immediate and long-range
needs of the United States and the world. Their recommendations,
though reflecting an uneasy compromise between harsh and lenient
views, did much to determine the course of the occupation and continued substantially to govern Japanese-American relations far into
the postwar years.[2]

The three most important documents which emerged from the
planning process were: 1) the Potsdam declaration of July 26, 1945,
an ultimatum reiterating the unconditional surrender formula and
containing broad hints as to the treatment Japan could expect; 2)

the United States Initial Post-Surrender Policy Relating to Japan (SWNCC 150/4/A), as altered by the Potsdam declaration and made public by President Truman on September 22 in the first weeks of the occupation; and 3) the Basic Directive for Post-Surrender Military Government in Japan Proper (JCS 1380/15), top secret military orders first debated by the Joint Chiefs of Staff (JCS) in August and formally approved in early November.[3] The initial drafts of the president's basic policy statement and of the Potsdam declaration had been hastily prepared at war's end in Washington by civilian and military planners who reported to the State-War-Navy Coordinating Committee (SWNCC), a body operating at the assistant secretary level under the leadership of the Department of State. There had been virtually no consultation with the Allies, although the British made some significant last minute changes in the Potsdam declaration. The policy statement, in turn, reached General Douglas MacArthur, Supreme Commander of the Allied Powers in Japan (SCAP), by cable on August 29, shortly before the official surrender ceremony in Tokyo Bay, and again in slightly revised form by courier on September 6, following President Truman's endorsement.

MacArthur's subsequent military directive from the JCS, which outlined in greater detail the political, economic, and military reforms he was to pursue in Japan, arrived almost three months after the start of the occupation but its probable contents had been known to him and his general staff in advanced draft form since late August, when they were about to leave the Philippines for Japan. Later drafts were sent for MacArthur's information and comment in early and mid-September. Moreover, separate SWNCC papers were forwarded as supplementary policy guides (or directives if bearing the JCS stamp of approval) on such diverse topics as disarmament, war crimes, censorship, media control, education, reorientation, governmental reform, the institution of the emperor, industry and trade, and agriculture and labor.[4]

Contrary to general belief, then and now, General MacArthur's role and that of his general staff in planning the initial goals of the Allied occupation of Japan were minimal.[5] What Washington wanted in Japan and how it viewed Japan in its larger postwar considerations were extremely important and would remain so despite continued preoccupation with the reconstruction of Europe. MacArthur, however much he chafed at guidelines and restraints, largely complied with his JCS orders in the opening stages of the occupation. Well informed about the personalities and politics behind the initial recommendations, the general's chief contributions in the crucial early days were in determining priorities and timing reforms, as he exercised in his highly assertive and colorful manner the usual discretionary authority of a theater commander and gathered essential information on conditions in Japan.

This paper will deal briefly with the planning process and decision making which produced the basic policy statement, Potsdam declaration, and military directive. It will touch on underlying assumptions and attitudes of American civilian and military planners, outline the conflict of opinion, and trace the resolution of the debate at middle and higher levels of Washington politics as the war with Japan abruptly ended in the late summer of 1945. Of special interest is the role of the government's country and area experts—Japan and East Asia specialists—in shaping the final documents and the nature and quality of their expertise. Did they reach a consensus, and how effective was their voice? What was their understanding of prewar Japan and of the causes of the Japanese-American conflict? How harsh or conciliatory was their approach to peace? What was their vision of postwar Japan? Were their loyalties somewhat suspect because of their specialized knowledge or supposed sympathy with the Japanese? Also relevant was their view of their own country and its recent history and culture.

Expert is an elusive term. It may be broadly defined to include world travelers, expatriates, sojourners abroad for business or professional reasons, or individuals with purely secondhand or book knowledge of a foreign culture. Or it may be strictly delimited to emphasize specialized training in a discipline and methodology, language facility (written or oral), and extensive firsthand acquaintance. Japan experts are here defined primarily as individuals with both language and area training and field experience but secondarily encompasses others with a significant period of residence in Japan.

Given the narrowness of prewar university education and the country's preoccupation with domestic concerns, Americans with Japanese language competence, whether spoken or written, were in fact only a handful when Pearl Harbor was attacked. Nevertheless, there was a surprising number of knowledgeable individuals with varying degrees of general and technical information about Japan, and they came to be scattered throughout the government as the war progressed. A good many had been Foreign Service officers, naval and military attachés, or university professors and were the prime recruits for postwar planning and research responsibilities. Others were missionaries or their children, foundation men, lawyers, journalists, bankers, and businessmen. Increasingly, the experts also came to include Americans of Japanese ancestry, the

Nisei or the second generation, who were either spared from or released from relocation centers to work in intelligence, psychological
warfare, or language teaching. The largest group of experts at war's
end were the instant or new experts—officers trained for civil affairs or military duties in accelerated language and area programs
run by the Army and Navy. To a considerable extent, it was these
men (and also women) who would carry out the policies and directives for occupied Japan at the operational level, undertake initiatives in the field, or act as translators and interpreters. Some of
them, increasingly fascinated by their former enemy, would go on to
deepen their knowledge in graduate school and help develop a
flourishing field of Japanese studies in the United States and a
postwar generation of Japan specialists.

Overview and Periodization

Overall planning for the postwar era began very early, if somewhat
hesitantly, in the American government—as far back as September
1939, immediately following the outbreak of war in Europe, and at
the initiative of officials in the Department of State. The United
States, they reasoned, might or might not be drawn into the shooting war but it would without doubt have a decisive influence on the
ultimate peace settlement and postwar reconstruction. Although
much influenced by Wilsonian internationalist ideals, they not only
had strong misgivings about the armistice and treaty with Germany
after World War I but were also critical of President Wilson's reliance in 1917–19 on the Inquiry. This was a group of experts,
mainly academicians, who had been assembled independently of the
State Department under the supervision of Wilson's closest adviser,
Colonel Edward M. House, to prepare the American case in advance
of the peace conference. Hoping to learn from history, officials in
1939 wanted not only to avoid repeating past errors leading to tensions and war but also to keep tight control by the State Department
over the formulation of postwar foreign policy. They retained much
faith, however, in the ability of scholarly experts to assist in the
preparatory work—to provide accurate information, make informed
studies and divine trends, and suggest sound principles conducive to
a better world order and an enduring peace.[6]

With a wary eye on the course of the war in Europe and Japan's
continuing aggression in China and in Southeast Asia, the Department of State with support from President Roosevelt created several
secret advisory groups, 1939–41, and solicited the opinions of other

departments and agencies. Their task was to collect data and grapple with questions about postwar international trade, monetary and banking systems, access to the world's resources, reduction of armaments, and permanent security. Since the department lacked an intelligence and research unit, it maintained semiformal contacts with several private organizations, such as the Brookings Institution in Washington and the Council on Foreign Relations (CFR) in New York (publishers of the journal *Foreign Affairs*), to assist and stimulate its thinking. In the realm of Asian affairs, the American Council of the Institute of Pacific Relations (IPR) was another useful forum.[7]

In February 1941, the State Department set up its first full-time research unit for the preparation of postwar foreign policy, the Division of Special Research (SR). It was under the direction of former Brookings Institution economist Leo Pasvolsky, since 1937 special assistant to Secretary of State Cordell Hull and author of many of the early proposals to study the problems of peace and reconstruction.[8] Once the United States entered the war in December 1941, the planning and policy development became increasingly comprehensive and systematic, first for Italy and Germany in keeping with the Europe first strategy, and then for Japan and East Asia, as attempts were made to define surrender terms, to anticipate the routine problems of military government, and to enunciate broader goals of security and reform.

After Pearl Harbor, there were essentially three stages of preparatory work for Japan, roughly paralleling that for Germany and corresponding to progress in the war. In the first stage, 1942–43, a time of research and preliminary position papers, the general framework for a new world order and basic principles for the treatment of defeated enemy countries, including a period of military occupation for demilitarization and democratization, were arrived at by the secret deliberations of President Roosevelt's Advisory Committee on Postwar Foreign Policy and its five subcommittees. Authorized by the president in late 1941 and headed by Secretary of State Hull as chairman of the parent committee, this complex planning hierarchy began its exploratory work in February 1942 and was comprised of influential private citizens, including members of the Council on Foreign Relations, and senior government officials, many of whom were in the State Department. To broaden the work, the representation was soon expanded to include high Army and Navy officers and congressional leaders. Although the Advisory Committee's formal recommendations, including the unconditional surrender formula, were transmitted to the president through the secretary and undersecretary of state (Sumner Welles), Roosevelt also met informally from time to time with other leading members. Pasvolsky's unit, SR, was delegated to provide the research staff, help draw up the agenda, and act as the secretariat. As news from the fighting front improved and the need for efficiency, confidentiality, and specialization increased, the work of the Advisory Committee was largely suspended in the summer and fall of 1943 and the postwar planning machinery was restructured.[9]

In the second period of more advanced work, extending from late 1943 to the end of 1944, when Secretary Hull resigned, Pasvolsky's staff and the older geographic units were joined by several new economic and cultural officers of the rapidly expanding Department of State to provide more regular and systematic intradepartmental consideration of the treatment of enemy nations. Previous recommendations for Japan were carefully reviewed under the supervision of senior officials, as the State Department attempted to place its stamp of approval on the initial and long-range postwar foreign policies of the United States. Serious differences, however, began to divide the political and economic planners. Moreover, because of the many practical problems and policy issues involved in the military occupation of enemy countries, other departments and wartime agencies increasingly played a role in the planning process— whether in defining basic questions and conducting basic research or in making operational preparations and modifying State Department positions. Of particular importance were the War and Navy departments, the Treasury (though more so for Germany than Japan), and the president's Executive Committee on Economic Foreign Policy. Also making significant contributions were the Office of Strategic Services (OSS), the Foreign Economic Administration (FEA), and the Office of War Information (OWI).

In 1945, the final year of the war and third stage of planning, SWNCC was set up to give broader and more efficient interdepartmental consideration to postwar policy formulation. By then, the secretaries of state, war, and navy (Stettinius, Stimson, and Forrestal) were also meeting frequently as the Committee of Three to deliberate on a host of international and security problems. The political solutions of the Japan specialists had gained wide acceptance, but new and more reformist ideas, some of them anathema to the Japan hands, entered the mainstream of planning and were incorporated into the final policy documents and military directive. In the last months of the Pacific war, military and naval planners and the civilian heads of the War and Navy departments, with security needs and the growing power of the Soviet Union very much in mind, had as much—if not more—to say about the treatment of occupied Japan as did the State Department, no matter how jealously the latter guarded its constitutional prerogatives and jurisdiction in the making of foreign economic and political policies. The era of a single defense agency and national security planning was dawning. Japan's sudden and unexpected surrender brought further alterations to the original calculations.

In all three stages, postwar planners took their cues from the dictates, speeches, and summit diplomacy of the president, whose network of friends and advisers was extensive and whose tendency was to bypass the State Department, or at least the uncongenial Secretary Hull, when he could. Whether they approved or not, Japan planners, like those for Germany, had to devise papers which accorded with the president's views—insofar as they could determine his principles and preferences.[10] To begin with, there were the Four Freedoms and the Atlantic Charter dating from 1941 and embraced by the United Nations in January 1942, with their call for disarmament, sovereign rights, and self-government, and cooperative international economic arrangements. Then at Casablanca in January 1943, following an agreement with Churchill, the president announced the policy of unconditional surrender, a concept which had emerged as early as the spring of 1942 during the deliberations of the Advisory Committee on the dangers of a negotiated peace. Roosevelt endorsed it, apparently at the advice of his friend and roving ambassador, Norman Davis, chairman of the Subcommittee on Security Problems and in private life president of the Council on Foreign Relations and head of the American Red Cross. The formula had already governed the first drafts of surrender terms for Germany and Japan as prepared in May by the army member of the Davis subcommittee, Major General George V. Strong, chief of military intelligence (until 1944), and it was further discussed prior to Casablanca by the president and the JCS.[11]

Thereafter postwar planners and propagandists for the war effort were plagued by the problem of how to interpret or change the policy. "The elimination of German, Japanese and Italian war power," Roosevelt had declared, "means the unconditional surrender by Germany, Italy, and Japan." This doctrine, he added, "does not mean the destruction of the population of Germany, Italy, or Japan, but it does mean the destruction of the philosophies in those countries which are based on conquest and subjugation of other people."[12] It is questionable to what extent Roosevelt foresaw in 1942 that rooting out an evil philosophy would lead to political and economic controls, decolonization, war crimes trials, purges, censorship, or wide-scale economic and social engineering. To Congress in January 1943, he argued that Germany and Japan must be disarmed and remain disarmed, and in a radio speech in February he said that unconditional surrender meant the punishment of "guilty, barbaric leaders." The Cairo declaration next announced in November 1943 that the Allies were fighting "to restrain and punish the aggression of Japan," and promised dismemberment of Japan's empire, a matter which had been thoroughly discussed by the Advisory Committee. In the fall of 1944, Roosevelt reminded Hull of the importance of eliminating monopolistic restraints in international trade, and his views seemed to take an even more punitive direction under the influence of Treasury Secretary Morgenthau's harsh pastoralization line for Germany. The Yalta communiqué in February 1945, which publicly proclaimed that unconditional surrender and military occupation of Germany required disarmament, punishment of war criminals, eradication of Nazism, and payment of reparations, foretold of similar plans for the treatment of Japan.[13] After the president's death in April 1945, the question was how much Truman and the men around him, especially James Byrnes, would embrace the postwar vision and plans of Roosevelt and what role they foresaw for Japan in East Asia.

The First Stage, Initial Planning, 1942–1943

When Pasvolsky and SR began their work in the State Department early in 1942 for the Advisory Committee, the old geographic-political units were fearful of losing power and prestige. There was an influx of scholars and professional men into the department—and into the government as a whole—as it expanded its role and functions, and career bureaucrats and Foreign Service officers grumbled that the academic men were naïve, innocent of practical experience, and all together ivory-tower types. The professors retaliated that the career men, however good they might be as political and economic reporters, were literally unable to sit down with a pencil and paper and make projections about the postwar world. Most of SR's growing staff came from private life, but there were a few transfers from the old units. Later on, in the fall of 1943, a solution was found in the creation of intradepartmental committees where experts of varying kind and degree could meet and exchange ideas regularly.[14]

Among the permanent bureaucrats, the most important initially was Secretary Hull's political adviser on Far Eastern affairs, Stanley K. Hornbeck, a China-centered East Asia specialist with a seat on most of the department's higher level planning groups. Trained at the University of Wisconsin before World War I as a political scientist, Hornbeck had a varied career as a scholar and technical expert before joining the department in 1928 as head of the Division of Far Eastern Affairs. Lacking facility in the Chinese language but widely read and intelligent, his pedantic manner and conservative views made him extremely unpopular with the younger generation of China hands, many of them trained language officers. To Japan hands, he was both a curmudgeon and an anti-Japanese bigot. After Pearl Harbor, Hornbeck was primarily absorbed with the China war effort, particularly questions of material aid to Chiang Kai-shek, and with ending extraterritoriality in American-Chinese treaty relations, but his ideas about postsurrender Japan carried weight with Hull.[15]

Under Hornbeck's close and often stultifying supervision was the Division of Far Eastern Affairs, headed from 1937 to 1943 by another China specialist, Maxwell Hamilton, and largely staffed by Foreign Service officers who rotated between field assignments in China and Japan and desk work in Washington. Hamilton's replacement in mid-1943, Japanese linguist Joseph Ballantine, displayed the same cautious tendency to identify with the views of his superiors. The repatriation in August 1942 of ambassador to Japan, Joseph Grew, and his counselor of embassy from 1937 to 1941, Eugene Dooman, added to the department's small roster of Japan hands, but at first there was difficulty in finding suitable assignments for them. Their warnings and advice from Tokyo had been largely ignored in the fall of 1941, and relations between Hull and Grew were at first tense. Those between Dooman and Hornbeck had never been cordial. Grew spent most of the next year and a half giving numerous speeches throughout the country under the auspices of the OWI, warning Americans that they faced a tough enemy in Japan and a long and difficult war in the Pacific and Asia. Grew was also preparing his diary for publication, *Ten Years in Japan* (1944). Dooman, considered to be the Foreign Service's chief expert on Japan, was assigned to the Moscow embassy as counselor, perhaps because of the presence of Japanese diplomats in Russia, but returned to Washington in 1943 for reasons of health and worked temporarily with the United Nations Relief and Rehabilitation Administration and as a liaison officer with intelligence units. Both Grew and Dooman would be drawn into the mainstream of the department's work in 1944 and begin to play extremely important roles in defining America's peace aims in East Asia and Japan and

in translating recommendations from the working level of specialists to the high policy of the secretary of state and the White
House.[16]

Others returning from internment in Tokyo who became involved
in presurrender planning were Frank S. Williams and Robert
Fearey. Williams, a longtime resident in both China and Japan, had
been commercial attaché at the Tokyo embassy in the 1930s.
Fearey, a young graduate of Harvard with a double major in history
and economics, had been Grew's private secretary in Tokyo for only
eight months when Japan declared war, and with Grew's strong
support he was almost immediately given a post in the department
as a divisional assistant and assigned with Williams to SR. Fearey
would remain in the department for the rest of his career, specializing at first in economic matters. Another returnee in 1942 but from
Manila was Cabot Coville, a Japanese language officer who had
risen to embassy secretary in the 1930s. After escaping from the
Philippines with the American high commissioners,[17] Coville was
loaned to Pasvolsky's planning unit in 1942–43 for a brief but important interlude.

In the meantime, while the East Asia staff was being assembled,
the first statements on major postwar problems in the Pacific area
were drawn up at Pasvolsky's request by Joseph M. Jones. An
economist with the United States Tariff Commission prior to entering the department in 1937, Jones had been assigned to the Division
of Far Eastern Affairs where he gained some expertise in United
States–East Asian economic relations. As he articulated the main
issue in February 1942, "The principal political problem in the
Pacific area at the end of the war will be the creation of a unified,
independent prosperous China." This entailed the end of special foreign rights and privileges and vast social reconstruction. Second to
that, he declared, was the problem of Japan. It must of course be
permanently disarmed, and other steps should be taken to guard
against its renewed aggression. But Japan, which he characterized
as an enterprising and energetic nation, must also be allowed to
support its "growing population in a rising scale of living" through
peaceful trade and industrialization. If Japan were denied access to
raw materials, foreign capital, and export markets, there could be
no enduring peace in the Far East.[18] These were themes which
would be accepted as axiomatic, needing only elaboration, by virtually all Japan hands, whether professors or diplomats.

As it turned out, however, the first serious and sustained research
and planning for postwar Japan was undertaken by recruits to SR
from the academic world. The two most important university profes-

sors were George Blakeslee and Hugh Borton, both historians. Later, other academic men would join the department and make significant contributions, as planning became more diversified and complex and the original Japan hands came to be viewed as primarily political experts and even generalists. Blakeslee, a close friend of Hornbeck, was then already in his late sixties and had behind him a distinguished career as a professor of history and international relations at Clark University and at the Fletcher School of Law and Diplomacy. He neither read nor spoke Chinese or Japanese, as was true of many prewar academicians specializing in East Asian studies, but he knew East Asia well—principally its intellectuals and elites, the right people (in 1929 he had been presented to the Japanese emperor)—from travel, lecture tours, and study. He was sensitive to Japan's aspirations while denouncing its territorial aggression and had considerable respect for Japan's modern transformation as a great power, calling it "the greatest achievement in modern political history." Blakeslee was acquainted with almost everyone of importance in the foreign policy field. Above all, as his government service once again showed, Blakeslee was a perfect committee chairman; he was skillful with people and knew how to organize research. To his detractors, he may have been "poor, dear Japan Blakeslee," but to his many admirers, he "kept the pot boiling."[19]

At Hornbeck's initiative, Blakeslee was brought to SR in August 1942 to help develop a specialized staff and policy questions for East Asia and the Pacific. Already on hand were John Masland, a political scientist trained at Princeton and teaching at Stanford; Amry Vandenbosch, a historian from the University of Kentucky whose interest was Southeast Asia, especially Indonesia; and Clarence Spiker, a veteran career officer with extensive experience in China. Cabot Coville and Robert Fearey were also soon added.[20]

Hugh Borton joined Blakeslee's little group in October as the last of the recruits on East Asia. Much younger than Blakeslee, Borton was a rarity in American universities, not only a professor of modern Japanese history but one who combined firsthand knowledge of the country with training in the language. He had begun his graduate studies at Columbia University but completed his doctoral work at the University of Leiden in 1937, writing his thesis on peasant uprisings in late Tokugawa Japan. A Quaker and pacifist, he had first arrived in Japan in the late 1920s to work for the American Friends Service Committee in Tokyo. It was then that he became acquainted with his lifelong friend, Sir George Sansom, commercial attaché at the British embassy, who was then completing *Japan:*

A Short Cultural History (first published in 1931). As Borton's mentor, Sansom helped to shape his view of the Japanese and deepen his appreciation of their culture. Returning to Japan in 1936 as a special graduate student at Tokyo Imperial University, Borton was an eyewitness to the Young Officers' Incident in February 1936. Perhaps because of these two periods of residence, he tended (in common with most prewar Japan experts) to contrast the good Taisho 1920s with the bad Showa 1930s, an interpretation of modern Japanese history which would have profound influence on planning for the occupation and on postwar American studies of Japan. Borton's knowledge of contemporary Japan, especially its political system and its politicians, was greatly expanded by the research he undertook in preparing a book for the Inquiry series of the IPR, *Japan Since 1931* (published in 1940). Largely factual, it was intended to acquaint the public with the basic issues in the East Asian conflict and Japan's trend toward "military fascism," a term which Borton dropped in his planning papers. When the war came, he was an assistant professor in the Department of Chinese and Japanese at Columbia. In taking up his new work with the government, Borton also became a lecturer in 1942 at the army's recently created school of Military Government at Charlottesville, Virginia, where he gained valuable insights into the practical problems of civil affairs officers in occupied countries.[21]

Borton and Blakeslee would remain in the State Department's various research units until the end of the war, giving coherence and continuity to planning at the working level. Within the framework already established by the Advisory Committee and Pasvolsky, they were instrumental in asking specific questions about Japan and in further refining the research agenda. Blakeslee tended to write papers on the general aims and objectives of the United States in East Asia and Japan and on the disposition of Japan's Pacific mandates, while Borton concentrated on political questions pertaining to the constitution, the emperor, and political parties. Both would continue in government service in the immediate postwar era, monitoring policies they had helped to formulate and framing new ones. Blakeslee became political adviser to the chairman of the Far Eastern Commission in Washington, and Borton advanced up the ladder of the State Department bureaucracy to become head of the Japan Division before returning to the academic world in 1948 to assist in founding the East Asian Institute at Columbia University.[22]

If the two men rather quickly arrived at basic approaches and conclusions, it was in part because they had previously formed an intellectual partnership and had been involved as private citizens in thinking systematically about postwar Japan and East Asia through their activities with the IPR and especially the Council on Foreign Relations, 1940–42. Their views remained substantially unchanged. The CFR had begun sending recommendations on war and peace aims to the Department of State in 1940–41, based on the work of five study groups in its War and Peace Studies Project, funded by the Rockefeller Foundation.[23] These dealt mainly with the war in Europe, but from November 1941 to April 1942, the council also sponsored six meetings of still another special study group, punctuated by the attack on Pearl Harbor, "Do Bases Exist for a Real Peace between Japan and the United States?" Blakeslee chaired the panels, and Borton, after satisfying the council that he was not pro-Japan, served as the rapporteur.[24]

At the first of the CRF sessions, held on November 3 and 26, 1941, the participants had speculated as to the peace terms which would be politically acceptable to the United States, China, and Japan—and took heart at the arrival of Kurusu in Washington to assist Ambassador Nomura. There was a consensus that Japan had been unfairly subjected to discriminatory tariffs and economic strangulation by the United States and Great Britain. Hugh Byas, longtime correspondent in Japan for the *New York Times,* confidant of Joseph Grew, and a special guest at the second meeting, spoke for several of those present in declaring that "Konoye is not Hitler." The Japanese, he hoped, would find a face-saving way back "to their old and only sound policy of friendship with the two naval and commercial powers, America and the British Empire, whose amity is essential to their security and whose trade is essential to their prosperity."

At the post–Pearl Harbor sessions, beginning in early 1942, discussants arrived at fundamental principles which they believed should govern a postwar settlement with Japan, following an agenda prepared by Blakeslee in February and March: reduction of the Japanese army and navy, dismemberment of the Japanese empire, reforms in the government, reconstruction of the economy, and peace keeping through a regional security system or police force. They were all in agreement on the necessity for a thorough defeat of Japanese militarism but rejected as unwise and dangerous any attempt to crush Japan in the subsequent peace. A few even spoke of the desirability of a strong Japan in postwar East Asia.[25]

For Blakeslee and Borton, who were involved in many other study conferences and discussions, the transition from academic and private debate to government research and planning in late 1942–43 was relatively easy. Their approach would remain basically con-

ciliatory and moderate; in this they were similar to their counterparts for Germany, principally David Harris, professor of Balkan
and Central European history at Stanford. They had no illusions
about Japan's militarists, recognized Japan's dependence for prosperity on international trade, and advocated limited political reforms. Both assumed that liberal elements existed in Japan, but
neither expected or spoke for social revolution. And as Borton wrote
to the editor of *Fortune* magazine in May 1942 on the never-ending
question of the emperor:

> On the matter of whether or not the Japanese Monarchy
> should or should not be overthrown, all my readings and con-
> tacts in the Japanese field lead me to the firm conviction that
> the monarchy can be used as a strong element of unity around
> which liberal Democratic elements can govern Japan. . . . Cer-
> tainly any nation or group of nations which forced the over-
> throw of the monarchy within Japan would arose violent
> animosity from the ordinary citizens. The vital problem, it
> seems to me, is to have effective checks in the governmental
> system over the armed services and over recalcitrant groups
> and I do not see why the overthrow of the Emperor would be a
> necessary prerequisite for this.[26]

This too remained a fixed conviction.

In January 1943, SR was divided into the Division of Political
Studies (PS) and Division of Economic Studies (ES), with Blakeslee,
Borton, and Masland assigned to the former and Fearey and Williams to the latter. By early March, the trio of Blakeslee, Borton,
and Masland had prepared a list of the major questions on postwar
Japan for consideration by the Subcommittee on Political Problems,
chaired by Undersecretary Welles. They were grouped under six
headings: occupational government, disarmament, internal political
problems, disposition of Japanese territory and Manchukuo, economic issues, and the ultimate status of Japan in regional or international security organizations. The underlying question, however,
was whether or not the United States (or United Nations) should
require social, political, and economic reforms in Japan—indeed
whether the victors had even the legal right to do so.[27]

It was by then understood that the Americans would play a predominant if not exclusive role in the military occupation of Japan,
just as they were bearing the brunt of the Pacific campaigns. The
questions therefore under occupational government were what
areas should be occupied, the combination of national forces to be

used, whether the forces should be military or civilian, and to what extent Japanese administrative personnel should be retained. General Strong's draft surrender terms for Japan had indicated only the occupation of points in Hokkaido. At this stage, the planners, though clearly aware of the administrative difficulties of governing Japan proper, had not come up with the solution of an indirect occupation, and in fact would not do so until the war had almost ended.[28] On arms limitation, they wondered if disarmament should be complete, extending even to the prohibition of merchant shipping and civil aviation. The third set of questions on internal political life were far-ranging and touched on the possibility of governmental changes.

> To what degree should the United States be concerned with the internal political development of Japan? Should the continuance of the Imperial House be favored? To what degree should the United States favor such changes in Japanese political institutions to assure such objectives as limitation of the power of the military, development of parliamentary government, extension of civil rights, and the decentralization of administrative authority?

Additional domestic reforms were contemplated. Should the United States "participate in measures to secure a change in Japanese political philosophy through supervision of the educational system and of other media of indoctrination?"

The Advisory Committee had already recommended dismemberment of Japan's empire, but should Japan's sovereignty be eliminated only from territories taken since the Sino-Japanese war of 1894–95 or since the beginning of World War I? Obviously, there was need for a set of papers discussing not only Taiwan, Korea, and Manchuria but also the Kuriles, Karafuto, the Bonin Islands, and the Ryukyus. The economic issues were extensive, beginning with the question of an indemnity or reparations. Next, as a counterpart to political reform, was the degree of pressure the United States should exert "to promote the reorganization and liberalization of Japanese finances, industry and agriculture." Should Japan retain its overseas investments, be given opportunities for emigration, or encouraged to develop specialized exports? And should the United States "encourage the economic rehabilitation of Japan on terms of equal access to raw materials and markets," or "promote the greater integration of Japanese economy into a broader system of international economic colloboration."[29] The sixth and last category, regional and international security, asked whether the United States should "favor the return of Japan as soon as possible to the international community on a basis of equality."

The research staff of ES and PS provided preliminary answers in the following months in papers written for debate by the Territorial Problems Subcommittee. The chairman was Isaiah Bowman, president of Johns Hopkins University and a member of the steering committee for the CFR's war and peace studies.[30] The fundamental questions—how much of the old Japan should or could be destroyed and to what extent the United States should directly or indirectly impose reforms—were handled by Blakeslee, who voiced the basically cautious approach of most of the old Japan hands, scholars and diplomats alike. He was opposed to the imposition of external controls by the military occupiers, using as an example education and the dissemination of information. "It might not be possible," he told Bowman's subcommittee in July, "to go much further than to require the freedom of the press and radio from governmental control." Continuing in this vein, he said that "it would be better not to insist on changes in Japan's constitutional regime, and four-fifths or nine-tenths of the experts on the question were agreed that it would be very unwise to attempt any change in the Emperorship."[31] Coville, who had been assigned the first full-scale papers on Japan proper, proposed a peace based simply on "rigid disarmament" and "economic viability," and believed the best solution to the institution of the throne was to humanize it.[32] Borton, too, in view of the ideals expressed in the Atlantic Charter, expressed reluctance to push for extensive interference in Japan's internal life, though less so in its political system than its economic and social organization, as his subsequent papers would reveal. He questioned the power of the victors to enforce through terms of surrender a preferred form of government on the Japanese. Perhaps all they could do was ask the Japanese to control their military and meet their international obligations. Another practical reservation, one noted by many of the planners, was the limited number of trained personnel who would be available to administer defeated Japan under military government. Therefore if changes, even of a limited nature, were deemed desirable, then the victors would have to find another way to bring them about, some form of encouragement or inducement short of coercion. Their answer, essentially, was to postulate the existence of moderates and liberals in Japan who could be expected, in the aftermath of defeat and humiliation of the military, to assume the basic responsibility for reforms.[33]

Blakeslee, in his summary that July for the Bowman subcommittee of the general principles which should guide a postwar settlement with Japan, began with dismemberment of empire and demilitarization, sufficiently extensive to prevent Japan "from again becoming a menace to international peace." This could be accomplished by eliminating Japan's sovereignty from Manchuria, Korea, and Formosa and depriving it of the "mandated islands and possibly of other strategic islands," accompanied by disarmament, military inspection, and temporary restriction of certain (as yet unspecified) economic activities. The economic and financial terms of the settlement, he next argued, should permit Japan, "within the framework of the restrictions necessary for international security (a qualifying phrase inserted in the revised draft of September by the Territorial Subcommittee), to share in the development of a world economy on a non-discriminatory basis, looking toward a progressively higher standard of living." Blakeslee was uncertain as to "the amount and kind" of reparations Japan should pay or the "desirability of permanent restrictions on specific categories of Japanese industry." The political goals, he wrote, should be to foster the creation of a Japanese government which respected the rights of other states. This would entail "constitutional and administrative changes" to end the privileges of the military, a freer flow of ideas (especially "intellectual communication with democratic countries"), and "other measures which will strengthen the moderate political elements in Japan." In other words, Blakeslee was not advocating thorough democratization.[34] The ultimate objective, he concluded, should be "to restore Japan to full and equal membership in the family of nations."[35]

Borton elaborated upon these points in several key papers which he wrote that summer and fall and also joined Blakeslee in defending them when called upon by Bowman's group to give expert testimony. Militarism he agreed, was Japan's curse, but since military control of policy was legal under the Meiji constitution, certain internal structural changes would be in order. Fortunately, it would not be necessary to make a complete break with the past to rid Japan of militarism, for there were politically moderate to liberal elements, at that time silenced by censorship or fear of assassination, who were capable of reforming Japan after the military authorities had been discredited. The real problem, as Borton saw it, was to strengthen democratic tendencies while eradicating militarist elements. As potential leaders in correcting abuses and instituting reforms, he named former premier Hiranuma Kiichiro,

Lord Privy Seal Kido Koichi, businessman Kobayashi Ichizo, Admirals Nomura Kichisaburo and Toyoda Teijiro, and diplomat Shigemitsu Mamoru. Prime Minister Konoye Fumimaro might be all right if he were surrounded by liberals. More questionable, thought Borton, was the political role of Japanese businessmen, particularly leaders "who have been identified with the powerful financial houses," for big business in Japan had been "basically willing" to support expansionism and had displayed deficiencies in "social consciousness." Possibly other business groups, that is the new moderates, with interests in international trade might support a reformed regime.

To assist Japan's political parties and civilian bureaucrats in establishing control and serving as more than simply a restraining influence, Borton recommended formal revisions of the constitution to destroy the privileges of the military, such as ending their direct access to the throne or right to sit in the cabinet, and to strengthen the Diet, specifically giving it control over the annual budget and the right to vote on treaties and making cabinet ministers responsible to it. Emperor worship and state support of Shintoism should of course be abolished, but the emperor as an individual and the throne as an institution should continue, he said echoing Coville, as part of a reformed government. To reinforce the point, Borton argued against the war guilt of Hirohito, saying that the emperor reigned but did not govern; if anything, the present emperor and his advisers had been a moderating influence in the 1930s. The institution of the emperor, if it were reformed as a constitutional monarchy, would very likely, he believed, be "one of the more stable elements of postwar Japan and provide help in establishing a stable and moderate government." Reforms would have to come from above, as they had in past Japanese history. Clearly, Borton did not expect Japan's military defeat to lead to a postwar revolution—neither a "great political upheaval" nor a widespread demand for abolition of the throne or for democratic government. Neither did he favor, as he explained again some years later, unleashing a revolution. "My answer to that always was, well, if you can guarantee to me that this is going to be a democratic revolution, fine. But you never can stop a revolution, and you can never be sure whether it's going to be completely Baptist or completely Communist or whatever."

Borton conceded that effective political reform was linked to changes in "the Japanese mentality," but such a transformation would take a long time. Since he and the others did not want a long military occupation, the only answer was to insist on freedom for the media in the surrender terms. Borton repeated the point that an unduly harsh economic peace, one which attempted to impoverish Japan, could not possibly be a permanent peace. "Not even the wisest and most temperate treatment of its political system can be expected to yield the results calculated if economic disabilities of a severe character are to be imposed on a defeated Japan." To induce Japan's postwar leaders to make the desired political reforms and improve their country's international behavior, the United Nations might offer reentry into the new world organization, specific help in rehabilitating Japan's economy, and increasing opportunity to develop "a progressively higher standard of living" through "access to markets and raw materials on a basis of equality."[36]

Fearey and Williams in their numerous papers on Japan's economy and recent Japanese-American trade relations, reiterated this last sentiment succinctly and eloquently: "A viable Japanese economy is to be considered a first prerequisite of lasting peace in the Pacific." It would only be self-defeating to destroy Japan's entire modern industrial plant in light and heavy industries, to cut off its foreign trade and liquidate its merchant marine, or force its reversion to an agricultural country. They were convinced that Japan could survive economically and perhaps even do better when shorn of its empire but only if it had access to world markets and raw materials. The best security against Japanese aggression, therefore, would be disarmament accompanied by a program of reform and rehabilitation directed at the revival of peacetime industry and trade and the regaining of a "tolerable living standard." Going a step further, they believed that reforms in industry and agriculture, whether undertaken by the Japanese themselves or by the United Nations, were necessary to expand the domestic market and move the farm population into new occupations. But above all, they believed and repeated:

> Certain basic facts must be recognized and accepted. These are: (1) The Pacific will never be pacific without a viable, contented and peace-abiding Japan; (2) Any attempt to crush 73 million energetic, patriotic, long-suffering, aggressive, industrious and productive Japanese people not only will be abortive, but will terminate in a festering sore which would contaminate and nullify any program designed to bring peace and prosperity to Asia; (3) A law-abiding and economically satisfied Japan can make many valuable contributions in many spheres of international activity, particularly those spheres centered in the Far East.

Separately, however, Williams made the point that consideration should be given to the people who had suffered from Japan's aggression. And Fearey took up the complex issue of the *zaibatsu,* Japan's powerful family concerns in big business and finance. He was to change his mind several times in 1943–44, first denouncing the concentration of wealth and income in the hands of a few combines and calling for their dissolution, but ultimately reversing his stand to credit the *zaibatsu* with playing a creative and constructive role in Japan's economic life and argue against alteration of the industrial system. As a protégé of Grew and Dooman, his youthful and passionate embrace of interventionism to mend and reform Japan yielded, in this instance, to more cautious admonitions.[37]

These views did not necessarily reflect the majority view in the State Department and did not go unchallenged in 1942–43. On the question of remaking Japan in the victor's image or leaving it alone, Hornbeck, while not exactly indifferent to Japan and its postwar internal development, did not think that its commerce was "essential to the welfare and happiness of the world" and attached little importance to its cultural and intellectual contributions. He was, moreover, not convinced that the great industrialists in Japan dominated politics in the same way as the Junkers in the German government; nor was Japan's economy as important to Asia as Germany's to Europe. Leadership in postwar Asia, in any event, should be assumed by China (he meant the China of Chiang Kai-shek) and by the United States. In disarming Japan, he did not think it would be necessary to ring the country with a series of military bases; probably export restrictions would be sufficient. Hornbeck was not prepared, he declared, after reading Borton's arguments, "to accept or endorse the concept that retention of the Emperorship is imperative." The debate should continue. The Japanese state, as he had earlier written to Grew, struck him as "a political anachronism. It is a deistic feudalism. The keystone of its arch is the god-emperor; how is it going to be possible to destroy the old arch while preserving the keystone." He could not help wondering if the military caste in Japan could be destroyed or discredited while continuing to treat the throne "as sacrosanct." Ignoring Borton's call for a reformed monarchy and an end to state supported Shintoism, Hornbeck asked how Japan could "have a government which is simultaneously 'based on democratic principles' and based upon a concept of a 'divine Emperor' and a God-given national destiny." He found that other assumptions and conclusions of Borton were "exceedingly optimistic." Although there might be "some able 'moderates' in Japan, who are capable of leadership, I still find lacking evidence that there exist *many* 'moderates' either in the upper ranks of the Japanese population or among the masses thereof." Arguing that Japan had not undergone a real revolution in 1868, Hornbeck suggested that it might be worth the risk to allow chaos in postwar Japan.[38]

Other critics were even less hesitant than Hornbeck. Captain H. L. Pence, the Navy's representative on the Security Technical Subcommittee, in several ugly speeches thumped for "the almost total elimination of the Japanese as a race." Why restore their economic life? Why not instead bomb them, so "the country could not begin to recuperate for fifty years"? Hamilton Fish Armstrong, editor of the CFR's journal, *Foreign Affairs,* insisted in somewhat strained logic at the last meeting of Bowman's group that the emperor was both "an impotent and dangerous symbol." Alger Hiss, then Hornbeck's administrative assistant and alternate on committees but soon to be charged with important preparatory work leading to the establishment of the United Nations, warned that a military defeat of Japan would not be sufficient. To win the present war and avoid future wars, Japan's national psychology and way of life, including the imperial concept, should undergo radical modification.[39]

Caught in the crossfire of the Japan experts and their adversaries, Bowman modestly summed up in December 1943 the tentative conclusions of his subcommittee on the postwar treatment of Japan: "To punish the military, insist that the emperor and other authorities (generals and perhaps the entire cabinet) sign the terms of surrender," decolonize the Japanese empire, and "sit on the lid for some time to come."[40] By then, the overall postwar planning machinery was being reorganized as was also the State Department's bureaucracy. Edward Stettinius had replaced Sumner Welles as undersecretary. Interdivisional country and area committees were being set up to draw upon the expertise of specialists throughout the department. And Pasvolsky's research officers were placed in the new Division of Territorial Studies (TS). Elsewhere in the government, military and naval planners were becoming restless with the seemingly dilatory leadership of the civilian planners.

Stage Two, Advanced Planning, Fall of 1943 to January 1945

On October 20, 1943, the Interdivisional Area Committee on the Far East (IDACFE) was created in the State Department to give more definite formulation and more extensive consideration to American

peace aims in Asia and policies for the occupation of Japan. Blakeslee took over the chairmanship when Hornbeck declined under pressure of business, and Borton became the secretary. At first a rather
small group, consisting of middle level research and desk officers,
IDACFE grew in 1944 as the State Department expanded its personnel and functions. The original working nucleus of Japan hands
from TS and the Division of Far Eastern Affairs was augmented in
1944 by economists, political scientists, and lawyers. Of special
significance, Dooman joined the deliberations regularly beginning
in March 1944, as did economist Carl (Charles) S. Remer. A professor at the University of Michigan before the war, Remer was a
China centered East Asianist, who, before shifting to the State Department's Division of Financial and Monetary Affairs (FMA) earlier that year, had been the first head of the Far Eastern unit of the
Research and Analysis Branch, OSS. In May, Grew became head of
the renamed Office of Far Eastern Affairs (FE), replacing Hornbeck,
who was under attack for his personality and views and had been
named ambassador designate to the Netherlands.[41]

IDACFE met frequently, in fact 221 times from October 1943 to
July of 1945, and generated numerous position papers for review by
assistant secretaries and divisional heads sitting in the Department's highest organ in postwar planning, the Postwar Programs
Committee (PWC). For Blakeslee, the task was to ensure a flow of
papers and to transform the preferred solutions of the Japan hands
into State Department and United States government policies. Borton has argued that "many of the recommendations" in the committee's 1944 papers "developed into the basic postwar policies for
Japan."[42] This is true, but it is equally important to note that many
were greatly recast in the tortuous process of amendment and compromise or even dropped. And additional ideas were successfully advocated by newcomers to the department or by other departments
and agencies. The final policy statement and military directive
would owe much to initiatives taken at this juncture by the War and
Navy departments, the OSS and FEA, and to a lesser extent the
OWI.

In the War Department, planning for military government in occupied areas was centered in the Civil Affairs Division (CAD),
headed by Major General John Hilldring. Within the Navy Department it was handled by the Occupied Areas Section, led first by
Captain Pence, and later, as the Military Government Section, by
Captain Lorenzo Sabin. By 1944, many lessons had been learned
from the surrender and occupation of Italy, planning for civil affairs
in Germany was well advanced, and the Army and Navy were devis-

ing a procurement and training program for military government in occupied Japan. They had agreed that 75 percent of the senior officers trained at the six civil affairs training schools should be Army and the remainder Navy. They understood that only a limited number of personnel could be trained and that mastery of the Japanese language would be considerably more difficult than German or Italian. Unhappy with the State Department's performance to date and in need of policy guidance to prepare military directives as well as military government officers, Hilldring and Pence forwarded a set of preliminary questions on February 18 for answer by IDACFE.[43]

Before drawing up their list, however, Hilldring and Pence had turned to the OSS, General William Donovan's new intelligence agency and another wartime organization dominated by professors and recent university graduates. In November, the Research and Analysis Branch (R&A) had prepared an "Agenda of Research Requirements for Civil Affairs Administration of Japan," with the intention of helping CAD "plan a rational allocation of research assignments" and provide documentation for guides, handbooks, and files for use by military government officers. R&A's questions were frank, direct, and important, revealing a mixture of great power calculations and international idealism. In summary, they were (paraphrasing mine):

1. What place did the United States want Japan to occupy in the American postwar world political system?
2. How weak did the United States wish Japan to be?
3. What was to be done with Japan's overseas territories and population? (This question was deleted after the Cairo declaration.)
4. What was to be Japan's industrial position? Did the United States "intend to maintain Japan as the industrial center of Asia; or to remove her heavy industries to other countries?" The decision would, so stated the OSS commentary, greatly influence the inclination of Japan's business groups to cooperate with the military administration of the victors.
5. At what standard of living did the United States wish the Japanese to support themselves?
6. Did the United States desire to preserve or to undermine the position of the emperor? This answer too would greatly determine "the degree of popular cooperation which can be achieved."
7. In what direction did the United States wish to influence Japan's political and social system? This, the authors con-

ceded, was a grave and unavoidable question, "even in a short occupation. The actions of civil affairs administrators in the selection and utilization of Japanese personnel, in enforcement or non-enforcement of existing limitations on free speech, assembly, and organized labor, in release of political prisoners, and in suppression of violence will strongly influence Japan's future political system."[44]

Hilldring and Pence obviously took note of this advice in framing their questions for the State Department. On the machinery of the occupation, they wanted to know which countries should participate in administering Japan, the composition of the national forces, what parts of Japan should be occupied, and whether there should be zones or unified control. On political issues, they asked about the treatment of the emperor as a person and the disposition of the imperial institution, the recall of diplomatic and consular officials, the "nullification of obnoxious laws," the dissolution of political parties, the establishment of freedom of worship, the best means of control at various levels of the Japanese government, and the designation of parties or agencies with whom the occupiers could deal "in the restoration of essential authority in Japan and its subsequent administration." The economic and financial matters which most concerned them were currency, taxes, pensions, relief and public works, unemployment insurance, labor unions, and reparations (later would come questions about banks, business combines and foreign trade, as well as education). The State Department had anticipated only some of these questions and had detailed comments ready at hand on only a few of them.[45]

R&A analysts churned out many studies in 1944–45 on the Japanese economy, political system, education, and media as back-up papers for civil affairs guides and handbooks. It drew up estimates of Japan's reformability and a survey of American aims and interests in postwar East Asia. One of its studies, written in July 1944 for internal discussion by the Staff Council of the Far East Division, once again warned that only a limited number of Americans and Allied personnel would be available for military government in Japan. The occupation authorities should therefore not assume responsibilities for functions they could not effectively manage and should make maximum utilization of Japanese administrative machinery and administrators. The Japanese collaborators would not be able "to retain popular confidence, and therefore any hope of sound evolution in a democratic direction" if they were "to be merely the tool" of the occupation or were "forced to be our agency in the exaction over a long period of economic terms which offer the Japanese no hope of economic improvement." The military occupation should be unobtrusive, with the troops kept off the city streets, the headquarters avoiding ostentation, and the Allied advisers barely noticeable. Policy decisions about reparations, foreign trade, and monetary matters should be carefully calculated, for "excessive economic demands or failure to keep inflation under control will jeopardize the position of any government chosen to collaborate with us."[46] As these remarks indicate, OSS/R&A officers were giving much thought to administrative concerns. Like the State Department, they postulated the existence of friendly Japanese and thought it best to work through them but more in the sense of controlling without seeming to control. Perhaps their most important contribution to the planning process was their willingness to view, more so than the State Department Japan hands, the occupation not only as a period of control for purposes of disarmament and demilitarization but also as a time of stringent reforms in the direction best suited to American interests.

The OWI, which had been created in June 1942 by President Roosevelt, would be drawn into the planning for Japan in 1944–45 through its propaganda functions of articulating war and peace aims and its involvement along with the OSS in psychological warfare. Its East Asia specialists had numerous insights into the operation of Asian societies and tended to be more reform minded than their counterparts in the State Department. They also acquired considerable experience as media experts and manipulators. Area III, or the Pacific Area, of the OWI's Overseas Branch was headed in 1943–44 by Owen Lattimore, a Central Asian specialist who was given to commenting broadly on all aspects of East Asian and Pacific affairs and was once editor of the IPR's journal, *Pacific Affairs*. His successor in 1944–45, George Taylor, and Taylor's deputy, John K. Fairbank, were both China specialists on loan from academia. Under them, however, at the Japan desk in Washington, and in field offices in San Francisco and Honolulu and operational units scattered on islands throughout the Pacific, there was a fair sprinkling of prewar Japan hands.[47]

Both the OWI rank and file and its head, former broadcaster and journalist Elmer Davis, became particularly interested in offering advice on postwar media control in Japan and the education and reeducation of the Japanese people—as they had previously for occupied Germany and Italy. In the view of Davis, reeducation was the central task of the occupation, a theme he reiterated from 1942 to 1945 and repeated in a letter to President Truman about Germany at war's end in July 1945.[48] Moreover, Pulitzer Prize-winning poet Archibald MacLeish, librarian of Congress, and one of the high level administrators of the OWI in its early days, became assistant secretary of state for public relations in early 1945. He would use his post as a spokesman for the policy of reorientation, by which he meant the transformation of the "national psychology," to use Hiss's phrase, of the defeated enemy peoples. Both the OWI and OSS were well ahead of the State Department's Japan planners in attaching importance and giving detailed consideration to the interrelationship between media control and educational reform.[49]

Another important point is that the policy of censorship of civil communications in occupied countries had already entered the planning process independently of the work of the Advisory Committee structure and was well advanced by the end of 1944. Both the old and revised military field manuals and General Strong's earliest drafts of surrender terms for Germany and Japan had references to censorship. This was conceived as a necessary, indeed an "imperative," activity, in essence an extension of the war effort, and was designed to assist counterintelligence and to further the aims of the occupation. The Office of Censorship and the State Department had authorized the War and Navy departments to proceed in this work in 1943. A separate unit was set up in the Division of Intelligence, Army Service Forces, of the War Department—the Special Overseas Planning Group—and it produced a preliminary plan by December 1944 for the training of civil censorship officers detailed to Japan. At about the same time, the JCS approved a directive to the Pacific theater commanders, including Nimitz and MacArthur, giving them sole administrative responsibility for civil censorship in their areas and ordering them to proceed with planning. In Japan's case, CAD anticipated that some type of control of civil communications "would be required for a considerable time after its defeat." It was first intended that the mails, telephonic and telegraphic facilities, travelers documents, and films and photographs would be subject to control. When the occupation began, newspapers, journals, books, and radio broadcasts were also added to the list.[50]

Despite its critics, the State Department was nevertheless to remain at the center of policy formulation for postwar Japan. Under Blakeslee's direction, IDACFE quickly prepared a large number of papers in early 1944 in answer to the questions from the military and naval planners. An additional set followed in the summer and fall in response to further questions. These papers were general and specific in nature and ranged over many topics: American postwar objectives in Japan, the duration and extent of the occupation, the national composition of forces to occupy Japan, the emperor and imperial institution, the political system and political parties, obnoxious laws, religion, war criminals, education, media of information, the economy, territories and mandates, diplomatic and consular officers, the abolition of militarism and encouragement of democratic processes, workers' organizations, and the underlying principles of the terms of surrender. Many of them were written within a few weeks or months of similar papers for Germany. All were subject to the scrutiny and review of the PWC. The revised papers, bearing PWC numbers, became State Department policy in December 1944 and were at long last sent to the War and Navy departments for comment and guidance in January 1945.[51]

Few of these PWC papers, however, touched on economic matters, for by that time there was a serious split between IDACFE's core of Japan hands and its economists, who had proceeded to form a separate subcommittee. The differences would continue in 1945 and have serious repercussions on occupation policies—and on careers. As a result, the general and political sections of the final policy statement and military directive would owe much to the thinking of the original band of Japan hands, but the economic and financial sections would be shaped by others in the State Department and elsewhere in the government.

The ascendance of Grew and Dooman in the planning for Japan and in State Department politics in 1944 help to explain the tensions. They too worked, but with more contacts and influence than Blakeslee, to retain control of foreign policy within the Department of State and to keep the cases of Germany and Japan separate in the minds of high decision makers. Both would become targets of intense criticism from China hands and from liberal journalists, beginning in the summer of 1944 and intensifying in the spring and summer of 1945. This was largely because of their supposed soft peace positions, which were likened to their appeasement stances before Pearl Harbor, and their generally conservative outlook.[52]

Grew and Dooman had formed a cordial and mutually respectful working relationship in Tokyo, 1937–42, Grew seemingly the perfect ambassador because of his long international experience as a career diplomat and Dooman the model counselor because of his fluency in written and spoken Japanese and his extensive knowledge of Japan's history and culture. Both men believed they could interpret Japanese character and psychology better than anyone else in the American government. Grew, of course, was not in the technical sense a Japan expert, for he had no claim to Japanese language competence and had only a superficial understanding of Ja-

pan's past. His ten years there had been spent largely with the rich
and powerful, and he relied heavily on Dooman for advice to the
department. Dooman's knowledge of Japan, while comprehensive if
not profound, similarly reflected a much more intimate acquaintance with elite culture and upper class life, including big business,
than of the grassroots and popular movements.

Both men were handicapped by alleged Japanophilism. Though
Grew in fact had much experience in several diplomatic posts and as
a high State Department bureaucrat, Dooman had spent almost all
of his career either in Japan and its territories or working on the
Japan desk of the Division of Far Eastern Affairs. The one exception
was a short term of service as secretary of embassy in London in the
early 1930s. As his widow later recalled, Dooman once ruefully
summed up the dilemma faced by all country and area experts: "The
trouble is that they sent people out to those countries to become
specialists and after they had been there long enough to be sufficiently knowledgeable of the country they said that you were too
sympathetic to that country." This indeed was the view of Hornbeck,
who believed that Dooman had forgotten that his chief purpose was
to serve the interests of the United States. There was some measure
of truth in the charge that Dooman was out of touch with recent
American life and problems; certainly he was very much out of tune
with what the New Deal had been doing in domestic and foreign
policy. His was the American conservative tradition, not its reformist impulses. He and Grew wished to restore postwar Japan as
quickly as possible as a friend of the United States and other Western capitalist nations, not only because they had a special feeling for
the country and respect, even affection, for its moderate leaders but
equally because of their dislike of Soviet communism, a deep-seated
prewar antipathy. Under attack as somehow unpatriotic or un-
American, Dooman would return the slings and arrows in vicious retribution several years later during the early days of McCarthyism.[53]

Handicapped or not, Grew and Dooman, by their maneuvering
and political skill, were instrumental in gaining acceptance for
many of IDACFE's recommendations by the PWC and Secretary
Hull in November of 1944 (and by Stettinius and his Staff Committee in January 1945). Japan planners displayed at the same time
some willingness to compromise as the planning advanced. They
continued to share a similar analysis of recent Japanese history and
to remain in close agreement, but the treatment they envisaged for
Japan became less mild and permissive. In May, Blakeslee reaffirmed American postwar objectives in Japan as demilitarization
during a period of stern military government, democratization dur-

ing a second period of "close surveillance" and "progressive" relaxation of controls, and a final period of Japan's reintegration into the world economy and the peaceful international community. Blakeslee had begun to speak more boldly about democratization. To win PWC approval, he had been forced to revise his original proposals of March several times and put more emphasis on the steps Japan would be expected to take in order to become peaceful and democratic. His earlier phraseology on economic aims had also been rejected. Rather than permit Japan "to share in the development of a world economy on a non-discriminatory basis, looking toward a progressively higher standard of living," the PWC preferred to say that Japan might "begin to share in the world economy on a reasonable basis."[54]

Blakeslee had also revised his paper to accord with another one drafted by Borton on "Japan: Abolition of Militarism and Strengthening of Democratic Processes," an important document for its underlying attitudes and methodology and one which might never have been written had not Assistant Secretary of State Adolf Berle persisted in asking probing questions and sent the first lot of IDACFE proposals back to the drawing board. What direct measures, he wanted to know, might be taken to eliminate militarism and foster a democratic transformation? In answer, Borton had listed freedom of the press, radio, and motion pictures and also freedom of discussion, but with the qualification that security not be endangered. He added liberalization of education and explanations through the media "of the meaning of personal liberties in a democracy." Films and dramas glorifying the military should be banned.[55]

This temporarily satisfied the PWC, and separate papers followed that summer, discussing for the first time in detail educational reforms and media controls. Courses, curricula, and textbooks were to be abolished or revised to root out ultranationalism, and the practice of venerating the emperor's portrait ended. There was no demand for removal of the portrait, recision of the Imperial Rescript, or decentralization of authority. Emphasis was given to broadening opportunities for all classes, and especially for women, and the training of teaching personnel with a new viewpoint. The use of school films and radio was urged to give students "a world outlook." The envisioned media control and censorship, though hinting at precensorship, seemed too mild to the PWC, and the recommendations were revised to ensure extensive indoctrination. Still, the basic attitude of the Japan planners was to be respectful of what the Japanese had accomplished and reluctant for the United States to assume responsibility for extensive structural changes.[56]

It proved relatively easy for IDACFE and PWC to arrive at recommendations for permanent disarmament: dissolution of the army
and navy ministries; dismantling of military and naval installations
not already destroyed by air attacks or combat operations; bans
against ultranationalist societies; periodic inspection to prevent
formation of an army, navy, and air force; policing from a ring of
bases; and economic controls to block the resurgence of an arma-
ment industry. No one had yet thought of insisting on a constitutional amendment to prevent rearmament or the use of military
force. Militarists should be removed from the scene, whether they
were political leaders or army and navy officers. Those guilty of
crimes should be dealt with by an international war crimes commission. This was about as close as IDACFE came to advocating purges
and public trials. On the more complicated problem of the causes of
militarism, they held to their conviction that the ultimate solution
was to give the Japanese a sense of economic security.

All of the Japan hands thought that the occupation should be
short in time and small in scale. On the mainly technical topics of
instituting and administering military government, they agreed
that the occupation forces should be stationed in several strategic
areas of the home islands, with the United States assuming the
major but not sole responsibility and naming the supreme commander. Although the forces would represent several countries, Japan
should be administered as one zone. The policy and law making organs of the Japanese government would have to be suspended, but
otherwise military government should make maximum utilization
of existing local and central administrative machinery. Retention of
Japan's centralized system would both economize on costs and take
advantage of the high degree of homogeneity and compactness of
Japan.[57] To Dooman, Japan was "a communalism, that is a graduated society, in which the top of the social structure formulated
purposes and objectives and the people down below conformed."[58]

The emperor remained a controversial topic in the State Department and with the American public, but the Japan planners had
little difficulty in reaching a consensus among themselves. Not only
should the present emperor be retained to sign the terms of surrender but also to ensure the cooperation of Japan's civil service with
the Allied occupiers. He should be "placed in protective custody,"
and then removed from Tokyo to a place easy to guard. There he
would be allowed access to his personal advisers and treated courte-
ously. Dooman, speaking for most of them, believed that allegiance
to the emperor kept the Japanese together as a social unit, for he
was "a living manifestation of the racial continuity of the Japanese

people." Without the throne the whole structure might fall apart, and the Communists, who were well organized, might even take over. On the assumption that the emperor would continue, or at least that the monarchy would in some form, the planners again pressed for political reforms aimed at strengthening the powers of the elected representatives in the Diet, including the right to initiate constitutional amendments, and to end the access of army and navy ministers to the throne should there be a future military establishment.[59]

The preferred economic solutions, as articulated in April and May by Fearey and Abbot Low Moffat, a newcomer to IDACFE from the Division of Liberated Areas, were, not surprisingly, very much in the same line of thought, for the drafters were really surrogates for Grew and Dooman. Since they attributed Japan's aggression to its domestic economic problems (overpopulation, limited land, few natural resources), the only long-range solution that made sense was to allow Japan equal opportunity to revive its economic life through continued industrialization and international trade. Moreover, Japan's economic rehabilitation would be in the best interests of the American economy. Therefore, leave Japan, they concluded, with sufficient industries and shipping tonnage to sustain its economic life and to pay reparations. Let the reparations be mild and come principally from the transfer of overseas properties. In the immediate period of military occupation, set up a program of relief in order to minimize disease and unrest.[60]

On workers' organizations, a topic which IDACFE discussed when the military planners brought it to their attention and assigned to a young man in the Division of Labor Relations, Dooman and others were willing for occupation authorities to permit, if not to encourage, the formation of labor unions and collective bargaining. On the *zaibatsu,* neither Dooman nor Ballantine were overly disturbed by the trend toward monopoly capitalism in Japan. As Ballantine remarked at one of the meetings, the concentration of economic power in the hands of a few was not unique to Japan or characteristic only of a feudal economy. IDACFE in 1944 did not recommend the breakup of the great financial and industrial houses, or indeed any other extensive interference in Japan's economy. "It is believed," concluded one of the drafts, "that, except as they may be specifically directed, the occupation authorities should not attempt long-range reform or reorganization of Japanese internal economy."[61]

This, then, was the modest reform program advocated by the Japan planners in IDACFE. Caught up in the problem of what was feasible, they were more ready to eliminate certain objectionable

and reactionary features of Japanese life, that is to provide a
healthier atmosphere for democratic growth, than to push for positive and direct measures to guide reform in Japan. Dooman was
perhaps the most skeptical of the ability or even of the right of
military government authorities to restructure by fiat Japan's political and economic life. Imposed reforms, he declared, could not be
far-reaching. If reforms were to be successful and long lasting, they
must have the support of key elements in Japanese society. At
Dooman's insistence, for example, the introduction to the final paper
on educational reform was revised by Borton to read:

> Modifications in the educational system imposed on the Jap-
> anese by military government can do little more than create
> conditions favorable to a change in the Japanese mental atti-
> tude towards religious, political and social problems; . . . there-
> fore military government should await the coming forward in
> sufficient numbers of cooperative Japanese, themselves propo-
> nents of liberal ideas upon whom can be placed the responsibil-
> ity for carrying to completion those fundamental educational
> reforms necessary for the elimination of ultra-nationalism and
> a militaristic spirit.

These moderate, friendly, or collaborationist Japanese, as Borton had
written a few months earlier, were expected to come from Christian
leaders, international businessmen, educators, political and social
reformers, and "the group of statesmen of the so-called Anglo-
American school who held political offices in the 1920s and who
have been conspicuous advisers of the Emperor." As long as the
Japanese were not military aggressors, ran this advice, the United
States should be prepared to get along with them.[62]

To others in the government, this amounted to a Sunday school
approach. Some critics were simply more interested in vengeance
and punishment. Others, more committed to reform, not only wished
to go further in removals by fiat but had greater faith in the power
of imposed innovations to produce behavioral and social change.
Within the State Department, most of the opposition came from the
economic divisions. The program outlined by Fearey and Moffat ran
into such a storm of protest that the PWC had not cleared any of the
economic recommendations when Hull resigned.

Only a few of the economists, like Remer, had any claim to
specialized knowledge of East Asian economies, but they believed in
the universal validity of their discipline and applicability of their
theories and methodologies. Many were antimonopolists and wished
to lower barriers everywhere to the free flow of goods and capital.

They insisted that Japan's economic mobilization for total war was led, financed, and manipulated by the great business combines. Internally, the *zaibatsu* structure was harmful to the working classes. The economists, too, spoke of Japan's ultimate reintegration into peaceful international economic relations, but first, and for some time, there must be a period of thorough and complete destruction of Japan's war potential (including civilian aviation) and of stringent reforms. It was not the responsibility of military government to rehabilitate Japan's industry, revive its economic life, or stimulate production. Certainly, the Japanese should not be promised a better standard of living than their neighbors. The economists wanted to hand Japan a substantial reparations bill, require it to do more to improve the lives of the working and farming populations, and force it to dissolve the combines.[63]

To resolve the conflict, Remer attempted to circumvent IDACFE by setting up a subcommittee to draft and consider economic papers separately before submission to the PWC. In the midst of this quarrel, during the summer of 1944, the Executive Committee on Economic Foreign Policy (ECEFP), a citadel of liberal antitrust beliefs, finished reviewing papers on short-term and long-range policies for Germany. When it asked to see comparable papers for Japan, the long-range work was assigned in September not to IDACFE but to Remer's division, FMA. The drafting was turned over to Oliver Lockhart, for many years a financial adviser to Chiang Kai-shek (1929–41) and assistant director of China's salt administration. "The attempt should be made," he declared, "to eliminate the forms of industrial and commercial organization within Japan which have been a factor in Japanese aggression and might again support a threat to peace and security." Japan's banking institutions should lend "more generously to small enterprise," new legislation should "encourage an effective labor movement," and, in general, "control should strive to open the door of economic opportunity to all classes."[64]

In the Commodities Division, Robert Terrill, head of the Business Practices Branch, and his colleague, Walter Rudolph, both antimonopolists, took an interest in the debate. They were completely convinced that Japan's monopolies were not only imperialistic and antidemocratic but also inefficient. The giant combines had distorted Japan's internal economic development. They were, therefore, incompatible "with a peaceful Japan which affords economic opportunity to all classes." In their view, "the activities of the Japanese monopolies have been similar to those of the German firms such as the I. G. Farbenindustrie. It is presumed that the U. S. policy toward them should be guided by the policy relating to the German monopolies in so far as the issues are parallel." Aware of the need to collect more factual and technical information for their policy papers and unwilling to rely on Fearey's research talents, the Commodities Division turned to the OSS for help. Late in 1944, Eleanor Hadley was transferred from R&A to Terrill's branch to undertake a study of Japan's international cartels and big business combines. The recent recipient of a master's degree in economics at Radcliffe, Hadley had spent a year and a half in Japan just before the war as a special graduate student at Tokyo Imperial University and had participated in the third United States–Japan student conference. A convinced antimonopolist, she believed along with her superiors that Japan's combines were "one of the architects of Japan's irresponsible government."[65]

The IDACFE papers on Japan's economy were either shelved or set aside. The new secretary of state, Stettinius, and his undersecretary, Joseph Grew, were forced to send the State Department's papers on Japan to the War and Navy departments in January 1945 without guidance on economic and financial matters. The impasse would continue well into 1945. Stettinius, himself a businessman and once head of the United States Steel Corporation, decided in the meantime to create the new position of assistant secretary of state for economic affairs and chose another big businessman and former assistant secretary of commerce, William Clayton, for the post. Edward Mason, a Harvard economist with strong antitrust convictions and head of the Monopoly Subcommittee of the ECEFP, was lured from his high post in the OSS to Clayton's office to advise on foreign economic policy, including the treatment of Germany and Japan, and to coordinate the work of the economic offices and divisions. Another important appointment in the State Department's reorganization of December and January, 1944–45, was Archibald MacLeish to the position of assistant secretary of public relations. Dean Acheson continued as assistant secretary of state but was shifted from economic policies to congressional liaison. Mason, MacLeish, and Acheson all had decided opinions about Japan, many of them in opposition to Grew. While these changes were taking place, Dooman began pressing IDACFE to turn to the drafting of the actual surrender terms for Japan. General Strong, senior member of the Joint Post War Committee, JCS, impatient to wait for the State Department's lead, had already succeeded in producing drafts of two versions of surrender terms.[66] It was obviously time to integrate political, economic, and military thinking.

Stage Three, Final Decisions, January–September 1945

In early 1945, planning accelerated for the occupation of Japan. Once the war with Germany ended, full weight would be given to defeating Japan, and military government would be instituted, either in the wake of combat or following unconditional surrender. In recognition of the great need for more extensive and efficient collaboration among the State, War, and Navy departments, at all levels from research to high policy, the three secretaries created SWNCC as the highest authority to formulate comprehensive policy statements for the president's approval and to provide guidance to the JCS in preparing surrender terms and military directives. To serve on the committee, they next selected Assistant Secretaries James Dunn (State), John J. McCloy (War), and Artemus Gates (Navy).[67]

One of SWNCC's first acts was to create the Subcommittee on the Far East (SFE), as it came to be called. Like the parent committee, it was interdepartmental, and its job was to review recommendations and generate position papers for Japan and Korea. Dooman was appointed to the pivotal position of chairman, and his senior colleagues were familiar names from the earlier planning days, General Strong and Admiral Harold Train. At the working level of SFE were Blakeslee and Borton, together with their counterparts from the planning staffs of the War and Navy departments. In the State Department, Undersecretary Grew was frequently also acting secretary, covering for Stettinius during his frequent trips away on business related to the launching of the United Nations. Japan hands, or the "Japan crowd," as the media dubbed them, were in a strategic position to define American responsibilities in East Asia.[68]

At SWNCC's request, Dooman and SFE quickly drew up a master list in February-March of "politico-military problems" (the SWNCC 16 series) in the order of their priority. At the top of the list for military government in Japan were disarmament, demobilization, and use of existing governmental machinery and personnel, followed by the treatment of the emperor, war criminals, administration of justice, and ending with social, economic, and financial questions.[69] Dooman's strategy was to gain SWNCC acceptance of the recommendations contained in the State Department's PWC papers. He had a large hand in deciding the agenda of topics, in formulating the precise charge to the drafting officers, and in determining which branch of the State Department would do the work. The results were mixed. In the end, the final drafts of the Potsdam declaration, the presidential policy statement, and the military directive were revised in the War Department under the close supervision of McCloy.

In the spring of 1945, when SFE had assigned only a handful of topics, the War Department once again took the lead in planning, as it had in February 1944. On April 6, General Hilldring sent an urgent plea to the State Department asking it for a "short policy statement" on Japan, so that CAD could move ahead in drafting general orders and a military government directive. The model Hilldring had in mind was the short statement for Germany which Roosevelt had approved in March to guide the final version of JCS 1067—General Eisenhower's directive for the American zone of occupied Germany.[70]

A few days later, the State Department supplied SFE with a "Summary of United States Initial Post-Defeat Policy Relating to Japan." Labeled "informal and without comment," and written in two parts, political and economic, it was the most important of the general policy documents up to that time. With a few changes by the military and naval representatives in SFE, the summary became SWNCC 150 in early June ("Political-Military Problems in the Far East: United States Initial Post-Defeat Policy Relating to Japan"). The first part, political, had no surprises. It drew heavily from the PWC papers in projecting three periods in the postwar treatment of Japan and repeating the general objectives of a limited, direct, and predominantly American occupation. The approved text in June added only two new emphases: 1) "permanent disarmament" of Japan; and 2) disbarment, in other words purge, of "flagrant exponents of militant nationalism and aggression" from public office and responsible positions in "public or private enterprise."[71]

Part two, economic, however, was much more interventionist and reform minded, and it owed very little to the 1944 IDACFE deliberations under Blakeslee. Added at the last minute, the economic section was chiefly the work of a New Deal economist named Edwin Martin, who was personally recruited from the OSS on part-time loan by his friend Edward Mason to work on Far Eastern economic affairs out of Clayton's office. Martin, whose prewar experience had been in the Office of Production Management, had little time to complete his assignment and no special knowledge of Japan or East Asia beyond what he had learned in OSS work. But he consulted broadly and read through all of the previous economic planning papers.[72]

Under an injunction to keep long-range objectives in mind (the as yet unapproved Lockhart paper, in other words), Martin proceeded to list as best he could the primary objectives of immediate post-surrender policy: meeting the needs of the occupation forces, preventing starvation and disorder, completing the economic disarmament of Japan, and arranging for reparations, restitution, and relief to the United Nations and liberated areas. To accomplish this would require extensive military government controls over Japanese currency, production, and distribution. Assistance, however, in the "restoration of the domestic economy," should be only "to the extent required to meet the needs of the occupation forces, of relief of liberated areas, and to provide a minimum level of domestic consumption." He advised that "no steps" be taken "which would provide a standard of living to the Japanese out of line with that of neighboring peoples" (a paraphrase from documents for Germany). Martin supported the encouragement of "voluntary associations, such as agricultural and industrial cooperatives and trade unions." His prescription for economic disarmament was detailed, and he asked for the establishment of a special commission empowered to make decisions as to which Japanese facilities should be destroyed, dismantled, or converted to civilian production. The Japanese should not be permitted to retain stockpiles of strategic items, and their research and engineering activities should be supervised. Martin favored substantial reparations but nevertheless believed, as did the Japan hands, that payments should "not be of such character or of such magnitude as to impair the ability of the Japanese economy to meet the needs of the occupation forces and minimum needs" or "to make the recipients thereafter unduly dependent on the Japanese economy."[73]

This first effort by Martin was severely criticized by IDACFE and SFE. General Strong, who tended to side with Dooman, called it "an utterly impracticable academic approach," particularly the part on trade unions, which he charged "showed an utter lack of knowledge of the Japanese Government and Japanese psychology." Dooman appointed a subcommittee to make revisions, after which he and Martin would correlate the economic and political sections. Martin again did most of the work and consulted even more broadly, talking to the State Department's economic officers, IDACFE and SFE personnel, and his friends in the OSS and FEA—and also reading the documents for Germany. The economic section of SWNCC 150 in June was subsequently much more succinct and better organized, but it was not much different in its main thrust. Extensive controls over Japan's economy were still projected for purposes of "continued economic disarmament" and provisions for reparations and restitution. It contained one important clarification. Somehow, Martin had obtained Dooman's acquiescence to the passage: "Military government shall encourage the development of democratic organizations in labor, industry, and agriculture, and shall favor a wider distribution of ownership, management and control of the Japanese economic system." Here was the entering wedge for the ultimate addition of *zaibatsu* dissolution, deconcentration of economic power, and the economic purge to the final documents. The passage also called for the promotion (not simply the allowance) of trade union activity and collective bargaining, but it was only vaguely addressed to the issue of land reform, a subject Fearey had already discussed in a preliminary fashion only to be squelched by Dooman and Japan desk officers in the Department of State.[74]

Although President Roosevelt's death on April 12 had undercut much of the political power of Treasury Secretary Morgenthau and his harsh economic views for Germany (and by extension for Japan), nevertheless the momentum was gathering for a more severe treatment of defeated Japan and a more extensive recasting of its social, political, and economic institutions than Grew, Dooman, and the older Japan hands thought wise. As the first of the SWNCC-SFE papers on various topics began to appear, so did these new emphases.

One of the most important of these was a draft policy paper on reform of the Japanese educational system, which was completed by Gordon Bowles on July 30. Born in Japan of Quaker missionary parents, Bowles had been with the Board of Economic Warfare and the FEA before joining the State Department's Division of Cultural Communications in October 1944. Trained as an anthropologist at Harvard, he had taught English at Japan's most prestigious higher school in the mid-1920s. The approach to reform which he expressed in the paper was very much in line with what would actually happen at the working level of SCAP in the early occupation period: a set of required negative changes (removals by fiat) to eradicate the bad features of the existing system and create healthier conditions for reform along liberal lines, followed by a set of positive measures (imposed reforms) which military government might properly initiate and supervise while waiting for (or going out and finding) friendly Japanese to take over the work and make the changes permanent. If not a root-and-branch call for revolution, it went beyond Borton's 1944 formula for eradicating militarism and strengthening democratic trends. New in the Bowles program of negative changes was the removal (again the word "purge" was not used) of objectionable teaching personnel and school administrators. His positive reforms included decentralization of government controls and expansion of the number of secondary and higher schools and of private universities.[75]

Moreover, on July 19, shortly before Bowles finished his paper, Artemus Gates, the Navy's representative on SWNCC, had urged the formulation of a comprehensive (his word was positive) program for the reorientation of the Japanese people. This was an exceedingly important document. It reflected not only the advice of MacLeish and Davis on the central task of reeducating defeated enemies but also the strategic and military concerns of Secretary of the Navy Forrestal, at the onset of the cold war, about the expanding power of the Soviet Union and the spread of its ideology. There were two menaces, militarism and communism. In short, changes in the formal schooling of the Japanese would be inadequate; the psychology or mentality of the entire population must be reformed along democratic lines, using all resources, including the media, at the command of the occupiers. The United States should take no chances about keeping Japan within its postwar global democratic capitalist system.[76]

Still another example of the new directions was the work for SWNCC-SFE on labor policy. Philip Sullivan, a newcomer in the State Department's Division of International Labor, Social, and Health Affairs, was given the task of reviewing and revising the PWC paper on workers' organi-.ations. He brought to the task much knowledge of East Asia, mainly China, having studied with Remer in the economics department at the University of Michigan and taught for many years at St. John's University in Shanghai. Military government, he recommended, should not only authorize but also encourage "the free organization of democratically managed trade unions" and collective bargaining. It should "prohibit strikes only in those industries whose uninterrupted operation is considered by them to be essential to their program." Sullivan also suggested that a labor section be set up within military government headquarters. While these ideas entered the mainstream of planning, Mason solicited the assistance of FEA's research staff in back-up papers.[77]

With the draft general policy statement in hand, SWNCC 150, the military and naval planners set about preparing a basic directive on military government. They found numerous ambiguities and inconsistencies in the document, and their work proceeded piecemeal over the summer as different working groups put together the three sections of the directive—general and political, economic, and financial. Their drafts were not integrated until August when SWNCC was making a final review of the general policy statement in the aftermath of the Potsdam conference and declaration.[78]

It is to that document we must turn, for among the purposes of the framers was that of restoring a moderate postwar program for occupied Japan—and of somehow conditionalizing unconditional surrender in order to induce a quick end to the war short of Russian entry and a costly invasion of the home islands.[79] The idea of making a public statement to the Japanese, clarifying the meaning of unconditional surrender, went back to IDACFE deliberations in the late summer of 1944; a similar argument about the wisdom of such a policy had of course been raging among the planners for Germany. The idea was picked up again early in 1945 by military and civilian officials and by the OWI, but it was Grew who took the first steps after victory in Europe and the devastating fire bomb raids over Tokyo in late May in trying to persuade the new president to make a statement to the Japanese. He had little difficulty in enlisting the support of Stimson and McCloy. All three men knew of the Manhattan Project (Committee of Three, May 8, 1945), and presumably were reading MAGIC intercepts and OSS reports.[80]

As so often in the past, Grew relied upon Dooman to draft the position papers for Truman and a proposed public statement. Both believed that the Japanese should be reassured on two points: retention of the emperor and a viable economic future. Dooman, however, perhaps because of the many public attacks on himself and Grew as soft on Japan, chose not to make an explicit pledge to save the emperor in the version which went to Truman. Instead, he quoted a radio address of Chiang Kai-shek made back on January 1, 1944, when the Chinese leader had remarked that the question of Japan's "form of government," once militarism had been destroyed, "can better be left to the awakened and repentant Japanese people to decide for themselves." As reinforcement, Dooman added a reference to the Atlantic Charter, which he apparently thought would subtly communicate the intended meaning to the Japanese, "nations shall be allowed to choose their own form of government." On the economy, he was stern, saying that it would "be demilitarized and those industries established to serve the manufacture of the implements of war will be destroyed. Economic control will be laid down to insure that there will be no rebuilding of war industries." Dooman changed this in early June to give wider assurances: "We would provide opportunity for the eventual participation of Japan in a world economic system on a reasonable basis."[81]

The famous proposed passage on the retention of the emperor which subsequently caused so much controversy and was deleted at Potsdam after Truman and his new secretary of state, James Byrnes, had consulted with the JCS, the British, and by cable with former Secretary Hull, was first drafted not by Dooman and the State Department but by military planners in the War Department, working directly under Assistant Secretary McCloy. Colonels Charles Bonesteel and James McCormack of the Strategy and Policy Group, Operations Division (OPD), put together a shorter form of the declaration in late June, one which was much closer than Dooman's to the final format. Japan's political system, they wrote, "may include a constitutional monarchy under the present dynasty if it be shown to the complete satisfaction of the world that such a government shall never again aspire to aggression." McCloy and Stimson, who subscribed to the Dooman-Blakeslee-Borton view that responsible Japanese liberals could be counted on to take over the government, made a few modifications in the text before sending it to Truman on July 2 but did not alter this passage. Dooman (in Grew's name) changed it on July 3, for delivery to Secretary Byrnes, to read, "This may include a constitutional monarchy under the present dynasty if completely satisfactory evidence convinces the peace loving nations of the genuine determination of such a government to follow policies which will render impossible the development of aggressive militarism in Japan."[82]

Within the State Department, as Byrnes was departing for Potsdam, Assistant Secretaries Acheson and MacLeish spoke against giving the Japanese any promise, veiled or explicit, to retain the monarchy when Grew read his version at a Staff Committee meeting, July 7. Pasvolsky wondered (as did General MacArthur a little later) how many troops would be necessary to occupy Japan if the victors deposed the emperor. Why, asked Assistant Secretary Dunn (who was also chairman of SWNCC), reinforced by the department's legal counselor, Green Hackworth, should not the statement be restricted to demanding an end to military control and permitting the Japanese to form a peaceful government of their own choosing. Hackworth was asked to write out "this suggested formula," and Dunn was requested to keep the Staff Committee's reservations in mind while at Potsdam.[83]

The Joint Strategic Survey Committee, JCS, a few days later debated sending a cable to the JCS at Potsdam recommending a substitution for the explicit reference to the emperor: "Subject to suitable guarantees against further acts of aggression, the Japanese people will be free to choose their own form of government." OPD, authors of the disputed phrase, objected, arguing that the proclamation should "state unequivocally what we intend to do with regard to the Emperor." They held out for: "Subject to suitable guarantees against future acts of aggression, the Japanese people will be free to choose whether they shall retain their Emperor as a constitutional monarch." The passage should be phrased in this way, explained Major General Harold A. Craig, acting assistant chief of staff, OPD, in a cable, July 14, to his superior at Potsdam, Lieutenant General John E. Hull, "to allay the fears both of the 'fanatical adherents' and the 'radical element'" in Japan. The American military, Craig declared, did not particularly fear Hirohito, for he was only "the titular head" of the Japanese.

> He is primarily a symbol and if we take over completely the actual government his influence would seem to be well under our thumb. Of course the final decision with regard to Hirohito is largely a political one in which full regard must be had of American public opinion which has been indoctrinated for the past few years with the idea that he should be eliminated. However, as I have said, militarily we do not fear him particularly.[84]

The political factors did prevail at Potsdam. The final text, as approved by Truman, Byrnes, Stimson, and the JCS, after consultation with the British, stated that occupation forces would be withdrawn when "there had been established in accordance with the freely expressed will of the Japanese people a peacefully inclined and responsible government." However, the preponderance of advice to Truman from the State, War, and Navy departments, and the JCS, was to leave Hirohito on the throne—to use him for the surrender of the military and the initial phase of the occupation, to treat him as a symbol, and to let the Japanese decide on the ultimate disposition of the monarchy. With all of the psychological warfare that surrounded the declaration, there was reason to believe that the Japanese leaders understood the underlying message.[85]

Otherwise, the Potsdam declaration informed the Japanese that, while there would be no enslavement or destruction of the nation, there would be a period of occupation and military government, punishment of war criminals, loss of empire, elimination of militarism, economic disarmament, removal of obstacles to democratic tendencies, and the establishment of fundamental human rights. Japan also would "retain such industries as will sustain her economy and permit exaction of just reparations, but not those which would enable her to rearm for war." This paragraph concluded in a manner satisfactory to Grew and Stimson and to the Japan hands. "To this end, access to, as distinguished from control of, raw materials shall be permitted. Eventual Japanese participation in world trade relations shall be permitted."[86]

To Dooman at Potsdam and to Blakeslee and Borton back in Washington, the declaration seemed to hold out the prospect not only of a more limited and indirect occupation but to open the door to a contractual interpretation of the surrender. The State Department's legal office disagreed, as did President Truman. Potsdam was not a final statement on all policies. Others in the reform camp of the State Department also noted the seemingly more moderate direction and worried that plans for the transformation of Japan might have to be watered down, since all high policy documents would have to conform to the language and tone of the declaration.[87]

The issuance of the Potsdam declaration, followed in swift order by the atomic bombings of Hiroshima and Nagasaki, Russia's entry into the war, and Japan's unexpected surrender, caught the planners off guard. Only a few of their policy and backup papers were in the final, polished versions. McCloy, immediately upon returning from Potsdam, sat down with the War Department's planners and called in former State Department economist Herbert Feis, then special consultant to the Secretary of War, to review the general policy statement and military directive. He and General Hilldring had all along been unhappy with SWNCC 150, and between August 14 (Japan's surrender) and August 22, it was rewritten at McCloy's direction. The document which emerged, SWNCC 150/3, was a compromise between the views of the Japan hands and their adversaries.[88]

There would still be a military occupation to effect the surrender terms and to ensure the attainment of the overall objectives. However, since the Japanese had surrendered with their government intact, the emperor was clearly cooperative, and a new cabinet was in the making, the planners made provision for an indirect occupation in which the character of military government would be supervisory.

> The authority of the Emperor and the Japanese Government will be subject to the Supreme Commander who will possess all powers necessary to effectuate the surrender terms and to carry out the United States policies during the period of his responsibility. . . . the Supreme Commander will exercise his authority through Japanese governmental machinery and

agencies, including the Emperor, to the extent that this satisfactorily furthers United States objectives.

To reconcile the arguments about the emperor, the new draft hedged
in artful circumspection:

> This policy, moreover, does not commit the Supreme Comman-
> der to support the Emperor or any other Japanese governmen-
> tal authority in opposition to evolutionary changes looking to-
> ward the attainment of United States objectives. The policy is
> to use the existing form of Government in Japan, not to support
> it. Changes in the form of Government initiated by the Jap-
> anese people or government in the direction of modifying its
> feudal and authoritarian tendencies are to be permitted and
> favored, even at the risk of civil unrest, so long as the unrest is
> not directed at the occupation authorities and does not imperil
> their objectives.

The JCS was worried that the Japanese might misunderstand or
deliberately distort this phraseology and use it as an excuse for
"mob violence." Accordingly, SWNCC deleted the phrase, "even at
the risk of civil unrest," and added a new sentence: "In the event
that the effectuation of such changes involves the use of force by the
Japanese people or government against persons opposed, the Supreme Commander should intervene only where necessary to ensure
the security of his forces and the attainment of all other objectives of
the occupation."[89]
An important new passage was inserted in SWNCC 150/3 explaining the international character of the occupation. It would be "in
behalf of the principal allied powers at war with Japan acting in the
interests of the United Nations." Therefore, "participation of the
forces of other nations that have taken a leading part in the war
will be welcomed and expected." All forces, however, would "be
under the command of a Supreme Commander designated by the
United States." In cases of differences of opinion among the allied
powers on policies, "the authority of the United States will be
decisive."[90]
The economic passages, though following the Martin formula for
extensive economic demilitarization and promotion of democratic
forces, were thoroughly revised. Policies favoring "a wide distribution of income and of the ownership of the means of production and
trade," were joined to those "deemed likely to strengthen the peaceful disposition of the Japanese people," and both were clarified to
include a purge "in the economic field" and "a program for the disso-

lution of the large industrial and banking combinations which have exercised control of a great part of Japan's trade and industry."[91] In resuming their peacetime economic activity, the Japanese were expected "to undertake physical reconstruction" and "deeply to reform the nature and direction of their economic activities and institutions." The Japanese themselves (as the Germans), and not military government, would be responsible for providing the necessary goods, services, and programs to avoid disease and unrest and "acute economic distress" and also for facilitating "the restoration of Japanese economy so that the reasonable peaceful requirements of the population can be satisfied," subject to the approval and review of SCAP. There would be eventual resumption of normal international trade relations, but in the interim the Japanese must make reparations payments and expect controls over imports and exports and foreign exchange. Equality of opportunity for foreign enterprise within Japan was stipulated. And finally, imperial household property was not to be "exempted from any action necessary to carry out the objectives of the occupation."[92]

Apparently, this version of the draft policy statement was immediately hand carried to MacArthur, along with a copy of the draft military directive. Almost simultaneously, the three parts of this directive had been hastily assembled in Washington under the auspices of the Joint Civil Affairs Committee, again with participation by McCloy. It was checked by August 22 for conformity with SWNCC 150/3 and then sent by special officer courier the following day to Lieutenant General Richard K. Sutherland, MacArthur's chief of staff, AFPAC, in the Philippines to provide helpful "preliminary information." As the covering letter from General Hull explained, "The basic concept of the application of military government to Japan, in a manner similar to that used in Germany, has been substantially changed by the Japanese surrender and the negotiations attendant thereto."[93]

In the explicit and highly detailed follow-up terminology of the draft directive, SCAP was told that the occupation would be an indirect one. He would not be establishing "direct military government" but rather exercising his power "so far as practicable through the Emperor of Japan and the Japanese government." SCAP was ordered not to "remove the Emperor or to take any steps toward his removal without prior consultation with and advice from the Joint Chiefs of Staff." A careful reading of the draft reveals that it added several other points in less veiled language than SWNCC 150/3. Among them was an extensive purge of political, educational, economic (industry, commerce, and agriculture), and police personnel.[94] It was much more open about media control and censorship, matters which were barely alluded to in the policy statement.

a. The dissemination of Japanese militaristic, National Shinto-istic, and ultra-nationalistic ideology and propaganda in any form will be prohibited and completely suppressed.

b.   You will establish such minimum control and censorship of civilian communications, including the mails, wireless, radio, telephone, telegraph and cables, films and press as may be necessary in the interests of military security and the accomplishment of the purposes set forth in this direc-tive. Freedom of thought will be fostered by the dissem-ination of democratic ideals and principles through the available media of public information.[95]

Both SCAP and the Japanese authorities were given a large share of the economic responsibilities. Military government was to impose extensive controls in order to prevent starvation and disease, fur-nish reparations, destroy Japan's economic potential for war, and "prepare the way for an ultimate restoration of Japanese economy to the extent that the reasonable peacetime requirements of the popu-lation will be met." But except for these objectives, SCAP was not to "assume responsibility for the economic rehabilitation of Japan or the strengthening of the Japanese economy." He was to hold Jap-anese authorities responsible for production, distribution, wages and prices, and even the dissolution of combines. The United States had "no obligation to maintain any specified standard of living in Japan." To further the policy of dissolution, SCAP was to "have a survey made of combines, pools, mergers, and semi-official com-panies and communicate the results of such survey to this Gov-ernment through the Joint Chiefs of Staff, together with your recommendations for the effective dispersion of the ownership and control of the industries concerned and for rendering ineffective the influence and controls exercised by the Zaibatsu."

This passage, which was closely modeled upon Eisenhower's di-rective for the American zone in Germany, had been in the draft since July 19. It was altered by November 3 to drop the word *zaibatsu* and to require the Japanese through a public agency to submit "plans for dissolving large Japanese industrial and banking combines or other large concentrations of business control." The complementary request in August for SCAP to make a survey of "rural land tenure" was mysteriously dropped in November. Fi-nally, SCAP was authorized to remove "all legal obstacles" to labor activity and advised to "prevent or prohibit strikes" only if they threatened military security or the aims of the occupation."[96]

In Manila, MacArthur's general staff officers and the embryonic Military Government Section proceeded to draft and redraft their plans and proclamations for the peaceful entry of occupation forces into Japan, in accordance with instructions from the JCS (Blacklist Operations).[97] Whatever MacArthur may or may not have said privately to his staff as they flew to Atsugi Air Base on August 30 and however much his underlings may have praised him later for understanding the so-called Oriental mind, Washington was the real source of most of his ideas. And whatever the Japanese-American war was all about, it had not been fought to allow generals to make policy. In the initial period of the occupation, MacArthur complied with his orders—tactfully characterized as the policies which would guide him. He indeed became so identified with them that it was difficult for him to shift gears a few years later when new ideas and politics prevailed in Washington. MacArthur tended to forget the warning at the beginning of all of the early basic documents, stating that the measures were only for initial purposes and not intended to serve as a final formulation of long-term policies or to cover all aspects of the occupation.

MacArthur knew before he ever met Japanese officials in early September that the occupation would be indirect but nevertheless far-ranging in its reformist aims and that he was to work with the older, nonmilitarist leaders while opening the door to a newer generation. His "statement to the Japanese concerning required reforms," issued to the new prime minister, Shidehara Kijuro, on October 9, following by a few days SCAP's instructions on civil rights, may be taken as a good indication of how he summarized the Allied mission and dramatized it for public consumption. The Potsdam declaration would require correction, as he phrased it, of Japan's "traditional social order" and "liberalization of the Constitution." He expected the Japanese government first of all to emancipate the women of Japan (for "the well being of the Home" rather than for feminist reasons). They were to encourage "the unionization of Labor" and end exploitation of children, to open "the schools to more liberal education," to abolish "secret inquisition," and to democratize the economy—by revising "monopolistic industrial controls" and by developing "methods which tend to insure a wide distribution of income and ownership of the means of production and trade."[98] Other things, which could not be mentioned openly, were already under way or under contemplation—censorship, media control, and purges.

Further instructions flowed from Washington to Tokyo. Planning
and policy making continued, since many of the papers for Japan
had not reached their final stages. Technical missions began to arrive in Japan, for the tasks of the occupation were numerous and
complex. Plans had to be adapted to the realities of defeated Japan
and the responses of the Japanese people and their leaders, who
were by no means passive or inert. All of this took place without
Grew and Dooman, who had left the government by September, and
Ballantine, who retired a few months later. Only Blakeslee and Borton of the major wartime Japan planners remained on the Washington scene. Dean Acheson replaced Grew as undersecretary.
China specialist John Carter Vincent took over from Dooman as the
chairman of SFE and from Ballantine as the head of the Office of Far
Eastern Affairs. In a final insult, or so it seemed, the State Department appointed George Atcheson, Jr., another China hand, instead
of Dooman or Ballantine, to the post of political adviser to MacArthur. To military strategists and foreign policy makers, China was
more important than Japan in American postwar calculations.[99]

Embittered, the old Japan hands continued their opposition to the
more extremist policies embedded in MacArthur's orders. As private
citizens, they gave talks, wrote letters, spoke to reporters and intelligence officers returning from Tokyo, and ultimately formed a
lobby, the American Council on Japan. In the belief that Japan's
restoration to stability (a code word for a nonmilitarist capitalist
order, led by the old Anglo-American school) was in the best interests of the United States, they wanted less destruction of the old
Japan and a less reformist line than MacArthur was implementing.
They were pleased with the continuation of the throne but worried
until 1946 that Hirohito might be in jeopardy as a war criminal.
They were unhappy with the thoroughness of the purge and the
methods by which it was done. It was absurd to bring forth new
leadership; the masses, said Ballantine, were "inert and tradition
bound." The "comprehensive recasting" of Japan's "economic organization" and the "sweeping 'reforms' in its political and social
institutions," only complicated Japan's return to stability, as the
"Japan hands knew," and made Japan's economic recovery, which
was also to the advantage of the United States and the world, much
more difficult. To those who called the old Japan crowd "fascist,"
they retorted that extremism in Japan was the product of "New
Deal economists, political scientists, and law graduates with little
experience in the world of practical affairs and none in Japan."[100]
There was almost no worse epithet than New Deal.

As the cold war advanced and postwar America turned more conservative, the Japan lobby picked up adherents within and outside the government, and they were an important element in the so-called reverse course (really a shift of emphasis and reassertion of older ideas) in economic policies in Japan, 1947–49. Dooman's subsequent accusations, however, that the basic documents for Japan were altered after his departure from the government in some kind of sinister New Deal or pro-Communist plot, or that John Carter Vincent and other former colleagues were primarily responsible for the turn toward an extremist or negative line, were totally erroneous. Instead, it was a Republican in good standing, John J. McCloy, corporation lawyer, future head of the World Bank and high commissioner to Germany, who worked out the partly punitive and partly lenient compromise for Japan—one which expressed thinking at the highest levels of the American government. American policy for early occupied Japan was a peculiar mixture of American liberalism and conservatism. It looked back in some anger at Japan but also ahead with great hope of making Japan cooperate again, in the words of no less than Herbert Hoover to President Truman, with Western civilization.[101] MacArthur had only a very short time to make sure that Japan underwent a social transformation but not a socialist revolution.

Chapter 2

Improvising Stability and Change in Postwar Germany

Earl F. Ziemke

Military government as it was installed in Germany during and after World War II was the servant of two masters. One of those was the armed force of which military government was a part, the other was national policy for which it was seen as being the executive agent. For the first it performed two elementary and useful functions: it relieved the tactical troops of concerns, other than romantic, with the civilian population and it carried out certain customary and legal obligations of a military occupation. The second, national policy, required it to serve as well a range of political, social, and economic purposes. As a result, its job, on the one hand, was to create stability in conditions verging on chaos and, on the other, to act as an instrument of change. It was, moreover, much of the time regarded as only minimally competent to do either one by those whom it served.

The purpose of this paper will be to look at military government in its dual character during the time it carried direct responsibility for governing a large part of Germany, namely, from September 1944 to June 1946. This was the period in which military government was both government and military. These twenty-one months, the bridge from the Third Reich to the postwar era, were also the ones in which the occupation had its most immediate impact on the German people.

The occupation of Germany began on September 15, 1944, when Detachment D8B1 set itself up in Roetgen, a small town on the Belgian border due west of Aachen. D8B1 was a civil affairs detachment, organized and trained to work in "liberated" territory, that is, in France, Belgium, or Luxembourg. The military government detachments were then still aboard ship off Utah Beach, and the first of them did not get into Germany until the 28th when Detachment

I4G2 took up its station at Monschau five miles south of Roetgen. The distinction between the detachments was not particularly significant and was mainly in the name, "military government" having been thought to have a stern ring that would be suitable for enemy territory. In three more weeks Aachen was taken, and Detachment F1G2 was installed there. F1G2 was a regional detachment designed to administer cities and substantial territory around them.

The military government detachments had been organized in England in July and August. The largest were the "E" detachments with twenty-six officers and thirty-five enlisted men. They were designed to take over the government of entire German states (*Länder*) and to supervise the other detachments, designated "F" to "I", installed within them. The smallest were the "H" and "I" detachments, five officers and ten enlisted men and four officers and six enlisted men respectively. Their assignments were to be in the rural districts and lesser municipalities. In September and early October it had looked for a time as if most or all of the detachments would soon be deployed in Germany, but the advance stopped at Aachen after only a slender wedge of German territory had been brought under American control.A few detachments found places in the occupied area, the others had to move into quarters in France and Belgium and wait. But military government in Germany had begun.

The road had been a long one, reaching back in time to early 1942 and in distance to the Military Government School at Charlottesville, Virginia, on the campus of the University of Virginia, to various Civil Affairs Training Schools on other university campuses in the United States, and to the Civil Affairs Center at Shrivenham, England. The military government officers who went into Germany were the product of more service schooling than any others in the United States Army, more than most wanted or thought they needed. They were also veteran subjects of controversy. Newspapers had dubbed the Charlottesville school a "school for Gauleiters." The president did not believe the Army was fit to conduct military government at all.[1] Strong opinion within the Army held that military government officers were culls and misfits and the enlisted men were mostly alumni of the mental wards. Some of both, no doubt, were, but the great majority were not. In 1943, the schools had accepted two out of twenty-five in-service officer nominees and one in fifty civilian applicants for commissions.[2] Their average age was forty years, substantially higher than that for the Army as a whole.[3] Many had pertinent civilian skills, and owing to their having spent long stretches of time in schools and other temporary organizations, most held ranks lower than they would otherwise have been entitled to by seniority. Sixty-eight percent of the enlisted men were in the AGCT (Army General Classification Test) categories I and II. The Army average was 41 percent. More than a few had training in law, teaching, engineering, police, or social work, and about one in three came from the ASTP (Army Specialist Training Program) and had received nine months of college instruction in foreign languages, an area in which the military government officers' training had been weak.[4] On the whole, the military government personnel were at least adequate and certainly better prepared than had been their World War I predecessors, who moved into Germany with no prior training at all.

When the first detachments moved into Germany in September 1944 the doubtful element was not the men but their mission, although considerable preliminary work had also been done toward defining that mission. The Moscow Foreign Ministers Conference in October 1943 had decided that all of Germany would be occupied and put under military government for some time, and it had created the EAC, the European Advisory Commission, which since January 1944 had been engaged in determining the boundaries of the zones and devising a control machinery. COSSAC, the Chief of Staff Supreme Allied Commander, predecessor to SHAEF, the Supreme Headquarters, Allied Expeditionary Force, had produced a guide called "Standard Policy and Procedure for Combined Civil Affairs Operations in Northwest Europe" which dealt with the forms and methods of military government.[5] And the CCS, the Combined Chiefs of Staff, had written a directive, CCS 551, in which it established political, economic, and relief requirements for the presurrender period. Using the COSSAC and SHAEF documents, United States and British military government field manuals, and doctrine developed in the military government schools, the SHAEF Germany Country Unit had by midsummer 1944 compiled a handbook that was designed to give the military government officer all the guidance on policy and procedure that he would need. While the handbook was austere in tone, particularly on the subjects of nazism and militarism, its intent was to give the Germans efficient, effective, and humane government.

In August, Secretary of the Treasury Henry J. Morgenthau, Jr., who already had misgivings about what he considered to be the softness of policy on Germany, had brought a copy of the handbook from London to Washington where it had two sudden and unforeseen effects.[6] One was the Morgenthau Plan for the so-called pastoralization of Germany. The other, more immediately important for the conduct of military government, was a memorandum from President Franklin D. Roosevelt to Secretary of War Henry L. Stimson in which the president characterized the handbook as "pretty bad" and asked to have all copies of it withdrawn.

When the first military government detachments entered Germany in September they did so without any approved guidance on policy. The president and Prime Minister Winston S. Churchill had reportedly adopted the Morgenthau Plan at the Quebec Conference (September 11–16, 1944), but both repudiated it shortly afterward. The directive known as JCS 1067 was being written, but it was a United States document and would require British concurrence before it could be put into effect during the period of combined operations. The handbook was in SHAEF G-5 being revised to try to meet the presidential objections. The customary first act of military government was to post a proclamation announcing the assumption of governmental authority, but that could not be done because the proclamation provided in the handbook had used the word "liberated" in reference to the Germans. A substitute had to be found, and it had turned out to be difficult to find one that did not have an inappropriate connotation when it was translated into German.[7]

In the midst of the policy turmoil the military government detachments in the field had work to do, and they did it. There were mayors and administrators to be appointed, people to be registered, curfews to be enforced, food supplies and rationing systems to be organized, weapons and other prohibited articles to be collected, public health and safety to be provided for, utilities to be restored and operated, debris and rubble to be cleaned up, and dozens of other jobs that had become the responsibilities of the occupying forces. The men in military government quickly realized that it was one thing to see the Germans from a distance in the abstract as Nazis, militarists, racists, and what not, and another to deal with them as flesh and blood people. As one officer put it: "The crossing of the German frontier is something of a shock. Even in Nazi Germany the cows have four legs, the grass is green, and children in pigtails stand around the tanks. Self-indoctrination by years of propaganda makes it a shock to rediscover these trivialities."[8] Military government always was going to be mostly a matter of trivialities that could not be quite harmonized with the grand sweep of policy.

The handbook was, finally, issued in October with numerous deletions and stern injunctions against tolerating Nazis or Nazi sympathizers in public office, importing relief supplies beyond the barest minimum needed to prevent disease and unrest, or taking any action that might tend to promote the German economy. The records do not show that the handbook particularly affected military government operations in any way. The detachments would have greatly preferred more leeway in handling the matters of nazism, relief, and the economy, but for the moment the strictures thereon were having less than full effect. The Nazis had almost all disappeared with the retreating German troops, the economy was at a dead standstill, and the magnitude of the impending food shortage was reduced because only about one-third of the normal population was present in the occupied territory. Nevertheless, winter was coming, and the people were going to have to be fed regardless of policy. Major General J. Lawton Collins, who as commanding general, VII Corps, bore command responsibility for military government in the occupied area, said that the Germans would have to be fed one way or another because the American soldier would not permit women and children to starve while he was well fed.[9]

The winter was hard. Under the snow, Aachen was, according to one description, "a fantastic, stinking heap of ruins."[10] Cabbage soup and potatoes were the standard diet for civilians, but that was about as good as was to be had most places in Western Europe that winter, and nobody actually starved. When the German Ardennes offensive, known to the Americans as the Battle of the Bulge, swept close, the civilians were terror-stricken but orderly and cooperative. The military government appointees, sure candidates for firing squads and concentration camps if the Wehrmacht returned, stayed on their jobs, even some prisoners of war who had been recruited as policemen. Throughout the battle United States troops and supplies passed through the occupied area in complete safety. By the turn of the year, military government had passed two tests: it had organized the occupation—at a low level to be sure—and it had demonstrated its worth to the tactical troops in a highly critical situation. Half a dozen detachments, incidentally, had been directly in the path of the German advance, one had been captured, and I4G2 had stayed in Monschau right on the edge of the battle throughout.

During the last week in February the front began to move again, first to the Rhine, in March over the Rhine and to the Elbe, and south through Bavaria in April. By V-E Day, United States Sixth and Twelfth Army groups held nearly half of Germany, all of the assigned United States zone plus an area almost as large in the British and Soviet zones.[11] For military government this was the mobile phase, the time of the spearhead detachments, H and I detachments that advanced with the front line troops posting proclamations, removing Nazi officials, and replacing them with non-Nazis, frequently in six or seven localities a day. E, F, and G detachments established themselves in the cities as soon as they were taken. Detachment F3G2 was doing business in Coblenz while German gunners in the Ehrenbreitstein on the east side of the Rhine were raking the streets with machine gun fire. The plan had been to lay what was called a "carpet" of military government detachments as the front advanced, but the area to be covered by the carpet turned out to be much larger than had been expected. Before the end of March, 150 detachments were deployed in Germany, almost two-thirds of the military government strength.[12] In April, the armies exhausted their allotments of trained detachments and resorted to organizing provisional detachments using antiaircraft artillery, field artillery, and signal personnel, some of which, fortunately, could be spared in the waning weeks of the war.

On crossing the Rhine, military government acquired another responsibility, the DPs, displaced persons. At first they numbered in the thousands, by mid-April over a million, by late April two million, eventually, including liberated prisoners of war, over five million.[13] French, Belgian, Dutch, Russian, Polish, and Yugoslav, they were to have been cared for by UNRRA, the United Nations Relief and Rehabilitation Administration, but UNRRA did not have the people or the resources to do that, hence the DPs became charges of military government. By definition they were victims of Nazi tyranny and German aggression, entitled to the best treatment available. As a practical matter, however, they were a mass of confused human beings cut adrift in a collapsing society who had to be fed, clothed, housed, supervised, and even entertained. They also had to be kept off the roads and, as far as possible, out of trouble. The Western Europeans could be sent home. The Russians, though, the largest single contingent, and the Poles became long-term guests of military government. Their governments were not prepared to receive them but more than ready, particularly on the part of the Soviet Union, to complain about shortcomings in their treatment.

The Germans were remarkably docile, relieved that the war was ending, apprehensive about the future, but far from being the incorrigible *Herrenvolk* the Americans had expected. They were not wards of the occupation as the DPs were, and the Army assumed no direct responsibility for their welfare. On the other hand, military government was charged with seeing to it that the Germans themselves maintained public services, economic controls, and rationing. Almost always the people who had performed those functions before the occupation were tainted with nazism and new ones had to be found, trained, and supervised. Those who were appointed seldom had more than rudimentary qualifications. The Nazi party had done a very thorough job of keeping nonmembers out of responsible posi-

tions. Nonfraternization complicated all dealings with Germans.
Since it was imposed on Americans, military government did not
have to enforce it, but it did have to observe it, which engendered an
awkward constraint on official contacts with Germans.

By the spring of 1945, JCS 1067, then in some official circles and
later more widely regarded as the Morgenthau Plan lightly dis-
guised, was approved United States policy for "the initial post-
defeat period." It was an austere document emphasizing the disease
and unrest formula for relief, a let-them-stew-in-their-own-juices
approach to economic affairs, and the so-called "three d's," denazification, demilitarization, and decentralization.[14] However, SHAEF,
a combined command, could not be given JCS 1067 as a directive
without British concurrence which had not been secured; consequently, policy, although no longer nonexistent, was technically
in abeyance. A SHAEF G-5 field survey conducted in late March
found a gaping deficiency particularly in political guidance, one that
it predicted "could have calamitous results in the not too distant
future." All military government activities, G-5 observed, had political implications, but the guidance from the top was so meager that
policy development—such as it was—was being left to the random
actions of detachments in the field. The SHAEF policy so far, the
survey concluded, was all negative, aimed at destroying nazism and
militarism with nothing having been said about what to put in place
of either one.[15] Those who knew the contents of JCS 1067—and not
very many did—saw it also as exclusively negative.

Lieutenant General Lucius D. Clay, who read JCS 1067 after he
arrived in Europe in May to assume his post as Deputy Military
Governor, told Major General John H. Hilldring, the director of the
CAD, the War Department Civil Affairs Division, that Washington
apparently did not have a clear idea of what conditions were like in
Germany and asked to have the directive revised to make it "flexible
and general."[16] Hilldring replied that his opinion on JCS 1067 was
similar to Clay's, but he believed it would be better "in the long pull"
to have an agreed and approved policy statement, which JCS 1067
was, than to begin over and possibly get nothing. He expected, he
said, that actual long-range policy would have to "bubble up from
the facts" that Clay discovered, and he added that he and Assistant
Secretary of War John J. McCloy had "planted the seed of this idea"
in JCS 1067.[17]

Facts were bubbling up. Certainly, by V-E Day the wartime conception of Germany as an automatic machine for generating preda-
tory power was not relevant to the country's current condition. The
people were not having to be shown that they had lost the war. They

knew it. And they were not plotting revenge. They were apathetic. Nazism was dead. The troops that had marched across Europe were in prisoner of war stockades and glad to be there. The economy was prostrate. This nation could not soon embark on another wave of conquest, but it could starve or become a permanent charity case. The latter, no doubt, General Clay had in mind when he asked for a more flexible directive.

The unconditional surrender resoundingly terminated German military and political hegemony in Europe; that also was a fact. But once the relief and joy of victory had subsided, which they did quickly, there was very little else left to celebrate. Europe was still tied to Germany in defeat. In May 1945, the Potter-Hyndley Mission, composed of United States and British solid fuels experts, predicted that in the coming winter northwestern Europe and the Mediterranean could experience a coal famine "of such severity as to destroy all semblance of law and order, and thus delay any chance of reasonable stability."[18] The coal to avert the famine would have to come from German mines, but they were producing only slightly more than enough to keep their own machinery running. Five million tons, about 20 percent of the tonnage needed, were stockpiled at the mines, but railroad tracks and rolling stock would have to be repaired before they could be moved.

According to the conception that had prevailed throughout the war, military government completed its main mission, support for the tactical troops, on V-E Day. What remained was a residual mission of carrying out United States occupation policy embodied in JCS 1067 for a short period, ranging from a few weeks to at most a few months, until a permanent civilian administration took over. President Roosevelt had said in 1942 and maintained firmly thereafter that governing civilians, including enemy civilians, was predominantly a civilian task.[19] His successor, President Harry S Truman, added in May 1945 that "the military should not have governmental responsibilities beyond the requirements of military operations."[20] At his first meeting with the army commanders on June 21, Clay told them that the War Department believed military government was "not a job for soldiers" and should, therefore, be "turned over to the political as soon as practicable."[21] But no civilian agency was ready to take over.

Consequently, military government stayed on the scene, still temporarily but also indefinitely. For other reasons it remained for more than two months after the surrender frozen as well in what continued to be called the mobile phase. Detachments were distributed across large parts of the assigned British and Soviet zones and all of the United States zone and future French zone. The governments were negotiating for the establishment of quadripartite control, but the Russians did not appear to be in any hurry and were making it clear that they would not enter into any agreements until they had full possession of their zone.[22] The British, on the other hand, wanted to use the territory in the Soviet zone as a lever for bargaining on some other unsettled matters between the Western Allies and the Soviet Union.[23] Meanwhile SHAEF, the combined command, could not be disbanded, and JCS 1067, which was still exclusively United States policy, could not officially be put in force.

The occupation, however, was an inescapably practical matter of the day-to-day existence of millions of people and could not be allowed to sink into a state of suspended animation. What was done in May and June could have catastrophic consequences in the months to come. On the march across Germany military government had observed large stretches of unplowed and unplanted fields. At the same time, SHAEF and army group surveys had indicated only that there *might* be enough food stocked in Germany to maintain a bare one thousand calorie per day ration until the next harvest was due. In April, May, and June, military government imported thousands of tons of farm and garden seeds, released *Wehrmacht* horses for farm work, set up farm machinery repair shops, and by these and other means brought the year's planting up to about 90 percent of normal. But the seed was put in late and the yield was likely to be reduced, which could be deadly serious since the SHAEF-occupied territory was at best no more than 60 to 70 percent agriculturally self-sufficient.[24] That the Germans would not be fed well was certain, but they could not be allowed to starve. As Brigadier General C. P. Stearns, the European Theater G-5, put it, "While we can say they brought it on themselves and to hell with them, the fact remains that the Supreme Commander ... will be forced to take at least minimum steps to prevent starvation."[25] In June, SHAEF began importing 650,000 tons of wheat for Germany. In July, military government campaigned to get the Germans to cut and store firewood because, even more than food, coal was certain to be short in the coming winter. These were affairs of the occupation that could not wait for quadripartite agreement or formal promulgations of policy.

In the second week of July the redeployment into the assigned zones was completed and the combined command was dissolved. SHAEF gave way to USFET, United States Forces European Theater. After the quadripartite Control Council was established in Berlin at the end of the month and military government in the

United States zone passed to the Eastern and Western Military Districts two weeks later, the occupation at long last entered the static phase. During the conversion, JCS 1067 became official United States occupation policy and, since much of it had been incorporated into the Potsdam protocol of August 2, 1945, also in effect quadripartite policy. In the minds of the Germans JCS 1067, when it was made public in August, was the Morgenthau Plan. To military government, accustomed to the hard language of the directive, amendments worked into the Potsdam protocol constituted the beginnings of a positive policy. Under the protocol, political rehabilitation, a dim and distant prospect in the original JCS 1067, was to be encouraged and democratic political parties and local self-government were to be established "as rapidly as may be justified."[26] Whereas JCS 1067 would not have permitted the German standard of living to exceed the lowest level in any one of the neighboring nations, Potsdam set the ceiling at the European average. At Potsdam also, President Truman had proposed a United States-financed relief import program for all of Germany and gave the War Department authority to procure imports for the United States zone whether or not a general program was adopted by the Control Council.[27]

At the beginning of the static phase the groundwork was laid for a long-term occupation that would not be exactly benign but would also not be vindictive. The bridge had been crossed. On August 6, General of the Army Dwight D. Eisenhower, commanding general USFET and the United States military governor, talked to the Germans by radio, not as the victorious commander but as a concerned and responsible administrator. He told them the months ahead were going to be difficult. Food would be short and there would be no coal for heating in the winter. The Army, he said, would help by using its trucks and drivers to bring in the harvest.[28] It was a bleak message, but it showed concern that would, in fact, continue in the months and years to come. Change, however, was also coming from other directions and much more quickly. Within weeks, the occupation was going to become the instrument of something approaching social and political revolution.

The ending of the Pacific war in mid-August 1945 had, among others, two effects: it terminated wartime censorship and it touched off a traditional American head-over-heels demobilization. The first of these brought an intense glare of publicity to play on what had all along been the occupation's knottiest problem, namely, denazification. From the outset, everyone had been agreed that Nazis and Nazi sympathizers should be eliminated from positions of authority and influence in public life. The trouble had been to determine who those persons were. The official definition embraced all party members, militarists, identifiable sympathizers, and individuals who had profited from the Nazi regime, which, strictly construed, virtually blanketed whole professions, such as law, public administration, police, medicine, and teaching.[29] Any German who, for instance, had been a small-town mayor or police chief after January 1933 was unemployable under the occupation whether he had belonged to the party or not, and actual party members could not even be employed as porters or scrubwomen in military government offices. On the other hand, military government had observed already in the early days around Aachen that the definition left mighty few persons with any ability, training, or recent on-the-job experience who could be employed. Nevertheless, the tendency was to enforce a strict interpretation even though it produced such organizational peculiarities as, for example, at Eichstätt, Bavaria, where when the sixty-four-year-old mayor had a stroke the only person eligible to replace him was his deputy who was over seventy.[30] In September, USFET reported totals of 82,000 Nazi party officials arrested and interned—where, incidentally, they subsisted considerably better on a 2,400 calorie daily ration than did most of the population at large—and 100,000 persons dismissed from public employment in the United States zone.[31]

But the press and the public were not convinced that a clean enough sweep had been made. Attention centered particularly on Bavaria where the appointed state governor was Friedrich Schäffer, who had not been a Nazi but had been a leader of a party which had collaborated with the Nazis in undermining the Weimar Republic during the 1920s. During the summer a strong and not ungrounded suspicion had developed that Schäffer was keeping people at jobs in his office whose antecedents were more dubious than his own.[32] The crisis came on September 22 when newspaper reporters, taking advantage of a recently lifted censorship prohibition on quoting general officers directly, questioned the military governor of Bavaria, General George S. Patton, and his response seemed to indicate that he saw no difference between Nazis in Germany and Democrats or Republicans in the United States.[33] Patton's remark appeared in newspapers across the United States the next day along with editorial comment questioning the whole conduct of the occupation. The questions raised concerned not only the thoroughness of denazification but the equity of it. A feeling had been growing in American—and German—public opinion for some time that the Nazis who had not taken party or government jobs were being left free to enjoy their positions and property. On September 24, General

Clay told his staff that he was dissatisfied with the progress in denazification and that "a decision has been made that we are going to denazify all phases of German life."[34]

Two days later, the newspapers and radio announced Military Government Law No. 8. It excluded Nazi party members from private as well as public employment in any capacity above the level of common labor.[35] The law engulfed the military government offices in a flood of work. Businesses were held responsible for purging themselves, but that forced military government into a running game of hide and seek with a sizable part of the German population as owners and managers attempted evasion by changing job titles and making deals. After the law took effect, military government property offices became trustees for thousands of establishments ranging from barber shops to factories. Since under the law doubtful cases could only be resolved by appeals, military government acquired the added job of appointing appeals boards and reviewing their decisions. Over 90,000 appeals were heard in Bavaria alone.[36]

In the midst of the intensive denazification the Germans were also given a crash course in democracy. On 16 September, Clay wrote to Assistant Secretary of War John J. McCloy, "If the Germans are to learn democracy, I think the best way is to start off quickly at the bottom."[37] Four days later orders went out to the German state governments to write election codes and to the military district commands to prepare for elections in communities of less than 20,000 population in January 1946 and in the larger communities in March and May.[38] As it turned out, elections were announced before any legal political parties existed. Although parties were authorized in the Potsdam protocol, none had yet been licensed in the United States zone. The thinking in military government had been—and for the most part continued to be after Clay's announcement—that the Germans ought to be subjected to an extensive preliminary period of education in democracy. To hold elections after only eight months and without the German character having been remolded in any significant way appeared to be either frivolous or cynical or both. Besides, the Germans themselves showed not the slightest interest in politics. Nevertheless, Clay refused to reverse his decision or delay its execution.

The elections added a heavy increment to the military government workload. To run a candidate in a locality a party was required to submit a license application signed by twenty-five sponsors each of whom had to fill out a *Fragebogen,* a questionnaire which inquired in detail into his political history. Then the candidates had to be investigated and checks made on the tone and content of their campaigns. Criticism of the occupation was prohibited as, of course, were any hints of nationalism or latent nazism. Actually, in the prevailing state of political apathy the real difficulty most often was in rousing the candidates to debate at all. Finally, the voters had to be registered and the rosters examined to eliminate Nazis and other ineligibles. Every step required reports, as did all other military government activities. In the month of October 1945, the average detachment dispatched 305 reports of one kind or another. One harried detachment commander figured this amounted to 1.3 communications an hour, eight hours a day every day including Sundays.[39]

For military government as it had thus far been constituted, denazification and democratization were not a new phase but rather the finale. Under the point system, 40 percent of the military government officers and 50 percent of the enlisted men were eligible for discharge before the year's end.[40] Most of the rest would become eligible in early 1946. The officers were committed to stay at least a year after the war ended, but many were having second thoughts. The rush to go home was on, and their competence was, if anything, being questioned more after the surrender than before. The newspapers criticized everything from lapses by local detachments to— particularly after the Patton affair—the whole concept of military government. Truman told Eisenhower that proper policies were not being carried out "by some . . . officers in the field."[41] Eisenhower complained about a "growing storm of discontent, even anger, among columnists and editors."[42] Eisenhower's chief of staff, Lieutenant General Walter B. Smith declared himself convinced that "the American people will never take kindly to the idea of government exercised by military officers."[43]

Again it was Clay who drew the ultimate conclusions. On October 1, he created OMGUS, the Office of Military Government (U.S.).[44] The word "military" in the title was meant to be purely vestigial. Clay wrote to McCloy that the object was to convert military government to a civilian operation and separate it from the military structure as soon as possible.[45] Eisenhower, in turn, told the army commanders, "The Army must be prepared to be divorced from military government responsibilities on twenty-four hours' notice."[46] Clay did not anticipate quite so much speed, but he did propose to turn over the whole top administration to a civilianized OMGUS by December 31.[47]

On October 4, Clay told USFET G-5: "We cannot expect the Germans to take responsibility without giving it to them. We are going to move a little fast."[48] The next day USFET ordered the local military government detachments to remove themselves from direct supervision of German civilian administrations by November 15 and the regional detachments to do so by December 15. After the elections and no later than June 30, 1946, the local detachments—comprising by far the largest personnel contingent—would be disbanded and replaced with two-officer liaison and security detachments charged with observing and reporting but having no authority, except in outright emergencies, to intervene in German governmental affairs.[49] Control from then on would be exercised by OMGUS and similarly civilianized officers of military government in the German states through the appointed state governments.[50]

After November, military government had one last service to perform: to see the country through what had for months been talked about as "the battle of the winter," a predicted struggle with hunger and cold that it was thought could engender uprisings against the occupation. In October, the detachments received orders to warn all German officials that they and their communities would be held accountable for acts against the United States forces.[51] The battle did not materialize. Fortunately, the winter was one of the warmest on record, and the coal shortage did not have the effect that had been expected. An added 300 calories in the daily ration—supplied from imported United States food stocks—was enough to keep the average consumer who did not have anything to trade on the black market from starving. A reverse flow of DPs from Eastern Europe, some new, others ones who had been sent home and did not like what they found there, put strains on food and housing; but an anticipated influx of millions of German expellees did not develop during the winter months. What disorder there was came almost entirely from DPs and American troops. Having turned over governmental affairs as ordered to Germans, the detachments spent much of their remaining time in protecting them from roistering Americans and from DPs bent on preserving the free and easy atmosphere of the early occupation—and, less successfully, in trying to persuade the tactical commands that since their strengths were down by two-thirds, they did not need all of the housing they had requisitioned six or eight months earlier.

In the spring of 1946 military government was on the way out. For those who had served in it the mood was probably more one of bitterness than of satisfaction. Their chief complaint was that they had not been allowed to perform what most believed ought to have been their principal function, namely to reeducate and reform the German people. The elections had been held, and over 85 percent of the eligible voters had turned out, but the suspicion was strong that they had done so in a spirit of accommodating the new masters as they had the old. A typical detachment comment was that the Germans had been given "a bum's rush into what passes for democracy."[52] OMGUS's own report concluded, "While the voting in the recent elections was gratifying, the fact remains that the average German does not yet recognize the personal responsibilities which go with political freedom."[53] Along with political responsibility, control over denazification had also passed to the Germans, and in doing so it had undergone a profound change. Where the American had seen it as the removal of Nazis from positions of power and influence, the Germans saw it as the lifting of the Nazi taint from individuals. In all but the very most aggravated cases, German denazification boards were restoring Nazis to full rights after letting them off with fines that were easily payable in inflated money.

If the war had been fought, as many believed it had, to work a grand transformation, that had obviously not been accomplished. On the other hand, the Germans had assumed substantial responsibility for their own governmental affairs without undergoing a social or political collapse and without any threat of a Nazi revival. Individual Nazis were escaping their just deserts in unduly large numbers, but the movement was dead and beyond revival, the latter not through social and political engineering but because the world in which nazism was born and had flourished had passed out of existence.

By June 1946, the two-officer liaison teams were in place. The shift to civilian control at the top levels, however, had not occurred because no civilian agency had the resources or the manpower to assume the job. The Army would continue as the executive arm in the occupation for another three years. But a major divide had been crossed. Behind lay the war and a trail of mostly meaningless ambitions and anxieties. Although the future was uncertain, one thing was apparent: it would not be anything like what had been expected a year ago or less. The world had changed, Germany had changed, and the rationale of the occupation had changed. The troops who had imposed the Allied will on the conquered country had gone home, as had all but a few of the military government officers and men who had accompanied them.

Discussion

Edwin M. Martin: I was chief of the Division of Japanese and Korean Economic Affairs, starting April 1, 1945, on a part-time basis as an advisor on this subject—then, in 1947 when Charles W. Kindelberger was moved over to the Marshall Plan on July 1st, they gave me Germany and Austria, as well, and the liquidation of the Enemy Assets Division. With respect to what Marlene Mayo has said, I think she has done, to my knowledge which is limited to the 1945 period and after, an excellent job. I have no quarrel from my recollection with any of the things she had to say. It was a long time ago and a lot has happened since, and I have not had many occasions to try to refresh my memory.

In particular I want to confirm one point, but then modify it a little bit. Dr. Mayo is quite right that, insofar as I represented the economic team, we were completely ignorant of Japan. In fact I had never been outside the United States. But the modification is that I was not operating alone. I represented a rather extensive amount of work which had been done in OSS, which she referred to very briefly: the Far Eastern Section of the Research and Analysis Branch. I went there in June of 1944 from being in charge of the priority system and the War Production Board. We completed our post–VE Day priority system and they wanted somebody to plan the bombing of Japan, but figured they could get nobody who knew about both Japan and war industry, and maybe I knew something about war industry.

But very quickly we had to set up a joint target group because we had so few experts and OSS could not do anything but transfer people like Charles Hitch and Russell Dorr from the European theater to the Japanese theater. So, after a short period of intelligence work, we started copying the people working on German occupation policy, both political and economic. We did have in OSS (and I became in December the deputy chief of that division) a chief, Charles Burton Fahs, who was a rather outstanding Japanese scholar and gave a lot of leadership to the work which we did in OSS. There were also some others there who were highly competent in this field, although not many strictly on the economic side; such people were scarce in the United States.

When I came over to the State Department, there was already another OSS transfer, Ed Mason, with whom I had done work in the Bureau of Labor Statistics back in the 1930s, who had been deputy to William Langer in OSS. He moved over in January of 1945, as I recall it, to be deputy to Will Clayton, the assistant secretary of state for economic affairs. So it was Ed Mason, in effect, that brought me over from OSS as another OSS person, first as advisor on Japanese and economic affairs (Far Eastern I guess it was) and then setting up the division.

The conflict between myself and Mr. Dooman was real; there is no question about it. I must say that I had the impression that Hugh Borton hewed more to a middle ground and that we understood each other a little better than Eugene Dooman and I ever did. I think this would be my impression of the situation. I would say, too, that Marlene Mayo is right that there was a great deal more planning on the Japan side than some people give credit for, although a lot of that particularly on the economic side was redone as the OSS influence moved into the State Department.

The real gap was that nobody ever thought of Korea and we had to start from scratch. That was a real problem and never very satisfactorily handled because, in the theater, MacArthur was interested in Korea only after all of Japan's needs had been taken care of, and he kept his hand on it but gave no attention to it. Even supplies did not get through to Korea. I recall about May of 1946, when I made my first trip to the Far East as the State Department advisor on the second poly-reparation mission, when we were in Korea there was nothing but cheese and hot dogs in the General Officers' Mess because there was a strike in San Francisco and what supplies there were were kept in Japan. It was only the surplus that got to Korea.

From time to time, having heard that I was involved in economic policy in Japan and Korea, in recent years people congratulate me on what a wonderful job we did in building a basis for the economic growth of Japan and Korea. If I am feeling honest, I confess that when I left the operation in 1948 we thought they were both hopeless economic cases.

Hugh Borton: I can verify that Korea business. They used to talk about the ramshackle planes that flew between Tokyo and Korea as something not fit to fly. In fact, they gave it the nickname of a one-way ferry. The day that I was due to come back, the plane was cancelled, implying that it had fallen somewhere in the Japan Sea.

Professor Ziemke has talked about JCS 1067 and you may wonder why 1067 did not also apply to Japan. The answer to that is that we saw to it that it did not. Members from the JCS and from the State Department came over and tried to persuade us. "Look, all you need to do is to cross out Nazi and put in Japanese and you can use this directive." We insisted that it would not work. Then, as Ed Martin remembers, in April of 1945 when we were in our last stages of approving the initial postsurrender policy statement, there was a section on finances which we said should obviously go to the Department of Treasury for their approval. But we also said that we would give them only two weeks to go over it so that they would not tear the whole document apart. At the end of the two-week period—I believe, Ed, you were the one who was communicating with the Treasury Department—we said what is their answer? In the meantime, President Roosevelt had died and Ed reported that they needed more time. Dooman, I believe, was at the time chairman of our subcommittee, and he said, "You remember our decision of two weeks ago?" Everybody said "Yes," and the document went on up as is. So, we knew all about 1067, but we did not like it.

Edwin M. Martin: My recollection is that the Treasury as individuals never really got into the Japanese-Philippines document operations, although I do not know how we kept them out.

Morris Amchan: I was formerly deputy chief counsel at Nuremberg. For Professor Ziemke: I noticed you stopped at June 1946. The Nuremberg judgment came out in October of 1946. In June 1946 did the Germans know of the atrocities, and what impact did it have on military government at that time, or was the full impact after the Nuremberg judgment came out?

Earl F. Ziemke: I think they probably knew in June 1946. There had been a lot of effort made to bring it to their knowledge. There had been information programs and what not put on. My own impression is that the judgment of Nuremberg may have influenced them in the opposite direction. They felt that this either settled the matter or had settled it in a way that was not the proper settlement. If they wanted to know, they certainly knew by June 1946 because there had, in fact, been other war crimes trials before that. A number of cases, Army cases, the Hadamar case—these were all com-

pleted already or were under way—the famous Malmedy case was
going on, I think. The Doctors' case, I think, also was going on by
then.

Jules Davids: Dr. Mayo mentioned that in 1945 Secretary of War
Stimson had quite a role in the matter of planning and policy in
Japan. I wonder if she could elaborate a bit on the role of Stimson.

Marlene J. Mayo: Yes, I will try. I despaired of getting that succinctly into a paper that was already overly long. The problem is
that in the Potsdam declaration—the role of the area committee
therein, and Grew, Dooman, Stimson—it was a problem of atomic
diplomacy and presidential politics and Allied politics. As many of
you probably know, Stimson was very important in keeping Kyoto
off the target list for the dropping of the first atomic bombs. He was
very, very sympathetic to the arguments of Grew and Dooman about
preservation of the emperor and the imperial institution for a variety of reasons, one of which was his worry that the Japanese armed
forces in China and Manchuria would not surrender unless there
was the cooperation of the monarchy. Then, like most of the Japan
experts, there was fear of antagonizing the Japanese people by
harming the emperor as a person or trying too soon to destroy the
imperial institution. So he accepted all of that. But he had a role
right from the start in the Manhattan Project, the development of
S-1, seeing it through to the end. I do not know to what extent he
confined all of his private thoughts to his diary. I do know that Martin Sherwin's excellent book, *The World Destroyed,* begins to break
apart at the point where Stimson comes into the picture in May,
June, July, and August of 1945. As best I can reconstruct it, and I do
not know the whole story either, Brian Villa has written a rather
instructive article which was published about a year ago in the
Journal of American History on the Potsdam declaration, the military and unconditional surrender. He paid little attention to the diplomatic documents in doing that paper but he, in turn, has dug up
some very fascinating things from the military documents. Nobody
has put together the whole story yet, as far as I can tell. Though
there is a good portion of it in Len Giovannitti and Fred Freed, *The
Decision to Drop the Bomb* (New York: McCann, 1965), there are not
careful footnotes in that book so it is a little bit difficult to know
where all of the material comes from or when the interviews were
sought with particular individuals such as Dooman.
     I think that Grew did know about S-1 some time in May. I cannot
quite get all of the evidence that would give me assurance on this

point, but I think Grew knew. Whether he knew how awful the weapon would be, whether he saw it in the apocalyptic way that Stimson and others did, I cannot be sure; nor whether he realized that there were plans to drop it on Japan. Well, I suppose he was not that dumb, he could have figured it out. On Saturday, May 26, 1945, he went to Dooman and they talked about trying to persuade President Truman to issue an early statement reassuring the Japanese that they could retain the monarchy and, of course, this would be a modification of unconditional surrender. This was going to be tied up later with an early warning about complete and utter destruction. But on May 26th, that Saturday morning, he said,"You give me something by Monday and I am going to take it to the president." Dooman went home over the weekend, taking with him all of these SWNCC and area committee papers. He had also had a blood and thunder draft memorandum put together by Douglas Fairbanks, Jr., then serving in the Navy, which became the preamble to the Potsdam declaration. Dooman had been talking to John King Fairbank and others in April and in May. So the area committee papers, the SWNCC papers, and Dooman's own ideas went into a statement prepared for Grew, who discussed it with the Assistant Secretaries of State Acheson and MacLeish that Monday, trying to get the ear of Truman. There were discussions with Stimson and with Marshall the 29th, the 30th. There were also additional discussions those days, secret discussions, involving the atomic bomb, invasion of Japan, mustard gas, and things like that—only a portion of which Grew was aware of. Anyway, he thought that he had the president's backing but everything was tabled for a while because of the atomic bomb.

There were more discussions in June, discussions in early July— apparently when Byrnes went off to Potsdam July the 6th he had a revised version of what Dooman had worked out over that weekend. In addition, he had a memorandum which Stimson had prepared July 2nd or 3rd which also argued for retaining the monarchy. These documents were taken along to Potsdam. Various people want to take credit for the ultimate document—Stimson seems to be taking credit in his memoirs, Grew wants to take credit, Dooman wants to take credit, and the area people who served in the State Department in 1944 and 1945. Brian Villa wants to give Marshall a lot of credit—he even singles out Winston Churchill for trying to modify unconditional surrender. As it turned out, the clause "let us retain the monarchy" was not included in the Potsdam declaration, July 26th.

Stimson came back into it again, to get back to your precise question, because he saw Truman three or four times between August 1st and August 14th, urging Truman to give the Japanese some kind of reassurance. Let the Japanese read between the lines, but let them know that we would not tinker with that imperial institution or do anything about hanging the emperor or accusing him of being a war criminal. So that was the role Stimson played; he wanted to soften the attitude of Truman—Truman was listening to James Byrnes.

Hugh Borton: One of the members of the State-War-Navy-Coordinating Committee, the Subcommittee, Colonel Fahey was here earlier. Is he here now and has he any comment to make on this?

Daniel Cox Fahey, Jr.: I thoroughly enjoyed Marlene Mayo's comments. As many of us were in those days, I was merely a civilian in disguise in uniform, having come into the Army through a reserve commission in the horse Cavalry—that dates me. In any event, just in listening I was amazed at how close Dr. Mayo came to the things that I lived with in the capacity of an errand-body, paper chaser—that is what we were. I had no position of authority but we had to occasionally produce pieces of paper and particularly argue with the State Department.

Eli E. Nobleman: I spent a number of years in military government from one of the earliest detachments that Professor Ziemke refers to, including the landing barges and everything else, all the way through to the Bavarian headquarters, first as chief of the German Courts Branch and then the Military Government Courts Branch. I want to compliment him on a superb summary of a great deal of detail.

In defense of the military government personnel: a great many of us had been put through a lot of schooling by the Army although we were already overeducated as Professor Borton so correctly stated. The first thing the Army did when we arrived in Manchester was to send us back to school. I was a legal and public safety officer at the time, and a lot of my time was spent in Scotland Yard's offices in Manchester as well as in the courts, but also in studying area and language. This, of course, stood us in very good stead later on—we had all our areas pinpointed and we had OSS information and material even on whom to arrest, and who would make a good *Bürgermeister.* Unfortunately, when we got to France, they simply shuffled the papers, and so none of us went to any of those places for which we had been carefully briefed. But that, of course, is standard procedure, and those of us who have been associated with the Army know that this is normal.

Hugh Borton: That reminds me of my lecturing out at the University of Michigan to a group of future civil affairs officers. When I was about finished, I said, "Now I must take five minutes and tell you something about Korea." All of their jaws dropped, and they said, "Korea, where is that?"

Robert Wolfe: I did want to respond to Morris Amchan's question about Nuremberg and its relation to German attitudes early in the game.

I have three vivid memories about the knowledge of war crimes and the effect on the German people. I think it was before war's end, I was standing in the newspaper plant in Heidelberg where we were printing posters showing the recent pictures taken in the Ohrdruf concentration camp, the first we had overrun and liberated. I hung back in the shadows because I was in uniform, so people talked quite freely. For the first time I realized that maybe they did not know, because in their conversations with each other they were shocked at the pictures they were seeing. Then, toward the end of that year and the beginning of the next year as an alternate witness in the executions of those convicted in the Hadamar asylum case and the Russelsheim "terror flier" case, I watched first five men and then three men hang. It was not pleasant and I thought only one of them really deserved to hang in the Russelsheim case. In the Hadamar case I had less question, but still it is something else again when you have to watch the consequences of your decisions. But the German people did not know much about those early cases.

Finally, when the IMT Nuremberg verdict was announced, I walked out of my office shortly after having heard it on the radio, headed for an elevator and met one of the German publishers we had recently licensed, who also had his office on the same floor. We were four floors above the ground floor, he had just heard the announcement, he had not been down in the street yet or talked to anybody, but he already told me what the *Volksmund* (public opinion) was saying about the Nuremberg IMT verdict: the three people who were acquitted were acquitted for the reason that Papen was going to forge the alliance for the war against the Russians, Fritsche was going to conduct the propaganda, and Schacht was going to organize the financing.

Hugh Borton: The general reaction that one got in Japan to the International Military Tribunal was: "Well, why do you go through all of this trouble? You know that you are going to convict them anyway." The purpose of trying to show that people will be responsible for their "crimes" just did not get across in Japan at all.

Second Session

The Realities of
Implementation

Introduction by Willard A. Fletcher

The papers of this session differ in content in the sense that one paper presents an analytical framework which is then matched with the actual situation in Japan; the second paper is an attempt at describing the interaction, so to speak, between the State Department and the War Department; the other two consist of reminiscences of a leading planner and a leading implementer of the occupations.

I wonder whether Professor Gimbel might not be too sympathetic to the Army. I saw some virtue, as a matter of fact, in the duality that was created by giving the State Department preeminence in the matter of policy formulation and by saddling the Army, as it were, with implementation and administration. I like to think that that provided the State Department with a certain amount of flexibility and freedom of action which it might not have had had it been much more directly involved in the affairs of the administration of the zone in Germany.

What I found puzzling about the two papers, and also in terms of what Mr. McCloy said, to which also one of the persons in the audience alluded, is this matter of perception, this matter of personality—I was first prepared to draw the conclusion that General Clay wanted to get out from under a job which was burdensome, which in a sense perhaps was even a bit unnatural to the usual preoccupations of an army. On the other hand, one gets the impression that General MacArthur enjoyed, so to speak, his reign over Japan. As a military person, Clay did not seem to have this desire and this preoccupation with military government over a conquered country.

What also intrigued me about this was the fact that General Clay, the more or less reluctant proconsul, faced in a sense a stiffer problem because he certainly had to face the dismantlement of an infrastructure, a dismantlement which was rather severe. And I am left with the conclusion that in spite of all these handicaps, and in spite of all his own personal reluctance to play the role he was asked to play, he made a remarkable success of the job.

With MacArthur, the situation seems to be a bit different in that there was not the dismantlement to such a great extent of the civil service. One has a bit of a feeling here that his was something of a principle of benign neglect, which turned out well in the case of Japan. But these are just my impressions.

I want also to suggest to the two panelists here that I missed in their papers concern with the so-called enemy opposites who were also very important to the success of the administration of both Japan and Germany. I speak here, in other words, of the civil servants and the politicians who came to the fore in Germany as well as in Japan. My interest in this, I suppose, stems in part from the fact that during the German occupation in Europe these people were working with the Germans and became tremendously controversial. I have often asked myself whether or not some of the German civil servants felt that they might in fact be risking their careers, in a sense, because who was to know how the whole thing would turn out.

I am sensitive to these matters because, as a student at the University of Brussels, one of my mentors was Charles Plisnier. He was one of those secretaries-general in Belgium who, under instructions from the Belgian government, had stayed behind, under orders to collaborate with the Germans to a degree so that the German interference in Belgian affairs would be kept at a minimum. These men took enormous risks, but certainly nobody in Belgium speaks of most of them as collaborators. Yet their careers, in a sense, were very badly hurt. Charles Plisnier after the war was not placed on trial; on the other hand, at the University of Brussels you have to view it as a demotion if you are sent back and asked to teach exclusively. Most of the faculty members in the faculty of law were, of course, government officials as well—highly placed civil servants. So I would like in my own way to suggest that perhaps when we talk about occupation we owe it to those who helped make it a success from the other side that perhaps they ought to be mentioned.

Chapter 3

The MacArthur Shogunate
in Allied Guise

Ralph Braibanti

*The Mikado kept his seat, the prestige of
antiquity and divinity, and the fountain of
authority at Kioto, while the Shogun,
or usurping general, held the
purse and the sword.*

Griffis, *Life of Commodore Perry* (1887), p. 327

The occupation of Japan, lasting for seven and a half years was probably the most significant effort to induce political change in a systematic way in modern times. It differed from the occupation of Germany, important for somewhat different reasons, in that the warp and woof of the social fabric which it sought to rearrange was outside the tradition of Western culture. Yet as different as the system was in cultural terms, it was unlike most new states made independent after 1945. Japan was an economic and political system of ancient lineage, great sophistication, philosophical coherence, and impressive efficiency.

In 1983 the controlled experiment in national reconstruction, which the occupation experience essentially was, would be called political and economic development, growth or modernization. The problems and the dynamics of change in that occupation parallel the contemporary experience of new nations in many respects. Yet that remarkable epochal transmutation has not been integrated with subsequent experience in foreign aid operations or academic analysis of the development of new political systems recently free of colonial rule.

The independence of new political systems starting with the end of the Second World War has given impetus to a subdiscipline known as political development or modernization. The notions or principles of this subdiscipline can be found in approximately 120 books published in the United States from 1960 to 1980, most of which were published during the shorter five-year period from 1966 to 1972. Since about one-half of these works are either collections of articles earlier published in journals or are textbooks, we are dealing with only some 60 original works. From these works we can abstract about 30 identifiable formulations or characteristics of a developed political system. These academic perceptions of the attributes of political development vary greatly. They are not all at the same level of sophistication, nor are they all of comparable analytical utility. Some were loosely designed as suggestive characteristics; others are more rigorously worked out as potential research designs. Some are the sterilized product of committee activity; others show flashes of brilliance by uncommonly creative minds. It is quickly evident that these formulations lack the conciseness, apparent elegance, and mesmerizing simplicity of analogous equations for economic development. This is because there are no clearly quantifiable criteria such as capital formation, per capita income, and gross national product which can be used to assess political development. The heavy value content of political systems and the intricate maze of relationships implicit in determining how those values are specified in particular cultures make the analysis of political development ambiguous and indeterminate.

One of the most critical deficiencies of political development analysis of the past quarter century is its total failure to reconsider and relate three great earlier experiences to contemporary developmental efforts. We can think of these as three major historical discontinuities between reality and rumination. The first is neglect of the experience of former colonial powers, especially Britain, France, the Netherlands and the United States in the construction of political systems within the context of imperial rule. The second discontinuity is the activity of Christian missionaries who had been at work inducing cultural change for more than a thousand years. One has only to study the work of Roberto di Nobili in India in the seventeenth century and of Matteo Ricci in China in the eighteenth century and the activities of a long line of Protestant missionaries for later periods to appreciate the relevance of this rich experience.

The third major discontinuity is directly related to the theme of this conference, namely, the military occupation of Germany, Japan, Austria, and the Ryukyus and the civil affairs administration of

Korea for approximately seven years after the end of hostilities of the Second World War. The Japanese, Korean, and Ryukyuan episodes were essentially American enterprises in inducing political change within the context of military control. In terms of overwhelming power of the victor over the recipient system, they resembled the earlier imperial experience. Although this occupation episode, spread over two continents, was rich in varieties of cultural experiences and produced a significant body of literature, the mode and language of analysis was entirely different from that used in subsequent political development analysis. One searches the occupation literature in vain for such expressions as modernization, development, emerging, less-developed country (LDC), third world, but the nearest equivalents found are democratization, denazification, and demilitarization. Yet political development is essentially what the occupation was about. The failure to transfer occupation experience to subsequent foreign aid operations and development literature is not surprising, even though several bridges facilitating such transfer existed. For example, the temporal sequence of the occupation and development operations was uninterrupted; hostilities ceased in 1945 and the occupations continued through 1952. Major nations such as India and Pakistan became independent in 1947 and the United States became involved in massive foreign assistance in the late 1950s. Thus the one experience flowed chronologically into the other. Moreover, a significant number of military occupation officers converted to civilian status and moved into foreign aid developmental activity. Finally at least two important parts of foreign assistance activity were originated in the occupations, although that genesis is now rarely mentioned and is all but forgotten. I refer to the exchange of persons or leadership programs which originated in Germany and the cultural information services which originated in Japan in the old Nitto Tea House in Tokyo.

Despite these bridges of transfer, the discontinuity was nearly total. Several reasons for this may be ventured. First was the ideological disdain of social science for the experience of empires, missionaries, and any activity of a military character. Second was the ahistorical bent of social science which, mesmerized by the new technology made possible by Norbert Weiner's cybernetics, turned its energies to computerizing the present rather than analyzing the past. Only in the last decade has there been disenchantment with the sorcerer's apprentice and a reconsideration of the utility of history. Thirdly, the speed with which new nations were formed seemed to make it essential to capture, study, and record the immediacy of these experiences rather than to relate them to a military past which appeared to be both repugnant and irrelevant. This haste was accelerated by the easy availability of research grants and jet air transportation. Scholars flew breathlessly from one system to another observing what they thought to be new and imagining that it had never occurred before. This analysis of new systems was made during a period when American social science reached the height of its intellectual arrogance. It presumed, and a large segment of its audience concurred, that the problems of mankind could be solved by the liberal disbursement of gifts of gadgets wrapped in pliofilm tied with ribbons of red, white, and blue. The preconditions prevailing in Germany and Japan were, to be sure, quite different from those found in the new states after 1947. Sophisticated infrastructures and technological competence existed in these two systems which had been sovereign and indeed imperial for some time. Yet this difference is not sufficient justification for total neglect of the occupation experience. Both systems were economically crippled, totalitarian ideologies had to be submerged if not eliminated, and new political structures had to be created.This was done in a context of latent force, but the task itself was not totally unlike the reconstruction of the new states from imperial rule to independence. Finally, whatever repudiation of military activity existed after the surrender was accentuated by the Vietnam experience when military prestige in scholarly circles reached its nadir. Other reasons for this discontinuity may be adduced, but the fact remains that military occupation, and the occupation of Japan particularly, has not been integrated into political development analysis of the past thirty-five years.

I shall attempt, in the remainder of this brief paper, to order some of the experience of the occupation of Japan in an analytical framework commonly used in contemporary political development analysis. This effort is meant to be tentative and preliminary, suggestive of further analysis rather than definitive. I have combined several characteristics taken from the thirty formulations mentioned earlier, and have subsumed them under four major headings.

A. Architectonics and the Correlative Problem of Polycommunality

What Cicero has called a "consensus of sentiment," and Ortega has defined as "dogmas about life and the universe, moral norms, legal principles, rules regulating the very form of the struggles," more recent analysts have called the crisis of national identity, national integration, community, or *civitas.* These concepts are subsumed in the term architectonics which refers to common agreement on a fundamental policy of the state—an overarching purpose that gives form, cohesion, and direction to all public action within a sensed community.

The achievement of national identity has been made difficult in new states by the rise of subnational groups demanding parity of esteem. This has been commonly called ethnicity, communalism, pluralism, confessionalism, consociational democracy, or pillarism. At a very moment in history when a new state must establish its identity, it must concurrently nurture the fissiparous tendencies which appear to work against that integration.

This problem was met in Japan in a variety of ways. There was no problem of cultural, linguistic, or religious heterogeneity. Japan was and had been for at least 300 years one of the most homogeneous societies in existence. The aboriginal Ainu became an isolated curiosity, the Eta were a depressed unmentioned class. Herbert Spencer's advice of 1892 to Baron Kaneko against intermarriage with foreigners was a regnant idiom. In sum, the polycommunal divisions which confront virtually all other systems except Korea and the Scandinavian countries and Iceland simply did not exist in Japan.

To this highly favorable base of an historically, culturally, racially coherent heartland were added several strengthening elements as a consequence of defeat and occupation. First, the severance of Korea, the Ryukyus, and the Kuriles eliminated peripheral divergent groups and reduced the country to its heartland of four islands which had historic coherence. This was an event somewhat comparable to the contraction of Turkey to its Anatolian heartland after the collapse of the Ottoman Empire. Thus its territory was made coterminous with its cultural-ethnic-religious sphere of validity which was Turkish and Islamic. Second, preservation of the imperial institution, presumably stripped of its mythology and secularized, was of critical importance in preserving psychic continuity with primordial sentiments reckoned by millennia rather than centuries. It preserved the self-respect and dignity of the vanquished. It connoted good faith thus removing symbols of defeat and humiliation and challenging the Japanese to accept a national polity—new, yet in unbroken psychic relationship with ancient tradition. Third, Japanese government continued to function. It was never superseded by American officials. In this respect it was markedly different from the pattern of control in Germany. There were no "military governors" in Japan; rather there were military government officers (*gunseikan*) who after July 1949 became civil affairs officers (*min-seikan*). Indeed, one officer was transferred out of Japan because his wife, writing a society column in an American newspaper, referred to her husband as a "military governor" and to herself (about to join him in Japan) as the prefecture's "first lady." Military government units posted in the prefectures exercised mere surveillance over local government.

Initially, small tactical units were stationed throughout Japan to be used in the event of resistance or disturbance. But it soon became evident that tactical troops were redundant and by 1947 most units were redeployed into larger units stationed in relatively isolated cantonments with no military government responsibility. The mode of operation was simple. The Supreme Commander for the Allied Powers (SCAP) in Tokyo issued directives (SCAPINS) to the imperial government. One thousand SCAPINS were issued from September 1945 to June 5, 1946, about three and one-third directives each day. The imperial government then issued instructions to the prefectures implementing SCAP directives. Military government units reported on such implementation to SCAP through the intermediate headquarters of the Eighth Army. Violations were reported by SCAP to the imperial government and the central-local communications pattern was repeated. Thus the Japanese government structure was constantly loaded, indeed overloaded, with activity. Some divergent patterns of American interference at local levels occurred, but they were sporadic largely because of the almost impenetrable complexity of the Japanese structure and naïveté and often ignorance of American officers in the field. In retrospect this deficiency in knowledge and competence appears fortuitous for it prevented us from making too many serious mistakes. Considering the almost total disintegration of the Japanese economy, the devastation of Yokohama, Tokyo, Hiroshima, and Nagasaki, and the repatriation of millions of troops, the resilience and effectiveness of Japanese government in coping with these conditions without being superseded by military government appears now as quite remarkable.

Finally, the 1946 constitution, cast though it may have been in the rhetoric of MacArthur, codified the new polity of Japan. Compared to constitutions of new states, it has been an eminently successful document. During the same period of time, Pakistan has had three constitutions, India's constitution was suspended for nearly two years, and the Philippines has had two constitutions. The stability of the Japanese constitution results not only from the difficulty of amending it, but also from its accurate reflection of the new policy for which Japan was prepared: popular sovereignty, parliamentary democracy, constitutional monarchy, expanded franchise, popular election of local officials, judicial review, renunciation of offensive war.

What then, can we conclude about the role of the occupation in meeting this first characteristic of development, namely architectonics or national identity? The occupation met a polity already well integrated and with a well-established identity. This characteristic was diminished somewhat by the disarticulation of war and surrender. Conceivably an occupation might have accelerated the loss of identity, thus increasing the polity's dependence on the occupying power. But, whether by accident or design, integration was enhanced by territorial consolidation, by continuity with tradition, and by the evocation of reconstructed political values embodied in a constitution, which preserved the psychic values of self-respect and national esteem.

B. Diffusion of Power and Institutional Capability

A second characteristic of development which has been given more attention than any other is the expansion of participation, by which is meant the involvement of the entire population in political life. This attribute has been variously termed participant society, social and political mobilization, power sharing, participant explosion, and channelment of mass society. Rapid diffusion of power to the periphery of the social order changes the nature and volume of political demands, thus increasing the strain on the capability of institutions to convert such demands into effective governmental action. This condition has been discussed in terms of "load," the "handling of crises," and the "demand-conversion crisis." The sequence or timing of the diffusion of power and the building of institutions are critical. Ideally rapid and effective institutionalization should precede rather than follow mass suffrage and the formation of political parties which are the principal structures for attaining power diffusion. But this sequence is rarely, if ever, put into practice by contemporary developing societies. Among non-Communist developing systems in 1977 probably only Iran, South Africa, Saudi Arabia, and Pakistan can be said to have tried to engineer such a sequence.

In the case of Japan an uncommonly strong institutional base existed at the time of the surrender. This was especially true of the economic infrastructure, the civil bureaucracy, the educational system, internal security, and religious institutions as embodied in

State Shinto. The basis for strong legislative institutions existed, but in effect legislatures were subordinate to the bureaucracy. The communications media, particularly newspapers, and the channeling of information through neighborhood associations (*tonari-gumi*) also were strong but were totally subservient to the civil bureaucracy. While it was not necessary to establish or to strengthen the institutional base of the polity, it was essential to convert already strong institutions to commitment to democratic ends. This was done first by the removal of hindrances to positive democratic reform through the instrumentality of formal written directives mandatory in application and generally detailed in scope. They were essentially negative if not punitive in directing the abrogation of certain restrictive laws or practices. The first thousand directives issued by SCAP during the ten-month period I referred to earlier were in this category. The directives, for example, demobilized the military establishment, released political prisoners, abolished government support of Shinto, abolished certain political parties and organizations, and required the emperor to "renounce his divinity." A second technique similar in its nugatory idiom to the first was the purge (SCAPIN 550: "Removal and Exclusion of Undesirable Personnel from Public Office"). These negative directives, designed to "eliminate the old order," were followed by a series of positive reforms the basis of which was the constitution promulgated on November 3, 1946, only fourteen months after the beginning of the occupation. This was followed by a series of some sixty new laws implementing the constitution and promulgated during 1947, the year after the constitution went into effect.

These constitutional and statutory instruments drastically changed the basis of power in Japan. The critical element was the extension of the franchise and the direct election of members of the Diet, members of legislative bodies of local government, and, most importantly, local government officials including prefectural governors who formerly were appointed by Tokyo. These, coupled with a modification of the imperial institution to a constitutional monarchy and elevation of the Diet as "the highest organ of state power" laid the basis for shifting allegiances and responsibilities in the direction of popular sovereignty. It should be noted that this participation explosion did not occur immediately at the beginning of the occupation. Indeed, the implementing statutes went into effect at different times during 1947. Thus, the full effect of massive participation was not felt until about two years after the surrender. During this time, the already strong institutions were sufficiently modified so that they absorbed the increased demands without breaking down. There is no doubt that even with this sequence, the strains on institutions were enormous. Indeed, strains for the first two years were largely those of processing the mass of SCAP directives and negotiating their implementation. But this type of demand tapered off after roughly three years and the relationship with SCAP changed to one governed by the exigencies of the Korean War and the diplomacy involved in the strategic necessity of building the strength of Japan as rapidly as possible.

Closely related to the relationship of institutions and participation is the principle Harold Lasswell has described as a self-sustaining level of power accumulation. This means simply that there must be a relative degree of stability and certainty as to legal norms and quantum of political power exercised in the total system. Thus, to rearrange subnational territorial boundaries, or to move powers from central to regional and local levels and back again too often invites conditions of stress and disarticulation. That did not happen in Japan. The traditional prefectural entities were retained, with only Okinawa added after its reversion in 1971 to Japanese rule. The distribution of powers prescribed by the constitution and the Local Autonomy Law (1947) remained basically intact.

During this initial time there were censorship restrictions on the press in Japan which were sharply criticized by the press in the United States. In a sense the very concept of *lèse majesté* which formerly had applied to the imperial institution now appeared to apply to the new shogun, MacArthur. During this period of censorship, criticism of occupation policies or of the Allied Powers was not allowed. From the beginning of the occupation in September 1945 until the end of 1949 prepublication censorship was exercised under the Press Code for Japan. This was succeeded by postpublication censorship except for certain subjects such as communism. In 1952 all press censorship ended. In retrospect it is doubtful if the occupation could have been as successful as it was had there been unlimited press freedom. It would now appear that the temporary limitation on press freedom was a small price to pay; certainly it had little adverse effect on the third estate of Japan which has evolved into one of the most vigorous, critical free presses in the world.

C. Adaptation

A third characteristic of development is not given explicit mention in development literature although it is a critical factor in the characteristic commonly called "legitimacy." The principal means of attaining legitimacy is to establish a polity which is in consonance with the social organization and traditions of the people administered. In the past few years, disenchantment with capital-intensive development strategies and with massive blueprints for social engineering introduced by foreign sources has given rise to a new appreciation of indigenous modes of behavior and attitudes. This appreciation is implicit in such new terms in development as "appropriate" or "intermediate" technology and moves towards a labor-intensive rather than a capital-intensive development strategy. The increasing emphasis in development economics of appropriate technology is simply a rediscovery of conventional classic economic doctrine which was earlier criticized as being too static. Appropriate technology means nothing more than the use of human and other resources at hand and the use of techniques compatible with a nation's culture, economy, historical circumstances, and psychic needs. The contribution of contemporary development economics to this analysis lies in the empirical validation of assumptions that labor-intensive methods and indigenous techniques can, in some cases, be cheaper and more productive than capital-intensive programs using exogenous techniques. It is not without significance that the ideas of E. F. Schumacher, once dismissed as harmlessly quaint because they had emphasized since the 1960s labor-intensity and intermediate technology, have now gained new respectability with the publication of his book *Small Is Beautiful*. Dissatisfied with the pejorative connotations of "indigenization," UNESCO at a conference on administrative reform in new states held in Tangier in September 1977 labeled this phenomenon "endogeneity."

In the case of Japan the issue of adapting high "hard" technologies such as agriculture, manufacturing, and engineering or high "soft" techniques such as commerce, administration, or education does not arise. The system has been able to utilize the highest technologies both "soft" and "hard" and indeed has been in the forefront of originating as well as absorbing technological change. However, the premise of the current idiom of intermediate technology is essentially that of adaptation. Hence if we are to appraise the occupation in terms of this third characteristic of development, the issue of adaptation must be raised. It was common during the occupation and for a long period after to criticize that enterprise as being one which sought to remake Japanese society in the image and likeness of the United States. The validity of this is extremely difficult to analyze simply because of the complexity of the processes of social change. After a third of a century, however, one does not find a Japanese polity which is a mirror image of that of the United States although there are striking institutional and attitudinal similarities. Certainly retention of the imperial institution and parliamentary democracy are not American.

In the earlier Meiji period of reform in Japan, a sophisticated apparatus was established for appraising Western institutions and adapting them to Japanese needs. I refer especially to the commission headed by Prince Ito Hirobumi which, on a world tour, studied deliberately various suggestions made, including those of Herbert Spencer and Lorenz von Stein with respect to reconstructing Japan's polity. In some instances comparable arenas of adaptation were in evidence in the occupation. Advisory commissions in education, police reform, labor, postal service, and other activities were appointed and they worked closely with counterparts in the Japanese government. This provided a means for the adaptation of reforms to traditional Japanese values. In other cases the Japanese simply refused to implement the reforms recommended. The most noteworthy of these was the Japanese insistence that the ideographic system of writing not be supplanted totally by the use of the Roman alphabet. This recommendation of the Educational Mission was based on an altogether too superficial view of the relationship of ideography to patterns of thought, to aesthetics, and to philosophical modalities—a relationship explicated in F. S. C. Northrup's *Meeting of East and West* and more recently in an essay by Martin Bronfenbrenner.

Even when external advisory committees were not appointed, the work of staff members of SCAP with or without the help of temporary individual experts was typically done in close collaboration with Japanese authorities. This was especially true of the local autonomy law and the judicial organization law. The local autonomy law, for example, shows the results of an adaptive process more clearly than others. While providing generally for decentralization of government power, it was peculiarly adapted to Japanese conditions especially in the respect that governors serve a dual capacity as elected executives of the prefecture and in some national activities as agents of the central government in Tokyo. The conditions of executive immunity and liability were made to vary with the nature of the responsibility. The limitations on executive power at the prefectural level included some trusted Anglo-American safeguards but there was also the ancient Chinese device of review of executive and legislative acts by an elected committee known as an inspection commission.

The question of adaptation and its relation to permanence of reform is one in which much additional research is needed. Each reform introduced during the occupation would need to be inventoried and correlations established between provisions for adaptation at the initiation of each measure and modifications made in the course of the last thirty years.

D. Leadership

Before the independence movements following the Second World War, it was common to think of epochal modernizing efforts in terms of dramatic leadership. Thus the Meiji reform of Japan, the role of Sun Yat-sen in China, Bismarck in Germany, and Kemal Ataturk in Turkey suggest almost immediately a congruence of personality and the substance of reform.

From the beginning of the occupation in September 1945 until its end by the peace treaty of September 1951, there were eight different ministries headed by five prime ministers (Prince Higashi-Kuni, Baron Shidehara, Katayama Tetsu, Ashida Hitoshi, and Yoshida Shigeru). Hatoyama Ichiro, about to become prime minister in 1946, was purged at the last moment by the provision of SCAPIN 919, May 3, 1946, directed exclusively to him. Yoshida, replacing him as president of the Liberal party, became prime minister in 1946 and headed three other governments from 1946 to 1955. Yoshida was the closest Japan came to widely accepted distinguished leadership. Even so, he was tainted by perceptions of being under the shadow of the new shogun, General MacArthur. Thus a vacuum existed in secular leadership. The sacerdotal role of the emperor was clouded by uncertainty. MacArthur, though a "barbarian from across the seas" seemed to be the resurrection of the shoguns of an earlier period. No better casting for this role could have been made.

MacArthur's leadership was characterized first by total control over the international groups whose representative he was supposed to have been. He effectively eliminated control by the Far Eastern Commission in Washington by ignoring their orders and reminding them that they knew little about the situation. He defanged the Allied Control Council in Tokyo by sending subordinates of lower rank than representatives of other nations to its meetings and by consulting the council at his discretion. Thus he avoided intervention by the Soviet Union, a stratagem he had already pursued by refusing to allow the Soviets to accept the surrender of Japanese troops or to occupy the country. The consequence of a contrary policy, conceived in desperation because of the shortage of our own troops, was seen in the truncation of Korea at the 38th parallel. Much to the distress of our Commonwealth allies, especially W. Macmahon Ball of Australia, the British Commonwealth Occupation Forces (BCOF) were limited to tactical garrison duty rather than given military government responsibilities. They were exhibited dramatically by providing the honor guard for the emperor's palace in Tokyo, where Sikh and Australian troops who seemed to be eight feet tall presented an awesome sight to Japanese crowds who watched the most spectacular changing of the guard Japan had ever witnessed.

By these stratagems, MacArthur clearly established the centralized, unilateral structure of his command. Like Commodore Perry nearly a century earlier, his personality and style fitted the Japanese temper. When the emperor crossed the moat to call on the new shogun, his Imperial Majesty was attired in striped trousers and cutaway coat. The shogun met him in khaki uniform with open collar and no insignia of rank. His aloof detachment from the masses, his brief, ambiguous, but inspirational messages, his unusual working hours from late morning to late evening: these were behaviors which had wide appeal among Japanese. The broad boulevard in front of his Dai Ichi Building headquarters was crowded each morning to witness his arrival. Trolleys stopped and passengers bowed as he arrived.

Joseph C. Grew, United States ambassador to Japan at the time of Pearl Harbor, wrote that to MacArthur must be ascribed "a high degree of statesmanship." "Few," he continued, "will question the assertion that both the United States and Japan were extraordinarily fortunate that a man of MacArthur's caliber, courage and vision was able to lead the occupation at this critical period in the Far Eastern arena." The same kind of evaluation was made of Commodore Perry a century earlier by Francis L. Hawks, editor of the official report on the Perry expedition, and Samuel Wells Williams, Perry's interpreter. MacArthur's later activities in the Korean War and his recall by President Truman should not obscure his quite remarkable leadership during the occupation. If indeed he was a twentieth-century shogun, he was in the tradition of Iyeyasu Tokugawa, the greatest shogun of all, whose Legacy advised: "The right use of a sword is that it should subdue the barbarians while lying gleaming in its scabbard. If it leaves its sheath it cannot be said to be used rightly. Similarly the right use of military power is that it should conquer the enemy while concealed in the breast."

Whatever relevance the occupation of Japan may have to contemporary developmental efforts of new states is based upon the characteristics or criteria of development chosen for the analysis. This is not the place to debate the comparative merits or the analytical utility of any single set of characteristics. My proposal at this point is that analysts of the occupation use any formulation or mixture of formulations by which the occupation experience can be analyzed. Is there any relevance of that experience to contemporary development efforts? No easy answer can be given.

Let us assume that there had been no occupation of Japan. Would not Japan have evolved in very much the same way, even without such occupation? This is an assumption commonly made by revisionist historians of a radical ideological persuasion who characterize the occupation as an essentially neo-imperialist activity, evil in intent, hence evil in outcome.

First, it must be said that speculation of this kind is scholasticism of very little utility. Had there been no American occupation, the Soviet Union, already pressing in on the Kuriles, would undoubtedly have occupied Japan. The political nature of the whole of East Asia—South Korea, the Ryukyus, as well as Japan would have been drastically altered. Communist influence would probably also have penetrated Taiwan and the Philippines. Without those American bases, it is doubtful that the United States would have intervened in Indo-China.

If we assume that Japan would have been left alone—with no occupation by any power—what kind of polity might have resulted? The likelihood is that the political system would not have been very much different from that which emerged under occupation tutelage. Forces conducing to secularization and a more participative democracy were powerful forces felt in all systems. Japan could not have remained isolated from such globally dispersed influences. There would, however, have been some differences. First, it is unlikely that Article Nine of the Constitution renouncing war would have become Japanese policy. In the absence of that provision coupled with the absence of a protective defense umbrella provided by the United States, it is likely that Japan would have emerged as a powerful military force in a decade or two. This would have strained economic rehabilitation greatly and might have necessitated a somewhat more authoritarian political system than eventually emerged under the occupation. It is likely that the imperial institution would have been retained, modified into the same constitutional monarchy which it is now. Perhaps not as much decentralization of power to prefectural and local levels would have occurred so soon after surrender. Perhaps, also not so much power would have been taken from the bureaucracy and assigned to the legislature. But these would probably have been differences in tempo, style, and degree rather than in basic substance.

Certainly it is clear that Japan was quite a different nation in 1945 than were most of the new states when they attained independence. Japan had an enormous reservoir of managerial skill, an ancient and coherent culture, a national pride which during the period of the war became a dangerous hubris, a strong commercial infrastructure, an industrial base, and above all, a Faustian will to achieve. Few, if any, of these preconditions were to be found in the new states established after 1945. Moreover, change occurred in the occupation under foreign guidance in accordance with a policy which at least was systematic if not always wise. In the wings was the latent military power of the United States acting nominally in behalf of victorious Allies. The sword was sheathed but lay gleaming in its scabbard. It may well be that the situation was so unique that it has no relevance to contemporary development. On the other hand, there is a kind of reverse relevance. The rapid reconstruction of Japan's polity shows the importance of such preconditions listed above. Thirty years have elapsed since most new states have attained their independence. Perhaps there are no more than six new states (Taiwan, South Korea, South Africa, Saudi Arabia, Singapore, Malaysia) with stable political systems capable of improving the life of their people. It is impossible now to replicate both the indigenous conditions of Japan and the unique forces of external control which governed the reconstruction of its polity for some seven years. It is likely that new states may take another thirty years or even longer before anything like these conditions can be attained.

Chapter 4

Governing the American Zone of Germany

John Gimbel

Not at all in accord with current popular beliefs about the nature of the military-industrial complex and the increasing "militarization" of United States foreign policy, the War Department was an extremely reluctant agent of the United States government for purposes of military government in Germany.[1] The United States Army did not want to administer a failure; to preside over hunger, cold, chaos, confusion, and possible revolution in Germany. Neither did it want to manage an expensive overseas operation that would require frequent appropriations from the United States Congress.[2]

Even before the Potsdam conference adopted detailed German policies, the Army balked at assuming politico-economic functions in Germany. In June 1945, during discussions in Washington on a presidential directive on coal exports from Germany, Assistant Secretary of War John J. McCloy insisted that the directive would cause the Army to have to do much more than simply police the Germans as an army of occupation. Undersecretary of State William L. Clayton agreed, but argued that United States interests in Europe required the Army to finance and procure supplies not only for the military occupation forces and to prevent disease and unrest in Germany, but also to provide relief and rehabilitation supplies from Germany for countries devastated by Nazi aggression.[3] In short, the State Department wanted the Army to be responsible for "all imports which serve the purposes of the United States government in Germany," and thus to finance and administer certain American economic foreign-policy operations from its bases in Germany. After much discussion of the opposing views, Secretary of War Henry L. Stimson advised Secretary of State James F. Byrnes, on July 4, 1945, that the War Department would finance supplies and imports into Germany to achieve the broad purposes envisioned by the State Department "only pursuant to policy established on a governmental basis and approved by the President."[4] Byrnes then took the matter to Truman, who resolved the interdepartmental dispute in favor of the State Department in two significant decisions. On July 16, 1945, Truman agreed to a proposal that the State Department be the policy-making agency for Germany and Austria, and that the War Department's functions be primarily executive and administrative.[5] Then, pressed by the State Department for another directive, Truman issued orders to Stimson on July 29, 1945, requiring the War Department to finance and procure all imports for which the United States "assumes responsibility" and to contribute the American share of any combined financing that might be undertaken by the occupying powers in Germany.[6]

Based on Truman's two decisions, the State Department made United States policy in Germany and the Army (in addition to its police functions as an army of occupation) administered that policy, sought funds from Congress for its implementation, and—in effect—bore the burden of defending that policy in the Congress and to the American people. Having thus been given a task by the president that it did not want in the first place, the War Department sought means, methods, and arguments to accomplish the early transfer of its political, financial, and administrative responsibilities in Germany to the State Department. Among other things, the Army did everything it could to complete its assignment in Germany as quickly as possible, essentially by trying to make military government a "going concern" from which the Army could then withdraw gracefully.

The Americans in Germany moved quickly to establish the four-power agencies that were provided for in the Potsdam agreement. In the first working session of the Allied Control Council (ACC) on August 10, 1945, the Americans proposed immediate creation of German central administrations headed by German state secretaries who would function under general directives of the ACC.[7] On the same day, General Lucius D. Clay appointed a German Standard-of-Living Board and instructed its chairman to have a report on reparations and the German postwar level of industry ready for the ACC's consideration within a month.[8] Simultaneously, the Americans began to recruit and identify German personnel for the proposed central agencies for finance, transport, communications, foreign trade, and agriculture, and they established a ministerial collection center in Kassel, where they assembled personnel, records, and documents that would be used by the central agencies.[9]

The determination with which the Americans moved to establish central German administrations reflects the Army's desire to reduce its day-by-day supervision of German affairs and thus to prepare for the transition from military to civilian control. Generals Dwight D. Eisenhower and Lucius D. Clay began immediately after the Potsdam conference to replace military personnel with civilians. Clay planned to cut his staff from 12,000 to 6,000 by February 1, 1946, and he said he expected military government to be a completely civilian organization by July 1, 1946.[10] The long-range purpose of all these activities is clearly stated in a United States Forces, European Theater (USFET) document of September 26, 1945, which outlined a plan for administrative reorganization and justified it as an effort to integrate United States agencies of military government with the central German administrative departments and thus prepare for the ultimate transfer of military government to United States civilian agencies, separate from military forces.[11]

While Clay reduced the size of his own staff, replaced military personnel with civilians, and reorganized military government for its ultimate transfer to a United States civilian agency, he also promoted German self-government at various levels. In October 1945 he established the Council of Minister Presidents of the American Zone (*Länderrat*) and assigned to its office in Stuttgart many of the functions and responsibilities that military government officers had performed since Germany's defeat. Early in 1946 Clay assigned new and greater responsibilities to the *Länderrat* for such things as food, agriculture, industry, transportation, and prices, so that it soon took on the character of a central government of the American zone. Concurrently, Clay scheduled elections in the American zone. Writing to Assistant Secretary of War John J. McCloy in September 1945, Clay said, "We can hardly withdraw the local detachments until officials appointed by us have been replaced by others selected by the Germans."[12] As it turned out the first elections were held in the villages in January 1946. These were followed by elections in the counties (*Landkreise*), the cities (*Stadtkreise*), and the states (*Länder*), all during 1946 and all in accord with a plan first developed in September 1945.[13]

Officials in Washington expressed concern at Clay's rapid personnel reductions; and German politicians and Clay's own advisers, including the political scientist James K. Pollock, thought Clay was moving much too fast on elections. Clay explained and justified his actions by referring to the wishes of congressional visitors, to certain features of the Potsdam agreement, to the American democratization objectives in Germany, and to the pragmatic value of teaching people to swim by throwing them into the water. Clay remembered telling Pollock that his actions were those of a hard-boiled soldier running a military occupation, and it is now clear that they were in accord with the wishes and plans of the War Department to convert military government in such a way as to make a case for relief from the political functions and economic responsibilities that Truman had assigned to the Army on July 29, 1945.[14]

While Truman was in Germany for the Potsdam conference, Secretary of War Stimson and General Eisenhower talked with him in Frankfurt about an early transfer of military government from the Army to the Department of State. After that the War Department campaigned with some of its heaviest guns for such a transfer. Eisenhower summarized the Army's arguments for Chief of Staff George C. Marshall on October 13, 1945. Reflecting the plans already being implemented in Germany, Eisenhower said that German governmental agencies would begin to function soon. Except for police functions, which the Army would continue to perform, the American presence in Germany would be essentially for the purpose of control and supervision of German officials and agencies. That was a civil function for which the State Department was better suited than the Army. In Eisenhower's own words, "The Government of Germany should, at the very earliest practicable moment, pass to a civilian organization."[15] In a two-front campaign, Secretary of War Robert Patterson next took up the issue with the secretaries of state (Byrnes) and navy (Forrestal) in the so-called Committee of Three, and Eisenhower went to Truman. Eisenhower reminded Truman of their discussion in Frankfort and said that organizational steps were already under way in Germany for a turnover of the Army's responsibilities to a civilian agency about June 1, 1946. The turnover, he argued, was in accord with "the American principle of keeping the Army . . . out of . . . civil government."[16]

Following preliminary discussions in October, the War Department formally proposed to the State Department on November 2, 1945, that the transfer of military government be accomplished in a series of steps to be completed "no later than June 1st." Secretary of State Byrnes had objected on October 23 when Patterson first suggested the transfer in the Committee of Three. On November 2 he said the Army's proposal was "bad news" and he hoped that a decision could be postponed for about eight or nine months.[17] Later Byrnes and his staff argued at various times that the State Department was essentially a policy agency without the operational experience that the Army had. The Army could use its existing organization to deal functionally with such things as transportation, industry, production, and procurement whereas the State Department would have to create new agencies to do so. But the Army was determined to get out of the occupation business, particularly after the War Department had studied the full implications and estimated the costs in dollars of the State Department's policy statement of December 12, 1945, on "The Reparation Settlement and the Peacetime Economy of Germany."[18] In any case, six days after the policy statement was released to the press Secretary of War Patterson met with Dean Acheson and others (Byrnes was in Moscow) and told them the Army was going ahead with plans to withdraw from the military government of Germany. Patterson also implied that the Army was now prepared even to abandon the steps-and-stages that it had proposed on November 2, 1945.[19]

On December 19, 1945, a day after Patterson had discussed with him the Army's plans to withdraw from Germany, Acheson went to Truman and convinced him that it was impossible for the State Department to take over the occupation there. Truman discussed the issue in the cabinet two days later and directed the secretaries of state and war to discuss it again after Byrnes's return from Moscow. Although he was convinced that Truman had already agreed with Acheson, Patterson wrote to Byrnes on December 29, 1945. He reviewed the history of the issue, mentioned the Byron Price report of November 9, 1945, which had also called for civilian control, and reviewed the Army's arguments. Later, Eisenhower saw Byrnes personally and found him to be "adamant and unbending" in his opposition to the State Department's taking over the administration of military government. Byrnes told Eisenhower that he would make clear to the president, the Congress, and the American people that the State Department could not handle the job. He also promised to support the Army's requests for funds from Congress, since many of the Army's expenditures would be for political rather than military purposes.[20]

The negotiations for a transfer of military government to the State Department remained stalled after January 1946. An Internal State Department memorandum of January 2, 1946, commented on the issue as follows: "The plain fact is that the Army became panicky over the idea that military government in Germany was becoming a liability. This is the basis for the War Department's desire to unload the job on the State Department."[21] What happened early in 1946 was that the Army changed tactics rather than strategy. It abandoned its *formal* efforts to shift military government to the State Department and shifted to a more indirect approach. At times on his own initiative, but always in accord with the War Department's larger objective, Clay undertook a wide range of activities in Germany to make the occupation a "going concern," either by unilateral actions in the American zone or by four-power agreement in Berlin.

Under American guidance and directives in 1946, Germans elected constituent assemblies in the *Länder,* drafted and ratified the *Länder* constitutions, elected *Landtage* (state assemblies), and established responsible ministries at the state level. As noted earlier, Clay and his staff increased the size and power of the office of the Council of Minister Presidents in Stuttgart. Throughout 1946 and continuing into 1947 the Americans in Germany encouraged the minister presidents of their zone to meet and confer with their counterparts in the other occupation zones, hoping thereby to lay a foundation for a national political development modeled after the Council of Minister Presidents of the American zone. The interzonal meetings began informally in February 1946, with a meeting in Stuttgart between officials of the American and British zones. After additional gatherings in Frankfurt and Bremen in February and March 1946, the program to encourage the minister presidents of the four occupation zones to work for unity developed a considerable momentum until it took a disastrous setback in Munich in June 1947. In Munich the Soviet zone representatives left the meeting after a dispute about the nature of the agenda, and the first four-zonal minister presidents' conference also became the last one.[22]

The Army's political initiatives were matched by economic ones. Anxious to organize the German economy in accord with the principles adopted at Potsdam, the Americans produced the basic studies and working papers and took the lead as the ACC developed the plan for reparations and the level of the postwar German economy. Within a week after the plan's adoption late in March 1946, Clay introduced additional proposals designed to deal with the interrelated problems of exports and imports, reparations, and central German economic administrations. Unable to get the French to agree, Clay suspended reparations shipments from the American zone on May 3, 1946, hoping that the resulting impasse would lead to government-level discussions on the failure of four-power control and to diplomatic and economic pressure on France to cooperate in Germany.[23] But no such pressure was applied from Washington, and the Council of Foreign Ministers (CFM) in Paris made matters worse rather than better. Byrnes had proposed a forty-year treaty of guarantees, with which he hoped to allay France's fears of Germany and thus induce the French to give way on their territorial and economic demands regarding the Saar, the Ruhr, and the Rhineland which had blocked the ACC in Berlin. But Byrnes's treaty generated little interest in France and Britain, and Molotov rejected it as inadequate and premature.[24] Byrnes also wanted the CFM to appoint special deputies for Germany, but that proposal was tabled until the next meeting of the CFM, which was scheduled for late in the fall of 1946.[25] Impatient for relief from the dollar costs of their occupation, the British notified the CFM in Paris that Britain would have to organize its zone in Germany to produce for export. Foreign Secretary Ernest Bevin said Britain "was unwilling to go on borrowing dollars to import food into Germany."[26] Britain's proposed unilateral action in the Ruhr threatened to foreclose the economic unity envisioned at Potsdam and to invalidate the ACC's level-of-industry and reparations plan of March 1946. Byrnes therefore sought indirect means to the same end by inviting all other zones to join with the American zone in economic unity. The British eventually accepted, but the French and the Russians did not, the Russians indicating, however, that they were prepared to proceed on a four-power basis as provided for in the Potsdam agreement.[27]

Clay and the Army hoped that union of the two zones would hasten the day the Army could withdraw from Germany. Significantly, on the eve of his trip to Washington, D.C., to help negotiate the bizonal financial agreement with the British, Clay went to Stuttgart to warn the minister presidents of the American zone that they would have to denazify more rapidly and more thoroughly. He told them denazification was a test of their commitment to democracy and of their ability to govern themselves and he threatened that unless substantial improvements were made within sixty days the Americans would intervene and see to it that Germany was purged of its Nazi influence.[28] Meanwhile, late in 1946, the two military governors (Clay and Sir Brian Robertson) created several German bizonal economic administrations and they developed a three year plan to make the bizone self-supporting by 1949.[29] But the State Department, which made policy for the United States in Germany, would not agree to economic policies in the bizone that impinged on its own priority for rehabilitating liberated Europe first. Neither would the State Department approve bizonal policies and practices that left France's expectations for German coal unfulfilled or threatened France's postwar recovery plans and political stability. Specifically, the State Department vetoed a bizonal policy that would have required Germany's customers to pay cash after January 1, 1947, for such things as coal, timber, and transit services, all of which Germany had been providing to France and other countries since 1945 without payment, in effect as covert or "hidden" reparations.[30]

Despite the early difficulties the State Department's vetoes caused for the bizone, a number of factors seemed to work in favor of the Army early in 1947. George C. Marshall, one of the Army's own, replaced Byrnes as secretary of state. The British government announced in January 1947 that it would increase German steel production, unilaterally if necessary, in the interests of a self-sustaining German economy. The leaders of the Republican party, which had won majorities in both houses of the Eightieth Congress, talked openly about cutting costs and some of them planned a thorough investigation of the "failure" in Germany.[31] Finally, Herbert Hoover went to Germany at Secretary of War Patterson's suggestion, and he returned in March 1947 to make public a report on "The Necessary Steps for Promotion of German Exports, so as to Relieve American Taxpayers of the Burdens of Relief and for Economic Recovery in Europe." It was a plan for building a "self-sustaining economic community" in Germany, and it included recommendations for rapid termination of such things as denazification and decartelization.[32] Hoover's ideas appealed strongly to the Republican leadership in the Congress, and Patterson announced that the Army's next budget requests to Congress would be based on Hoover's recommendations.[33] Responding to these and other pressures, Marshall agreed with Bevin privately on April 18, 1947—while the two were in Moscow for the meeting of the Council of Foreign Ministers—to push rapidly for bizonal self-sufficiency by 1949. Specifically, Bevin and Marshall agreed to reorganize the separate bizonal economic administrations into a more effective, efficient, and unified structure and they agreed to raise the German level of industry and thus reduce Germany's reparations deliveries and coal and timber exports.

For reasons that are not altogether clear, Marshall soon decided that his and Bevin's agreement to rehabilitate the bizone would have to be broadened to include Germany's neighbors as well. Perhaps his discussion with Clay at Tempelhof Airport on the way back from Moscow convinced him.[34] Perhaps John Foster Dulles and State Department functionaries, such as H. Freeman Matthews, influenced him. In any case, on the first day of his return from the Moscow CFM he called George F. Kennan to his office and told him to organize the Policy Planning Staff in the State Department, to work up a recommendation on Europoean economic recovery, and to avoid trivia.[35] Kennan's committee had its first report ready on May 23, 1947, and the report's most specific recommendation was for a "coal for Europe" program: a plan to increase German coal production and insure "its movement to the places of consumption in Europe."[36]

The Army and the War Department had objected to excessive and cheap German coal exports for two years and it was clear that they would not accept the "coal for Europe" program without a struggle. Exporting large quantities of German coal threatened to set back the three year plan for bizonal self-sufficiency and prejudiced the revision of the level-of-industry that Bevin and Marshall had authorized for the bizone in April 1947, and which the two military governors were already working on in Berlin.[37] It is therefore probably not a coincidence that Marshall wrote to Patterson on May 23, 1947—on the day that Kennan completed the Policy Planning Staff's initial report—and suggested that the two departments begin formal discussions on the transfer of responsibility in Germany from the Army to the State Department. Unlike Byrnes and Acheson, who for two years expressed the State Department's terror at the prospect of assuming administrative and financial responsibility for military government, Marshall apparently decided that the economic foreign policy that was being developed in the State Department could not be implemented with the Army in command in Germany.

Marshall's decision to transfer military government from the Army to the State Department gained acceptance at State only gradually. Only a few days before Marshall's letter went to Patterson, H. Freeman Matthews recorded his great disappointment at OMGUS's unwillingness to buy Iceland fish for $2 million, noted that the incident was typical of others, and concluded that "OMGUS will only cooperate under extreme pressure." In June 1947, State Department functionaries "believed that under the plan for recovery of Europe" Germany would have to be treated as another European country, rather than an American enclave, and that General Clay would have to deal with German problems on that basis. By July, a member of Matthews' staff thought it was time to "force Clay" to cooperate. He argued that a "mere instruction" to Clay to cooperate was not enough. Something had to come from the secretary of war or "preferably from the President."[38] Finally, by August 1947, James A. Stillwell, a special assistant to Undersecretary Clayton, recommended that the State Department take over civil affairs in Germany, relieve Clay as military governor, and replace him with a high commissioner "directly responsible to the State Department." Stillwell's argument was that Clay was "still operating on disease and unrest and economic self-sufficiency ideas," whereas the "main objective of our occupation policy henceforth is to direct the German economy so it will be able to play its rightful share in the Marshall Plan for Recovery of Europe." Stillwell argued that the coal and industrial production of the Ruhr were too important to European recovery to allow the Army or the Germans to determine how they would be allocated and used.[39]

The Army's position in 1947 was not much different from what it had been in 1945. When the State Department delayed publication of the revised bizonal level-of-industry plan that Clay and Robertson had drafted in July 1947, in response to the Bevin-Marshall agreement in Moscow, Clay threatened to resign, saying, "I think we are facing disaster in Germany and I don't like to head a failure which I can do nothing about. Under present conditions, it seems to me War Department should disdain further economic responsibility and insist now on a civilian takeover by State."[40] Less than a month later, after Clay had threatened once again to resign over a number of issues, such as coal export prices, the level of industry, and a decision to negotiate with France on these and other things, Secretary of the Army Kenneth Royall assured Clay that the Army was "again trying to induce State to take over Military Government . . . and if State does not take over promptly, I will seek approval of a broad directive to that end," presumably from Truman.[41]

True to his promise to Clay, Royall discussed the State Department's take-over with Marshall late in August 1947, and there is evidence that he talked about doing it with a stroke of a pen.[42] On September 3, 1947, the Army made a formal proposal, suggesting October 10 as the deadline for the appointment of a high commissioner and November 1 as the deadline for the transfer of functions, personnel, budget balances, and responsibilities.[43] As it had always done when it faced the prospect of implementing the policies it would have preferred to "force" Clay and the Army to implement, the State Department recoiled. Marshall having already agreed to the transfer in principle, however, this time State Department functionaries objected to details and specifics, arguing especially that they could not meet Royall's rigid deadlines. The discussions continued, however, and Marshall and Royall eventually agreed informally to plan for the State Department to take over by July 1, 1948, but to withhold announcement of the decision until after the London CFM adjourned in December 1947. But after the London CFM, the State Department still wanted to avoid a public announcement of the decision or the target date, claiming that a world crisis might require an embarrassing reversal later. Royall finally went ahead anyway on January 27, 1948. As if to prove that the

State Department was correct, on March 23, 1948—three days after
the Russians walked out of the ACC in Berlin—Truman announced
that after a review of the situation in Europe he had decided not to
make any changes in the administrative arrangements in Germany.
Clay would remain as military governor and commander of American military forces in Europe.[44]

Truman's press release of March 23, 1948, said that the decision to
keep the Army in control would not change American policy to develop German self-government and administrative responsibility.
The Army, Clay in particular, used that promise as a lever to encourage, promote, and literally force the rapid creation of a West
German government which could assume the responsibilities the
Army did not want anymore—and which it had exercised unwill-
ingly since the early summer of 1945. The accounts of Clay's role in
the London Six-Power Talks of 1948 on the future of Germany, of
how he convinced and pressed the minister presidents of the three
Western zones to accept the Frankfurt Documents in July 1948, and
of how he influenced the development and ratification of the Basic
Law are too long and complicated to present here. There is little
doubt, however, that the most decisive support for German self-
government and for the Basic Law came, *in the first instance,* from
Clay and the American Army, who saw in the creation of a German
government a means to be relieved of some of the Army's political
and economic responsibilities in Germany.[45] Thus, the newborn
West German government of 1949, which rose out of the ashes of
military defeat, was conceived and delivered by the American
Army. Ironic as it may be, for the second time in the twentieth century, Germany's democratic development was heavily influenced by
a military establishment, albeit not by the same one.

Chapter 5

Proconsul of a People, by Another People, for Both Peoples

Lucius D. Clay

It is most important to recall how we really began to drift away from Russia. There is no question in my mind but that the total Marshall Plan would never have resulted if Russia had been more amenable at the end of the war. It could have been done internally. I think that the Cold War was inevitable, but that it came so quickly was unbelievable. At that time we had nothing but warmth for the Russians.

Although the Cold War without any question speeded up our understanding and accommodation of German needs, I doubt whether in the long run it made much difference. We are not a nation that carries hate and vengeance for any long period of time. We do not like to see disorder; we do not like to see chaos; we do not like to see lack of economic progress and growth anywhere, really, and particularly if we have anything to do with it. Just like Herbert Hoover said, you cannot let hunger occur where you have the American flag flying.

When we took over Germany, we adopted as a general principle the eventual return of the German government to a democratically chosen government. I do not think we thought much beyond that, in terms of how you prove that it was such a government.

Actually, after World War I, Germany was a democratic country in the sense that its officials were truly elected by the German peo-

This paper consists of passages pertinent to this conference excerpted with kind permission of the McCloy Fund and the Conference Group on German Politics from a July 1977 interview of General Clay by George K. Romoser and Robert Wolfe. That interview and interviews with John J. McCloy and others are being prepared by the interviewers for prospective publication under the tentative title "Founding Principles of the Federal Republic of Germany: Retrospective Views of Some American Co-Founders."—Ed.

ple and were held responsive to an elected parliament. On the other hand, there was no effort made at that time to bring about any kind of an economic recovery. This first venture, after World War I, into democracy took place at a time of economic want, and it therefore appeared to be a failure to the very people who had established it. This enabled the power-grabbing political leaders of the period to come in and take over, to forget about democracy, using the economic chaos as their reason.

Perhaps we would have had the same thing occur after World War II except that we did have the power to prevent that from happening. If there was any seizure of power to develop the economic side, it was not done by Germans. It was done by the occupying powers.

In my own case, nobody talked to me about what our policies were in Germany. They just sent me over there. I did not want the job. After all, we were still fighting a war, and to be the occupying deputy military governor in a defeated area while the war was still going on in the Pacific was about as dead-looking an end for a soldier as you could find.

I had been in the tag end of World War I; I did not get over again except on an after-the-war visit. I did see the inflation. I did see the difficulties under which the new German government was attempting to establish itself. Of course, there was no destruction in Germany. There was no physical chaos. There were no hundreds of thousands of prisoners that had not been returned. The situation was, from the viewpoint of the German people, nowhere nearly as bad after World War I as after World War II, with one exception. We participated in a military government after World War II. If it had not been for that, I do not know where Germany would be today.

A foreign group cannot establish a successful revolution. All we would have done if we had backed Germans politically would have destroyed them. It was my contention that we tried to observe complete political neutrality.

We were criticized a lot because the British were more or less backing the Social Democrat party. They had their own Labor government which was a socialist party, and they were backing the German Social Democrat party to a certain degree, I am sure. That had much to do with Adenauer being moved out as the mayor of Cologne. We had put him in. The British moved him out; they told him because he was too old, which was sort of belied by what he did afterwards. But we tried to maintain complete neutrality, thinking that whatever happened in the creation of a democracy, if it did not come from the Germans, if it came by order, it would not last, would not endure at all.

I had no policy given to me as to what kind of a democracy we wanted. I did not have very much experience in the field myself, never having voted at that time. I came from a state where soldiers were not allowed to vote; because of the fact that they had voted for Hayes in the Hayes-Tilden election, the state of Georgia had passed a law prohibiting the vote of soldiers. Actually, one of the prime reasons that I started local government elections at a very early date, against the advice of some of the local experts on our staff, was that I felt the Germans had to have experience in taking responsibility. If they established local governments and got them going before you had state controls, you could avoid the state power which had always made the local officials in Germany very secondary.

I think this did help. In the first place, the voters were voting for people they knew. When they voted in local elections, they were voting for Bill Smith or Tom Jones or somebody they knew. In state elections, as a rule, they voted for people they had never even heard of except as they would publicly state their positions.

So one of our prime purposes in getting Germany back into a self-governing state was to create, or to attempt to create, this sense of local responsibility. And we followed that up, of course, with state governments. I think these state governments have zealously tried to maintain some of their responsibilities.

By and large we went to the universities for our political leadership. A number of our *Länder*-presidents and officials we got right out of universities. We very carefully checked the fact that they had resisted the increase in power in the central government as one of the reasons why we picked and selected them. I think even Chancellor Erhard had come out of one of the German universities. Geiler, Heuss—all of these people were well-known intellectuals, and their power and strength was such that we felt that it was their job to bring about in the universities the reforms that were necessary. And tô some degree they did.

One of the things that I insisted on, with great difficulty, was that none of our administrative units could carry out reforms that went beyond those we had in the United States. That was why, particularly with the Civil Service people and the break-up-the-trusts people, who wanted to put in the kind of reforms in Germany that the liberals had tried to but had never been able to enact in the United States, I said this was way beyond our mission. In a general sort of way, the people to whom I reported also felt this way. I do not think that Mr. McCloy, for example, to whom I reported and wrote letters and gave accounts of how things were going, ever would have thought of carrying any reform in Germany beyond the stage that we had been willing to enact in the United States.

I remember when we were in Moscow for the Foreign Ministers Conference, 1947, I guess it was. General Marshall had just taken over. Foster Dulles was there, and Ben Cohen, and quite a group from the State Department. I can remember when we were getting ready, preparing for various and sundry issues, that we spent one whole day disagreeing on a definition of democracy. This was entirely within the American delegation. We could not agree on any common definition for democracy. I doubt if you could get any ten people in a room that would today.

Of course, the very re-creation of dictatorial government in East Germany made it just that much easier for the West Germans to really want a democracy. I think it makes it more difficult to judge when you see two peoples, one on one side of a border that very calmly, apparently, accepts a dictatorial government, and the one on the other side that has achieved, at least in every outward sense, a democratic government.

The answer to that lies, I suppose, in the fact that they are more accustomed to strong central governments than a democratic government, and the East German did not go through the experience of having control of his own affairs, which the West German government people did, and they like it. Now, if a people really learned to like democracy, it is going to be very difficult to take it away from them.

You also have to remember that in this particular stage, with the Marshall Plan, the currency reform, and other factors, there was an upward surge of the German economy, and they began to see hope for the first time. This, combined with their assumption of local responsibility, gave democracy a chance—better than it would normally have. Right now they are getting some economic prosperity in East Germany, and I think as a result their regime is not quite as dictatorial as it was. Hungry people do not give a damn about politics.

When I was sent over to be General Eisenhower's deputy for military government, knowing General Eisenhower, I knew that he would delegate that authority to me, keeping as he always did in close touch, but nevertheless he delegated authority. On the other hand, not having wanted the job, not having given any thought to preparing for it, I really did not have any fixed views. I did not get the American declaration of policy until after I had been over there several months.

Of course, when we got that [JCS 1067]—as a matter of fact, that is when Lewis Douglas decided he would not stay because he was not going to try to operate a financial situation when the instructions were he was to do nothing—it was obvious to me even at that stage of the game that an economic vacuum in the center of Europe meant economic chaos in Europe. So, from the very beginning, I realized that we had to do something in the economic field in spite of JCS 1067, and succeeded in getting something done on the basis of relieving the United States from the several hundred million dollars a year that it was costing us for food and other things.

We were creating a situation that was hopeless. We were preventing, not helping, the recovery of a country we had defeated, but at the same time paying for its deficits to keep it alive. This was a hopeless situation unless we got some sort of an economy going. So I think this is what made the economic recovery a goal, which indicated perhaps that we had developed a friendly interest in Germany, which was perhaps not the case at all. We were trying to get it off our backs and also into the total picture of recovery in Europe. If you remember rightly, politically the Communists were almost everywhere in Europe the most powerful single party at that stage of the game. I had no fixed feelings with respect to the Germans one way or another.

Let us look back on it as it occurred. The Germans surrendered. Our tactical forces were occupying a very substantial part of Western Germany, much more than was to be a part of our zone of occupation. They had picked somebody here or somebody there to be a local *Bürgermeister,* a local official, without much screening and without much time to screen. There was no interconnection. The mails had broken down. Food distribution was very difficult, but we had fortunately brought in hundreds of thousands of tons that we had built up because we knew the situation was going to exist.

Well, what do you do? The first thing you do is to pick something which you can do. The first thing we had to do, even before we had moved into our final zone of occupation, was to go to work with the British to get the railroads running. Then we went out to determine as we moved back into our own zone of occupation, what we would do about government at the local level. We had to establish military government units, take over from the tactical troops. The tactical troops did not want to give up, because as long as they were in charge they could commandeer houses, and whatever they wanted, and they liked that sense of power.

This was quite a problem, getting the control out of the hands of the tactical troops into the military government units. The preparations for all of this that had gone on before, while they had been done on a very high intellectual plane, were all based on the theory that we were going to take over existing ministries. But these existing ministries did not exist. This is the first thing I saw, that this (preconception) was just a lot of foolishness, that we were going to have to be the government ourselves and build from the bottom up. Otherwise, we would have been violating all of our rules about Nazis in government, because if you were not a Nazi, you did not hold a high post in the Third Reich, that is certain.

In the second place, it was obvious to me then that it was going to take a long time before the four occupying powers, three at that time, could agree on who would be the German ministers. Political questions had already arisen. I cannot imagine me as a deputy military governor sitting there agreeing to 50 percent of the ministers being Communists. I do not think I would have lasted very long. Not that that was important, but the fact remains we would not have liked that at all back here.

So we had innumerable problems and what we were trying to do was to solve each problem as it arose. Eventually we began to get within our military government a German government.

We had several hundred thousand refugees, arriving ten and twenty thousand a day, some of them fleeing from communism, others being ousted by the Communist governments, like the Silesians and the Sudeten Germans. I think there were about three million of these refugees that had to be accommodated in a country that was in collapse. Fortunately, they were needed later on.

We began to realize that, just like any other people, not all Germans were bad Germans or bad people. For example, in '46, I think it was, when Secretary Byrnes came to make his speech in Stuttgart he was terribly impressed with our minister-presidents. They were really very down-to-earth men. You could not dislike them. They mostly were nice people. Now, I was very careful and kept at arm's length from all of the Germans of that time and period. I did not have a German friend. Not because I could not have liked many of them, but I was afraid I would taint them. I was afraid I would destroy any effectiveness they might have in the Germany of the future. I think that was wise, because my friendship with Adenauer and Erhard and others was a development after I left Germany, not while I was there.

On my eightieth birthday I got telegrams from the president and the chancellor, the leader of each political party. It was heartwarming. They were all expressions of friendship, not for me, but fundamentally for the relations between our two countries.

For a long period of time my real contact was my monthly visit to Heidelberg. Also I met with the German minister-presidents in our zone and the so-called parliament each month, and I guess it was unique for me; I would go in before them and answer all their questions. Sometimes my answers were pretty short, when they would ask questions about why we did certain things, like making them take care of refugees. But, in any event, it was these meetings, I think, that created the give and take between occupier and occupied. That was very important particularly in the days when we were trying to get the Basic Law adopted. These were very interesting meetings because fundamentally the German political leader is a better educated man than in most countries. I really believe that it was this experience, particularly as we did this in our zone with our four states, that made it possible for the constitutional assembly, or whatever you want to call it, "Basic Law Assembly," to adopt a federal type of government.

In the meetings which the three military governors held with the representatives of the constitutional assembly, whose leaders were Adenauer and Schumacher of their respective parties, it became quite evident to me that the Germans themselves hardly knew what we were talking about when we were talking about federal government. Then I found out that neither did Washington! I could never get a strict definition for what they really intended me to do to create a federal government, and even in the last few days when the Germans would want to put something through that I thought was vital, Washington would usually weaken and say,"Let them have their own way." We did not, because they did not order me to. They just suggested it. But I think we have a peculiar idea of our government being perfect without knowing really and truly how it works. Very few people, when you really get down to it, have any firm ideas about what is meant by federalization. Certainly we have left a lot of it behind us.

The give and take was a fact, that here were these states giving and taking their position, not only with the central authority (we being the central authority), but with each other. So that at least you had the opportunity of finally coming up with a consensus. Now, a consensus was obviously what was ordered by military government, but military government was fairly careful in trying to come up with a consensus unless it was in conflict with some deep-seated principle.

To tell you the truth, I do not know how much of the Basic Law was German and how much of it was American inspired. The principal advisor to the Basic Assembly was a Harvard professor by the name of Carl J. Friedrich. Carl was, of course, born in Germany, but he had become very much imbued with American political tradition, and he was a very important off-the-record figure with his advice at that constitutional assembly. His fluent German and his knowledge of German history and previous constitutions also made him an expert on the question. So, whenever I had thoughts or ideas about what now, he was the one I always talked with and went to, never asking him to take a position because I did not want to destroy his value. He was not there except to be available. But the fundamental requirements as laid down for the general subject of federalization and so forth were not unacceptable to the Germans.

I think the division of Germany is going to influence German thinking for a long, long time, and I think that as the world situation eases, the desire of the Germans to go back together will become stronger again than it appears at the present moment. If you go back and look at the history of Poland and see how many years Poland was divided, and yet the desire to reunite was always there and finally expressed itself. I think this is going to be true in Germany, and I do not think that politically any German political leader could afford to take any other position. I do not think that you could ever get the West Germans to accept the fact that the separation was necessarily permanent and to be accepted as such. They are always careful to put in language that indicates that this is not permanent in their thinking and in their minds.

As far as how the German people would react, and how you test democracy, I cannot give you an answer except in these terms. In the final analysis, the American people never make the wrong decision. When it comes to a really major decision in this country, they will change political leadership, they will adopt positions, and they have always been proved right on the major issues. They have not had a crisis like this in Germany yet, and so we cannot really answer. I could not tell you what I think about German democracy until I see it go through a crisis.

I was very unhappy that they had a coalition government so long—the Grand Coalition—because I felt that to really learn democracy you had to have the play of two big political parties. I welcomed in my own mind, as an advantage in their gaining democracy, a two-party system which they still now have. Matter of fact, I do not like to see a small minority party exercising the influence that the small minority party does in Germany, because it is far beyond its actual strength with the German people.

For example, I do not think we are going to suffer in this country the full ill effects of an inflation which we seem unable to stop. Because somewhere along the line the common sense of the American people is going to take over, and they are going to say, "Let's get this place of ours in shape." Now, can Germany do that if the same situation develops? If this can happen, then it has truly, in my opinion, become a democratic country.

I think that you have to remember that they did stick to a parliamentary form of government which we do not have. There is one place where I would have liked to see their president have more power, more authority. That is one place where the British and French really disagreed with us. They were so afraid of a strong central authority, the result was that the president became pretty much a state representative and not one who was carrying any authority. The result was, of course, minority political parties became more powerful. They also became more powerful because of the fact that there was such a close division of strength between the Christian Democrats and the Socialists. On the other side of the picture the price that you pay for any other way of government would have been very, very difficult.

With the German people there is no question that it was the airlift that made them look on not only me but Americans as people who had saved them, and as friends. It did a great deal to create that kind of atmosphere. On the other hand, I think our relationship with the Germans (through the military government that we established) who did become the political leaders of their country with the constitutional assembly—our relationship with the thinking German was a very good one.

The fact is that they appreciated that they could never have done a currency reform, and they also appreciated the fact that it had to be done. I think this is the kind of thing they realized we were taking on our shoulders to save them from that particular agony and problem. They realized the fight that we put up to get them accepted in the European Recovery Program, which none of the Western European countries really wanted and some of our own people were lukewarm to. Fortunately, Paul Hoffman and Averell Harriman were big enough men to realize that if you did not do something in Germany you were not going to succeed anywhere. But the fact remains that we had to put up a very big fight; they realized that this was how it had to go. So I think amongst the German leaders—now they are gone, most of them, but they have been there up till now—our military government and our American government stood in very high repute as having done the best we could for a defeated country.

What actually happened [in the currency reform of 1948] was a movement in Washington at the time to defer our own actions, to wait to see if there were any signs of the Russian willingness to go ahead. My own view was that we could no longer wait. If the Russians wanted to come in under proper conditions, we would have had to accept them, in my opinion. But to have delayed the currency reform at that stage of the game would have been absolutely and completely destructive. It would have leaked out; the whole story would have been known; we would have backed away—it would have been terrible. It would have been a complete disaster.

We said [to the State Department] "Please take it"; we really did. My whole philosophy from the time I landed was to get responsibility for the U.S. zone into the hands of civilians so that it was not an army matter, but that the State Department would take over.

In the first place, victorious troops, tactical troops, have no business running a country. This is not said in any lack of high respect for our forces, but you look upon yourself as a conqueror. You cannot avoid it. In the second place, the military establishment had long before given up its old-time role as the keeper of territorial possessions. As you remember, back in the old days Cuba, the Philippines, all that had been part of the War Department, had been transferred to the State Department to take over after we had established what we called law and order.

You have got to have civil affairs reserve units. They are being trained more realistically today than they were in my day because they really are being trained primarily for running local governments and technical administration. You cannot train people for the political role, whatever it may be, because you do not know what it is going to be. You have no idea.

You have to start from wherever you are and whatever you are. Of course, in the chaos and disorder following the war, it is only the army that is on the ground and who has the talent and the administrative experience within its ranks to do the job, so they do not have any choice.

You are told to go in and run a town; you go in and run it, period. If you try to find somebody else over in America, you get fourteen different reasons why they can or they cannot. If they want the job, they are probably not the one you want, and if they do not want it, you cannot get them. So, if we had not had our army officers to call for originally, and then to persuade to stay as civilians, I do not think that we could have ever staffed the occupation. For those were immediate, chaotic days. It was hard work, and it was not fun. Looking back in retrospect, I never worked so hard in my life as I did for the Germans.

Capitalism certainly had not proven the success in Europe that it might have been. But the very fact remains that if you are going to represent your country in a foreign country whether it is as a military governor or whatever, you had better by a damn sight represent the convictions of your country and not theoretical convictions, if you want to be supported. We had to get two or three hundred million dollars out of Congress every year from the GARIOA [government and relief in occupied areas] budget.

I am terribly sorry I did not make that [Americans as Proconsuls] Conference. I wanted to very much, but could not physically take a conference.

Chapter 6

From Military Government
to Self-Government

John J. McCloy

As you can imagine, listening to these papers and discussions so far prompts many memories both from the Japanese and the German occupation. Let me say a word or two about the Japanese. It so happened that somewhere along the line in 1944 or early 1945, I was told to prepare the surrender terms for General MacArthur. They were the terms that were signed on the *Missouri*. I took no papers with me when I left the government—they are all down in some Maryland warehouse now—but I recall very definitely a sort of a précis of what the concept of the Japanese occupation was to be. It was all centered around and related to the concept of a constitutional monarchy.

There was a big question that came up in the early days of the Truman administration as to what the next steps were to be in the conduct of the war against Japan. There was a meeting of all the bigwigs in the White House and, in the course of it, I think that was the first time in any such assembly that anybody ever mentioned the word "atomic bomb." It was just anathema to do it—you should not mention Skull and Bones on the campus at New Haven—so you should not mention atomic bomb. But it came up at that point because they were determining whether or not the authorization to attack the main Japanese Honshu Island was to be given by the president. It ended up by agreeing to go forward with Kyushu but not Honshu. Since the issue was momentous—that is, what options there were in considering the next step in the war against Japan—the president would not let anyone out of the room until he had stated his position. I said, "I think we ought to talk about this thing." And, I said we ought to have our heads examined if at this point, where we have such an enormous superiority, we did not try to seek a political settlement.

When the words "political settlement" were mentioned, somebody said what do you mean by political settlement? The first words that came out then were "constitutional monarchy." The underlying issue in this question of what next to do about Japan was whether or not to preserve the Mikado. I suggested, for one thing, that we ought to notify the Japanese about the bomb. After the sweep across the Pacific which we had just completed, it was hard to find another battleship to bomb or another town to destroy. It did seem as if we ought to try to get somewhere with a political settlement and we ought to tell them that we had the atomic bomb and about its devastating effects. There was a good bit of dissent about that and also what to do with the Mikado. The Japanese would never accept our branding their emperor a war criminal and being deposed. At that stage, though, there were some (including apparently Secretary Byrnes) who felt we should get rid of the Mikado. A lot of others (including myself) felt that you would have a simpler problem in the postvictory situation in Japan if you did maintain the Mikado under a constitutional monarchy. Then the question came: what do you mean by a constitutional monarchy and how do you want to spell it out? That was the genesis of a good bit of the memoranda that were prepared as to what the type of the occupation of Japan should be. I remember it said something about allowing the Japanese access to raw materials but preventing their control of them. (The Japanese had rationalized their wartime aggression by accusing us of boycotting their access to essential raw materials.) There were also comments on the establishment of the Mikado and on the expansion of the electorate which you referred to.

When the victory did ensue in Japan, I do not recall why, but I was told to draw up those surrender terms and I did. I remember that when the surrender documents came back from the *Missouri,* there was a sort of meeting at the White House with all of the admirals and generals, all the factors in the victory. The phone in my office rang and President Truman, with whom I had worked a good bit in connection with the Japanese terms, said they were going to take a picture here, "but we are not going to take it until you come along." I wish I could remember what wisdom I put down in those surrender terms, but I was very much impressed with the fact that Mr. Truman insisted that I get in the picture.

Thereafter, on a number of occasions, I did go out to Japan and attempt to give guidance to the "Shogun." One time I went out there and it was a rainy, mean day and that road from the airport into Tokyo—when you get a little rain, how slippery and how inadequate as a means of transportation it was. Three times we went into

the ditch—twice I fell over on MacArthur, and then the third time
he fell over on me. By the time we got back, he was very sorry that
he had come out to the airport to welcome me at that point—
particularly as I had some other criticisms I wanted to make.

I remember in those days it was a little awkward—I went all the
way around the world the other way as a cover plan so that no one
would know that I was going out to talk to General MacArthur
about occupational policies. But I must say that he was most impressive as he talked about the future and the forces that were playing around the Orient with which he was quite familiar. With that
corncob pipe and shaking his matchbox throughout, he laid out to
me then what he thought the future of the Orient was going to be
after the victory. He was a man of tremendous discernment, a man
of great quality. But, as you indicated, we needed a Mikado at that
point and he took the role of the Mikado. I was there on several
occasions when he arrived on the scene in front of his headquarters
where all the Japanese there were knocking their heads in the
ground as he came and went. I think that the concept of his personality and his demeanor had a good bit to do with the authority and
the respect with which our occupation policies were carried out.

Of course, my role was primarily in Germany. Some time in 1944,
President Roosevelt called me to the White House, and the war was
in full flight with no victory either in Germany or Japan at that
point. As I came into the office, he held up his hand in a Hitler salute
to me and said, "Heil, Hochkommissar für Deutschland!" I had no
more idea of what he was talking about than a man in the moon; it
was just so much Greek to me.

You must bear in mind that Mr. Roosevelt was rather intrigued,
and attached, and very much interested in Germany. In his youth he
had bicycled through Germany and, as the assistant secretary of the
navy after World War I, he had gone over there in connection with
the liquidation of some of our bases and general facilities abroad. He
had spent a considerable amount of time in Germany and he had
definite ideas as to how we would treat Germany after what he assumed, even then, was to be our victory. Shortly after the adoption
of the Atlantic Charter—he went up there on the battleship and
talked with Mr. Churchill at that point, and came out with the so-
called Atlantic Charter. From time to time he did refer, particularly
with Mr. Stimson—once when I was present—about his theories in
connection with the occupation of Germany, and it was by no means
a *vae victis* concept. It was rather benign (maybe "benign" is not
quite the word, but certainly enlightened)—there was no such thing
as pastoralization in his mind at that stage.

He was thinking in more enlightened terms because a number of us in the Army who had been in the German occupation in World War I, including myself—I had been up in the Koblenz bridgehead billeted in Trier, then attached to the Regular Army—had experienced the bitterness of that occupation. And it was in the minds of all of us—the recollection of the reparations issue, and the reoccupation of the Ruhr, and the harrassments, and the agitation, and the irritations on which Hitler so greatly capitalized later when he came into power. And even that early (and I am talking of the relatively early part of World War II), Mr. Roosevelt did have the idea of the redemocratization of Germany; how were we going to treat with it.

Twice in his lifetime and mine, due to this antagonism between France and Germany, we had to move across the Atlantic with our blood and treasure, and it was getting a little bit tiresome every generation having to go over and fight another war because of Franco-German antagonisms. The center of his thinking was a rapprochement between France and Germany. It had not reached at that stage the concept of a European community, but it was not such a great step from what he was thinking about to that thought, with the idea of encompassing Germany after this victory into a community which, from the point of view of security, would cause people not to fear a recrudescence of German militarism. And that was, I thought, a very significant thing and it was not until very much later, at the stage of the so-called Morgenthau Plan (which I will come to in a minute) when this so-called *vae victis* concept arose. Up to that time Mr. Roosevelt had not been, it seemed to me, at all in that mood; he was thinking in terms of the rejuvenation or the redemocratization of Germany, and the elimination of the old Franco-German antagonisms.

When he gave me that salute, and after I understood what he was talking about, I said I thought it would be a great mistake to put a civilian in charge of the occupation of Germany immediately after the victory. In the first place, the generals and the field marshals and the soldiers would be marching and counter-marching at that time, and it was also a matter of keeping body and soul together; it was not a matter of the reconstitution of the constitution at that point. It was something in the nature of what I call a "Mississippi River disaster," and I think you have got to put the military in charge because a civilian would be lost that quickly after the close of the hostilities, and while all of the generals were in occupation, the great military leaders of the war. It was only appropriate that the Army should carry on at that stage.

He said that was all very well, but he did not know any soldier

that could do it. I said that I knew one—because when I used the
term "Mississippi River disaster" I had thought of an engineer—
and I then mentioned Clay to him. I said, "Well, I know one, Lucius
Clay." He should have known Clay but he did not seem to—Clay
was then a subordinate of General [Brehon] Somervell, but Clay already at that point had a real record. He had been a page boy in the
House of Representatives and was the son of a former senator. That
intrigued the president, so he said, "Go down and talk to Jimmy
Byrnes about it." Well, Jimmy Byrnes was then sort of the "assistant president" and had a room down the hall, and I went down to
talk to him about it. And he said, "You are absolutely right; you go
back to the Pentagon and get General Clay promoted and I'll take
care of the boss." That is a little insight on how Clay came to be the
first military governor.

Then, later on, I was in the World Bank at the time, and I got
another call to go to the White House. This time it was Truman.
When I came in he said, "McCloy, I have made up my mind and I am
going to appoint you the first high commissioner to Germany; we are
going to put it into the State Department." I said, "This is not the
first time it was offered to me." He did not know a thing about the
earlier affair. And I said, "Well now I think the time has come"—
although bear in mind by this time Clay had not only been the
military governor, he had been a real constitutional innovator. He
was very much involved in the drafting of the Basic Law and his
concept of starting out with the *Länder;* he had some real political
acumen, and he had gotten things moving up to a point where the
so-called high commissioner had quite a good base upon which to
operate from a political background.

As a matter of fact when I went over first, I was a full year there as
military governor, and we continued on with the programs and policies that Clay had instituted; the further invigoration of the governments and the *Länder* and the denazification period and so forth.
By that time he had been operating under the famous JCS 1067.
There had been papers drafted and concepts created as to what the
occupation policies ought to be. I do not know whether the documentation that exists shows where they are. There was, of course, a
handbook of military government that we prepared in some consultation with the British. We were pretty far along with that and had
some ideas on it coming from the other side, from Eisenhower. I
would like to take another look at it; I have not seen it for a long
time but I think it would stand the light of day today not in terms of
its softness, but in terms of its reality. Then suddenly the roof fell in,
and down from Quebec came the so-called Morgenthau Plan. It

should not be called the Morgenthau Plan; I think it could justifiably be called the Churchill Plan, because Churchill drafted it. Mr. Stimson upbraided the president for it because he said, "This is a shocking document; it will impair your place in history." At the same time he was getting the same sort of comments from Eden who was shocked by it. Mr. Roosevelt said, "Harry, I don't know what you're talking about." And Stimson said, "Yes you do, Mr. President, don't dissemble with me, I'm talking about the pastoralization letter." "Oh," he said, "that was one of Winston's whimsies, I would never have thought of the word *pastoralization*." And I think that's true, I think "pastoral" was a little too graphic, almost a Churchillian word, that Mr. Roosevelt would probably not have used. That document was pretty stark in the language used, but it was something of a studied affair because Lord Cherwell—"the Prof"—who was with Mr. Churchill, concocted this idea of the pastoralization of Germany—the complete deindustrialization of the entire nation. Looking back now, it was sort of a silly concept—it would have been impossible to do and would have made Germany vulnerable to Soviet domination—and the president realized it was, and somewhere along the line all copies of it were buried. I do not think you can find a copy of it in his papers.

Out of that and the reaction to that, the negotiation of a new directive to the armed forces in Germany and the occupation people emerged, and that was so-called JCS 1067. It was rather Draconian—it was not as bad as the Morgenthau Plan—but it was pretty negative in the sense of "do not do anything really, to restore or reinvigorate German industry, with nothing in the way of rehabilitation." It was obvious that you could not function living amongst the Germans and being responsible for their welfare and peace and the necessity of feeding them. You could not very well carry that out in its literal form. It gave rise to the "disease and unrest" exception on which a good many developments were connected, and you will find, I think, if you look through JCS 1067 throughout most of the paragraphs there is some part of a provision there which I thought was sort of realistic—in case we were to get down to a pinch, generally speaking, do not do anything that is very substantial in terms of trying to reinvigorate German industry, but do what you can to keep body and soul—and that was about the way which they functioned for some length of time.

There has been a good bit of criticism of JCS 1067. My then brother-in-law Lewis F. Douglas, who was over there with General Clay on his staff for a while, got very excited about JCS 1067. General Clay was not so excited; he thought he could function under it. I think he several times said he thought that this was a document under which he could very well progress. The emphasis upon JCS 1067, if you look at it, was that it was temporary. The word *temporary* was used in the introduction to it, and throughout the temporary aspect of it was stressed. I do not think it really interfered with the development of Germany. It certainly did not bring about any drastic or Draconian applications.

As time went on and just in the ordinary operation of keeping things going and the necessity of getting coal—I remember the early priority was "pit-props." Nobody could find pit props for the mines and there was a great question as to whether or not under JCS 1067 they could get pit-props out of the Scandinavian companies and bring them down into the mines, so that they could hold the mine up, so that we could get enough coal to keep people warm. Maybe some of you were there, but I remember they moved from one priority to another, and rationalizing from one step to another, both on the political and the economic line.

The occupation did move ahead. We talk a great deal about the miracle of the German recovery. It was to some extent miraculous. In many ways, however, the Germans were quite fortunate; not only did they have the advantages as we went along with the massive benefits that the Marshall Plan and the counterpart system played. But because of the dismantling program, which was then in full force, there was a certain inconsistency about dismantling at the same time we were trying to press heavy reparations from the Germans. The result was that the reparations out of the west zone were not very substantial, certainly at the beginning. Perhaps it enabled us to meet some of the demands that the Soviets were making for a rather heavy and a very oppressive reparations policy, because it seemed rather inconsistent to be trying to move in the negative way we were, at the same time we were trying to generate the reparations which could only be produced with a vigorous industry.

I come back again to this question of the rapprochement with Germany and France. I remember the night that Adenauer was elected chancellor by one vote, and it was his vote—he voted for himself. He came down to see me at Bad-Homburg, and said, "You had something to do with running this country, for a little while, so tell me what you think is the chief imperative that you would pass on here as what you think is the priority." And I mentioned that I thought rapprochement with France was the main thing. He was very receptive to that, of course. As you know, he was quite a Francophile. To him it was only the day before yesterday that Charlemagne ruled in Aachen. The Holy Roman Empire was a thing of reality to Adenauer. Remember, after World War I he had a little arrangement with France, so that it did not take a great deal of urging on the part of Adenauer to work out his understandings and his relationships with France. He found de Gaulle a very sympathetic figure.

I have talked about the genesis of JCS 1067, the effect of the Morgenthau Plan on our occupation at that stage; and I look back on the whole affair with a good bit of satisfaction. I think in terms of the rehabilitation, for whatever reasons—they were not all due to the wisdom of American occupation or the wise policies. You have to give the accolade to Ludwig Erhard, who just died a week ago, for his determination to free up the economy; that together with the currency reform, of course. Erhard insisted over our objection—we thought he was going too fast—on removing the controls. But he had a good discernment and a good touch for it, it came at the right time, and the Germans were there—skilled workmen—who knew how to make the things that the world was athirst for at that time. This was another factor.

Through it all, I think there was a certain discernment on the part of our decision-makers that resulted in the rather spectacular reconciliation with our former enemies and the stability of Europe, and the rehabilitation of Europe on which, at least up until recently, has been a rather substantial and a more important factor in maintaining the recovery of Europe and the preservation of our freedoms and the preservation of the peace.

I do not think that it would be helpful for me to talk about the specifics as Mr. Gimbel pointed out these steps which were somewhat familiar. You must bear in mind there was a period there where I had nothing to do with the German scene. It was not until later that I came on the scene, and we began to really talk then in terms of German relations with the other countries, the establishment of NATO, and the finer elements of the constitutional processes in Germany.

I was very much impressed always in Germany with the quantity of individuals there were around that we could find without too much trouble. With all the denazification business that went on, everyone said that we could not carry on that denazification program without eliminating all of the people who had been in government, all the *Mitläufer* and others, but we did get rid of anybody of any real Nazi significance, barring a few exceptions that slipped through. We did get rid of that strata, and we were able to reach down and pick up people who had been either in the resistance or close enough to the resistance (they may not have been the great heroes or heroines like some of the names that come to mind).

I just heard, for example, that Kaisen of Bremen just had his ninetieth birthday the other day—a very good man and a stalwart amongst those minister presidents; Brauer, of course, from Hamburg, was another one; and Ehard from Bavaria. But all around, together with those that we could work out who were real members of the resistance, a good many of whom are still alive even with all of the vicissitudes that they have gone through, there were enough people to supply the officials for the *Länder* and later on to produce the statesmen or the members of the *Bundestag* who were able to carry on those early stages of government. The debates in the *Bundestag* were of a dignified character, and they were of a rather high order. That was an entirely new group, really, that came in, and they were not tainted with the Nazi business. There was a very substantial element of talent and quality and integrity that we could rely on.

I have one or two other thoughts that I would like to refer to before I have to run. Another element was the spur which we always had at this stage—the fear of the Soviet Union, the fear of the Russians. There they were, across the way in Berlin, pressing. In those days we were always on an alert—always reports were coming down the line that a column was coming toward our eastern borders. Would they come through? We had constant alerts that never got into the papers, but there was a *qui vive* there that extended throughout the whole zone, not only as it did later in Berlin, that kept everyone on their toes and there was a sense of fear and a sense of cooperation with the occupational authorities—very little irritation and very little unpleasant incidents. In those days, we were treated in the zone pretty much as we were treated a little later in Berlin when the pressures were down in Berlin and, in a way, we could do no wrong up there because the importance of showing ourselves in Berlin was so apparent to the Berlin population that it was almost a delight to go up to Berlin where we could do no wrong, while down in the zone we were apt to be criticized.

I think that the general tone, the political vigor—the miracle, if there was anything of a miracle—I think in the postwar period, it was the speed with which the completeness of the new political system and really a democratic system, with now and then some threats coming from the neo-Nazis, none of which ever prevailed, all of which were repudiated in whatever elections that took place. The speed with which that took place, and the vigor with which the

German Federal Republic picked up its constitutional and political responsibilities, if anything, was the miracle, in view of the fact that a short time before that, from minister president to dogcatcher, every job was held by a Nazi. There was a real thorough housecleaning which seems to have taken hold, and that, together with the good sense and the general industry of the German people, together with I won't say a brilliant occupation, but I think a quasi-enlightened one.

I think that is probably as much as I can do without going into further specifics, but if anyone has any questions while I have got some time, I would be very glad to try to answer them.

Discussion

Carl G. Anthon: Mr. McCloy, to what extent did reeducation and reorientation still play a major role in HICOG policies?

John J. McCloy: Oh, I think it played a very major role. We had a number of people on our staff who had been educated in Germany, and who knew the university system pretty well. We spent a good bit of time down with the universities, we had these seminars with the universities, and we had some very elaborate reports, of course, as to what the make-up of the faculties were at that time. We knew where the Nazis and *Mitläufer* were in the educational system. Early on, as you know, this exchange system was created, and there was a constant flow of professors and teachers, particularly starting in the higher education area, not only from the United States, but from Great Britain and France, and gradually the rather notorious figures that had overinfluenced the German higher educational system were eliminated. We pressured for the removal of a good many of the rectors that we felt had rather bad records, but the quantity and the excellence of the teaching that we had in the higher educational individuals that came over from the United States and from England began to exert their influence very early. Shepard Stone [OMGUS 1945–46; HICOG, 1949–52], my HICOG media adviser, who had a lot of wide German contacts, was one of those that stimulated it. We did get around and talk to the universities a good bit—I am talking about my staff. It was a very conscious effort on our part; some places we ran into a little resistance, but generally speaking, we were very well received.

Carolyn Eisenberg: I wanted to ask some further questions about the tensions between the State Department and the War Department in the period between 1945 and 1946. I have been reading through government records, and I am very struck by what seems to be a quite abrasive correspondence between Mr. Acheson and Mr. Patterson; specifically over the question of the extent to which the State

Department would put pressure on the French to collaborate in setting up central agencies in Germany, and the War Department was contending that the failure of the State Department to put pressure on the French was making it impossible to implement the Potsdam accords. I am wondering what your analysis is of the consistent refusal of the State Department to exercise that kind of leverage over the French.

John J. McCloy: I was not there then, so I cannot talk about it as a matter of direct knowledge. There has always been an interagency rivalry — it is nothing new; it is still going on between the Pentagon and the new State Department building. It may have reached some rather heated interchanges between Bob Patterson and Dean Acheson, both of whom were rather strong-minded and eloquent individuals. I should not be talking about it because I was not there then, and I do not know what that was. I do know I have suffered and my head has been bowed from time to time over the so-called interservice rivalry that not only exists in the Pentagon, but sometimes reaches across the river. But I am aware of what has been said heretofore about how reluctant the State Department was to take on political responsibilities.

I think one of the things that scared them off was Mr. Roosevelt's attitude in this regard. He had the feeling that there was going to be a great deal of unrest in Germany, and that we were going to have to put in a rather punitive sort of system in order to take care of the rioting that would come perhaps not by reason of any particular animosity toward the Americans, but just because there would be people that were hungry and there would be danger. He was also fearful of the Communist menace at that point. That was one of the reasons why he was so insistent upon the American forces getting near the ports, so that if difficulties arose we could get out quickly without getting involved.

I think there was a general feeling in the State Department, I think quite rightly, that they were not as well equipped to do the operating as the Army was. The Army is the only one that can really go in and operate in a situation like that. They are in the field, they know how to set up the tents, and get the trucks, and get things moving, and the instinct of the State Department to confine themselves to policy was a natural one. On the other hand, the difficulty that you have with the Army accepting authority while they have the responsibility for operating, having to look to somebody else for leadership, is not too pleasant an occupation on the part of a soldier.

I think that it is one of these human irascibilities that is not too significant.

Robert Donihi: Mr. McCloy, I am Robert Donihi. I did a research job for you in your immediate office in [the I. G. Farben Building in] Frankfurt some years ago, compiling for you a couple of footlockers full of documents pertaining to your administration in Germany. I am wondering whether or not you plan to do anything about writing on your administration or whether these documents might be available to scholars.

John J. McCloy: I do not know where they are now. I did not take anything with me. But where the I. G. Farben records are, I just do not know. To answer your second question—whether I considered writing memoirs on this area—I really have not. I have been rather busy doing other things. If I thought I could distill out of my experience something that I thought was really well worthwhile in preserving that would tend to be a guidance to our future foreign policy, I would go to work and try to do it. But that distillation has somehow eluded me up to this point. It does not do to just say, "Now it can be told: I said this to Churchill; Churchill said this to me." Reminiscence is not very good and, besides that, there is a lot of work involved. Dean Acheson told me, "Don't ever try it, Jack, unless you can take three years out." It is true, your memory plays you tricks and you have really got to do an awful lot of careful thought and research. I have sometimes wondered if it was worth the while. But if I could, as I said, really come to the conclusion that there was something worth preserving, I would try it on.

Dale Hellegers: Mr. McCloy, I was tantalized by your few brief comments regarding your meeting with General MacArthur in October of 1945. This was a difficult period for the general since he was under a lot of fire for a soft occupation in Japan, mostly from the American press, and since the State Department was involved in negotiations with the Soviet Union over securing that country's entry into the Far Eastern Advisory Commission. I wonder if you might perhaps amplify a bit on your comments regarding Mac-Arthur during the time you met him. You were the highest government official, after all, in that period to have a meeting with MacArthur and I assume that you brought him something of information from the War Department and from the United States government as a whole. You mentioned that you had some critical comments to make to him but you did not give us the benefit of what those were. Could you perhaps indicate on one hand the message that you brought to MacArthur and on the other what he told you about his perceptions of the occupation at the time—where it was going, what he intended to do, and what he thought the American government should do?

John J. McCloy: Well, I wish I could—I have got somewhere those notes on that conversation I had with MacArthur. All I can recall at this time (I did not come prepared to talk about that because I did not realize we were going to talk about Japan), all I can say is what I did say, and I forget at this moment precisely what point of criticism I had—there was something that was going wrong with the occupation or we thought was going wrong with it and I was sent out there to put it straight and we did get it straight. There was some misunderstanding, but I cannot for the moment recall precisely what it was. As to his philosophy in regard to the forces that were playing around the East, I said how impressive he was. He saw the Communist menace. He was very much interested in what was going to happen in China. He had been a real student of the Orient and the winds that blow around the Orient and when he got going he was very eloquent as you know. I cannot remember exactly now what were the most pungent and discerning things he had to say, but I got the very strong impression in listening to him that he was a very thoughtful man, he was not just a poseur. He was a man of considerable penetration of mind and thought and he had given a great deal of thought to what the future of the Far East was going to be and our relation to it, with very, very sage comments and foresight as to the ambitions and objectives of the Soviet Union. They were thoughtful—I do not mean to say that he was intransigent, but he was thinking in terms from the point of view of history what their objectives were apt to be and how they would attempt to apply them. And considering all of the circumstances of the handicaps and restrictions that flow with the democratic form of government we had, whether we could be in a position to exert our influence against the dictatorships. I think I can go no further than that because it is rather vague in my mind. As I say, I think I have some notes somewhere and it would be helpful if I had them at this moment, but I do not have them.

Joseph Langbart: I think perhaps you may have an answer to why MacArthur's position in Japan was different than our military governor's in Germany. After all, MacArthur was reenacting a role; he had been a military governor once before. He had spent almost ten years in the Philippines in effect being the shogun of the Philippines. So it was in his nature, perhaps to be the political ruler rather than the military ruler.

Jacob D. Beam: I would like to ask Dr. Gimbel about the Basic Law. Was there any pressure brought to bear from our side, from the Americans, on the Germans to adopt proportional representation?

John Gimbel: No, just the opposite, in fact. The Americans worked very hard to try to get the concept of single member districts put into the Basic Law, and there was a controversy, and you know that in the first elections they worked out a compromise where there were certain deputies elected, proportional representatives, and certain single member district ones. But the American position—Hans Simmons, Joseph Panuch, Clay—these people were essentially in favor of a sort of single member district type election as I recall the details. I have not been back to the material for some time.

Kurt Glaser: I wonder if Dr. Gimbel would like to comment on the German situation from the point of view of bureaucracy and bureaucratic groups. I have first in mind the fact that you have a duality not only in Washington where the State Department makes policy, transmits it to the War Department where the civil administration transmits it down through War Department channels to the commander, in this case, General Clay; but on the local level you also have the United States political advisor or US POLAD who is a State Department official usually with a rank of ambassador whose function it is to give political advice on the local level. So on the local level he is supposedly staff to the military governor. There a complication arises because in the Department of State directives are developed and sent over to the War Department where they have to be processed and it may be several days before they get down the line. The State Department, however, has its own radio system so US POLAD gets them in Berlin at least two days before they come through War Department channels. So Ambassador Murphy would sometimes go to General Clay and say, "Look, this is what you are going to get day after tomorrow." And Clay, I think, very much rejected the idea of getting orders from one of his own staff people. I think there is an ambiguity there, and this led to Clay creating his own special POLAD which was the Civil Administration Division which actually took over the political advice functions that US POLAD was supposed to do, including giving most of the advice on putting together the Federal Republic. I am not sure how much that situation existed in Japan, but I suspect there was very much the same thing. From my own research on the papers, I get the impression that orders from Washington were frequently distorted or ignored in the carrying out in the field.

Now, so far as proportional representation is concerned, we have a lot of political scientists that managed to get into military government and were anxious to try out their own ideas. Officially, yes, we were in favor of single member districts. It happens, however, that the head of the Political Parties and Elections Branch, namely Richard Scammon, came from being head of the Minnesota Proportional Representation League. So what is good for Minnesota must necessarily be good for Germany. I suspect that our pressure for single member districts was not as strong as it could have been, although you may perhaps disagree.

There were several other ideas, of course, that we wanted to try out. We wanted them to disestablish the church—to separate the schools from the church. Another one we had was abolishing the distinction between *Beamter* [official] and *Angestellter* [employee]. We did not put that over. So there were attempts to put over certain ideas which did not always work. But the thing that I think is most significant is this structural conflict which seems to be built into the situation.

John Gimbel: I will try to make it brief. On the Clay-Murphy relationship there is a good deal of material in the OMGUS records about the problems that were caused. There are, of course, times when Murphy got information before Clay did. But they had a good personal relationship as I have been told by Clay and Murphy themselves, and I can verify it from the records. They had a good personal relationship, and when Murphy heard about something that Clay was going to get two days later, it gave Clay two days' lead time to prepare an answer, which he often wanted to do. And so they often collaborated in trying to get changes in directives that way. So it worked both ways.

Your comment about Clay setting up his own political advisory function I think is extremely accurate. This could be in part because Murphy deferred to him. I hope Murphy will not take this as an offense if someone tells him that. I think Murphy in a sense deferred to Clay at that point for whatever reasons I do not know. But there is no question that, beginning after the London Six Power Talks in 1948, Clay's office took over the function of United States political advisor. Even though Murphy was in Berlin—in fact, Clay brought James Pollock back, he brought Carl Friederich back, Ed Litchfield filled up his Civil Administration Division with people out of the academic world of this country, and they were running all over Germany in the summer of 1947 advising Bavarians, Hessians, and Württembergers and, if they could get into the French zone, they advised them, too. At any rate, I think you are on the track when you see this function being taken over by Clay, but I do not think there is anything subversive about it. I think Murphy knew what was happening, I think Clay knew what was happening, and they simply decided that that was the way to get the job done.

Eleanor M. Hadley: I would just observe as we speak of MacArthur and his enjoying his shogunate reign, that he likewise, however, possibly for quite different reasons, very much favored a short occupation. He was in 1947, really illegally in terms of the division of responsibility, doing peace treaty work and that was not part of his responsibility. But there was work being done in the occupation in 1947, because he very much felt that to maintain the vitality of the occupation, you could do this quickly, and if it stayed on, it rapidly went into the various weaknesses and abuses of power.

Ralph Braibanti: There were those who said you could not accomplish anything in a two-year period. It is remarkable, when you look back on it, to find that most of your accomplishments did occur within more or less of a two-year period. But MacArthur did talk about two years.

Carolyn Eisenberg: Dr. Gimbel, I would like to follow up the question that I asked Mr. McCloy about the relationship between the State Department and the War Department in the handling of France. I am now working on a book on the breakdown of quadripartite cooperation in Germany. I am very struck by the centrality of the whole issue of how France was handled for the breakdown of four power harmony. The question that I am struggling with right now in my own work is to try to analyze what the State Department was concerned with, and why they so systematically refused to give support, first to General Eisenhower, and then General Clay in Germany when they asked for help in reinforcing the American position. To make my question a little more specific, I wonder whether you feel that the State Department's position simply reflected a reluctance to exert pressure on the French because of the realities of French domestic politics—whether you think it was in part an expression of some hesitation in the State Department to establish the four power agencies that had been agreed upon at Potsdam.

John Gimbel: I was wondering if you would ask me that question. I can avoid a lot of detail if I ask you if you have read my book on the origins of the Marshall Plan. You will find an answer in there, but let me, for the benefit of those who do not want to read that book, say that it is a complicated question. I would say at the very superficial level the State Department was staffed with pro-French people. The European Desk was full of French sympathizers: H. Freeman Matthews, John Hickerson—I wish John Hickerson were here because I found a beautiful quotation in one of his letters in which he summarized for some of his colleagues in SWNCC the American position regarding France. This was in December of 1945—John Hickerson said it is American State Department policy in Europe to make France the bulwark of democracy in Europe, which I think summarizes a lot. There is, of course, a feeling that the French deserve our sympathy and the Germans do not, and I am not quarreling with that idea. There is also an economic thing. I think that once you abandon the Morgenthau Plan and go toward a German level of industry, the French had a plan for how to handle that by transferring German industry to France under what became the Monnet Plan. A great many State Department people were very intrigued by that possibility. You could kill two birds with one stone—you could take care of the German deindustrialization, and you could take care of the French Monnet Plan all with one program. That had a certain attraction. There are minutes to show this to be the case.

Then, of course, there is the problem of the Communists and the socialists in the French provisional government. Byrnes in particular was absolutely terrified at what might happen if you put too much pressure on the French, that somehow Bidault was going to go down the tube or something was going to happen. Particularly during the elections in 1946 there was a problem. I found any number of instances where Byrnes said we cannot do this—pressure on the French—because we have got to keep them as stable as possible. There is the fear that any kind of French instability would threaten the American supply lines to Germany. So there are all kinds of reasons why.

But on your comment about Acheson and Patterson and the intensity of their exchanges in late 1945 and early 1946—the reason for that, I think, is not simply the issue we are talking about here, but that the Army got saddled with a job it did not want. Then, when they wanted to do it right, the State Department said, "No, you cannot do this." The Army said, "We cannot send twenty-five million tons of coal out of Germany by April 1, 1946," and the State Department said that Truman had put out a document that says "you have to." And the question was how much we charge for coal that is exported. The Army said to charge the going rate, $16.00 FOB Poland–$22.00 American coal landed in France. What did they come out with? They got $8.60 a ton which would not even pay for it anyway. But the Army then was saying they could not do the job unless they got some pressure on the French and pressure on the State Department and that is why Patterson was so angry with Acheson in the fall of 1945 and early 1946. I tried to allude to some of that—it is a rich topic and I say, "God bless you, you've got lots of work ahead of you."

Thomas W. Burkman: I have a question for Mr. Braibanti. You use the word "shogun" in your title, as you indicated, reluctantly, but since you accepted it I would like to ask you to deal with it. Was this indeed a title which MacArthur used? Did he conceive of himself and articulate the term "shogun," and did the Japanese people at the time speak of his role in terms of "shogun," or is this something that has been sloppily applied by westerners in later years? I think this is important in terms of the indigenous institutionalization that the Japanese people were willing to accord him.

Ralph Braibanti: I do not know of any instance in which he used the term to describe himself, but then he was a General of the Army and I was a captain, so I did not have much access to him. On the other hand, it was (I will not say widely) fairly commonly used in certain Japanese circles at that time, when Japanese often referred to him as "Mikasa Shogun." I say it was fairly widespread, but I think probably your latter comment is the one which is the most applicable—that is, it has been applied in a sense in a rather sloppy and a rather careless way, after the fact, with that exception that it was used by a few people.

Hans H. Baerwald: I have a question for you, Dr. Braibanti. I liked your elegant four categories and I was wondering if you were aware of the fact that the Japanese at the moment are developing a whole school of thought that really the occupation did not have anything to do with what happened to their society subsequently. One can use your four categories and make a case on their behalf. MacArthur, hidden away in the Dai Ichi Building, etcetera etcetera. I was wondering if you would care to comment on this.

Ralph Braibanti: First of all, I think you cannot view an experience of seven and a half years which includes massive penetration or infusion of foreign ideas and foreign influence, and simply write it off. This is manifestly impossible in any kind of experience. Any more than you can write off the equivalent amount of time with respect to British rule in India. You can haul down the statues of Victoria and you can take down the statues of Commodore Perry and so on, but this is denying the validity of seven and a half years of life. So I would say manifestly this cannot be done, and this kind of revisionism, I think, simply does not correspond with the social change generally, with contact between civilizations, and with impact of ideas as they circulate and are rediffused.

Now, on the other hand, you can look at it somewhat like this: Suppose for a moment that the occupation were not there, that Japan had surrendered and would have been left totally alone, without this kind of American influence. How would the government have developed? Well, obviously this is very reckless and almost useless kind of speculation. In the first place, of course, it is not conceivable that Japan could have developed alone. Had we not stepped in, undoubtedly the Soviet Union would have and the development then might have been quite different. That is the first observation to be made. But suppose, again to be quite reckless, the Soviet Union had not stepped in and that Japan would have been in a vacuum—again something manifestly impossible in the context of that particular time. But let us assume that had happened. Then I suspect that there was enough latent impetus for change moving in this general direction that the polity would have developed pretty much as it did under occupation control. But having said that, in effect, is saying nothing, because it is denying almost totally the context of that particular time.

Unidentified Questioner: Professor Braibanti, my question is a rather narrow one. In your talk, a minor point, perhaps, that you made was that there was press censorship of some sort of the Japanese press during the time the directives were coming down. I could not ask you what they complained about, but I would like to know what the mechanisms for censorship were and, in your opinion, does not this run contrary to many of the other things that we were trying to do at that time?

Ralph Braibanti: The mechanisms of censorship were two kinds. In the first stage it was actual precensorship—that is to say prepublication censorship—that is, it had to be submitted actually to American censors in CI&E. It then, after a few months, moved into a different kind of censorship; namely, a censorship simply of responsibility. Those were the two phases. As to the second part of the question, yes, it is contrary but in a sense obviously military occupation is contrary to many things.

Willard A. Fletcher: On your behalf and on my behalf, I should like to thank our panelists for their contribution to the program and I herewith close the formal proceedings.

Third Session

Reparations, Economic Reform, and Reconstruction

Introduction by Jacques J. Reinstein

I find myself in a strange position as chairman, or moderator, or perhaps umpire of this session. I was a drafter or a codrafter of, and often a dissenter from, many of the documents of which use is being made in our discussions, beginning with the State Department's Reparation Committee Report in 1943 to which Mr. Backer refers, the critical telegrams from Washington after the Potsdam agreement to Clayton and Collado, the early Policy Planning Staff papers, and many others.

However, unlike you, I had not read them as history. They remain in my mind as events through which I passed, usually dramatic and often vivid in my memories of the time. As the events were happening, I often thought that historians would have an enormous job in attempting to reconstruct the truth out of the mass of documents we were accumulating and the body of understanding and practice which emerged from our discussions, often not recorded. I am glad to be a participant in your efforts to discover that reality.

In initiating this part of our discussion, I will confine myself to a few general observations which I hope will be helpful in directing it to major points rather than innumerable matters of detail which one might discuss for days.

In his extraordinary and scholarly volume on the origins of the Marshall Plan, John Gimbel correctly states that there was no "Marshall Plan" in June 1947. He is quite correct. But it is not true that there were no plans of any kind against the background of which the evolution of the European Recovery Program took place.

An American statesman slightly older than I once said in my presence: "My generation fought two world wars and suffered the worst depression in the world's history. Our foremost objective is that this shall never happen again!" That generation set out deliberately to create a new world order, to ensure peace through the United Nations and a stable economic order through the International Trading Organization charter and the International Monetary Fund. Though its plan, if it can be called that, was shaped in the heat of national and individual differences, it was an international plan and it exercised a profound influence on the development of subsequent action, or improvisation if you prefer, as the events of the immediate postwar period unfolded.

The conceptions were admittedly Western. The two world wars were viewed by us as European civil wars in which the Americans had been forced to intervene twice at great cost in blood and treasure. The economic system which had broken down was a Western system, developed over centuries. Whatever its imperfections, we thought it was the best available system for the efficient use of resources and the general diffusion of economic well-being, if we could make it work well. It was recognized that some bridge would have to be constructed to the Soviet Union, a mysterious entity operating on different principles, which would no doubt be a difficult partner but with which, at least initially, it was assumed that some manageable relationship would have to be worked out as a practical matter.

My second general comment is that both we and the British grossly underestimated the damage which the war had caused to the structure and functioning of the European economy and the social structure of Europe and had grossly overestimated the strength of the British economy. I have found it odd that the papers I have reviewed for this conference apparently make no reference to the United Kingdom loan nor the effort to restore the early convertibility of the British pound as a means of promoting European recovery.

My third comment, made as someone who was in and out of German affairs from 1943 to 1958, is that in the discussion of our European economic policy, undue weight is given to the role of Germany in early policy formulation in the Executive Branch and inadequate attention is given to the role of Congress in focusing on the importance of Germany as a key element in the revival of the European economy. While there were many complex German problems, I rather question that a coherent American policy toward Germany began to emerge until the late 1940s and I think that our policy continued to remain somewhat ambivalent for almost half a decade later. Concern regarding the division of Germany and Europe long haunted American foreign policy, as a potential source of another world war.

One final comment concerns Germany and Japan. I find a strong consistent thread in the concept in American thinking that the concentration of economic power is an enemy of democracy. We tried to export that idea to both Germany and Japan. And I do not think that we intended to let the large American combinations from whom we had so recently wrested power on our own soil in the 1930s establish it on occupied territories under our rule.

Chapter 7

From Deconcentration to Reverse Course in Japan

Eleanor M. Hadley

In the occupation of Japan economic reform was undertaken as underpinning for political reform. In 1945 the United States was of the view that its security interests would not be adequately protected with mere proscription of army and navy and with the payment of reparations, that nothing less than fundamental political restructuring would meet its security needs. Just as the prosecution of each war brings changed standards—the distinction between combatants and civilian population dropped away in World War II—so political reform was added to the price of defeat.

The occupation, in my judgment, succeeded in bringing about fundamental political, economic, and social change in Japan. I would join those who favorably compare, in scale of change, the occupation to the Meiji period. Under the occupation, the locus of sovereignty was changed from the person of the emperor to the people, and in this change ministers were made responsible to the Diet and the Diet to the electorate, which was expanded to include the other half of the human race. It was held among those architecting this change—specifically the assorted levels of the State-War-Navy Coordinating Committee (SWNCC)—that sovereignty residing in the people could have no meaning if economic power was concentrated in but a handful of business families. SWNCC reached the need for deconcentration by this back-door route.

The decision to undertake economic deconcentration was a contested one. Within the State Department there were sharp differences of view between the Japan desk and the economists in one of the newly created economic divisions. (Given our notion of the pervasiveness of economic issues in foreign policy today, it is noteworthy that economic divisions were not added to the department until World War II.) The economic division in question was the

Commodities Division which contained a unit called the International Business Practices Branch. It was the economists in this unit who led the struggle to have United States policy require dissolution of the *zaibatsu* just as they earlier had successfully committed the United States to deconcentration in Germany.

While, broadly speaking, the Japan Basic Directive took shape as a reflection of the Germany surrender instrument, the Japan desk officers argued in the case of the *zaibatsu* that Japan was unique and that inasmuch as the *zaibatsu* were staunch friends of the United States, it would be a dreadful mistake to call for economic deconcentration.

The economists of the International Business Practices Branch were unconvinced and argument escalated to higher levels. The new-to-the-department economists won the day, but having won, made the discovery that they had no one on the staff with familiarity with Japan. Economists can go a long way on analysis, and it was on the basis of analysis that they had argued that there could be no development of democracy in a country where the economy was highly concentrated, but to prepare a research/policy paper spelling out the existing concentration, they recognized facts were necessary.

To overcome this deficiency they asked the Research and Analysis Branch of the Office of Strategic Services if someone could be lent for purposes of preparing such a paper. I was at the end of one assignment, had not started the next and chanced to be the person lent. Subsequently I transferred to State.

How did one write a paper on the *zaibatsu* in the United States in 1944? American library resources were as scarce as our national ignorance was profound. However, as it later turned out even Japanese were woefully ignorant of the facts of these structures for, much as with the oil companies in the United States today, there was no one with sufficient political clout to insist that information be made available to the government. The information which the Headquarters required the *zaibatsu* to submit in the occupation was the first detailed glimpse that Japanese had as to how these business structures operated.

To return to the question as to how such a paper was written in the United States in 1944, the answer is it was largely written from a corporation directory—a 1940 one as I remember—which, for the major companies, gave liabilities and assets, major shareholders, principal officers, profit rate, and a synopsis of corporate history. However, oftentimes, even the skeletal amount of corporation-directory information was not available for under "principal shareholders" or "principal officers" the entry would simply read "not available." Oland Russell's *House of Mitsui* (1939) was avidly read as was the authorized *The House of Mitsui,* published by the Mitsui Gomei in 1933, which gave heavy emphasis to the combine's charitable undertakings following, as it did by but one year, the assassination of the managing director of the holding company, Baron Dan.

In any event this paper prepared under the direction of Walter Rudolph, a former Stanford faculty member in the International Business Practices Branch, with Corwin D. Edwards serving as consultant to the unit, was deemed to establish what the economists had known from the start, that concentration was great and that a policy of deconcentration was clearly indicated.

Let me add an aside. While there was no difference of view among the economists of this unit that Japan's economy was concentrated, not all economists shared or share the view. Japan's concentration had been achieved by an unusual path. Monopoly in a strict sense of that expression was exceedingly rare in Japan. Japan's business houses built their empires by linking significant market positions across the gamut of industry, finance, and commerce. Thus, for example, the Mitsui *zaibatsu* accounted for 35 percent of coal production, 13 percent of ammonium sulphate, 53 percent of calcium cyanamide, 53 percent of dyestuffs, 21 percent of cement, 25 percent of heavy electrical equipment, 81 percent of paper, 5 percent of shipbuilding, 14 percent of ordnance, 14 percent of warehousing, 20 percent of rayon staple yarn, 14 percent of commercial banking, 22 percent of trust accounts, 5 percent of life insurance, and 6 percent of casualty insurance.[1]

The strength of the combine lay in joining together these and other—to use jargon—oligopolistic positions to build a single whole. The whole was a "conglomerate." Japan invented conglomerates, which, in the United States in the sixties, became quite the thing. However, the whole training of economists is to analyze micro problems in single market terms. To this day, economists do not have a good grasp of how to analyze simultaneous positions in diverse markets.[2] Accordingly, it was possible to have the State-War Mission on Japanese Combines, which was invited out to the theater by MacArthur to assist in translating through his directive, "dissolve Japanese combines," write in the analytical part of the report: "Something has been seriously wrong with the social system of Japan. . . . The excessive concentration of economic power in Japan is, however, one of the more important factors."[3] And, to have the eminent British economist on the Japanese economy, G. C. Allen, contend, "At first sight it seems perhaps surprising that competitive conditions should flourish in a country where the large scale trades

are dominated by a few groups and where the state has had historically a large role; yet if the true nature of Japan's political and
economic system is appreciated the apparent inconsistency dis-
appears."[4] However, since it was the United States which was
dominant in the military defeat of Japan, American views were
dominant—and under MacArthur became even more so—in the
occupation.

During the first two and a half years of the occupation when
United States policy was being guided by the Basic Directive for the
Japan Occupation, GHQ-SCAP attempted to carry through the
terms of the Basic Directive. I quote from that directive. In paragraph 25 it was stated:

> It is the intent of the United States Government to encourage
> and show favor to:
>   a) Policies which permit a wide distribution of income and
>   of ownership of the means of production and trade.
>   b) The development of organizations in labor, industry and
>   agriculture organized on a democratic basis.
>
> Accordingly, you will:
>   1. Require the Japanese to establish a public agency
>   responsible for reorganizing Japanese business in
>   accordance with the military and economic objectives of
>   your government. You will require this agency to
>   submit, for approval by you, plans for dissolving large
>   Japanese industrial and banking combines or other
>   large concentrations of private business control.
>   2. Establish and maintain surveillance, until satisfactory
>   plans for reorganization have been approved, over the
>   Japanese business described in subparagraph (1) above
>   in order to ensure conformity with the military and
>   economic objectives of your government.
>   .   .   .   .
>   7. Require the removal of all legal hindrances to the
>   formation of organizations of employees along demo-
>   cratic lines.[5]

In paragraph 23, SCAP was informed:

> You will prohibit the retention in or selection for positions of
> important responsibility or influence in industry, finance, com-
> merce, or agriculture of all persons who have been active expo-
> nents of militant nationalism and aggression, of those who

have actively participated in [specified organizations] and of any who do not direct future Japanese economic effort solely towards peaceful ends. (In the absence of evidence, satisfactory to you, to the contrary, you will assume that any persons who have held key positions of high responsibility since 1937, in industry, finance, commerce or agriculture have been active exponents of militant nationalism and aggression.)

In paragraph 28 he was informed,

You will assure the execution of programs of reparations in kind and of restitution of identifiable looted property in accordance with decisions of the appropriate Allied authorities transmitted to you by the Joint Chiefs of Staff.

In paragraph 22, MacArthur was informed:

Serious inflation will substantially retard the accomplishment of the ultimate objectives of the occupation. You will, therefore direct the Japanese authorities to make every feasible effort to avoid such inflation. However, prevention or restraint of inflation shall not constitute a reason for limiting the removal, destruction, or curtailment of productive facilities in fulfillment of programs for reparations, restitution, demilitarization, or economic disarmament.

The occupation was a bold experiment in which to have participated, and notwithstanding its crudeness, its lack of balance, the fits and starts with which it moved, I would say in 20/20 hindsight that it made a profound contribution to Japan politically and economically. Even those groups who at the time were keenly critical of the deconcentration program now are likely to say it made a very real contribution to the country. But before taking up assessment, let us note the main outlines of the deconcentration program.[6]

Holding company dissolution. Holding companies are companies which do not produce goods and services but exist to steer other companies. The term "holding" refers to holding stock in other companies for the purpose of directing the company as one would wish. The top holding companies were the nerve center of the *zaibatsu* groupings. Under the *zaibatsu*-dissolution program eighty-three holding companies were designated for dissolution. This does not indicate there were eighty-three *zaibatsu*. In the case of the largest *zaibatsu,* key subsidiaries of the top holding company oftentimes had important holding functions in addition to their production and service activities. The number swelled to eighty-three by inclusion of certain of these key second-level holding companies and by designation of certain unimportant *zaibatsu* groupings. Fifty-three of the eighty-three designated companies were either reorganized or dissolved. With the exception of the two trading companies, Mitsui Trading and Mitsubishi Trading, no operating company or operating functions were dissolved. Where a company combined operating and holding functions, it was only the holding functions that were dissolved. The other thirty holding companies were untouched.

It was the intention of the program to accord full respect to property rights. Thus there was to be no confiscation of *zaibatsu* property; the owners of the top holding companies, primarily the *zaibatsu* family members, were compensated in bonds. Since it would make no sense to provide them the wherewithal to turn around and buy back their position of dominance, their bonds were made nonnegotiable for a ten-year period. In fact, however, the program turned out to be close to confiscation, given the virulence of the inflation which overtook the economy.

Capital-levy tax. While this tax of November 17, 1946, was quite separate from the *zaibatsu*-dissolution program in conception and administration, it nevertheless had a fundamental bearing on the program. Personal capital assets were taxed at steeply rising rates starting with 25 percent on assets above 100,000 yen and rising to 90 percent on assets over 15,000,000 yen. The tax was not applied to corporations.[7]

Economic purge. The economic purge was one of the most contentious issues of economic reform. Although the Basic Directive directed MacArthur to remove persons holding "positions of important responsibility . . . in industry, finance, commerce, or agriculture . . . who have been active exponents of militant nationalism and aggression" and stated that "in the absence of evidence, satisfactory to you to the contrary, you will assume that any persons who have held key positions of high responsibility since 1937, in industry, finance, commerce or agriculture have been active exponents of militant nationalism and aggression," this order was unfelicitously phrased. By tying together positions of high responsibility with "active exponents of militant nationalism" it created unnecessary antagonism and failed to call attention to the real issues. The real point of the economic purge was that one of the key *zaibatsu* control devices was personnel. If the point of the *zaibatsu*-dissolution program was to sever the ties which bound company after company into single wholes, then clearly it made sense to have a change of personnel. But being bitterly contested within the Headquarters, execution was delayed a year from the start of the political purge, and a year

later the political climate was not as amenable. Further with dis-
sention within the Headquarters, leaks to the press abounded and a
certain news magazine made it a cause célèbre. By this time it
reached the Congress where certain Republicans in particular ex-
coriated those responsible for such misguidedness or worse, wooly-
headedness, which they claimed played into the hands of the
Russians. Piteous tales were reported.[8]

The facts? The purge removed[9] 639 officers from some 240 companies with some 896 resigning in anticipation of being removed.
Thus some 1,535 officers were affected. The purge did not deny to
the Japanese economy the benefits of this talent. The purge proscribed such persons from occupying top designated positions in designated key companies, leaving "purgees" free to take nondesig-
nated positions in designated companies or any position elsewhere
in the economy. For example, Mandai, chairman of the board of
Mitsui Bank who was purged by virtue of holding that position
within the designated dates, moved to chairman of the board of Sony
where his distinguished talents were put to splendid use.

*Split of companies deemed excessive concentrations of economic
power.* It was this legislation forced through the Diet December 1947
which was the straw which broke the camel's back. What this legislation was directed to was the dominance which certain single companies wielded after their *zaibatsu* ties had been cut, that is to say,
dominance so great as to make difficult the possibility of competitive
conditions in such markets. It paralleled legislation called for in
Germany a year earlier (OMGUS 56), and the text of this law had
been cleared by MacArthur with the Army Department.[10] Further
MacArthur informed the Army in detail how the Headquarters
planned to proceed under their legislation.[11] MacArthur informed
the Department of the Army that companies designated would be
grouped by 1) industrials, 2) service and distribution, 3) insurance,
and 4) banks.

The initial designations under industrials numbered 257, those
under service and distribution 68 making a total of 325.[12] While
there were clearly many "respectable" designations in this collection, it is evident—especially in hindsight—that a fraction of this
number would have been far better. MacArthur got no farther than
initial designation of groups 1 and 2.

The whole climate of opinion was changing. Relations with the
Soviet Union were beginning to go sour. Furthermore, the future of
China, on which United States postwar Far Eastern policy was pred-
icated, looked increasingly uncertain. In addition, businessmen

were only beginning to get a clear idea as to what was occurring in Japan in late 1946. They were admitted to the theater for the first time in August 1947. To criticize effectively one needs facts. They now were in a position to acquire them and many were horrified. Excerpts from a confidential report by James Lee Kaufman, who was serving as a consultant to the Department of the Army, were published in the December 1, 1947, issue of *Newsweek* under the heading, "A Lawyer's Report on Japan Attacks Plan to Run Occupation . . . Far to the Left of Anything Now Tolerated in America" and constituted the opening public salvo. On December 19, 1947, Senator Knowland opened the congressional debate, having acquired a copy of the classified document FEC 230, the designation given the policy recommendation of the State-War Mission on Japanese Combines, upon submission to the Far Eastern Commission.[13] The Deconcentration Law was based on these recommendations but was considerably less extreme than the recommendations.

As I wrote in *Antitrust in Japan:*

> The senator was shocked by the Deconcentration Law, . . . the procedures for dismantling holding companies. . . . He was dismayed that the U. S. could be calling for divestiture and removal from positions of responsibility of those who had exercised a "controlling voice" in the large business organizations. . . . Senator Knowland [stated]:
>
> > Mr. President, it was unbelievable to me that such a document could be put forward as representing the policy of the government of which I am a part. . . .
> >
> > Mr. President, the Congress and the country should be told who the originator of this proposal is. . . . The country and the Congress should be informed as to whether General Douglas MacArthur was consulted in advance . . . or whether he has been given directives.[14]

The next move was that of Secretary of the Army, Kenneth Royall, who in a January 6, 1948, speech stated:

> It is clearly understandable . . . that in 1945 the main purpose of occupation should be protection against an enemy which had viciously attacked us. . . .
>
> Since then new conditions have arisen — in world politics and economics. . . .
>
> The Japanese Government has been directed to prepare

legislation prohibiting international cartels. Stringent antitrust and deconcentration has been prepared and passed in
part. . . .

While the various steps were being taken, new developments
were arising, and old factors were changing in importance. . . .

Both the Department of the Army and the Department of
State . . . realize that for political stability to continue and for
free government to succeed . . . there must be a sound and
self-supporting economy. . . .

We also realized that the United States cannot forever continue to pour hundreds of millions of dollars annually into relief funds for occupied areas. . . . Earlier programs are being
reexamined.[15]

If the premise of the program is granted that political democracy
could not be developed in a highly concentrated economy, the matter
of costs should be carefully weighed. World War II is estimated to
have cost United States taxpayers $330 billion of which $100 billion
is attributed to the Pacific Theater.[16] The costs of the Japanese occupation were primarily borne by Japan which provided office space,
heat, housing, transportation, and recreation which costs accounted
for some one-third of total government expenditures in the beginning years. The United States taxpayers paid for salaries of occupation personnel and their food. Relief to Japanese people—primarily
food and fertilizer—from August 1945 through December 1946
amounted to $194 million; from January to December 1947 to $404
million.[17] Thus, Mr. Royall was discussing expenditures in the case
of Japan of close to $600 million over twenty-six months against a
war which had averaged $25 billion a year. (It will be noted that
Mr. Royall in discussing costs shifts from costs arising out of the
Japan occupation, the topic of his remarks, to costs "for occupied
areas.")

Further in assessing the Deconcentration Law of December
1947—and in my hindsight judgment, its far too many designations—it must be borne in mind that the reorganizations contemplated under the legislation were not occurring in the context of a
normally functioning economy but one undergoing reorganizations
from multiple causes—one of the most traumatic of which was cancellation in October 1946 of war indemnity payments owed private
corporations by the Japanese government, variously estimated in
the 80–100 billion yen range (in yen of 4–6 to the dollar). Therefore,
in calling for reorganization of operating companies representing
excessive concentrations of economic power these standards would

have been added to the standards being employed to meet bank-
ruptcy problems in general and cancellation of war indemnification
in particular.[18]

Unfortunately, the public debate over United States deconcentration policy in Japan took on an increasingly strident, emotional tone
and moved to question the integrity of those who had authored it
and/or who supported its continuation. While antitrust is about as
American as apple pie, Senator Knowland in a continuing attack on
the program in Japan asserted (January 19, 1948): "Either originating among doctrinaire New Dealers who found their activities limited in Washington and signed up for overseas occupation service, or
finding its fountainhead in the Far Eastern Commission . . . certain
activities are open to serious question by both Congress and the
people."[19]

MacArthur responded to growing criticism publicly through a letter to Senator Brian McMahon read to the Senate on February 17,
1948,[20] and confidentially by proposing to the Department of the
Army January 1948 establishment of a Deconcentration Review
Board in order, as I expressed it in *Antitrust in Japan:* "to determine
whether the plans of reorganization under the Deconcentration Law
would, in the opinion of an independent group of observers, have a
retarding influence on Japanese economy recovery. Apparently
MacArthur assumed the critics were concerned with the impact of
the Deconcentration legislation on recovery rather than, as we shall
see, using the question of impact merely as a device for scrapping
the entire combine dissolution program."[21]

In his letter to McMahon, MacArthur observed,

> In any evaluation of the economic potential here in Japan, it
> must be understood that tearing down the tradition pyramid of
> economic power which has given only a few families direct or
> indirect control over all commerce and industry, all raw mate-
> rials, all transportation, internal and external, and all coal and
> other power sources is the first essential step to the establish-
> ment here of an economic system based upon free, private com-
> petitive enterprise which Japan has never before known. . . .
>
> The Japanese people, you may be sure, fully understand the
> nature of the forces which have so ruthlessly exploited them in
> the past. They understand this economic concentration not
> only furnished the sinews for mounting the violence of war but
> that its leaders in partnership with the military shaped the
> national will in the direction of war and conquest. . . .
>
> These things are so well understood by the Japanese people

that apart from our desire to reshape Japanese life toward [a] capitalistic economy, if this concentration of economic power is not torn down and redistributed peacefully and in due order under the Occupation, there is not the slightest doubt that its cleansing will eventually occur through a blood bath and revolutionary violence. For the Japanese people have tasted freedom under the American concept and they will not willingly return to the shackles of authoritarian government and economy or resubmit otherwise to their discredited masters.[22]

Notwithstanding such bold words, the "reverse course" had been set in motion. On March 12, 1948 the United States withdrew its support for FEC 230 and MacArthur recognized that large-scale releases of companies under initial designation under the law were in order. On May 1 it was announced that 50 companies were being released outright while in the case of 144 other companies they were deemed to have such minor problems that they could continue under surveillance or concurrently with making certain changes.[23] On July 1, 31 additional companies were released outright making a total of 225 out of the original 325.[24] Further releases were to await the views of the Deconcentration Review Board.

By September 1948, the Deconcentration Review Board had developed its criteria—which had nothing to do with the terms of reference under which the board had been brought to the theater[25]—and the new climate of opinion became further evident. In a September 11 meeting between the Holding Company Liquidation Commission, Headquarters staff, and the Deconcentration Review Board, the board's criteria were explained. The newspapers were not slow to grasp the change.[26] The September 14 *Asahi Shimbun* reported, "Deconcentration—to be Liberalized on Great Scale. Reinvestigation for Those Already Decided." On September 17 the Central News Agency of China transmitted the following dispatch from Tokyo: "The economic deconcentration law . . . is on its way to the scrap heap." The 325 companies in the original designation were ultimately reduced to 11 for structural reorganization plus 8 companies where the board recommended adjustments of assets, subsidiaries, or the like.[27]

As an aside, it is noteworthy that while as we have seen there was an uproar over the Deconcentration Law of December 1947, a few months preceding that legislation MacArthur had taken action on his own which was far more drastic than anything in the Deconcentration Law for which there was not even a murmur of criticism. On July 3, 1947, MacArthur directed the Mitsui and Mitsubishi Trading Companies be dissolved, the first and only instance in the deconcentration program of dissolving operating companies. Further, the terms concerning successor companies were harsh indeed. SCAPIN 1741 read:

2c. Prohibit any persons who have been officers, directors, advisors, branch managers of foreign or domestic branches, or department or section heads of said companies, during a period of ten years prior to the date of this memorandum, from associating together to form a new company, or more than two being employed by or advising any one existing company or company hereafter formed.

2d. Prohibit any group of employees in addition to those specified in paragraph c above, being employed by any one existing company, or any company hereafter formed, without permission of the Holding Company Liquidation Commission or such other agencies as may be designated. The Holding Company Liquidation Commission or such other agencies shall grant such permission only if it shall conclusively appear that a possibility of re-creation of the dissolved companies or other monopolistic combinations shall not result.

2e. Prohibit any trading company in which any officers or employees of both said companies shall be employed from occupying any office now used or formerly used by either of said companies as a business office, and further prohibit any company from using the firm name Mitsubishi Trading Company or Mitsui Trading Company or any resemblance thereof.[28]

As I speculated in *Antitrust in Japan* on this odd contrast:

Was the absence of criticism to be explained by ignorance of the event; endorsement of dissolution over reorganization; disapproval of trading companies; or the loyalty of Republican critics to a fellow Republican? The decision to call for dissolution was taken within Headquarters itself. It is not clear to the writer how to interpret this seemingly strange behavior. It is difficult to believe that critics were unaware that dissolution had been ordered, and it is difficult to believe that critics favored dissolution over reorganization. It is doubtful that the critics so disapproved of trading companies that they would endorse their dissolution. Seemingly, the only explanation is that supporters of MacArthur did not wish to embarrass him in a situation where responsibility was clearly his alone.[29]

The program to bring about a "right of enterprise" in Japan proved controversial within the Headquarters, within the Executive Branch, within the Congress, and naturally within Japan. In the palace politics of the Headquarters, General Willoughby, chief of G-2, viewed criticism of the program as a means of dislodging General Whitney, chief of the Government Section, from his first-place position in the pecking order of those advising MacArthur. In consequence of supporting economic deconcentration, the economic purge, land reform, and encouraging a labor movement, General Willoughby accused General Whitney of being pink and harboring pinks in his division.[30]

Within the Executive Branch it led to sharp differences of view between departments and within departments. George Kennan in his *Memoirs, 1925–1950,* writes critically of the efforts during the occupation to bring about economic deconcentration. On the broad reversal of United States policy in Japan he comments, "I consider my part in bringing about this change to have been, after the Marshall Plan, the most significant constructive contribution I was ever able to make in government."[31]

In Japan four-times Prime Minister Yoshida was highly critical of the program. In the *Yoshida Memoirs,* Yoshida commented on a question at a press conference with foreign correspondents the purport of which was

> that, since the financiers had been behind the war, the strictest measures should be taken against them. I answered that it would be a great mistake to regard Japan's financial leaders as a bunch of criminals; that the nation's economic structure had been built by such old-established and major financial concerns as Mitsui and Mitsubishi, and that modern Japan owed her prosperity largely to their endeavors, so that it was most doubtful whether the Japanese people would benefit from the disintegration of these concerns.[32]

In a 1955 Mitsubishi Economic Research Institute publication, entitled *Mitsui-Mitsubishi-Sumitomo: Present Status of the Former Zaibatsu Enterprises,* the observation occurs in the Mitsui Section:

> With the ruinous diminution of the Mitsui families' wealth, the dissolution of Mitsui Honsha, Ltd., the complete democratization of the shareholding system of Mitsui companies and the retirement of Mitsui family members and former executives, the powerful organization of Mitsui enterprise has been thor-

oughly dissolved as a business concern from the point of view of both capital and personnel. . . . This is one of the main reasons rendering Japan's postwar economy very weak and making its reconstruction exceedingly difficult.[33]

However, in the mid-sixties when I interviewed a high Liberal Democratic party official who has been in a number of cabinets, asking his retrospective views of the program, he saw it as an enormous plus for conservatism. The LDP was able to go before the people without, as he expressed it, "the albatross of the *zaibatsu*."

In a 1971 meeting with two colleagues from the then United States Tariff Commission (now International Trade Commission) with the president of the *Keidanren* and other top officials of that organization, Uemura, the then president, associating me with that program, volunteered, "The deconcentration program has been a major factor in postwar Japan's strong economic performance." In my own view Japan's postwar growth, over double its prewar average, cannot be explained without introducing the increased rivalry in the economy. The quest for increased market share has been one of the driving forces.

Further, the concept of antitrust has taken root in Japan. In 1973 Japan hosted an international competition policy under Organization for Economic Cooperation and Development patronage with antitrust experts from most of the industrial countries plus representatives of less developed countries. In 1975 the Miki cabinet endeavored, as an anti-inflationary measure, to introduce strengthening amendments to the Antimonopoly Law enacted in 1947 which was designed to keep the economy deconcentrated. The amendments passed the Lower House but failed in the House of Councillors. When such amendments were introduced into the Diet in 1977—in close to identical form—they passed in May. Is Japan the first major economy to use antitrust as an anti-inflationary weapon?

It has for some time seemed exceptional to me that so keen an observer of international affairs as George Kennan would take so critical a view of the reform aspects of the occupation. I now perceive a probable part of the explanation to have been that he was heavily influenced in his judgments by William Sebald who in turn was influenced in his judgments by his brother-in-law, Charles A. Willoughby. Sebald was the top State Department representative in the Japan occupation from 1947 to 1952, heading the Diplomatic Section during these years. Thus when Kennan came out to the theater on a sensitive mission of assessment, February 1948, it was natural

that he would place particular credence in the views of William
Sebald whom he greatly respected. Kennan writes of him,"an able
and experienced officer with a deep background in Japanese affairs"
(p. 370).

Kennan's assessment of the occupation as revealed in his *Memoirs*
differs little from Willoughby's as indicated in *Shirarezaru Nihon
Senryo* [The unknown Japanese occupation] with a foreword by William J. Sebald. In assessing the land reform program, industrial
reorganization, and the purge, Kennan writes (pp. 387–89):

> The land reform, in itself constructive and desirable, had af-
> fected about one-third of the arable land of the country and had
> led to the purchase by the Japanese government of a very large
> part of this property with a view to its redistribution. Only
> about one-seventh of what had been purchased had, however,
> been resold up to that point. The result was a situation of great
> confusion and instability in the relationships of agricultural
> land ownership.
>
> A similar situation existed on the industrial side. SCAP had
> embraced with an almost wild enthusiasm the trust-busting
> ideals that already commended themselves so powerfully to the
> antitrust division of the Department of Justice in Washington.
> Some two hundred and sixty Japanese companies, including
> some of the most tremendous industrial concerns, had been
> designated as "excessive concentrations of economic power."
> Their securities had in many instances been taken over by the
> Japanese government at SCAP's direction and were theoret-
> ically awaiting resale—to whom was not clear.[34] The com-
> panies, meanwhile, existed in a state of uncertainty which
> could not help but interfere seriously with initiative and con-
> fidence of management.[35] The ideological concepts on which
> these measures rested bore so close a resemblance to Soviet
> views about the evils of "capitalist monopolies" that the mea-
> sures themselves could only have been eminently agreeable to
> anyone interested in the future communization of Japan.[36]
> Their relation to the interests of Japanese recovery was less
> apparent.
>
> Most serious of all, as I saw it, was the situation created by
> the wholesale "purging" of people in government, in education,
> and in business who were suspected of having had militaristic
> sympathies or of having abetted Japanese aggression in earlier
> days. Here SCAP had proceeded on a scale, and with a dog-

matic, impersonal vindictiveness, for which there were few examples outside the totalitarian countries themselves.[37] Seven hundred thousand people had already been involved, at the time of our visit, in the attendant screenings. Just in the educational establishment alone, some 120,000 out of a half million teachers had been purged or had resigned to avoid purging. Nor was there any visible end to this process. SCAP had decreed that checks should henceforth be run under its supervision on all new governmental employees, so this sort of screening was apparently intended to go on indefinitely. The program, furthermore, had taken on a wholly unfathomable complexity. Orders, regulations, and institutions relating to this process had been piled on top of each other in appalling profusion. To the ordinary Japanese, as I later wrote in my report to the government, ". . . the operation of the purge must be thoroughly bewildering. I doubt, in fact, whether many persons in SCAP . . . could explain its history, scope, procedures and purpose." All useful punitive psychological effect had been lost amid the confusion of ordinances, directives, and programs. The indiscriminate purging of whole categories of individuals, sickeningly similar to totalitarian practices, was in conflict with the civil rights provisions of the new constitution that we ourselves had imposed upon the Japanese. It had had the effect of barring from civil life many people who could not be regarded on any reasonable standards as exponents of militarism and whose only crime had been to serve their country faithfully in time of war. Important elements of Japanese society essential to its constructive development were being driven underground. Pressures were being engendered which, if not promptly relieved, were bound to come to the surface someday in extremely unhealthy ways. Particularly strange and unfortunate was the regularity with which the purge had seemed to hit persons known in the days before the war for their friendly attitude toward the United States. It was as though pro-Americanism, especially among upper-class Japanese, was particularly suspect. Here, again, the policies of SCAP had brought Japanese life to a point of great turmoil and confusion, and had produced, momentarily at least, a serious degree of instability.[38]

To sum up: Notwithstanding the crudity of the deconcentration program, its excesses, and its deficiencies, I believe the original

United States policy was wisely conceived. When I say "wisely," I imply it was a policy which has not only brought inestimable benefit to rank and file Japanese but has brought benefit to the United States in furthering political democracy in Japan and in encouraging those political forces which the majority of Americans like to see encouraged, conservative political forces.

Chapter 8

From Morgenthau Plan
to Marshall Plan

John H. Backer

Although the younger generation knows little of America's recent history, Morgenthau and Marshall plans are familiar concepts. It is generally known that the Morgenthau Plan aimed at the elimination of Germany as an industrial power and that the Marshall Plan was directed toward the reconstruction of Western Europe after the Second World War. This is as far as the general knowledge goes. As to details, one finds even in learned circles a great deal of oversimplification and occasionally a misinterpretation of facts.

For instance it is little known that actually there were three so-called Morgenthau plans which differed in important respects. There was the Treasury draft memorandum of September 1, 1944, *Directives for the Occupation of Germany;*[1] there was Morgenthau's top secret memorandum to the president for Quebec, *Program to Prevent Germany from Starting World War III;*[2] and most important there was the so-called "pastoral letter," the Quebec memorandum which Churchill and Roosevelt initialed.[3] Whereas the first document envisaged the creation of three German states including a South German state in customs union with Austria, an internationalized Ruhr area, and the annexation of the Saarland by France, the second paper concentrated on the deindustrialization of the Ruhr and suggested an early withdrawal of American troops to be replaced by Russian, French, Polish, Czech, Greek, Yugoslav, Norwegian, Dutch, and Belgian soldiers. The Quebec memorandum finally did not mention the suggested division of Germany into several states nor the annexation of the Saarland by France, but it placed the latter together with the Ruhr under international supervision. Moreover, it spelled out very clearly the aim of making Germany "a country primarily agricultural and pastoral in its character."

Secretary Stimson relates in his memoirs how President Roosevelt under the influence of an aroused public opinion was soon obliged to repudiate his signature.[4] Nevertheless, as documents in the Foreign Relations Series of the United States show, Morgenthau continued not without success to pressure for a highly restrictive policy and the often cited directive for the occupation of Germany, JCS 1067 reflected his influence.[5]

As to the eventual substantive impact of Morgenthau on the occupational policies in Germany no systematic analysis has been made. Nor has the application of his policy as a contributing factor in the emergence of the Marshall Plan concept been duly appraised. Earlier writers on the subject contended that JCS 1067 was simply a slightly modified version of the Morgenthau Plan, that during the first two years of the occupation a spirit of revenge prevailed and that there were numerous representatives of the United States Department of the Treasury in key positions in Germany who did their level best to implement the ideas of their former boss. According to this interpretation, the change of policy took place in the summer of 1947 when JCS 1067 was replaced by JCS 1779 and the concept of a European Recovery Program emerged. It is worthy of note that these views found support in the memoirs of General Lucius D. Clay[6] and of Ambassador Robert Murphy,[7] who for reasons of their own stressed the handicap of JCS 1067 under which they had to operate.

Subsequent research challenged this interpretation; it exposed its numerous oversimplifications and demonstrated the need to separate the economic and political aspects of Morgenthau's initiative. As a result, three key elements—the economic "hands off" policy, denazification, and reparations—have been identified and will be discussed. It also will be shown that the first policy was promptly abandoned, that the second—with questionable results—was vigorously implemented and that the third, in its ultimate consequences, triggered the creation of two Germanys.

General Clay in his memoirs drew attention to the text of the Potsdam agreement[8] which, whenever in conflict with JCS 1067 superseded the latter.[9] The directive stipulated that "no steps will be taken a) looking toward the economic rehabilitation of Germany; b) designed to maintain or strengthen the German economy." At Potsdam these "hands off" provisions were replaced by the instruction that "measures were to be taken promptly to effect essential repair of transport, to enlarge coal production, to maximize agricultural output and essential utilities." Moreover, Potsdam ordained that "in working out the economic balance of Germany the necessary means must be provided to pay for imports approved by the Control Council in Germany." These provisions were promulgated on August 2, 1945, and one can therefore conclude that JCS 1067 in its original harsh form was less than three months in effect. The second important factor softening Morgenthau's revanchism was the so-called "Disease and Unrest" formula which the War Department lawyers under the leadership of John J. McCloy had inserted over the active resistance of representatives of the Treasury. The latter were, of course, fully aware of what the War Department boys were up to. Nevertheless, Morgenthau's efforts to substitute the more specific language of *"epidemic* disease and *serious* unrest" were unsuccessful and the War Department's escape clause prevailed.[10]

It would seem that Lucius Clay, who was trained to implement unambiguous military orders, first did not fully grasp the significance of this loophole, but once its purpose became clear to him, he used it freely and extensively. Two months after the end of hostilities, three-fourths of the railroad tracks in Germany had been rebuilt; 25,000 railroad cars brought into Germany by the American army were turned over to the German railroad administration; and more than 10,000 trucks were made available to the German economy through sale on a deferred payment basis. In a similar vein, there was a sustained effort to expedite the reactivation of the German communication system with the result that three months after the surrender telephone lines had been repaired and post offices operated again normally. Moreover and most important, the "Disease and Unrest" formula provided the rationale and the legal basis for the large food supplies which were brought into Germany during the first three years of the occupation. The immediate efforts of OMGUS to revitalize the German export industries, finally, were prompted by the understandable need to reduce the burden on the American taxpayers.[11]

There is now documentary evidence available which invalidates Clay's comment on the restrictive role of JCS 1067. When the War Department on President Truman's instructions in December of 1945 asked for proposals how the directive should be amended, Clay cabled back that without JCS 1067 he would not have been able to accomplish his mission. Moreover, the amendments which OMGUS eventually suggested were technical and of minor importance.[12]

The above-cited provisions of Potsdam in conjunction with the "Disease and Unrest" formula provided the technical justification for a constructive approach to the problem of Germany's economy. But even in absence of these instructions the occupational authorities could not have stood idly by. The realities of the situation were spelled out when Howard Peterson, the assistant secretary of war, in the course of the GARIOA hearings testified before a House Appropriations Committee. "What would happen," a congressman asked, "if we don't appropriate funds for continued food supplies?" "We would have to send more troops," Peterson replied, "and troops we don't have." He added, "We also could move out completely." Whereupon the questioner concluded, "Then somebody else would move in!"[13]

Clay himself, in one of his last interviews before his death, succinctly described the early abandonment of Morgenthau's "hands off" policy. "If you followed JCS 1067 literally," he said, "you couldn't have done anything to restore the German economy. If you couldn't restore the German economy, you could never hope to get paid for the food that they had to have. By virtue of this sort of thing it was modified constantly; not officially but by allowing this deviation and that deviation et cetera. We began to slowly wipe out JCS 1067. When we were ordered to put in a currency reform, this was in strict contravention of a provision of JCS 1067 that prohibited us from doing anything to improve the German economy. It was an unworkable policy and it wasn't changed without any discussion or anything by those of us who were in Germany. It was done by gradual changes in its provisions and exchanges of cablegrams, conferences and so on."[14]

One final comment on the spirit of revenge which allegedly prevailed during the first two years of the occupation and which supposedly was kept alive by employees of the United States Treasury stationed in Germany. On the working level of the economic division where this writer served, the Morgenthau concept was not even an object of discussion because the economic recovery was the clearly defined goal. Since civil servants like other Americans were subject to draft for military service, peacetime employees of the United States Treasury as of most federal agencies could be found among OMGUS staffers. However, as everybody familiar with the workings of America's bureaucracy knows, it would have been most unusual for a federal staff to have consistently and uniformly supported the policies of a temporary political appointee at the helm of an agency. As a case in point, the example of Jack Bennett, the head of the Finance Division of OMGUS and Clay's principal financial advisor, may be cited. Although on the Treasury's payroll, he took his orders from the War Department. As he told this writer, he hardly knew about the existence of a Morgenthau Plan.[15]

In contrast to the quickly passing economic restrictions, both de-nazification and reparations policies were fully upheld for several years. But although the secretary of the treasury and his immediate associates played an important role in the drafting process, it would be erroneous to put the blame for the unfortunate results exclusively on Henry Morgenthau's doorstep. Both policies enjoyed the full support of the nation's political leadership and of America's public opinion at large. Accordingly the paragraphs of JCS 1067 dealing with denazification contained no escape clauses and had to be rigidly enforced. Since there were 3.5 million registered party members in the American zone alone, the chaotic consequences of the required mass round-up were predictable. General Clay's denazification advisors repeatedly urged concentrating on the prosecution of the estimated 100,000 Nazi leaders, but the deputy military governor remained adamant.[16] As he read his instructions, he had no leeway. The Patton incident and the continued inflammatory reports of the American media, moreover, also necessitated a rigorous and all-encompassing denazification program. Of course the Jewish element guided by Morgenthau played in this respect an influential role, but Americans in general, once involved in the war, became crusaders and their crusading fervor could not be easily contained. The resulting irrational, emotional, and even contradictory denazification process in conjunction with its questionable legality not only damaged America's prestige in Germany but it also left many of the guilty leaders to go scot free. Some qualified observers therefore had a point when suggesting that the handling of the program actually had prompted a "renazification" of the country.[17]

Morgenthau's influence on the reparations question was equally unfortunate. In its ultimate consequences it led to a paradoxical situation because it accomplished precisely the opposite the secretary of the treasury had planned, namely the freeing of the Federal Republic of Germany of a meaningful reparations burden. On the other hand, since the Soviets insisted on reparations from production as concession for the establishment of a unified German government, the division of their country was the price the Germans had to pay.

In the State Department an Interdivisional Committee of Reparations, Restitution and Property Rights had begun to examine the problem of reparations as early as November 1943. It was able to utilize in its considerations two earlier studies, one conducted under the auspices of the Council of Foreign Relations, the other completed by a British governmental bureau that worked with John Maynard

Keynes. Both papers challenged the popular view that the history of the twenties had demonstrated the impossibility of collecting reparations. As they correctly pointed out, the unwillingness of the victors to accept large amounts of German goods had been the main reason for the breakdown of the reparations settlement after Versailles. Whereas huge monetary transfers were indeed not possible, payment of reparations through deliveries in kind was entirely feasible. The Interdivisional Committee in its final report included a detailed economic study which the Federal Reserve had undertaken for the State Department. Taking Germany's net national output and its uses from 1925 to 1938 as a basis, the paper estimated that Germany would be able to pay $30 billion over a period of twelve years. A few months later an independent study by the Research and Analysis Branch of the Office of Strategic Services indicated an even larger German potential for reparations, namely about $6.5 billion annually.[18]

Both papers were based entirely on economic considerations. The secretary of the treasury, on the other hand, introduced a political element when rejecting German reparations from production because they presupposed the existence of a strong industrial base. Instead he proposed the large-scale dismantlement of German industries. While Morgenthau wanted a greatly weakened Germany, his adversaries in the State Department were more concerned about the consequences of excessive Soviet power. As they saw it, Germany should not be weakened too much so that it could continue its role as a balancing element and counteract Soviet influence. The legend that only American loans had enabled Germany to pay reparations after the First World War had been widely accepted. It also became the principal argument of the anti-Soviet faction and brought an element of domestic policy into the debate. The final result of the controversy was that for very different reasons the two opposing sides subsequently found common ground. The policy directive which was eventually issued put a priority on dismantlement and minimized reliance on reparations from production.[19]

When hostilities ended, the first superficial inspection of Germany's heavily destroyed cities seemed to lend support to a policy which excluded reparations from production. But already at Potsdam Molotov told Secretary Byrnes that according to Soviet intelligence estimates about 85 percent of Germany's industrial capacity had remained intact and a systematic examination of industrial installations by the United States Air Force's *Strategic Bombing Survey* soon reached the same conclusion.[20] It was not physical destruction, but a suppressed inflation, Western inability to cope with it, and German reactions thereto which were responsible for three years of economic paralysis.

After the First World War, Germans had put their full trust into the inherent value of their currency until it was too late. When they finally realized what inflation had done to the country most people had suffered great losses and the entire middle class had been virtually wiped out. By 1945 every German had learned how to cope with the problem. For the manufacturer, the farmer, and the businessman it meant to sell as little as possible at official prices and to barter the rest. For blue and white collar workers it meant to exert oneself as little as possible in order not to burn up irreplaceable calories. It was wise to work two or three days in order to earn the small sum of money needed to buy rationed goods at official prices. The rest of the time was used to go out to the farmers in an effort to barter some wares for essential food items.[21]

In the Soviet zone of Germany this problem was greatly reduced because on the first day of the occupation the Soviet military government had frozen all bank accounts. Subsequently, only payments of RM 300 were permitted to depositors whose total account did not exceed RM 3,000. Depositors with larger amounts were considered undeserving capitalists and received no funds. All financial claims and liabilities of financial institutions were voided along with the Reich's debt which served as their main backing. As a result of these ruthless measures, the economy in the Soviet zone was drained of nearly 80 percent of its monetary assets; in part this action was compensated by the issuance of an occupation currency but nevertheless the purchasing power of the population was drastically reduced, inflationary pressures eased, and work incentives reestablished. The consequence was that during the first years of the occupation production in the Soviet zone recovered much more rapidly than in the West. Soviet coal output in 1946 for instance reached 98 percent of the 1936 level while output in the Ruhr area was only 53 percent.[22] A fateful by-effect of the economic paralysis in West Germany was the miscalculation of the country's economic potential and the refusal even to examine the feasibility of a reparations settlement with the Soviet Union.

At Yalta the Big Three had agreed that in addition to taking German foreign assets whenever possible, there would be three sources for reparations: dismantled equipment, current production, and labor. At Potsdam already a different political atmosphere prevailed and the three Allies concentrated on the first category. It was agreed that economic experts would establish within six months a ceiling for the peacetime German economy. All the industrial capacity above the ceiling would be available for reparations.[23] Although reparations from production were not mentioned in the Potsdam agreement, the American "reparations ambassador" Edwin Pauley reported to the president that this question would be taken up once the future industrial level of Germany had been determined.[24]

At the Paris Council of Foreign Ministers Conference in June 1946, however, the United States raised the ante by contending that Potsdam had superseded Yalta and that, since reparations from production were not mentioned, there would be none. The Soviet Union never accepted this position and insisted that Potsdam had not superseded but implemented Yalta and for that matter it had only implemented it in part.[25] There is now documentary evidence available which would seem to lend support to the Soviet point of view.[26]

It also seems that General Clay was one of the few who foresaw the eventual consequences of this feud, but his recommendation for a careful investigation of Germany's economic potential was disregarded.[27] Accordingly, the Soviet proposal at the Moscow Council of Foreign Ministers Conference in March–April 1947 to proceed simultaneously with a reparations settlement and the establishment of a German government was rejected. As a consequence Germany was split and two German nations eventually emerged. The term "economic miracle" was later used to explain the swift emergence of an economically strong West Germany. In fact, however, its economy after the currency reform of June 1948 showed almost the same pattern of recovery that had been observed twenty-six years earlier in the Soviet Union. When in connection with Lenin's New Economic Policy a new currency had been introduced, the economy reacted promptly and dramatically. In both cases, prewar production levels were reached within less than four years.[28]

A significant consequence of these developments was the freeing of the Federal Republic of Germany from a meaningful reparations burden. According to German estimates, West Germany paid about $600 million in the form of dismantled equipment.[29] This may be compared with the $4.5 billion extracted according to conservative estimates by Russia from the DDR;[30] and also with the sum of 9 billion 1928 dollars or about 15 billion in 1946 dollars taken from Germany after the First World War. A cynic might therefore suggest that a Morgenthau plaque ought to be unveiled in Bonn's Ministry of Finance. By insisting on dismantlement in lieu of deliveries from current production, the Secretary of the Treasury de facto had been instrumental in bringing about a very favorable result for the occupied country. By the time the reparations issue was to be re-examined, American-Soviet tensions had increased and the pendulum of public opinion in America had swung so far that the welfare of West Germany had become much more important for the United States than that of the Soviet wartime ally.

If one now turns to the connecting links between Henry Morgenthau's and George Marshall's policies, one recognizes that the application of the former hastened the activation of the latter. Already Truman's coal directive of July 1945 ordering General Eisenhower, the American commander in chief in Europe, to make available for export from the German mines a minimum of ten million tons of coal in 1945 and of an additional fifteen million tons by the end of April 1946, threw the original Morgenthau recommendation to close the German mines out of the window.[31] The question whether these shipments—as after the First World War—should go on reparations account or as commercial exports was initially left open. In the absence of a viable German currency, the coal directive brought the question of German exports and the problem of payment modalities to the fore.[32] Although Morgenthau's "hands off" policy was gradually discarded, this did not mean that the time for a vigorous all-encompassing assistance such as the European Recovery Program had come. When William Draper, Clay's economic advisor, in the spring of 1946 proposed one million dollars in imports in the form of industrial raw materials, Clay had to tell him that such support was not in the cards.[33] The German economy, Clay said, had to be pulled up by its bootstraps.

Accordingly, an Export-Import Section of OMGUS was given the responsibility to generate exports. Its task was not an easy one because how does one promote exports when there is no mail service and no telephone communications with foreign countries; when German businessmen cannot travel abroad because of security considerations or the lack of foreign currency; and when foreign buyers cannot visit Germany because of lack of housing and feeding facilities? The answer was the establishment of a temporary foreign trade monopoly similar to the one found in Communist countries.[34] Not only was all foreign trade conducted by a central office, but in absence of a meaningful cost basis, prices had to be set by government fiat. This meant that a small group of government officials with limited access to the outside world was given the task of determining world market prices for hundreds of export goods. The unavoidable result was that progress was slow and foreign trade initially developed at a snail's pace.

Pricing in the case of bulk commodities was easier, since world market prices could be quickly determined. But the question in what kind of currency foreign trade should be conducted still had to be settled first. With Swiss francs and American dollars the only convertible currencies at the time, Clay and his advisors concluded that all German exports—just like bread grains and other vital imports—also had to be paid for in dollars.[35] It was a decision which left open the question how dollars could be collected when practically none of Germany's traditional European customers had any hard currency reserves. The resulting international controversies permeated the foreign relations of the United States for several years and only subsided after the German currency reform had offered a solution to the problem.

In a similar vein, the dollar question became a bone of contention between OMGUS and the Department of State which tended to take the side of the liberated countries and often intervened on their behalf. As Clay, who was responsible for the War Department budget for the occupation, saw it, however, the State Department's intervention amounted to an attempt to make European policy at the expense of Germany. The pricing of coal was a case in point. Since coal had to be exported by fiat and nobody had dollars to pay for these shipments, the initial emergency solution was to make the deliveries against quantitative receipts. Later, after the United States had made dollar loans to the European countries, some of these funds were used to pay for the German coal. But it still was not a fully satisfactory solution, because on State Department insistence the export price for coal was kept artificially low, thus giving substance to the charge that the underpricing was tantamount to hidden reparations.[36]

The debate about German coal provided the first demonstration that the German economy could not be rebuilt in isolation. There were similar vocal and protracted feuds regarding the use of the Dutch and Belgian ports, the importation of vegetables from the Netherlands, of fruit from Italy, and regarding transit charges for freight to and from Czechoslovakia. While Clay in each case fought for the conservation of scarce War Department dollars for the German economy, the State Department took the opposite side thus making it abundantly clear that a new approach was needed.

It came in the form of the Marshall Plan, whose long-range impact eliminated the European dollar problem. The general public remembers the plan as a magnanimous foreign aid program, although its political implications are also recognized. In today's terminology, it might be referred to as a recycling of the world's monetary reserves. The change of policy is correctly seen as an about-face from a spirit of revenge to one of cooperation and reconstruction. The incremental nature of the transition, as described above, was hastened by the vestiges of the Morgenthau concept. Its influence reflected in JCS 1067 contributed to the unduly long period of suppressed inflation and the absence of a German currency. The result was a protracted controversy within the Truman administration as well as between the United States and its European allies. This dilemma showed in dramatic clarity the need for an all-European solution which the Marshall Plan provided.

Discussion

Diethelm Prowe: Dr. Backer, it was my impression after listening to your speech that the assumption that the currency reform is really the key turning point in terms of economic development of postwar Germany, clashes head-on with Werner Abelshauser's book [*Wirtschaft in Westdeutschland 1945–1948* (Stuttgart: Deutsche Verlags-Anstalt, 1975)] which argues that the economic upswing really comes after the starvation winter of 1946–47, and was well under way by the time the currency reform came. Could you comment on that?

John H. Backer: I know the study that you mentioned, and I was pleased to see that Dr. Abelshauser came to the same conclusion I did in my first book, and apparently without any reference to my book—I think his research was entirely independent, based on German sources. So, the fact is, as I hope I explained, we cleared the underbrush. We actually put the whole transportation system back. We put the communication system back and we kept the Germans alive. Moreover, we started the foreign trade going. When the currency reform came about, we had trade agreements on behalf of Germany with practically all European countries. So we really prepared the ground, we cleared the underbrush. There was a very slow increase but the final push came with the currency reform.

Up to that period the Germans participated slowly, understandably disinterested, and so on. I can give you one practical example. I was in export promotion and we had actually a two-front fight, if I may use that term. We had, first of all, to convince the countries abroad to buy German goods. Most of these countries, which were traditionally German customers, had been occupied by the Germans and they were reluctant to start buying German merchandise though they needed it. On the other hand, the German manufacturer was unwilling to export for the simple reason that all he got in exchange was worthless Reichsmarks which were put in his account, but he did not know what to do with this money. So you had this built-in resistance which only was (of course, you had a similar problem domestically) that the people were just not willing to trade, as I tried to explain in my paper, until they really knew they got money with which they could do something. So you had a so-called "cigarette economy"; and you had actually two compartments of the economy: one compartment where official prices were still meaningful, but pertained only to the small food rations which they could buy, to utilities (the telephone and so on), and maybe to rent, and the other compartment where everything else was spent. You had, indeed, a slow starting of the economy, but the decisive up-turn came, of course, in 1948, when within a few months production jumped by about 60 percent.

Morris Amchan: I was formerly a deputy counsel at the Nuremberg trials. Dr. Backer, I was interested in your Morgenthau Plan comment, but are you aware of the fact that at the I. G. Farben case at Nuremberg, we presented the detailed plan of the German government, the "New Order," which was a sophisticated Morgenthau Plan to deindustrialize all of Europe? The essence of that plan was, and I. G. Farben and the Economic Ministry worked together on it, that they detailed the production capacity of every occupied country in Europe. They set out by detail what each country would be permitted to retain—the central thesis being that no occupied country in Europe should be permitted to have an industrial capacity that could create war material, or any civilian goods that were convertible to war materials. So my question to you, sir, is: Do you think it would be a fair historical balance whenever you discuss the Morgenthau Plan to present the equal type of plan that the Germans had? Now you will find all of that plan at the National Archives in the record of the I. G. Farben trial.

John H. Backer: I think I have to ask you a question before I can answer you, because I did not quite follow you. Did you mean to say that one aspect of the Morgenthau Plan pertained to the deindustrialization of other countries than Germany? And number two, what secret plan are you talking about?

Morris Amchan: The "New Order," which was introduced in the I. G. Farben trial at Nuremberg, contemplated a detailed plan of the German government that every country in occupied Europe was not to have any industrial capacity to manufacture war materials or civilian products that were convertible to war use. My question is that are you aware of that, and is it not fair as historical statement or research to mention that fact when you are discussing the Morgenthau Plan?

John H. Backer: Thank you. Actually, in sum, you are stating that Morgenthau had good reasons for his plan. I mean, that is what you are saying—because the Germans actually wanted to do worse to the rest of Europe than Morgenthau wanted for Germany; is that what you are saying?

Morris Amchan: No, it does not follow because that would depend upon whether Morgenthau knew of the German plan at the time he was doing it. But, assuming he did not know it, what I am suggesting to you is historical fact—that the Germans, independent of Morgenthau, had the same concept of how to deal with the new Europe—as they called it, the "New Order."

John H. Backer: I have not found any evidence that Morgenthau was aware of this plan, but that he did not expect any good from a German victory I think can be taken for granted.

Robert Wolfe: There is a similar German "mirror image," I think we would call it, of some of our thinking about German national character. Hitler's view of what had gone wrong in the First World War in one respect, was that the Allied propaganda in that war was unfair because it was untrue—"Belgian nuns" and all that. Hitler said that the main mistake the Kaiser and Hindenberg and Ludendorf made was not to be ruthless enough to win the war, and that he would not make the same mistake—he would do everything necessary in order to win the war. Now we have just heard a "mirror image" here; although the program that I. G. Farben and the *Wirtschaftsministerium* were proposing never got that far, it made very good documentation for the prosecution at Nuremberg, and might even justify the Morgenthau Plan in retaliation. To that I think there is a simple rebuttal: *We* are not Nazis.

Orville J. McDiarmid: I had a brief spell in SCAP in 1945–46 in the Economic and Scientific Section; subsequently I was with the Young and Dobbs Mission to Japan, and for the last several decades I have been ensconced in the World Bank. I would like to return the discussion for a moment to the Far East on the two subjects which Eleanor Hadley addressed—the purge and the *zaibatsu* program—for neither of which, I might say, I have at any time had any great regard.

I believe the basic difficulties of the purge were with the mechanical operation, as I think Dr. Hadley pointed out: removing certain categories and individuals who not necessarily had connection with the Japanese and militaristic adventures. I think the highlight of the purge in my mind was the purge of Finance Minister Ishibashi about a year after he had become finance minister of Japan. He was an ardent Keynesian and he might have been purged on those grounds at that time in Japan, but I believe he was purged primarily because his degree of sophistication in economics so far exceeded that of the generals with which he conferred, that they felt it best to get rid of him. That might be a libelous statement, I do not know.

On the *zaibatsu* issue, I think the great error was in confusing concentration of economic power with older, radical integration of the economy. If they had taken action to divest the industrial giants of their financial affiliates, namely the leading banks in Japan, I think there might have been some justification in their action. I believe the effect of the *zaibatsu* program was to shift economic power in Japan from industry to finance and it has rested there ever since. My real question on this is: Do you really think, Dr. Hadley, that this program had any real effect on Japan for better or for worse? It is true that the top layer of the *zaibatsu* companies were removed or put into retirement; however, the new giants that have emerged in Japan: Sony, Tokyo Shibaura and so on, would have emerged in any case—*zaibatsu* program or not—and therefore I think that the whole program of the *zaibatsu* which, in some mystic connection, was linked with militarism was a mistake and an unproductive one.

Eleanor M. Hadley: I think I would join you in saying that it was distinctly unfortunate to have linked the *zaibatsu* program with militarism. Actually, there was more of a connection than Prime Minister Yoshida and a number of other spokesmen wanted to make. The *zaibatsu* benefited very greatly in their relative position during the Pacific War. The Big Four, at the beginning of the war, accounted for 12 percent of paid-up capital; at the end of the Pacific war they accounted for a quarter of paid-up capital. But I would not argue the merits of the program on that line, and I think basically it was confused, and was just unnecessary.

I, myself, would argue the merits of the program entirely on the issue of whether or not one can grow political democracy in an economy which is highly concentrated, where business families can perfectly easily buy elections. If we go back to the 1920s, when Japan did have some party government before the Manchurian In-

cident and on to the China incident and on to the Pacific war, at that
time Mitsui bought elections for Seiyukai and Mitsubishi for Min-
seito, and whoever won had the coal contract for the national railroads. Even though I think there is a connection, I would not argue
the case on the military. I would argue the case on was it a worthy
objective for the United States to have attempted to create a democratic form of government in Japan, if it were agreed that it was
important to have a democratic government. Mr. Reinstein was
speaking in the case of the feeling after two world wars in Europe—we in 1944 and 1945 kept using the expression "Japan's program of aggression," from Manchuria (there was the Shanghai
Incident and the China Incident, both Manchuria and China being
full-fledged wars) and then on to French Indo-China, as it was then
called, and then on to the Pacific war. So, it was the program of
aggression that we were addressing, and we said it was important
for the security interests of the United States that Japan be democratic, on the grounds that a democratic government was not as
likely to be territorially expansionistic, so we thought, as an authoritarian government. Personally, I think that is the way to look
at the program of whether or not democratic forces can be grown
when one has very high concentration.

I also think that it has been difficult in a public sense—you, Mr.
McDiarmid, are a sophisticated observer—but for persons who are
not familiar with Japan and they see the same names: Mitsui, Mitsubishi, Sumitomo—now as then—what is the difference? Is not
everything just the same? Actually the name stays the same, but
when you greatly diminish the links which tie Mitsubishi heavy industry to Mitsubishi chemicals to Asahi glass to Mitsubishi mining
and so on, we really did create a much looser, more rivalrous business environment. I think it is the greatly increased business rivalry—and I think this is what Mr. Kogoro Uemura, the president of
the *Keidanren* was speaking of—the much greater rivalry in the
postwar economy. They are giants, right, but there is a lot more
rivalry than I think was the case under the *zaibatsu* system where
I would describe, to use vivid jargon, as cordial oligopoly—one did
not challenge the market positions in the same way because one
thought in terms of the combine as a whole. One did not go at it,
shipbuilding against shipbuilding, mining against mining. One
viewed one's market strategy in terms of the whole.

Just to make a couple of other comments: You are certainly quite
correct in observing that the purge in the case of Japan was mechanical. Though, in a very interesting book on the Japan occupation by
the late Professor Callwey, *Japan's American Interlude,* he con-

cludes that, as mechanical as it was, it really got the whole thing over more rapidly and cleanly than trying to do it through a judicial procedure. I have not done enough work in the area myself to have an opinion, but I think there is that to be said on the other side of the mechanical.

On Mr. Ishibashi, that is a singular case; I would suggest that your hypothesis may have something to do with it. I think he had the misfortune to criticize certain things about the Headquarters, but it was not an example really of the way overall the purge was run.

On your point of shifting—and really doing nothing very much more than to shift—the locus of economic power from industrials to finance, I entertained that thought for a time myself as I was starting to work in this area. But I really do come out after a long time feeling that, although names have stayed the same in major corporations, and although no bank was reorganized, simply because there are more credit sources today and because these links from the bank to the trading company to the heavy industries, the chemicals and so on were cut, I do believe myself that a considerably more rivalrous environment has been created. It is the keenness of that rivalry which has been one of the elements causing a postwar growth rate which is over double the rate Japan had prior to the Pacific war.

Jacques J. Reinstein: I must share with you an aside that Dr. Backer suggests that perhaps the finance minister was purged for being a Keynesian, and might be purged more readily now than then.

Hans H. Baerwald: It so happened that I was one of those who helped draft the memorandum that purged Mr. Ishibashi. What we could do, Mr. McDiarmid, I suppose is reactivate the Economic and Scientific Section government section divisions over the viewpoint concerning the purge, *zaibatsu* reform, and related matters. As a matter of fact, Ishibashi, as Dr. Hadley quite correctly pointed out, illustrates one of the things that can happen when you do not use the categorical approach; because Mr. Ishibashi did not fit under any of those criteria that had been developed, a very special case had to be concocted against him, involving, for example, his writings, his editorship of something called *The Oriental Economist,* which was a very important journal (still is, as a matter of fact), and the positions that the journal had taken during the years that Japan had been engaged in conquest and expansion. I am not sure that it was the proper thing to do—I think, as Dr. Hadley quite correctly pointed out, it is probable that Ishibashi's purge was the result of his having criticized certain directives from Headquarters, having gotten himself into some arguments with those who felt that his policies were excessively inflationary and were damaging to the reconstruction of the Japanese economy. Nonetheless, one can also make a case—it is a difficult case—and I hope at some point all of those documents will come to light. I have not seen them yet.

John Gimbel: I would like to comment on Jacques Reinstein's statement about the underestimation of the British and the Americans on the amount of damage Germany had suffered. That idea is prevalent in the literature, but I would argue that, although they may have underestimated the amount, they were very worried that they had made a mistake. As a matter of fact, my study of the records of Edwin M. Pauley's reparations mission in Moscow makes very clear that Pauley was concerned about the twenty billion dollar figure that was mentioned at Yalta, and he talked about maybe twelve billion. He did not know; nobody knew at that time, and everybody admitted that they did not know how much Germany could afford to pay. The point I would like to make here, in this audience, is that after the Pauley mission in Moscow adjourned to the Potsdam conference in July of 1945, the twenty billion dollar figure was, in fact, abandoned by the Russians as well as everybody else. There are revisionist historians, Bruce Kuklick and Gabriel Kolko and others, who are writing today, as though the Americans somehow sandbagged the twenty billion dollar figure afterwards. The Russians admitted that the twenty billion dollar figure was simply pulled out of thin air, and the Potsdam agreement on reparations, imperfect as it was, because it let the Russians go in their own zone and what-not; but the Potsdam agreement on reparations would be in the form of residues—what was left over—and there was no attempt made at Potsdam to discuss twenty billion, twelve billion, fourteen and one-half billion. The only thing that was agreed at Potsdam was that the Russians would get at least half. There was no question about that—that the Russians would get half. Now, what was supposed to happen after Potsdam was that within six months the Allied Control Council was to work up the German "level of industry" and the reparations plan, which meant that Germany would have a general level of industry equal to the average of the European countries except Britain and Russia, and that all industrial capacity over and above that average would go as reparations—and that is the residue.

I do not really have a question; I simply wanted to comment on this since reparations is so important to all of this, and since there is in the revisionist literature a tremendous amount of accusation back and forth about who sandbagged Potsdam, and who sandbagged Yalta, and who dropped the reparations ball, and what-not. There is a tremendous amount of misunderstanding about Germany's capacity to pay and so on.

I notice that John Backer wants to refute everything I have said now. Maybe I should not quit until you are all tired.

Jacques J. Reinstein: Let me clarify a point. I was not speaking about the underestimate of the damage to Germany. What I was talking about was the underestimate of the damage to the economy of Western Europe and of the social structure of Western Europe: of France, of Belgium, the low countries, Denmark, Norway, Italy. As a vast number of you did, I worked on Italy. Italy was left absolutely fractured. When the Germans retreated, they left every single generator damaged. They put a hand grenade at every single place they could. The country was completely fragmented. Had it not been for that extraordinary genius of the Italians, who can take almost anything and make something out of it, Italy would never have recovered at all. As a matter of fact, if it were not for the extraordinary genius of many of the other Western European countries, they would not have been able to put it together either. Thank God they got some help. At any rate, I was not just talking about Germany and reparations.

John H. Backer: I would like to refer to John Gimbel's comments here. Now, the Soviets at Yalta asked for ten billion dollars of German reparations and then they threw in, "Well, you get the same amount." Obviously they were not interested whether the West received ten billion dollars or no reparations. They were interested in ten billion dollars. This ten billion dollar reparations claim, to my knowledge, was never dropped. It was maintained very emphatically in Paris in the summer of 1946, and it was again brought up in Moscow in the spring of 1947, and at the London Conference, and so on. So the Potsdam agreement only dealt with one item—the dismantlement. At Yalta it was pointed out, as I mentioned earlier in my paper, three sources of reparations—dismantlement, production, and use of labor. Now, as to the use of labor, the United States said very early that we are not interested in that and, for all practical purposes, every country used German labor as it saw fit. France used German labor, the Soviets used German labor, and the British used it to a certain extent. So the key question which finally brought crucial impact on American-Soviet relations was the question of reparations from production. Now, reparations from production were not mentioned in the Moscow document. Therefore, as of June 1946, the American position was: it is not mentioned, therefore, it is dropped. In the meantime, there was one public speech by Ambassador Pauley, a report to the secretary of state by Ambassador Pauley, and a report by Ambassador Pauley to the president of the United States, in which he was very clear that the question of reparations from production could, for commonsense reasons, only be solved after the question of dismantlement has been settled. Obviously, there is no point talking about reparations from production unless you know what is going to be left to produce. So, it was a very commonsense position, and there is now documentary evidence available that there was an oral agreement between the United States and the Soviet Union on the so-called fair charge principle, which stipulates that *first* come exports to payment for imports, and *then* come reparations. This agreement, which is part of the Potsdam agreement, did not apply to reparations. If you want to know more about this fine point, I am afraid you will have to wait four or five months when my second book will be coming out, because it has the documentary evidence.

John Gimbel: I definitely want to rebut. I agree with 90 percent of what John Backer says. The thing I disagree with is that the Russians never gave up on the ten billion dollars. If you read again (and I do not have it here now, I wish I did) the final protocol of the agreement on the American reparations position at Potsdam, Stalin said in the presence of Attlee and Truman that he agreed to the American position. And then somebody (I forget who it is, but I could look this up) said, "Do you agree that we are not going to mention a dollar figure?" and Stalin said, "Yes, we agree on the American position." In my estimation, that is an admission by the Russians that they are not going to go for ten billion dollars, but for the residue that the Americans suggested. Now Molotov came back at Paris on July 9, 1946, and reopened the twenty billion dollar figure. But my suggestion is that the reason that he reopened it is because Clay stopped reparations on May 3rd, and Molotov smelled a rat.

Tristan E. Beplat: I was in SCAP from 1945 to 1948 in finance. I would agree with Dr. Hadley's remarks on the horizontal splitting up of the banks and the other companies who weigh in the *zaibatsu* holding companies. But I do not think enough has been said, or enough has been discussed about it, and she alludes to the fact that because of that it really was instrumental in bringing about the financial strength of Japan and bringing it back again. But I think that was only a very small part of it.

The fact remains that the Finance Division in the beginning took a very strong position that they had to provide an alternative to breaking up banks. And the alternative to that was to create new banks, new competition. And, as a result, when Japan went into foreign trade instead of the four banks that used to monopolize all the finance, all of the credit, eight other banks were brought in. So, initially, there were twelve foreign exchange banks in Japan, and four of those banks had never been in the business before, and today they are some of the largest banks in the world. As a result of that, we created long-term money and this money was used for the development of Japanese industry. Today, these banks rate among the largest international banks in the world with billions of assets.

The third area was in developing and encouraging the provincial banks such as the Saitama Bank and the Hokuriku Bank and others. So, today Japan has one of the strongest and well-balanced financial institutions, and these institutions are able to finance the 60 billion dollars of Japanese trade every year in addition to taking care of the domestic trade. Today anyone in Japan can get the credit they need and they are not tied in anymore to the four big *zaibatsu* banks. As a matter of fact, firms like Mitsui and Company now have to go maybe to the Fujuii Bank to get extra credit because they find that banks like the Mitsui are no longer large enough to take care of their credit needs, and so Mitsui and Company now has many of its principal banks other than in the Mitsui group. I wanted to bring you up to date on that and I am not sure whether or not you want to comment, Dr. Hadley.

Eleanor M. Hadley: I share your view that strong financial institutions are indispensable for buildng a strong recovery. I have just a few points: for example, Mitsui Trading, up until 1937, primarily financed itself through the big five of the city of London, so there *had* been a pattern. Trust banks began in Japan in 1927, if I recall correctly. But to the extent that one can build additional credit sources by bringing additional banks into creation or prominence rather than severing or cutting up, I share your view that that is a better approach. What had been contemplated—and this got caught up in that excessive concentration of economic power law, or debacle we might almost say—was that instead of the Mitsui (so-called in technical jargon) "city banks," instead of being able to have branches all over Japan, it was being played around with in the Headquarters that what would be done would be to maybe divide the country up into five sectors and they could have branches within one sector of one-fifth of Japan but they could not have branches in all of Japan as is the actual situation.

A fascinating point which I have not done enough research on: Japan has financed this phenomenal postwar growth rate majorly out of bank credit rather than out of the capital market. And a question which keeps coming back to my mind, again and again, is really whether you can have possibly higher growth when you do it that way rather than when you do it our way, which is through the capital markets. I am most ready to grant you that while (I do not want to overemphasize the significance of the deconcentration program) there are lots of factors affecting this—freedom from the burden of armaments when you have no war machine that you are financing is a tremendous assist to the economy if we are talking about commercial, economic development.

In my view, the reason one has this much higher postwar investment rate than before is tied to the more rivalrous state of the economy. Companies in the postwar Japanese economy have madly pushed for first position in the market and, in my view, when one was dealing with the prewar *zaibatsu,* one did not have that scale of challenge. For example, shipbuilding and coal: Mitsubishi was much stronger in shipbuilding than Mitsui; it was weaker in coal than Mitsui. My argument would be, analytically looking at the situation, Mitsubishi would tend not to push its strength in shipbuilding because it was vulnerable to the same conglomerate in coal; therefore, it was live and let live. If one looks at markets, year by year, and who was in first position and second position and third position, there has been tremendous rivalry in this high postwar growth rate. The first firm this year is not necessarily the first firm next year.

Speaking of Sony, I should mention that I had an interview with Mr. Ibuka and my whole question was directed to entry—whether under the *zaibatsu* system there could have been a Sony. Mr. Ibuka looked very soberly at me and said, "I'm not that old."

Jacques J. Reinstein: We started twenty minutes late and we have gone fifteen minutes beyond what we had planned to go. I think this illustrates the fascination that we have for not only these two extraordinary industrial giants, but the curiosity we have about our own role in making them what they are. We have not answered those questions, but we have had an extremely stimulating discussion and I think we owe our panelists a vote of great thanks.

Fourth Session

Purging the Body Politic

Help or Hindrance to Reorientation and Rehabilitation?

Introduction by Eli E. Nobleman

As panel moderator for "Purging the Body Politic: Help or Hindrance to Reorientation and Rehabilitation," my instructions are to devote a few minutes to lay down the premise and then to take time to describe military government courts in Germany and the role they played in the democratization of the German people.

Over a period of years as a prosecutor and judge (not in the same case, of course) in the summary, intermediate, and general military government courts in Germany, I tried some one thousand cases in a year. You may not think that is much when you hear the statistics of a ten-year period with more than half a million cases just in the United States zone, and these do not include war crimes. These were criminal courts which were later given some civil jurisdiction. I also served as legal and public safety officer in a number of detachments throughout Germany. Of course, when you were a public safety officer you were also charged with responsibility for what our British colleagues call "Special Brawnch," which was the denazification and intelligence program. So I have processed several thousand *Fragebogen* (you will hear more about *Fragebogen* from Elmer Plischke).

Laying down the basic premise here, we speak of *purging* in Japan and *denazification* in Germany. The objective was the same — it was, in fact still is in some circles, the most highly controversial program, much criticized, but nevertheless one of the principal objectives of the United States and its allies. The German program cannot really be equated, other than in objective terms, with the program in Japan, which was a miniprogram by comparison. I do not mean to derogate Dr. Baerwald's account, but the volume in Germany was so much greater and it was perhaps more difficult to reorient thinking and the environment generally through democratization in Germany than in Japan. I do not know very much about the Japanese purge, but I can tell you that the task in Germany was a twenty-four-hour a day never-ending task, and at least half the time mistakes were made and injustices occurred. Unfortunately, a lot of people got through who should not have gotten through—that was inevitable.

Chapter 9

United States Military Courts in Germany

Setting an Example and Learning Lessons

Eli E. Nobleman

Military government courts began to function in Germany in September 1944. Although originally established under international law for the sole purpose of protecting the allied forces and punishing offenders against the military government as well as against German law, it is my judgment that probably no other military government operation in the field had a more signal effect on the so-called democratization of the German people than the operation of these courts. That is my basic premise and my basic thesis. To those of us who have been brought up in Anglo-American traditions, that should not come as any surprise, because we have long recognized that civil rights and civil liberties, privileges, and immunities become meaningless unless we have an independent court system—an independent judiciary which is available at all times to dispense impartial justice according to law.

Military occupation courts, as such, are not new to United States legal history. We have used them since the 1830s. In fact, during the one hundred and thirty years in which we have engaged in thirteen major occupations, we have always established military courts to maintain law and order and to protect the interests of the occupying force. But we have never had as elaborate a system as we had in Germany in World War II. Normally, our forces have established military commissions or provost courts, manned by military personnel most of the time, not by trained lawyers.

During World War I we had some experience with these commissions, but the local courts were open. They handled local civilian, civil, and criminal matters, and our military courts were limited to the normal functions of military courts.

A major development occurred during World War II planning for Germany. Eleven years of National Socialism and five years of war had virtually reduced the German judiciary to such a feeble and corrupt state that it could not under any circumstances be trusted, at least at the outset, to resume operations. It was also apparent that the reconstruction of a denazified German judicial system based upon democratic principles would require a considerable period of time. Later, one of my assignments was to reestablish in Bavaria (*Land Bayern*) the German judicial system, and the denazification program gave me a great deal of trouble in trying to do this. Because of the state of the German judiciary, it was obvious that we would have to establish a much more elaborate system of military courts which would be able not only to perform the traditional functions, but also to replace completely the German system for the time being in maintaining law and order in general.

As the first American troops came into the Rhineland, we immediately established these courts, and began to operate in the field. I am not going to burden you with their jurisdiction but the procedures we followed were a combination of United States Army courts martial, the German legal system (that is the Roman legal system), and the Anglo-American system. The idea was a complete innovation, a complete departure, and was based on the theory that at the outset, at least, we would not have enough lawyers, and the courts would have to be manned by lay officers who were not legally trained, other than the usual training in military justice. We later tightened it up so that intermediate and general courts would have to have at least one lawyer, and if there was one legal officer there he could handle the matter alone, at least in the intermediate court.

We then promulgated Ordinance No. 2 which provided that certain fundamental rights were to be afforded to all persons appearing before these courts; these were printed in German on the reverse side of every summons. In addition, the charge sheet included the right of every accused to have, in advance of trial, a copy of the charges, be present at his trial to give evidence and examine or cross-examine witnesses, be represented by counsel of his choice or court-appointed counsel, bring material witnesses, have an opportunity for adjournment to prepare the case, have the proceedings translated, and to appeal conviction. In other words, German defendants were afforded traditional basic rights that we afford in our own courts.

Many of these rights, of course, existed in pre-Nazi Germany and many of them were used or at least granted by the courts and protected by the courts, but that was all in pre-Nazi Germany. It appears that of all the German institutions in existence prior to the advent of the Nazi regime, the courts probably suffered the greatest impact of the National Socialist program, because it was particularly in the courts that the fullest realization of the loss of their rights came to the German people. Rights guaranteed by the Weimar constitution and various state constitutions were rendered meaningless by the inability of the citizens to enforce them before nazified tribunals. This accounts, perhaps, for the complete bewilderment of the average German defendant during legal proceedings before our courts. We noticed this from the first days, and I collected many reports about how amazed that particular generation was when they saw the care with which our military government judges protected the rights of defendants before them.

In a very considerable number of cases which I tried, we had a little problem with the plea. First of all, translating it in German, and then when we asked "How do you plead?" they would say "I was never in the Party." Now the charge was carrying a gun or contraband of some kind, anything from a curfew violation to a serious violation, because we sat first as committing magistrates to determine which court was the proper level court for the particular offense charged. A defendant would say, "I did it, but am not guilty; the victim had it coming."

Another reply to a request "How do you plead?" was "Yes I was in the Party but just a dues paying member." Thus, it was difficult to convey our concept of a plea so that the people would understand that our concern was not with party membership, but with the charge.

I found early in the game that we had to get advice on German law, although we had good summaries and texts, and many of us were trained in it. But this was not adequate, because there are a lot of peculiarities which we did not know about. The trick was to find a retired local or district judge. We found such a gentleman who was very helpful and I advised others to do the same because it was a very valuable aid.

The classic example is a *Fragebogen* falsification: a woman applied for the position of head of the school district. One of the questions on the questionnaire was "Are you or have you ever been related to a member of the leadership corps of the Nazi Party?" She had written "No," but it turned out that she was married to a very well known Nazi in the very top hierarchy of the party, who had since been taken prisoner by the Russians. We had begun to prepare a case against her when the *Anwärter* (advisor) advised me that under German law a husband is not a relative of his wife. That gave us a little food for thought.

Between the fall of 1944, when they began to function, and July 1945, when the combat phase ended and the permanent occupation began, three hundred and forty-three military government courts had tried in excess of fifteen thousand cases in the United States zone alone and new cases were coming in at the rate of approximately ten thousand a month. Although the courts functioned effectively from the standpoint of protecting the security of the occupying forces, I must admit that many excesses were committed by the officers manning these courts. In many respects, defendants were treated no differently than they would have been in the old Nazi courts and, unfortunately, when they began transferring into the courts combat officers who had been through a lot of combat, the attitude of a regimental commander who was now operating as a court officer was: "Well, the hell with them—we were supposed to kill every German from the Rhine all the way east—so obviously he is guilty, he's German." This made it very uncomfortable for me, as a junior officer and the only lawyer on these courts, with a colonel on each side since I was a first lieutenant at the time. Fortunately, the review process enabled us to correct a lot of these errors. Ultimately, when I took over as chief of the Military Government Court Section in Munich, I was able to review and right some of these wrongs because I had the reviewing officers under me at that point. We had a rather informal arrangement—when good cases came along I got off the bench and prosecuted. Eventually, I developed a sixty-five circuit riding organization for the whole of Bavaria, in which I had teams of judges and prosecutors traveling around. Again, the reason was that we did not have enough lawyers. The Army had always put them all on KP and they wanted to get out as quickly as possible.

With the onset of the permanent occupation, we began to get official directives concerning how these people were to be handled, and how these courts were to operate. On July 16, 1947, OMGUS issued a directive setting forth the fundamental principles: "It is desired that military government court proceedings and all essential points conform to the traditional procedures of American law which apply whenever the life, liberty or property of an individual is subjected to penal procedure. Likewise, every effort must be made within the objectives of the Occupation to respect the guarantes of personal rights provided by German constitutions. The sole function of every military government court is to give justice in every case before it according to the law and the evidence." It then continued at some length with a basic checklist of safeguards, requiring all persons connected with military government courts to observe these, with an implied threat to the officers concerned if they did not. Under the provisions of a later ordinance, Germans, whose personal liberty was restrained, were authorized in appropriate cases to have what is the equivalent of a habeas corpus to determine why they were held in custody.

Although basic rights were guaranteed until 1948, we had a bad situation because the local commander not only appointed the judges and the prosecutors but was also the reviewing authority. This was not a permissible system under our theory of government.

In the summer of 1948, OMGUS established an integrated zone-wide court system based on our own system at home. Thus, the prosecution function was separated from the adjudication function; a three tier trial system was established; and a complete system of judicial review replaced the administrative procedure.

The key point I want to make is that American military government courts have probably played a more important role in demonstrating democracy in action to the German people, and its advantages to them, than any of the more obvious military government operations. These courts, which began as a device to protect the interests of the occupier, eventually became a guarantor of the fundamental rights of the inhabitants of the occupied area.

There were three factors: first, military government courtrooms, and this is at the grass-roots level, were at the all-important *Kreis* level. Many of you gentlemen here dealt at the top policy levels. We were dealing as local military governors, local proconsuls, on a *Landkreis* (county) level, on a *Regierungsbezirk* (district) level, with the German people on a day-to-day basis. It was cold in various parts of Germany and the courtrooms were always well heated so lots of people came to watch, largely because they had nothing else to do; but they came to watch. Another point was that this was one of the few places where the average German, who was not an official, had an opportunity to watch Americans at work—to see what our thoughts were, what our theories were, how we operated. Germans of all classes and strata of society came in. Another thing: when we promulgated these various ordinances guaranteeing fundamental freedoms, the average German took it with a grain of salt: he did not give us much credence, so the court procedures were very important because they gave an opportunity to the average man on the street, who had some problems with the law, to test these fundamental rights, these newly acquired so-called democratic, natural rights and safeguards, whether they afforded real protection.

We had a problem in getting defense counsel for the more serious cases because most of the German lawyers were put out of business since nearly all of them had been in the Nazi party—they had to be in order to practice law. We found one old gentleman who was not, so he represented everybody, like a public defender. I said to him one day, "You must be making a fortune," and he replied, "I am doing a lot of work but nobody is paying me." Well, I could understand why—there was really nothing worthwhile to pay with at the time.

Between September 1944, when the courts were established, and August 1948, when they were reorganized, these courts tried almost 400,000 cases, and if you add the period through 1955, over 600,000 cases. If you think in terms of the audience, the number of witnesses, the defendants—in large areas we used the regular courtrooms whenever we could; some of them could seat 300, 400, or 500 people—you get an idea of the impact. Also, we developed a system—I started it in my *Landkreis* earlier in the game—every time we had a court day, we printed and posted all through the county the entire calendar: the name, charge, and what the sentence was. You would be surprised how crime went down in our *Landkreis* but it went up correspondingly in the *Landkreise* on both sides of me, because they did not know what the penalty was going to be over there. This was the problem with the whole system, just as it is in our own system here, where there is a serious disparity in sentencing; but we are working on it here and have been for a hundred years or so.

One of the things that came out of all this was the fact that I persuaded the American Bar Association to establish a standing committee on the law of occupied areas, which we later extended to extraterritorial defense areas. We have a large volume of reports and written material which are helpful.

The basic point is that I am not sure that any occupying country can ever reeducate or democratize people—in fact, I have grave doubts that this can be done effectively—especially in a culture that is many generations, a thousand years if you will, older than our own, but from which many of us have come. The fact is that it sounds good on paper, but when you are charged with performing the task it is quite a different matter. I think that we did not really understand what it was all about, until we were there for a couple of years, and had worked on these problems on a daily basis. You really have to win the confidence of the people, change the environment, boost the economy—there are a lot of different things that have to be done. I still maintain that the role of these courts throughout the United States zone played a really major part in this work.

Another thing is that it had a real impact ultimately on the American Bar because all of this work was being performed by American lawyers, especially on the civilian courts which took over in 1948. Many of the judges were sitting judges from state courts in the United States who had been trained, and these courts operated exactly like our own courts, and I think quite successfully.

Chapter 10

The Purge in Occupied Japan

Hans H. Baerwald

Thirty years ago, we were all young. We were also optimistic, self-assured and goal-oriented. The Potsdam declaration (July 26, 1945), the State-War-Navy Coordinating Committee (SWNCC) "United States Initial Post-Surrender Policy for Japan" (August 29, 1945), and the Joint Chiefs of Staff's "Basic Directive for Post-Surrender Military Government in Japan Proper" (November 3, 1945) all included stern policy prescriptions regarding Japan's wartime leadership.

In each of these documents, there is at least one sentence concerning wartime leaders deemed ineligible to hold positions of public trust and responsibility in occupied Japan. Potsdam required eliminating "for all time the authority and influence of those who have deceived and misled the people of Japan." SWNCC required the removal and exclusion from leadership of "active exponents of militarism and militant nationalism." The JCS, after reiterating this policy, also ordered that those "who manifest hostility to the objectives of the military occupation" not be allowed to hold positions of public or private responsibility.

By the time I arrived in Tokyo in the early autumn of 1946, the occupation had already been under way for about a year. In the interim, the basic policies regarding the removal of Japan's wartime leadership had been translated into a far-reaching directive to the Japanese Government entitled "Removal and Exclusion of Undesirable Personnel from Public Office" (SCAPIN 550, January 4, 1946).

It was this directive that provided the basis for the "purge." As John Montgomery has pointed out in his *Forced to be Free: The Artificial Revolution in Germany and Japan* (Chicago: University of Chicago Press, 1957), "purge" is an unfortunate word. Politically, it brings forth visions of vicious reprisals, possibly ending in death. Physiologically, it has inelegant connotations, at the very least. Lest there be any misapprehensions, no one was killed, and no one was forced to drink any castor oil.

Whatever the program was called, its impact was substantial. Over two hundred thousand individuals were removed or barred, for a few years at least, from specified positions of responsibility. Recently, a Japanese colleague pointed out to me that this statistic is incorrect because it does not include the members of a "purgee's" family, who were also affected; if they are included, the proper number is closer to one million. In either case, the purge cut a wide swath through Japanese society.

Initially, higher policy ordered the removal of Japan's wartime leadership. What was expected to be achieved? Paragraph 6 of the Potsdam declaration put it succinctly by noting that the intention was to usher in a "new order of peace, security and justice" which cannot be established "until irresponsible militarism is driven from the world." "Militarism," then, was the principal target. SCAPIN 550 translated this requirement into seven major categories: war criminals, all career military and naval officers, leaders of ultra-nationalistic organizations, leaders of the Imperial Rule Assistance Association and its affiliates, officers of companies involved in economic colonialism, governors of occupied territories, and a catchall clause encompassing "additional militarists and ultranationalists," rather vaguely defined. If nothing else, the new leadership was intended to be pacifist, or at least nonmilitarist and nonexpansionist, either economically or politically.

The contradictory elements in these policies were generally overlooked. Almost from the onset the purge's clearly stated objective of demilitarization was entangled with the goal of democratization; speculation concerning what the Japanese people would tolerate resulted in some important compromises with the stated goals of the program; and in the last two years the JCS instructions to remove from leadership those persons deemed hostile to the occupation became paramount over the objectives of demilitarization and democratization. In the beginning, however, SCAP's public relations hyperbole was comforting and thus rarely challenged. The complexities and contradictions were swept away by the assumption that to the extent that Japan's wartime militaristic leaders had been antidemocratic, to that extent would Japan's new nonmilitarist leadership be prodemocratic. This assumption was epitomized in the official press release issued with SCAPIN 550, January 4, 1946: the purpose of the directive, it proclaimed, was "to strike the shackles from the efforts of the Japanese people to rise toward freedom and democracy." At that moment, alas, rhetoric overcame reason.

Some of the serious consequences flowing from the juxtaposition of goals had their source in administrative decisions regarding the criteria and their application. On the one hand, the criteria determining who was to be purged required that an individual be declared fit or unfit on the basis of the position that he (or, in a few instances, she) had held during the years that Japan had been at war, the period generally defined as having begun with the outbreak of the "China Incident" in 1937. On the other hand, those who had not held such positions were deemed to be eligible, and by definition thereby to be among those who would lead Japan toward "freedom and democracy." There were few appeals in the beginning, but the concepts of "real" versus "formal" responsibility were recognized albeit without consensus of opinion on which took precedence.

Inevitably, a host of anomalies resulted, a few of which will be cited for illustrative purposes. Under the Meiji constitution, all formal government actions were undertaken by the emperor. Chapter I, article IV states "The Tenno [emperor] stands at the head of the Empire, combining in Himself the rights of sovereignty and exercises them, according to the provisions of the present Constitution." If "formal," as opposed to "real," responsibility was to be the basis for defining the purge categories, the emperor should have been included as the first purgee. He was never designated for a variety of compelling reasons, most of which revolved around the desire that tranquility should prevail. Those rationalizations were deemed sufficient in his case, but not in a myriad of other instances, at least until the appeals process was seriously undertaken in the waning years of the occupation.

A second controversial issue involved the last-minute removal of Hatoyama Ichiro on the eve of his becoming prime minister in the spring of 1946. Hatoyama was one of Japan's senior parliamentarians, having first been elected to the House of Representatives in 1915. His designation as a purgee—specifically ordered by SCAP— was based on a complex line of reasoning that added up to his being among the "additional militarists and ultranationalists" not covered by the explicitly categorical criteria defining who should be purged. On the other hand, his replacement as president of the Liberal party and prime minister was Yoshida Shigeru. Yoshida had held at least equally responsible positions of authority, but he had been a career official in the Foreign Ministry. In effect, a bureaucrat replaced a parliamentarian, whatever else might be said about them. This substitution had far-reaching consequences in strengthening the hands

of the Japanese government's officialdom at the expense of the people's elected representatives. Quite possibly this unintended consequence was a built-in product of earlier decisions to exercise control
through the existing structure of the Japanese government, unlike
the direct government that had been instituted in Germany. Any
claim that a career bureaucrat—no matter how "antimilitarist"—
would be more equipped to guide the newly democratic Japan than a
long-tenured member of parliament was bound to create at least
some confusion.

In the final two years of the occupation, the criterion that the
purge was to be an instrument of SCAPIN 550, paragraph 1a—the
instruction to remove those who resist or oppose the occupation
forces—became paramount. Throughout the winter and spring of
1950 the Japan Communist party's leadership had become increasingly provocative and hostile to occupation authorities; this was a
direct response to the Cominform's stinging criticism that it had
been excessively subservient to "the imperialist occupiers in Japan."
After a series of verbal warnings, SCAP ordered the purge of senior
party leaders and the editorial board of *Akahata* [Red Flag]; concurrently, substantial numbers of "leftists" were fired from their jobs in
the private sector. While these actions reflected sentiment that was
being expressed back home in the United States, it would be impossible to square them with the goal of removing "militarists and ultranationalists"; after all, the JCP's leaders and their sympathizers
had been in jail, in hiding, or in exile as opponents of Japan's
militarists.

Using the purge against Japan's "leftists" coincided with the successful appeals expanding the grounds justifying reinstatement for
many who had been purged under the earlier criteria. Many of these
reinstatements were justifiable because the removals had been
based on excessively rigid adherence to categorical criteria. However, the removal of "leftists" and simultaneous return to public life
of "rightists" emphasized that shift in overall occupation policy that
is often referred to by the Japanese as the "reverse course."

If basic policy and the criteria for removal or disbarment were
sometimes contradictory, what about the process whereby policy
was implemented? During the first year, SCAP—that is, Government Section, with some initial assistance from the chief of staff G-2
(Intelligence)—carefully controlled the actions of the Japanese government. This supervision included the translation of the SCAP
purge directive into Japanese law as well as reviewing the Japanese
government's decisions in individual cases. For example, it was in
this period that SCAP overruled the Japanese authorities by deter-

mining that prime minister-designate Hatoyama should be purged. Nonetheless, the process of enforcement was in Japanese hands, by and large.

Possibly even more important, SCAP officialdom early decided that the entire process was to be administrative rather than a series of judicial proceedings. Selecting administrative action had far-reaching consequences, not the least of which was to place into the hands of decision-makers powers that could almost be called untrammeled. Holders of or applicants for public and important private office had to fill out lengthy questionnaires which were reviewed by "screening committees" that were established by the Japanese government. A committee's discretion was circumscribed to some degree by SCAP supervision, but even more tellingly by the character of the criteria on the basis of which an individual was declared to be eligible or ineligible.

This set of constraints was crucial if the purge was to remain within the parameters of occupation policy and not become a capricious tool whereby those who held the levers of power could rid themselves of political rivals. At first, the criteria were relatively broad, but SCAP supervision was continuous and regular. In the second year (1947), the purge ordinances were expanded from the national to the local levels of government as well as into the realms of business, industry, and banking, and the public information media. Doing so required extensive elaboration of the criteria which, understandably enough, took a good deal of time. Furthermore, with each passing month, the purge became the object of increasing opposition from other SCAP staff sections and from certain elements within the Japanese government, and subject to criticism in the United States. One consequence of these cross-pressures was to complicate the defining of the criteria, in turn making the end product more and more specific.

Concurrently, since the single national committee could not possibly accomplish the task of screening all local appointive and elected officials, new committees were established in each of the prefectures and large cities. This task was not easy because it required finding individuals who were presumed to understand what the purge was all about and who could be dispassionate in accomplishing the delicate task that they faced. Once again, the increasingly detailed character of the criteria provided much needed controls; so much so, in fact, that the Japanese authorities—with SCAP approval, of course—"provisionally designated" all those individuals as purgees whose careers had included the holding of specified offices covered by the purge criteria.

This procedure, in effect, made the screening committees superfluous. It also meant that it was the criteria that became central to the determination of eligibility or its opposite rather than the administrative procedures engaged in by the screening committees, national or local. Either one had been a career officer in the army or navy, an important official in the Imperial Rule Assistance Association, an important official of a designated ultranationalistic society or business or newspaper and so forth, and so forth, or one had not. If one had held a position designated under the purge criteria, one was removed or barred. If one had not, one was free to pursue one's career. It was almost as if the more rigid and well defined the criteria became, the more elaborate—and futile—the screening mechanism had become. Undoubtedly, "provisional designation" helped speed up the process of determining who was to be purged, but it also drastically reduced the discretion that might have been exercised by the purgers. It was only after the "appeals boards" came to be established, in the third and fourth years of the purge, that extenuating circumstances could be effectively taken into account. However, initially the mandate of the appeals boards too was quite narrow and it was not until occupation policy made its dramatic about-face that these became empowered to undo what the purge had sought to accomplish.

While important and time consuming, defining the purge criteria and designating those who were caught in their web did not complete the program. After all, the initial policy had required that the influence and authority of those who were purged should be removed. Monitoring the activities of purgees, in many respects, proved to be even more difficult than specifying criteria and officially determining that all designated individuals had been either removed or barred.

Some kind of investigatory machinery was required if the surveillance of purgees' activities was to be meaningful. In this connection, it is worth emphasizing that purgees were not jailed, with the exception of those who had been indicted as war criminals and were awaiting trial by the International Military Tribunal for the Far East. Furthermore, SCAP officials repeatedly emphasized that the purge was not punitive, which comments were generally recognized as being disingenuous; the truncation of a career—even if it eventually turns out to have been temporary—can be a form of punishment.

At the height of the purge, roughly from the summer of 1947 until the autumn of 1948, there were approximately 200,000 individuals who were ordered to desist from exercising their influence in government, in politics, and in certain segments of private business and the press. How was this policy to be achieved? Government Section, the SCAP special staff section that had responsibility, had no investigatory powers—nor did it have the personnel. G-2 (Intelligence), did have trained operatives, especially in the Counter Intelligence Corps (CIC). However, General Willoughby, G-2's chief officer in SCAP, had early questioned the wisdom of the purge because of its possibly destabilizing consequences. His demurrers turned into outright opposition to the thrust of Government Section's orientation in general, and most particularly the purge. Hence, any expectation that he would assist in tracking down purgees who were engaging in illegal activities would have been unrealized.

Meanwhile, rumors circulated that one or another purgee was continuing in the exercise of power. There had been only vague admonitions in the purge's first year of implementation concerning what a purgee could not do after his designation. Only with the expansion of the purge categories in 1947 did the Japanese ordinances include a list of proscribed activities. Some of the hearsay was probably exaggerated in a deliberate attempt to discredit the purge. If large numbers of purgees were still manipulating events from behind the scenes, then public confidence would be shaken in the tortuous process of the purge itself. In any case, it was this apprehension that provided the impetus for adding a new dimension to the entire program.

Government Section officials, in private discussions with their Japanese government counterparts, began to urge the creation of a Special Investigation Bureau. Initially established in the Ministry of Home Affairs, it was subsequently transferred to the newly created Attorney General's Office which had previously been—and has again become—the Ministry of Justice. Attorney General Suzuki Yoshio, a moderate member of the Socialist party, was sympathetic to the project and found a partner in his law firm (who had been jailed for antimilitarist activities during the 1930s), to be the first director of the bureau.

Despite a willingness to undertake the unpleasant tasks of surveilling purgees' activities and prosecuting alleged infractions of the law, it took almost one year to create the beginnings of an effective investigatory organization. The usual trivialties of establishing a bureaucratic structure presented seemingly insurmountable obstacles. Office space had to be found, budgetary appropriations had to be allocated, and—most important of all—experienced investigators had to be located. Many of the best political intelligence operatives had received their training as special higher "thought control"

police officials, and quite a number of them had been purged; furthermore, their background, training, and experience raised doubts
about their willingness to do SCAP's bidding.

All in all, overseeing the activities of purgees was never fully
achieved. Nor, in all likelihood, could it have been effectuated without reintroducing the practices of political control and repression
that had been exercised by the wartime rulers of Japan, and which
SCAP had pledged itself to eradicate. In the end, as might have been
anticipated had we not been so intent on controlling the purgees, the
Special Investigation Bureau became the reincarnation of a police
agency whose purpose was to ferret out subversives. By then, too,
SCAP had decided that the danger to Japan's nascent democracy
was primarily from Communists and their sympathizers rather
than militarists and ultranationalists. Once again, initial occupation policy had been stood on its head.

I have stressed some of the dilemmas and problems that we encountered in conducting the purge in Japan. Among the most salient
of these was that if the criteria determining who was to be purged
were defined in rigid categories, then there was little room for administrative discretion to incorporate extenuating circumstances.
Conversely, if the criteria were relatively broad, then allowance
could have been made for factors other than whether a particular
individual had actually held a position, the holding of which was
sufficient proof to have rendered him ineligible. However, loosely
defined criteria that were subject to varying interpretations could
have provided the purgers with a ferocious weapon against their
political opponents, who may—or may not—have been the intended
victims of the purge.

These dilemmas were ultimately less significant than the problems that arose in attempting to control the activities of those
deemed inimical to the new order. One possible solution to this issue
would have been incarceration, but that alternative was ruled out
and would have required judicial proceedings if it was not to have
violated every tenet of due process, which SCAP was also seeking to
propagate. Yet, not to supervise the activities of purgees, or at least
not to attempt to do so, could readily result in the purge becoming an
exercise in futility. So, an agency was created that had as its initial
goal the investigation of unlawful activities of purgees (militarists)
but—when the winds of politics and policy started shifting—ended
up pursuing opponents of parliamentary democracy at the opposite
end of the political spectrum (Communists). The "Lord High Execu-
tioner" could once again scrutinize the activities of his traditional
enemies.

The purge did achieve some of its stated objectives. By far the largest group that was affected was the military. My reading of the statistics—which are themselves open to various interpretations—is that four out of every five purgees belonged to this category. In the years since the end of the occupation (1952), the Japanese military establishment has remained marginal in its capacity to influence the course of politics. Of course, the purge was not the only instrument that SCAP used. Article IX of the new constitution, aided by a strongly pacifist public opinion, has also been consequential. Nonetheless, the purge came closest to reaching its goal in helping to reduce—substantially and significantly—the influence of this group as a decisive force.

By contrast, the purge was least effective in altering the personnel of Japan's civilian bureaucracy. This outcome was probably inevitable as soon as the decision had been made that SCAP would rule through the existing structure of the Japanese government. Occupation authorities needed the kind of expertise that only experienced bureaucrats could offer. Furthermore, it was these government officials that assisted in translating SCAP directives into Japanese law. Under the circumstances, it is somewhat surprising that any bureaucrats fell afoul of the purge criteria.

National and local politicians—elected or appointed—had their ranks thinned by the criteria encompassing those who had held positions of leadership in the Imperial Rule Assistance Association (IRAA) and its affiliates. I believe that this aspect of the purge was ill-advised. At the national level of government Japan lost its most experienced parliamentarians. At the local level, the criteria ensnared many mayors whose only contribution to the war effort had been to serve as IRAA branch chiefs in an ex-officio capacity. This application of rigid categories was among the earliest to be reconsidered by means of the appeals. Until appeals were recognized, considerable damage had been done to public acceptance of the purge. Finally, the original rationale of the purge was forgotten when the purge was turned against leaders of the JCP.

Close to two thousand captains of industry and about twelve hundred press lords, publishers, and managers of the entertainment industry also were briefly removed from positions of leadership in their enterprises. This phase of the purge was the last to be implemented—prior to the reverse course—and the most cumbersome, primarily because defining the criteria was endlessly complex and controversial. These criteria sought to establish the point that those who had supervised Japan's wartime industry and had manipulated public opinion should be held accountable as political leaders. While undoubtedly within the scope of the original goals, it was unbelievably difficult to effectuate.

Any forced removal by foreign victors of such a broadly defined political leadership raises fundamental issues of political theory, for example, the use of authoritarian means to achieve liberal democratic ends. Does this mean that we should have refrained from using the purge? Possibly, but without the purge, Japan's entrenched leadership would have had limitless opportunity to undermine positive reform programs. Removal of that leadership could conceivably have been accomplished by free elections. This alternative overlooks the inherent advantages that are available to incumbent vested interests.

In retrospect, it is easy to find deficiencies in the Japanese purge. It should have been accomplished more quickly and broadly, instead of incrementally. Conversely, an appeals machinery should have been created as soon as possible in order to consider extenuating circumstances in specific cases. Finally, the criteria should have been based on the premise that the "old" leadership was being removed so that a "new" generation could come to the fore, instead of trying to justify each category on the basis of necessarily vaguely defined notions of "war guilt." None of these suggestions resolves the issue of utilizing authoritarian means for achieving presumably democratic goals. That issue remains irresolvable.

Chapter 11

Denazification in Germany

A Policy Analysis

Elmer Plischke

Assuming the axioms that one ought to learn from history and that there is merit in self-evaluation, and recognizing the advantage of looking back on past experience with the advantage of a generation of hindsight, the devisement and implementation of what turned out to be an integrated program for denazifying the German Reich constituted a major role of Americans as proconsuls in Europe at the end of World War II.

Various approaches may be used to examine this American venture in military government. One would be a simple descriptive chronicling of purposes, policies, and programs—reviewing the facts, the institutions, the principles, and the procedures involved. Some literary attention has been devoted to such treatment and is readily available. An alternative treatment would be largely judgmental—whether legalistic, moralistic, political, or psychological. All major and some other analyses of the subject provide assessments and adjudgments, and they range from condemnation and ridicule to apology and vindication. Even central participants take umbrage at the constraints, complexities, and uncertainties that disaffected particular elements of the program.

A third approach would be to concentrate primarily on systematic policy and program reanalysis, examining the functioning and timing of the decisional process and the nature and consequences of its determinations. This entails scrutiny of not only denazification policy and its application, but also of the objectives sought and the bureaucratic mechanism whereby decisions were made. If this analytical method were employed in depth, reasonable alternatives would need to be identified, their advantages and disadvantages would be weighed, and certain readily identifiable appositional components would be accorded attention, including bureaucratic versus rational (or intellectual), query versus options extrapolation, probatory versus assessory, and pragmatic versus normative analysis. This brief policy review posits basic options, summarizes the program—objectives, policies, and performance—and assesses the experience in terms of immediate outcomes and long-run consequences.

The fundamental issue following the defeat and unconditional surrender of Germany in 1945 was its treatment in the immediate post-hostilities period and the management of its eventual revival in the community of nations. As a policy matter, this problem was applicable to Germany as a country and, as is the case following major wars, it involved matters of territorial disposition and the country's international power posture, including such more specific matters as territorial fragmentation, political decentralization, and termination of alliance arrangements. It also applied to the treatment of the German people (*das Volk*), and in the likelihood that they were not to be enslaved or subjected to total migration and resettlement, the problem involved issues of mass or selective punishment, management, and reorientation. Finally, the basic question applied to the treatment to be accorded the Nazi system, for which a vigorous cleansing program was devised.

As it turned out, all three—the patrimony, people, and political party system—were made the targets of United States and joint occupation policy. The overall program formulated was both negative and positive. Among its principal negative ingredients were such matters as demilitarization, depoliticization, decentralization, deindustrialization, decartelization and deconcentration (of industry), and denazification,[1] and on the positive side were democratization and self-determination.[2] Collectively these were sometimes referred to unofficially as the "de-program."

Denazification often is misunderstood. Generically, it is referred to as a policy, a program, or a process. Functionally, it has been identified largely with the arrest, detention, and removal from office of Nazis. Rather, as will be seen, it was a comprehensive and complex undertaking which introduced a revolutionary approach to occupation law and practice—regarded by its framers as warranted by the unusual circumstances of the defeated country and its unorthodox ruling regime. Regardless whether it is deemed to be "a revolution by legal means,"[3] or "an artificial revolution,"[4] or no revolution at all, it did help to clear the decks for substantial modification of German governmental organization, policy, and leadership. In this respect it possessed both destabilizing and reformative qualities designed to undo the past and facilitate change for the future.

To place denazification in proper perspective, in terms of both importance and timing priorities, the first order of business was the defeat of Germany, and the second was its treatment following the war. Total war, if winning was to result in genuine defeat, necessitated more than the annihilation—or surrender—of the *Wehrmacht* and the destruction of the German warmaking capacity. It also required the liquidation of nazism as a sociopolitical system which, in turn, meant the dissolution of the Nazi apparatus, destruction of its institutions, elimination of its leadership and symbols, abrogation of its legal foundation, and reform of the philosophy and psychology imbedded in German culture that engendered and nurtured nazism. In terms of viable options, as in 1944 and 1945, even with the hindsight of three decades, it is not possible to frame more reasonable alternative objectives. As at the end of the war, today variation is more a matter of degree than of kind.

Objectives and Initial Basic Policy

All policy analysis requires examination of both ends and means—of the objectives sought as well as the courses of action devised to achieve them. In keeping with traditional national goals, early statements of American leaders specified World War II aims as embracing the reestablishment and maintenance of peace, the preservation of security, and the promotion of human welfare, including the self-determination of peoples. With respect to Nazi Germany, these were more precisely related to the destruction of Nazi tyranny and German militarism. These objectives were alluded to on several occasions—as in the Atlantic Charter (even before Pearl Harbor),[5] the Moscow Foreign Minister's Declaration on General Security of November 1, 1943,[6] and the declaration subscribed to at the Teheran Conference the following month,[7] together with the individual policy statements of President Franklin D. Roosevelt, Secretary of State Cordell Hull, and other American policy framers.[8]

In terms of functional components below this amorphous level of generality and, as applied to the overall treatment of Germany, United States objectives came to entail its demilitarization and denazification. So far as the latter is concerned, in summary, these aims were extrapolated to embrace the extirpation of the Nazi party, its subsidiary and affiliated agencies, and its leaders, memorials, and symbols, and the liquidation of their property, assets, and archives.

Consideration of American objectives was handled by the President's Cabinet Committee on Germany and by the allied heads of government at the summit conferences at Quebec, Yalta, and Potsdam in 1944 and 1945. The Cabinet Committee, created by President Roosevelt and composed of members of the State, Treasury, and War Departments, together with Harry Hopkins, commenced meeting in September 1944 and dealt with policy planning for the Quebec and Yalta meetings. It considered such matters as the partition of Germany, the punishment of war criminals, demilitarization, political decentralization, reeducation, restitution and reparations, and denazification. The president met with the committee on several occasions to discuss objectives and proposals, primarily as outlined in separate State, Treasury, and War Department plans.[9] As is well known, that of the Treasury came to be called the Morgenthau Plan.[10] For a diagram of the denazification policy-making mechanism, see Figure 1.

In part because the meeting at Quebec in mid-September 1944 was primarily concerned with military affairs,[11] few presidential decisions respecting the specific State and Treasury Department proposals were made prior to Roosevelt's departure for Canada, nor were they negotiated and agreed upon at the summit sessions. Nevertheless, the proponents of harsh treatment of Germany influenced the president to promote and initial a joint British-American memorandum designed to establish a "program" for eliminating German "war-making industries" in the Ruhr and the Saar and for "converting Germany into a country primarily agricultural and pastoral in its character."[12]

With hindsight, it may seem strange that the Treasury Department assumed such initiative in developing concrete proposals for the postwar political treatment of Germany,[13] and that the president paid them as much attention as those of the Department of State. It also is interesting to observe the workings and consequences of the bureaucratic process of policy-making and the interrelations of the president and cabinet members in this matter.[14]

Reaction to the Morgenthau Plan as embodied in the Quebec Conference agreement was widespread and lingered for months.[15] It is reported that Secretaries Hull and Stimson "burned with rage and disgust" when they learned of it,[16] British Foreign Minister Anthony Eden disapproved it,[17] and it was publicly characterized as a "policy of revenge."[18] Edward R. Stettinius confirms that the sec-

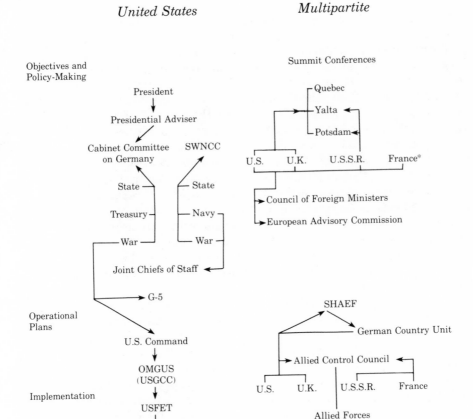

United States   *Multipartite*

Objectives and
Policy-Making

Summit Conferences

President

Presidential Adviser

Cabinet Committee
on Germany   SWNCC

Quebec
Yalta
Potsdam

U.S.   U.K.   U.S.S.R.   France*

State   State

Treasury   Navy

War   War

Council of Foreign Ministers

European Advisory Commission

Joint Chiefs of Staff

G-5

Operational
Plans

SHAEF

German Country Unit

U.S. Command

Allied Control Council

OMGUS
(USGCC)

Implementation

U.S.   U.K.   U.S.S.R.   France

USFET

Allied Forces

Land (State) Offices of
Military Government

U.S.   U.K.   U.S.S.R.   France

German Administration

Denazification Ministries
Local Boards
Denazification Tribunals

Key:
G-5   Civil Affairs Administration
OMGUS   Office of Military Government, U.S.
SHAEF   Supreme Headquarters, Allied Expeditionary Forces
SWNCC   State-War-Navy Coordinating Committee
USFET   U.S. Forces, European Theater
USGCC   U.S. Group, Allied Control Council

*Originally U.S., U.K., and U.S.S.R., and France added later.

Figure 1. *Denazification policy-making mechanism*

retaries of state and war were convinced that the president failed to realize the extent to which he had committed himself and that, although Secretary of the Treasury Morgenthau continued to press for his plan, by October 1944 the president had decided not to accept it.[19] Apparently Secretary of War Henry L. Stimson was able to influence the president against the Quebec agreement,[20] and it was not reconfirmed at either Yalta or Potsdam.[21]

What the leaders actually agreed to at Quebec was not the comprehensive Treasury Department program for the post-surrender treatment of Germany referred to earlier,[22] which was top secret at the time, but rather the sweeping economic proposals for the deindustrialization and pastoralization of the country.[23] Nevertheless, even though the president ameliorated his position on this matter, the spirit of Quebec permeated Washington planning for some time in refining goals and devising policy for the occupation program for Germany, including the determinations of the Joint Chiefs of Staff.

The initial basic plans of the State and Treasury Departments differed somewhat respecting the items they included and in their severity. The differences pertained more to matters other than the question of denazification, however. Thus, the Treasury Department proposal called for creating an International Zone in the industrial Ruhr, other specific territorial amputations, the partition of Germany into two states (north and south), and political decentralization. The Department of State plan was silent on these issues or, as in the case of partition, it recommended deferral. Another basic difference was that the Department of State suggested a subsistence economic level for Germans, whereas the Treasury Department later came to insist on sub-subsistence levels. On denazification, on the other hand, the two plans were generally in agreement respecting arrest and detention, dissolution of the Nazi party and its affiliates, removal and exclusion of Nazis from office, amendment of Nazi laws, and prohibition of propaganda and control of German communications and education, although the Treasury Department proposals tended to be more precise and inclusive, and its later version added prohibition of parades and the display of Nazi insignia and uniforms.[24]

Between the Quebec and Yalta conferences, in a memorandum to the president, Secretary Hull revealed the inability of the Cabinet Committee to agree upon a consensual statement of United States objectives and policies, registered opposition to the Morgenthau proposals, and reiterated the Department of State plan.[25] In responding, the president appeared to be surprisingly unconcerned with any urgency in defining denazification and other occupation goals in any precise way, although he did subscribe to the general precept of dissolving the Nazi party and its affiliates. Apparently he was then more concerned with basic economic than with detailed political policy,[26] and it has been reported that he regarded the Department of State as too soft in its attitude toward the treatment of Germany.[27] Also, the documentation suggests that the distinction between defining objectives and detailed programs was not clearly expressed or understood in Washington at this early stage, and this delayed refinement of not only detailed policy development but the purposes as well—except for the general goals of eliminating German militarism and nazism.[28]

Nevertheless, the Department of State proceeded to prepare the Yalta Conference Briefing Book Paper on the post-hostilities treatment of Germany. Aside from calling for demobilization, disbandment of the German armed forces, dissolution and prohibition of military and paramilitary agencies, seizure and destruction of German armaments, and the like, it provided for the destruction of "the Nazi tyranny," "dissolution of the National Socialist Party and its affiliated and supervised organs," "abrogation of the Nazi laws which provided the legal basis of the regime," "abolition of Nazi public institutions," "the elimination of active Nazis from public and quasi-public office and from positions of importance in private enterprise," and "the arrest and punishment of the principal political malefactors and war criminals."[29] In this encompassing proposal, long-range and short-term objectives and policies were distinguished, or at least rendered distinguishable, although they were dealt with summarily rather than in detail.

At the Yalta Conference in February 1945, which dealt with political as well as military matters,[30] the Big Three agreed to fundamental denazification objectives as well as a number of other joint occupation principles for dealing with Germany. As summarized in the Crimea Declaration, these included determinations "to destroy German militarism and Nazism and to ensure that Germany will never again be able to disturb the peace of the world," to "disarm and disband all German armed forces," to "eliminate or control all German industry that could be used for military production," to "bring all war criminals to just and swift punishment," and more precisely on denazification, to "wipe out the Nazi Party, Nazi laws, organizations and institutions," and to "remove all Nazi and militarist influences from public office and from the cultural and economic life of the German people." In short, they affirmed their determination to destroy nazism and German militarism.[31]

High level unilateral refinement in Washington and full extrapolation of denazification objectives by multipartite agreement was not achieved until Harry S Truman succeeded to the presidency and after the German surrender. By this time the Department of State had reassumed leadership in developing United States postwar political policy,[32] and the Joint Chiefs of Staff, responsible for policy determination for the military during the occupation period, as noted later, engaged in designing operational plans for the occupation. High-level interdepartmental policy coordination was undertaken by the State-War-Navy Coordinating Committee (SWNCC, or "Swink"), created in December 1944 at the assistant secretary level, which had a separate subcommittee to deal with German affairs, and which superseded the Cabinet Committee on Germany.[33]

At the Potsdam Conference in mid-1945, among other things,[34] the Big Three specified their joint purposes as including the destruction of the Nazi party and its affiliates, dissolution of Nazi institutions, prevention of Nazi and militarist activity and propaganda, abolition of Nazi laws, arrest and punishment of war criminals, arrest and internment of Nazi leaders, influential supporters, and high officials in Nazi organizations and institutions, and removal from office and positions of responsibility in important private undertakings of all members of the Nazi party who had been more than nominal participants.[35] Progressively, denazification objectives thus were being prescribed more definitively, but not until the Potsdam Conference was the panoply proposed in the Department of State plan made multilaterally official.

Denazification Program and Planning

Devisement of an operational denazification program, based on such generic and more specific policy objectives, constitutes the third stratum of this survey, and analysis entails juxtaposing participants, coordination and implementation processes, and historical progression or timing. Although it might have been expected that the fundamental determinations agreed to at the summit meetings would have been projected into a systematic schedule of functions and responsibilities, because of the physical separation of the SHAEF (Supreme Headquarters, Allied Expeditionary Force) and Soviet commands and the exclusion of France in early negotiations, little overall pragmatic and detailed multipartite coordination was achieved until after the German surrender. Nevertheless, some responsibility was coordinated trilaterally (and quadrilaterally after Yalta, when France was added as a fourth occupation authority), and somewhat greater program development was achieved with the British, initially during the SHAEF period and again later (1946–48) during the Bizonia years.[36] However, events intervened so that much of the program that eventuated was handled unilaterally in the American zone.

At a high diplomatic level, the European Advisory Commission (EAC) was created in 1943—a tripartite policy development agency located in London and consisting of a member of the British Foreign Office and the American and Soviet ambassadors, with their staffs. Although many matters relating to the occupation of Germany were discussed and a dozen papers were negotiated, it did not produce an overall occupation plan. President Roosevelt expressed some reservation concerning its work,[37] and ultimately it perfected only three papers that were approved by governments and put into effect. These included a draft unconditional surrender instrument,[38] a protocol on zones of occupation, and an agreement on Allied control machinery.[39]

At the operational level, for a time in the West, occupation affairs were dealt with jointly by the United States and the British in SHAEF. One of its subsidiaries—the German Country Unit, established early in 1944, and made responsible for planning the nonmilitary aspects of the occupation—prepared a *Handbook for Military Government in Germany,* to be readily available not only at headquarters, but also to operational detachments in the field. Its third draft, the first to contain specific stipulations regarding the liquidation of the Nazi party and the arrest of its leaders, was completed shortly before the Quebec Conference. Although Washington had been delinquent in furnishing other than the most amorphous guidelines, Secretary of War Stimson approved the *Handbook.*[40] Nevertheless, because pressures from various sources, especially those of the Treasury Department, peaked at this time, President Roosevelt—who took the position that the German people should be taught the lesson that they had lost the war[41]—rejected the *Handbook* plans as too "soft." After some revision, and following the dissolution of the German Country Unit, the *Handbook* was eventually published, though "unofficially," late in 1944.[42]

When SHAEF was dissolved in July 1945, American and British planners were freed to develop their own occupation and denazification programs. It was not until after the Potsdam Conference, however, when the four-power Allied Control Council for Germany was established in Berlin—consisting of the four military governors and their staffs—that the United States pressed for more definitive joint arrangements for all of Germany. In the following months, some action was taken and common military government laws and directives were adopted, but unilateral interpretation of objectives and the devisement of practical measures by the four occupying powers produced differing prescriptions and results, as noted later.

In the meantime, so far as United States operational policy was concerned, much initial planning was handled by the Joint Chiefs of Staff and the War Department in Washington. Even before the leaders met at Quebec, the Joint Chiefs engaged in drafting a unilateral directive to the American commander in Germany to define the American program.[43] Ultimately approved by President Truman, it was issued as JCS 1067 (classified secret) shortly before the Potsdam Conference, and it prescribed American occupation policy for the crucial period from May 1945 to mid-1947.[44] Being a military-oriented document reflecting the period of the Quebec Conference and the president's attitude toward the Morgenthau Plan rather than the post-Quebec position of the Department of State, it prescribed harsh treatment for Germany, and it contained detailed stipulations relating to denazification.[45]

Following the dissolution of the German Country Unit, United States military government operational planning in Europe was turned over to the United States Group, Control Council (USGCC) in the summer of 1944—later superseded by the Office of Military Government for Germany (OMGUS), established in the fall of 1945, which functioned until the latter part of 1949.[46] OMGUS, located in Berlin, had the dual responsibility of representing the United States in the quadripartite control machinery, and of supervising military government activities in the American zone. The function of coordinating denazification policy and directives was assigned to the Political Affairs division—or the Office of the Political Adviser POLAD to the military governor.[47] This agency prepared a coordinating document, completed in April 1945, which incorporated the operational plans developed by the various implementing units.[48] Designated "ANNEX XXXIII" to the "Basic Preliminary Plan: Allied Control and Occupation of Germany," it encompassed all of the components of the policy plans for dealing with nazism, and it first introduced the integrating term "denazification."[49]

Subsequently, aside from the Allied Control Council and OMGUS, the major policy developments involved the Council of Foreign Ministers (CFM) and the Joint Chiefs of Staff. By 1947 much of the denazification program was either accomplished or well under way, as noted later. The Council of Foreign Ministers, established by the Big Three at the Potsdam Conference,[50] meeting in Moscow in its fourth session in April 1947, took up the question of denazification coordination in the four zones of occupation. It directed the Control Council to hasten the implementation of the process, to complete as soon as possible the arrest and trial of war criminals and the removal from office programs, and to turn responsibility for their administration over to German authorities.[51] In Washington thought was being given to amending United States operational policy direction, and on July 11, 1947, JCS 1779 was issued (superseding JCS 1067). Fixing United States policy for the next two years, unlike its predecessor, it dealt with denazification in a single sentence, which simply required the institution of the Council of Foreign Ministers' recommendations.[52]

In summary, although a number of American, bipartite, and multipartite agencies and forums wrestled with denazification objectives, policies, and plans, the major documentary basis of the program included the general agreements reached at the summit conferences and by the Council of Foreign Ministers, JCS 1067 applicable in the United States zone (later JCS 1779), the *Handbook* prepared by the German Country Unit, the Basic Preliminary Plan with its annexes, and the determinations of the Allied Control Council. Because of the lateness of some of the major decisions concerning objectives and delays in policy planning, what eventuated was applicable primarily in the postsurrender period.[53] For a diagram of denazification administration, including policy-making and implementation levels and components, and their interrelations, see Figure 2.

Program Analysis

The denazification program that emerged may be analyzed systematically in a number of ways. Two of these, distinguishing between the making and implementation of policy, or between unilateralism and multilateralism—aspects of which have already been broached—are relatively simplistic and require little additional comment.

A third approach, delimiting the program solely to United States policy and action within its zone of jurisdiction, is to review developments in terms of primary chronological phases keyed to imple-

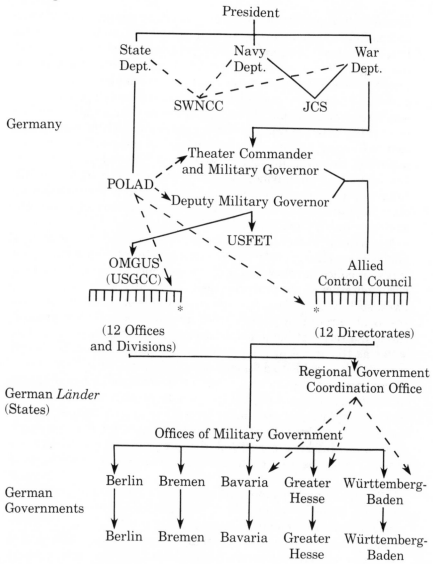

Washington

Germany

German *Länder*
(States)

German
Governments

Key:
*   Political Affairs
JCS   Joint Chiefs of Staff
OMGUS   Office of Military Government, U.S.
POLAD   Political Adviser
SWNCC   State-War-Navy Coordinating Committee
USFET   U.S. Forces, European Theater
USGCC   U.S. Group, Control Council

Sources: Designed from chart prepared by OMGUS and from Department of State, *Occupation of Germany: Policy and Progress* (Washington, D.C.: Government Printing Office, 1947), p. 12.

Figure 2. *Denazification administration*

mentation responsibility. These include the initial period of military occupation, the conversion to civil occupation while the United States continued to exercise sole responsibility, the period in which the United States was supported by German law and action, the period in which German authority took over under United States guidance and review, and, finally the period in which responsibility was turned over completely to the Germans. Certain functional aspects of the program were generally consummated before the transition to German governmental agencies, but the residual phases of several of the more important were not completed until after the United States relinquished its active participation. A major difficulty with this method of analysis is that not all of these phases are applicable to all components of the program, and rates of progression and timing varied considerably.

A fourth method of treatment, employed to some extent by most analysts and clearly preferred by some, is to hinge review chronologically on policy development and change reflected in the basic legal documentation of the program. Beginning with initial policy directives, such as JCS 1067, and the stipulations of the *Handbook* and the Basic Preliminary Plan with its annexes, analysis proceeds through a series of implemental documentary stages. For example, so far as the arrest of Nazis and their removal from office is concerned, it is possible to delineate some half dozen such stages.[54] The disadvantage of this approach is the risk of superficiality if applied to the denazification program as a whole or, alternatively, its confusing complexity if treatment is both inclusive and segmental, because in its operational stages, differing legal documentation applied to different aspects of the program. However, this approach might be useful in analyzing individual components of denazification.

A final, and perhaps the most useful and satisfying approach is to structure analysis on the basis of the spectrum of major distinguishable functional elements.[55] As suggested by the objectives determined at high levels and as originally planned under the directives and policy guidance mentioned, it consisted of some dozen primary components (see Table 1).

The advantages of using this method of analysis are obvious. A major difficulty is also clear—in coping functionally with such a complex network of items, serious problems of chronological development ensue. In part, these may be ameliorated by grouping and synthesizing elements on the basis of logical compromise among such factors as importance, substantive interrelation, timing, and longevity.

Table 1. *Denazification Program*

1. Liquidating the Nazi party.

2. Dissolving affiliated and subsidiary Nazi organizations, including the SA (*Sturmabteilung*), SS (*Schutzstaffel*), and HJ (*Hitler Jugend*).

3. Arresting and punishing war criminals.

4. Arresting and detaining Nazi leaders, influential Nazi supporters, and other persons dangerous to the Allied occupation or its objectives.

5. Removing and excluding from public office and from positions of responsibility and importance in quasi-public and private enterprise of members of the Nazi party who had been more than nominal participants in its activities, active supporters of nazism, and other persons hostile to Allied purposes.

6. Eradicating nazism from German legislation, decrees, and regulations and, more specifically, abolishing Nazi discriminatory laws and decrees.

7. Seizing, holding, and disposing of the premises, property, funds, and loot of the Nazi party and its affiliated and subsidiary organizations, and of individual Nazis subject to arrest.

8. Seizing and holding the archives of the Nazi party and its affiliated and subsidiary organizations.

9. Prohibiting Nazi privileges and benefits and payment of Nazi pensions and emoluments.

10. Prohibiting German parades and the wearing of uniforms, the public playing or singing of Nazi anthems, and the public display of Nazi flags and other party insignia and paraphernalia.

11. Changing the names of streets and public ways, parks, institutions, and buildings named after persons or things associated with nazism and German militarism; removing movable monuments and statues associated with nazism and German militarism; and removing Nazi emblems, insignia, and symbols from statues, monuments, and edifices not amenable to removal—pending their eventual disposition.

12. Preventing Nazi propaganda in any form, and removing nazism from German information services and media—including the press, radio, the theater, and entertainment—and also from education and religion.

Program Implementation and Results

Most of these dozen aspects of the denazification program could be consummated by legislation and other summary action. This was the case with the following:

Dissolution of the Nazi party and its affiliates[56]	Items 1 and 2
Eradication of Nazi legislation and decrees[57]	Item 6
Seizure of Nazi premises, property, assets, and loot[58]	Item 7
Seizure of Nazi archives[59]	Item 8
Elimination of Nazi privileges, benefits, and payment of Nazi pensions and emoluments[60]	Item 9
Elimination of Nazi uniforms, parades, flags, and symbols[61]	Item 10
Altering names of streets and parks, and removing monuments and statues, and Nazi insignia from immovable edifices[62]	Item 11
Elimination of Nazi propaganda[63]	Item 12

Implementation of these nine categories was legislated piecemeal by United States military government headquarters and the Control Council. Once the liquidation of the Nazi organization, the seizure of property and assets, the changing of street names and insignia, removal of monuments and statues commemorating Nazis and militarists, and the like, were achieved, these matters required little additional positive action by occupation authority. Much of the program, however, was not so easy to consummate. Some programmatic elements, such as identifying and superseding Nazi laws and decrees, determining the future of Nazi property and assets, and deciding on the disposition of certain Nazi and military memorials and statues took some time. Other components, including prohibition of the wearing of uniforms and insignia, of parades, and of the ferreting out, custody, and disposal of Nazi archives, and the prevention of the use of Nazi anthems and engagement in Nazi propaganda, though legislated at the outset, remained continuing occupation functions.[64]

Three elements—the apprehension and punishment of war criminals, the arrest and detention of Nazi leaders, and the removal and exclusion from office and other positions of responsibility—engendered the most intricate programs, took the most time and energy to implement, caused the greatest difficulty and controversy, and came generally to be identified with the concept of denazification.

Arrest applied to both war criminals and Nazi leaders, but procedures for trial and the legal consequences differed for the two groups. Under the Potsdam agreement and later Allied Control Council direction,[65] American authorities arrested two types of Germans. The first included those who fell within certain prescribed arrest categories and who were arbitrarily apprehended simply by virtue of the positions they had held in the Nazi party system or the German government, not the culpability of the particular individual. The second type represented those who were prescribed in the Allied Arrest Blacklist and they were individually sought out by name. Many Nazis, of course, fell into both groups.

In general, automatic arrest was originally required of all persons who held office in the Nazi party organization, down to a low level, who held commissions in the paramilitary organizations down to and including the equivalent rank of major, who served as officers and senior noncommissioned officers of the SS (Schutzstaffel), and who had been appointed to the higher ranks of the German civil service. A revised mandatory arrest directive, issued February 4, 1946, reduced the scope of the program. It designated seven groups of Nazi and military leaders for arrest and detention.[66] Penalties, as noted in part in Table 2 at the end of this section, included imprisonment, internment, forced labor, loss of civil rights, loss of property, fines, removal and exclusion from office, restrictions respecting employment, and "deprofessionalization" (such as disbarment of lawyers and judges).[67]

This denazification arrest program was coordinated with the war crimes trials. The prosecution at the major trial at Nuremberg argued for conviction of six indicted Nazi groups, including the Nazi leadership corps, the Reich Cabinet, the German General Staff and High Command, the SA (Sturmabteilung), the SS (Schutzstaffel—including the Sicherheitsdienst or SD), and the Gestapo (Secret Police). These had an aggregate membership exceeding two million, and it was estimated that approximately half of them would be made liable for trial if the groups were convicted.[68] In its decision the International Military Tribunal convicted three of them—the Nazi leadership corps, the SS (including the SD), and the Gestapo. The other three were acquitted of collective war crimes charges, but this did not relieve individual members of such groups from conviction and punishment under the denazification program. Members of

the three convicted groups, on the other hand, were subject to apprehension and trial as war criminals by the national, military, and
occupation courts of the four allied powers. Moreover, even though
an individual member of these convicted groups might be acquitted
of war crimes, he nevertheless remained subject to trial under the
denazification program.[69]

The most discussed and criticized aspect of denazification was the
so-called removal-from-office program, prescribed in both the Potsdam agreement and JCS 1067.[70] According to the American implementing directive—entitled "Removal of Nazis and Militarists"—
dismissal applied to Nazi party members who were "more than nominal participants," to "active supporters of Nazism or militarism,"
and to "all other persons hostile to Allied purposes."[71] Understandably, difficulty arose over defining the meaning of several
of these terms, despite attempts to delimit their meaning and
applicability.[72]

Under the initial American directives, removal from public and
semipublic office was either mandatory or discretionary. Mandatory
dismissal was required for the upper levels of Nazi leadership, including the officials of the party and its affiliated organizations, for
those who received prescribed Nazi party decorations, and for certain higher levels of the German civil service. The quantity of Germans affected by this mandatory program naturally was much
larger than the number subject to arrest. Other groups were rendered subject to removal at the discretion of military government,
based on individual investigation of the particular merits of the
case.

The removal procedure involved a deliberate system of vetting
and screening. All persons employed by the American occupation
forces were required to fill out a detailed six-page personnel questionnaire called the *Fragebogen,* containing some 130 questions intended to reveal the individual's personal history, employment record, experience, military service, membership and role in various
types of organizations—especially the Nazi party and its affiliates,
writings and speeches beginning in 1923 when Hitlerism was being
organized, income and assets since the party first achieved political
power, travel and residence abroad, and the like. This had to be
signed and certified, it being understood that falsification constituted a punishable offense. More than 1,650,000 Germans—approximately one out of every ten persons in the American zone—were
processed under this arrangement within a year, by June 1, 1946,
when a new procedure was adopted. By that time, of the cases examined, 373,762 (roughly 23 percent) resulted in removal or exclusion

from office. But these figures reveal only part of the story because, as Nazi agencies were dissolved or simply evanesced, many thousands of Germans were subjected to automatic group removal.[73]

Those who registered were classified in the following five groups:

Class 1. Major offenders (*Hauptschuldige*).
Class 2. Offenders (*Aktivisten*)—or Activists, Militarists, and Profiteers (that is, active participants or supporters, or recipients of excessive or unjust profits).
Class 3. Lesser Offenders (*Minderbelastete*)—or probationers.
Class 4. Followers (*Mitläufer*)—those who, though party members, were nominal Nazis.
Class 5. Non-offenders (*Entlastete*)—or persons exonerated.

This categorization was applied to both the arrest and removal from office programs.[74]

Inasmuch as United States policy applied not only to removal but also to exclusion from office and other positions of importance, including those in private enterprise, action was taken on September 26, 1945, by promulgating Military Government Law No. 8 to ban the employment of all members of the Nazi party and its affiliates—whether active or nominal—in business enterprises otherwise than "in ordinary labor." Thereafter it was illegal for private enterprise to be managed or owned by those who had not passed the *Fragebogen* process, and German employers were rendered criminally liable for failure to abide by the law.[75] This sweeping and much criticized practice was intended to prevent former Nazis from exercising direct or hidden influence in the economic life and development of Germany at this critical juncture.

In the course of time, as difficulties were encountered and experience was gained, as enforcement was turned over to German administration, as regulations were amended, and as amnesties were granted, the applicability of the arrest and removal from office practice was moderated. In March 1946, under American guidance, the German *Land* (state) governments enacted a common "Law for the Liberation from National Socialism and Militarism," under which all adults were required to register and be vetted. This revised arrangement, monitored by American authorities, was administered by German denazification ministries, local boards, and appeals tribunals operating under German law.[76]

Much of the public commentary on and criticism of denazification focused on the application of these arrest, detention, and removal aspects of the program, both by those who regarded enforcement as too sweeping and severe, and those who objected to amelioration.

Nevertheless, overall, eventually more than one-fourth of the total population of the United States zone was affected. More than 13,400,000 Germans over eighteen years of age were required to register, of which nearly 3,700,000 (28 percent) were charged under the law. Of the latter, about 70 percent were amnestied without trial in 1946.[77] According to official reports, by May 1949 some 945,000 were tried by German denazification courts (of which one-third were amnestied), nearly 130,000 were found to be "offenders" of various categories, 147,000 were declared ineligible to hold public office or were confined to restricted employment, and 635,000 other sen-

Table 2. *Status of Denazification Proceedings*

End of May 1949
United States Zone

Type	Percentage	Thousands
Total registrants	100.0	13,180.3
Not chargeable cases	73.8	9,738.5
Total chargeable cases	26.2	3,441.8
Chargeable cases completed	26.1	3,432.5
Amnestied without trial	18.9	2,487.3
Trials completed	7.2	945.2
Chargeable cases to be completed	0.1	9.3
Findings: Cases completed by denazification tribunals		945.2
Found as major offenders		1.6
Found as offenders		21.9
Found as lesser offenders		106.1
Found as followers		482.7
Found as exonerated		18.3
Found as amnestied or proceedings quashed		314.6
Appeals received		90.5
Appeals not accepted for decision or withdrawn		12.4
Appeals adjudicated		70.2
Appeals pending		7.9

tences were meted out, including assignment to labor camps, confiscation of property, and fines—as indicated in Table 2.

Evaluation

By comparison with other United States occupation policies and practices in Germany at the end of World War II, such as disarmament and demilitarization, denazification evoked a high level of criticism. Objection was directed less at the basic goal of destroying nazism than at the policies and implementation procedures to achieve it. There were those who complained about both too soft and too harsh treatment of Germans, about laxity or delay, and about overreactive enforcement. Other criticisms ranged from the intricacy of the policy-making mechanism to the uncertainty and tardiness of decisions, from the motives, dedication, and inconsistency of

Table 2. *Status of Denazification Proceedings* (*continued*)

Type	Percentage	Thousands
Cases completed by denazification tribunals which are finally and legally valid		924.7
Sanctions imposed*		
Sentenced to labor camps		9.6
Fined		569.0
Ineligible to hold public office		23.0
Restricted in employment		124.2
Sentenced to special labor but not imprisoned		30.4
Subject to confiscation of property		25.8
Internees, number of		0.4
Internees serving sentences imposed by tribunals		0.4
Internees awaiting trial		0.05

*In many cases more than one sanction has been imposed on a single individual.
Source: U.S., Department of State, *Germany, 1947–1949: The Story in Documents* (Washington, D.C.: Government Printing Office, 1950), p. 111, as augmented.

those responsible for implementation to the comparative positions taken by our allies, and from the effects of amorphous Morgenthauism to the specific treatment or mistreatment of particular local German officials or businessmen. Among the more memorable specific cases are the Aachen[78] and Patton[79] incidents, but equally important are Ambassador Robert Murphy's questioning of the wisdom of requiring American agencies to function for so long under the constraint of secret directives from Washington,[80] and allegations of resort to illegal Nazi-like practices to achieve denazification.

Difficulties

Naturally many difficulties were encountered in designing and applying such a massive and complicated program. Those who led the vanguard joked at the outset that it was impossible to find any Nazis in Germany. Among the most obvious problems were the physical destruction and social disorder in areas of hostilities and immediately following surrender, the confusion of military and political objectives and programs, and of priorities among them, and the training, mobility, and retention of qualified operational personnel. A good many other difficulties were more subtle. Representative are such matters as the struggle for policy influence between Treasury Department agents and military and State Department officials, not only in Washington but also overseas, and the problems that arose over the interpretation of important concepts such as Nazi party "affiliates," "nominal Nazis," "positions of responsibility" in private enterprise, and persons who were "dangerous to Allied objectives." Still others included the necessity of concentrating more manpower on administering denazification than had been intended—and at the very time that American opinion at home clamored to bring the troops back to the United States, and the inhibitions that emphasis on denazification imposed on the institution of other, sometimes more constructive, programs.[81]

Another major difficulty, sometimes underestimated, was the problem of aligning American policy and action with those of three allies. The United States had the options of coordination with them or going its own way in its area of jurisdiction and naturally, in the absence of joint decisions, it applied United States policy. Cooperation was close with the British at all levels, but negotiations with the Soviets and French were difficult and often frustrating—in the European Advisory Commission, the Council of Foreign Ministers, the Allied Control Council, and the Kommandatura for Berlin. As a matter of fact, Ambassador Murphy, political adviser to the American military governor, concluded that France was our Number 2 problem in dealing with the German occupation following surrender, exceeded only by the problem of secrecy accorded to basic policy documents.[82]

Except for the degree to which United States and British plans were developed during the SHAEF period, joint denazification objectives and policies agreed to at the summit conferences were not perfected in operational determinations until the Control Council was established and it produced its quadripartite laws and directives. By that time hostilities had ended, military government was in control throughout Germany, and much of the denazification program had already been launched by each of the occupants in its zone of control. Even though all the occupying powers were intent on destroying nazism, they differed on the means and methods to achieve this. As a result, operational practices varied in the four zones of occupation. In summary, the British and United States programs were similar and even when the British acted under their own unilateral mandates from London, denazification was not seriously affected.[83] On the other hand, the French and Russians dealt with some aspects of denazification—especially the arrest and removal from office programs—in their own way.[84]

The French, regarding their culture as superior, it has been said, emphasized educational and other positive goals rather than denazification, they preferred to deal with Germans as individuals rather than as members of arbitrary categories, they occupied an area of Germany that was among the least nazified, and they suffered what they regarded as an affront to their historic prestige resulting from their defeat by Germany and their liberation by Americans.[85] As a consequence, they elected to act independently, they were less prone to emphasize denazification as assiduously as did the United States, and they refused to subscribe enthusiastically to the removal and exclusion principles initiated in the American zone, although they did accept the ameliorated version approved by the Control Council in October 1946.[86]

In the Russian zone, the situation was quite different. Denazification played a subordinate role to the destruction of capitalism. Soviet authorities proclaimed that they were less concerned as to whether an individual had been a Nazi than whether he was an active one—that is, whether he was guilty of crimes or helped forward the criminal policies of the Nazi regime. They moved quickly and vigorously against those they wished to eliminate and spared those they could convert to their purposes. Their nebulous, subjective formula enabled the Russians and German Communists to exercise considerable flexibility in arresting, punishing, and removing or employing whomever they chose, and these aspects of their program could therefore be more rapidly completed.[87]

Policy Machinery

It is clear that United States designers of the postwar treatment of Germany did not produce in advance a grand design for the machinery to define objectives, policies, and operational plans as they had for military operations. This is understandable, and much of the military mechanism naturally became involved in occupation and posthostilities planning. However, because the future of Germany and its status in the international community was bound to become a primary long-range issue, political considerations were as important as the military, necessitating the participation of the Department of State, both centrally in Washington and overseas. In addition, because the eventuating treatment of Germany was the concern of the United Kingdom and the Soviet Union (and, following liberation, also of France), multipartite negotiations and machinery were needed.

As a result the military occupation and postsurrender policymaking mechanism was broadened and supplemented. In such matters, layering is natural, and involvement of presidential, cabinet, subcabinet, diplomatic, and operational levels was to be expected. Coordinating facilities were essential, and these were provided by the Cabinet Committee on Germany and subsequently by SWNCC at the subcabinet level. Although alternatives might have been considered, these interdepartmental agencies were logical and served useful purposes. The problems that arose resulted less from the essence of the machinery than from the decision to include the secretary of the treasury in the Cabinet Committee and the presidential attitude toward its role and accomplishments.

For coordinating intergovernmental policy planning, the European Advisory Commission also was a reasonable forum. Its deliberations were affected more by the difficulties caused by Soviet representatives, the president's attitude toward it, and high level determinations respecting its usefulness than by its intrinsic nature as a diplomatic instrument. A primary alternative might have been to elevate it to the ministerial level by convening more frequent *ad hoc* foreign ministers' meetings (like that at Moscow in 1943), or by creating the Council of Foreign Ministers at an earlier date. This may have altered the presidential disposition, but, in all probability, much of the deliberative work would still have had to be handled at the subministerial or diplomatic levels, or both.

During the SHAEF period, it also was natural that operational planning for the treatment of Germany went hand-in-hand with military affairs. It was not unexpected, therefore, that a joint Anglo-American agency like the German Country Unit should be created to commence such consideration. Whether under the circumstances it might have been structured or focused differently, or should have been accorded greater seniority, priority, or authority, is difficult to determine. It is clear, however, that being a military agency concerned primarily with the initial military government period, it lacked diplomatic personnel and perspective, political direction, and continuity when the country unit was terminated at a crucial period.

Later, when the Allied Control Council and the United States component (OMGUS) were created, the latter continued American operational planning and coordinated policy with the allies in the Control Council system. With Robert Murphy serving both as POLAD and as head of the Political Affairs division of OMGUS, and he and his staff handling United States interests in the Political Directorate of the Control Council, the policy and positions of the Department of State were directly and widely represented. Again, while it is possible to conceive of other institutional arrangements, those established, in essence, were neither unmanageable nor unreasonable.

So far as United States and joint mechanisms for denazification policymaking were concerned, therefore, they reflected the needs of the mission and the realities of the times. Structurally they were generally adequate to their tasks, and criticisms would need to be attributed to other causes. Although it is not difficult to envision improvements, changes that one might suggest with hindsight, such as greater preplanning, may not have been feasible under conditions pertaining at the time. As with all sociopolitical institutions, if there is a will to make them work, ways can be found to employ the machinery, despite its faults, to make it succeed.

Functional Program

Functionally considered, the basic objectives and policies of the United States to achieve denazification comprised a comprehensive spectrum of possibilities. The most important policy-analysis questions are whether some aspects of the program might have been excluded or treated in a different way. Little commentary has emerged

respecting inclusion or exclusion of specific programmatic components, and all of the twelve that emerged are individually justifiable
and were substantively interrelated.

The most noteworthy problems related to policy-making included
confusion in distinguishing among objectives, policies, and operational programs, and aberrations in timing relationships among
them. The processes by which they were framed were not systematically designed in advance, nor were matters clearly preplanned respecting responsibility—and this pertained both to levels and to
agencies. This resulted in a degree of policy development in advance
of objectives determination, and of program planning prior to policy
formulation. As a consequence, policy refinement and implementation were functionally uneven, action in the field sometimes preceded direction, and programmatic components emerged piecemeal
rather than as preconceived integral parts of a cohesive master plan
or grand design. Much the same conclusion may be drawn for the
correlation of denazification and other occupation policies, except for
the alignment of distinct programs for the treatment of war criminals and other Nazis and militarists.

The functions of arrest, removal, and exclusion, as noted, caused
the greatest difficulty. Little question has been raised concerning
their basic purposes, and in this respect the United States differed
little from the other three occupying powers. The issue, therefore,
was a matter of degree rather than kind. Early reaction tended to be
more critical of laxity and "softness,"[88] although some objected that
these matters were dealt with too harshly,[89] and others criticized
inconsistency and unevenness of enforcement, arbitrariness of categorization, implementation from the bottom up rather than the top
down, and the very propriety if not legality of the process itself.

In assessing the implementation of these aspects of denazification,
the crucial question is not so much whether all individual cases
were dealt with equally and expeditiously, or even whether the results were minimal or maximal, but rather whether Nazi leadership
and institutions were adequately dealt with to destroy the Nazi system. Consciousness of the difference between vindictive punishment
and redirection, as well as other factors, contributed to substantial
modification of the program between 1944 and 1950. In any case, in
terms of the personal dispositions of commentators at the time, the
issue as to whether these aspects of denazification did not go far
enough, went too far, and were too inconsistently applied, is not
likely to be resolved to their satisfaction. Some of those involved,
however, have had second thoughts, and generally those who review
the program with hindsight tend to conclude that, if anything, the

removal and exclusion program was too massive and might have preferably and more rapidly been dealt with from the top down.

The propriety and legality of these aspects of the program have also been raised. It has been alleged, for example, that denazification was an "undemocratic procedure,"[90] that the denazifiers were placed in "unresolved paradoxes and dilemmas of their own democracy" and "democratic popular rule was at odds with democratic civil rights, and virtue,"[91] that denazification caused the "greatest single damage to faith in American purposes in Germany,"[92] and— most damning—that it was itself a "Nazi practice."[93] The issue whether the rule of law was violated ceased being moot—if it ever was—as soon as Military Government and Control Council laws and regulations were issued. Additionally, when in the spring of 1946 the Law for the Liberation from National Socialism and Militarism was promulgated, arrest and removal of Nazis and militarists were made a matter of German law as well. The issue, therefore, was not whether the Allies applied the law, but rather whether the authority to make the law was itself lawful, and this is not generally questioned.

More fundamental, perhaps, is the question whether the American concept of human rights was violated. Allegations have been made that the arrest and removal programs contravened traditional concepts of Anglo-Saxon jurisprudence in three respects, namely: a person could be considered guilty until he proves his innocence, he could be arrested automatically simply on the basis of arbitrary categorization, and if suspected he could be held indefinitely without hearing or trial.[94] Given the objective of eradicating nazism and the exigencies of total war, the niceties of legality and propriety may have been compromised at the outset, but as the program was refined and turned over to systematic administration by courts, legal and judicial processes were instituted to complete the program. Moreover, if principle is to be argued, the fundamental quality of impropriety or illegality would have been as applicable to the treatment of the most serious Nazi offenders as against the less culpable. In view of the circumstances prevailing at the time, therefore, there scarcely were more viable or acceptable alternatives.

Looking back on the denazification venture in Germany—branded "the most extensive legal procedure the world had ever witnessed"[95]—it is impossible to ascribe a meaningful yardstick for exact qualitative measurement of either positive or negative results. Like most decision-making experiences and policy formulations, perfection is elusive, and value tends to be more relative than absolute. Adjudgments may be abstract, or in relation to historical

conditions, or simply in terms of consequences—and each may lead
to different conclusions.

A number of important generalizations may nevertheless be
made. In assessing overall American policy for the treatment of
Germany after World War II, given the immutable objective of eliminating nazism and militarism, the principal difficulty emanated
from the specter of Morgenthauism. Even though the agreement
made at Quebec was neither directly nor explicitly related to denazification, and despite the fact that it was short-lived, the ghost of
the Morgenthau Plan survived for several years and tainted the
policy-making atmosphere with an attitude of vindictive negativism
in the treatment not only of the Nazi system but of Germany as well.
Although, in all probability, demilitarization and denazification
programs would have been instituted without either the Morgenthau proposals or the Quebec agreement, the spirit in which they
were devised, the manner in which they were implemented, and
especially the extent to which they were carried may have differed.
Objection is more attributable, therefore, to the historic accident of
Morgenthauism per se than to the compulsion for denazification,
with which it has come to be confused.[96]

It also is clear that, given the circumstances, the occupying powers were convinced that there was no escaping the obligation of
diagnosing the cancer of Germany as nazism and performing major
surgery to excise it from the German body politic. As usual with
such an operation, equally important with the technique to be employed is the probability of outcome—that is, how the patient will
endure the procedure, whether he will recover, and what aftereffects
will follow—and usually these cannot be foreseen. Whatever the
outcome, it is apparent that the surgical experience reflected the
guiding imprint of American policy and leadership.

In terms of fulfilling short-range Allied objectives, the facts are
that the Nazi system was shattered, its institutions were dissolved,
its laws were repealed or superseded, its symbols and trappings
were removed from public display if not consciousness, and many of
its leaders were arrested, interned, dispossessed, fined, and removed
from positions of public trust and importance. These aspects of the
program were sufficiently enforced to end the Hitler regime and the
Nazi era. Some individual functional components were implemented
expeditiously and thoroughly, while others took more time, but
early action under them also contributed to satisfying the most immediate of purposes.

More important, however, is the matter of long-range goal fulfillment. If the eradication of Nazism meant its nonrevivability as well

as immediate dissolution, the denazification record is equally able to withstand scrutiny. There is little evidence that postwar Germans have wanted to resurrect the Nazi system, and the magic of Hitlerism appears to have vanished. A new system based on the rule of law, parliamentary government, judicial review, and the sanctity of human rights emerged in West Germany to replace the Third Reich. It has flourished for more than three decades—which exceeds twice the lifetime of either the Weimar Republic or the Thousand Year Nazi Reich, and it has endured a good many years longer than the two combined. Within it, the Nazis have disappeared and their organized power has evanesced, political extremes have been reduced to relatively weak minorities, political and economic viability and stability have thrived under democratic principles, and such leaders as Konrad Adenauer and Helmut Schmidt were maintained in office by free elections for a longer tenure than that of Hitler. In addition, militarism lost its militancy, nationalism was moderated by internationalism, and the public policy process was reoriented to look forward to new horizons rather than backward to tarnished glory. One analyst, contemplating this transformation within but a single generation, concludes: "Few would have believed this possible in 1945. For all its faults and follies, denazification may have helped to achieve this admirable end. But in history, there is no end."[97]

This being the case, as Lucius Clay prognosticated in his last report on the subject in 1950: "In the final analysis, Nazism will stay out of German life only if the German people reject it and continue to ban it even when the occupying powers are gone."[98] Therefore, if nazism should ever revive in West Germany, the denazification program can scarcely be faulted, for Americans could only have guaranteed permanent nonrevival at the cost of permanent occupation— and even this is questionable.

Chapter 12

War Crimes Trials and Clemency in Germany and Japan

John Mendelsohn

United States policies for a democratic reeducation of the German and Japanese peoples included as an essential element war crimes trials and clemency for war criminals. Vigorous prosecution of war criminals and stern sentences brought home the lesson to the Germans and Japanese that the Nazi government in Germany and the militarist rulers in Japan were criminal and that the creators and executors of the orders alike would find themselves subject to harsh punishment if found guilty. On the other hand, perhaps because of the intense concern to prosecute, the planners of the trials either at the diplomatic or military levels gave little thought to posttrial treatment of the defendants at that time. As a consequence, all paroles and clemency extended to convicted war criminals resulted from executive clemency or parole and not from judicial appeal. At times, particularly during its initial phase, executive clemency had the appearance of mass clemency. Nonetheless, the main concern of the planners of the trials focused on prosecution and conviction of war criminals and not on their posttrial treatment. The trial or punishment phase of the reeducation program for Germany lasted through 1948, although some of the United States trials at Nuremberg, the twelve subsequent proceedings, dragged on until 1949 (see Figure 1). In Japan, several of the trials lasted as late as October of that year.

In Germany, three United States jurisdictions prosecuted Nazi war criminals. From November 1945 to October 1946 the International Military Tribunal (IMT) tried, with strong United States participation, several organizations and the twenty-four major German war criminals including *Reichsmarschall* Herman Göring, Hit-

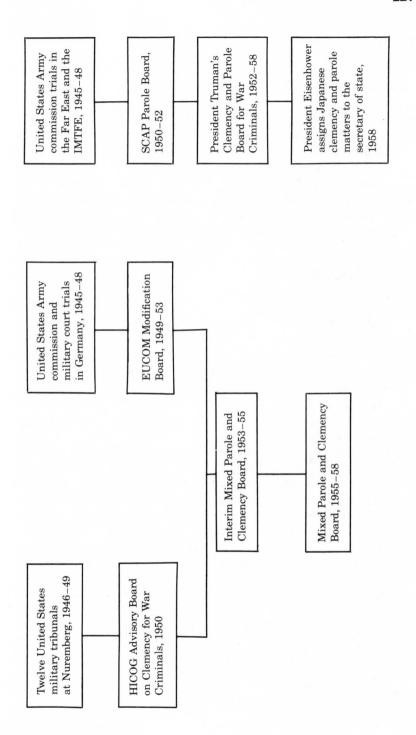

Figure 1. *United States clemency and parole boards for war criminals in Germany and Japan*

ler's deputy Rudolf Hess, and Foreign Minister Joachim von Ribbentrop. The IMT sentenced most of the accused to death or to extensive prison terms and acquitted three. The Allied Control Authority denied all clemency appeals and with the exception of three medical paroles[1] the convicted war criminals either met their fate at the rope's end or served their prison terms in full in Spandau Prison in Berlin. Today it has a prison population of one, Rudolf Hess, by now an octogenarian, who remains the only war criminal tried with United States involvement who still languishes in jail.

At Nuremberg, 185 additional individuals stood trial as war criminals before United States military tribunals in twelve separate proceedings, grouped either by type of crime or by organization.[2] These consisted of four cases in which the defendants belonged to various branches of the SS, Hitler's notorious security and extermination organization led by *Reichsführer SS* Heinrich Himmler. Officials of three industrial organizations were prosecuted: the I. G. Farben company, the Krupp works, and the Flick combine. The tribunals also tried three cases of German generals, and the remaining two cases indicted mainly members of former German ministries.

The United States Army tried another 1,672 persons in 489 proceedings before military commissions or special and general military government courts divided roughly into four categories: parent concentration camp and subsequent concentration camp cases, as well as flier and miscellaneous cases (see Figure 1). The first two groups embraced over 250 cases with over 1,000 defendants, including staff members and guards of the six main camps: Dachau, Buchenwald, Flossenburg, Mauthausen, Nordhausen, and Mühldorf including out camps and branch camps. Military tribunals tried over 200 flier cases with about 600 defendants for the killing of nearly 1,200 United States citizens, mostly airmen. The final category included a few cases such as the Malmedy Massacre trial which indicted over seventy SS men for killing large groups of surrendered United States prisoners of war; the Hadamar murder factory case, which tried Hadamar Asylum staff members for killing about 400 Russian and Polish nationals; and the Skorzeny case, which acquitted members of the German Armed Forces for participating in the Ardennes Offensive wearing United States uniforms.[3]

In Japan, the International Military Tribunal for the Far East (IMTFE) convicted twenty-five major or Class A war criminals including former prime ministers Hideki Tojo and Koki Hirota, sentencing most of the condemned to life imprisonment, several to death, and a few to lesser prison terms (see Figure 1). In addition, the United States Army in Japan and in the Pacific area tried over

1,300 individuals in so-called Class "B" and Class "C" cases (see Figure 1). In many of these trials the prosecution charged suspects with the ill treatment of prisoners of war and civilians, but also with committing ceremonial murder and senseless illegal medical experiments on involuntary human guinea pigs.[4]

The earliest war crimes tribunals after World War II frequently meted out the most severe sentences. As war crimes became more remote in time and the cold war period accentuated the differences between the Allies, trying military leaders in Germany and in Japan and at the same time attempting to reestablish national military forces or seek other defense contributions in these countries also became more difficult. Consequently, the severity of sentences decreased.[5] Sometimes, however, the nature of the crime committed precluded the defendants from obtaining lighter sentences as in the case of the *Einsatzkommando* (mobile extermination unit) leaders at Nuremberg who received stiff sentences as late as April 1948 for the crime of mass murder.[6] On the other hand, the perpetrators of the most atrocious crimes had their trials often but not always early during the punishment period, so that chiefly lesser offenders remained for trial as the proceedings wore on. Still, a fair number of suspects in major crimes awaited trial in cases where evidence collection was difficult.

Two major concentration camp cases known by Army authorities as mass atrocities cases may serve as an illustration that as time progressed, sentences often became lighter. A military tribunal heard the earliest of the cases, the Dachau case, late in 1945. Of the forty individuals tried, the military court sentenced thirty-six to death while the remaining four received life sentences or ten year prison terms.[7] Another military court tried the Nordhausen case in late 1947, resulting in only one death sentence, fourteen prison terms, and four acquittals.[8] Although circumstances varied in the two cases, nonetheless the tribunals pronounced lesser sentences in the Nordhausen case for offenses punished more severely in the Dachau proceedings.

As in Germany, United States military tribunals punished earlier cases often more severely in Japan. Perhaps the best known of the early trials dealt with the command responsibility of General Tomayuki Yamashita. The proceedings held in Manila in 1945 have caused a good deal of discussion subsequently, largely because of their controversial findings and because of the harsh judgment rendered. The general commanded the Fourteenth Japanese Army Group in the Philippines toward the close of belligerent operations in that area. The prosecution charged him with having failed in his duty as a military commander properly to control his troops who committed hundreds of instances of rape, murder, looting, and other atrocities during the United States reconquest of the Philippines. Yamashita defended himself by stating that he did not command the Japanese forces in the Philippines, particularly naval forces in Manila, who committed many of the atrocities. He emphasized furthermore his inability to coordinate his widely dispersed and scattered units under conditions of generally poor communications. Despite these defenses, the military commission conducting the trial found Yamashita guilty as charged and sentenced him to death by hanging, stripped of his medals.[9]

Yamashita petitioned the Supreme Court of the Philippines for a writ of habeas corpus which the court denied him. He then petitioned the Supreme Court of the United States for writ of habeas corpus and certiorari which the majority opinion of the court, delivered by Chief Justice Stone, also denied.[10] Justice Rutledge and Justice Murphy wrote dissenting opinions.[11] Yamashita's case belongs among the earliest war criminal trials heard in the Far East with the arraignment taking place already on October 8, 1945, while the Supreme Court of the United States handed down its decision early in February 1946. In his final review of Yamashita's sentence, General MacArthur stressed that the Japanese general had failed utterly in his duty as a soldier and that "the transgressions resulting therefrom as revealed by the trial are a blot upon the military profession, a stain upon civilization, and constitute a memory of shame and dishonor that can never be forgotten. . . . It is appropriate to recall here," he concluded, "that the accused was fully forewarned as to the personal consequences of such atrocities. On October 24— four days following the landing of our forces on Leyte—it was publicly proclaimed that I would 'hold the Japanese military authorities in the Philippines immediately liable for any harm which may result from failure to accord prisoners of war, civilian internees or civilian noncombatants the proper treatment and the protection to which they of right are entitled.'"[12] A few days after General MacArthur had confirmed the sentence of the military commission, they hanged General Yamashita.

Telford Taylor, the United States chief of counsel for war crimes, felt that the Yamashita case had important consequences for the development of the doctrine of command responsibility in the United States Armed Forces, particularly in Vietnam, as evidenced by the trial of Lieutenant Calley for his part in the My Lai incident.[13] Thus, after the Yamashita case, today the field commander is responsible to a much larger extent for the actions of his troops than

1. Proconsuls prepare for liberation and occupation at the School of Military Govern-
ment in the Law School of the University of Virginia, Charlottesville. Commanding
officer Brigadier General Cornelius W. Wickersham, center, *with members of his fac-*
ulty and staff in August 1943.—United States Army Signal Corps photograph SC
177775

2. Shogun *and* Tenno. *Supreme Commander Allied Powers, General Douglas MacArthur, with Emperor Hirohito in the United States Embassy in Tokyo on September 27, 1945. This visit, presaging renunciation of imperial divinity on New Year's Day, 1946, symbolized the relative power of these two leaders.—United States Army Signal Corps photograph in NA RG 208 N-46403 (PU 125J)*

3. *General Douglas MacArthur accompanied by his senior aide, Colonel Herbert B. Wheeler, leaves his headquarters in the* Dai Ichi Seimei *(Number One Life Insurance) Building, Tokyo, on Christmas Day, 1945.—United States Navy (USS* Antietam*) photograph in NA RG 80 G-418660*

4. Captain Ralph Braibanti of the Yamanashi Detachment, 32nd Military Government Headquarters Company, IX Corps, Eighth Army, with staff interpreter Aiko Enomoto in 1946. In 1983, Ms. Enomoto was the principal of a women's Christian college in Japan. — Photograph courtesy of Ralph Braibanti

5. Mayor Hichiro Kihara of Hiroshima receives advice on rebuilding his city in January 1946 from Lieutenant John D. Montgomery of the 76th Military Government Company, Eighth Army, a former city planner from Kalamazoo, Michigan. In the background are the ruins of an industrial arts museum which have been preserved as a memorial. — United States Army (Eighth Army) photograph by T/4 Charles De Marce

6. *Hugh Borton, chief, division of Japanese Affairs, State Department, in 1946.*—*State Department photograph US-106-46*

7. *Eleanor M. Hadley,* left, *celebrating in Tokyo in 1947 the birthday of her colleague in the Government Section, GHQ-SCAP, Alfred C. Oppler,* center, *who directed revision of the Japanese legal codes. Cyrus H. Peake,* right, *chaired Government Section's committee which drafted that part of the new Japanese constitution dealing with the cabinet.*—*Photograph courtesy of Osborne I. Hauge, chief of GHQ-SCAP Public Affairs Division, 1946–51*

8. *Assistant Secretary of War John J. McCloy, during a round-the-world trip to learn first-hand the problems facing occupation theater commanders, at a Tokyo airport with General Douglas MacArthur and Lieutenant General Robert L. Eichelberger, October 22, 1945.—INS photograph in (public domain) NA RG 208-PU-127A-10*

9. *United States High Commissioner for Germany John J. McCloy, left, attends a* Richtfest *(roof-raising bee) at Schuldorf Bergstrasse in Seeheim,* Landkreis *Darmstadt on June 26, 1952, with Land Commissioner (and former military governor) of Hesse James Newman. Seeheim's "school village" was the brainchild of Kenneth A. Bateman, who served as teacher education adviser in Hesse.—Photograph by K. Kopp, courtesy of Kenneth A. Bateman*

10. *United States High Commissioner for Germany John J. McCloy returning to Frankfurt's Rhein-Main Airport from a foreign ministers' meeting in London on May 15, 1950. Descending the ramp behind him is McCloy's political adviser, James W. Riddleberger of the State Department.—New York Times Frankfurt Bureau photograph in (public domain) NA RG 306-NT-316-K-2*

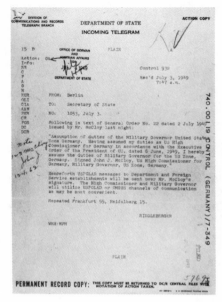

11. Telegram received in the Department of State on July 3, 1949, from James W. Riddleberger, political adviser to OM-GUS, announcing that John J. McCloy had assumed the duties of military governor of the United States zone in connection with his assignment as United States high commissioner for Germany. —NA RG 59 740.00119 Control (Germany)/7-349

12. Abortive attempts at Allied proconsular government of Germany. United States and Soviet delegations at an Allied Control Council meeting in Berlin on February 11, 1948. James W. Riddleberger sits between General Lucius D. Clay, extreme left, and Major General George P. Hays; Marshal Vassily Sokolovsky sits at the extreme right. The British and French delegations, completing the other two sides of the hollow square seating arrangement, are not seen here.—NA RG 260 OMGUS photograph 121-1/17, folder 210 no. M44

13. *Self-government under military government. General Lucius D. Clay addressing the* Länderrat *(Council of Minister Presidents of the United States Occupation Zone) at its headquarters in the Villa Reitzenstein, Stuttgart, on January 8, 1947. Seated on the dais, left to right, are Clay's principal American subordinates: Political Adviser Robert Murphy; Deputy Military Governor Frank Keating; state military governors Colonel James R. Newman, Hesse; Sumner Sewall, Württemberg-Baden; General Walter J. Muller, Bavaria; Forest Davis, War Department observer; Coordinator of Regional Government Colonel Charles D. Winning. At the table in the foreground, left to right, are elected leaders of the German states of the American zone: Wilhelm Kaisen, Bremen; Erich Rossman,* Länderrat *general secretary; Dr. Hans Ehard, Bavaria; Christian Stock, Hesse; Dr. Reinhold Maier, Württemberg-Baden.—NA RG 260 OMGUS Box 22, folder 563, photograph L-57*

14. *Entrance to United States Military Government Headquarters on* Clay-Allee *in Berlin-Zehlendorf. This scene, pictured sometime during the occupation period, except for foliage growth remains virtually unchanged in 1983, much as has the divided city's status.—Photograph from NA RG 260 OMGUS 121-1/17-179*

15. *Publication Control officers Robert Wolfe, left, and Conrad M. Mueller of the Heidelberg branch of Information Control Division, Office of Military Government for Württemberg-Baden, review the proposed book and periodical publishing program of German licensee Adolf Rausch, standing, who was also an elected Social Democrat member of the Heidelberg city council, March 19, 1946.—United States Army Signal Corps photograph SC 231846*

16. *Memorandum by Robert Wolfe responding to a Dial Press request for translation rights to Karl Jaspers'* Die Schuldfrage *[The guilt question], a rare reversal of the military government program to secure for German licensees nominal-cost translation rights to American works deemed useful for "reeducating" the Germans. Jaspers designated Hannah Arendt as his American agent in America; her first postwar publication in German was in the short-lived intellectual magazine,* Die Wandlung *[The transformation] from the same United States–licensed publisher as* Die Schuldfrage, *the Lambert Schneider Verlag of Heidelberg.—NA RG 260 OMGUS 245-2/5, ISD Publication Control Branch, Subject File*

MILITARY GOVERNMENT - GERMANY
SUPREME COMMANDERS AREA OF CONTROL

Militärregierung - Deutschland
Kontrollgebiet des Obersten Befehlshabers

Public Notice No. 5

Öffentliche Bekanntmachung Nr. 5

By order of the Military Government.

Im Auftrage der Militär-Regierung.

17. *Military Government poster announcing sentences meted out by United States Military Government Summary Court Bogen sitting in Mittelfels courthouse on August 17, 1945.—Poster courtesy of Eli E. Nobleman*

18. *Lieutenant Eli E. Nobleman reopening under German jurisdiction the Bogen county court in Mittelfels town in Lower Bavaria, October 8, 1945. Left, Judge Kolber, recalled from retirement to replace ousted Nazi judges; right, County Commissioner Zettler.—Photograph courtesy of Eli E. Nobleman*

19. Lieutenant John H. Backer, somewhere in Europe as an intelligence officer with the 82nd Airborne Division, 1945.—Photograph courtesy of John H. Backer

20. Jacques J. Reinstein, director, Office of German Economic Affairs, State Department, 1949–50.—State Department photograph US-123-64

21. John Gimbel, arrow, *with other members of Detachment G-34, 2nd Military Government Regiment stationed in Friedberg, Hesse, in early 1946.—Photograph courtesy of John Gimbel*

22. *Lieutenant (jg.) Elmer Plischke of the staff of the United States Group Control Council for Germany quartered in the I. G. Farben building in Höchst near Frankfurt in July 1945, shortly before that Group moved up to Berlin. On the desk to the left is a copy of the* Handbook for Military Government in Germany.—*Photograph in NA RG 260, OMGUS 122-1/17 No. 364*

MILITARY GOVERNMENT OF GERMANY

Fragebogen

A. PERSONAL / A. Persönliche Angaben

1. List position for which you are under consideration (include agency or firm). — 2. Name (Surname). (Fore Names). — 3. Other names which you have used or by which you have been known. — 4. Date of birth. — 5. Place of birth. — 6. Height. — 7. Weight. — 8. Color of hair. — 9. Color of eyes. — 10. Scars, marks or deformities. — 11. Present address (City, street and house number). — 12. Permanent residence (City, street and house number). 13. Identity card type and Number. — 14. Wehrpass No. — 15. Passport No. — 16. Citizenship. — 17. If a naturalized citizen, give date and place of naturalization. — 18. List any titles of nobility ever held by you or your wife or by the parents or grandparents of either of you. — 19. Religion. — 20. With what church are you affiliated? — 21. Have you ever severed your connection with any church, officially or unofficially? — 22. If so, give particulars and reason. — 23. What religious preference did you give in the census of 1939? — 24. List any crimes of which you have been convicted, giving dates, locations and nature of the crimes. —

1. Für Sie in Frage kommende Stellung: Dirigent eines Männergesangvereins

2. Name ~~————~~ 3. Andere von Ihnen benutzte Namen

   Zu-(Fam...n..)name   Vor-(Tauf-)name

   oder solche, unter welchen Sie bekannt sind: keine

4. Geburtsdatum ~~————~~ 5. Geburtsort ~~————~~

6. Größe 1.68   7. Gewicht 56kg   8. Haarfarbe schwarz   9. Farbe der Augen grau

10. Narben, Geburtsmale oder Entstellungen keine

11. Gegenwärtige Anschrift Fulda. Schloss-Str.10

    (Stadt, Straße und Hausnummer)

12. Ständiger Wohnsitz Fulda. Schloss-Str.10

    (Stadt, Straße und Hausnummer)

13. Art der Ausweiskarte Deutsche Kennkarte Nr. _____ 14. Wehrpaß-Nr. keine 15. Reisepaß-Nr. keine

16. Staatsangehörigkeit deutsch 17. Falls naturalisierter Bürger, geben Sie Datum und Einbürgerungsort an.

18. Aufzählung aller Ihrerseits oder seitens Ihrer Ehefrau oder Ihrer beiden Großeltern innegehabten Adelstitel keine

19. Religion r.kath. 20. Welcher Kirche gehören Sie an? r.kath. 21. Haben Sie je offiziell oder inoffiziell Ihre Verbindung mit einer Kirche aufgelöst? nein 22. Falls ja, geben Sie Einzelheiten und Gründe an _____ 23. Welche Religionsangehörigkeit haben Sie bei der Volkszählung 1939 angegeben? r.kath. 24. Führen Sie alle Vergehen, Uebertretungen oder Verbrechen an, für welche Sie je verurteilt worden sind, mit Angaben des Datums, des Orts und der Art keine

B. SECONDARY AND HIGHER EDUCATION / B. Grundschul- und höhere Bildung

Name & Type of School (If a special Nazi school or military academy, so specify) Name und Art der Schule (Im Fall einer besonderen NS oder Militärakademie geben Sie dies an)	Location Ort	Dates of Attendance Wann besucht?	Certificate Diploma or Degree Zeugnis, Diplom oder akademischer Grad	Did Abitur permit University matriculation? Berechtigt Abitur od. Reifezeugnis zur Universitätsimmatrikulation?	Date Datum
Volksschule	Nieder-leih	1909-1917			
Präpar.Anstalt	Fritzlar	1917-1920			
Lehrerseminar	Fulda	1920-1923			

25. List any German University Student Corps to which you have ever belonged. — 26. List (giving location and dates) any Napola, Adolph Hitler School, Nazi Leaders College or military academy in which you have ever been a teacher. — 27. Have your children ever attended any of such schools? Which ones, where and when? — 28. List (giving location and dates) any school in which you have ever been a Vertrauenslehrer (formerly Jugendwalter).

25. Welchen deutschen Universitäts-Studentenburschenschaften haben Sie angehört? keiner

26. In welchen Napola, Adolf-Hitler-, NS-Führerschulen oder Militärakademien waren Sie Lehrer? Anzugeben mit genauer Orts- und Zeitbestimmung. in keiner

27. Haben Ihre Kinder eine der obengenannten Schulen besucht? nein Welche, und wann?

28. Führen Sie (mit Orts- und Zeitbestimmung) alle Schulen an, in welchen Sie je Vertrauenslehrer (vormalig Jugendwalter) waren in keiner

C. PROFESSIONAL OR TRADE EXAMINATIONS / C. Berufs- oder Handwerksprüfungen

Name of Examination Name der Prüfung	Place Taken Ort	Result Resultat	Date Datum
keine			

23. Pages one and three of the six-page Allied Military Government Fragebogen (Questionnaire) as filled out by a conductor of a male chorus (name, date of birth, and place of birth deleted), showing membership in the Nazi party and its formations or affiliated organizations, the SA (Storm Troop), NSV (welfare association), and NS-Lehrerbund (teachers' guild).—NA RG 260, Records of OMGUS

E. MEMBERSHIP IN ORGANIZATIONS / E. Mitgliedschaften

48. Indicate on the following chart whether or not you were a member of and any offices you have held in the organizations listed below, the lines 41 to 95 to specify any other associations, society, fraternity, union, syndicate, chamber, institute, group, corporation, club or other organization of any kind, whether social, political, professional, educational, cultural, industrial, commercial or honorary, with which you have ever been connected or associated. — Column 1: Insert either "yes" or "no" as such line to indicate whether or not you have ever been a member of the organization listed. If you were a candidate, disregard the columns and write in the word "Candidate" followed by the date of your application for membership. — Column 2: Insert date on which you joined. — Column 3: Insert date your membership ceased if you are no longer a member. Insert the word "Date" if you are still a member. — Column 4: Insert your membership number in the organization. — Column 5: Insert the highest office, rank or other post of authority which you have held at any time. If you have never held an office, rank or post of authority, insert the word "none" in Columns 5 and 6. — Column 6: Insert date of your appointment to the office, rank or post of authority listed in Column 5.

40. In der folgenden Liste ist anzuführen, ob Sie Mitglied einer der angeführten Organisationen waren und welche Aemter Sie darin bekleideten. Andere Gesellschaften, Handelsgesellschaften, Burschenschaften, Verbindungen, Gewerkschaften, Genossenschaften, Kammern, Instituten, Gruppen, Körperschaften, Vereine, Verbände, Klubs, Logen oder andere Organisationen beliebiger Art, seien sie gesellschaftlicher, politischer, beruflicher, sportlicher, bildender, kultureller, industrieller, kommerzieller oder ehrenamtlicher Art, mit welchen Sie je in Verbindung standen oder welchen Sie angeschlossen waren, sind auf Zeile 96—98 anzugeben.

1. Spalte: „Ja" oder „nein" sind hier einzusetzen zwecks Angabe Ihrer jemaligen Mitgliedschaft in der angeführten Organisation. Falls Sie Anwärter auf Mitgliedschaft oder unterstützendes Mitglied oder im „Opferring" waren, ist, unter Nichtberücksichtigung der Spalten, das Wort „Anwärter" oder „unterstützendes Mitglied" oder „Opferring" sowie das Datum Ihrer Anmeldung oder die Dauer Ihrer Mitgliedschaft als unterstützenden des Mitglied oder im Opferring einzusetzen.
2. Spalte: Eintrittsdatum.
3. Spalte: Austrittsdatum, falls nicht mehr Mitglied, anderenfalls ist das Wort „gegenwärtig" einzusetzen.
4. Spalte: Mitgliedsnummer.
5. Spalte: Höchstes Amt, höchster Rang oder eine anderweitig einflußreiche, von Ihnen bekleidete Stellung. Nichtzutreffendenfalls ist das Wort „keine" in Spalte 5 und 6 einzusetzen.
6. Spalte: Antrittsdatum für Amt, Rang oder einflußreiche Stellung laut Spalte 5.

	1 Yes or No Ja oder nein	2 From von	3 To bis	4 Number Nummer	5 Highest Office or rank held Höchstes Amt oder höchster Rang	6 Date Appointed Antrittsdatum
41. NSDAP	ja	15.33	gegw.	umbek.	Memb.	
42. Allgemeine ₩	nein					
43. Waffen-₩	nein					
44. Sicherheitsdienst der ₩	nein					
45. SA	ja	10.6.33	19.4.35		keine	
46. HJ einschl. BDM	nein					
47. NSDStB	nein					
48. NSDoB	nein					
49. NS-Frauenschaft	nein					
50. NSKK	nein					
51. NSFK	nein					
52. Reichsb. d. deutschen Beamten	nein					
53. DAF	nein					
54. KdF	nein					
55. NSV	ja	13.34	gegw.	umbek.	keine	
56. NS-Reichsb. deutsch. Schwest.	nein					
57. NSKOV	nein					
58. NS-Bund Deutscher Technik	nein					
59. NS-Aerztebund	nein					
60. NS-Lehrerbund	ja	13.34	gegw.	umbek.	keine	
61. NS-Rechtswahrerbund	nein					
62. Deutsches Frauenwerk	nein					
63. Reichsbund deutscher Familie	nein					
64. NS-Reichsb. f. Leibesübungen	nein					
65. NS-Altherrenbund	nein					
66. Deutsche Studentenschaft	nein					
67. Deutscher Gemeindetag	nein					
68. NS-Reichskriegerbund	nein					
69. Reichsdozentenschaft	nein					
70. Reichskulturkammer	nein					
71. Reichsschrifttumskammer	nein					
72. Reichspressekammer	nein					
73. Reichsrundfunkkammer	nein					
74. Reichstheaterkammer	nein					
75. Reichsmusikkammer	nein					
76. Reichskammer d. bildend. Künste	nein					
77. Reichsfilmkammer	nein					
78. Amerika-Institut	nein					
79. Deutsche Akademie München	nein					
80. Deutsches Auslandsinstitut	nein					
81. Deutsche Christen-Beweg°ng	nein					
82. Deutsche Glaubensbewegung	nein					
83. Deutscher Fichte-Bund	nein					
84. Deutsche Jägerschaft	nein					
85. Deutsches Rotes Kreuz	nein					
86. Ibero-Amerikanisches Institut	nein					
87. Institut zur Erforschung der Judenfrage	nein					
88. Kameradschaft USA	nein					
89. Osteuropäisches Institut	nein					
90. Reichsarbeitsdienst (RAD)	nein					
91. Reichskolonialbund	ja	Aug. 38	gegw.	unbek.	keine	
92. Reichsluftschutzbund	nein					
93. Staatsakademie für Rassen- u. Gesundheitspflege	nein					
94. Volksbund für das Deutschtum im Ausland (VDA)	ja	Sept. 38	gegw.	unbek.	keine	
95. Werberat d. Deutsch. Wirtsch. Others (Specify) andere:	nein					
96.						

24. Colonel William R. Swarm, left, commandant of the Civil Affairs School, with Major General William F. Marquat, chief of Civil Affairs–Military Government, Office of the Chief of Staff (chief, Economic and Scientific Section, GHQ-SCAP, 1946–52) and Richard M. Scammon, State Department political advisor (OMGUS, 1946–48; State Department, European Research Division, 1948–54), during the annual two-week Logistics Exercise 196 at Fort Lee, Virginia, May 5, 1955.—United States Army Signal Corps photograph 69 LX 61-18/A1-55

25. Colonel William R. Swarm, right, commandant of the United States Army Civil Affairs School at Fort Gordon, Georgia, greeting Major General J. Strom Thurmond, (res.) assistant chief of Civil Affairs, during his visit to the school on October 13, 1961. Senator Thurmond served on the First Army G5 staff during the World War II European campaign.—United States Army Signal Corps photograph 09-057-751-2/AJ-61

26. *German and American members of the OMGUS microfilming project and families, including John Mendelsohn,* standing second from the left, *and James J. Hastings,* holding child, *at a picnic held shortly after the "Americans as Proconsuls" conference, as demonstrated by the salvaged registration sign in the center foreground.* —Photograph courtesy of John Mendelsohn

27. *Speakers and program staff during the "Americans as Proconsuls" conference on the Mall in Washington, D.C., with the Museum of Natural History of the Smithsonian Institution in the background, May 20, 1977.* Left to right: *Hans H. Baerwald, Ralph Braibanti, Milton O. Gustafson, Hugh Borton, Captain Robert H. Alexander, Brigadier General James L. Collins, Jr., Jack A. Siggins, Eleanor M. Hadley, James J. Hastings, Marlene J. Mayo, Alfred F. Hurley, Silvio A. Bedini, Arthur H. Funk, John Mendelsohn, Donald S. Detwiler.* — Smithsonian Institution photograph 77-7559-18A

28. Speakers during the "Americans as Proconsuls" conference on the balcony of the National Museum of American History of the Smithsonian Institution, May 20, 1977. Left to right: Earl F. Ziemke, Willard A. Fletcher, William R. Swarm, Harold Hurwitz, John D. Montgomery, Forrest C. Pogue, Elmer Plischke, John H. Backer, Jacques J. Reinstein, John J. McCloy, Carl G. Anthon, Robert Wolfe, Jacob D. Beam, Eli E. Nobleman, John Gimbel.— Smithsonian Institution photograph 77-7559-16A

29. John J. McCloy, center, during a pause at the "Americans as Proconsuls" conference in conversation with, left to right, Robert Wolfe, Jacques J. Reinstein, Elmer Plischke, and Jacob D. Beam.—Smithsonian Institution photograph 77-7559-5

before the trial of Tomayuki Yamashita. General Taylor also felt that at Nuremberg Yamashita would not have received the death sentence.

Awareness of sentences with varying degrees of severity for similar war crimes was one of the determining reasons that prompted United States Army officials in Germany and in Japan to create clemency and parole boards for the purpose of equalizing and modifying sentences for war criminals (see Figure 1). The high commissioner for Germany, John J. McCloy, also created a clemency board for war criminals convicted by the twelve subsequent proceedings at Nuremberg falling under his jurisdiction. These boards and their successors made recommendations which led to the dismissal of all war criminals confined in the two major war criminal prisons, Landsberg and Sugamo, by the end of 1958.

Many military government and other United States officials did not accept the change from punishing war criminals to cancelling their sentences gracefully, but the realities of the cold war made this shift smoother. Other factors that hastened the development of a parole and clemency system for war criminals, particularly in Germany, included the disputed sentence reduction of the notorious Ilse Koch.

A United States Special Military Court tried Ilse, the wife of the former Buchenwald Concentration Camp commander, Karl Koch, together with thirty camp staff members and sentenced her to life imprisonment for atrocities committed against non-German nationals at Buchenwald.[14] One of the charges in this trial that shocked the world concerned Ilse's alleged complicity in the production of lampshades from human skin. Upon reviewing the sentences, General Clay, the United States military governor of Germany, reduced these for twelve individuals, shortening Ilse Koch's prison sentence to four years. The general's decision endorsed the findings of his review board,[15] consisting of nine lawyers, who reexamined the evidence and who agreed on the reduction of the sentence.[16]

As the Army delayed the announcement of the reduction, the decision resulted in serious questioning of the Army's handling of sentence review. Consequently, a subcommittee of the Senate's Committee on Expenditures in the Executive Departments under the chairmanship of Senator Homer Ferguson of Michigan, investigated the trial and sentence reduction of Ilse Koch and reported its findings on December 27, 1948.[17] The report declared the reduction of her sentence to four years improper.[18]

The Army had tried Ilse Koch solely on charges involving atrocities committed against non-Germans. General Clay suggested, therefore, to the president of Bavaria, Erhardt, to consider trying her by a German court on charges of atrocities committed against German nationals. This recommendation—the general felt—would not violate the principle of double jeopardy on the one hand, and on the other, it would take the wind out of the sails of some of the most severe critics in the United States of the Army war crimes program.[19]

As a result, a German court in Augsburg tried Ilse Koch and sentenced her again to life imprisonment. She was not present in the courtroom when the sentence was pronounced for she had fled into what the court physician described as a simulated mental disturbance.[20] Subsequently, Ilse Koch entered the large women's penitentiary at Eichach, thirty-five miles northeast of Augsburg where she eventually committed suicide.[21]

The Ilse Koch affair resulted in considerable media involvement, consisting largely of condemnation of her and the Army's conduct. The media gave even heavier coverage to the improprieties which occurred during the Army investigation of SS officers and men charged with the perpetration of the Malmedy Massacre.

In July 1946, the so-called Malmedy Massacre trial took place at the Dachau War Crimes Trials Enclosure.[22] A military tribunal tried seventy-three SS men including SS *Oberstgruppenführer* Sepp Dietrich, the commander of the Leibstandarte SS Adolf Hitler, one of the elite units of the SS, and Colonel Joachim Peiper, commander of the SS Battle Group Peiper, for complicity in the killing of approximately seventy unarmed United States prisoners of war and numerous Belgian civilians.[23] Most of the killings took place in December 1944 during the Ardennes Offensive in various places in Belgium including Malmedy Crossroads, Büllingen, and Ligninville. The Malmedy Massacre stands out as the largest single atrocity committed by the Nazis against United States citizens. The tribunal convicted all of the defendants, and sentenced forty-three to death, twenty-two to life imprisonment, and eight to terms of ten, fifteen, and twenty years.[24] During the trial the defendants testified about their mistreatment either by threats and other forms of psychological or physical violence. In fact, during the investigation of the charges preceding the trial, the investigators moved the defendants from the Dachau War Crimes Trials Enclosure to a jail in Schwäbisch Hall, a thriving town of about 25,000 inhabitants in Württemberg, Germany. There, the pretrial investigators used various means not normally condoned in civilized countries in order to obtain confessions from the battle-hardened SS men. These included the use of hoods placed over the heads of the prisoners, mock trials staged to obtain confessions, and other forms of duress.[25] Critics have thought of the trial as weighted in favor of the prosecution conducted by Army officers who frequently were not trained lawyers.

As a consequence, the Subcommittee of the Senate Armed Forces Committee, authorized by Senate Resolution 42, investigated the conduct of the Malmedy trial and presented its report on October 13, 1949, after exhaustive investigations in the United States and in Germany during which some altercations between Senators Joseph P. McCarthy and Raymond Baldwin, the chairman, occurred.[26] The subcommittee affirmed in its report in isolated instances the physical brutalization of German prisoners, but refused to acknowledge this was a general practice. The subcommittee recommended also that the United Nations should work out methods and procedures of trying war criminals, that investigators of future trials should have enjoyed United States citizenship for at least ten years, and urged the utilization of more trained lawyers in these proceedings.[27] The subcommittee also noted that a movement existed to discredit the whole war crimes program in Germany. In the wake of these proceedings authorities executed none of the death sentences and released all prisoners eventually, among the last, Hubert Huber and Joachim Peiper.[28]

In contrast to the Ferguson Committee which had criticized Army actions and found improper Ilse Koch's sentence reduction by General Clay, the Baldwin Committee refrained from any direct critique and stated flatly that there existed a conspiracy to discredit United States military government in Germany. Although the abrasive treatment of the Army by Senator McCarthy undoubtedly contributed to the somewhat defensive findings of the Baldwin Committee, the result of the well publicized hearings and media reporting tended in fact to discredit the war crimes trial program of the Army and prepared the public for absorbing the clemency phase.

The establishment of an independent commission, the Simpson Commission, convened by the secretary of the Army, Kenneth C. Royall, in the summer of 1948 for the purpose of analyzing the war crimes program, particularly the Malmedy case, constituted a more crucial event for the development of a clemency and parole system for war criminals. The Simpson Commission, consisting of Colonel Gordon Simpson, Colonel Edward L. van Roden, and Lieutenant Colonel Charles W. Lawrence, Jr., recommended commutation of a number of sentences and the establishment of a permanent clemency and parole board.[29] This recommendation opened the road for the Army to proceed toward the end of 1949 with the creation of such a board, the EUCOM Modification Board (see Figure 1).

Meanwhile, in order to aid him in extending pardons, paroles, clemency, or to release prisoners early, High Commissioner McCloy convened an Advisory Board on Clemency for War Criminals (see Figure 1) in March 1950, in Washington.[30] The board consisted of David W. Peck, its president, the presiding judge of the Appellate Division of the New York Supreme Court; Frederick A. Moran, chairman of the New York State Board of Parole; and Brigadier General Conrad E. Snow, assistant legal advisor of the Department of State.[31] The board met in Washington and Munich, and a board member interviewed inmates at the Landsberg war criminals' prison. The board submitted its final report and recommendations to the high commissioner on August 28, 1950.[32]

The clemency board did not consider the sentences of sixteen defendants in two of the industrialists cases, the Flick and Krauch cases, because the defendants had served their sentences or awaited their impending release, but acted on the remaining ten cases tried by United States military tribunals at Nuremberg.[33] The high commissioner extended commutations and paroles to seventy-nine of the eighty-nine Nurembergers remaining at Landsberg.[34] He did not grant clemency to five individuals sentenced to death, because the enormity of their crimes precluded this. SS Major General Otto Ohlendorf, SS Colonels Paul Blobel, Werner Braune, and Erich Naumann convicted in the *Einsatzgruppen* Case, and SS Lieutenant General Oswald Pohl tried in the SS concentration camp case were eventually executed at Landsberg.[35] McCloy denied clemency to Field Marshall Wilhelm List and General Walter Kuntze because of their responsibility in taking and shooting excessive numbers of hostages in the Balkans. Nonetheless, he pointed out in his clemency decision regarding these two officers, "The board suggests that List and Kuntze, both elderly men, may have such physical infirmities as to raise the desirability of further medical examination to determine whether any medical parole is appropriate."[36]

A military tribunal tried the remaining three generals—Hermann Reinecke, Hans Reinhardt, and Hermann Hoth—in the von Leeb case, one of two military cases.[37] Reinecke received a life sentence for complicity in the ill treatment and shooting of prisoners of war, while Reinhardt and Hoth drew terms of fifteen years, chiefly for transmitting the "Commando" and "Commissar" orders, which authorized the ill treatment and killing without trial of raiding parties and Communists.[38] With the exception of these ten individuals to whom the high commissioner had denied clemency, February 3, 1951 represented a red letter day in the lives of the Landsberg inmates. On that day Landsberg Prison authorities released thirty-two prisoners with reductions to time served.[39] Most of these had received original terms of ten years, three served terms of fifteen years and four served terms of twenty years each.

With the actions of the HICOG Clemency Board and the approval of sentence reduction by the high commissioner, the period of punishment in the treatment of Nazi war criminals had officially come to an end. As General Clay had granted clemency in only three instances to the Nurembergers during the period from 1946 to 1949, the sentence reductions recommended by the HICOG board, in contrast, was the most sweeping clemency action extended to prisoners held at Landsberg.

Many pressures contributed to the change in attitude toward war criminals. September 1949 saw the establishment of the Federal Republic of Germany and her relationship with the occupying powers placed on a contractual basis. The Office of the High Commissioner for Germany, created three months earlier, in June of that year, had an interest in beginning this new relationship on a good footing and consequently extended clemency to the convicted Nuremberg war criminals wherever this seemed possible. Unfortunately, these actions did not have the desired results and rather than mollifying the various segments of German public opinion which had clamored for clemency, the massive amount of sentence remissions tended to produce a cynical attitude among many of those Germans who had advocated greater leniency toward the convicted.[40]

Also, in the United States, public opinion regarding Germany and war criminals underwent a process of transformation. The valiant stand of the West Berliners during the Berlin airlift and their firm adherence to the West could not fail to win the admiration of the press and media. It impressed upon the people in this country who had struggled so hard to put down the Nazi menace that Germany could be trusted again and that a revival of national socialism did not appear likely. At the same time congressional investigations of the conduct of war crimes trials tended to discredit some of the activities of our military authority in Germany.[41] In the United States, these events helped to bring about a more positive attitude toward clemency for war criminals.

Executive clemency as practiced by the HICOG clemency board and by the high commissioner for Germany acted as a trigger device on the slower moving European Command (EUCOM) Modification

Board. This board, under Army direction, seems to have had greater difficulties at first in leaving behind it the period of punishment for war criminals and in propelling itself into the new era of commutations. Of course, the problems confronting the EUCOM board often differed from those facing the HICOG board. For example, the EUCOM board dealing mainly with prisoners confined at Landsberg under Army jurisdiction considered over five hundred cases, whereas the HICOG board had deliberated over less than one hundred.

The EUCOM Modification Board, created in 1949, could build on established review procedures. In the initial phases of the Army war crimes program, the Army commanders exercised review authority. Upon consolidation of the program under the deputy judge advocate for war crimes in 1946, this office reviewed the records of each completed case and issued a review and recommendation which the judge advocate general forwarded with his recommendation to the theater commander. In order to arrive at a decision in a certain case, the theater commander sometimes created his own additional boards of review.[42]

The EUCOM board was established in direct response to the recommendations of the Simpson Commission and to the pressures caused by Congressional hearings. EUCOM commander in chief, General Thomas Handy, successor of General Clay, appointed the Modification Board, consisting of five senior EUCOM officers, on November 29, 1949, for the purpose of submitting to him any recommendations on war crimes cases.[43] The convening authority chose the designation "Modification Board" over clemency board so as not to convey to prisoners the notion that they could expect clemency or had a right thereto.[44]

At the first, the board decided not to hear individual prisoners or their attorneys except in unusual circumstances; however, they could file petitions or briefs. This soon changed, largely because of the prisoners' complaints that Nuremberg prisoners were treated better than the Dachauers (most Army cases were tried at Dachau), and the board, holding its sessions at Landsberg, saw prisoners and their attorneys in order to determine clemency and paroles in accordance with a docket based on a set of priorities.[45] Each of the prisoners received at least thirty days' notice prior to his hearing. The EUCOM board established the date when the sentence of the prisoner commenced, extending thereby to many Landsberg inmates considerable sentence reductions. Also, from August 1950 good conduct time increased to ten days per month instead of the customary five days.[46] Both HICOG and EUCOM boards agreed to grant to prisoners compassionate leave at the impending death of a close personal relative.[47]

The board confined its recommendations mainly to individuals serving prison terms. Prison authorities had executed most death sentences and the board recommended commutations to lesser terms in only 13 instances of maximum punishment. Other suggestions included reductions of 20 life sentences, shortening over 200 prison terms, and 150 remissions to time served. In about 120 cases the board recommended no remission. The EUCOM commanding general approved two-thirds of these recommendations, some with changes, and disapproved the remaining third. Around Christmas 1951, the prison doors opened up for a large number of short-term prisoners as the result of a Christmas amnesty which left 313 prisoners under Army jurisdiction in Landsberg.[48]

Both HICOG and EUCOM boards prepared the groundwork for the final acts in the drama of United States war crimes trials in Germany. The first step in this spadework centered around the creation of the Interim Mixed Parole and Clemency Board (see Figure 1) the IMPAC Board, with two German members, and finally the evolution of the Mixed Parole and Clemency Board, the MPAC Board, with binding decisions in cases of unanimity, which disposed of the remaining Landsberg Prison population.

The IMPAC Board, established on August 31, 1953, became operational when Chancellor Konrad Adenauer stated in a letter to High Commissioner James B. Conant that the Federal Republic of Germany would agree to the terms of the order establishing the board including cooperation in enforcing parole conditions. The United States appointed the five members of the board with two individuals nominated by the Federal Republic. The board could not question the fairness of the tribunals that had tried those convicted at Landsberg,[49] but it could compare the severity of sentences and it could consider a variety of factors in determining both clemency and parole. These included, for example, the nature of the crime committed by the confined war criminal and his previous record. Other important points encompassed age, physical and mental condition of the individual, his employment opportunities upon release, and the condition of his family.[50]

As with the EUCOM Modification Board, the vast majority of cases considered by the IMPAC Board resulted in parole recommendations rather than conditional or unconditional clemency. At the time of the creation of this board, Landsberg Prison confined thirty-one Nurembergers and 281 Dachauers. Since the high commissioner and the commanding general in Germany approved most of the recommendations of the IMPAC Board, by August 1955 only seven Nurembergers remained and the number of Dachauers, too, had shrunk to thirty-four.[51]

As amended by the Paris Protocol of October 23, 1954, the Bonn Conventions of 1952 became effective on May 5, 1955. The conventions established the Mixed Parole and Clemency Board (MPAC, see Figure 1), which became operational in August 1955. It had six members, three Germans and one United States, British and French member, each. Unanimous recommendations from the new board caused the release of prisoners under both State Department (HICOG) and Army jurisdiction. The MPAC Board emptied Landsberg of its remaining war criminal population by May 1958, and the last individuals released included four prisoners who left on May 9, 1958. These consisted first of Otto Brinkmann, serving a life sentence for participation in mass atrocities in Nordhausen Concentration Camp, and second, Ernst Biberstein, Adolf Ott, and Martin Sandberger, officers in the SS *Einsatzgruppen,* sentenced to death in the Ohlendorf case at Nuremberg.[52] After that date, the United States Army restricted its activities at Landsberg to remitting the unserved portion of the sentences of a number of prisoners released on parole, and the transfer of the war crimes facilities to German authorities.

While United States authorities in Germany struggled with the problem of how to handle properly the fate of these convicted war criminals, the British authorities in Germany had tried 749 war crimes suspects in their zone of occupation. By 1953 they had released all of those serving prison terms except thirty-one individuals, by 1955 there remained seven, and by 1958 these, too, were released. The British did not have a system of parole and prisoners were released on good behavior after having served three-quarters of their sentences.[53] The French, who continued to try Germans for war crimes for several months after the British and United States Army had concluded their war crimes trials, convicted 1,639 individuals, and sentenced many to five years' imprisonment or less. They discharged most of the prisoners on a good conduct release after serving two-thirds of their sentences. The French had seventy-two convicted war criminals left in prison in 1953 and by 1955 they had reduced this number to eighteen. They released the last war criminals tried in the French zone of occupation in 1958.[54]

Circumstances under which authorities tried war criminals in the Far East and under which their condition improved as they received clemency and parole often differed from those prevailing in the European theater. Although many war criminals in Japan languished at first in the prisons of the victorious Allies, as in Europe, eventually most stayed in the Tokyo War Criminals Prison, Sugamo. Those confined there included mainly Japanese nationals sentenced by the International Military Tribunal for the Far East (IMTFE), United States military tribunals in Yokohama, Manila, Guam, Shanghai, and Kwajalein, as well as by military tribunals established by France, The Netherlands, Great Britain, China, and Australia. Sugamo Prison also housed suspects and hostile or friendly witnesses.[55]

On March 1, 1950, for example, Sugamo confined 1,670 individuals. In the course of the next few years many of the nations that had tried war criminals in the Far East transferred their convicted war criminals to Sugamo Prison upon the request of the Japanese government. Yet by the end of 1958 the prison population, which at one time exceeded 2,000 individuals, had vanished in the wake of world events and more particularly the clemency, parole, and early-release programs instituted by the Supreme Commander Allied Powers (SCAP).[56]

Although more Japanese participated in the administration of the prison from the start than did their German counterparts at Landsberg, control of the treatment of the inmates at Sugamo rested almost entirely in the hands of the United States.[57] As early as Christmas Eve, 1949, SCAP announced a clemency program extending to convicted war criminals credit for pretrial confinement and for good time. At the same time a parole board was established.[58]

SCAP Circular No. 5 of March 17, 1950, entitled "Clemency for War Criminals," implemented the clemency program for the Far East. SCAP extended presentence confinement credit to all convicted war criminals. This credit did not consider, however, detention in a prisoner of war status. Sentenced war criminals with good prison records received time off for good behavior ranging from five to ten days per month in length.[59]

The circular also established a parole board (see Figure 1) with three civilian members. Moving rapidly, the board held its first official session on March 17, 1950, submitted its first recommendation to SCAP in April, and continued to meet, normally once a week, until its termination in April 1952 when the Japanese Peace Treaty went into effect. During this period the SCAP Parole Board met a total of 120 times, generally in either the Teikoku or Meiji Building in Tokyo.[60]

The board considered the trial record of a prisoner and particularly the severity of the crime which he committed, but the board members placed greater weight on personal factors including the housing situation, the physical and mental health of a prisoner, his prison record, the status of his family, and his opportunities for rehabilitation in the outside world. A show of remorse by the prisoner for the actions for which he was convicted seemed of some importance to the members of the board. Moreover, the board displayed eagerness to learn new facts which would reflect more favorably upon the prisoner.[61]

One murderer of a United States prisoner of war confessed his remorse to the board by pointing out that "at that time I acted [on] my seniors' orders just as mechanical as a cog in the wheel but since the day of my sentence I recognize that my offense was grave and I have been earnestly serving with a sense of remorse and atonement praying for the repose of the sufferer's soul."[62] This rather typical expression of remorse among the many contained in the records of the SCAP Parole Board led to the parole of the prisoner.

As in Europe, a prisoner became eligible for parole generally after he had served one-third of his sentence. SCAP did not extend parole automatically, but required the prisoner's formal application to the authorities. If SCAP approved the recommendation of the board, the supreme commander issued a parole certificate to the prisoner which normally listed the conditions of the parole. According to these, the prisoner had to report to his parole supervisor within eight days of his release from Sugamo Prison. He had to telephone or write on the fifth day of each month and keep the supervisor informed of all changes of address. The parolee could not undertake trips exceeding eighty kilometers without the supervisor's permission. The supervisor, in turn, recorded all these changes.

The Japanese government administered the parole system. The National Offenders Protection and Rehabilitation Commission, known as the NOPAR Commission, carried out these functions. The NOPAR Commission submitted lists of parole supervisors to the SCAP Parole Board and reported all changes of addresses and other facts pertaining to a parolee to the board.[63] The parole system for Japanese war criminals thus differed from its counterpart in Europe in that it utilized from the start the existing Japanese parole system administered by Japanese nationals whereas German nationals entered the system only gradually. The NOPAR Commission began to recommend clemency and paroles to the various powers, following the effective date of the Japanese Peace Treaty in April 1952.[64]

The parole board received nearly 1,200 applications for parole and heard the personal pleas of over 900 applicants. Prison authorities had released the remaining applicants before they could have a hearing or had established eligibility for parole. In the cases of the

900 applicants heard by the board, denial of parole was suggested for only twenty-six individuals; for all other pleaders the board recommended parole. SCAP approved all these recommendations.

On September 4, 1952, President Truman established a Clemency and Parole Board for War Criminals (see Figure 1) for the purpose of recommending clemency and parole for war criminals in Japan. In the case of IMTFE prisoners, the board required a majority of the nations represented on the bench in order to grant parole or clemency while, with all other prisoners, consent of the nation pronouncing the sentence sufficed. The board, consisting of three members, one each from the State, Defense, and Justice Departments, met generally once a week in the chairman's office in the Department of State.[65]

In January 1958, President Eisenhower abolished the Clemency and Parole Board for War Criminals established in September 1952 by President Truman, and ordered the secretary of state "in general to accept the recommendations of the government of Japan if they are accompanied by findings made by a responsible non-political board" (see Figure 1).[66] This meant, in effect, that the United States had turned over the release of war criminals to the Japanese government.

Following the personal request of Japanese Premier Nobusuka Kishi, himself a war criminal suspect as former minister of commerce in the Tojo cabinet but never tried, on his visit to the United States in 1957, unconditional freedom, that is, removal of parole conditions, was granted to ten individuals sentenced by the IMTFE.[67] Finally, on December 31, 1958, there appeared the following item in the *New York Times:* "United States authorities freed today the last group of war criminals held in Sugamo Prison here. The United States informed the foreign minister [of Japan] it was terminating the sentences of eighty-three prisoners. Sugamo thus ceases to be a prison for war criminals."[68] The end of the year 1958 saw the formal ending of direct United States involvement in war crimes trials in Germany and in Japan.

In conclusion, then, it is fair to say that a good many similarities but also contrasts existed in the operation of clemency and parole granted by United States authorities in Germany and Japan to war criminals. As we have seen, military authorities established boards to make recommendations to the commanding generals in the European Command and of Eighth United States Army in Japan at about the same time. In fact, the EUCOM Modification Board began operations less than a month before the SCAP Parole Board. Three months later, in March 1950, the HICOG Clemency Board came into existence. The EUCOM Modification Board moved slower and the commanding general of EUCOM disapproved many of its recommendations. On the other hand, the HICOG board recommendations were of a more sweeping nature and High Commissioner McCloy approved these with some exceptions. SCAP also tended to confirm the recommendations of its parole and review boards. Thus, in the two years of its existence, the SCAP Parole Board recommended paroles for 892 prisoners which the commanding general of the Eighth United States Army or SCAP approved.

The Japanese had not resorted to the theory of racial superiority resulting in the extermination of countless people; they had no organization comparable in viciousness to the SS or the Gestapo. As a consequence, war crimes of the Japanese consisted largely of waging wars of aggression or committing murder and brutalities against prisoners of war and civilian populations; but nothing existed in Japan approaching the unspeakable horrors of Auschwitz, Sobibor, or Treblinka.

Perhaps the following scenario delineates and illustrates quite well the differences pertaining to war crimes trials and clemency that grew out of the fact that Japan retained her sovereignty, whereas Germany did not. In the summer of 1955 two old men met in a suite in the Waldorf Towers in New York City. One, the seventy-five-year-old hero of the Pacific campaign whose statement "I shall return" won immortality and whose recent dismissal from his position as SCAP by his irascible president, Harry S Truman, filled media headlines, confronted sixty-eight-year-old Marmoru Shigemitsu, who had signed the friendship pact between Germany and Japan.[69] He became ambassador to Germany and in 1943 Japanese foreign minister. He signed the Japanese surrender on the *Missouri* and the IMTFE sentenced him to seven years' imprisonment for participating in the planning of aggressive war. After serving four and a half years of his sentence, Sugamo Prison authorities released Shigemitsu and he assumed again an active role in Japanese politics. Later, Japan appointed him to the position he had held in World War II, that of foreign minister and also deputy prime minister (1954–56). Now in New York he discussed with General MacArthur the release of all Japanese war criminals to which the general agreed in principle.[70]

The scenario for Germany differed considerably from that for Japan. The IMT at Nuremberg tried Nazi Foreign Minister Joachim von Ribbontrop, sentenced him to death, and executed him in 1946. The tribunal also sentenced his predecessor, Konstantin von Neurath, to fifteen years' imprisonment, but released him for medical reasons before the expiration of his term. A United States military tribunal tried the two deputy foreign ministers, Ernst von Weizsaecker and Gustav Adolf Steengracht von Moyland, in the "Ministries Case" resulting in short prison terms.[71] None of these three top Foreign Ministry officials who survived into the fifties gained prominence in public life in the Federal Republic of Germany and no convicted war criminal ever gained high political office there.

Punishment and clemency phases in the treatment of war criminals compare with initial occupation and reverse course. Realities of the cold war period provided the general framework that prepared the ground for the early release of war criminals, but other factors such as the desire of the Army to equalize sentences, congressional investigations of the war crimes program, and media pressure had an equally important role. The Japanese people often viewed the convicted war criminals as martyrs while few in Germany did likewise. If our goal included removal from public life of war criminals, one is tempted to conclude that the program succeeded to a remarkable degree in Germany and only partly so in Japan. There can be little doubt, however, that a number of convicted war criminals achieved signal successes in the economic sphere in both countries, and such individuals as Albert Speer earned distinction as writers.

Fifth Session

Reeducation for Democracy

Introduction by Carl G. Anthon

It may seem redundant for me to point out once again after all these panels and discussions that Germany was different, indeed, from Japan. The German problem was obviously very different from the Japanese problem. As was pointed out yesterday, the Japanese were regarded as bad but the Germans as downright evil. Or, as many intellectuals and especially psychiatrists in this country thought (and perhaps not just in this country), the Germans were sick. There was presumably a collective paranoia about them which required a radical therapy to be carried out by American doctors, of course, in our occupation.

Was this concept limited to the Anglo-Americans in the time of fighting; was this a war psychosis on our part? I think we should call attention to the fact that there were many Germans, too, who believed that, while there was perhaps not a collective guilt, there was need for radical reeducation. We could call attention to people like Thomas Mann in this country, and many other émigré intellectuals, who felt that Germany needed reeducation—people like Paul Tillich and all those who were associated with advisory groups on what to do with Germany during the early 1940s. And inside Germany, as well, there were intellectuals and religious leaders who thought likewise. Friedrich Meinecke, for instance, who can certainly not be classified as a leftist or radical historian, also felt there was a genuine need to go back to the true German humanistic heritage, and he said quite plainly in his *Deutsche Katastrophe* that there will be need for reeducation and Germany's former enemies will assist in this process. Thus the American reeducation effort was actually anticipated and to some extent approved by many Germans.

Of course, it is the method, how is it to be done, that is the big question. I might here call to your attention the dictum which I think Franz Neumann wrote somewhere: "It is difficult to educate, it is more difficult to reeducate, and it is downright impossible to reeducate a whole foreign nation."

So there is the problem; but here, too, we can say that there were many German leaders who were ready to help in this process, whom we could turn to for ideas, for advice, for initiative, and for implementation. I would like to suggest that it is not only the American reorientation officials whom we must look to here for information and for reminiscences, which is all very pleasant (I see here two or three people who were involved in the reeducation programs in Germany and also in the postreorientation activities subsequently). Perhaps we will hear from them. But my specific feeling is that there is another side to the whole story which we have not heard this whole weekend; namely, that of the occupied population—what did they think of our operations? Perhaps we can include this perspective in future deliberations. But I do see several German visitors here and if they are inclined to express their views on how it felt to be occupied and to be reoriented and reeducated, I think that would add to our understanding of the problem.

Chapter 13

Civil Censorship and
Media Control in
Early Occupied Japan

From Minimum to Stringent Surveillance

Marlene J. Mayo

American and Japanese students new to the study of the occupation of Japan, especially a younger generation with little or no memory of World War II in the Pacific, are invariably startled and perplexed to learn that Americans engaged in extensive censorship of Japan's civilian communications and gave considerable guidance to Japan's mass media. Why should this be so, they wonder, if one of the reasons for fighting the war, as first expressed in the Four Freedoms and repeated in the Potsdam declaration, was to encourage free speech and free inquiry in the postwar world. Civil censorship and propaganda are obviously necessary in time of war, but why practice them in time of peace? How could the Allies, particularly the Americans, who were the predominant occupying power, expect to set a good example for the Japanese and foster democratization of the information and entertainment media if they replaced Japan's wartime controls of press, radio, and films with their own—and possibly equally stringent—set of controls?[1]

This paper was commissioned to provide a Japanese parallel to the immediately following paper, "Comparing American Reform Efforts in Germany: Mass Media and the School System," by Harold Hurwitz. Presented at the Columbia University Seminar on Modern East Asia, March 11, 1983, it is a substantially recast version of pertinent portions of the author's "Psychological Disarmament: American Wartime Planning for the Education and Re-Education of Defeated Japan, 1943–1945," in Thomas Burkman, ed., *The Occupation of Japan: Educational and Social Reform* (Norfolk, Va.: Gatling Printing and Publishing Co., 1982).—Ed.

The answer, put very simply, was that the occupation came in the aftermath of war. Japan was a defeated enemy country. The new controls, while more severe than first intended, did not necessarily have the same purposes or operate in quite the same ways as Japan's own prewar and wartime regulations. The victors, determined to avoid another war with a resurgent Japan, believed they must censor and guide Japan's media until their enemy could get rid of wrong ideas and acquire better ones—replace militaristic and aggressive ideas with democratic and peace-loving ones. The occupation also came at the beginning of the cold war, and Americans felt impelled to combat communism together with nazism, fascism, and militarism. The controls therefore would continue until the occupiers could trust the Japanese, reestablish friendly relations, end the occupation, and leave (or largely leave) the country. The nature and extent of American censorship and guidance would be shaped as much by Japanese behavior and compliance with occupation directives as by the needs of military security and the idealism of the victors. These controls, moreover, reflected a larger effort at war's end, though Congress was skeptical and parsimonious with funding, to continue overseas information services as a permanent instrument of American foreign policy and to expand existing international education programs. Cultural foreign policy was viewed as necessary to clarify the aims of the American government and to project, particularly through short wave radio broadcasting, a favorable image abroad of American life and institutions.

As in all matters pertaining to the occupation of Japan, General Douglas MacArthur, both as commander in chief of United States Army Forces in the Pacific (CINC/USAFPAC) and as the supreme commander for the Allied Powers in Japan (SCAP), received extensive initial and long-term policy guidance from Washington on Japan's media, including emergency guidance for the first fifteen days. Moreover, MacArthur and his chief staff officers largely accepted the recommendations. They had the added benefit of the problems encountered, techniques utilized, and mistakes made in efforts to control information in the American zone of occupied Germany.

Contributions to MacArthur's guidelines came from the State Department, the War and Navy departments, the Office of Strategic Services (OSS), and the Office of War Information (OWI), 1942–45. The final plans drew heavily upon policy preparation for Germany, which, given the priority of the European theater, usually preceded by weeks or months comparable papers for Japan. Despite the best efforts of the Japan experts working in the various regular departments of the federal government and its wartime agencies to focus on the special characteristics of Japan, the final policy also reflected the tendency of officials at higher levels, victims of their own wartime propaganda or general ignorance, to lump Japan together with Italy and Germany in a blurred vision of the war as one of the democracies against the totalitarian systems. Eliminating militarism in Japan, however, did not necessarily present the same problems as eradicating fascism and nazism in Italy and Germany; nor was the analysis of militarism always precise and cogent. Should distinctions be drawn between authoritarian and totalitarian states? This was compounded by the difficulties of countering communism in different settings.

The abrupt end of the war with Japan in mid-August 1945 had, it is true, caught civilian and military planners in Washington very much off guard. They were still in the midst of refining a host of draft policy papers touching on all aspects of Japanese life and also revising the overall Basic Policy Statement and Basic Military Directive for the initial administration of civil affairs in Japan. Extensive thought, research, debate, and compromise, however, had already gone into these papers as they made their way from lower specialized levels to higher interdepartmental committees and ultimately to the president and Joint Chiefs of Staff. In most instances, they depended only on reports about conditions in Japan for their final form and wording. In the case of censorship and control of Japan's media, a preliminary policy paper had been approved in late 1944 and reworked again in the summer of 1945. Its purpose was twofold: 1) to eliminate militaristic indoctrination, and 2) to promote the dissemination of democratic ideas. The first function was thought of as negative, requiring expurgation, deletion, or suppression of any vestiges of aggressive and ultranationalistic sentiments. The second function was seen as positive, calling for the insertion of approved democratic themes into the flow of entertainment and information. Both were geared to the large, more grandiose goal of reorientation and reeducation—fundamental and lasting changes in Japanese thinking. Ideological disarmament was as essential as military demobilization and disarmament. The planners had in mind a comprehensive program not only for the education of Japanese youth but also for the reeducation (indoctrination) of the entire population, children and adults alike. New attitudes had to be fostered, ostensibly those acceptable to the United Nations but in reality those approved by the United States. The reorientation program was conceived as a defense against any ideologies, whether belonging to recent allies or defeated enemies, which might threaten the security of the United States and its economic, political, and social system. It could not be effected without sophisticated utilization of the mass media or careful coordination with national propaganda.

This paper will briefly trace the evolution of policy formulation in wartime Washington for Japan's media and indicate why civil censorship and media control were deemed necessary for all wartime theaters of operation, not just Japan. It will further attempt to explain why the concept of relatively lenient control was quickly replaced in early occupied Japan by maximum surveillance. At all times, American policy planners and makers were acutely aware of the contradiction between their democratic values and censorship requirements. It was another of the necessary evils emerging from brutal and dehumanizing total war and from fears of another even more horrible war.

From the beginning of the planning process, the American government made provision for the censorship of civilian communications in liberated and occupied enemy territories. This was treated as one of the mandates of war and occupation. Americans were also censoring themselves by voluntary compliance with press and radio codes. As early as May 1942, General George V. Strong, head of Military Intelligence, War Department, touched upon the question in a preliminary draft of "Conditions for Japanese Surrender to the United Nations." Intended for the deliberations of the Security Subcommittee of President Roosevelt's secret Advisory Committee on Post-War Foreign Policy (a carefully selected cross-section of prominent private citizens, congressional leaders, and public officials), it stated, "The United Nations will exercise censorship of the press and means of communication within the occupied areas of the Japanese Empire." At that time, Strong envisioned only the occupation of Japan's northernmost main island, Hokkaido. In September 1943, a draft directive for Hokkaido, prepared as an exercise by naval planners, also included media control. "You," it ordered the theater commander, "will institute necessary control over dissemination of news or information by radio, telegraph, or cable, or in any other form."[2]

In addition, there was already in existence a military government manual (1940) based on the limited experience of Americans in the occupation of German territory following World War I. The revised edition, *The United States Army and Navy Manual of Military Government and Civil Affairs* (December 1943), declared as a general principle, "To the extent that military interests are not prejudiced, freedom of speech and press should be maintained or instituted." Under the specific heading of censorship, which was defined as one of the functions of civil affairs officers, the manual further explained:

> Censorship of civilian communications is effected in order to accomplish two objectives: the protection of security, both military and civilian; and the obtaining of intelligence information. It will normally be established in the very earliest phases and continue throughout the period of occupation. Thus, its operation by civil affairs will require close liaison with the military intelligence staff for the area from whom censorship policies and directives emanate.[3]

Security and intelligence would remain constant as the desired ends of censorship, expanding later to overlap with guidance in reorientation. The duties of censorship, however, highly complex and specialized, required separate training and would in the end be assigned to counterintelligence officers.

The manual was in accord with important deliberations at much higher levels. In July of 1943, in response to initiatives taken by Byron Price, director of the United States Office of Censorship, the Combined Chiefs of Staff (American and British) had ruled for the European and African theaters that censorship of civilian communications in territories occupied by the forces of the United Nations was a military responsibility. The State, War, and Navy departments all concurred that questions relating to the institution and operation of censorship in areas taken by United States forces were of primary interest to the War Department. In a subsequent memorandum, the War Department further characterized censorship as "imperative" in gaining information vital to the prosecution of the war, enforcing the terms of surrender, assessing public opinion and morale within the occupied territories, reinforcing policing and military security, and collecting political and economic intelligence. Civil communications were defined as the mails, telephone, telegraph, travelers' documents, radio, press, films, and photographs. In a passage prophetic of what would happen to Japan, the memorandum declared "in the case of occupied enemy territory . . . the system of control should be based primarily upon severe restrictions on freedom to communicate in order to reduce the censorable matter to proportions which can be handled by personnel recruited exclusively from United States or Allied sources." Censorship would extend to both external and internal communications. Postal censorship, it was suggested, might be exercised by random sampling, telegraphic control by withholding facilities from hostile or subversive civilians, and telephone calls beyond local areas by imposing a total embargo.

Control of radio broadcasting should be strict. Press releases for local consumption should be scrutinized in cooperation with public relations officers. The public should view only commercial motion pictures made for entertainment. No person, except those on official business, should be authorized to enter or leave the territory. In follow-up communications, commanding generals in the European and African theaters were all directed to appoint a civil censorship officer to undertake the necessary preparations.[4]

All of this was relevant for Japan. In the summer and fall of 1944, the American Joint Chiefs of Staff formally applied the same principles to the Pacific and Asiatic front, again acting after nudging by Price. Civil censorship, they determined, should be the sole responsibility of the supreme commander in the various theaters. A basic corollary planning assumption at this stage of the war was that the civil administration of Japan, including civil censorship, would be primarily a United States responsibility since it was bearing the main burden of the fighting. The Civil Affairs Division (CAD) of the War Department was the senior planner for postwar civil affairs administration in Japan but was collaborating closely with the Navy Department's Office for Occupied Areas. Other interested parties were military and naval intelligence officers. Although still very general and tentative, civil censorship plans were proceeding in Washington on the basis of four areas—Southeast Asia, Southwest Pacific, Central Pacific, and Central Asia. As Admiral William Leahy, chief of staff, stated in a report to chief American censor Price in June, the largest civil censorship undertaking "by far" in the Pacific and Asiatic areas would be for Japan, "both because of the complex nature of communications, including the language, and also because it is apparent that some type of military control including censorship will be required in Japan for considerable time after her defeat."[5]

Until the early spring of 1945, Japan proper was considered to be in the Central Pacific category. The original planning responsibility in the war theater on this matter was therefore charged in 1944 to Admiral Chester Nimitz, commander in chief of the Pacific Fleet and also of the Pacific Ocean Areas (CINCPAC/CINCPOA), who in turn delegated authority to one of his subordinate Army commanders, Lieutenant General Robert C. Richardson, Jr., commanding general, United States Army Forces in the Pacific Ocean Area. Adjustments of theater boundaries with consequent transfers of plans and planning staffs were anticipated by Washington, no doubt because of the jurisdictional jealousies and command disputes of Nimitz and MacArthur. The first civil censorship guidance in the

Pacific had in fact gone informally to MacArthur the previous May (1944), when the War Department sent secret instructions for the Southwest Pacific area. This was in anticipation of campaigns in the Philippines and the Netherlands East Indies. The enclosed guidelines were very close to the CCS memorandum for European commanders but did not mention press and radio censorship, an oversight which Price noted but which was never completely corrected before the ending of the war.[6] The reasons are unclear, but perhaps this was because MacArthur censored press and radio combat news releases through his public relations staff.

The next step was to define more thoroughly the aims, objectives, and functions of civil censorship and to recruit and train a force of censors. Major General Clayton Bissell, Strong's successor as head of G-2, military intelligence, requested in August that a small planning staff be created as soon as possible to develop broad plans and "make appropriate recommendations for the procurement and training of the necessary personnel" and the requisition of technical equipment. He estimated that it would be necessary to train approximately 300 officers and 1,500 enlisted men with "a working knowledge of Japan and its language" and eventually to add civilian examiners who were fluent in the language.[7]

In November 1944, the JCS formally decided upon a civil censorship policy (JCS 873/3) and sent it to the Asian and Pacific theater commanders as a directive. In familiar language, it stated that the "scope and duration" of civil censorship would be governed by military security and by information requirements necessary to prosecute the war and enforce the peace. Civil censorship would continue, therefore, "during the period of occupation of enemy territory after the conclusion of hostilities." Clarifying jurisdiction, the JCS ordered each theater commander to "operate censorship of civil communications as a military measure through agencies under his direct control. Normally, he will exercise this responsibility through the intelligence division of his staff." At his discretion, he might modify the "scope and degree" of civil censorship but was not to terminate it without the prior approval of the JCS. Guidelines almost identical to those issued to MacArthur in May 1944 were enclosed but with the addition of "publicity media" to the types of censorable communications. These were not identified, although advice was given on radio control. "In all probability no telephone or radio broadcast communications to points outside the area would be permitted except monitored materials from previously censored script." Internal or local broadcasts should be subject to similar restrictions. Finally, the directive repeated the warning that in enemy territory, "local inhabitants could seldom be used because of their inherent hostility." Censorship examiners must be recruited from the armed forces and possibly from "civilians of adjacent United Nations territories" (Korea, China, the Philippines).[8]

The War Department set up a small planning unit—the Special Overseas Planning Group—under the director of intelligence, Army Service Forces, to work on basic recommendations. By late November, a general plan for civil censorship in Japan had been prepared, and by the end of December it was approved and ready for implementation. This became the controlling document (along with JCS 873/3) for recruiting and training censors in the United States and for detailed operational planning in the theater. As was true of other documents of this nature up to July and August 1945, it was based on the assumption that an invasion of the Japanese home islands would be necessary to effect surrender. Censorship operations therefore would be set up in the wake of combat, with or without an indigenous government in existence. The plan carefully set forth "the authority, mission, jurisdiction, basic assumptions, and basic functions of the Civil Censorship organization for Japan," and it gave revised estimates of the total number of officers, enlisted men, and civilian personnel required to conduct effective surveillance.

Stated succinctly, the mission was "to control and examine communications and to collect and disseminate such information contained in those communications as will be of value to the United Nations." Censorship personnel, operating out of headquarters in Tokyo, were to direct their main intelligence efforts toward the following wide variety of subjects:

a. Defeat of any enemy forces still resisting the United Nations.
b. Enforcement of all terms of the Surrender Agreement and any subsequent agreements, including peace treaties if any.
c. Detection of secret military and political organizations and other subversive elements.
d. Security of troops of occupation.
e. Maintenance of order in Japan.
f. Disarmament of Japan and prevention of rearmament.
g. Apprehension and conviction of war criminals.
h. Recovery of property stolen from other nations by the Japanese.
i. Prevention of black market and hoarding activities.
j. Obtaining full knowledge of Japanese espionage and counterespionage systems.

k. Determination of Japanese political and economic policies both within and outside Japan proper.

l. Appraisal of Japanese propaganda activities in other nations and of the activities of Japanese organizations among Japanese in such countries.

This intelligence function continued to be central both in the planning and training phases and later in the execution of the mission in Japan.

Should Japan capitulate rather than resist invasion step by step, civil censors were to prohibit temporarily all external and internal communications. Upon restoration, internal mails and phone calls would be subject to spot checks; a fixed percentage of radiograms and telegrams would be examined at control points; and external communications would be placed under total censorship. In the postcombat and stabilized periods, restrictions would be removed gradually.

The plan directed the War Department to procure and train censors for Japan from Army and Navy officers and enlisted men, United States civilians (including Japanese-Americans), and, in a departure from previous thinking, also indigenous civilians—approximately 400 officers, 1,500 enlisted men, and 2,500 civilians. Navy officers and enlisted men were to specialize in electrical communications; the Army was responsible for most of the remaining duties, utilizing Women's Army Corps officers whenever possible. All Army and Navy officers were required to take three months of training in civil censorship, followed by six months in a Japanese language and area training program, comparable to that being given to prospective civil affairs officers. "Fluency will not result from this course, but the basic language requirement will be met"— and so, presumably, the basic culture requirement. Supervising officers were to meet still higher standards of fluency and be "highly qualified" in the language. In February 1945, the War and Navy departments began sending the first contingent of officers specially selected for such duties to the Civil Affairs training schools at the University of Michigan and the University of Chicago. Also, enlisted men were chosen for separate language, area, and censorship instruction under the Army Specialized Training Program. Plans for screening and clearing indigenous personnel were developed later. The emphasis on recruitment of Japanese nationals in subordinate positions was an obvious recognition of the language barrier. But it also reflected another basic policy decision to work through friendly or cooperative Japanese in carrying out the aims of the occupation.[9]

Still in question is how the mass media came to be included under the jurisdiction of the civil censorship mission in occupied Japan, for the War Department's plan made no explicit provision for newspapers or for radio broadcasts.[10] Equally important is how censorship for purposes of security and intelligence, standard practice in wartime and in the early stages of transition to peace—and commonplace in wartime Japan and its empire—broadened to include assistance in Japan's ideological reorientation. How did the dual functions of civil censorship and media guidance in occupied Japan come to be exercised by two quite different arms of the SCAP bureaucracy, the Civil Censorship Detachment of the Civil Information Section and the Information Division of the Civil Information and Education Section?

Civilian planners in the government were instrumental in shaping the outcome in 1945. The Army's civil censorship preparations showed signs of coordination with civilian agencies and deference to civilian controls. Of particular interest as the planning process matured and the papers for Japan became more detailed and elaborate, 1943–45, are the views of the State Department insofar as it gave firm leadership under the Constitution in advising the president on postwar foreign policy and defining American peace aims. Its functions embraced guidance to the OWI, the OSS, and the military in national propaganda themes and psychological warfare.

In March 1943, East Asian experts attached to the State Department's Division of Political Studies, a secret research and postwar policy planning unit, raised a crucial question in a lengthy prospectus on Japan which they had drawn up for the Political Affairs Subcommittee of Roosevelt's Advisory Committee on Post-War Foreign Policy: "To what extent should it [the United States] participate in measures to secure a change in Japanese political philosophy through supervision of the education system and of other media of indoctrination?" The authors—George Blakeslee, Hugh Borton, and John Masland, all recent recruits from universities and specialists in the politics, history, or international relations of Japan and East Asia—were then in the beginning stages of their work and sorting out the various issues which they believed were most likely to concern the United States in postwar East Asia.[11]

Blakeslee and Borton, who remained with the Japan planning process throughout the war and into the postwar period, were not enthusiastic about extreme interference with Japan's institutions, including the media. Essentially moderate and cautious reformers, who took the Atlantic Charter seriously, they questioned the lasting qualities of externally enforced reforms and had qualms about the victors infringing upon the sovereign rights of the defeated. Blakeslee believed that "it might not be possible to go much further than to require the freedom of the press and radio from governmental control." In other words, he would set the media free and let the Japanese say and write whatever they wished. He had not yet addressed the question of whether or how to foster changes in Japanese thought other than possibly changing the school system. Borton argued that the shock of defeat would in itself do much to discredit militarism and totalitarianism, though he conceded that the Japanese would require additional education in the advantages of democratic government and their responsibilities as world citizens. There should be some indication, he added, in the terms of surrender of United Nations policies on censorship and control of the media.[12] Borton's prescription at this midway point during the war in effect was: 1) elimination of propaganda controls imposed by Japan's militaristic government, and 2) initiation of "unprejudiced dissemination of news and information" by requiring free speech and inquiry in a Japanese bill of rights. This early formula was challenged and considerably recast before adoption of the final policies in 1945.

By early spring 1944, planning in the State Department had been reorganized and many more papers on Japan had been produced, most of them by the Interdivisional Area Committee on the Far East (IDACFE), a group chaired by Blakeslee and composed of Japanese-language Foreign Service officers, Japan experts in the postwar research unit, and specialists from various economic and cultural divisions. When the Postwar Programs Committee (PWC), one of two high policy committees in the State Department, first sat in judgment on the preliminary drafts, the members were highly critical of several of the recommendations, labeling them too lenient and sending the experts back to their drawing boards. Assistant Secretary of State Adolph Berle, for example, declared that too much attention was being given to changes in the political machinery. He insisted that the Japan planners focus "on the ideas and principles which would guide the Japanese political structure into desirable channels. To this end," he explained, "we should discover what liberal thought and forces exist in Japan for altering the direction of emotion and thought of the Japanese people and ascertain the means through which these forces could be used most effectively." In essence, he was asking IDACFE to think through the question of ideological reorientation.[13]

The PWC was then also debating recommendations on the elimination of aggressive nationalism in Germany by effecting "fundamental" changes in and attitudes "toward war and ultranationalism." A paper of May 4 on German reeducation was to have implications for Japan. It stated that long-term United States security rested as much on reform of the German outlook as on the imposition of military and economic controls. The victors "should attempt to bring about the psychological disarmament of the German people as rapidly as possible through a carefully planned program of reeducation." This program was conceived as "a positive reorientation of German thinking, through internal reconstruction aiming toward democratic experience and through the revival of the finer aspects of the German tradition." This required effective utilization of the press, cinema, and radio, not for indoctrination, said the authors, but rather for "the widest possible dissemination of accurate information for free discussion, and for the renewal of untrammeled cultural activity."[14] Even this, ultimately, would not be seen as sufficiently positive.

Borton was handed the Japan assignment, producing in early May a new paper, "Abolition of Militarism and Strengthening of Democratic Processes." On the media, he stated:

Liberal thought and democratic processes might be strengthened by:
1. Freedom of the press, radio and motion pictures except for ideas subversive of the aims of the United Nations.
2. Freedom of discussion except as it might endanger security.
3. Elimination of restrictions on liberal education.
4. Explanation through press, radio and motion pictures of the meaning of personal liberties in a democracy.

At about the same time, Blakeslee for consistency also expanded and rewrote a paper for IDACFE on general postwar objectives of the United States in occupied Japan to incorporate the "encouragement of democratic thought through the press, radio, cinema, and schools." This time, both papers were approved by the PWC.[15]

The basic ideas, still vague and general, were further developed in a separate IDACFE paper on the media of public information and expression. Drafted in early July by an experienced Japanese-language Foreign Service officer, Beppo Johansen, it too retained the cautious approach. Mindful of the overall goal of promoting freedom of expression in Japan, Johansen recommended that controls over Japan's media—identified as the press, radio, motion pictures, and drama—be held to a minimum. Referring specifically to "censorship," he said it should be limited to ideas "clearly dangerous to security or subversive of the aims of the United Nations" and coupled with assurances to the Japanese that a cooperative attitude would lead to a rapid relaxation of controls. Under appropriate supervision and censorship (Johansen was not explicit about the mechanics), Japanese newspapers should continue to publish. Later on, when the occupiers had established proper surveillance, periodicals, which Johansen characterized as less important to the general public than newspapers, might resume publication. Japanese laws which prevented freedom of the press should, of course, be eliminated. And measures which encouraged writers and publishers in the expression of liberal opinions (the accent was on liberal) should be instituted. The victors should directly operate radio broadcasting facilities, the most important means of communication in the early stages of the occupation, in order to give the Japanese people essential information and instruction at fixed hours. They should also remove restrictions against the use of short-wave receivers in Japan. The showing of films and the staging of plays, though necessary for relaxation and entertainment, should not be authorized without prior clearance by the military government.[16]

Here, in embryonic form, were notions of precensorship. Johansen, however, did not conceive of censorship and control as broadly as they were subsequently practiced by SCAP. He and IDACFE were not calling for sweeping interference with the flow of ideas. Nor were they making clear distinctions between the functions of guidance and censorship. In all of the papers, security needs were recognized as paramount. By mid-1944, civilian planners had accepted the necessity of a certain amount of censorship and news control in occupied Japan but were also aware, sometimes painfully, of the conflict with advocacy of civil liberties. Whatever the contradictions and tensions, this policy was deemed to be preferable to Japan's existing forms of thought control and intellectual isolation.

The moderate tone of the planning papers was noted with disfavor by other officials in the Department of State and by specialists in other departments or wartime agencies—the War and Navy departments, the OWI, and the OSS. Within the War Department, John J. McCloy, assistant secretary of war, was following closely the planning process for postwar Germany and would later do the same for Japan. He had been important, together with Secretary of War Stimson, in revising and toughening the State Department's preliminary plans for Germany, while rejecting the pastoral line of Treasury Secretary Morgenthau, and he favored stringent controls

over the German press, communications, and education in order to
bring about "fundamental reform in German objectives and public
opinion."[17]

The OWI, similarly, having gained considerable experience as the
propaganda agency of the American government, wished to offer
advice on postwar information and cultural programs in defeated
nations—both the content of the programs and measures to operate
them. Its intelligence analysts believed that "the information and
ideas given to Japan immediately after defeat" through radio, censorship, news service, and adult education "will be more potent in
the long run program of education" even than reforms in the schools.
Claude Buss, head of the San Francisco office of the OWI, spoke in
1944 of the need "to debunk Japanese spiritual policy." The OWI's
director, Elmer Davis, a well-known journalist and radio commentator before the war, was passionately convinced of the need to use
the radio and other media, "the prime instruments of psychological
and political warfare," to reeducate defeated peoples, preserve the
peace, and build a better world. He repeated these convictions in
correspondence with the secretary of state and Presidents Roosevelt
and Truman. As the war was ending, Davis had a strong ally in
Archibald MacLeish, librarian of Congress, who was appointed assistant secretary of state for public and cultural relations in the
departmental reorganization of December–January, 1944–45. Mac-
Leish was intent upon retaining an American information program
in the postwar world and became deeply involved in general and
technical questions related to reorientation as a means to combat
fascism, an ideological crusade he had embarked upon as head of the
short-lived Office of Facts and Figures, 1941–42, and as an assistant
director of the OWI, 1942–43. Political and moral reeducation was
the chief task of the occupation of Germany, he wrote to the new
secretary of state, James Byrnes, in early July 1945, at almost the
same time that Davis was telling President Truman, "The central
problem of Germany is the reeducation of the German people, without which our other measures may be no more than temporary pal-
liatives."[18]

In the Research and Analysis Branch of the OSS, an analyst had
pointed out in October 1944 how few structural changes the State
Department's Japan planners seemed willing to make. This included a failure to face the necessity of "indoctrination of school
children with the glories of democracy as such" through radio, film,
and recordings or to deal with "the crudities of direct propagandizing." The policy for the press was "to maintain things as much as
possible." An OSS prospectus for a civil affairs guide on public rela-

tions and education, which was drawn up for an interdepartmental editorial committee in the fall of 1944, characterized public relations and education programs as "parts of the same problem" and described them as aiding in the maintenance of public order, the security of the occupying forces, the countering of Japanese propaganda, and "the reorientation of Japanese attitudes toward war and militarism."[19] This vision of the Research and Analysis Branch was close to MacArthur's later establishment of the Civil Information and Education Section (CI&E) in SCAP General Headquarters, with its dual functions of educational reform and information guidance.

In late 1944, under prodding from PWC, the State Department's planning paper on the Japanese media was rewritten to express a stricter approach. The revised version was more explicit about preventing and eliminating ultranationalist propaganda in Japan and utilizing the media to convey acceptable ideas, in essence liberal thought. At this stage all of the State Department's planning papers for Japan as approved by the PWC (and reendorsed by its successor body, the Staff Committee, under the new secretary, Edward Stettinius) were forwarded to the War and Navy departments for further study of the military implications and for guidance in work on a basic civil affairs directive for the theater commander. In addition, the State-War-Navy Coordinating Committee (SWNCC) was set up at the beginning of 1945 to coordinate and review planning at the assistant secretary level. SWNCC, in turn, appointed a Subcommittee on the Far East, chaired by Eugene Dooman, the leading Japanese-speaking Foreign Service officer and counselor of embassy under Ambassador Joseph Grew in Tokyo, 1937–41. The Grew-Dooman connection remained very close and was of extreme importance in 1945 when Grew was undersecretary and acting secretary of state.[20] These changes led to closer scrutiny of plans, rethinking, further debate, and some new conclusions.

As the war with Germany was drawing to a successful close in the spring of 1945 and island fighting in the Central Pacific, together with MacArthur's land campaigns in the Philippines, brought the Americans and Allies closer to Japan, there was a push for more concrete preparations in Washington and in the combat theaters. Even then, the war with Japan ended too suddenly for the adoption of final, detailed plans. In early April, SWNCC's Subcommittee for the Far East asked the State Department to prepare a new policy paper on the "Control of Media of Public Information and Expression in Japan," attaching an explicit request for a discussion of the characteristics of the Japanese media and of measures to prevent the dissemination of subversive ideas while conveying information about the United Nations. This time the assignment was given not to Japan hands in the research division or to Foreign Service desk officers but to John Begg, head of the Division of International Information, which fell under the supervision of MacLeish. Begg was quite willing to cooperate informally with the OWI in drawing up recommendations. In May, MacLeish held a State Department conference on reeducation, with prominent educators as consultants. They concluded that reorientation, to be successful, must be part of an integrated, comprehensive program for Germany's rehabilitation and should utilize the mass media. Working with MacLeish in organizing the conference and writing the papers was Gorden Bowles, an anthropologist who was born in Japan. Bowles, who had recently joined the Division of Cultural Cooperation, was shortly given the task of writing SWNCC's planning paper on educational reform. And in August, together with Borton, he was asked to prepare recommendations on reorientation of the Japanese. About the same time the OSS set to work on a detailed study of public information in Japan—its national censorship policy and measures for disseminating official news.[21] What Americans later attempted to do in Japan was conditioned by their understanding of the existing system of thought control and its damaging effects on the Japanese mind.

The military planners were also moving ahead. The JCS, while reviewing their plans for an invasion of the Japanese home islands, made Japan into a separate theater of operations. In early April, they created a new command for MacArthur—CINCAFPAC, Commander in Chief, United States Army Forces in the Pacific—and directed him to make preparations for the campaign in Japan, beginning with Operation Olympic, the invasion of Kyushu in November 1945. In early May, he was put in charge of military government for Japan and a few weeks later formally assigned all responsibility for civil censorship; any existing plans were to be transferred to him, whether from Washington or from Nimitz' headquarters. By then, MacArthur's officers had accumulated considerable experience as civil censors in the Philippines. A Civil Censorship Detachment (CCD) had been organized under the jurisdiction of military intelligence, USAFFE (United States Army Forces Far East, MacArthur's prior command), headed by Lieutenant Colonel Donald D. Hoover, the theater's civil censorship officer. It was Hoover, a former newspaperman, who drew up the preliminary plans for Japan in April and in July, and who devised the press and radio codes for the Japanese in September during the first weeks of the occupation.[22]

Hoover's preliminary plan for Japan, dated April 20, even before the formal transfer of planning authority to MacArthur, was based on JCS 873/3 and on guidance from the War Department and the United States Office of Censorship. He anticipated revisions and expansions. His draft also drew from the plan for Germany, but was "considerably more strict," and covered all civilian communications—the mails, telegraph and telephone facilities, and travelers' documents but exempting "the censorship of press communications or radio broadcast scripts which in this theatre are the responsibility of the Public Relations Officer, GHQ." There was a cryptic reference to censorship of press and radio information by appropriate authorities before passage through civilian communications channels. As before, the mission was defined as military security, counterespionage, and collection of intelligence. Though the measures would be strict, they were "of a nature comprehensible to the Japanese, who imposed similar controls in the Philippines; and presumably in other occupied areas." A "Special Report on Japanese Censorship in the Philippines" had incidentally concluded that Japanese civil and military censorship there had been more restrictive than the American. "It was controlled by the notorious Kempei Tai, and was imposed on mail, telecommunications, newspapers, periodicals, motion pictures and the educational system."

Hoover expected to employ "a considerable number of civilian nationals" as translators, "in positions where they would not have access to classified material." Officers in the advance units in Japan would come from the CCD, "supplemented by officers now in training in the United States and elsewhere." Other officers and enlisted men might be reassigned from the Allied Translator and Interpreter Service. The plan frankly declared, "Inasmuch as Civil Censorship will be operating in an enemy country, rigid controls will be imposed." Externally, a ring would be drawn around Japan. Internally, all communications making mention of "troop movements, criticism of Allies, codes, politics, rumors, any subject disturbing public tranquility" would be destroyed. These forbidden topics were standard in all censorship plans, apparently, and not peculiar to conditions in Japan. Violations would be punishable by a military tribunal.[23]

Hoover went to Washington for further consultation with the War Department and the United States Office of Censorship. Back in Manila, he drew up a revised plan, July 10, based on these discussions, AFPAC's "Basic Plan for Civil Censorship in Japan." It was more precise about recruitment of personnel and the procurement of technical equipment and supplies, but the mission in Japan was exactly the same and CCD was to carry it out through three projected periods of hostilities, posthostilities, and stabilization. There were some interesting new touches. In making use of indigenous civilians, Hoover was counting on an estimate that at least five percent of the total Japanese population could read English. To simplify the task of American censors in reading the mails, all letters were to be written only in *kaisho* or complete block form. The cursive styles, *gyōsho* and *sōsho,* were forbidden. If Japan capitulated, all types of communications would be prohibited, to be resumed only when staff was available to establish district stations. Since MacArthur had also been ordered by the JCS in June to make plans for Japan in the event of sudden surrender or capitulation, Hoover began working on contingency planning, known as Blacklist Operations, to set up a skeletal organization in the field immediately. Little progress had been made, however, when Japan actually surrendered. Furthermore, Hoover's plans had omitted the media, though Washington policy makers clearly intended that they be censored, if not by CCD then by some other segment in MacArthur's organization.[24]

The basic policy documents for Japan—MacArthur's bible—were in draft form by June 11: SWNCC 150, "Statement of Initial Post-Surrender Policy for Japan," primarily the work of the State Department; and a military government directive prepared by the Civil Affairs Division of the War Department. Both contained brief passages on information control, and the CAD directive, in addition, made overt references to censorship. SWNCC 150, drawing upon the language of the old PWC paper, simply required termination of the "dissemination of ideas subversive of the United States"and the substitution of "information and knowledge of the ideas and concepts in which the United States believes." There could, of course, not be termination of subversive ideas without censorship; and similarly there could not be substitution of approved ideas without information guidance. As the problems became clearer over the summer and gaps in the planning were spotted, this wording was revised and expanded. The initial policy of the United States, as endorsed by President Truman and sent to MacArthur in early September and made public on September 22 (SWNCC 150/4/A), was to encourage the Japanese "to develop a desire for individual liberties and respect for fundamental human rights, particularly the freedoms of religion, assembly, speech, and the press." Since this was a public document, the only reference to information guidance was oblique. "The Japanese people shall be afforded opportunity and be encouraged to become familiar with the history, institutions, culture, and the accomplishments of the United States and the other democracies."[25]

CAD's draft directive of June 11 was more explicit as was the ultimate version. The theater commander was ordered to prohibit "the dissemination of Japanese militaristic, National Shintoistic, and ultranationalist ideology and propaganda in any form." In accordance with JCS 873/3, he was specifically to "assume control of censorship of the press, printing, publications, radio, telephone, or cables" as were necessary for military security and to render Japan a peace-loving nation. Subject to these considerations and to the requirements of military security and maintenance of law and order, he was to "permit freedom of speech, press and religion." The Army and Navy planners in Washington tinkered with the phraseology in June and July and made some changes but without altering the thrust. A more advanced secret draft directive on civil affairs, hurriedly assembled in three parts (general and political, economic, and financial) after Japan's surrender, was sent by courier to MacArthur's headquarters in Manila on August 25 to assist theater planning for an occupation which was soon to begin. It added little to the original sections on information control and censorship except to emphasize that controls should be kept to a *minimum* and to define more extensively what was meant by the media.

> You will establish such minimum control and censorship of civilian communications including the mails, wireless, radio, telephone, telegraph and cables, films and press as may be necessary in the interests of military security and the accomplishment of the purposes set forth in this directive. Freedom of thought will be fostered by the dissemination of democratic ideals and principles through all available media of public information.[26]

MacArthur was presented with a difficult balancing act, but in an enemy country the requirements of security would take precedence over freedom of information. Also, the press, films, and radio were included in civil communications. MacArthur would have to decide where and how in his organization he would handle Washington's requirements.

The third chapter in MacArthur's bible, the Potsdam declaration of July 26, clarified unconditional surrender to include the removal of "all obstacles to the revival and strengthening of democratic tendencies among the Japanese people." Specifically, "freedom of speech, of religion, and of thought, as well as respect for fundamental human rights shall be established."[27] Nothing explicit was said

in this public document about civil censorship and information guidance other than the reference, again oblique, to the establishment of
respect for human rights. But the declaration was not all-inclusive,
and MacArthur was to receive and interpret his ultimate orders
not only as an Allied proconsul but also as an American theater
commander.

The fourth chapter, perhaps the most crucial policy guidance
given to MacArthur, though it did not arrive in final form as a directive from the JCS until early 1946, was the "Positive Policy for
Reorientation of the Japanese." It was first proposed by the Navy
member of SWNCC, Artemus Gates, on July 19 while most of
Washington's high policy makers were away at Potsdam. In essence,
Gates wanted preparations to begin immediately for an integrated
and comprehensive program aimed at making changes in Japanese
ideologies and attitudes of mind. The occupiers were to see to it that
Japan's feudal mentality and chauvinism, its belief in divine mission, and its "extensive racial consciousness" were transformed into
wholesome, democratic, and peace-loving attitudes. Gates did not
propose "to recast the culture of the Japanese, but rather to use it, as
far as possible, in establishing new attitudes of mind conforming to
the basic principles of democracy and fair dealing." Perhaps "older
ethical standards of Japanese home and family life" could be emphasized. To gain the support and understanding of women, who
might otherwise resist out of conservatism, they should be given
equal educational opportunities. Moreover, such reeducation would
"only be effective as it goes hand in hand with some gradual improvement in the economic conditions of the ordinary Japanese."
Therefore, "the encouragement of appropriate agrarian and economic reforms should constitute an integral part of the program of
reeducation." To reach everyone and make the points effectively
would require utilization of all of the media, "including books,
textbooks, periodicals, motion pictures, radio, lectures, discussion
groups and the school system," and advance preparation of suitable
materials. Failure of the United States to develop an integrated
program for Japan might lead, Gates warned, to "prolonged unrest
and civil strife, coupled with the development of a political hegemony inimical to the best interests of the United States and the
future peace of the world." He alluded to the chaos existing for two
years in Italy and to criticism of American military government in
Germany. General Eisenhower had been given a similar assignment, more succinctly, for the American zone in Germany but had
not benefited from detailed advance preparations: "An affirmative
program of reorientation will be established designed completely to

eliminate Nazi and militaristic doctrines and to encourage the development of democratic ideas." Japan hands in the State Department, including Eugene Dooman, were inclined to scoff at the Gates memorandum as grandiose and idealistic, but in August Borton and Bowles were set to work on follow-up papers for SWNCC.[28] Couriers were constantly going back and forth between the War Department and theater headquarters and there can be no doubt that MacArthur saw these and other recommendations in their earlier as well as final versions.

In the meantime, the gaps and omissions in AFPAC theater planning for press, film, and radio controls were noted by Brigadier General William Crist, who had been selected as MacArthur's chief military government officer for Japan. He arrived in Washington from Okinawa in mid-July for a briefing from the War Department on civil affairs planning for Japan. On July 23, he cabled Manila, asking about the status of AFPAC's planning for control of the Japanese information services (as distinct from civil censorship), including press, radio, and entertainment. He pointed out that in the European theater the Psychological Warfare Division of Eisenhower's headquarters, an outfit which integrated personnel from the OWI, had been converted into the "Information Control Division of Theater Headquarters." Did MacArthur, he asked, intend to follow the European pattern "by projecting your Psychological Warfare Branch into post-hostilities period," or did he wish information control to be an activity of military government—and fall therefore under Crist? General Crist recommended the European pattern, together with close reliance upon a small OWI planning staff to set up operations in Japan.[29]

If Crist's advice were followed, information control in Japan would fall under Brigadier General Bonner Fellers, MacArthur's military secretary, who had doubled since late 1944 as head of the Psychological Warfare Branch (PWB). Fellers was trusted by MacArthur, having been his military aide in the prewar Philippines. Fellers had also served a tour of duty in Japan in the late 1920s. During the Philippines campaign, he and his chief executive officer, Colonel J. Woodall Greene, had worked closely with OWI operatives in waging combat psychological warfare. Fellers had decided views about the continued utilization of the Japanese emperor and the imperial institution and about Japanese military psychology, and he seems to have exercised considerable influence over MacArthur at the end of the Pacific war and the beginning of the occupation. Like MacArthur, he was interested in Republican politics back home.[30]

MacArthur, however, was at first inclined to place information control under military government. But while he pondered the advice, his staff continued working on the Blacklist Operations for postsurrender entry into Japan and the establishment of direct though limited control over the Japanese government. Both MacArthur and Washington favored maximum utilization of Japanese governmental agencies, but the planners had to prepare for any eventuality, including the possibility of collapse of the Japanese government. MacArthur activated the Military Government Section (MGS) on August 5, before Crist returned to Manila, and the original organizational charts made provision for public information functions. The Military Government Annex, August 6, to Blacklist Operations, which was drafted in Washington and brought to Manila as a model for the fledgling Military Government Section, contained several passages on information control. Following faithfully the language and intent of SWNCC 150 and the CAD draft directive, it prohibited the dissemination of militaristic ideologies and propaganda "in any form." For the purposes of substituting American propaganda to destroy Japanese militarism and its supporting ideology, the annex contemplated broad controls by occupation authorities over every conceivable kind of Japanese information, news, and entertainment media and meeting place, ranging from radio, press, news agencies, telephone, telegraph, and wireless facilities to publishing and printing plants, paper stock, public libraries, concert and opera halls, film and live theaters, assembly points, shrines, restaurants, geisha houses, and picnic grounds. Freedom of speech, press, religion, "and (eventually) freedom of assembly" were, however, to be permitted "as soon as practicable," subject to the requirements of security and law and order. The Cabinet Board of Information (the official propaganda agency of the Japanese government) and Dōmei (the government controlled news agency) would either continue under regulation or be partly abolished, whatever best suited the immediate needs of the occupation.

Manila's handling throughout August of contingency plans for military government is of interest in revealing the predilections and attitudes of MacArthur and his staff and their compliance with instructions from Washington. It also indicates the degree of their knowledge about Japan. For some of MacArthur's men, it was hard to believe that after such a brutal war it would be possible to walk into Japan without combat or fanatic resistance. The plans further show jockeying for position and power on MacArthur's staff during the coming period of occupation. There was a constant review and revision of theater documents, including operations instructions and annexes, as drafts and final versions of research and policy papers arrived from Washington and as estimates were made of the situation in Japan. Gradually, the distinctions between missions of civil censorship and of propaganda were sorted out.[31]

Both in Washington and in Manila, OWI officials were greatly concerned about proper machinery for the postcombat control of information in Japan. John Embree, in prewar life an eminent sociologist and the author of a classic study on a Japanese village, was on temporary assignment in the Pacific for the OWI. In a letter of August 2 to his chief in Washington, George Taylor, he suggested, "If MacArthur takes over all psychological warfare and consolidation work in the Japanese area, something really effective should be done in Washington to enforce a United States Government rather than a local theater line in American information programs directed to Japanese populations." The fundamental problem Embree alluded to was the reorganization of the wartime OWI into a peacetime international information service located in the State Department and following approved national propaganda lines. The OWI became the Interim International Information Service (IIIS) on August 31, and a few months later was succeeded by the permanent Office of International Information and Cultural Affairs (OIC). Several Japan specialists in the OWI—and also the OSS—transferred at this time to the State Department as information and intelligence experts.[32]

While waiting for instructions, OWI personnel in the Philippines had already begun assembling approved films and publications in early August for shipment to Japan and were attempting to arrange for rebroadcasts of OWI programs produced in San Francisco and Honolulu (a Voice of America for Japan). They were considerably bolstered by the presence of Bradford Smith, chief of OWI's Central Pacific Operations and a prewar Japan hand, and by Harold Vinacke, member of the Japan desk in Washington and senior OWI representative in the Far East. Smith, who had once taught English in Japan, and his colleagues produced in mid-August an operational plan covering all of the media and turned it over to General Fellers.[33]

It was at precisely this point, as Japan formally surrendered, that Fellers decided Crist and the European theater had the right idea about information work. He prepared a brief paper on August 15 ("Dissemination of Information in Japan") in which he recommended using PWB personnel for such responsibilities. "The aim of PWB," he said, "would be to turn over to Japanese the dissemination of information as rapidly as can be justified, subject only to military censorship." In a subsequent version of August 22 ("Basic Military Plan for the Control of the Dissemination of Information in Japan")—and by then a Japanese team had been to Manila to discuss surrender formalities and preparations for MacArthur's entry into Japan—Fellers called for the continued operation of broadcasting agencies, news agencies, and visual media by Japanese personnel under the supervision of the converted PWB, which he wished to redesignate as the Information Control Section. This time, Mac-Arthur, who was beginning to receive much more detailed and specialized guidance from Washington, including the JCS draft directive and an emergency directive on information control, agreed. On August 27, even before the occupation officially began, the Information Dissemination Section (IDS), AFPAC, was set up under Fellers. This was a direct forerunner of the Civil Information and Education Section (CI&E), SCAP, and represents the first of several diminutions of the functions of MGS until it was dissolved on October 2.[34]

There were still unsettled questions about the mission, functions, and jurisdiction of civil censorship. Who would take charge of the press, radio, and film censorship ordered by the JCS draft directive? Apparently, Brigadier General Legrande A. Diller, MacArthur's chief public relations officer, had been toying with the prospect. By August 18, he had prepared a guide for censoring the press and radio releases of army and naval forces in the Pacific, but it applied to foreign correspondents and not to the activities of Radio Tokyo, the Japanese press, or Dōmei. All information about troop movements, major events, or plans for the occupation of Japan, for example, must come from authorized SCAP sources. Secrecy would be maintained on such technical information as the atomic bomb. Japanese military and civilian personnel were not to be identified as war criminals without clearance by General Headquarters. President Truman, who was already suspicious of MacArthur and contemptuous of the general's grandstanding ego, ordered competitive news coverage of the formal surrender ceremony. Further thought and additional guidance must have convinced MacArthur that the job of monitoring Japan's media was much too big and complex for the public relations staff. That assignment would go shortly to CCD, which had been placed since July under the Office of the Chief of Counterintelligence, G-2, General Elliot Thorpe.[35]

MacArthur's ultimate arrangements in late August and early September as the occupation began were based upon a continued, if fitful, flow of recommendations from Washington and by the ability of the Japanese government to remain in existence. The final formula for information control in early occupied Japan was twofold, embracing 1) the negative aims of ridding the Japanese of objectionable ideas (as determined by the United States), eliminating objectionable or unfriendly Japanese from operation of the media, and dissolving prewar and wartime Japanese government controls over the press, publications, radio, and films; and 2) the positive goals of providing approved radio scripts, books, and other publications and phonograph records, which contained concepts of democracy and of individualism and information about the history and culture of the United States. This left room, it was believed, for a freer flow of information than in wartime Japan, including the import of publications from the European democracies and the Soviet Union. Specifically, the final recommendations to MacArthur drew heavily upon the reeducation and reorientation thinking in Washington, research by the OSS, emergency guidance by the OWI, and last-minute State Department and SWNCC policy planning papers on the Japanese media.

If the Japanese system was to be changed, by what model should it be altered? How much was known about prewar and wartime Japanese journalism or the internal operations of the film and radio industries? What did American analysts understand of thought control in Japan? Did the good 1920s and bad 1930s interpretation apply? The OSS, in outline notes on the media drafted in May and circulated to civilian and military planners, had focused on the dominant role of the Cabinet Board of Information in the dissemination of official news and determination of propaganda lines. Censorship controls were described as repressive and extensive, covering the press, radio, motion pictures, phonograph records, and the theater. The Japanese press was subject, for example, to prepublication censorship by police censors attached to newspaper offices. Publishers of magazines were required to send postpublication copies to the Home Ministry for scrutiny. Radio scripts were checked prior to broadcasts, and films before screenings. The notes, while stressing the pervasiveness of controls from 1937 to 1941, also pointed to more liberal news policies under the Koiso cabinet. "In recent months," for example, "the Japanese public has been fairly well informed as to the true situation." In June, a source judged highly reliable by the OSS, reported relaxation of press censorship by the new Suzuki cabinet. "Publications, public speeches and even government controlled radio" give news surprisingly near the truth, "including the extent of air raid damage," and political writers were expressing their personal views.

By August, the OSS was finishing a mammoth research paper on "Public Information in Japan." Rich in detail, it further described the formulation of public opinion in Japan, both by the exercise of government controls and the activities of private groups; the operations of the Cabinet Bureau of Information under the General Mobilization Law; the general characteristics and history of the press; the controls over the publication of books, magazines, and pamphlets; and basic features of the Japan Broadcasting Corporation and its radio audience and of the motion picture industry, including entertainment films, cultural films, and newsreels.[36] This kind of technical information was useful to those who drafted the final policies and orders, both before and after Japan's surrender, and later to MacArthur's staff in dismantling Japan's wartime controls.

Hastily, two drafts of a media paper were produced in quick succession in early August and under the auspices of SWNCC's Subcommittee for the Far East, "Control of the Media of Public Information and Expression in Japan." More comprehensive than the old PWC paper, the August 10 draft was probably the work of John Begg's division in the State Department and owed much to the current obsession with reorientation of the Japanese mentality. In the usual SWNCC format for policy papers, it provided relevant remarks on the Japanese press, publishing industry, radio broadcasting, and film-making to back up its statement of the problem and policy recommendations. It commented, for example, that the large metropolitan dailies were "comparable to large Western papers in news coverage, equipment, and public service activities," but had always been subject to various kinds of government control. In the period before 1941, books and magazines were published in greater numbers in Japan than in the United States, and, at one point, more feature films were produced in Japan than in any other country. Radio broadcasting was a government monopoly, and the central stations were believed to have excellent facilities. Not only did radio scripts fall under precensorship, but offensive programs could be cut off while on the air.

In view of these facts and the overall purposes of the occupation, the paper cautioned that any information program designed for Japan should be feasible and operational. The main task of military government would necessarily be supervisory (a reference to the language problem), and considerable reliance should be placed on cooperative Japanese personnel and existing channels of information. The media specifically were to be utilized for: 1) the immediate objective of communicating orders and explaining to the Japanese people the purposes of the occupation; and 2) the long-range objective of eliminating militarism, reorienting the Japanese toward a more international outlook, and creating the conditions for continued freedom of expression in the postoccupation period.

To accomplish these aims, the occupation authorities in the initial emergency period (an invasion was still a possibility) should provide information directly through available Japanese facilities while identifying trustworthy Japanese personnel. In the postemergency period, reliable Japanese should be allowed to operate the media but under supervision and guided by appropriate regulations. Only vague clues were offered as to the content of this guidance: ban anything prejudicial to military security or to the aims of the occupation. Enforcement might be by pre- or postproduction censorship, suspension, confiscation, or fines. "However, these regulations should be progressively relaxed." In the case of the press, suitable and willing Japanese should be allowed to reestablish publication of the dailies, at first under military government direction and later by a system of licensing cooperative publishers. Dōmei should be allowed to resume its domestic news operations, subject to censorship, after cooperative leaders were found, but it should be freed from government control, converted into a private press association, and cut off from government funding. Competitive news services, both domestic and foreign, should be allowed to develop. Military government should take over radio facilities immediately, giving the Japanese people information and instruction "at fixed hours" and withdrawing only when suitable Japanese personnel could be licensed to operate the system. Bans on owning short-wave sets should be lifted. The paper was noncommittal on breaking up monopoly broadcasting, a reform which Begg had been pushing. Films were to be placed under stringent rules. In the initial period, only the military government was to supply, distribute, and exhibit approved foreign and Japanese feature films, documentaries, and newsreels. Later on, even when the Japanese took over, preproduction and predistribution censorship of films was to continue.

The paper concluded with a set of approved information themes to guide military government officers in preparing materials for the Japanese media: compliance with military government, the role of militarism and aggressive nationalism in bringing ruin and suffering to Japan, the need for reorientation of political thinking to nonmilitaristic and international outlooks, the true story of the war as seen by the United Nations, American life and institutions, and the importance of international organization and agreements.[37]

Concurrently, with surrender now imminent, the OWI and State Department, with assistance from Army and Navy planners, began working on a Draft Directive for Emergency Information Control in Japan. After revision and clearance, it was cabled to MacArthur on August 22 "for such guidance as you may desire." It reflected Washington's major shift in emphasis from limited military government to an indirect occupation (SWNCC 150/3). Since Japan had formally surrendered without an invasion, there would be no initial period of direct takeover of the media. The new policy was to maintain and utilize the existing Japanese information services and personnel (insofar as possible "trustworthy pro-democratic civilian information personnel") for a period of about two weeks—that is to adapt the Cabinet Board of Information, Dōmei, and the Japan Broadcasting Corporation (NHK) to the needs of the occupation. The press was to operate under postcensorship, and American censors were to monitor broadcasts. Films, however, were temporarily banned. For world news and pictures, MacArthur's Headquarters and OWI files were to be "the sole and exclusive source." Several negative guidelines were recommended for censorship of domestic news: no publication of items "prejudicial to public order and safety," such as criticism of the surrender terms and Allied control measures; no suggestion of disunity among the Allied powers toward Japan; no praise or pity for Japanese taken into custody; no attribution of promises to the Allied powers "save on the basis of direct textual quotations from official documents reported without comment or interpretation." MacArthur was to use his judgment in adopting measures for libraries, theaters, rallies, and periodicals.[38] Obviously, MacArthur would have to make provision very soon somewhere in his Headquarters for censorship of the press, radio, and films.

MacArthur concurred in the recommendations, except for a misunderstanding about the banning of films, which was intended by Washington to be in effect only for the emergency phase of about fifteen days. "Under proper control of censorship," MacArthur replied, "motion pictures are not only a vehicle of education and propaganda but have become such a medium of relaxation that their stoppage would tend to transfer the interest of the population to the more sinister forms of activity." He concluded, revealing his own thinking about Japanese psychology, "The introduction of American films would be one of the best methods of combating mysticism and fanaticism of this people." Colonel Hoover, in a prompt response to the latest policy change, told his advance CCD units preparing to enter Japan not to seize or stop communications "unless expressly directed."[39]

Washington was so concerned about Dōmei, which had scooped the world with the story of Japan's surrender, August 10, and was embarking, as MAGIC diplomatic intercepts revealed, on national atomic bomb propaganda in its overseas news service, that it sent additional guidance a few days later, August 28. Dōmei's managing diector was to be made personally responsible to SCAP for obeying orders, and its personnel were to be carefully screened. The cable further stated that censorship requirements had the "highest priority" and were to prevail over "all information control directives when conflicting."[40]

At the end of August, then, just as MacArthur was about to leave the Philippines for Atsugi Airfield in Japan, he had received the latest revisions of the presidential basic policy statement and JCS draft directive, which conveyed the essence of all of this thinking at higher levels. And he had received explicit policy guidance on civil censorship and information control. But as these crosscurrents indicate, Washington and SCAP were still sorting out and differentiating the range and functions of media censorship and direction. In clarification, MacArthur notified the commanding generals of his supporting armies and air units, August 28, of the change in the concept of military government. The occupation would take place without combat and violence, and the Japanese government, together with imperial headquarters, would be utilized to effect the surrender and demobilization of Japan's armed forces at home and overseas. The occupying armies would become SCAP's agent to enforce orders and directives to the Japanese authorities. Civil communications would continue without interruption. "It is desirable that all commanders," he said, "take steps to ensure that in the occupation of Japan the priority rights of the Japanese are scrupulously respected. Actions contrary to universal standards of human behavior such as looting, pillage and rape will be severely dealt with. The behavior and conduct of our troops must be such as to instill in the minds of the Japanese people that the occupation is orderly, firm and lawful."[41]

Colonel Hoover arrived in Japan with his advance party about September 1 and began setting up minimal operations. His superior, General Elliot Thorpe, was also soon on the scene. SCAP instructions to the Japanese government on September 3 (SCAPIN 2) ordered it to keep communications facilities intact and in good repair, to utilize existing personnel in continued operations, and to provide access to this network for censorship or supervision. Already it was clear that the jurisdiction of CCD should increase to include the press, radio, and films. That same day, General Thorpe, in response to verbal instructions from MacArthur, formally assumed responsibility as chief of counterintelligence for censoring the mass media in addition to the mails and telecommunications. His advice in a memorandum to MacArthur was to tell the Japanese journalists and broadcasters what subjects were forbidden. Thorpe's preferences were to keep prohibitions to a minimum and to punish violations by suspension. He was comfortable with press censorship on a post-publication basis and radio censorship by spot checks. Dōmei would require close scrutiny. It was important that censors be "schooled carefully in what constitutes 'information that disturbs public tranquility,' which in the last analysis will be subjects the Supreme Commander does not desire discussed." Further explanations to the Japanese on forbidden themes might be given later at a meeting of representatives of publishers, editors, and broadcasters. Thorpe even entertained the notion of asking the emperor to issue an imperial rescript banning news which might disturb "public tranquility."[42]

The censorship organization, however, was not at full strength and had limited means of implementation. During the emergency period of the first two weeks, the Japanese press, radio, and Dōmei were allowed to continue domestic operations, as Washington had recommended, with CCD making only modest efforts to monitor the press and radio while simultaneously taking steps to impose controls over the mails and telecommunications and to impound prewar and wartime nationalistic publications. Dōmei also sent news dispatches overseas, and Radio Tokyo (technically the central station of NHK, Nippon Hōsō Kyōkai, Japan Broadcasting Corporation), though ordered on September 3 to stop foreign language broadcasts, simply switched to the English language for international programs. Allied correspondents began grumbling to MacArthur's press relations staff that Dōmei enjoyed unfair advantages in getting and sending news while they were subject to censorship. By this time, the Cabinet Board of Information had announced (August 28) that it would suspend wartime restrictions. The prime minister indicated the government would not strictly enforce repressive legislation, pending repeal by the Diet. With many of the old controls supposedly in abeyance and the new controls not yet operational, the Japanese media seemed to enjoy unaccustomed freedom as the occupation began. A controversial question ever since, and one worth careful research, is how well they handled their responsibilities. SCAP officials and foreign correspondents saw a reactionary, even duplicitous, press. But a recent study argues that it had begun to set a peaceful and constructive tone and was returning to its traditional role "as the guardian of the public good."[43]

On September 10, as occupation troops were moving into and securing Tokyo, a CCD inspired SCAPIN, which was very much in accord with the desires of Washington policy makers, gave the mass media new guidance along the lines of Thorpe's suggestions. This ten point press and radio code decreed "an absolute minimum of restrictions upon freedom of speech," but at the same time ordered the suppression of news "through newspapers, radio broadcasts, or other media of publication which fails to adhere to the truth or which disturbs the public tranquility." Other prohibited subjects were Allied troop movements, "false or destructive criticism of the Allied Powers, and rumors." The penalty for noncompliance, warned the SCAPIN, was suspension. The categories, though fairly standard and predictable, would also give CCD wide latitude for potential abuse. In a separate communication, September 10, NHK was again told to conduct only domestic operations and ordered to restrict broadcasts to "a single original outlet at Radio Tokyo." Initial programming was limited to news, entertainment, and music.[44]

To carry out CCD's expanded mission, a new unit was established in the organization on September 10—the Press, Pictorial, and Broadcast Division (PPB). Censors immediately began systematic postpublication surveillance of major Tokyo newspapers and prebroadcast censorship of Radio Tokyo news scripts. They moved into Dōmei's offices and took over part of the NHK building. As a result, within a matter of days, Dōmei was jolted by an overnight suspension for violating the code and transferred to precensorship. Within a week, two newspapers were briefly shut down as further examples to the press. CCD was furious with Dōmei, for example, for implying in its news service at home and overseas that the emperor had been more responsible for ending the war than Allied military superiority, for hinting that Japan had not surrendered unconditionally and therefore could negotiate with the Allies as an equal, and for spreading stories of misbehavior by American soldiers. An even more stringent set of censorship controls than originally anticipated by Washington was put into effect by November, when SCAP concluded that the Japanese were being deliberately uncooperative, irresponsible, and subversive.[45]

Most worrisome to SCAP, Dōmei's overseas news had begun attacking, as mentioned, the atomic bombings as the acts of a barbaric government. There was evidence that this was part of a conscious propaganda policy of the Japanese government to counter American stories of Japanese atrocities and to temper the harshness of the occupation. From MAGIC intercepts of Japanese diplomatic dispatches, American intelligence had learned that Japan's minister in Stockholm had warned the Foreign Ministry on August 29 about widespread distrust of Japan in Anglo-American public opinion as expressed in the European press. Yet Anglo-American opinion was also, he added, "deeply shocked at the use of the atomic bomb," and on the whole disapproving. He concluded that "the deep-seated suspicion of Japan on the part of the enemy makes it appear that rather severe measures will be taken in the handling of Japan." In his opinion, they should turn the situation around by exploiting atomic bomb sentiment. "Since it is difficult to justify the heavy damage inflicted and the massacre of hundreds of thousands of innocent people, there is an opportunity—by making use of the Diet, the radio, and various other means—to play on enemy weakness by skillfully emphasizing the extreme inhumanity of the bomb."

On September 10, the intercepts disclosed that the Japanese minister in Lisbon had characterized use of the atomic bomb as "a crime against humanity unparalleled in the pages of history." Japan had "adequate grounds for exposing" President Truman and Prime Minister Churchill "as violators of the laws of warfare." On September 13, Foreign Minister Shigemitsu Mamoru, MAGIC next learned, had advised Japan's legations in Sweden, Switzerland, and Portugal that:

> The newspapers have given wide publicity to the Government's recent memorandum concerning the atomic bomb damage in Hiroshima and Nagasaki, and the sending of an imperial messenger, the daily-rising count of dead, and the like. . . .
>
> All these reports have been sent abroad by Domei, in full detail. To what extent have they been carried by the newspapers and other media in your place?
>
> Since the Americans have recently been raising an uproar about the question of our mistreatment of prisoners, I think we should make every effort to exploit the atomic bomb question in our propaganda. If necessary, we shall telegraph further details. Please let me know by wire whether that would be desirable.

In reply, Berne and Stockholm told Tokyo, September 13 and 14, to avoid creating the impression that Japan was deliberately conducting an atomic bomb propaganda campaign. This same end could be accomplished unobtrusively, suggested Stockholm, by 1) having "announcements made exclusively for home consumption" and getting Anglo-American news agencies (UP, AP, INS) to "carry these announcements," and by 2) having "Anglo-American newspapermen write stories on the bomb damage and thus create a powerful impression abroad." MacArthur, who was on the receiving end of MAGIC intercepts, responded by restricting Dōmei on September 15 to the distribution of news inside Japan. The ban on Radio Tokyo's overseas broadcasts continued. When Tokyo newspapers proved reluctant to print an official statement on Japanese war criminals or use a release on Japanese atrocities in the Philippines, they were ordered to do so. MacArthur's public relations officers closely checked the dispatches of foreign correspondents. And a few weeks later, at the end of September, SCAP cut the Foreign Ministry's overseas radio communications.[46]

Stories about troop misbehavior were a cause of great alarm and brought further punishment to Dōmei. CCD learned of Dōmei reports in early September of numerous cases of rape, looting and robbery by American soldiers, of insults to the Japanese police, and of general rudeness. These items, in turn, were picked up by major newspapers and Radio Tokyo and spread throughout Japan. Such incidents had occurred, but in SCAP's view the Japanese media was magnifying sporadic or minor outbreaks into a crime wave. General Willoughby's official history labeled them "canards." Allied correspondents similarly charged that some of the incidents were alleged or even faked. MacArthur had taken the precaution on September 6 of issuing new orders to his commanders demanding disciplined troop behavior. And on September 9 he released a public statement calling directly upon the troops to respect the persons and property of the Japanese. "The occupation of Japan must take place without unnecessary violence, without undue oppression. Looting, pillage, rape and other deliberate violations of the universal standard of human behavior would but stain your high honor." The victors should practice the principles for which they fought. Dōmei nevertheless made new accusations on September 13. Obviously, until all points in Japan were secure and the temper of the Japanese people more fully ascertained, SCAP was anxious to avoid anything that might lead to civil unrest. Whether or not the stories were true or exaggerated, Dōmei was suspended for twenty-four hours on September 14, charged with disturbing public tranquility. Upon resumption of operations, it was placed for this and other indiscretions under complete precensorship along with the English language newspaper *Nippon Times*.[47]

As Dōmei's suspension was ending on September 15, Colonel Hoover gave a selected group of Japanese media people a tongue-lashing for ignoring instructions and not adhering to SCAP's code and announced that MacArthur had therefore ordered a more stringent censorship. He began by accusing the Japanese of publishing untrue statements and furthermore of knowing they were doing it. The news was so "colored" that the public was acquiring false ideas of the relative positions of the Japanese government and the Allied Powers. MacArthur, he declared, was extremely displeased. As Hoover proceeded to explain:

General MacArthur has decreed that there should be an absolute minimum of restrictions upon freedom of speech and discussion of matters affecting the future of Japan. His limitation was that this discussion could not be untrue, that it could not disturb the public tranquility and that it not be harmful to the efforts of right-thinking Japanese to help their nation emerge from defeat. Freedom of the press is very dear to the Supreme Commander, and it is one of the freedoms for which the Allies have fought.

You have demonstrated that the latitude provided in the directive cannot be entrusted to you. You have not met this responsibility co-operatively. In the days since your surrender you have revealed your lack of good faith in handling the news. Therefore, the Supreme Commander has directed a more severe censorship. Domei News Agency was suspended yesterday at 1729 hours, for the dissemination of news which disturbed the public tranquility. . . .

General MacArthur desires that it be clearly understood that the Allied Powers do not regard Japan as an equal in any way. . . .

The Supreme Commander will dictate orders to the Japanese government. . . . He will *not* negotiate with it. . . . The slanting of news must be discontinued immediately.

You are upsetting the public tranquility in that you do not give the truth to your people; you are creating an inaccurate picture of the true status of Japan.[48]

Frustrations with the Japanese press mounted. *Asahi Shimbun,* Tokyo's leading daily, was a serious problem to CCD. In stories, headlines, and editorials, it had minimized Japan's war guilt and was critical of the United States and of occupation authorities. It questioned accounts of Japanese atrocities in the Philippines, asserting that Japanese soldiers, as good husbands and fathers at home, could not have behaved so cruelly abroad and implying that American GIs in Japan were the ones capable of outrages. CCD got tough again. On September, the *Asahi* was closed down forty-eight hours for, in effect, inflammatory, false, and destructive reporting. On September 19, the *Nippon Times,* soon retitled the *Japan Times* as less "militaristic" and, of course, easier to scan for precensorship, was punished for attempting to publish an editorial alluding to "cases of petty criminal acts" by American troops, even though the incidents were described as "few and isolated." It was suspended for twenty-four hours.[49]

Colonel Hoover had in the meantime begun developing more elaborate press and radio codes (in conformity with ethical practices followed by American journalism), and these were approved as SCAPINs on September 19 and 22. They further explained what was banned: anything untruthful, disturbing to the public tranquility, tainted with propaganda, falsely critical of the Allied powers, or distorted by omission of facts or by editorial opinion. These stricter rules covered editorials, news stories, and advertisements in the press and applied to news, entertainment, and educational programs on the radio. CCD enforced the point again on October 1 by confiscating the September 29 issue of the prestigious weekly journal *Tōyō Keizai Shimpō* [Oriental economist], owned and edited by Ishibashi Tanzan, subject of a famous purge in 1947 and a future prime minister. It had contained an unsigned article charging that Americans would lose the respect of the Japanese because of "depraved" individual soldiers. They were a small number, perhaps, but still many more than the anonymous author thought safe or permissible. SCAP was spurred in its continuing crackdown by the attempt of the Japanese government on September 30, again in violation of SCAPINs, to confiscate copies of three major Tokyo dailies carrying an interview by two American reporters with the emperor and the famous photograph of General MacArthur in shirt sleeves and open collar, looming tall beside an uneasy Emperor Hirohito attired in morning coat, at their historic meeting a few days earlier.[50]

A revised plan for civil censorship in Japan was ready by September 30, stating what was by then a *fait accompli* — civil communications included the press, radio, pictures and films. Otherwise, it was close in basic principles to the original AFPAC draft of July, with an emphasis on full postcombat procedures to censor and control the flow of information to Japan, from Japan, and within Japan through civil facilities. A secret PPB manual, dated the same day, gave as the objectives of the division not only the determination of prohibited topics and the conduct of precensorship and postcensorship but also "the education of press, publishers, producers, and the people of Japan in the functions, advantages, and responsibilities of a free press." The mission of CCD had come a long way from military security and counterintelligence to incorporate Japan's reorientation and would precipitate rivalries with other SCAP officials, especially Civil Information and Education Section officers. On October 2, CCD was formally placed under the Civil Intelligence Section, one of several new special staff sections of General Headquarters, SCAP, which were created to replace the abolished omnibus Military Government Section.[51]

As SCAP's view hardened and PPB's personnel increased, systematic precensorship of the major vernacular newspapers in Tokyo was begun in early October, and the list shortly expanded to include several metropolitan dailies in Osaka and ultimately in Sapporo. Censored items had to be rewritten without any signs of deletions or excisions. The number of major precensored periodicals steadily increased, October through December, with particular interest displayed in publications of lesser circulation leaning toward ultranationalism or communism. The remaining newspapers and periodicals were postcensored. All books (except school texts being revised by CI&E) were added to the mandatory precensorship list in late October. Feature films and newsreels were brought under precensorship by demanding preproduction scenarios, as were theatrical performances, phonograph records, musical scores, artwork, and lantern slide shows by either hearings, screenings, or synopses. Ultranationalistic, militaristic, and feudalistic themes and scenes were taboo in motion pictures. As of January 1946, no film could be exhibited without a censorship identification number.[52]

While all of this was happening, Dōmei had decided to dissolve voluntarily, apparently fearful of SCAP's intentions, September 24, in ordering the separation of the Japanese press, news agencies, and radio broadcasting from government controls and suggesting that private enterprise should challenge the "present monopoly" in news distribution. Whatever the reason, Dōmei was succeeded in October by two private news services (Jiji and Kyōdō) which had no ties with the government. They nevertheless were monopolistic and employed many of the same personnel. Like their predecessor, these agencies, too, fell under complete precensorship. Although censorship of foreign correspondents through MacArthur's public relations staff ended on October 6, the Japanese press could not freely make use of materials it received from foreign news agencies.[53]

Two additional SCAP directives, inspired by Washington and initiated by CCD's staff, ordered the abolition of all wartime and peacetime restrictions imposed by the Japanese government on "freedom of the press and communications" and of "compulsory organizations of publishers and writers" (September 27) and the elimination of government barriers to freedom of speech in the motion picture industry (October 16). These particular SCAPINs, argued Willoughby's official report a few years later, "constituted the foundation for freedom of speech and press in postwar Japan." It was "neither paradoxical nor accidental" that civil censorship took these steps but was rather "a graphic demonstration" of its "fundamental character and actual objectives"—assistance in the gradual transplantation of full freedom of expression in Japan. According to this interpretation, the Japanese had their own hostility, incompetence, and immaturity to blame for three years of pervasive and thorough precensorship by occupation authorities. While the Japanese media were freeing themselves from "tyranny self-imposed" and the public was finding release from "years of indoctrination with ultra-nationalistic and militaristic concepts," CCD provided a necessary "incubation period" for the development of civil liberties by temporary prepublication censorship. CCD's action was, in other words, "a maternal screen for democratic media" and "a police force against anti-democratic propaganda." Without it, the official historian dramatically proclaimed, the civil rights mandated by the Potsdam declaration and granted by SCAP's directives "would have either been still-born or would have gone unexecuted for a long period."[54] There is no hint in this polemic of the contribution of Japanese journalism and broadcasting to their own reform and development of professional standards, but it captures precisely SCAP's rationale.

The dangers of civil censorship by an occupying military power, no matter how well-intentioned, were evident. John Embree, writing from Honolulu for the *New York Times Sunday Magazine,* September 9, predicted that the "provisions of the Potsdam proclamation for freedom of speech and of thought will remain mere formalisms so long as all Japanese media of communication are under strict army control. Paradoxically, there is likely to be less criticism permitted of our Army administration than the Japanese Government permitted of itself in the Japanese Diet." Captain Alfred L. Dibella, the first head of PPB, cautioned in early November that "the sound judgment of the censoring officers is the basic necessity." There must be self-awareness, but mistakes would be made. "The problem of censorship of the Japanese press and other media is one which is extremely sensitive." The existing policy, he believed, was "one of extreme liberalism in all respects," requiring that CCD not use censorship "as a force to propound any propaganda aims into the newspapers, even though those aims may be admirable." As examples of the kinds of criticism the Japanese could make, as long as it was "not *destructive* criticism," he gave: articles about President Truman's policies, solutions to the atomic bomb question, or policies of the occupying powers in Germany.[55] This was the tone Dibella wished to set, but would such power be exercised wisely or circumspectly, and how soon given up?

John J. Costello, Jr., Dibella's successor, 1946–48, and an editorial writer before the war, conceded when reminiscing many years later that mistakes were made but often in favor of the Japanese because of the time demands and physical difficulties of looking at so many materials. "I'm a newspaperman. I'm not a censor. I'm not an Army officer. My basic instincts are to be as little of a problem as you can, to do what you had to do, but make it as simple as possible, make it as easy as possible for people to get by the censorship. And there were very few taboos." All the rules really "boiled down" to two in practice—don't criticize the occupation (and "MacArthur would typify the occupation") and don't criticize the Allied Powers. Real precensorship in a country Japan's size would have taken an army of people. The limited amount PPB did do was necessary but transitional. For the Japanese press, "the system was set up," he said, "to pass stuff, not to stop stuff, because with the daily newspaper and the wire service, you cannot hold up copy without destroying [the news value]—they've got to have it fast." Also, the press people had become "pretty canny about censorship because we weren't the first censors." They had lived a long time with Japanese government restrictions and had learned a few tricks about getting things through. In addition, they subscribed to the services of three American news agencies, AP, INS, UP. If they had trouble printing one of the wire stories, the Japanese would run back to the American source, get leverage that way, and complain that occupation censorship was delaying an American story—not a Japanese story. "So we didn't get flak" from the Japanese. "We'd get flak from the AP, UP," or someone in the American press corps might file a story back home about MacArthur's press tyranny. A bad censorship decision would then lead to MacArthur's "catching hell" in the United States. There was in Costello's mind, through the "blur" of time, a memory of how much got through, not how much was banned. There was considerable free discussion in the newspapers and periodicals, he believed, despite censorship. "You've got to let some diversity of opinion," or there would be explosions. "So our job was a very, very sensitive position, and, as I say, we were not a politically indoctrinated group. You know, we were mechanics, and basically our job was to get the stuff out." Was the Japanese press, however, not only canny but also cautious and discreet? One wonders why the need was felt, if censorship was basically mild in intent or nominal, to ban as detrimental to American interests the following *haiku* (a poem in seventeen syllables) with its positive imagery of vegetable gardens in the ruins of a city: "Small green vegetables/Are growing in the rain/Along the burned street."[56]

But censorship was only half of the job of information control; another arm of the occupation *was* propounding propaganda themes into the newspapers and other media as well. General Fellers had begun developing the mission of information guidance in early September, though the Information Dissemination Section was to remain under his control for less than a month. If his guidelines for psychological warfare during the Philippines fighting were any precedent, there would be as much skillful manipulation of the media to protect and enhance MacArthur's image as to provide materials for reeducation. Fellers had ordered, for example, "no blackout on any accurate news" but with the reservation that "in our dissemination of information, news should be shaped and weighted so as best to serve the policy of the Commander-in-Chief." Fellers very early directed his executive assistant, Colonel Greene, to retain OWI and PWB personnel in the new section. One such person was Bradford Smith, who arrived at the IDS headquarters in the Customs House, Yokohama, September 7, from the OWI Manila outpost. Another was Lieutenant Colonel Harold Henderson, in prewar life a professor of Japanese language at Columbia University and during the war a specialist in propaganda leaflets and a member of Fellers' leaflet executive committee in the Southwest Pacific campaigns. IDS, in short, began with a handful of veteran psychological warfare and information officers who knew prewar Japan quite well.[57]

IDS objectives, as defined by Fellers on September 10 in a staff study (the same day that MacArthur sent CCD's first censorship code to the Japanese government) were: the preparation of programs for the Japanese press and radio, the provision of films for release through a central exchange, and the outlining of "new courses in liberal government for the schools." This initial policy embraced both education and reeducation and was clearly derived from SWNCC-JCS guidelines and OWI field experience. As Henderson later recalled, "his first job" in IDS "was to be the re-education of Japan," and he set about making contacts with his prewar Japanese friends—presumably the friendly or cooperative Japanese singled out in the policy papers. Others met with the Cabinet Board of Information and with editors, publishers, writers and filmmakers. The

War Department cabled its approval of IDS and told MacArthur
to give it "all necessary priority" in allocating personnel and
facilities.[58]

IDS moved to the Radio Tokyo building, September 13, shortly
after SCAP's flag raising ceremony at the Tokyo Embassy, but like
CCD was hampered by a lack of equipment and personnel. Smith
was upset with Japanese reporting. He thought Fellers' information
program was "innocuous" and Greene much too passive in simply
suggesting subjects and treatment to the Japanese press and radio
instead of issuing a positive "statement of guidance." Looking
ahead, he sent cables to Washington asking for suitable films, books,
magazines, pictures, and recordings in order to create a foundation
for future information libraries. As more consideration was given to
problems of information dissemination and reorientation, in essence
thought reform and propaganda, MacArthur decided to create the
Civil Information and Education Section (CI&E) on September 22
and to put a new officer in charge, Colonel Kermit (Ken) Dyke, soon
to be promoted to brigadier general. In setting up CI&E, MacArthur
brought the functions of educational reform, reorientation, and
media control closely together. The section was, in addition, to advise him on policies relating to religion, arts and monuments, and
social and cultural problems. Its information objectives were to
spread democratic ideas and principles through the mass media
(making the Japanese desire, it had been said, what Americans
wanted them to desire) and to confront the public with the facts of
the war and war guilt of its leaders. MacArthur reestablished CI&E
on October 2, without change of mission, when he set up GHQ,
SCAP.[59]

Dyke seemed to be an excellent choice to head CI&E. In prewar
civilian life, he had been vice-president for promotion and research
at NBC radio, and his specialty was advertising. After Pearl Harbor,
he had first worked for the OWI, and then in 1943 upon receiving his
Army commission, had joined MacArthur's headquarters in the
Southwest Pacific. As head of troop information and education,
Dyke's job was to bolster the morale of American soldiers and keep
them mentally alert and well informed.[60] His appointment was a
signal that the Japanese would begin to receive more extensive direction in reeducation and that it would be highly flavored with
American salesmanship techniques.

Bradford Smith, who served as Dyke's general adviser until November in the dual capacity of head of the Division of Plans and
Operations, CI&E, and senior IIIS representative in Japan, was de-
lighted with the change. The staff was still too small, but at least

CI&E's "sights were set." He found Dyke to be "a man with ideas, energy, organizing ability, and a good background in the business of information." Smith expected Dyke therefore to do a much better job than the earlier IDS military officers "who had been created media experts overnight" and had not pushed "a vigorous policy of controlling and guiding the Japanese press and radio." Since the occupation had not yet set up adequate press analysis, Smith further complained, the Japanese had been going their own way. "By emphasizing American strikes, overplaying stories of the misbehavior of American troops, and ignoring its responsibility to inform the people regarding war criminals," the press was in effect conducting "a successful propaganda campaign under our noses." Moreover, the old guard was trying to argue that the biggest danger in Japan was communism, not militarism, even persuading some members of the foreign press corps to fall for the line. Disappointed that Dyke stopped the plan to rebroadcast IIIS programs originating in Honolulu and San Francisco on grounds that SCAP did not have sufficient control over the contents, Smith was equally critical of Radio Tokyo's output.[61]

While civil censorship officers were devising press and radio codes for the Japanese media and determining categories for deletions and suppressions, CI&E's information specialists were wondering how best to shape news and entertainment programs and to insure the insinuation of approved ideas and themes into Japanese minds. Not unexpectedly they evolved a philosophy of selling democracy. They dubbed the average Japanese citizen Moe-san, the counterpart of the American John Doe. Moe-san "was a typical citizen, of whom 43% were tenant farmers." He had about eight years of primary schooling and could probably read about 1,500 characters. His literacy was "about the level of sixth or seventh grade grammar school" in America. Moe-san had been successfully sold militarism. His history, geography, ethics, and morals texts had been "warped" since the Meiji period and had served as a vehicle for "militarism and nationalism." This average citizen "realized the Occupation also has something to sell." As much as possible, he was to "be given the facts, the truth, without such censorship as to make the truth unintelligible," and he should feel that the occupation was fair even if tough. In propaganda, it was best not to go beyond the truth, Dyke believed. For example, how could faith be created in a new Japanese government if its members were not worthy of that faith?[62]

To enhance their efforts, CI&E's information officers continued to seek out their Japanese counterparts and check their records for signs of moderate views and willingness to cooperate. By the end of

September, they had designated a small group of Japanese writers and artists who were considered sufficiently trustworthy "to interpret news positively and creatively for the Japanese public." In film work, David Conde, chief of the Motion Picture and Theatrical Branch and an old OWI hand, called high industry representatives to his office to discuss the principles they should follow in making feature films, documentaries, and newsreels. Feature films, he advised, should dramatize stories of Japanese soldiers returning to civilian life, ordinary people discussing political problems, labor unions engaging in peaceful organization, and famous Japanese historical figures who worked for freedom and democracy. In newsreels, politicians should make speeches attacking war criminals. Upon investigation of film files, a CI&E inspired SCAPIN in mid-November called for the elimination of undemocratic motion pictures, decrying such "nationalistic, militaristic and feudalistic concepts" as "conformity to a feudal code, contempt for life, creation of the 'warrior Spirit,' the uniqueness and superiority of the 'Yamato' (Japanese) race, the 'special role of Japan in Asia.'" It attached a list of over 230 films, banning their distribution, sale, and exhibition, and directed the Japanese to round up all prints and negatives for storage. Producers of new films were told to submit plans and scenarios to CI&E for suggestions. Similarly, Kabuki plays in CI&E's judgment smacked too much of the samurai spirit and values, and few were deemed acceptable for public performance.[63]

In radio work, new programs were started in late September, prompted by CI&E advice, such as "Voice of the People," "Man on the Street," and "Woman's Hour." Advice soon followed on format, contents, themes, and production of news and entertainment programs. The head of the Radio Branch told NHK in October it should lengthen its hours on the air, give the public what it wanted, and set up advance weekly program scheduling so that regular audiences might develop for particular shows. NHK's non-news programs were "too serious," he said, and would have higher "entertainment value" if presented in a "dynamic manner." Play modern music, he added, and not neoclassics. Surveys taken later of listeners' preferences would lead to quiz shows, talent contests, and musical and variety productions and to uninterrupted programming, but not all of the bright, snappy ideas of CI&E would be to the taste or liking of the Japanese.[64]

According to Smith's official report, it was he who urged Dyke to remind MacArthur to comply with the Potsdam declaration in granting civil liberties to the Japanese. Accordingly, CI&E's officers were asked, almost overnight, to prepare a SCAPIN to the Japanese government on October 4, popularly dubbed the Civil Liberties Directive. Among its many provisions were orders for the removal of restrictions on political, civil, and religious liberties, the release of political prisoners, the suspension of the propaganda activities and organs of the Home Ministry, and abolition of the censorship apparatus of the police. The Japanese were encouraged to speak and write freely about the emperor, imperial institution, and the Japanese government. Angered by the contents and abrupt manner of the orders, the Japanese cabinet resigned and SCAP began casting about for more amenable leaders. Smith, still unhappy with superficial press accounts of Japanese atrocities and war crimes and suspicious that the media were deliberately exaggerating food shortages and the danger of communism, persuaded Dyke to authorize a CI&E project on the history of the war, stressing Japan's guilt. He pressed for "decisive action" at MacArthur's level in naming Japan's "real war criminals—the top men"—as the best way to encourage Japanese liberals to speak out and to elicit cooperation with the occupation's goals. Improved press analysis would enable CI&E to watch trends. Removal of the big bureaucrats at NHK—a media purge in embryo—would help create a better atmosphere for reform.[65]

Materials began arriving from the United States in mid-October, and CI&E persuaded Japanese liberals and released political prisoners to speak on the radio. Smith finished the first draft of a history of the war. Nevertheless, when he left Japan in early November, he felt there had been a "slow and silent sabotage" of the Civil Liberties Directive "by the men who run Japan." He and his colleagues had barely managed to scratch the surface, he lamented. The information program was scarcely thorough in Tokyo, and there was nothing to speak of outside of Tokyo. Once again, Smith urged Washington to send competent press and radio people. Moreover, a projected research unit in CI&E would need personnel to conduct public opinion polls and community analysis surveys.[66]

Smith had also advised Dyke to summon a conference of newspaper editors and publishers and radio broadcasters to discuss their general responsibilities. Dyke did so on October 24 and proceeded, as had Colonel Hoover in September, to scold the Japanese for continuing to peddle militaristic propaganda and for failure to develop a free and independent press and radio. He accused them of ignoring important subjects like the Civil Liberties Directive in their columns and scripts; of avoiding a "full and frank discussion" of war criminals; and of suppressing negative remarks about the emperor. He asked them "to report domestic and foreign news fully and truthfully"; to "explain adequately the aims and activities of the Occupation forces" to the Japanese people; "to permit and encourage discussion" of important ideas; and to allow "all segments of responsible public opinion" to use the media. Dyke's lecture was released to the public and was probably intended to illustrate SCAP's problems with the Japanese while undercutting criticism that MacArthur was coddling the Japanese. This was the beginning of many sessions for the instruction of Japanese editors, reporters, and columnists, and radio heads, and of a series of carefully orchestrated press conferences for the release of occupation news.[67]

Dyke remained uneasy about the effectiveness of the information program. In early November, he told Professor Owen Lattimore, then in Tokyo with the Pauley Reparations Commission, that psychology was playing an important role in American-Japanese relations but added that it was "a two-way process." The people who used to run Japan and who were still running it, he confided, echoing Smith's sentiments, had retreated somewhat but were regrouping. He feared that they were in a better position to "observe our lines and dispositions" than the occupation was to control them and they might soon begin "experimenting how to throw us off balance." Did the Japanese, he was asking, understand the Americans better than the Americans understood them? As Lattimore recorded their conversation:

> We are affecting their minds, and they are affecting ours. They are in a position to do a better job. They have far more people who know what makes Americans tick than we have people who know what makes Japanese tick. . . . He [Dyke] has high professional respect for the way the Japanese are feeding their stuff into the American press and radio, creating confusion of mind among us and differences of opinion both between American groups and between the Americans and our allies.

Lattimore, a scholar of Inner Asian and Chinese relations with decided views about Asia generally, was something of a media expert himself, having edited *Pacific Affairs* in the 1930s for the Institute of Pacific Relations and headed the Pacific Branch of the OWI in 1943–44. His book *Solution in Asia,* published in early 1945, had favored drastic reforms in Japan, including abolition of the emperor institution, and he was undoubtedly sympathetic to CI&E's plight.[68]

Dyke's fears were somewhat assuaged after he received aid from Washington. When Colonel Bruce Buttles, head of the Propaganda Branch, G-2, War Department, and another contributor to SWNCC's reorientation policy planning paper, visited Japan in mid-November with a State Department representative, he and Dyke discussed ways to place "affirmative propaganda" in the Japanese press and on the radio and to induce the media to criticize militarists. A round table discussion sponsored by CI&E that month on the emperor met with mixed reaction, but the format was retained for further political reeducation broadcasts. To expand the radio network, SCAP issued orders for the Japanese to encourage the manufacture and distribution of home radio receivers. And to guard against the monopoly of paper stock by bigger and wealthier newspapers, the Japanese government was made responsible for equitable allocation of supplies. In early December, MacArthur named top men as class A war criminals, not only generals, admirals, cabinet bureaucrats, and imperial advisers, but also a few media people. On the list for arrest, detention, and interrogation were Shōriki Matsutarō, owner of the newspaper *Yomiuri-Hōchi,* whose workers had already formed an independent union in an effort to oust him; Furuno Inosuke, wartime head of Dōmei; and Shimomura Hiroshi, poet, former vice-president of *Asahi,* and president of NHK until his appointment in 1945 to head the Cabinet Board of Information under Prime Minister Suzuki.[69]

In conjunction with these arrests came the inauguration of a radio and press series, using items planted by CI&E. The Tokyo dailies began running in installments on December 8 (timed obviously for the anniversary of Pearl Harbor) stories on Japanese wartime atrocities, with supporting documents and photographs supplied by SCAP. On December 9, a radio program, "Now It Can Be Told," which had been previewed by Dyke and Japanese consultants, began its run three times a week. Heralded as the "first radio version of the true account of Japan's aggression, atrocities and defeat to be heard in Japan," CI&E claimed it was a popular program. A Japanese critic remembers it rather as "the most unpopular radio program of the day." Though it was a "necessary and edifying program for the Japanese," who did not know the facts about the battles of Midway and the retreat in Burma, they did not relish listening to it. "Part of its lack of popularity," he says, could "be attributed to the obviously poorly translated material, the bossy and pushy attitude and style of the narrator, and the hasty choice of subject matter." Beyond this "was the strong emotional reaction of the public who simply did not wish to be told any more about the truth of what was over and done with." Joining in the condemnation of CI&E dominated radio, an American account charged that the program's " 'March of Time' style confused many Japanese with its changing voices, slam-bang pace, and loud music." And in general, these first "radio programs sounded like direct translations of American scripts, with none of the nuances of Japanese thought patterns. Listeners were snapping off their radios in disgust, saying the information programs were nothing but foreign propaganda." The Japanese audiences were weary of any propaganda. Americans were zealous but not subtle or sophisticated. Imported Hollywood movies would meet with a much more enthusiastic reception in 1946.[70]

Part of the problem of informational work in early occupied Japan was jurisdictional—how to incorporate civilian advisers into a military organization and coordinate SCAP's work in Japan with approved United States information and propaganda policy throughout the world. In late November, after Smith's departure, Don Brown was sent to Japan. He too was an experienced Japan hand, having spent the 1930s in Tokyo working on an English language newspaper, the *Japan Advertiser*. During the war, he had joined the OWI, working both in New York, close to the national media centers, and in the Pacific on leaflets for psychological warfare. Shifting to the State Department after the war, he took over CI&E's Information Division while continuing on the payroll of the department's Office of International and Cultural Affairs, permanent successor to the OWI. To satisfy MacArthur, OIC transmitted its approved information themes to Brown through the War Department, but Brown, technically, was a propaganda officer of the American government assigned to Japan and not a Department of the Army civilian working for SCAP.[71]

By December 1945, then, the Press, Pictorial, and Broadcasting Division of the CCD had developed a stringent policy for the suppression of undemocratic, militaristic thinking or other objectionable ideas in the Japanese media. It was telling the Japanese what they could not do. The Information Division of CI&E had evolved into the propaganda and reorientation arm of the occupation. It was telling the Japanese media what they should and must do. Both protected zealously the image of MacArthur. And both considerably expanded their activities in 1946–47.

To what extent these increasingly stringent controls were justified by the behavior of the Japanese media early in the occupation and by the immediate needs of a relatively small military force in the fall of 1945 to ensure security and collect intelligence, or were simply a matter of timing, or reflected insensitivity and ignorance on the part of Americans, are important topics for further research. Only parts of the censorship story have been told. There is much need for content analysis of the Japanese press in the summer and fall of 1945 and for larger studies of modern Japanese journalism and the film and radio industries. Equally, a study of American and Japanese wartime propaganda for truth and accuracy or for distortion and disinformation are in order. SCAP, it should further be remembered, had the additional responsibility of keeping Japan firmly within the American orbit in East Asia even while punishing the Japanese and eradicating wartime chauvinism. From the start, reorientation meant not only the elimination of militarism but also resistance to Communist ideology. It was reorientation to traditional and current American values. Democratization in the early stages, as NHK's official history succinctly summarizes the proposition, had as its "ultimate objective" the enlightenment of "the Japanese people towards the promotion of American world policy so as to make this country a better supporter of the United States."[72]

Until detailed analyses appear of the occupation years, a few remarks should be made in a concluding overview. SCAP's tactics changed and CCD's mission expanded as MacArthur became more sure of the situation and felt freer to act. To curtail the Japanese media too drastically at first, when it was necessary to convey information quickly about the aims of the occupation, would have been contrary to sound military thinking. To conduct even the maximum censorship permitted under the initial orders of minimum surveillance required a sizable establishment. The conditions MacArthur found in Japan, added to fears about international communism, hastened his timetable. "Occupation authorities," insisted the official report five years later on censorship operations, "could not gamble that Japan's docile surrender was not an elaborate cover for an extensive program of sabotage and resistance" by militarists. Moreover, there was a positive job of democratization to carry out. In the end, the censorship organization in Tokyo and in the field grew quite large. At its height in 1948, the authorized strength was 66 officers, 63 enlisted men, 225 Department of the Army civilians, 148 foreign nationals, and 5,658 Japanese nationals. CCD employed almost twice as many Japanese nationals as the planners had anticipated back in 1944, mostly as low level checkers and screeners under American supervisors. The turnover was great since the Occupation's pay scale was less than in private Japanese industries, and the replacements were frequently less able. It was hard also to find and keep the ideal American censor: a "paragon" of "better than average intelligence," who was willing to work long hours at routine assignments, was "bilingual, with an intimate knowledge of Japanese customs and culture, and of current events and conflicting political ideologies and issues" and possessing "a broad background in such unrelated subjects as journalism and propaganda, radio

transmission, postal mechanics and cryptography." PPB censors
were guided by the general press, radio, and pictorial codes authorized by SCAP and distributed to the media, and by a more detailed secret operational manual and changing set of key logs which
at the end of 1946 had as many as thirty categories of deletions and
suppressions with brief explanations. These ranged from criticisms
of SCAP, the war crimes trials, the United States, and SCAP's authorship of the constitution, to references to divine descent propaganda or the overplaying of starvation. One key log ordered, at the
request of the Government Section in 1947, "that general statements that General MacArthur is maintaining a hands off policy on
selection of the Japanese cabinet" be passed and "statements that
new cabinet must have approval of U.S. Government and FEC [Far
Eastern Commission]" be suppressed.[73]

Under the early rules, PPB by January 1946 had already deleted
686 items after examining 37,924 pages of press proof. This included
censorship of the wire dispatches of foreign news agencies prior to
republication in Japanese. In March, SCAP issued the first orders
for the withdrawal of prewar and wartime nationalistic and militaristic publications from bookdealers, warehouses, and bookshops,
though not from libraries and private ownership, a program which
continued until 1948 when over 9,000 titles had been reviewed and
7,738 removed as propagandistic. And while PPB was finding publications, plays, dances, and movies to be unfit, other arms of CCD
were busily opening internal and external mail, listening to phone
calls, and examining telegrams and cables. CCD precensored and
deleted an even longer list of press and radio material and had spot
checked more mail traffic by June 1947 than June 1946—monitoring 6,400 broadcasts in 1946, for example, and 8,600 in 1947; pre-
censoring 40 dailies in 1946 and 69 in 1947; and examining
3,999,000 pieces of mail in 1946 and 5,910,000 in 1947. In June
1948, 140,854 news items were precensored, 148 films, 15 books, and
464 broadcast scripts. In four years of existence, CCD checked an
amazing figure of 330 million pieces of mail and telecommunications
and monitored 800,000 phone conversations. The Japanese were
perhaps more greatly antagonized by American spying on their private correspondence than by any other form of censorship.[74]

The Kabuki theater was in serious trouble with the censors,
1945–47, with most of its repertoire judged as feudalistic and offensive. An early PPB guide attached much importance to Japanese
theater "as the medium best adapted for the portrayal" of desirable
national characteristics. "Kabuki is the glorification of the Bushido
spirit of the past," and its "plots are punctuated with murder, sword

play, death, and hatred." Unfortunately, "almost any selection" of a Kabuki play has elements which make the minds of the audience "receptive to the ideals of the old order." And yet Kabuki was rescued in 1947 by a friendly PPB censor, Faubion Bowers, who was a prewar aficionado and postwar scholar of Japanese drama, and by self-censorship. The popular *Chūshingura* [Forty-seven rōnin] was once again performed in November 1947, starring leading Kabuki actors.

Literary censorship temporarily stopped publication of atomic bomb literature—poems, stories, eyewitness accounts, and essays—and lamentations for the dead, such as the prose poem, *The Battleship Yamato,* which was dismissed by the censors as militaristic propaganda. Film shot by a Japanese camera crew of atomic bomb damage in Hiroshima and Nagasaki was impounded by SCAP officials in 1946 and not returned to the Japanese until 1967. Copies of banned prewar and wartime feature films were ordered destroyed by SCAP with negatives and four prints to be stored for future disposition. Photographs of the emperor in military uniform were removed from public places as were paintings glorifying Japan at war. Graphic stills of dead Nazi war criminals, "shown with their tongues hanging out and eyes bulging," came through the wire services while the Tokyo trials were still going on, but were killed as inflammatory and too gruesome for Japanese consumption. A Japanese could see "his own guys in the same position."[75]

In one celebrated case in the summer of 1946, a documentary made by a Japanese company, Nichie, at the instigation and with the help of CI&E's David Conde, *Nippon no Higeki* [The tragedy of Japan], tracing the rise of militarism, was subsequently censored by CCD for incitement to unrest in a reversal of an earlier decision. This was done upon the intervention of General Willoughby but with the connivance of Prime Minister Yoshida Shigeru, who did not like its irreverent attitude toward the emperor. This was just when Chief Prosecutor Joseph Kennan of the International Military Tribunal for the Far East had announced that the emperor would not be tried as a war criminal. Showings ended (there is a debate about the enthusiasm of the audience response), and CCD ordered that all of the prints be confiscated. The producers lost an estimated $600,000 and were later forced into a merger. In 1947, a film by Tōhō productions, *Sensō to Heiwa* [War and peace] ran afoul of the censors and suffered several cuts in scenes and the deletion of one song from the soundtrack. The director in both cases was the same person, Kamei Fumio. Considered to be a Communist by occupation authorities, he had trouble finding another job. When Kamei tried in 1948 to speak of the trauma of his experience at a roundtable discussion sponsored by a leftist journal, some of his remarks ("I was disappointed that my film was suppressed against my belief in the revival of the world of liberty," translated PPB's censor) were struck from the published discussion.[76]

Although SCAP forbade any references to censorship after the initial press releases and allowed no indications in printed texts or films of deletions, the practice was well known to the Japanese. From time to time, American reporters harshly condemned it in newspapers and national magazines back home, providing examples of stupid, arbitrary, or unjust decisions. The "censorship is not mild and perfunctory," declared Paul Vincent Miller in an indictment published in *Commonweal* (April 1947); "it is carried out with such methodical diligence that even a people as patient and subservient as the Japanese are obliged to wince at it." If it were necessary in the beginning, and he conceded that it was, the "danger" had passed. Censorship coincided neither "with our professions or our ideals as a democratic nation." Functioning with less quality in the districts than in Tokyo, it was turning "fascistic." Roger Baldwin, director of the American Civil Liberties Union, checked into complaints on a trip to Japan and Korea in the spring of 1947 as an independent consultant to SCAP on civil liberties in Japan, but was relatively mild in his public censure. "The general is a charming, wise, witty, most unmilitary man with a strong sense of mission," he wrote privately to the Board and its friends, "a genuine democrat who sees his role in large historic outlines, and with great confidence in the Japanese." Publicly he stated that censorship could be relaxed. "The controls were necessary in the early days to insure against anti-democratic forces," he wrote in the *New Leader,* but "democracy is working well enough now to relax them without danger of releasing hidden anti-democratic forces of right or left." He may have had some impact, for Undersecretary of the Army William Draper wrote MacArthur in October, after a conversation with Baldwin, that "it may well be that the time has come when you would consider" the possibility of eliminating precensorship of the daily papers and of certain magazines and substituting postcensorship.[77]

In keeping with promises to relax and eliminate restrictions gradually as the Japanese became more responsible, SCAP progressively ended precensorship of the media in several stages, 1947–48, beginning with puppet theater or Bunraku in May 1947, radio scripts in August (except for programs directly relating to the Allied Powers or to the progress of the occupation), Kabuki theater in

June, and Nō plays in September, and extending to most book publishers in October, phonograph records in November, periodicals in December, and the press and news agencies in July 1948. Publishers of extremist newspapers, books, and magazines (left and right) remained on the precensorship watch list, and postproduction surveillance continued of all media. The program to locate and censor presurrender films lasted until 1948. Eventually over 21,000 titles of films were reviewed and over 7,800 titles were suppressed or suffered deletions; precensorship of new Japanese films and of foreign imports was maintained to 1949.[78]

This transfer to almost complete postcensorship was part of a general shift of emphasis in Washington's policy, 1947–48, from progressive reforms to security issues and economic reconstruction. A Department of State intelligence report commented in October 1947 that censorship, however narrow in scope, contradicted the mission of democratization. In limiting the practice of free expression, it had "the effect of continuing the authoritarian tradition in Japan." Were the acquiescent Japanese really accepting the new principles or deferring to their conquerors and slanting news to win approval? "One prominent newspaper publisher expressed the view," said the report, "that the Press now has more freedom than at any time since the military revolt of February 26, 1936; less than at any time before it." The censorship policy of SCAP raised a very basic question—were the media "being effectively groomed to contest possible attempts at renewal of Japanese government interference with the freedom of expression and information in the future"?[79]

The need to retain censorship controls was also questioned by George Kennan, head of the State Department's Policy Planning Staff, after a trip to Japan in March 1948. In his opinion, "Censorship of literary materials entering Japan should be conducted with a minimum of delay and precensorship of the Japanese press should cease. This should not operate, however, to prevent SCAP from exercising a broad postcensorship supervision and from engaging in counterintelligence spot checking of the mails." William Sebald, chief of SCAP's Diplomatic Section and acting political adviser, had already concurred, telling the secretary of state in February that CCD "should be abolished." It had "overstayed its usefulness in Japan," and was doing more harm than good as a "discomposing and doubt-raising factor" in Japan. "It would appear that the permanently necessary contribution of the censorship to intelligence can readily be absorbed by the continuing intelligence agencies." These views are embodied in a National Security Council policy statement,

"Recommendations with Respect to United States Policy toward
Japan" (NSC 13), which was endorsed by President Truman that
fall.[80]

In Japan, CCD until its demise at the end of October 1949 shifted
primarily to intelligence and analysis, using postcensorship to develop information leads and tips in black market cases and subversive activities and to gauge public reactions to occupation policies.
The press and radio codes technically remained in effect, and foreign
broadcasting was not resumed until the end of the occupation. To
Costello, postcensorship was "not censoring. You can call it anything you want, but believe me, it isn't censoring." Surveillance of
extremist publications and activities was very real, however. In late
1949 and accelerating in 1950 with the outbreak of the Korean War,
SCAP was back in the censorship business, helping the cabinet of
Yoshida Shigeru to suspend and close down Communist publications
and expel Communists from positions in the media and elsewhere in
public life.[81]

To charges that the American censors were racist and indifferent
to Japanese cultural mores and values, John Costello recalls his
Japanese house away from other Americans and his box at the
Kabuki theater, and points out that the Japanese were in a sense
censoring themselves. The majority of the censors were Japanese
nationals who did the initial screening. While they needed the work
badly, they "were probably in sympathy with the occupation." They
were bilingual, fairly well educated, and made the crucial decisions
to pass something or question it. If they passed it, that was usually
"the end of it." But one might ask how many American censors truly
respected Japanese customs, or whether Japanese censors were
being unduly conscientious in order to keep their jobs and not necessarily out of ideological commitment. There was also, as previously
indicated, the problem of turnover of Japanese nationals. From 1945
to 1949, there were no beatings; few arrests, trials, and jailings; and
only some suspensions and fines, but there were many admonitions
and reprimands (some of them written), and considerable harassment. No one's life was endangered by American censorship, it is
true, but one's livelihood might be at risk. Not all of the onus for
censorship, incidentally, should fall upon CCD, for often it was expected to stop items which other staff sections found objectionable or
embarrassing. William Coughlin, the first to provide a comprehensive account of the occupied press, was careful to point out many of
the inconsistencies and dangers of censorship but nevertheless concluded that it was a necessary evil, justified by a "reactionary,
irresponsible" Japanese press reception at the beginning of the oc-

cupation. It did no "permanent harm" and indeed may have helped to create a more professional, middle-of-the-road Japanese journalism. The Japanese press in 1952, he believed, was a strong watchdog of Japan's "infant democracy." Others, like Eto Jun are convinced that civil censorship did lasting harm to Japan's collective consciousness and severe psychological damage to individuals.[82]

If the Japanese media were traveling safely in the middle of the road but going in an American direction in 1952, this was as much attributable to the efforts of CI&E as CCD, although the two cooperated only infrequently and informally. Even the State Department's intelligence report when questioning the wisdom of continuing censorship in 1947 recommended the "infusion of informational materials and educational guidance in the principles of the media of information in a free society." Propaganda activities in Japan expanded and became highly specialized after 1945, and the War Department set up a Reorientation Branch in the Civil Affairs Division to facilitate the work and coordinate with the State Department. But the thought molding programs of CI&E in films, radio, press, books, and plays have often been confused with the role of CCD or not well publicized, and may be among the least known and studied aspects of the occupation.[83]

The stiffened stance in information work, 1946–47, was justified by familiar arguments—the Japanese were captives of feudalistic and reactionary concepts but were rescuable. They were also increasingly desirable partners in Washington's global policies. Cultural imports to occupied Japan could enter only under SCAP auspices. The Information Division of CI&E helped select and distribute foreign feature films, documentaries, and newsreels, favoring of course American productions. There could be no direct mailings; all foreign printed materials sent to Japan had to be addressed through CI&E and the Army Post Office for delivery to Japanese recipients by the Ueno Imperial Library. Under measures and criteria adopted in December 1946, CI&E regulated the import of foreign books and periodical subscriptions by licensing only those considered not detrimental to the purposes of the occupation. Don Brown told the Japan Publishers Association what foreign books might be published. He favored *Tom Sawyer* and biographies of Lincoln, but was not so keen about John Hersey's *Bell for Adano* or *Hiroshima,* or Erskine Caldwell's *Tobacco Road.* Books from Germany, France, and Britain seemed to be more popular than American ones, and CI&E inaugurated in 1947 a gift book program to encourage the influx of American publications. By October 1949, there were seventeen CI&E information centers in Japan, including one at each major university, stocked with 5,000 to 10,000 books and subscribing to 400 periodicals; ten additional centers were planned for the future. CCD had censored a Japanese translation of the *Kama Sutra* as possibly disturbing to public tranquility, but in 1947 referred obscenity cases or pornographic materials to CI&E for correction through educational measures rather than by censorship (obscene literature was not covered in the press code). In dramatic presentations, CI&E was supportive of productions of Thornton Wilder's *Our Town* and Lillian Hellman's *Watch on the Rhine*. CI&E also prepared interpretive and factual materials for Japanese consumption. More than 20 million illustrated and annotated copies of the SCAP-authored constitution were distributed under SCAP's watchful care. Photographs were recommended of the emperor in a business suit and talking to farmers and workers or relaxing at sports events.[84]

With new recruits and changeover in personnel, 1946, CI&E continued to suggest ideas for film scenarios and to supply themes for new and existing radio programs. Japan's film industry had not yet recovered in 1946, and Japanese audiences seemed to like Hollywood's brand of entertainment, though some American observers worried that the quality of American imports was inferior to British and Russian selections. The important consideration was that Hollywood present American life and values in a positive manner. A Time-Life documentary, *Modern America,* featuring color panoramas and requiring special equipment, was shown to an estimated half million Japanese in 1949. CI&E's Radio Branch worked mightily to make the radio more appealing and interesting to Japanese listeners and exploit the airwaves to illustrate the meaning of democracy. It started permanent information programs on numerous topics, such as agricultural cooperatives and land reform, labor movements, the food situation, and women voters. Its own directly originated programs occupied more than ten percent of the air time. Improving upon its earlier roundtable format, the Radio Branch launched the "National Radio Forum" in April 1946, featuring speakers discussing subjects from several points of view and taking questions from an at first passive studio audience. In October, it offered "Liberal Thinkers," casting Japan's most popular film and theater actors in stories about prewar Japanese liberals. "Bells of Freedom," in February 1947, attempted to dramatize freedom of religion, speech, and assembly. In November 1948, "a typical month," SCAP had its information material on the air 944 times in 468 separate programs, with political information and education as the predominant topics. "Man on the Street," begun in September 1945, was continued, although the precaution was taken of recording interviews to prevent any unexpected criticism of the occupation. Gradually, the Japanese became more enthusiastic about the format, and in June 1947, when Prime Minister Katayama Tetsu answered questions about economic stabilization to a crowd, they were eager to participate. "The problem was not to make them talk but to shut them off." CI&E further encouraged candidates in the first postwar elections of April 1946 to campaign on the radio, following up with a new "Diet Roundtable" program. In 1947, radio time was made available in local elections, although reportedly a candidate in the April mayoral election in Hiroshima was cut off the air by an alert censor for making references to the A-bomb. In 1949, CI&E added still another new program, this time based on *Primer for Democracy,* a textbook written by CI&E's education officers with Japanese consultants for secondary and adult education and published by the Education Ministry in 1948. More than two and a half million copies were distributed to classrooms or commercially sold, 1948–49, and a large audience existed for the program. In one assessment, "the radio was an effective means of suggesting rather than ordering change." And soap operas were started, which "appealed instantly to housewives, because they dealt with modern and mundane affairs. But in the background was the familiar music of classical Japanese drama. The information programs were geared to Japanese, but each included at least one woman 'expert.' " Radio became more enjoyable and more influential.[85]

CI&E's wide ranging activities included pressure on the Japanese media to adopt new ethical codes and professional practices, such as less mixing of reporter-editorial opinion in the news. The techniques employed were conferences, speeches, personal contacts, admonitions, and rebukes—and further circulation of American publications. CI&E became deeply involved in the reorganization and rehabilitation of the film and radio industries and in the union activities of media employees, along with other special staff sections, but backed off from the early policy of promoting labor agitation against the old guard management as giving too much support to Communist organizers. At the opposite end, it joined with the Government Section in 1949 to prevent the Yoshida cabinet from making use of a new law, in violation of the constitution, to interfere with press freedom prior to an election. After travel bans were relaxed, 1948–49, CI&E helped send students, scholars, technicians, scientists, and professional men to the United States for advanced training and research and further exposure to American life. SCAP allowed only limited travel to Japan for cultural purposes until late in the occupation, citing problems of food, housing, and maintenance, but made exceptions for missionaries and trade representatives.[86]

In September 1949, Lieutenant General George Stratemeyer, commanding general of the United States Air Force in the Far East, perhaps not fully acquainted with CI&E's endeavors, urged that "vigorous measures" be taken to defeat Communist penetration in Japan. He complimented CI&E for its success in reorienting the older generation but believed the Communist party was gaining a significant hold on Japan's youth in the schools with arguments that the United States was exploitative and imperialistic. He wanted funds to be made available to purchase American books and periodicals and hire trained youth workers who could "acquaint the leadership potential of Japan" with democratic principles through study groups and seminars. "It is my opinion that any program should be directed toward the positive goal of promoting Americanism rather than suppressing Communism. The American ideal of life, liberty and pursuit of happiness is still as revolutionary in the Orient today as it was in the West in 1776." If presented properly, it would be more attractive to the Japanese "than the Communist theses of hate, class warfare and Stalinism." Undersecretary of the Army Tracy S. Voorhees had noted the same problem on his trip to Japan, and in 1949–50 CI&E redoubled its efforts to approach university students and run public lecture tours. Former CCD officers, then transferred to psychological warfare, helped coordinate the efforts.[87]

To truly reeducate the media and change the leadership and structure, SCAP had demanded a purge in 1946–47, as it had in politics, business, and education. This meant using cooperative Japanese to remove undesirable personnel in newspapers and news agencies, radio broadcasting, magazine and book publishing, and film and theatrical production. After several false starts, the Japanese government embarked on an expanded media purge in late 1947, screening persons for ultranationalistic and militaristic activities during the years 1937–41 on the basis of positions held at that time. Owners and presidents, managing directors, editors and editorial writers, and heads of research bureaus were in purgeable categories. Publications with circulations as low as 10,000 were affected. Top media figures who had earlier been placed on the Class A war crimes list were released from Sugamo Prison in 1947 but were prime candidates for the purge. In the end, by May 1948, out of 2,295 persons screened or provisionally designated, 1,066 were purged. This was in comparison with overall totals of 200,000 barred from public positions. Most of those affected in the media (857 individuals) had resigned or retired before the screenings in a self purge. Their exile did not last long, and many were reinstated in a depurge of 1950–51 that had Washington's blessing. In the meantime, the number of Communists who lost their jobs in the media after the Red purge of 1950 was about 700.[88]

In ending American wartime censorship, Byron Price wrote President Truman in August 1945 that "everything the censor does is contrary to the fundamentals of liberty." He invades privacy, delays mails, restricts the exercise of free public discussion. Censorship should "come into being solely as an instrument of war" to keep dangerous information from the enemy or to collect intelligence, and should not be used to "suppress criticism of the government," to "conceal government blunders," or to restrain editorial opinion. Elmer Davis had earlier reminded a congressional committee that there would be extended internal censorship in Germany. "As General Eisenhower advised the president, 'We are not going to lose the peace by giving license to racialist Pan-Germans, Nazis and militarists so that they can misuse democratic rights in order to attack democracy, as Hitler did.'" Occupied Japan, like Germany, was still at war in a sense with the United States, and MacArthur's logic had much in common with Eisenhower's. American monitoring of foreign telecommunications and of international mail was extended into peacetime as national security measures, even as the Truman administration was promoting the cause of freedom of information throughout the world.[89]

By one set of standards, civil censorship and propaganda dissemination in occupied Japan were highly successful in the overall reorientation goal of transforming Japan into a friendly and reliable but not unquestioning junior partner in the Pacific—and in rehabilitating the media. But the endeavor was beset by contradictions and hypocrisy. How could SCAP uproot deep-seated beliefs held by nearly all Japanese, including even friendly intellectuals, that there was considerable validity to Japan's aims of economic viability and resisting Western imperialism? How could an American military figure convincingly tell the Japanese that their own military people had misled them? Led them to defeat, yes, but misled them? To use capitalist rhetoric, could Americans without undue advantages sell their ideas better in the free marketplace of ideas than the Russians or the homegrown nationalists? What harm would a tough and extended period of censorship and propaganda guidance of the Japanese do to American ideals and self-knowledge and to the Japanese collectively and individually? Why not allow more criticism of the occupation? Some Americans, including censors and propagandists, underwent a reverse reorientation from arrogant conquerors to humble seekers of Asian wisdom. But the tension between the goals of freeing and manipulating the flow of information was never quite relaxed from the beginning to the end of the occupation. For the Japanese, this would serve both to release but also to inhibit creative and intellectual expression, and to raise doubts from the start about American wisdom, sincerity, and compassion.

Chapter 14

Comparing American Reform Efforts in Germany

Mass Media and the School System

Harold Hurwitz

In his studies[1] of United States military government and the Marshall Plan John Gimbel has drawn two conclusions that we cannot afford to overlook if we want to study the motives, efforts, and effects of American attempts to promote the development of democratic institutions and of political culture in Germany during the occupation period.[2] By showing that OMGUS' predominant consideration was not the intention to "reeducate" or "democratize" Germany but rather America's own national interests,[3] Gimbel compels us to ask how much and what kind of room was there left for a motivation that he elsewhere describes as having been zealous and idealistic throughout: "to go in and make the changes."[4]

The question for which American and German scholars will continue to seek an answer is: how much and what kind of democracy was permitted, supported, or curtailed by the emerging and changing perceptions of American interest in Germany? This is, of course, a question about which orthodox defenders of United States policy and revisionists will continue to disagree. However, Gimbel's most recent study about how, in a not altogether rational process, America's long-term interests in Germany were "clarified," can flush birds of all feather out of the trees. We should all have trouble mending our nests after so much evidence that in 1945 and 1946 Lucius Clay felt he had substantial cause to hope that the multipartite experiment in Germany might work with the Russians, though not with the French, that neither Bizonia nor the Marshall Plan originated in response to Soviet obstruction, that fear of communism, as a danger anticipated for Western Europe, did define what came of these initiatives, with anticommunism, gaining more and more weight of its own because it proved to be the handiest possible argument for selling the Marshall Plan to a Republican Congress.[5]

Such findings are relevant to current academic discussions of the question confronting us in this session: democratization by American proconsuls. It is important to bear in mind the context of this dispute: the charge made by American and German revisionists that the Western occupation powers—and some do extend that charge to include the Soviet Union—prevented German anti-Nazis of the Left from taking the political initiative in 1945,[6] and that subsequently American policies in Germany, having been anti-Communist and anti-socialist from the outset, by means of Bizonia, Marshall Plan, and currency-reform *systematically* set the stage for the restoration of capitalism and a pseudo- or inadequately democratic order in West Germany after 1949.[7] Gimbel's fastidiously researched findings compel this kind of criticism to be more discerning. For example, he has pushed up by at least two years—from 1945 to 1947—the myth of an American imperialist conspiracy in Germany from the outset.[8] On the other hand his study might impress an orthodox historian or two with the importance of distinguishing between the rational, justifiable, and manageable dimensions of response to a Soviet presence or a Communist threat and dimensions of response that are irrational, self-deluding, and unmanageable.

It is not my present task to make such distinctions. What I do find relevant to our theme is, however, the fact that evidence of American duplicity—and self-deception—in connection with the origins of the Marshall Plan may encourage an unwarranted measure of doubt and oversimplification when approaching the subject at hand. There did indeed exist a problem of compatibility between anticommunism and democratization efforts in Germany at a time when the influence of national socialism was fresh and the bitterness of defeat an open wound.[9] It is well to bear in mind that there are different traditions for anticommunism; some are democratic, others are not. Yet here only evidence can help, and in the face of the record it is difficult for young German scholars, who have access to the facts, not to be impressed by the progressiveness of certain reforms that Americans sought to bring about during the occupation of their country. However, did not this democratization effort slacken, was it not perverted by the turn to anticommunism, in a grand design combining West European recovery with a policy of containment that helped to divide Germany? This is what one German scholar, impressed by the anti-Nazi and democratic quality of United States radio broadcasting between 1945 and 1948, but loyal to her New Left principles, recently asked.[10] Barbara Mettler mended her nest in a fashion that I expect to become characteristic after Gimbel's latest monograph. Clarification of how limited, uncertain, and contradictory official perceptions of the United States national interest in Germany were in 1945–46 was taken to mean that "progressives" found opportunities to work effectively only in the early years. Undoubtedly the periods from Moscow conference to London conference to Berlin crisis—in which a consistent policy emerged that was anti-Communist and can be called separatist—can be worked into a more or less monotonic explanation of why reform efforts were dropped or why they failed.

Superficially the period can be construed to coincide with proclaimed phases of OMGUS' democratization program: the changes from control to services, from "reeducation" to "reorientation" allegedly coinciding first with emphasis on reform and then with its abandonment, as emphasis shifted to turning West Germany into an anti-Communist bulwark of the "free world." However, the record of reform efforts does not correspond with this scheme, neither neatly in point of time nor happily in terms of expended energy. A major connection did exist between democratization programs and the new policy, but it was not a monotonic relationship in one or the other direction, and its complexity reveals much more about the problems of directed institutional change in Germany under American tutelage and the cold war than either the apologists or the revisionists, thus far, seem to have grasped. I hope to point this out by demonstrating the value of relating the goals and comparing resources, instruments and also the effects of different American reform efforts: here with respect to the German press, radio, and public schools.

No matter how individual beliefs—and politics—came to differ about the way change in the occupied country might, if at all, be brought about, whether by operational direction and control, whether by guidance that was backstopped with veto power and intervention, or only through exposing the defeated people to the "four winds" stimuli of opportunities to learn and choose, each occupation power tended to see reeducation in Germany in terms of the way it conceived itself to be a democratic country. The negative perception they tended to have of Germany, as an authoritarian, hierarchical caste society that was disposed to collectivism, strongly encouraged American reformers and reeducators to emphasize liberal and egalitarian aspects of their own traditions. Apart from a self-righteous moralizing rigorism, the reform program of United States military government did have a strong accent of liberalism American style.

Where information media were concerned the liberal goal meant providing German journalism with the status of the "fourth estate," independent of government but, as the watchdog of truth, just as indispensable to the public interest in controlling state and economic power as parties, the legislature, or the judicial branch can be. This concept called for developing a whole bundle of core and flanking measures from 1945 until 1952.[11] First, it meant putting German information media into the hands of reliable anti-Nazi individuals. Information Control handled the screening of licensees, editors, and reporters for press and radio with greater severity than was applied anywhere else in American military government. This entailed retraining the editorial personnel, promulgating as new journalistic practice the strict separation of news from commentary, emphasizing detailed reporting of the facts and standardized routines for designating sources—these being practices that were honored more exactingly by journalism in Britain, the United States, and Scandinavia and which, greatly modified, have become standard practice in the Federal Republic. It was assumed that, if so edited, German newspapers and newscasts could educate the people to make knowledgeable judgments on their own. For this reason sensational journalism was discouraged. Political engagement was encouraged, but not party partisanship. Carefully screened anti-Nazis were likely to have party affiliations, so the Americans made two, three, or even more licensees with different political backgrounds jointly responsible for the same newspaper. The effort to prevent a partisan development by politically balancing personnel extended to editorial staffs and radio commentators.

It was considered highly important that the new information media be equipped to defend their *independence,* above all against government influence and harassment, after military government would end. This called for new standards and habits of intercourse between government authorities and the media: establishing the right of journalistic enquiry into all public matters, insisting upon impartial treatment of rival media, regular press conferences, and so forth. Above all, however, it was considered necessary that new press laws and radio laws be passed[12]

Finally, steps had to be taken to provide the newspaper licensee who had "made good" with every opportunity to obtain permanent possession of publishing facilities that were adequate to his needs. Private property was involved that had first been requisitioned and later mandatorily leased to licensees. The major activity of the United States High Commission on behalf of former licensed newspapers was organizing a Press Fund to help them buy and equip their own plants.[13]

The American effort to reform German information media depended upon a new elite, but it also involved changing structures and norms. What were the chances and the limits of such a reform? Where the press was concerned the owners of fifty-nine new newspapers were provided an opportunity to become very wealthy men. If this motivation was not enough to combat successfully the interest groups, which Western occupation powers knew they only temporarily could inhibit, the Americans were prepared to provide the new media an unusual measure of protection and assistance for some time to come.

The interests to be combatted were many and varied. *Altverleger* (former publishers) were not only Nazis and nationalists; they included owners of a great many very small provincial and some big city papers which had been politically colorless and easily manipulated before 1933; their owners had had little choice but to serve the Nazis after 1933. However, quite a few newspapers—the party press of the SPD, Zentrum, and KPD, high-quality liberal daily newspapers with nationwide distribution, and some provincial clerical papers—did have strong anti-fascist records until they capitulated, were taken over, or forbidden in 1933.[14] The revival of such papers was also prevented by United States military government—although the French and British made concessions here. In the case of party newspapers, although the State Department urged permitting them in 1945, and although the Information Control Division (ICD), as well as German licensees, supported doing so in the following years, General Clay stubbornly and skillfully evaded giving in to the democratic political parties.[15]

Obviously America's refusal to model the new German media along pre-Nazi lines not only served the denazification purge; the promotion of a new structure was considered necessary to protect the "fourth estate" against other institutions that belonged to a new liberal democratic order: against control by the state, by parties, by the churches. However, by taking an undiscriminating stance in this matter, Clay provoked antagonism to the American reform effort along an unbroken front which unfortunately included most anti-Nazis. Whether social-democrats or conservatives, as party leaders or as government officials, they felt that they had every justification—traditional, legal, and moral—especially after the Nazi experience, to utilize the information media in their difficult

struggle to establish a new legitimacy for their parties and governments in a social environment that was still ridden with alienation
and hostility toward them.

The press model that Americans hoped would remain dominant
after controls had been lifted was a system of privately owned regional newspapers that should be strong enough to counteract concentration of ownership or domination by matrix syndicates.[16]
Beyond this point little attention was given to problems of how
commercial interests impinge upon freedom of the press in a free-
enterprise economy.[17] Non-attention extended to the difficulty of
clarifying the difference between the roles of journalists and of publishers in the "fourth estate," that aspect of press freedom that man-
ifests itself in the obligation of editors to investigate matters and
express views that do not conform with a publisher's economic or
political interests. The early effort of a few licensees to convince ICD
and other newly privileged colleagues that their newspapers should
be transformed into public foundations ended in failure and hardly
left an echo[18] until years later, when these problems acquired an
urgency that they did not yet seem to have before currency reform
and the end of licensing controls.

However, when it restructured German radio, Information Control did take stronger measures to safeguard a plurality of opinion in
the future. German radio stations had always been organized under
government dominated corporations, and although during the Weimar Republic political neutrality became a maxim and radio time
was given to rival parties, political responsibility was so atomized
between two Reich ministries, *Land* governments, and the parties
in power that the authoritarian chancellors Brüning and von Papen
had proceeded to make radio-programming an instrument of central
state policy even before the National Socialists did a thorough job of
it.[19] Hence, the long-range problem facing United States military
government in 1945 was to provide for the autonomy of German
radio stations at some later date.

Whereas the French and British occupation powers organized
radio in 1945 on a zonal basis, United States Information Control set
up separate stations in each Land of the zone as well as in Bremen
and in the American sector of Berlin. Direct management of German radio by the Americans was exercised more strictly and lasted
longer than was the case in the British zone.[20] Naturally enough,
when facing the problem of turning over *independent* stations to
Germans, the solution that Americans first considered was privatization,[21] to make way for free enterprise and competition between
rival networks. As far as I know, no researcher has yet described the

process by which American authorities were influenced to drop a model that accorded with their own national experience for one that might have seemed socialistic, a revised BBC concept of radio as a public service institution that was independent of government.[22] Henceforth, the Americans wished the *Land* radio stations to be governed by an autonomous body (*Rundfunkrat,* or radio commission) representing a cross section of the varied elements in the community. The number of government representatives was not to exceed a small minority and, in distinction to the BBC, the political parties were not to be represented.

It is noteworthy that when American authorities issued instructions to German *Land* governments to draft radio legislation along these innovative lines, the date was November 1947, and the early cold-war period was underway;[23] it was the period in which Washington outran even General Clay in doing everything possible to inhibit socialist experiments in the West German economy,[24] when the military governor dressed down decartelization to a size that could not get in the way of rapid reindustrialization,[25] and when, probably for the same reason, that embarrassing failure, Clay's technocratically managed denazification effort, was hastily laid to rest.[26]

These changes in economic and denazification policy have made it easier to assume that this was also the time when "anticommunism" ended a phase of the United States occupation, during which it still could be considered in the American interest to try to influence German political culture by introducing institutional innovations of a democratic nature. To test the validity of the proposition that the cold war put a stop to democratization efforts, it is useful to include, for comparison to ICD's reform program, the attempt by OMGUS to reform the German school system.[27]

Apart from negative objectives, to purge teaching staffs and textbooks of Nazi and chauvinist influences, American educators conceived school reform to be an attack against one of the most important institutions for preserving traditional class privileges in German society. Instead of separating "class" from "mass" as fourth-grade children in the traditional three-track school system, the reformers proposed a unified, comprehensive and fluid system where differentiation would begin after the sixth grade, but even then not be complete or final. Instead of training primary-school teachers on a separate lower plane, they too should be educated by the same university faculties as secondary-school teachers. Education should be compulsory for at least nine years, and those who left school at this point for employment or apprenticeship training should be required to continue in school part-time until they were eighteen years old. Tuition fees should be abolished and textbooks free, coeducation introduced, social studies emphasized, small country schools merged into larger units, the quality of education in private schools controlled. While parochial schools should be tolerated if parents wanted them, they no longer should be encouraged. Student self-government and parent participation in the planning process was supported, but in keeping with United States advocacy of federalism in Germany, the school system was to be organized, as it had been until 1933, on a *Land* basis; apart from the influence of parents on curriculum, no serious emphasis seems to have been laid on the principle of decentralizing the planning and control of schools to the local community level.[28]

Land jurisdiction over education would help conservatives to block the execution of significant reforms everywhere in West Germany, except in city-states like Bremen, Berlin, and Hamburg where there were Social Democratic majorities. All told, this school reform program constituted a larger-scale, emotionally more aggravating challenge to the vested interest of class, of the churches, of private industry and commerce, and of traditional politics in agrarian areas than were American efforts to "democratize" German information media, government structures, or political party and trade union organization. The bitterness of opposition to educational reform in the West zone, as well as the not very passionate support it was given by the Social Democratic party and the trade unions, provide evidence for the thesis that under the conditions of economic and social jeopardy that prevailed in early postwar Germany, class antagonisms were acutest among those whose property, privileges, and status were being threatened by the consequences of defeat, and that social aggressiveness was far more likely to be directed from the top downward, against traditionally underprivileged groups, than vise versa.[29]

Americans did not, of course, intend to overcome class stratification in Germany, but rather to weaken and modify its rigid hierarchical structure through land reform, decartelization, freedom to engage in a trade or profession, and school reform.[30] The liberal egalitarian concept stressed in the field of education was consistent with America's positive perception of its own experience, expecting school reform to open up the German caste system by promoting social mobility and by achieving, with the help of this perspective, that kind of social concensus which is beneficial to democratic sociality in a free enterprise system. However, in the case of school reform the American program coincided point for point with reform programs that some liberal and many socialist educators in Germany had developed and begun to implement during a brief period of prosperity under the Weimar Republic[31]—a fact that OMGUS experts frequently stressed. Beyond this, the American program was also compatible with the thinking of the British, Soviet, and French educators in Germany at that time. Although ACC Directive No. 54 left open such questions as control by the German states or by a central government, promotion of a unified school system, and regulation of religious instruction, it clearly bore the stamp of American influence and gave quadripartite approval to the changes that American educators wanted to bring about.[32] In the end American efforts to reform the German school system were a confessed failure, whereas important institutional changes could be effected in the German press and radio. To explain the difference one must go back to the very different initial circumstances, and to the resources and instruments that were available in each case.

The transition from psychological warfare with the German language media to the promotion of new German press and radio institutions under direct tutelage by military government involved a continuity of organization and of large-scale operational experience, which American units responsible for education completely lacked. Robert McClure, the chief of PWD/SHAEF and of Information Control Division/USFET, was not only a professional general officer whose rank was equal to Clay's, his influence in the military sufficed to postpone merger of his organization with military goverment until February 28, 1946, and, henceforth, to protect his very civilian-spirited and intellectual "outfit" from outside encroachments. After ICD/USFET and the military District Information Control Command (DISCC) units were incorporated under OMGUS, the designation "Information Control" was retained on all levels until August 1948 when they were renamed Information Services Division (ISD) and Branches (ISB).

By contrast, education was a notoriously neglected step-child of United States Military Government. That was the case from the moment the Anglo-American preparatory staff, the German Country Unit, was dissolved in the late summer of 1944. In the United States Group Control Council and in OMGUS, Education and Religious Affairs (ERA) remained understaffed, underrated, and submerged as a section of branches and divisions that had no relationship to its mission[33] until "widespread criticism in education circles in the United States" finally brought a "drastic change" in 1947 and 1948.[34]

A special obstacle to permeating German education with reforming influence from the start lay, of course, in the vast number of schools and the urgency of opening them. Unlike newspapers and radio stations, schools could not be run at first as overt American undertakings. Screening personnel to license newspapers and political parties was a smaller task than purging the whole teaching profession and stopgap measures like training replacements in newly created teachers' colleges. Yet the French and Russians did take this and other direct actions to introduce radical changes of the German school system almost immediately.[35]

American education officers had misgivings about reopening schools or universities for the sake of expediency before something had been done about providing for textbooks and new teachers, but security considerations prevailed;[36] it was considered not only necessary to get children but also former officers "off the streets." Clearly the motivation to reform the German educational system was not very strong in the upper echelons of OMGUS in 1945 and 1946. This is all the more significant in light of the emphasis given to the "reeducation" of Germany in American discussions of postwar planning ever since 1942 and the lip service use of that phrase, by military government spokesmen.

That OMGUS devoted so little attention to "reeducation" in dollars and cents terms was at least partly due to Clay's deprecating attitude. It might have seemed logical to merge ERA with ICD, which is what did occur under HICOG, and would have even happened beforehand if counterpart-servicing offices in Washington and New York would have had their way. In the Berlin headquarters of OMGUS that would have unduly strengthened McClure's organization.[37] More important, probably, was Clay's parsimonious view of public spending in view of the uncontrollable occupation burden and his watchful sensitivity for the political scene at home. Clay's understanding of priorities found expression in the formula he used when rejecting a War Department admonition that he should apply for more funds to buy reorientation supplies in 1947 than he had requested for1946: "We still believe full bellies to be a first requisite to recapture minds."[38] Requesting dollars to import paper for German textbooks was, he felt, out of the question. This kind of thinking had already made it impossible to realize reorientation plans that ICD and ERA had hoped to implement during 1946. Clay was never a party to the New Deal enthusiasm that revived under military government—although, in keeping with the Fair Deal scene, his communications to Washington frequently did refer to the "liberal" nature of America's mission in Germany, at least until Republican victory in the congressional elections of November 1946 seemed to predict a conservative administration after 1948.[39] Ironically it was the grand design, seeing West Germany as the cornerstone of an anti-Communist bulwark, that justified military government to a conservative Congress and provided liberal reorientation programs, which had long been planned, with more support than Clay had ever asked for or even now considered to be justified.[40] Only in October 1948, after the currency reform had liquidated ICD's domestically earned assets, did Clay request an additional 2.4 million dollars, until the end of that year, to purchase materials for servicing the very same kind of information and educational projects for which he had refused to ask more than 1 million dollars per year in 1946 and 1947.[41]

By the fall of 1947, from which time anticommunism is said to have introduced a drastic negative change in reorientation programs, ICD had been engaged in directly influencing the reform of German media for over two years, whereas a serious effort by military government to reform the German schools had gotten under way only a short time before. Having forsaken direct control of education at the outset, the only way to effect school reform was to influence German legislation. That was also a crucial task facing Information Control, but operating radio stations and licensing newspapers had provided ICD with instruments that education officers did not have.

In practice, there never had been a clear distinction between negative and positive phases of "reorientation." When institutions had to be launched that were so patently political, military government could neither withhold permission very long nor fail to supervise them closely when they got started. This applied to information media, parties, and trade unions. The screening involved in licensing, in staffing the media, and in clearing elected officials constituted denazification in a positive sense. Of course, information media lent themselves more readily to close, continuing control—and patronage—than did parties and trade unions. In the latter cases, after a phase of direct interference in 1945–46, OMGUS' reorientation efforts shifted to the higher plane of influencing policy, government structures, and law-making. By contrast, ICD press and radio officers were still attending to the anti-Nazi and "reeducational" content of what was daily published and broadcast when they broadened their tasks to include the problem of press and radio legislation by *Land* parliaments in 1947 and 1948.

It is a task for future research to show how that "drastic change" was brought about in the status of ERA (becoming the Educational and Cultural Affairs Division of OMGUS), which made possible a

serious effort to reform the German school system. It seems to have
required interaction lasting nearly two years, between frustrated
educators in military government, interested officials in Washington, and parts of the United States educational establishment.[42] The
reforms called for by the Zook Commission of prominent American
educators, who were sent to Germany in August 1946, provided authoritative support to programs that ERA had previously advocated;[43] decisive was the commission's recommendation that ERA be
granted a status high enough to compel General Clay's attention
(additional personnel was another corollary of such status). New
was the finding that the present policy of limiting action to friendly
advice, moral and material support, a policy that justified noninter-
ference and a modest staff, would not suffice: veto power was necessary to reform German educational structures.[44] Yet it took nearly
another year until a "big name" had been found for the assignment
in Herman B. Wells, president of Indiana University, whom Clay
felt was equal to the job and a partner to be respected.[45] It was characteristic of the strong-minded military man Clay, when finally
convinced that a change of direction was necessary or inevitable, he
would support the new policy just as stubbornly as he had the old.

Lucius Clay has written that "the German inability truly to understand democratic freedom" manifested itself most clearly when
the military government tried "to obtain adequate legislation" for
school reform and for guaranteeing freedom of the press and of
radio.[46] However, especially at this juncture, when it was intended
to replace reform by fiat with a more complex interactive process
that should involve negotiation and compromise, enticement, and
the proconsul's veto power, did it become apparent that the difficulties were due to more than German inability to understand
democracy.

The potential for democratization in Germany at any given time
was as Leonard Krieger later pointed out, "not identifiable as definite qualities, groups, or institutions but as a process," an interactive process, I would add, in which the cognitions and expectations
Americans and Germans had regarding each other helped to determine how much and what kind of change was possible. To Krieger
the "moral for planned political change" by military government
was that in this process "the planners must not only measure
continuously the changing tendencies of their charges, but take continuous account of their own measuring rod as well."[47] The measuring rod for planned political change that Americans applied was,
indeed, altered by the advent of the Marshall Plan and the cold war

to include anticommunism as a part of the democratization concept. But what detracted from the democratization effort was another effect—the great haste now called for in creating a West German government under a High Commission which retained only minimal powers to interfere. However, where General Clay's military government was concerned, the tendency to withdraw was not born at the outbreak of the cold war. Since the turn of the year 1945–46 German politicians had been given cause to assume that while some Americans were pressing for directed institutional reform, others higher up were seeking justifications to terminate direct controls by a military government altogether.

Yet, during the entire period military government *was* attempting to carry out what John D. Montgomery called an "artificial revolution," one which Leonard Krieger later pointed out was based upon deprecation of the past and present capacities of German democratic forces.[48] These, however, were the very forces needed to carry out reforms once OMGUS had forsaken legislating by command. Prejudices that underrated the domestic German democratic potential bolstered autocratic attitudes native to military government; they worked hand in hand with a maximum of nonpartisan neutrality, where German politics was concerned, that did not prevent OMGUS from preparing the ground for a capitalist development of the West German economy, but did hamper American reformers, who were trying to liberalize political and social institutions in a fashion that policy called for.

In the case of school reform nothing was done to explain and popularize among parents a reform program that was as much German as American in origin;[49] nor were German supporters encouraged to organize, to coordinate their actions on a zonal basis and across party lines. By refusing to license party newspapers OMGUS made it less likely that *Landtag* members would counteract the authoritarian inclinations of coalition government officials when ICD tried to get legislation that would prevent encroachment upon freedom of the press.[50] In fact General Clay preferred restoring influence to German governmental elites, expecting them to influence legislatures and parties rather than vice versa. American programs to promote "grass roots democracy" in Germany were the most artificial of all because they never involved a serious effort to encourage citizens' action on genuine political issues. Hence, instead of systematically stimulating whatever popular democratic potential did exist, instead of discreetly encouraging the self-organization of different pressure-group networks and joining forces with them selectively, from issue to issue, OMGUS relied heavily on the autocratic practice of formally submitting guidelines and formally rejecting the draft laws that failed to take guidelines adequately into account.

That the problem could be handled differently by the military government of a Western democracy is indicated by the success the British had in paving the way for legislation that would reform German local government in Lower-Saxony and North-Rhine-Westphalia along English lines. With patient determination and subtlety, they promoted, among diverse groups and across party lines, the emergence of common interests in the introduction of institutional changes that would long outlive the occupation period.[51]

In the four *Länder* of the United States zone a sparring match ensued in which the weaker party could win points simply by holding out longer. In each area discussed here—press, radio, and school reform—the Americans had first called for acceptable legislation in 1946, long before the cold war could interfere, and in each area, whether German governments were dominated by parties that wanted liberal reform or wanted to prevent it, they all dragged their feet long enough on the new policy to make it easier for them to get whatever they really wanted.

In the case of school reform only one state government (Hesse) enacted a constitution in the fall of 1946 that called for schools with the democratizing functions that ERA considered essential.[52] Between April 1, 1947, and the spring of 1948 each state was required to redraft its reform laws three times before America's shrinking list of minimum requirements had been more or less adequately taken into account. The impression that successful resistance by Bavaria would impede reform in Württemberg-Baden and even in Hesse induced General Clay to act autocratically.[53] On November 18, 1947, he made it clear to the Bavarian Minister President Hans Ehard that his minimal wishes *had to be* heeded in a third draft. Yet, even then, Clay probably realized that, in a showdown, he no longer would be in a position to remove from office Alois Hundhammer, the ultraconservative minister of culture who was blocking reform in Bavaria.[54] Moreover, it had become apparent that if state governments insisted that the United States-approved laws could only be implemented by passing further legislation, then it would be less likely that these reforms, and agreements in principle, would, after all, ever be carried out.[55] Characteristically, Clay imagined that this problem could be solved by inducing the state governments to circumvent their parliaments by issuing executive orders to enact the reforms.[56] He even clung to this illusion after Hundhammer and Ehard disavowed responsibility for their obedient compromise in public—Hundhammer by attacking free textbooks and coeducation in the *Landtag* on January 29, 1948, the day before he submitted that law, his "compromise," to the Americans for approval.[57] Of course, state governments did insist on bringing in their legislatures; Bremen also did so, although Bremen was the only state that would implement a school reform that lived up to the expectations of the American and German reformers.[58]

With the end of military government in view, OMGUS had reduced its program by the spring of 1948 to pressing for only those reform measures that it imagined could be carried out by the end of 1949: in Bavaria this meant having free tuition and textbooks by September 1948 and introducing a fifth year of grammar school as well as university-level training for elementary school teachers by the fall of 1949.[59] However, when the *Landtag*, before adjourning, seized upon the post–currency reform fiscal squeeze as a reason to postpone providing for free tuition and school materials, Clay *commanded* Ehard not to charge fees or sell textbooks in the forthcoming school year.[60] Not even Social Democratic and liberal supporters of reform were willing to excuse an affront like that by the military governor. The drama ended in a promise, to eliminate tuition fees step-by-step until 1950–51, that would not be kept.[61]

Bavaria continued to have grammar schools with only four classes, in a public school system dominated by parochial schools and, as a token, adorned by a one-hour required course in social studies. Characteristic were the consequences of military government's having refused to support a modest comprehensive-school proposal by the liberal CDU minister of culture in Hesse; henceforth, this weakened his chances of influencing his own party in a reform direction. By 1951 the tide of conservative sentiment regarding education had become so persuasive that a new government based on a strong SPD majority abandoned its commitment to introduce a unified comprehensive school system, although this had always been a central concept of that party's reform program for education. By 1957 even Bremen restored a system whereby children could again enter the *Gymnasium* after spending only four years of grammar school in the company of the lesser privileged.[62]

An anti-Communist change of policy and political climate had influenced this development, but we have seen that it did so in a reinforcing but also quite contradictory fashion. Clay's belated but bitter last-ditch effort to compel democratization of the German school system may well have been motivated by a compensatory desire to prevent restorative forces from taking advantage of the new situation.[63] He was impeded both by his own autocratic inclina-

tions,[64] and by the encouragement that German conservatives opposed to school reform received from influential Americans, under
the impulse of that kind of anticommunism that encourages oppor-
tunism and irrationality. Hundhammer was in Washington on February 18, 1948, for the Senate hearings on Germany of the Case
Committee, and he felt encouraged by them.[65] Credited with having
"saved the humanistic Gymnasium in Bavaria" was Bishop Alois
Muench from Fargo, North Dakota, who, in addition to being vicar
general to the Armed Forces, represented both the American hierarchy and the Vatican in Germany.[66] Muench repeatedly persuaded
Cardinal Faulhaber to oppose aspects of the school reform in Bavaria that were obviously not religious issues.[67] "What he did not
agree with he randomly characterized as 'Nazi,' 'communistic,' 'socialist,' 'undemocratic' or even 'un-American.' "[68] This applied not
only to using the liberal standards of the American educational system to influence change in Germany but also to the intellectual sec-
ularism of Der Monat, a highly successful monthly magazine (edited
by "a N.Y. Jew," Muench often repeated), which had been launched
as part of General Clay's overt anti-Communist information program. Muench "did everything in his power to close it down," and
when American financial support for the magazine did terminate in
1954, he "claimed responsibility for the action."[69] There was nothing
even remotely anticlerical about Der Monat. Since Clay had tried
and failed to get rid of Muench in October 1947, he was unwilling to
attempt it again seven months later, when the Land director for
Bavaria, Murray D. Van Wagoner, asked him to do so during the
school reform controversy.[70]

During the battle of words that accompanied the demolition of the
West German school reform into the 1950s, its opponents found it
equally useful to denounce it as an impertinent American imposition as to claim that this was the very system Communists had introduced in Eastern Germany[71]—although after 1949, when East
Berlin introduced a rigid, genuinely Communist school system more
along Soviet lines, the similarity no longer did exist.[72] Of course all
of the reforms that were dropped were revived by the German school
reform movement of the late sixties.

Far more successful were American attempts to provide for the
independence of press and radio, although at least where legislation
was concerned, these efforts too, were hampered in 1948–49 by the
stampede to liquidate controls in the wake of the new anti-Communist containment policy. This applied far less to radio than to
press legislation. It took over two years before state legislatures in
the United States zone had passed radio laws which guaranteed the

decentralization and the safeguards against government control or party influence that Information Services Division (ISD) insisted upon.[73] In Mettler's judgment, had the Americans not been so persistent, state monopoly of radio would have been reestablished in Bavaria and in Württemberg-Baden.[74] In the years to come, *Land* governments and political parties would accept the BBC-type innovation, with radio and television being directed by representative public-service bodies; however, within this framework, they succeeded in gaining ever more influence: either by placing more power in the hands of a smaller administrative committee (*Verwaltungsrat*), where influence by government could more easily be imposed,[75] by increasing *Landtag* representation in the *Rundfunkräte* (this provoked a public debate between a powerless *Land* commissioner and the president of the Württemberg-Baden *Landtag* in 1951),[76] or, indirectly, when parties influenced trade unions, churches, and chambers of commerce to appoint their men to these bodies. The principle of decentralization in the federal structure had been firmly enough established in law to prevent Konrad Adenauer from reorganizing or creating new media under the control of the federal government.[77] What could not be prevented was that the system of checks and balances that had been institutionalized to counteract government control of radio would fall prey to the German system of closed-party parliamentarianism.[78] The problem plaguing radio and television journalists since the 1950s lies in the fact that for the control commissions, the "neutrality" or "objectivity" of a program is assessed solely according to the criteria of party politics and not by the standards of an independent and critical investigative journalism in the public interest.[79] Yet this cause has been stubbornly defended by German radio and television journalists since the occupation period. For them the freedom of criticism that British and American radio officers tolerated is more than a warm memory.[80]

Anticommunism was not especially detrimental to American reform policy where German radio legislation was concerned. During the blockade, objections were raised to turning over so important an asset in the cold war to several German public commissions, but these misgivings were overruled. Ironically, an important reason why the High Commission opposed Adenauer's first attempt to make the federal government responsible for the stations in 1950–51 was the American argument that West German radio required advantageous wave-lengths for reasons of military security, and that the Allied powers would continue to be in a far better position to secure them than any German government.[81]

The case for anticommunism having been detrimental to America's reeducation effort where press and radio were concerned rests primarily on what surely was a political purge of German and American personnel—all of whom were not Communists or fellow travelers. Careful study is still required to judge the justification and impact of this pre-McCarthy activity in occupied Germany. Secondly, the case is argued with an assertion that emphasis on anti-Nazi reorientation was weakened *because of* an anti-Communist change in programming. Apart from the general problem of how anticommunism could be made compatible with democratization in Germany after Nazism, I think that the thesis will be difficult to support empirically, once content analysis and study of power struggles for influence in the media have been conducted in a comprehensive and systematic fashion. The fact that the mismanaged denazification program already had lost all effectiveness before the cold war called for a coup de grâce would lead one to expect that journalism, too, was already giving problems of *Vergangenheits-bewältigung* (coping with the Nazi past) less and less attention— this was, indeed, doubtlessly true of the Communist party press in East Germany.[82] At the same time pressure by conservatives to gain positions of influence on editorial staffs was apt to become more successful as ISD relaxed its controls, and that was inevitable. Anticommunism would make it easier for them—and could more likely become an illiberal and undemocratic weapon in their hands. Finally, cognizance must be taken of the fact that the "operation back talk" program of ISD's newly created Political Information Branch (PIB) was a long overdue defensive response to Soviet propaganda attacks;[83] even before the Berlin blockade ended, the thrust of PIB's activities was redirected away from exposing communism in a "battle of ideas" and information. The office was transferred from Berlin to the Frankfurt area in order to promote integration of a West German state in a West European community and to develop public relations type information programs about America's policies and way of life.[84] The German radio time that OMGUS and HICOG reserved for the "Voice of America" and official spokesmen was also devoted to this kind of information. The modulation and redirection of "reeducation" and "democratization" themes in United States information programs was not so much anti-Communist in thematic content as it was pro-Western and pro-American. After reduction in force (RIF) had decimated the OMGUS staffs to be taken over by HICOG, all that was left of anti-Communist information programs that PIB had created were two publications for intellectuals, *Der Monat* and *Ostprobleme*.[85]

All this suggests that in order to appraise the chances and effectiveness of American attempts to liberalize German political and cultural institutions one must distinguish, on one hand, between the contradictory aspects of anticommunism's impact on American intentions and efforts, while, on the other hand, discerning how the revival of an old and dangerous propaganda slogan affected German behavior in the process of regaining self-determination and a comeback by conservative social forces. It is noteworthy that, whereas these developments destroyed the chances of liberal reform of the school system, they did not do so where German mass media were concerned.

In the case of the licensed press, once it had become certain that it would not be possible to do as General Clay wished and turn controls over to the Germans in 1946,[86] ICD/ISD was able to continue its careful tutelage until September 1949. This meant that for more than a year after currency reform, the newspaper licensees were able to accustom themselves to free market conditions before being submitted to the test of real competition with party and *Altverleger* newspapers.[87] ISD arranged this by declaring that the passage of acceptable press laws was a contingency for ending controls and yet waiting until October 1948 to formally instruct *Land* governments to begin drafting this legislation. The state press laws which OMGUS finally approved in the summer of 1949 were a disappointment to ISD.

Since 1945 all kinds of chicanery and attempts to muzzle or to penalize newspapers had shown widespread unwillingness by local and state governments to acknowledge that freedom of the press constituted an independent public service. Conflicts with newspapers had been especially bitter in Württemberg-Baden;[88] its government acted now as the pacesetter for resistance to press legislation. It gained negotiating leverage for itself by having the *Landtag* enact a special penny culture-tax on all commercial publications including newspapers. In the cycle of rejecting and redrafting the law, ISD finally did obtain a basic concession: the press was defined as a public institution. However, the state Supreme Court declared the penny-tax constitutional—pointing out that when military government had rejected the conservative Reich Press Law of 1874, it had failed to exempt a paragraph which did prohibit special taxation of the press. This court decision was approved by the OMG for Württemberg-Baden, and ISD/OMGUS could not convince the Military Government Legislative Review Board to suspend the press law until a paragraph was included that corrected its oversight.[89]

Outmaneuvered, ISD was neither able to eliminate nor correct the press law's so-called rebuttal clause, which obliged newspapers to print factual counterstatements by a public authority or private person who felt misrepresented by press criticism;[90] a paragraph of the original draft had stressed that the author of a rebuttal was legally liable if he forced a newspaper to print false information, but the government had dropped this passage from subsequent drafts.

Had OMGUS not been so hard-pressed to end its responsibilities, ISD would doubtlessly not have been compelled to accept a law which press officers feared would not protect newspapers from certain forms of government repression, including the ability to prosecute a journalist who refused to reveal his source of information. On the other hand, especially in light of diverse punitive clauses that military government had been able to delete from the German drafts, the reform press laws were clearly progressive. Each had established the basic principle that news media were public institutions; each obligated governments to provide information to investigating journalists.[91] Reduced was the danger of arbitrary confiscations, a problem that had plagued press freedom in Germany throughout history. More significant, however, is that subsequent German press legislation was not regressive, as in the fields of education, but tended, rather, to protect press freedom from the kind of encroachments that ISD felt it had failed to secure remedy for in the 1949 legislation. The existence of strong rival parties contending for a popular mandate to govern helps to account for the entrenchment of press freedom in the Federal Republic. Some credit, however, is due to a new generation of journalists that were trained during the licensing period.

Although they emerged nearly unscathed from the press war with *Altverleger* in 1949–50 and were subsequently provided by HICOG with substantial legal and financial assistance to procure the capital equipment many of them needed, licensee-owners' political commitment often proved weaker than their personal interests. There were mergers and sellouts to *Altverleger* and many conventional accommodations. However, generally, the former licensed press remained fairly, if not aggressively, critical of authoritarian developments during the 1950s and 1960s. Moreover, the regional expansion of a few liberal urban dailies that have retained their original political character as well as the expansion and perseverance of quite a few provincial ones, whose political commitments have faded or changed, are factors that have set limits, in the former United States occupation zone, to the expansion of West Germany's largest press-monopoly, the Springer concern, which now controls the greater part of the Northern German and West Berlin newspaper markets. Party owned or controlled newspapers, licensed by the British and French, rarely did as well. Hence the American decision to rely on the kind of motivation that private ownership could induce even among anti-Nazis of socialist persuasion seems to have contributed some diversity and independence to a medium that still practices a slightly Americanized style of journalism. Otherwise free enterprise's West German press is characterized these days by a lack of investigative power and by a colorlessness that contrasts, perhaps significantly, with the critical standard which journalists are still able to produce in German radio and television—under a system of pluralistic public control which has protected and stimulated freedom of the press to a limited, but less-limited, extent.

Combined Discussion

[*This section covers the material of the fourth and fifth sessions of the conference.* —Ed.]

George K. Romoser: Could I ask a technical question first? I think many of the themes that were brought up this afternoon at the earlier session are related probably to the evening session. I do not know what is going to go on at the evening session; whether it is to be a general discussion, or papers presented. So I, personally, would prefer to make some comments now, but I am not sure whether this is the most appropriate time, or whether it might be better in the evening.

Robert Wolfe (presiding): Well, I would say, if we are tired now, we may be even more tired in the evening. So here is your chance to ask questions.

George K. Romoser: This is somewhat complicated at least in form, I am sure not in substance—it is probably oversimplified in substance. I first want to ask a question just to get something straight since I did not hear the whole of Professor Hurwitz's paper. Would it be fair to say that the thesis of your paper was that the records show that policy with regard to Germany was influenced by two things: first of all influenced by a linkage between anticommunism and notions of what democracy involved—that the democratization of Germany came to be overshadowed or at least accompanied by an anti-Communist mentality, and that this affected how much democracy was achieved. Also affecting this were what I think you designated as certain conservative attitudes of General Clay. Would this be fair or is this an oversimplification?

Harold Hurwitz: That is an overstatement, of course, and not what I intended. I mentioned that there is a relationship, and there must be a relationship when the initial concept of denazification and reorientation is formulated in quadripartite agreement terms, and when you know that Goebbels' Nazi propaganda was anti-Communist, that anticommunism has a tradition in Germany which is not only democratic but a tradition that was explicitly fascist, and a conservative view of East European culture and Russia that also constituted a problem. I was in the Political Information Branch when this occurred, and I was a member and an active participant in the program. In Berlin in this situation, we had no difficulty in translating this program into democratic terms. But the ISD people in the *Länder,* and people in other branches of OMGUS/ISD, including the Publications Branch at that time—I recall the views expressed were worries that anti-Communist slogans would arouse and release motivated judgments and prejudices that would be prejudicial to a democratic development. I consider that a problem; a problem that has to be solved by thinking it through and judiciously applying the program.

General Clay was very much aware of this in the early period. There is plenty of documentation between November 1947 and March 1948 showing his reticence in regard to the implementation of this program. The reason why I brought this up was because German scholars and "new left" scholars, take the view that you simplify. But when they work on the documents, they have to adjust this concept. Essentially there are two arguments—one, a personnel argument: there was a purge of personnel including a number of people who were not Communists or fellow travelers, including a number who were active anti-Communists, during the summer of 1948 and 1949, also involving a number of Germans who were independent leftists. The type of removal that occurred before 1947 was of a different nature. There was a sort of stampede after the blockade: a number of Americans, who were later rehabilitated, were dismissed at this time, who had been very active observers in an anti-Communist frame of reference in Berlin from 1946 to the period when the Germans were carrying the ball of resistance.

So I say that this is a very complex affair that has to be looked at in detail. One of the arguments is personnel, and the other is content: did the content of our media change? And I think the content analysis will show that it had been changing—that is, a weakening of the strong, hard emphasis on denazification was already under way. I think the whole thing has to be looked at very closely and you will find that there is a compensatory aspect.

There is also another interesting aspect that certain programs that had been neglected before are suddenly emphasized, definitely in terms of the liberalization-democratization concept in the later period, particularly in education, but it also applies even under HICOG to such cases as police reform and democratizing the German civil service. This fact that these things are emphasized at a later date contradicts the expectation that anticommunism had destroyed our democratization program. I think it complicates it considerably.

George K. Romoser: The theme or question I think I am getting at is not really directed at you, alone, but the general theme is really the relationship between the use of records and the perspective of people who use the records. You said, for example, that the current "new left" would have to make revisions in their views based upon documents. Could you just give me an example of that?

Harold Hurwitz: I think a very good example is the study by Barbara Mettler [*Demokratisierung und Kalter Krieg* (Berlin: Verlag Volker Spiess, 1975)], who is a serious researcher, and the extent to which the generalizations that you heard before the documents were available, and the manner in which she treats the problem of content in radio broadcasting and the problem of the purge. With the documentary information, she is much more differentiating and her effort to understand things in her frame of reference is very much revised and not at all pro-Communist, is identifiable as an interpretation that has not been verified. The experience is academic, it is serious, it is qualified and it is very helpful for discourse.

Robert Wolfe: It was precisely because I saw the bias of young German writers who thought they were taking an honest historical view, but were hampered by the unavailability of the basic contemporary records in Germany, that I pushed my own government toward recognition of the importance to us of German researchers and writers getting early access to the records of the occupation. But I would also like to reorient this discussion a little bit—using the word "orient" advisedly—Professor Baerwald wanted to talk to this subject from the Japanese side and I think that might be enlightening. And if you would like to rest, Professor Romoser, I promise you the microphone back when the time comes.

Hans H. Baerwald: I will try to be very brief. We faced precisely this same problem in Japan as apparently was faced in Germany. I mentioned the reverse course in my talk this morning—actually, that particular phrase was first developed by the Japanese. There are still Americans who are not willing to accept the fact that there was a reorientation, if you will, a redirection of American policy toward Japan. Those who do not accept the fact that there was a reorientation of American policy during the occupation generally look to the cold war as the triggering device. There are many of us who served in the occupation in Japan who believe that this is totally incorrect. That, as a matter of fact, there were certain reorientations that took place long before the cold war became a salient issue. It so happens that a dissertation is being written at the moment by a Ph.D. candidate at UCLA—she is teaching at the moment in Texas. I think that her book will at least reopen that whole debate and present a good deal of new evidence thanks to the opening of certain archives. I just thought it might be worthwhile to mention that to the extent that the issue was salient in Germany, it was very much a factor in Japan.

One final comment—I am not quite sure that I understood you correctly, Professor Hurwitz, when you spoke of personnel removals. Did you mean Americans?

Harold Hurwitz: Americans and Germans.

Hans H. Baerwald: I think that some very key individuals were removed from the scene in Japan, in Tokyo. The records of that are still not available. I would dearly love to see some of that come to light, at some point, to determine what really happened. The usual explanation was that they had participated in black market activities, but so did everybody else, which does not, therefore, provide an explanation.

George K. Romoser: In addition to the archivists' interests and the persons who do concrete research, we also have to understand in dealing with the subjects of the occupation and with the theme "Americans as proconsuls," and looking at the current literature on that subject, that there has been a change in the notion of democracy as well as there has been new research and new records used. This is the real issue, looking at it from a political scientist's or political theorist's point of view. That is something that should be linked up with the research that goes on in the history of the occupation and the history of the immediate postwar period. We have to relate changes in the concept of democracy and democratization, today, to the understanding of democracy and the self-understanding of people at that time as to what they were doing. To achieve an overview of what had actually gone on, it is not sufficient for us to simply speak of terms like denazification and democratization, as if these were acceptable terms. As a matter of fact, their meaning at that time, and their meaning in the self-understanding of someone like Mr. McCloy, one encounters constantly. The understanding is rather self-evident on the part of these people, but it is not a reflective understanding. I am simply saying that this is a theme which must be central. The research on the period has to be self-reflective itself, that is the point.

Robert Wolfe: In my ringmaster's opening statement, as I lined up the elephants for you in the order in which they were going to appear, I suggested that, from my own experience, our understanding of the meaning of democracy, and the absence of democracy and the need for denazification has, through our own experience and maybe growing up with some of our own problems, changed in our own minds.

George K. Romoser: No, I am saying that today the understanding of democracy includes vast realms of culture. For example, in Germany, it includes realms of culture such as education, and not only education but many other spheres. People refer to this as needing democratization and this is a phenomenon of our time. I do not believe it was necessarily understood in the late 1940s that democracy implied a democratization of culture in this sense. It implied many procedures.

Hans H. Baerwald: I am sorry; I disagree. If you look at the SWNCC policy papers they paint a very, very broad picture of what at least those people had in mind when they spoke of democratization. Now, once it got to Japan, certain things happened; but certainly those who provided the policy documents thought very presciently in terms of the kinds of things that you have in mind.

Harold Hurwitz: Surely the study of planning will show that the problem of cultural disposition, the concepts of political and social psychiatry, problems of normative socialization processes were discussed, not only by émigrés, but in American educational circles. This was a frame of reference in which expert planning occurred. If you look, as Carl Anthon said this morning, at the German resistance movement, there was a very strong left and right, including even the Communists, particularly the conservatives, who learned during the resistance experience the acknowledgment of the necessity to reeducate. Now you find very peculiar manifestations of this. The conservative group that learned the most, the *Kreisauer Kreis,* had a concept of economic change which is very close to Morgenthau's plan of pastoralization; a utopian rejection of industrialization. You have a tradition in Germany where the concept itself of democracy is rejected, not only as parliamentary democracy on the extreme left, but the enemies of the Weimar Republic, who supported the Nazis at the last moment and then lived to regret it. Their thinking also in the Third Reich was not explicitly democratic, and in the early postwar period you have an identification on their part with decentralization, or "federalism equals democracy." So you have a problem here of clarification, and we got into this with our own federalist policy, without knowing what we were encouraging. I think that this is a very complex process, and hard for us to deal with at the moment, but I think that definitely people were aware of it at the time.

George K. Romoser: I agree with you. I think the problem, though, is that I am very familiar with the revolutionary conservatives you are referring to and with their successors, whom I would classify as the *Kreisauer Kreis.* But this is all a literature and an outlook of cultural crisis. This is a viewpoint of cultural crisis which is reappearing, perhaps, today in the new left under certain different auspices. But in any case the point is this: however much discussion there may have been, one has to sort out in research on this period the difference between this sort of cultural discussion, and the practical decisions that were made and probably had to be made by the acting figures, by the chief figures. I am not saying that to deny this, but this is one central theme. There could have been discussions about cultural factors, socialization and what-not. One of the central themes is what is the relationship between that discussion and the actions of political figures?

In Germany very soon after 1949, the charge of restoration arose. I can remember this, as a student in Germany, being charged in the mid-1950s, that there had been a restoration. What was really being complained about was that some sort of notion of a cultural, social, general Western crisis had not really been faced up to, that the restoration had not dealt with the really essential causes of national socialism. This led a sort of half-life until the mid-1960s when it was brought to the surface by the new left.

Robert Wolfe: In the context of some of the things that were said here, it is worth paying some attention to Willy Brandt, who as an exile writing in socialist newspapers in Sweden, made some harsh suggestions for the native country he had to flee. But he changed his mind after a while, and has even been himself accused of restoration.

I also remember in the America Houses there were German students and even professors in Heidelberg sitting and listening while some rank amateurs like yours truly and Dolf Sternberger debated with Professor Walther Jellinek and Captain Donald Bedard from American military government about proportional systems of voting as opposed to voting for individuals. I also lectured in *Amerika Haus* in Heidelberg about the American federal system. The Germans were interested in learning about our federalism but, of course, when we talked about federal powers and state's rights, they were talking about federal versus central; there is a fundamental semantic confusion.

And finally, in 1969, I was in Germany visiting a cousin, and one of his friends was the Heidelberg lawyer who had rabidly defended Heidelberg student-rebels. When he found out I had been in military government in Heidelberg at the time we supposedly cleaned out Heidelberg University, he jumped me immediately for having done a poor job. I was used to, by that time, being accused of meddling in things of which we ignorant, uncultured Americans had no understanding. But now to be told that it had been our duty, and that we had failed to reform Heidelberg University when the Lord knows our own universities were having a good deal of trouble, makes me wonder whether the Germans, in some cases, are not carrying out their own generational battles and even the battle between capitalism (which we are supposed to represent) and socialism, and whether we are not, by making history relevant, warping what really happened, and reading into the past what was not then in our minds—our collective minds.

Morris Amchan: Dr. Mendelsohn, on your discussion of clemency, could you please amplify the organizational set-up of the Nuremberg tribunals and the military tribunals that also had concentration camp atrocity trials? The reason that I ask this question is this: take the case of Ilse Koch. She was tried by a military tribunal, not by the International Tribunal sitting at Nuremberg. There was in the United States Congress a substantial evidence of coercive actions on the part of the prosecution which led many people to reexamine those trials. Now some people have the impression that what happened at the military court-martial trials also happened at Nuremberg. It is for that reason that I ask you if you would please amplify the organizational set-up between the Nuremberg trials of major war criminals and [lesser] war criminal trials that the Army conducted. In that connection, could you also direct your attention, if the evidence shows it, to clemency. Was clemency, as you see the records, predicated on a concept that the clemency board was going to review whether or not the particular individual received a fair trial and, if so, were they going to correct it by changing or mitigating the sentence; or, along with that or apart from that, did they also take into account on an overall basis that clemency in some cases would be applied because of a political act and a changed political situation?

John Mendelsohn: As far as the organizational set-up of the various trials is concerned, there was one International Military Tribunal at Nuremberg and twelve United States military tribunals, the so-called subsequent proceedings. Although several cases at Nuremberg dealt with concentration camps peripherally, there was only one case among these thirteen trials that dealt specifically with the concentration camp issue—that was the subsequent proceedings Case No. 4, *United States of America* v. *Oswald Pohl*. That is what we normally refer to as the Concentration Camp Case of the subsequent proceedings. Now the Army had many proceedings against concentration camp guards. They were held originally at the Third Army and Seventh Army War Crimes Trials enclosures at Ludwigsburg or Frankfurt, and later on moved to Dachau; all generally referred to as the Dachau Trials. In the Dachau Trials, there were proceedings against the guards and personnel of six major concentration camps. In addition to that, there were over 250 proceedings against personnel of out-camps and work camps of these six major camps, totaling over a thousand individuals. It was the largest segment of the Army's trials. The other large segment dealt with the so-called flier cases. These were cases against German nationals who mistreated, mutilated, or killed American airmen who parachuted over Germany.

As far as clemency was concerned, General Clay was under a good deal of pressure. He was a stern proconsul, which I do not think has been brought out so far: he was very stern in regard to the war criminals. He did not mitigate, he did not change any heavy sentence except one, and two very minor ones, of individuals tried and convicted at Nuremberg.

When High Commissioner McCloy took over there was a complete and total change. Quite suddenly there was clamor for clemency; clemency was in the air. McCloy appointed an advisory board on clemency, and this board operated according to certain procedures.

It included three members; one was a judge, another was in charge of the New York State parole system; and they applied generally procedures that were used in New York, of course. Frederick A. Moran, who chaired the New York parole system, went around talking to the prisoners. He went to the German Ministry of Justice to get some background information on the family conditions of the individuals, and went so far as to arrange for each one of these war criminals psychiatric and medical examinations in order to be able to get rid of a number of them on grounds of a medical or psychiatric parole. Mr. McCloy said that he thought that there were so many differences in sentences—whether the judges were too harsh in some cases or too lenient in other cases, I do not know, but the judges in these United States subsequent proceedings had impeccable judicial backgrounds. They were generally from state supreme court benches, including a few presidents and chief justices, and about three-quarters of the remaining judges. There was a panel of three judges that decided on each case—in some cases there were four judges.

General Clay was constantly under a great deal of pressure. There was the Ilse Koch case which created a whole lot of bad publicity for him. She had been convicted and given a life sentence for crimes against humanity including having tattoos from human beings made into lamp shades. It was an allegation never proven in court. A group of nine lawyers, advising General Clay in his clemency decision, told him that the woman was not even there when the tattooing process allegedly took place. General Clay, interviewed on video tape, which I had occasion to look at, asserted that it was not even human skin, but goat's skin! Following his reduction of Ilse Koch's sentence from life to four years, there was an outcry in the United States. Along with the outcry over the Malmedy case, described in my paper, this predisposed Clay in all probability against further commutations.

So Clay left him, as Mr. McCloy told us yesterday, a very nasty problem. Although he wanted to leave McCloy a clean slate, he was unable to do so.

Morris Amchan: The only point that I wanted to make was that the Nuremberg Trials were not part of the occupation. They were totally independent. And the point I was asking you to make, which I think you did make, is that the military trials were separate and apart from the Nuremberg Trials, and the coercion that was found to exist with respect to the military trials did not exist in the Nuremberg Trials, and that point I think you made effectively and I thank you.

Sixth Session

Source Materials
for the History of
American Military Government

Introduction by Mabel E. Deutrich

We are well into our second day of listening to some very interesting papers relating to the occupations of Germany and Japan following World War II. These papers, however, could not have been produced without documentation. Important questions, then, are: Where is this documentation? How extensive is it? How accessible is it? And when we talk about accessibility we need to think in terms of restrictions on the use of the records, the arrangement of the records, and the availability of finding aids.

Assembled here is a panel of experts to talk to you about source materials for the history of American military government in Germany and Japan. Since the largest groups of documents in the United States relating to the occupation of these two countries are among the holdings of the National Archives and Records Service, it should come as no surprise that three of the panel members are my colleagues from the National Archives and Records Service.

Although the largest volume of occupation records are in the National Archives and Records Service, there are significant collections elsewhere. To reply to questions about these records we have Captain Robert H. Alexander, director of the MacArthur Memorial Library, and Dr. Fred L. Hadsel, executive director of the George C. Marshall Research Foundation.

The two basic tools of an archivist servicing federal records are a knowledge of the administrative histories of the organizational elements that created the records, and a knowledge of their record-keeping systems. This holds true whether the research relates to the occupation of Germany and Japan or any other subject. This knowledge must extend far beyond a knowledge of the system itself. It must include information on how a particular agency or organization interpreted or implemented the system. Most War Department agencies filed the bulk of their records according to the WD decimal filing system. But Mr. Hastings states that the Joint Chiefs of Staff classified much of its documentation relating to occupation planning under the decimal number 383.21 which stands for "military government" while the Joint Affairs Committee used 014, the number meaning "civil affairs."

But even this explanation is too simple. There are few documents that relate strictly to one subject and so the various agencies usually adopted guidelines for the classifiers of the documents. To give you just one simple example, the Office of the Chief of Engineers had a rule that said that if you had a document that related to money for a particular item or activity, you should never classify the document under the number for money if you knew what the money was for. Thus a document relating to money for the construction of a road would have been classified under 611, the number for roads, instead of 121.2, the number for funds. The Office of the Quartermaster General took the opposite view. This, of course, is where the archivist comes into the picture. He or she has knowledge of these variations.

Whereas a knowledge of the administrative histories is of great importance to the researcher using federal records, the names of people is of basic importance to the researcher using personal papers or manuscript collections. The questions for which you need answers are: Who were the key people involved in the undertaking? Where are their records? Some of the personal papers containing information on the occupation of Germany and Japan are in our presidential libraries; many are in other repositories.

All of you are aware of the desirability of exploiting published sources, both primary and secondary, before using original records. I am not going to discuss published records except that I do want to refer to the *Foreign Relations* series produced by the State Department. An examination of these volumes is a prerequisite to research in the original records. Not only does use of these volumes provide the researcher easy access to basic documentation, but the footnotes and editorial notes provide references to other related documents. When referring to related documents that were not published, this fact is generally noted. This is extremely helpful because the researcher knows he or she must go to the original records to find the document(s).

There is one thing, however, that the State Department does not do that would be a great boon to researchers; it does not mark the original documents to indicate that they have been printed in *Foreign Relations*. Because of this, Dr. Gustafson suggests that researchers prepare a list of the printed documents to prevent a waste of time in doing archival research. This is, of course, good advice. But think of the time it takes to prepare such a list! Furthermore, each researcher must go through this laborious task! If the State Department could see its way clear to neatly stamping the documents that are published, the archivists and historians using the records would applaud its efforts.

Chapter 15

State Department Records in the National Archives Relating to the Occupations of Germany and Japan

Milton O. Gustafson

My topic today is State Department records in the National Archives as source materials for the history of United States military government in Germany and Japan, 1944–52. It is getting harder and harder for me to give a speech like this because the State Department is transferring more and more records to us, and I have an ever-increasing amount of records to talk about. Many of you have used State Department records in your research, and have talked to our reference archivists. They are still the best source of information about records in our custody. You must talk to them again, because I cannot hope to describe adequately in a few minutes everything that I would like to mention.

I would like to begin with a general discussion of access to State Department records in NARS, advise how a researcher can prepare for a research visit and best use his time during that visit, and then briefly describe several dozen unique groups of State Department records that specifically relate to our topic today.

First, I want to emphasize that State Department records in the National Archives are open to all researchers (from all countries) on an equal basis. No longer is there a period of "limited access," whereby American scholars applied to the State Department for a security clearance to gain privileged access to certain records, took notes only (no copies allowed), and then submitted those notes for review by State Department officials. Now, no one will review your notes, and, if you wish, you can obtain a copy of any document you use.

There are, and there always have been, some documents that have been removed from the boxes because they are still security-classified or are otherwise restricted. Our system for handling such material is much better now than it used to be. Before, we had to remove categories of documents that the State Department wanted us to remove; now, the Freedom of Information Act prevents us from removing documents unless they fall under one of nine specifically exempted categories. Before, documents were removed and the researcher had no way of knowing how many documents were removed and how important they might be to his topic; now, whenever we remove anything from a box we must insert a withdrawal notice, identify the document or file, and list the reason for its removal. Before, there was nothing the researcher could do about the documents that had been removed; now, the researcher can make a request under the Freedom of Information Act for a special review. If the documents must remain security-classified, a State Department official at the rank of deputy assistant secretary (or someone at equivalent rank in another agency for information from the other agency) must make that determination in writing. If the documents are unclassified but otherwise exempt from release, the assistant archivist for the National Archives must make that determination in writing. In both instances, the requester may follow administrative procedures to appeal the agency decision, and if the appeal is denied, sue in a federal district court.

Freedom of Information requests are time-consuming, and the results are not always worth the effort (and taxpayer's dollars) that must be expended to handle them. So, we prefer to work with researchers and advise them about keeping their requests reasonable. What kinds of documents, for example, are withdrawn from State Department files? The largest category is records that are still classified, for which agencies have not given us declassification authority. Within this category, most of the withdrawn documents are those which reveal information classified by a foreign government and furnished to the United States government in confidence. Second are those intelligence documents which reveal sources and methods of intelligence.

Let me move on to my second point—how can a researcher prepare for a research visit? A key research tool for anyone using State Department records is the documentary publication *Foreign Relations of the United States*. Many of the most important documents

have been printed there, and researchers should study those volumes carefully. It is a waste of time to read and take notes on original documents that have already been printed, and there are no
marks on the originals to indicate they were printed. The file citation for each document that was printed also serves to identify the
file that may contain other documents on the same subject that were
not printed.

Naturally, before using archival sources, a researcher should be
well versed in other published primary and secondary sources—
particularly memoirs and biographies, and congressional hearings
and other items in the serial set. An archivist cannot perform research for the researcher, but if the researcher fully explains his
topic, the archivist can save the researcher's time by directing his
attention to the most significant archival sources for his topic.
Briefly, that is what I plan to do now.

I will talk about records in the four National Archives record
groups that have State Department records relating to the occupation of Germany and Japan. There are two kinds of finding aids for
these records—those prepared by the State Department at the time
the records were indexed and filed, and those prepared by the National Archives after the records were accessioned.

There are over 19,000 cubic feet of records in Record Group 59,
General Records of the Department of State, divided into over 900
separate series, and described in a preliminary inventory of 311
pages, including nine appendices and an index, published in 1963. It
is out of date, and is being revised, but it still will not be of much
help because approximately half of those 19,000 feet of records are
in only one of those 900 series—the Decimal File, the most important series for most research topics.

The decimal file is a subject filing system in which all possible
subjects are assigned a number according to a decimal classification
scheme. It was the central foreign policy file for the State Department. For the period from 1910 to 1963, most State Department
records—correspondence between the department and its diplomatic and consular officials in the field, other government agencies,
foreign governments, Congress, the president, and the public, dealing with practically all activities of the department, plus internal
memorandums and reports—are all in the decimal file. In order to
find what you need, a researcher must turn to the first kind of
finding aid—those prepared in the State Department at the time
the records were filed.

Besides the published classification manual, which gives the subject for each decimal file number (available as microfilm publication M600), there are three other finding aids. The first is the subject index—in purport books from 1910 to 1944, and purport cards after July 1944. Each document is described—from, to, date, file number, subject, and a sentence of substantive information about the document; the subject index is arranged the same way the records are arranged—by decimal file number. The second index is the source card index—the same information but arranged according to the source of the document and thereunder chronologically. The third index is a selected name card index.

There are four major segments of the decimal file for occupation policy for the 1945–49 period. Files beginning with the number 894 (8 is for internal affairs of states and 94 is the country number for Japan), are in 65 boxes, and there are hundreds of subtopics—after the decimal point—for political affairs, the constitution, military affairs, social matters, economic and financial matters, manufacturing, transportation, and communications. Files beginning with 862 (internal affairs of Germany; 62 is the number for Germany) are in 187 boxes.

The decimal filing system was too inflexible to cope with a subject as big as a world war. After 1939, everything related to World War II was filed under 740.0011 (which means general political relations of Europe), and other digits and words were added to the decimal file number. The other two main files, then, are 740.00119 Control (Germany), in 174 boxes, and 740.00119 Control (Japan), in 20 boxes. Finally, documents of interest might be located in many other decimal files—those I have listed are only the largest—and can be found through use of the indexes and cross-references.

Records in the decimal file for the 1950–54 period are still in the State Department. It would be impossible to separate those dated 1950 from those dated 1951–1954, and so the records of the 1951–1954 period will be transferred to the National Archives only after the State Department can also transfer to us the authority to declassify its records through 1954. The transfer of such a large quantity of records, and the page-by-page review for items that must be withdrawn, will create enormous problems for us, but the opening of records in a five-year block will be a tremendous boon to researchers.

The other records I want to talk about are called "lot files" by State Department historians, a term that loosely describes everything not in the central decimal file. During World War II and the postwar period, many offices in the State Department began to keep important documents and series in their own office files instead of sending them to the records service center for indexing and filing in the decimal file. State Department offices seldom created finding aids for their own office files, although we do have some lists of folder labels. Many of these lot files have been recently transferred to the National Archives, but they are not yet included in any published inventory. They are listed in *Prologue,* and other scholarly journals, as they are accessioned, and we have prepared a unique kind of in-house finding aid for them called a "List of Special Files," which we make available to researchers.

Among the lot files specifically dealing with the occupation of Germany are the records of Philip E. Mosely, United States political adviser to the European Advisory Commission, 1943–45 (36 boxes), records of the meetings of the Council of Foreign Ministers, 1945–49 (384 boxes), and records of the Allied Control Council, 1945–50 (57 boxes). Among the records of the State Department's Central European Division, 1944–53, are 5 boxes of records relating to the work of the German Branch.

Lot files specifically relating to the occupation of Japan include records of the Far Eastern Commission, 1945–51 (249 boxes), records of the Allied Council for Japan, 1946–52 (27 boxes), and reports on the Japanese Economy, 1938–46, gathered by Corwin Edwards, later chief of the State Department's International Resources Division.

Dean Acheson has written that proliferation of meetings is an inevitable product of weak leadership and administration, and that when the Department of State was run by meetings, committees, or soviets, it was not run at all. Nevertheless, we do have an abundance of State Department committee records. Much of the material on postwar planning committees was assembled by Harley A. Notter, which we list as the Notter File. Committee records in this file (327 boxes) include the Advisory Committee on Post-War Foreign Policy, the Policy Committee, the Postwar Problems Committee, various interdivisional country and area committees, and the Executive Committee on Economic Foreign Policy. There is another large lot file (150 boxes) consisting of various committee records maintained by the central secretariat of the department. Perhaps the most important of these is the Secretary's Staff Committee, which met 207 times from December 1944 to January 1947. The records of this committee have just become available as a National Archives microfilm publication (M1054, 5 rolls).

Another important committee for occupation policy was the State-War-Navy Coordinating Committee (SWNCC), later State-Army-

Navy-Air Force Coordinating Committee (SANACC). Although SWNCC documents are scattered in many different files, most of the official records of SWNCC were transferred as one lot file. The records include numbered SWNCC documents in 402 separate subject files (in 70 boxes), 18 boxes relating to the work of the Subcommittee for the Far East, two boxes relating to the Informal Policy Committee on Germany (IPCOG), four boxes relating to the Subcommittee for Europe, and 23 boxes of separate subject files.

There are several lot files relating to the activities of the secretary of state. Edward Stettinius kept a record, a weekly diary of his activities, for the period from December 1944 to July 1945. For George Marshall, we have copies of his memos to the president, arranged chronologically. For the Acheson period, we have several series of records of the Executive Secretariat, including summaries of the Secretary's Daily Meetings, and several series relating to the staff meetings conducted by the undersecretary of state. Another lot file kept by the Executive Secretariat is called Daily and Weekly Summaries of Current Foreign Relations, prepared for distribution to various levels in the State Department and the White House.

One lot file that is getting more use because of a subject card index recently made available, is the State Department's collection of intelligence reports prepared by its Research and Analysis Branch, which was under the Office of Strategic Services during World War II. There is one series of reports, numbered from 1 to 8506, dated from 1941 to 1961, in over 500 boxes. We also have a collection of 138 research reports prepared by the Historical Office of the State Department, 1944–50, but more important are the numbered policy studies prepared by the Policy Planning Staff, 1947–49. There are other records of the Policy Planning Staff, however, that we have not accessioned because the State Department cannot yet give us the authority to declassify them.

Other records, of more specific importance to occupation policy, are 15 boxes of records relating to wartime conferences, from Moscow in 1943 to Potsdam in 1945; 111 boxes relating to the reparations missions of Edwin Pauley, 1945–48; 7 boxes of records of the Office of the Assistant Secretary for Occupied Areas, 1946–49; 4 boxes of records of Arthur Gardiner, 1947–49, relating to the European Recovery Program and trade negotiations with Germany and Japan; 12 cubic feet of records maintained by the political adviser in Frankfurt and Berlin; and 34 cubic feet maintained by the political adviser in Tokyo.

Finally, I want to mention briefly the records of the Office of Public Opinion Studies, 1943–63, which consist of special reports and studies of public opinion in the United States on foreign policy questions, including special reports on Germany and Japan. Also valuable for public opinion research are the verbatim records of State Department press conferences, 1929–70, prepared for departmental use, but not otherwise available to researchers until now.

Chapter 16

United States Military Records in the National Archives Relating to the Occupations of Germany and Japan

James J. Hastings

As World War II drew to a close, the American military establishment in Washington and the United States forces in the field found themselves having to think about more than just winning the war. By late 1944, they were under great pressure to determine what was to be done when the Allied armies entered the defeated nations. As diplomatic officers discussed the shape of the postwar world, military officers planned the administration of the areas to be occupied. By autumn of 1945, the administration of the occupied areas became the primary responsibility of the American military. In the course of this massive military venture of occupying Japan and Germany, thousands of people produced an enormous amount of paper records. This mass of paper remains as a legacy of the American proconsuls.

Even if we had the time and patience, the military records pertaining to the two occupations could not be described in fifteen hours. Because we have only fifteen minutes, this presentation is merely a brief overview of the files, presented in the hope that this introduction will assist individuals contemplating a visit to the National Archives. Only a personal experience with the records can provide a full appreciation of what Earl Ziemke describes in *The U.S. Army in the Occupation of Germany* as "an archival smorgasbord."

The military records in the National Archives pertaining to the two occupations can be divided into two broad categories; the records of the Washington-based military headquarters, and the records of the military field commands in Japan and Germany. The diversity of the files at both the Washington and the field levels presents a bureaucratic maze that can bewilder an unprepared researcher. Those of us who were not involved with one of the occupations must depend on secondary sources for explanations as to who was responsible for particular aspects of the American proconsular venture. The researcher who comes to the National Archives with a reasonable understanding of the administrative structure of the occupation bureaucracy will be at a distinct advantage. The following paragraphs will introduce the researcher to the pertinent records in the military chain of command.

Washington Headquarters

In the hierarchy of the exclusively military agencies in Washington (below the civilian secretaries and assistant secretaries of war and navy) the Joint Chiefs of Staff was the highest ranking organization. The Joint Chiefs of Staff consisted of the Army chief of staff, the chief of naval operations and the commanding general of the Army Air Force. As the military policy development organization, the JCS was involved with all phases of strategic and operational planning. Its responsibilities included planning for the occupation of the defeated nations and, in this capacity, it worked closely with the State-War-Navy Coordinating Committee. As in most high level organizations, much of the policy formulation occurred in committees and lower level organizations, namely the Joint Civil Affairs Committee, the Combined Civil Affairs Committee, and the War Department Civil Affairs Division and Operations Division.

The records of the Joint Chiefs consist of the central files of the JCS which include documentation from the lower levels. The documents from the lower levels provide background to the formal papers of the JCS, thus constituting a significant series of records of occupation policy formulation. The files are arranged by the War Department decimal system with geographical subdivisions. The principal designation for occupation related materials is 383.21 (Military Government).

The Joint Civil Affairs Committee maintained separate files and these records remain as a rich source on occupation policy through 1946. The arrangement is also according to the War Department decimal system, although the clerks in the JCAC opted to file documents relating to occupation activities under 014 (Civil Matters).

A notch below the Joint Chiefs level in the military hierarchy was the War Department, in particular the War Department General and Special Staffs. Of these the Civil Affairs Division and the Operations Division (later Plans and Operations Division, Department of the Army) and the Office of the Provost Marshal General were the organizations directly involved with the occupations. The Office of the Director of Intelligence (G-2), although not directly engaged in occupation activities, did gather a great deal of information on occupied Germany and Japan and these records should be noted.

Although there were no military offices in Washington concerned exclusively with occupation matters, the Civil Affairs Division of the War Department directed most of its effort toward this end. The CAD was established in 1943, to advise the commanders in the field on procedures in administrating captured territory. In addition, the CAD provided supporting information to the Joint Chiefs for use in policy formulation. The files, therefore, include documentation that reflects activities in the field as well as documentation of JCS and SWNCC internal policy matters. The records include items such as case files, reports, correspondence, guides, and other fundamental materials. Although the CAD was not involved in all high level aspects of the occupations, there is significant documentation on many subjects such as economic recovery in Japan and reeducation in Germany.

The Operations Division also communicated directly with the commanders in the field as well as the higher authorities in JCS and SWNCC. The division's responsibilities were broader in scope than those of the CAD in its capacity as the principal strategic, logistical, and operational planner in the War Department. The Operations Division was a "super" agency, with responsibilities that touched on all aspects of military activities. Its involvement with occupation activities stemmed from its status as "special assistant" to the Army Chief of Staff and its concern with strategic implementation of policy in the field. Topics of interest included among the OPD files are constitutional revision in Japan and plans for bizonal economic cooperation in Germany.

Among the responsibilities of the Office of the Provost Marshal General (PMGO) was selection and training of military government personnel. The PMGO established the School for Military Government in Charlottesville, Virginia, in 1942, and the records of this unit provide insight into the planning for the occupations. The records consist of files of the PMGO and the School for Military Government and include various reports, lectures, handbooks, and similar documentation reflecting American preparation for posthostility military government.

The Office of the Director of Intelligence was responsible for gathering and reporting information on military, political, economic, and social developments in all parts of the world. For the period of 1944–52, there are thousands of reports dispersed among the files that relate to Japan and Germany. The reports were prepared by Army Intelligence officers as well as by other military and civilian intelligence agencies.

Research in
Washington Headquarters Files

The records of the Washington military headquarters document official policy formulation and direction and are an indispensable source. Because the military was involved in all aspects of postwar Japan and Germany, Washington could not direct every activity in the field. Consequently, the Washington headquarters files do not provide documentation specifically related to every occupation topic. Even when not directly involved, Washington provided the foundation for activity and the records, therefore, have at least a tangential pertinence to all topics. The orderly arrangement of most of the records makes it relatively easy to locate files relating to many areas.

There has been a great deal of progress in the declassification of the military headquarters records within recent years. Most of the records dated prior to 1950 are now declassified. Those not declassified present declassification problems because they include material protected under the national security or privacy exemptions of the Freedom of Information Act. The authority of the National Archives and Records Service to declassify such records is therefore limited. Particularly affected are records of the Department of the Army intelligence (G2) and operations (G3) staffs.

Field Commands

All of the records to this point have two characteristics in common; they are central policy making files of relatively modest volume, and they are rather well arranged and described. As we move to the records of the field commands, modest volume and adequate descriptions no longer apply. The files maintained in the field are administrative records that accumulated during the day to day activities of the occupations. They are not central files but widely diversified office and individual files, with arrangements ranging from ingenious to nonexistent.

The records of the Supreme Headquarters, Allied Expeditionary Forces (SHAEF); United States Forces European Theater (USFET); the European Command (EUCOM); and the Office of Military Government for Germany, United States (OMGUS) document the occupation of Germany. For Japan the records of American Forces, Pacific (AFPAC) and the Supreme Commander for the Allied Powers (SCAP) are the files of the occupation.

Field level planning for the military occupation and government of Germany is relatively well documented in the SHAEF files, in particular the G-5 (Civil Affairs) Section. The records of other general staff sections and the Secretary General Staff also include files relating to occupation activities as do the G-5 sections of the numbered armies attached to SHAEF. Reports of lower level military government detachments are dispersed through the SHAEF records.

SHAEF was terminated on July 14, 1945, and its occupation responsibilities in the United States zone of Germany were inherited by the United States Forces, European Theater. The USFET Secretary General Staff files include material on the transitional stage of the occupation prior to the creation of the Office of Military Government for Germany, United States, on October 1, 1945. The records of OMGUS constitute the administrative files of the occupation of Germany and include the records of its predecessor, the United States Group Control Council.

The abrupt end of the war in the Pacific caused the American military to be less prepared for the occupation of Japan than Germany. Consequently, the records of AFPAC pertaining to the occupation are sketchy. SCAP was created on September 2, 1945, with broad instructions to administer the occupation of Japan. Because of the circumstances, most of the planning was *ad hoc* reaction.

Although SCAP and OMGUS differed in some administrative aspects, the records of the two organizations are similar in arrangement, physical condition, adequacy of finding aids, and declassification.

The arrangement of OMGUS and SCAP records is hierarchical, roughly according to the organization of the two administrations at the end of each occupation period. Both occupation authorities were organized into functional units. In Germany the highest headquarters functional unit was the division and thereunder the branch. Below the headquarters level were the military governments of Bavaria, Hesse, Württemberg-Baden, the Bremen enclave, and the

American sector of Berlin. The administrative organization of the lower level military governments was patterned on the headquarters model. In SCAP the section was the highest functional unit, followed by the division and then the branch.

While administrative details such as this may be dry, it is essential that the researcher have an understanding of the administrative history because, in keeping with standard American records keeping practice, there are no central files of the occupations. Each section, division, office, and most individual officers maintained separate files for daily use. The key to finding pertinent material, therefore, is a knowledge of which administrative unit was responsible for specific functions.

The volume of the OMGUS records is 8,000 feet; SCAP is 10,000 feet. When the records were prepared for shipment to the United States, screening teams in Japan and Germany stuffed the files into footlockers and made lists of the folder titles. When the files arrived in the United States they were reboxed but the records remain in the same unprocessed condition and the shipping lists are the only finding aids. Because these are administrative files, the researcher often encounters records concerning personnel actions, routine housekeeping matters, travel authorizations, and press clippings in addition to more valuable documents. The shipping lists provide an indication as to the contents of a folder but only a vague, and sometimes misleading, indication of the nature of the specific record.

Most of the records of SCAP and OMGUS are declassified. Prior to this declassification, researchers needed a clearance from the Army to use the files. This is no longer the case, indeed the Army no longer grants clearances to use these records because of the declassification. Although most of the records are declassified, the staff of the National Archives must screen the files for material that is restricted for reasons other than security classification, such as an investigative document which if released could be considered an invasion of an individual's privacy.

Research in SCAP and OMGUS Records

The complex arrangement, the unprocessed physical condition, the inadequate finding aids, and the need for screening are all inhibiting factors and may be enough to frighten timid researchers into reconsidering their career goals. Indeed, the volume of the SCAP records alone prompted Professor John Dower to comment in the

February 1975 *Journal of Asian Studies:* "Most scholars could not walk the length of the collection let alone read it."

Nevertheless, significant research has been done in SCAP and OMGUS records and a great deal remains to be done. The files lend themselves to work in all aspects of the occupations except for official policy planning for Japan, which, as Milton Gustafson noted, and Marlene Mayo has amply demonstrated, are more heavily documented in State Department files. A few examples should serve as an indication of the potential of these records. The records of the Government Section of SCAP provide the background to the constitutional revision in Japan; those of the Civil Information and Education Section, Women's Affairs Branch, document the development of American policies toward the women of Japan. The Economic and Scientific Section records provide minute detail into the elimination of *zaibatsu* control, and the records of the Civil Affairs Section illustrate the activities at the prefectural and local level in the later years of the occupation.

Representative samples of OMGUS records include the Manpower Division's files on the formulation of trade unions; the decartelization files of the Finance, Economics and Legal Divisions; documentation of the publications control activities and public opinion research of the Information Control Division; several files concerning the establishment of zonal boundaries among the records of the Adjutant General; and, at the local level, detailed observations of all aspects of life in the American zone. The records of OMGUS are more detailed and voluminous at the local level than the records of SCAP.

Although the SCAP and OMGUS records provide ample research opportunities, there are limits. Because these are administrative files and consist of such an enormous volume, research topics within the files should be well defined and, if possible, should be confined to the records of one functional section, division, or branch. The administrative nature of the records also tends to blur the record of activities of particular persons involved in the occupations, making biographical research very difficult.

Special Records

The records of the Washington headquarters and the files of the field commands are not the only sources of military records of the occupations. The National Archives Collection of World War II War Crimes

Records includes the trial records of the International Military Tribunal at Nuremberg, and of the International Military Tribunal for the Far East, including the records of the International Prosecution Section, and the files of the twelve subsequent proceedings of the United States tribunals at Nuremberg. The records of the Office of the Judge Advocate General include copies of United States trials in Germany and Japan as well as clemency petitions. Class B and C war crimes transcripts are among the records of SCAP.

Also of possible interest are the records of the United States Strategic Bombing Survey. The purpose of this organization was to determine the effects of aerial attacks on Germany and Japan. The reports of USSBS constitute a significant source for conditions in Japan and Germany immediately after the war.

Future Use

Although research in the military records concerning the occupation of Japan or Germany is a time consuming and difficult task, researchers should not be discouraged. Thorough scholarly work is possible in the files, as evidenced by the papers presented in this conference. In addition, the international importance of the records has sparked ambitious description and reproduction projects.

As mentioned previously, the Bundesarchiv (Archives of the Federal Republic of Germany), the Institut für Zeitgeschichte (Institute for Contemporary History), and various other public and private institutions in Germany have embarked on a joint program with the National Archives to make the records of OMGUS more accessible to scholars in Germany as well as the United States. The three to five year project involved detailed folder descriptions of each folder in the massive records. The folders were described by teams of German archivists and historians who selected as much as 50 percent of the records for reproduction on microfiche. The reproductions are deposited in the Bundesarchiv as well as in the National Archives. We hope that the descriptive material will be computerized for a future, ultramodern finding aid.[1]

A joint project is also in progress for the Japanese records. The National Diet Library in Tokyo and the National Archives have reached tentative agreement to describe and reproduce SCAP records.[2]

Records of the occupations of Japan and Germany have received enormous use in the past few years. The description and reproduction projects now under way will make the records even more accessible. Perhaps research in the records of the American proconsuls has reached the point that Vergil's rumination in the days of the original proconsuls no longer applies. The Roman bard in his *Georgics* pondered that "happy is the man who plucks the fruits from the branches that the fields willingly yield; and avoids the iron laws, the mad court, and the public archives."

Chapter 17

Resources of Presidential Libraries for the History of Post–World War II American Military Government in Germany and Japan

Benedict K. Zobrist

The presidential libraries, now spanning from the Hoover through the Johnson administrations, present to the scholar almost boundless resources on nearly every aspect of American life and world affairs during the middle years of the twentieth century.[1] As with most broad subjects, major aspects of the history of American military government in Germany and Japan can be found in these libraries.

Indeed, one recent writer on American military government has flatly stated that "the word which best describes the source materials available on the post-World War II occupation of Germany is *awesome*." I would add the adjectives "extremely diverse and scattered" as well. In addition, the very subject presents extreme complexities and ramifications because of the wide scope of government involvement ranging from the White House down to a bewildering array of commissions and committees, to say nothing of the United Nations' involvement and civilian relief organizations. The writer of that volume also commented that the groups of records pertaining to the occupation "defy categorization" and asserted that "individually and collectively they are an archival smorgasbord."[2] This description coincides completely with the findings of my survey of the resources of presidential libraries for the study of American military government in Germany and Japan.[3]

The exploration of this labyrinth starts logically with the Franklin D. Roosevelt Library at Hyde Park, New York. A considerable amount of material relating to the establishment of military governments in Germany and Japan is in the President's Secretary's File, the Official File, and the Map Room File of the Roosevelt papers. Discussions concerning the political treatment of occupied areas as well as initial concerns and controversies over the degree of military as against civilian control and the organization and training of military government personnel are documented in these collections. Also included is an extensive file on the Charlottesville School of Military Government. Intimately related to these policy matters is considerable correspondence concerning the United Nations Relief and Rehabilitation Administration (UNRRA) and the potential political side effects of the distribution of food and supplies in occupied territories. Much of the material in the Secretary's File and the Official File deals with the domestic side of these issues while the Map Room papers include documentation of military viewpoints and exchanges with foreign governments, particularly Great Britain.

Similar materials, found in several other collections in the Roosevelt Library, describe advance planning for occupation in far greater detail than do the White House files and carry the story forward into the occupation period after President Roosevelt's death. Most closely related to Roosevelt's papers are those of presidential advisor Harry L. Hopkins. The Hopkins papers contain files on postwar planning, supplies for liberated areas, and refugees in occupied areas. Extensive background files prepared for conferences such as Yalta and Moscow detail American planning for occupation, and reveal the American positions as they were argued by staff planners before such conferences.

At the Roosevelt Library the most voluminous files relating to military governments are to be found in the papers of Henry M. Morgenthau, Jr., Roosevelt's secretary of the treasury. In the so-called Morgenthau diary there are hundreds of entries for "post-war planning" and "military government," as well as files on the Morgenthau Plan, American fiscal planning for occupation, reparations, financing the occupation, and UNRRA. Morgenthau's papers reflect his interest in limiting the industrial reconstruction of Germany so as to ensure that Germany could never again wage war, as well as his deep concern for the plight of refugees in occupied Europe.

Papers of two members of the Board of Economic Warfare (BEW)—Oscar Cox and Louis Bean—have files on BEW planning for postwar Germany and Japan, and for their occupation. The Cox papers have, in addition, files on "Aid to Reoccupied Countries," "End of War Thinking," UNRRA, and the various conferences where postwar settlements were discussed. Cox's files also have his personal correspondence with General Lucius D. Clay, head of Allied military government for Germany.

Isador Lubin was associate representative of the United States on the Allied Reparations Commission. His papers have files on the commission and its activities, as well as Lubin's correspondence with the United States Group Control Council, various members of the military governments for Germany and Japan, and a file on European economic recovery.

Charles Fahy, solicitor general of the United States from 1941 to 1945, was involved in the planning for military governments and was legal advisor for the one established in Germany. There are many files in his papers on the legal problems of that government during the year he served in that position. The Fahy papers are presently restricted and require Judge Fahy's permission for access.

Among several collections of secondary interest at the Roosevelt Library, the records of the War Refugee Board contain some correspondence relating to German refugees, particularly the necessity to provide supplies. These records cover the period up to the termination of the board on September 15, 1945. In the papers of Herbert C. Pell there is a small amount of scattered correspondence in connection with Pell's position with the War Crimes Commission. The correspondence of Myron Taylor includes letters written by him as United States representative to the Intergovernmental Committee for Refugees. Recently opened papers of Mordecai Ezekiel, economic advisor to the secretary of agriculture, contain a small amount of material on food problems and refugee resettlement in occupied areas.

At the Truman Library, Independence, Missouri, the papers of President Truman yield relatively little material on American military government during the postwar period. Of significance, however, are the papers of Abijah U. Fox, who was deputy director of the finance Division of the American military government in Germany, and those of J. Anthony Panuch, advisor to General Clay in Germany during the years 1947–49. The papers of Edward A. Tenenbaum have just been acquired by the Truman Library, but not yet processed. In 1945 Tenenbaum joined the Finance Division of the United States military government in Germany where his main responsibility was in negotiating, planning, and executing the German currency reform of 1948.

In the papers of Secretary of State Dean Acheson, transcripts of the so-called Princeton Seminars, recorded in 1953–54, include discussions of the problems which arose in establishing military government in Germany. Oral History inverviews with individuals such as General William H. Draper, Jr., chief of the Economic Division of the United States Group Control Council for Germany; John D. Hickerson, assistant secretary of state for United Nations affairs; General Charles Saltzman, assistant secretary of state for occupied areas; and James W. Riddleberger, political advisor to the high commissioner for Germany, also deal with the subject of military government. Extensive interviews with one of yesterday's participants, Jacques J. Reinstein, State Department special assistant for economic affairs and chief of the Division of German Economic Affairs, 1946–50, will soon be completed by the Truman Library.

Voluminous Herbert Hoover postpresidential files housed in his presidential library at West Branch, Iowa, reflect his views and those of his correspondents concerning major events of this era. During the spring of 1946, Hoover conducted a 52,000 mile world famine relief survey for the Truman administration and became intimately involved with the food problems of the occupied areas. His postpresidential subject files include substantial information gathered on this trip. In February 1947, again at President Truman's request, Hoover conducted a special survey of Germany and Austria.

In addition to his involvement with official government recommendations and policies, Hoover was active in several private relief agencies aiding occupied areas. His subject files on the American Field Service, CARE, and other agencies provide substantive information on conditions in the occupied countries and the progress of the relief effort.

Hoover corresponded with many individuals about the occupation and postwar policies. Perhaps the largest and most interesting correspondence file is that with John O'Laughlin. O'Laughlin, editor of the *Army-Navy Journal,* kept Hoover well supplied with information from the Washington scene.

Other materials of interest at the Hoover Library regarding occupation policies can be gleaned from related collections. Of particular interest are the diary of Maurice Pate, director of the United Nations International Children's Emergency Fund (UNICEF); the papers of Robert E. Wood, president of Sears Roebuck & Co.; papers of William R. Castle, undersecretary of state; and the papers of Felix Morley, editor of the *Washington Post.* It should also be noted that the Hoover Institution on War, Revolution, and Peace at Stanford University has a substantial portion of Hoover's records concerning postwar relief, as well as many other collections dealing with occupation policy.

Papers of General Dwight D. Eisenhower located at the Eisenhower Library in Abilene, Kansas, contain scattered references to American military government in Germany as do the papers of Charles D. Jackson, who headed the Psychological Warfare Division of Supreme Headquarters, Allied Expeditionary Force. The occupation of Japan is touched on by the papers of Naval Captain William W. Outerbridge and General Charles W. Ryder, commanding general of IX Army Corps. Although largely duplicated or microfilmed from National Archives sources, the General Walter Bedell Smith Collection of World War II Documents and various United States Army collections for this period are quite extensive and pertinent.

Even the John F. Kennedy Library, Boston, Massachusetts, contributes significant holdings on American military government. Walter W. Heller, President Kennedy's economics adviser and chairman of his Council of Economic Advisers, served as the chief of internal finance for the United States military government in Germany during 1947–48. In addition to the Heller papers, the personal files of James V. Bennett, director of the United States Bureau of Prisons, reflect his assignment in 1945 to organize civil prisons in Germany.

The John Kenneth Galbraith collection contains a fair amount of incidental material dealing with the economics of the postwar period. Leon B. Poullada's assignment as chief counsel at the Dachau War Crimes Trials and Drexel A. Sprecher's work as counsel at the Nuremberg Trials as well as his correspondence and reports of the Farben case and his editorship of the fifteen-volume *Trials of War Criminals before the Nuernberg* [sic] *Military Tribunals* are reflected in these respective collections.

And to pique your curiosity into exploring uncharted sources, I mention the James P. Warburg papers at the Kennedy Library. Although his official involvement in the war effort was limited to service with the Office of War Information, Warburg was throughout his life an avid and well-connected student, writer, and critic on American foreign policy with a special interest in Germany, the country of his birth. Warburg's "name file" contains extensive correspondence with a number of prominent figures in American foreign policy during this period, including Acheson, Bowles, Dulles, Eisenhower, Harriman, and Stevenson. He also wrote and spoke extensively on foreign policy in general and Germany in particular.

This survey is by no means exhaustive. Many small but significant collections have, of necessity, been omitted from this limited analysis. However, highly trained archivists, who are specialists in their period, as well as published listings and finding aids are available to assist the researcher at each of the presidential libraries.

A systematic study of the post–World War II occupation of Germany and Japan is still to be written. Whether the problem is that neither the military historian nor the political historian consider the subject to be in his domain or the sheer difficulty of mastering the voluminous materials, the fact remains that the record has been preserved and we look forward to serving our colleagues.

Discussion

Mabel. E. Deutrich: Frank J. Shulman, who with Robert E. Ward prepared the valuable bibliography entitled *The Allied Occupation of Japan, 1945 to 1952,* is in the audience. He has offered to describe pertinent materials in the McKeldin Library at the University of Maryland.

Frank Joseph Shulman: The East Asia Collection at the McKeldin Library, University of Maryland, College Park, contains what is probably the single largest collection of published materials in Japanese from the years 1946 through 1949. These consist of tens of thousands of books, magazines, and newspapers including suppressed and censored materials from the files of the Civil Censorship Detachment. They cover all subjects ranging from the social sciences and the humanities to the technical sciences, agriculture, and forestry, even children's literature. The present status of these holdings may be summarized as follows: There are approximately 10,000 titles each of newspapers and magazines from the occupation years. For certain titles we may have only one or two items—for others we may have a complete run. The magazines are in order, alphabetically, by title and chronologically by date of publication.

A catalog is to be published ultimately. Researchers and scholars interested in using these magazines at the McKeldin Library are welcome to use them. By the end of the summer we hope to have finished processing all of the magazines. The newspapers, on the other hand, are only one-third processed, and because of their very fragile nature they are not readily accessible. Nonetheless, to the extent that researchers have identified very specific issues of newspapers and wish to use them at the McKeldin Library, special arrangements can be made. These include censored newspapers where there are deletions and suppressions that never appeared in print. Approximately 11,000 books out of an estimated 40,000 books have been catalogued and, for the most part, are available on interlibrary loan. The remaining publications are arranged, more or less, by broad subject category, and interested users are welcome to come and browse the shelves and select the materials that are of use to them.

The censored files contain unique, irreplaceable documentary information concerning the intention of SCAP in censoring information within the Japanese press and in Japan as a whole. These contain the actual galley proofs, manuscripts, page proofs, with the deletions or suppressions and, in many cases, the English language working papers that explain the reasons for censoring materials, translate the objectionable passages, and often contain correspondence relating to specific deletions that proved controversial. These holdings, then, are available to a certain extent for researchers to use. However, they are neither microfilmed nor available in paper copy. There is no published catalog—researchers must come to College Park to make use of them. We are open Monday through Friday from eight in the morning to six in the afternoon, but special arrangements frequently can be made to accommodate the researcher's needs for evenings and weekends. The materials are available for those who read English without reading Japanese to the extent that working papers for the censored materials exist within our files. For the most part, however, our holdings are in Japanese and have not been translated and probably never will be translated into English.

Why is the collection unique then? First, whatever was actually deleted or suppressed is available nowhere else. Second, it represents the single largest collection in the West and, in some respects, the single largest collection anywhere in the world, Japan included, of materials from these years. Our newspaper holdings in particular are not found anywhere else.

Mabel E. Deutrich: Thank you very much. Having very magnanimously suggested that the State Department should mark the documents published in *Foreign Relations of the United States,* I think it is only fair that we give somebody a chance to comment. I wonder if Arthur Kogan would be interested in commenting.

Arthur G. Kogan: The idea of such a stamping procedure would be good, but we have to consider its practicality. One of the greatest difficulties in carrying out such a scheme would be that for many years our compilers have worked not from the original but from copies. A compiler looks at the material, a microfilm is made, and he works from that microfilm and blow-ups of that microfilm. He no longer sees the original documents. Another reason is that during compilation it is by no means clear what the ultimate product will be—how many documents may be eliminated in the process of reviewing at various levels, clearance problems of information furnished by foreign governments, and some technical considerations—so in the end, there is no final selection until actually the volume has been page-proofed. So what it really would entail would be a separate operation not in any way related to the work of the compiler; that would be extra work, we would run into great manpower problems. I just do not know how it could be done as part of our regular working procedures. Perhaps the technology of the future may allow it—but at the moment it is not feasible.

Mabel E. Deutrich: I am aware it would be a tremendous amount of extra work on your part. I am looking at it, of course, from the standpoint of researcher after researcher having to go through this laborious task of making a list of the documents that were published.

Eli E. Nobleman: There is a considerable amount of source material in the form of documentary material and published works at Fort Bragg, North Carolina, at the John F. Kennedy Center for Military Assistance where they have the Special Warfare School, the Civil Affairs School, and other training facilities. A large library has been set aside for material originally collected by Colonel Swarm when he was commandant of the United States Army Civil Affairs School, at Fort Gordon, which has been transferred to Fort Bragg, and has been catalogued and organized. In addition, there is what is known as the Marquat Library. Major General William F. Marquat was the first postwar chief of civil affairs and military government of the Army staff, and this library is dedicated to his own materials as well as other types of related materials. It is an excellent source, particularly with respect to Germany, and almost as good with respect to Japan. General Marquat served on General MacArthur's staff before he came back to the Pentagon. I think Marquat Library materials are easily available through interlibrary loan, and are worth your consideration for further research.

Brewster S. Chamberlain: Mr. McCloy mentioned yesterday that he at one point had made a lot of notes during his tenure as high commissioner in Germany but he has not the faintest idea where they might be. I am wondering where not only McCloy's notes are but what the condition of the HICOG records as such might be. [For a listing of HICOG records see Archival Sources: HICOG.—Ed.]

James J. Hastings: The records of the United States high commissioner for Germany are still in the jurisdictional control of the Department of State and are stored in the Washington National Records Center in Suitland, Maryland. They are under the control of the Department of State and open for research only with special permission of the Historical Office of the Department of State.

Arthur G. Kogan: One of the problems with the records of HICOG is that, to the best of my knowledge, there is really not one separate HICOG collection which would parallel the records of the Office of Military Government. This is the knowledge which we, in the Office of the Historian, have of this problem. I think the records of HICOG are scattered over several files in the Department of State. There are files of the posts in Frankfurt and Bonn and Berlin, and also retired files of the Office of German Affairs, and some of these files are in Suitland like most of the department's foreign service posts records, but I do not think that there was any comparable structured file of the United States high commissioner which would parallel the Office of Military Government for the period prior to 1950. So, in addition to all the questions of classification, there is the sheer problem of locating and identifying the records which can be classified or described as records of the Office of the United States High Commissioner.

Jacques J. Reinstein: Perhaps Dr. Kogan has answered my question. I have been curious as to what has happened to various collections of State Department documents, some of which I originated and some of which I or my colleagues have had occasion to use from time to time. Some of them were in Washington—for example, I put something like nine to fourteen cabinets of records in what was the warehouse up at M Street at one time. I suppose that is now in Suitland. I do not know whether they still exist as a unit. I am curious as to what happened to the records of the delegation to the German Debt Settlement negotiations in London which were carefully assembled over a period of three years, and which were needed for international arbitration proceedings that we had going on with Germany. Apparently these records have not been located. I gather that the only record that exists was kept in my office, rather inadequately at the time, in Washington. I am also rather curious as to what happened to all the records of the task force that sat during the summer of 1947 working up the material (I notice there is no reference to it in John Gimbel's book on the Marshall Plan) under the chairmanship of Willard Thorpe. In the evenings, about four nights a week, we developed material for our consultations with the Europeans when they came for friendly advice, and also organized ourselves for the inevitable meeting with the Congress. I just wondered where these records are to be found, and are there any inventories for them?

John Gimbel: I want to comment about Arthur Kogan's previous answer. I have trouble imagining that there are no HICOG records as such. I was at HICOG in 1953 and 1954 as a researcher before researchers were expected. I worked there for about two and a half months in the HICOG office there and they showed me a lot of files that they had in boxes there. They simply gave me special permission to use them. But there were at that time definitely HICOG files. Do you mean to tell me that those boxes were broken down and the files were put in other files afterwards? I saw these files at HICOG headquarters. And I would like to add to that—we have talked about this before, Arthur, and I know that you believe what you are saying but I do not think it is right.

Again, long before researchers were expected in those records, I was agitating for some access, and one of your predecessors, E. Taylor Parks, told me that there were eighty archives boxes. I forget (I have it in correspondence) whether he said footlockers or boxes. Anyway, eighty boxes of archives material were in a warehouse in Alexandria, Virginia, which he was willing to open up to me on a selected basis. This was just before Dr. Parks died, so I was never able to follow up, because after he was gone there was nobody else who would open them up for me. At any rate, I really have serious doubts, Arthur, that your answer is adequate. I am sorry to do this here but you asked for it.

Arthur G. Kogan: Well, the question has come up before, and all I can say when we have an occasional question from people who want to know something about HICOG records, it is the opinion of all of our people who have done extensive research in those files in the preparation of the *Foreign Relations* volumes. They said there are certain HICOG files, but they are split up in various portions of several other files, so there are subcategories. You find some HICOG files in Frankfurt post files, some in Bonn post files, some in German Affairs lot files, so that is the answer which I have always received from our colleagues who did the research with these records and worked with them on the preparation of the volumes. There could be some other separate groups of records—those that were in Alexandria would now be in Suitland, but I just do not think there is really a comparable collection to OMGUS, to the best of my knowledge.

If you saw them in Germany in the 1950s, a lot of changes take place in the transfer of records and it could very well have happened—before they were sent they may have been merged with other records—that is not unknown. So that would not necessarily be proof that the same collection is here, but if it exists in Washington, I do not know where. Again, Parks might have thought that he could put his finger on certain HICOG records, but it may have been within some other larger file group.

Milton O. Gustafson: I would like to make just one comment about the first question and about the later question of John Gimbel, too: I think one of the problems with State Department records and the problem of finding records is that the State Department, unlike the War Department and other executive agencies, was considered to have a central filing system. Every document that was ever created was supposed to go into the central filing system so that all of the files that were kept within an office—when you had to gather together documents from a lot of places to create a working file for a particular problem, the originals would all be in the central files where they belonged. So for many years the State Department's records officers and people believed that the items of importance were all in the central files and that the office files were not that important. When State Department historians began to do research for *Foreign Relations,* they discovered that many things that they really wanted were not to be found in the central files; they had to go to the office files. The problem now is trying to locate the HICOG files. When those office files were transferred to the records center in Suitland, or to some place, to try to keep track of all these transfers of records is a very difficult thing because you do not even know what was in those transfers. No one ever considered that those records had permanent value until much later when the historians got into them. That is a rather simplified answer for what happened to the things that you asked about, but we have recently accessioned a small group of records relating to European Recovery Program planning, which was one of the things that I left out, and it may be the very thing that Mr. Reinstein mentioned.

Sherrod E. East: With respect to the discussion about HICOG records, while I personally have not handled State Department records, the answer to the question lies in GSA's system which differentiates between the National Archives itself and the Federal Records Center system. Generally speaking, records in the Federal Records Center are still controlled, as far as access is concerned, by the agencies retiring them. In general, a plan was devised by Dr. Grover and Dr. Bahmer when the records center system was set up and they liquidated the intermediate depositories of the several agencies of the government, notably the Department of Defense. The plan was that at some time in the future, periodically perhaps, at twenty year intervals or as occasion demanded, the staff of the National Archives would select from the masses of material in the records centers those series deserving permanent preservation in the National Archives. This is one of the problems that we face now, but I will say this for the Federal Records Center system: Ned Campbell, who was administering the Region Three Federal Records Center which formerly was in Alexandria and is now in Suitland, had and they now have a very good control of accessioned collections *series by series*. If you would examine their control records of accessions from the Department of State or, incidently, from the Department of the Army after 1954, you would be surprised to find listed the new locations of these collections which you have seen (you, who participated in their creation or have used them during previous periods).

Now, with respect to Mr. Hastings' statement—I was a little surprised, if my hearing serves me rightly, he started with the Joint Chiefs of Staff. Secretaries Knox and Stimson might turn over in their graves if the records of their respective offices had not been referred to as sources on this subject under discussion. For instance, in the files of the secretary of war are the files of his several assistants, and there are some very good McCloy files there.

One other comment with respect to the Marshall Library and some six hundred reels of microfilm. The late Eugenia LeJeune, who was assistant to Dr. Pogue, developed what, in my judgment, is one of the best cataloging systems for controlling the selected documents included in that six hundred reels of microfilm, the bulk of which happens to have been taken from War Department records while Miss LeJeune and her staff were stationed in my office in Alexandria. This is simply to say that the so-called Marshall source materials relating to the occupations, insofar as they were covered in the files of the chief of staff himself (and, of course, in this period General Marshall was wearing two hats in that he was chairman of the Joint Chiefs and chief of staff for the War Department)—these files are replete with documentation which can be located through Miss LeJeune's cataloging system.

I would like to say that some of you who may have done some of your research during the period referred to by Mr. Gimbel and his special relationship with Mr. Parks might be happy that you did so rather than to go through the process afforded you by the Freedom of Information Act. One of my duties was to implement the Eisenhower policy on access to records, established in 1948 when he was chief of staff of the Army and which I was invited to forget about on many occasions—notably the McCarthy era—but that policy was one which afforded access to classified material for background purposes which made it possible for the production of some of the finest writing by unofficial historians at the same time that the official historians were preparing their products. I do not have to name them to this group. Suffice it to say now that that policy, as it was applied by the State Department under the regime of Dr. Noble and Mr. Parks was comparable to that followed by the Army through its Departmental Records Branch, and made possible a great deal of early substantive research.

Dean C. Allard: Since the Navy thinks it had something to do with making the occupation possible and certainly in supporting the occupation, I would like to mention that the records of the two forces that supported the occupation in Japan and in Germany, that is, United States Naval Forces Japan or United States Naval Forces Far East, and then United States Naval Forces Germany, are in the Archives annex at Suitland. So, if anyone were interested in the naval aspects of the occupation, those sources would be there. They were part of the so-called Flag Files that were accessioned several years ago out of the limbo of the Records Center to the Archives annex. Also, in case anyone is interested in the training of military civil affairs officers, the Naval History Division's archives, with which I am connected, does have some materials on the Civil Affairs School run by the Navy at Columbia and Princeton which could be of interest. We also have the papers of Captain Pence who was the head of the Occupied Territory Section of the Office of the Chief of Naval Operations. I might also mention that the Navy's main role in military government after the war had to do with what became of the Trust Territory of the Pacific Islands which the Navy administered until 1951. We do have the records of the Island Governments Branch of the Office of Chief of Naval Operations, which monitored that program.

Dagmar Gunther-Stirn: I have a very brief question for Mr. Hastings. I understand that there are records of Army commanders who participated in the occupation of Germany which are available at

Carlisle Barracks in Pennsylvania. To what extent are these records part of the OMGUS files and are they available for research?

James J. Hastings: The Carlisle Barracks is still a part of the Department of the Army and Dr. Deutrich knows more about it than I. I do not know which commanders' records are there. Essentially the function of that historical unit is to hold records that somehow do not fit into the purely governmental records that would be in the National Archives, and yet are not purely personal files that people can walk off with. Other than that, I really cannot help you as to which ones are there. I suggest that you contact Carlisle. I know that they are interested in business.

Mabel E. Deutrich: I think what Mr. Hastings said is correct. The Military Historical Records Collection of the Military History Institute is under the Army Center for Military History (ACMH), but it is not intended to be a repository for official federal records. It is quite appropriate for personal papers to be deposited there; it is quite appropriate for valuable records, but not the official records of the federal government.

John Mendelsohn: I have just a very brief comment on the HICOG records. We have about five feet of records of the Advisory Board on Clemency of High Commissioner McCloy in the National Archives. These have been incorporated in Record Group 238, the National Archives Collection on War Crimes Records, and are open for research.

Seventh Session

Impact of the Proconsular Experience on American Foreign Policy, National Security, and Civil Affairs Doctrine

Introduction by John D. Montgomery

This panel was not given one of those elegant titles devised by Robert Wolfe. "The Impact of the Proconsular Experience on American Foreign Policy, National Security, and Civil Affairs Doctrine" sounds like the subject of a master's thesis. In spite of the uninspired quality of the title, the questions which we plan to address are in some ways perhaps the most interesting of the conference, at least to those of us who think that what happens next in the world is more important than what happened a while ago. We are going to try tonight to explore the articulations between the past and the present, and to look a little to the future.

The set of questions we plan to discuss can find only fragmentary answers, but we hope that their mere posing will help us all examine our national experiences in the occupations in the search for wiser policies in the present and the near future. For we are not likely to go through another world war or mount another occupation of Germany or Japan. That bottom line question then has to be an extrapolation from the past. What did the occupation do to the United States itself in ways that "matter" in our present and perhaps our future? Most of our discussion in this conference has centered about the issue how did we get "there"? Did we, in fact, get to a particular "there" as a result of these occupations, or were there several "theres"? Were there also several "we's"?

There are many ways of thinking about this question. Tonight we
consider three of them: First, what was the effect of the occupations
on American foreign policy? How did the experience in Germany
and Japan, for example, affect our perceptions of the role of the
United States in Europe and the Far East? Second, what was the
effect of these experiences on the armed forces? To what extent did
the participation in an act sometimes thought of as reconstruction
affect the military's perception of its role in the world and its participation in the making and execution of foreign policy? To what
extent is the Army now capable of carrying out corresponding ventures that it might be charged with in the future? The third question
is more provocative still: Was there an accretion of American pride
and sense of mission that produced a direct line from Germany and
Japan to the Marshall Plan, Point Four, Lebanon, the Dominican
Republic, and Vietnam?

I am sure that our panelists will be relieved to hear me say that
none of us expects them to offer definitive answers to these questions. But we are expecting some interpretations of the facts presented at this conference, so we can draw, if not the bottom line, at
least a preliminary statement of the accounts.

Chapter 18

Impact of the Proconsular Experience on American Foreign Policy

An Engaged View

Jacob D. Beam

Actually, I am going to talk primarily about the division of Germany and the lessons we learned from the events that led up to it. I started, not quite at the beginning but in 1943, with the European Advisory Commission. I had spent two years as private secretary to Ambassador John Winant, who was chief American delegate to the Advisory Commission. He appointed me to be his observer. It was a very distinguished group of people—George Kennan, who was Winant's deputy; Philip Mosely was also on the commission; and we had two or three others: General Wickersham, and an Air Force colonel, and a Navy admiral.

We started in 1943. Of course, a lot of work had been done in the Department of State, but no zones had been drawn. We did not know how the occupation of Germany would be sorted out, as and when victory would be won. We and the British were not even on the Continent in September 1943. The British came through with a diagram outlining three zones—American, British, and Soviet (the French were not sovereign at that time). We looked it over very skeptically and so did the Russians. We thought that it was not too bad, considering the fact that we had not yet landed in Europe. The Russians, I am sure, looked it over from the standpoint of "You'll probably never get that far, why should we give you anything?" In due course this zone program was accepted at Yalta, together with a set of surrender terms—I think there were thirteen points.

When we finally reached the Continent, people forgot about this planning, and military considerations came first. When the surrender finally came, the terms which we had drawn up and had been approved at Yalta had somehow been forgotten. I think the United States Army's excuse was that it was a Combined Chiefs of Staff document which had been communicated without specific authorization of the United States Joint Chiefs of Staff. The resultant "short surrender terms" were actually improvised by Winston Churchill and General Eisenhower late at night. On May 7, they scared up a Russian general to sign these terms. Thereafter, that signatory, General Souslaparov, disappeared completely. Following the surrender, the terms which we drafted in London were finally proclaimed and became the basis for our legal actions in Germany.

At Potsdam, of course, the Allied Control Council was set up and Eisenhower was our representative, General Zhukov for the Russians, Sir Brian Robertson for the British, and General Koenig for the French. Our people made a real effort to get along with the Soviets to run Germany as a unified country, and Zhukov was very amiable, but we soon found out that he was not the man in control—it was a General Sokolovsky, so initial goodwill did not get us very far.

In the meantime, the State Department was underrepresented in Germany, although it was well served by Ambassador Robert Murphy. Mr. Byrnes was not greatly interested in Germany itself, and was more concerned with general European questions. The United States Army, quite rightly I think, went ahead in taking care of their needs in Germany and dominated the scene more and more. A rhetorical enquiry addressed to the secretary of state, Mr. Byrnes, as to whether General Clay would obey orders, evoked the reply that he probably would not, and so what of it?

The Army had to do all the work, they had the resources, and they knew very well that since they had to get the appropriations, this gave them power which would justify their doing pretty much as they wished. General Clay, who was assigned to the supply side during the war (he never had a command), enjoyed great influence with Congress. The State Department was simply not equipped to take over the operation of Germany at that time. To his great credit, General Clay went ahead quickly in establishing in the Germans a sense of initiative and patterning our organization to fit in with their local groups.

In the meantime, by late 1945, it became quite clear what the Soviets were doing. They stripped their zone while receiving a certain amount of reparations from our zone. Stories leaked back into West Germany of "atrocities," the way they treated the civilians in their zone.

Also, the matter of the Berlin elections came up, and despite every maneuver the Russians made, the Social Democrats won. But the Soviets tried to beguile us. Not all of our people knew a great deal about Germany in those days. I was sent to give our commandant some political advice. I remember the first thing he said was, "The Russians accuse us of putting up a man named [Ernst] Reuter who has a terrible record, he was with the German Army in Hungary and we just cannot have this man." I said, "Well, he is the best man we have." He was accepted and proved to be one of the very best mayors that Berlin ever had. This was the beginning of our learning about the Russians and also the Germans learning about the Russians.

The Germans could not comprehend our concern with denazification and this feeling seems to have been shared by Mr. Hull when he was secretary of state. On one occasion he told Mr. Murphy he had a very easy solution—let the Germans kill their own people, let us drop knives behind the lines, and then there would be no need for denazification when we get there. The War Department did not like that, the CIC said it would endanger our troops, so they entered into a much more elaborate plan.

General Clay had to take a number of political and economic initiatives just to keep the zone going. He had an active staff of educators, denazification people, and constitutional lawyers. I must say that sometimes they got in our hair, but also they got in his hair even more and he wisely paved the way for turning their responsibilities over to the Germans.

General Clay was also deeply interested in the economic reorganization of Germany and in upholding freedom of the press.

In 1946, it was fairly clear that reunification was a long way off, if it was possible at all. Mr. Murphy asked me and my staff to get up a theoretical study—if the Russians agreed to the reunification of Germany, how we could put the two pieces together, East and West. We came to the conclusion that such a feat was absolutely impossible. It was just about a year or so after the surrender. Everything in the Soviet zone was different, the laws were different, the social organizations were different, inheritance and currency were different, and it would have taken a very long time with the best of will to reunify Germany.

As regards the Germans, I think some of them were becoming less and less interested in reunification. The Bavarians did not wish to get together with the Protestant or "atheistic" people in the North, nor did the Rhinelanders. The people who were more interested than anybody else were the Berliners. The French, of course, were completely unenthusiastic. As the story goes, some Frenchman said, "We love Germany so much we want two of them." And they seemed to be having their way.

Meanwhile, Secretary Byrnes and British Foreign Minister Ernest Bevin, after the New York meeting of foreign ministers in December 1946, had signed an agreement to combine our zones and build them up. Supplemented in 1947 by the Marshall Plan, it formulated an enlarged concept: we were to seek a solution beyond Germany, but with our part of Germany, calling for the integration of Germany within the new European Community. The Germans understood this and appreciated it, and it gave them an inspiration.

The Council of Foreign Ministers met again in Moscow in March 1947. General Marshall had become secretary of state. This meeting began under rather poor auspices because the Truman Doctrine was proclaimed two days after it opened, and it was clear that the meeting would end in failure, which it did. We brought up our proposal again for the forty year treaty guarantee of the reunification of Germany, combined with guarantees to the Russians and the Western Allies against German aggression, but it got nowhere at all. The decisive meeting of the Council of Foreign Ministers was in London during November and December 1947. We got absolutely nowhere with the Soviets.

Immediately thereafter the Western commanders and foreign ministers got together in London and decided that we had to combine the three zones and run them as a unit after taking certain further steps—one of the most important of which was the reform of the currency. That brought us, of course, to the point where we ran right up against the Soviets. I remember that after long debate, a decision was made that we should introduce reform in Berlin. I had to sign off on this paper for the State Department with Charles Hilliard for the Treasury Department. In January 1948, a new currency was introduced in Berlin, the Russians marched out of the Control Council in March, and the blockade started.

Then there was all hell to pay around the State Department. General Marshall wanted to know who signed the paper and attempted to fix responsibility. We reminded him that this was a proposal approved by the foreign ministers and occupation commanders after the London conference. As we succeeded in carrying out the blockade, everybody was somewhat happier.

My intention has been to show that we learned European affairs through experience, and that with the Marshall Plan (which was a great achievement) we succeeded in bringing the Germans along with us.

Chapter 19

Impact of the Proconsular Experience on American Foreign Policy

A Reflective View

James W. Riddleberger

Although the principle of attaching political advisors to command-ing generals had been established early in World War II, the pri-macy of military considerations was early recognized and observed. Furthermore, it was often convenient to the military to let their political counselors assume the responsibility for decisions unpopu-lar in the United States, for example, Ambassador Robert Murphy and the recognition of Darlan in the North African campaign. But with the signing of the European armistice in May 1945 and the advent of the occupation of Italy, Germany, and Austria, the State Department sustained some rude shocks. These were not so evident in Italy, where a peace treaty had been worked out in 1945 and where military government was relatively short-lived. In Germany

Because of his long and unique experience in dealing with German affairs for the State Department, Mr. Riddleberger was invited to expound on lessons of the occupa-tion. Prevented by prior commitment from participating in this conference, he pre-pared this paper with the benefit of access to papers and transcripts of discussion from this and other sessions of the conference. He also drew on his recorded responses to pertinent questions put to him by Robert Wolfe during an interview in Washington, D.C., on March 7, 1980, conducted by Wolfe and George K. Romoser for the Confer-ence Group on German Politics, assisted by a grant from the McCloy Fund. That and two other interviews with Mr. Riddleberger, along with interviews of John J. McCloy, General Lucius D. Clay, and others, are being prepared by the interviewers for pros-pective publication under the tentative title "Founding Principles of the Federal Re-public of Germany: Retrospective Views of Some American Co-Founders."—Ed.

and Austria, however, where prolonged military governments were the rule, the difference in outlook of the Pentagon and the State Department became painfully evident. The same situation evolved in Japan, but that case will not be discussed here.

In the State Department and the Foreign Service, a highly centralized system is the norm with decision-making authority vested in the secretary of state. Because of a myriad of conflicting interests and policies in countries with which the United States maintains relations (good or bad), the process of policy decisions must necessarily be central and closely related to domestic concerns as well. This process is well recognized in the professional foreign service and no matter how important and urgent a recommendation may be, no embassy expects to "win them all." This system may lead to great disappointment on the part of political appointees but eventually they, too, must conform to their instructions. Foreign countries maintain embassies in Washington and, if the State Department is not satisfied with the presentation of its own ambassador, it can quickly rectify it by making its position clear in Washington.

In the military establishment, however, the authority of the theater commander is far-reaching. Once the overall mission has been established by the Joint Chiefs of Staff, the secretary of defense, or the president, the method of execution devolves to a high degree upon the commanding general. He is given a high degree of authority and the primary responsibility for execution devolves upon him. There are excellent reasons for this modus operandi as a moment's reflection upon the vicissitudes of combat will demonstrate. Logical and necessary as this method may be, it could be called the antithesis of diplomatic procedures. Thus it was inevitable that these two concepts would clash. Once General Clay was established in Berlin with JCS 1067 as his guide, clashes were bound to come. JCS 1067 was a purely American directive, had not been negotiated with any of the wartime allies, and could in effect only be executed in the American zone of occupation. The Potsdam agreement did not embrace French agreement and was also full of ambiguities. Thus the scene was laid for conflict between the Departments of State and War already operating on different concepts.

One of the early differences of opinion between the State and War Departments had to do with channels of communication. Both Ambassador Murphy, as political advisor, and I, as chief of the Central European Division, were adamant in our decision to maintain our own line of communications between him and the State Department. This principle had been established before the end of the war and was continued as long as General Eisenhower remained as

commander in chief and military governor in Germany. Generals
Eisenhower and Clay worked out early the division of functions between them, that is, all communications which dealt with civil
functions should be sent to Berlin for Clay's action, with the understanding that he would take up with Eisenhower such matters
as were sufficiently important to require a commander-in-chief
decision.

So much for the internal military communications, but the problem of State Department communications was more complex. In
November 1945, Clay cabled the War Department a proposal essentially as follows: a) The military government was prepared to receive instructions from either the War or State Department and
fully recognized State responsibility; however, b) State Department
instructions should come either through the War Department or directly to the Military Governor rather than through State Department representatives in Berlin. Clay had no objection to exchange of
information between political advisors and State, but wanted instructions sent directly to him. In simple terms, the channel of instructions to the military governor should follow the chain of
responsibility.

This cable posed a very real problem for the State Department. It
was most unwilling to give up its communications with Murphy
which it regarded as essential in dealing with the host of questions
raised by other governments respecting occupation policy. But the
funds were provided from War Department appropriations and the
State Department was neither staffed nor equipped to deal with a
myriad of purely logistic problems involved in *military* government.
The upshot was that instructions were sent through the War Department, but the State Department could make suggestions through
the political advisor.

In practice, this system worked well enough, although the State
Department officials often chafed under the necessity of persuading
Clay they had a valid case. Part of the difficulty stemmed from a
difference in systems. State Department cables carry the name of
the secretary, as do embassy cables with the name of the ambassador. In the War Department, thousands of cables are exchanged
with merely divisional indications of origin. Important messages
originate with the JCS or the secretary of war. Clay contended that
under the State Department system all messages seemed to have
the secretary's approval and he could not distinguish the important
from the routine. He obviously resented the fact that signing officers
in the State Department (which could descend as low as assistant

division chiefs) could send him instructions. I always responded that while he had a point, this could be remedied by slight modifications whereby messages intended for him could be identified as coming from the secretary or undersecretary, but Clay was not entirely convinced this idea would work.

On the whole, however, the system worked fairly well. Instructions to Clay were transmitted through War Department channels. Suggestions from the State Department were sent through the political advisor in Berlin. Clay was meticulous in keeping the political advisor informed and we, in turn, always explained the reasons for a suggested line of policy. As the personal relations were good and as the political advisors were experienced officials with long backgrounds on Germany, Clay came to rely on them in dealing with many complicated questions. The political advisor and his staff, for example, were all fluent in German and French (while many military government officers knew neither) which facilitated Clay's contacts with the German officials and the French contingent in military government. Although there were excellent interpreters, for informal discussions the State Department officers played a most important role.

Yes, the communications and coordination of military-diplomatic collaboration in making and implementing policy for the government of the United States zone of Germany worked tolerably well, if not without occasional friction. But the real measure of success is not the process but the results, short and long term. Both the popular and expert consensus is that our occupations of Germany and of Japan have resulted in notably prosperous and stable democratic societies, which was the proclaimed goal of the American government and its proconsuls.

Nevertheless, in view of our subsequent failures at direct and indirect attempts to inculcate democracy and prosperity in other places, indirectly through military and economic aid, or directly through military incursion on behalf of allies, it behooves us to reexamine how and whether our policies and processes in Germany accomplished the acclaimed result.

It was a success for two or three very fundamental reasons. Although it took us two years to admit, we all agreed that there had to be an economic revival of Germany in order to bring about the economic revival of Western Europe. I do not think anyone contests that any more. Also, we successfully withstood a high degree of Soviet pressure on Berlin. Yet, when we reflect on what there was in the zone in the way of Western Allied forces, to say nothing of their large number of dependents as potential hostages, we know there were scarcely enough troops to serve as a minimal tripwire. There was then no NATO.

In the meantime, we have remedied that lack; we have a North Atlantic alliance now. I know full well that the French in some ways wrecked the military structure, but the alliance as a force, nonetheless, continues to exist. If I sat in the Kremlin and looked around the periphery and saw some of the forces that could also be brought to bear against them, I would think a long time before I got too venturesome. So, therefore, I would think that the moral, political, and military renascence of Germany is a great accomplishment.

Why this accomplishment? Was it something we did, or did we just "luck in" in both Germany and Japan? Well, I think it was a combination of things. In the first place, Americans by nature and experience tend to be more optimistic than the Europeans. Maybe because I have spent most of my adult life in Europe, I still think it is arguable whether there has been any moral progress in the world whatsoever in the last 2,000 years. I think as a thesis that can be argued. So, therefore, maybe my outlook is more European than American. But I do think Americans had the self-confidence, and the faith, and the initiative, and the push to decide that something could be done. I do not have to tell you the picture in Western Europe in the winter of 1946–47 was not something I would care to look upon again in the near future. I do not think anybody knew what was going to happen.

Now, you do not have to bring know-how to teach the Germans how to make steel or the French how to make lace. But we had to have the willingness to sacrifice in order to bring them the raw materials and the food so that they could get back into their productive state. I do not know that you can really use the term "teach." I think the Germans profitted from the extant possibilities, especially American material help, American example, and the willingness of people like Clay to take risks.

We have tried the same process in other places since Germany and Japan with far less success. But there are only a few places in the world with what one might describe as the intellectual and educational base for political and economic self-development. And, God knows, I say this as an ex-director of the Foreign Aid program! When I became director, of course, the Marshall Plan was *schon vorbei* (already past), so I caught all the "underdeveloped Third World" countries. The very success of the Marshall Plan led us to believe that the same technique could be applied in underdeveloped parts of the world with the same degree of success. Frankly, I never thought so, but I had to try.

Most experienced Foreign Service officers shared my skepticism, but we are a government in which the president exercises enormous power. Since our presidents are not necessarily persons whose foreign experience is anything to write home about, advisors from the State Department who keep telling the White House what it would rather not hear can always be changed quickly.

Chapter 20

Impact of the Proconsular Experience on Civil Affairs Organization and Doctrine

William R. Swarm

1. World War II and Before

1. Organization and Doctrine

Prior to World War II there was no identifiable organizational capability in the United States military for conducting Civil Affairs and Military Government[1] (CAMG) operations; the last such capability was terminated by the post–World War I withdrawal of United States occupational forces from the Rhineland. Similarly, official doctrine for CAMG was practically nonexistent.

By 1939, Field Manual 27-10, *Rules of Land Warfare,* was published by the Judge Advocate General's office. This manual did not enter into questions of CAMG policy and organization, with which CAMG officers had to be familiar, although it did include treatment of some CAMG legal questions. Several Army field manuals touched on the nonlegal aspects of CAMG, but at the beginning of 1940 no doctrinal manual existed which dealt with CAMG systematically and exclusively.[2]

During 1940, however, JAG published FM 27-5, *Military Government,* premised almost entirely on United States Army experiences in the post–World War I occupation of the Rhineland.[3] A revision was published in December 1943 as Army FM 27-5 and Navy OPNAV 50E-3. The latter manual clearly defined the broad principles and policies of MG, which at that time was the all-inclusive term for both CA and MG. It specifically covered: military necessity, supremacy of the commanding officer, flexibility of plan, treatment of population, retention of existing laws and customs, retention of local government departments and officials, and so forth. The military government responsibilities of the services were touched on lightly: The Army was responsible for land operations, the Navy for islands. Supervision of MG functions was stressed.[4] The necessity for development of proclamations and orders was emphasized.

Thus, these manuals (FMs 27-5 and 27-10) provided the basic CAMG doctrine for training and operations during the World War II combat period; they were supplemented by area studies, area handbooks (such as the *Handbook for Military Government in Germany Prior to Defeat and Surrender,* SHAEF, December 1944) and theater-army-corps-division proclamations, ordinances, plans and directives that provided operational guidance to CAMG staff officers and detachments.

2. Training

Training during World War II in the United States was provided for two categories of CAMG officers: a) officers already commissioned in the military service, and b) officers commissioned directly from civil life primarily for their expertise in a specific CAMG function. The training was conducted in three institutional arrangements: a) the School of Military Government (University of Virginia), Charlottesville; b) the Provost Marshal General's School, Fort Custer, Michigan; and c) the Civil Affairs Training Schools (CATS), some seven to ten of which were affiliated with selected civilian colleges and universities.

The training consisted of three main segments: a) principles of MG; b) study of the geographical area to which officer students would subsequently be assigned; this training included governmental structure, banking system, educational system, customs and mores of the people, and so forth; and c) language study, which tried to develop in the student as much fluency as possible.

2. Post–World War II

1. General

To assess the impact of the proconsular experiences on the CAMG organization and doctrine, we must first appreciate the effect that participation in CAMG had on some of our top proconsular leaders. General Eisenhower's reactions were typical of those voiced by many of us, no matter how far down the chain of command we operated. In a 1942 letter, he expressed his sentiments to General Marshall: "The sooner I can get rid of all these questions that are outside the military scope, the happier I will be. Sometimes I think I live ten years each week, of which at least nine are absorbed in political and economic matters."[5]

During the North African campaign, responsibility for government activities was divided between nonmilitary agencies and the War Department. But the proliferation of civilian task forces in Washington led to confusion over authority, duplication of effort, and lack of coordination with military operations. Writing again to General Marshall, Eisenhower declared, "I am having as much trouble with civilian forces behind aiding us as I am with the enemy in front of us."[6] He recognized the need for a single centralized military authority over CAMG matters, and so advised General Marshall.

Subsequently, General Marshall picked Major General John H. Hilldring to establish the Civil Affairs Division (CAD) in the War Department in 1943 with responsibility for administering all aspects of United States civil-military relationships. Hilldring supervised the CAD and its guidance to United States forces throughout most of the World War II occupations. He became a foremost exponent for developing a permanent CAMG capability within the Army. In 1946 he was the prime mover in organizing the Military Government Association (now the Civil Affairs Association), an organization that is still dedicated to preserving CAMG expertise and improving CAMG training and doctrine.

Service in CAMG had a similar effect on a large segment of those officers involved at lower levels. The problems were complex, the organization unwieldy, but there were many opportunities for improvement. Actions to initiate improvements were motivated by the conviction that results would be mutually beneficial, to the indigenous populations and to our United States national objectives.

Thus, the proconsuls, command and functional staff officers alike, contributed to the improvement process. Their impact on CAMG was gradual but it had a cumulatively profound effect on all aspects of United States Army and Joint CAMG organization and doctrine.

They added considerable knowledge within the CAMG functions, particularly relating to judicial and court procedures in the Legal function; nutritional, immunization, and sanitation matters in Public Health; currency controls and inflationary pressures in Finance; extent to which traditional school systems could be democratized in Public Education; press control and public opinion surveys in Civil

Information; handling of refugees under the Displaced Persons function; and other necessary functions.

But the greatest effect was on CAMG planning, training, organization, deployment of units, and operational techniques. This impact was generated by the proconsuls—CAMG policy formulators, CAMG operations directors, and CAMG advisors to indigenous governmental officials—who were determined that the United States would never again have to cope with a war situation without benefit of an in-being CAMG readiness capability.

2. CAMG Organizations

A. *Organization of CAMG United States Army Reserve Units.* After the cessation of hostilities in Germany and Japan, as well as in Austria, Trieste, Okinawa, and Korea, the Civil Affairs Division, located in the Office of the Chief of Staff of the Army, became involved in Joint and Army strategic and capabilities planning for future military contingencies. Development of the CAMG annexes for the entire family of military plans became the responsibility of CAD, because the Army had been appointed by the JCS as executive agent for CAMG matters.

These plans generated a requirement for CAMG staff sections and units to carry out the CAMG responsibilities of the military commanders. By 1949 the Army had created, for the first time, 70 peacetime United States Army Reserve CAMG units based on an official Table of Organization and Equipment (TO/E 41-500) to meet these obligations. This CAMG reserve consisted of 14 groups each composed of 50 officers, 2 warrant officers, and 52 enlisted personnel; and 56 companies, each composed of 66 officers, 2 warrant officers, and 166 enlisted personnel; 70 units in all.

Soon these units were supplemented by the activation of reserve Special Units. This additional reserve consisted of: a) several CAMG Area Headquarters units, designed to supervise or assist the indigenous government of a country, or to be employed as a CAMG staff section of a theater headquarters; and b) several CAMG school units to provide for rapidly expanding the CAMG training capability during a general wartime mobilization.

B. *Organization of Active Army CAMG Units.* Additionally, three active Army CAMG units were created about this time (1948–49) consisting of the 95th Group and the 41st and 42nd Companies. For the first time in history, these units provided the Army with the capability of instantly deploying CAMG units as part of the strategic Army force to trouble spots anywhere in the world.

It is significant to note that although doctrine in the 1954 FM 41-15, *Civil Affairs Military Government Units* specified that the Area Headquarters units were designed to administer a nation, the group to administer a state, and the company to administer a number of substate-level government entities such as counties, flexibility of deployment options was retained by specifying that the mission of these units was similar; namely: 1) to support military operations, 2) to conduct CAMG operations, and 3) to further United States national and allied policies.

C. Establishment of the MG Department, PMG School. By the middle of 1950, Major General Edwin P. Parker, the provost marshal general of the Army, was under great pressure to provide resident and nonresident training for the 4,700 officers that were serving with the CAMG United States Army reserve and active duty units. These units had been brought into existence by the World War II occupational experiences, the experiences of the "proconsuls" adapting to the military.

General Parker had suitable training facilities at the PMG School located at Camp Gordon, Georgia, which was then devoted to training Military Police officers and enlisted personnel. He obtained a total of five officers from the Department of the Army personnel source to undertake the job—a job that later proved of much greater magnitude than anyone envisaged at that time. Four of these officers were experienced "proconsuls," the author of this piece as the chief of the MG Department had CAMG experience in the European theater. He was assisted by Lieutenant Colonel Irvin Harlow, Infantry, European theater; and Majors Leroy E. Wade, MP, Far East, and Clyde Hertz, Infantry, Far East. This nucleus was completed with the addition of Major Floyd Spencer, staff specialist, who had served on Department of the Army and Department of Defense staff assignments in the field of public information and on special intelligence assignments in Greece and Africa.[7]

By the middle of 1952, due to the wide scope of the CAMG activity, the MG Department was expanded by the addition of nine officers and eight "Scientific and Professional Personnel."[8] The officers were: Majors Eldon Dye (Europe); Harry Apple (Europe); Gerald Knight (Far East); and Captains Anthony Auletta (Europe); James Hyndman (Far East); Bruce Abbot (Far East); and Clement Petrillo (Europe). Editorial support from the MP Board was furnished by Dr. Solomon Lebovitz who was commissioned while serving with an MG detachment in Europe.

(1) Training Considerations. The significant difference between World War II CAMG individual training and post–World War II

individual training lay in the fact that World War II training was relatively simple because the specific geographic area of assignment for the officer being trained was known; for instance, if he were going to Europe he would be trained in the customs, government structure, economy, and so forth, of that area—France or Germany. In post–World War II we had no idea where our officer trainees might ultimately be deployed for the conduct of CAMG operations. The sheer magnitude of the task precluded us from training them at the MG Department of the PMG School in the backgrounds of all the countries in the world. It thus became clear that we must provide them with a set of techniques and doctrine that would enable them to conduct CAMG operations wherever and whenever deployed (see par. 3, C, [6] below).

Area training was not neglected. It was continued as a CAMG unit activity during regular drill periods throughout the year; each USAR CAMG unit was designated a geographical area of specialization, with the result that a wide range of area-oriented units became available for deployment as required.

Similarly, we could not make the post–World War II officer trainees fluent in all languages in the world; so we came to the conclusion that the objective of CAMG language training would be for familiarization, with reliance on graduates of the Army language school system to provide necessary language fluency within the CAMG organization.

(2) *CAMG Courses of Instruction.* The first CAMG course of instruction was conducted early in 1951 by the MG Department of the PMG School for CAMG officers. It was a general course of four weeks duration, applicable to all grades from colonel to second lieutenant. Later, as the refinement of doctrine progressed, we developed two separate four week courses —one for field grade officers, the other for company grade officers. Each course stressed matters appropriate to those grade level responsibilities. The courses were subsequently subdivided into two-week segments, thus enabling us to reach more reserve officers by presentation of the material in a time-frame convenient to their fifteen-day active duty training periods.

D. *Establishment of the CAMG School and CAMG Board.* By 1951, the split responsibility between OCAMG and OPMG for CAMG matters precipitated a Department of the Army study[9] which recommended that all CAMG activities be merged into a single element in order to insure better supervision and coordination of the many aspects of CAMG. Consequently, the CAMG responsibilities of OPMG, which included the MG Department of the CAMG USA

Reserve units and the CAMG Active Army units, were transferred
to the direction and control of the chief, OCAMG at Department of
the Army level. Thus, the MG Department of the PMGS became the
nucleus for the first separate CAMG school; Lieutenant Colonel
Leroy E. Wade was assigned as the first school commandant and
under his supervision a smooth transition was accomplished in
1955.

The following year saw the establishment of the CAMG Board,
another first, as an integral part of the CAMG School, dedicated to
the development of doctrine. This, in accordance with the organizational arrangement at that time pertaining to all Army schools, required school faculty and board members to work closely on doctrine
development and provided the opportunity for the doctrine to be
school-tested on resident course students.

*E. CAMG Branch, Insignia, and Career Specialization Program
Established.*[10] Until 1956, officers assigned to CAMG staffs and
units were commissioned in a basic branch of the Army, such as
Infantry, Artillery, Transportation Corps, and so forth. It became
increasingly apparent that some means would have to be devised to
insure the availability upon mobilization of these bank presidents,
industry executives, school superintendents, and so forth, and pre-
clude their withdrawal from CAMG reserve units for duty with their
basic branches. The result was the establishment of the CAMG
Branch in the United States Army Reserve in 1956, soon followed by
the adoption of the CAMG Branch insignia. A corollary provision
was made by establishing a CAMG career pattern for active Army
officers who preferred to specialize in CAMG.

3. CAMG Doctrine

A. General. Development of comprehensive CAMG doctrine became
inevitable for the MG Department of the PMG School from the moment we began preparations for our first course of instruction. For
instance, in preparing instruction for teaching CAMG principles
and policies, which we assumed would be a repetition of the World
War II teaching process, we found that the 1947 revision of FM 27-5
contained major deficiencies. Examples of these deficiencies included unworkable doctrine for deployment of units, imprecise staff
and command guidance, and lack of a method for guaranteeing that
officers serving with CAMG reserve units would be made available
by their basic branch (infantry, artillery, and so forth) for CAMG
duty upon mobilization.

As these doctrinal inconsistencies surfaced, a rethinking process over the next six months resulted in the development of a concept paper by this writer entitled "Fundamentals of the MG Activity," which was published as a school text in 1951. In effect, it provided an outline body of CAMG principles and techniques essential to the development of a system for influencing the population in a theater of operations.

Lesson plans for resident courses were prepared and refined in order to obtain consistency; student reactions assisted greatly because most had served as proconsuls in CAMG World War II operations. The need became apparent for additional field manuals to supplement the general FM 27-5, *Civil Affairs Military Government,* of 1947. Drafting of a revision of FM 27-5 was begun, shortly followed by creating the initial drafts of a field manual, *Civil Affairs Military Government Operations,* to provide staff and unit operational guidance, and a field manual, *Civil Affairs Military Government Units,* to deal with CAMG unit organization, internal administration of units, and training of both units and individuals.

By the time these manuals had gone through the review process, CAMG had been assigned, for the first time, a number to identify its publications. That number was, and still is, 41.

Concurrent with the drafting of the field manuals, the MG Department submitted doctrinal comments to the Command and General Staff College for including the Army mission of population control in the basic Army doctrinal manuals, FM 101-5, *Staff Organization and Procedure,* and FM 100-5, *Operations.*

Subsequently, all of these manuals embodying the new CAMG concepts were officially published as follows:

FM 41-5, *Joint Manual of Civil Affairs/Military Government,* 1958

FM 41-10, *Civil Affairs Military Government Operations,* 1957

FM 41-15, *Civil Affairs Military Government Units,* 1954

FM 101-5, *Staff Organization and Procedures,* 1954

FM 100-5, *Operations,* 1954

B. Publications.

(1) CAMG Special Texts. During 1950–53 and prior to official publication, the MG Department used the newly developed concepts in both resident and nonresident instruction in its effort to develop a meaningful body of CAMG doctrine that could stand the scrutiny of logic. As an interim measure and to meet the need for making

CAMG case studies available to the students, the following material, almost totally drawn from experience of the "proconsuls," was published by the MG Department of the PMG School in coordination with the Office of the PMG. It should be noted that the MG staff of OPMG included Colonel Albert Bowman, JAG; and MPC Lieutenant Colonels Wendell W. Perham, James Case, and Robert H. Slover,[11] all European theater proconsuls.

(2) Occupation Forces in Europe Series 1945–1946; Originally Prepared by the Historical Division European Command:

Training Packet No. 50, Public Safety
Training Packet No. 51, Civil Affairs
Training Packet No. 53, Displaced Persons, 1945–46
Training Packet No. 54, Displaced Persons, 1946–47
Special Text 41-51-55, Displaced Persons, 1947–48
Training Packet No. 56, United States Military Government in Germany; Operations During the Rhineland Campaign
Training Packet No. 57, United States Military Government in Germany; Operations from late March to Mid-July 1945
Special Text 41-26-59, Financial Policies and Operations
Special Text 41-10-62, Planning for the Occupation of Germany
Special Text 41-20-69, Domestic Economy
Special Text 41-10-70, The Terms of Surrender
Special Text 41-20-50, The Bizonal Economic Administration of Western Germany; Ph.D. diss. of Dr. (then Lt. Col.) Robert H. Slover, Harvard University, 1950

(3) Materials Developed or Sponsored by the MG Department PMG School:

Special Text (unnumbered), Fundamentals of the Activity (1951)
Training Packet No. 58, Military Government Under General Winfield Scott
Training Packet No. 4, Unit Supervision of Selected Government Functions
Training Packet No. 5, Principles of Government
Training Packet No. 6, General Problems of Military Government
Training Packet No. 7, Case Studies on Field Operations of Military Government Units (Originally published by the Civil Affairs Division, Department of the Army, February 1949)

Training Packet No. 11, Legal Aspects of Military
Government
Training Packet No. 52, Military Government Courts in
Germany; JSD diss. of Dr. Eli Nobleman, June 1950

(4) CAMG Research and Development Is Initiated. By 1951 it became clear that deeper research into the political and social science aspects of military operations was necessary for the development of sound doctrine. Such a request was made by the chief of the MG Department to the PMG and resulted in an exploratory visit by two members of the Operations Research Office undertaking research projects for the Department of the Army: Darwin Stoltzenbach and John Montgomery. Up to that time, Army research and development had been in the "hard" science areas. As the result of this visit, the first research into the political science area was initiated, culminating over the next ten years in some twenty studies involving CAMG subjects. Among those engaged in making the CAMG studies was Henry Kissinger. These studies leaned heavily on CAMG documentation produced by the proconsuls in both Europe and the Far East.

C. CAMG Doctrinal Concepts Officially Adopted. Some of the more important doctrinal concepts that were initially proposed by the proconsuls and that subsequently were officially adopted by the United States Army and the JCS are discussed below. How they finally appeared in the official doctrine is indicated by the noted references.

(1) CAMG Controls Population. Fundamentally, the CAMG organization is the military commander's means for getting the people in his area to respond favorably to our national policy objectives. In a military government situation these objectives may be announced through posting of ordnances and proclamations. In a civil affairs situation the objectives may be spelled out in a status of forces agreement or in an agreement drawn up at an intergovernmental level between representatives of our Department of State and a friendly government in exile. Implementation of such agreed objectives may become exceedingly complex in the heat of combat conditions which are usually accompanied by a disrupted and disoriented population, as well as extreme shortages of food, transportation, and shelter. Whatever the condition, the commander relies on his CAMG organization to exercise control of the population. References: FM 41-10 (1957), pars. 1 and 51a.[12] FM 100-5 (1954), pars. 2 and 8; (1962), par. 15.[13]

(2) CAMG Has Responsibility for Carrying Out Whatever Policies

Are Transmitted by Proper Authority. Within the constraints of the Laws of Land Warfare, the Geneva Conventions to which the United States is signatory, and any other commitments to which the United States has subscribed, the CAMG G5 staff officers and CAMG unit commander are responsible for carrrying out whatever policies are transmitted by their duly authorized commanders. Compliance is facilitated because the CAMG organization is composed of a wide range of governmental, public facility, economic, and special functions; functional specialist personnel are drawn from public administrators, civil engineers, bankers and economists, news editors, and so forth; the CAMG personnel are mature, have demonstrated managerial ability, are highly educated in their functional specialties and trained in military staff skills appropriate to their grade; they provide a wide range of flexibility to cope capably with the most complex civil-military problems. Reference: FM 41-10, par. 51c.[14]

(3) CAMG Advises Higher Headquarters as to How and Why Policies Should Be Changed. It is the responsibility of CAMG personnel at lower echelons to forward fully substantiated recommendations to higher headquarters on how and why policies or operational directives should be changed in order to improve operations or obtain the desired objective. It is likewise incumbent upon CAMG staff and command at higher echelons to give serious attention to recommendations from lower echelons and cause appropriate implementation of those recommendations which will improve CAMG operations. When a subordinate unit deviates from policy guidance, for military necessity or otherwise, it promptly advises the higher echelon as to the reason and probable duration of the deviation. By following these principles, the in-depth analysis of a problem by the many functional specialists on a CAMG unit can be made available to the higher command, and the recommended options for improvement can receive consideration. Reference: FM 41-10, pars. 44 and 51c.[15]

(4) CAMG Combats Enemy Action. The CAMG organization provides the commander with an agency for combating enemy action. Enemy action does not necessarily have to take the form of "shot and shell." In modern warfare the enemy more and more turns to less tangible but nevertheless very effective means of combating our forces. Some of these enemy actions are willful and planned—such as carrying out a "scorched earth" policy, forcing refugees through our lines to delay and confuse us, infiltrating into or leaving behind in our area saboteurs and guerrillas for the purpose of destroying us. We encounter other unplanned conditions which result from both our own and enemy action. These conditions combine to delay us in accomplishing our mission or taking our objective in as real a sense

as if they were imposed by a curtain of enemy fire. Thus, deployment of CAMG units assumes a tactical implication, since they are designed to counteract actions taken by the enemy or to counteract conditions which result from action against the enemy. Reference: FM 41-10, par. 51b.[16]

(5) CAMG Regulates the Social Processes of the People. The social processes are the changing ways in which human beings relate themselves to one another. Since CAMG is concerned with the regulation of peoples, their economy, and their institutions, it is concerned with the regulation of the social processes. These processes constitute a most complex and unpredictable medium. CAMG, therefore, deals with social relationships, which differ from an exact science in the same manner that the study of mathematics differs from the study of civics. Just as the sociologist strives to reduce the social process into a scientific pattern, so the student of MG attempts to reduce the art of government to a science as his knowledge of the subject increases. Reference: FM 41-10, par. 51d.[17]

(6) CAMG Uses Administrative and Judicial Control Techniques. In order to obtain the degree of influence or control necessary to carry out authorized goals and policy objectives, CAMG officers must be knowledgeable in the techniques that can assist in that effort. These techniques are general and adaptable to all CAMG functional activities. They are commonly used techniques in normal day-to-day conduct of government and business management throughout the world.

Intelligent application of techniques appropriate to the specific situation enables the CAMG functional specialist officer to obtain the desired objective in the most effective manner. Whenever possible, noncoercive controls are employed as opposed to coercion. The techniques are as follows:

Noncoercive Administrative Controls

Declaration of Policy	Conferences
Declaration of Legal	Conciliation, Mediation,
Obligations	Arbitration
Establishment of Standards	Purchase of Consent
Setting of Examples	Submission of Reports
Demonstrations	Review of Records
Educational Campaigns	Compliance Through Publicity

Coercive Administrative Controls

Licensing	Apprehension of Violators
Investigations	Taxation
Inspections	Summary Action

Coercive Judicial Controls

Adjudication	Injunction
Fine	Writ
Prison Sentence	Reparations

Reference: FM 41-10, par. 124.[18]

(7) CAMG Staff Established as G5. Clausewitz states, "Warfare has three main objectives: (a) to conquer and destroy the armed power of the enemy; (b) to take possession of his material and other sources of strength; (c) to gain public opinion [at home]." Frequently military commanders emphasize (a), the "destructive" viewpoint, and it tends to dominate their point of view. During combat the CAMG advisor is primarily concerned with points (b) and (c) in order to bring about (a). He presents the "constructive" viewpoint to the commander. For the purpose of furthering the military mission, his responsibility is to insure that the commander does not neglect any opportunity to utilize fully the resources of the occupied area. The CAMG units carry out this task for the commander in such a way as to gain public opinion at home. It is therefore mandatory that the viewpoint of the CAMG advisor be presented to the commander in order that the commander can make an intelligent decision based on a presentation of both the "destructive" and "constructive" points of view. The CAMG advisor must be on the same level with the other advisors to the commander, else the "constructive" point of view will become absorbed in the "destructive" point of view en route to the commander, and consequently not be presented for the commander's consideration. Since G3 represents the "destructive" view, the CAMG staff officer must be at general staff level also—G5. References: FM 41-10, pars. 36 and 37.[19] FM 101-5, par. 21.[20]

(8) CAMG Plans. The CAMG activity involves strategic planning on a large scale because of the necessity for coverage of the area in *depth*. The concept of the skirmish line is not applicable to this activity because the commander's CAMG responsibility extends *throughout* his area. The strategic implication of the MG activity involves making plans, using military forces and equipment for the purpose of gaining and keeping the advantage over the enemy in combat operations, and includes distribution, transportation, and employment of troops and supplies *according to a study of the entire combat area*. The headquarters having responsibility for execution of a military operation is responsible for preparing and supervising the implementation of the overall CAMG plan. The CAMG plan

provides for control of an area in extended *depth.* Localities to be controlled or supervised by CAMG units are designated in the overall plan. This plan furnishes the basis for the conduct of the CAMG operation, as well as the basis for the CAMG unit and personnel requirements. Reference: FM 41-10, par. 42.[21]

(9) CAMG Estimate of the Situation. The necessity for developing a CAMG estimate of the situation prior to making a CAMG plan was identified, the format created and consequently taught as MG Department doctrine in 1952–53. The format for the CAMG estimate first appeared officially in the 1954 edition of FM 101-5. References: FM 41-10, par. 41.[22] FM 101-5, par. 21.[23]

(10) Operational Control of CAMG Units. A significant change was necessary in the doctrine pertaining to the control of CAMG units. A study of FM 27-5 (1947 edition) revealed the unreliability of using "combat" and "post-combat" time periods as the criteria for establishing the type of chain of command for controlling deployed CAMG units. An analysis indicated that the applicable criteria was not a "time period," but rather whether or not the military tactical situation would be "moving" or "static." It was determined that a "moving" front line favors delegation of CAMG area responsibility and consequently control of CAMG units to commanders down to division level, in order that decisions can be made quickly without going through various higher headquarters. Conversely, a slow moving or static situation favors consolidation of CAMG area responsibility at the highest headquarters level as soon as possible in order to insure uniformity of policy throughout the widest possible area. References: FM 41-5, par. 31,c.[24] FM 41-10, par. 56.[25]

3. Conclusion

World War II Civil Affairs and Military Government policy was developed at the national and international levels, then handed to the military to carry out; it was then that the proconsuls—the CAMG officers—became involved in the policy modification process, such as the case of the Joint Chiefs of Staff Directive 1067 which envisaged an agrarian Germany.

The impact of these modifications was generally confined to the respective geographical areas we have been considering—Germany and Japan—and involved details of the MG functional activities, such as the level of economic development *or* democratizing the education system.

But the impact of the proconsuls on development of CA doctrine and organization came later, with their return to assignments in the CA Division of the Army in the Pentagon *or* with the Provost Marshal General's Office in Washington *or* his school at Camp Gordon, Georgia—all of which were involved in creating a peacetime capability within the Army to conduct CAMG operations as an integral part of United States military forces.

To assess the impact of the proconsular experiences on the CAMG organization and doctrine, we must first appreciate the effect that participation in CAMG had on some of our top proconsular leaders. General Eisenhower's reactions (quoted early in this paper) were typical of those voiced by many of us.

For practical purposes the United States had entered World War II unprepared doctrinally and organizationally to carry out its CAMG responsibilities. The proconsuls, command and staff officers alike, saw many areas of CAMG that needed improvement. They were anxious to initiate the improvements, motivated by the conviction that the results would be mutually beneficial, to the local populations and to the accomplishment of our United States national objectives.

It is noteworthy to point out that not all CAMG doctrine was initiated by the proconsuls. Doctrine pertaining to CAMG principles and policies was published in the original United States Army manual solely dedicated to CAMG, the 1940 edition of FM 27-5 entitled *Military Government*. That was long before our World War II occupations of Germany and Japan were operationally deployed. These aspects of CAMG doctrine were based generally on United States Army experience in the World War I occupation of the Rhineland, but it took into account United States CAMG experiences in previous wars.

The proconsular impact on CAMG organization and doctrine was gradual, but it profoundly influenced United States CAMG activities, generally between 1946 and 1960. The high point was probably attained during the 1954 to 1957 period when the first official doctrine, initiated and developed by the MG Department of the Provost Marshal General's School, began to be published in Army field manuals. The momentum of this influence continued, although at a diminishing rate after 1960 due to innovations in both CAMG doctrine and organization designed to counter insurgency and guerrilla activity in Southeast Asia. However, the proconsul-based doctrine continues to provide the matrix of United States Civil Affairs doctrine up to the present time. It is regarded by the military forces of the free world as the authoritative standard on which their counterparts are modeled.

Organizational and doctrinal creations derived from World War II experience provided the CAMG organizations mobilized to meet several contingencies—Korea in 1951, the Berlin Crisis in 1962, and the Dominican Republic in 1965. It has provided CAMG personnel for numerous Mobile Training Teams to NATO, SEATO and other countries; and it has supported numerous Army and Joint Field Exercises. Of greatest significance is the capability it provides to State Department and military planners for including CAMG in whatever strategic and contingency plans may be developed. In brief it provides a capability for managing the foreign policy responsibilities of the military—wherever and whenever it may be required.

4. Epilogue

The foregoing account recites the Civil Affairs developments largely initiated and accomplished by the former proconsuls during the 1944–52 time frame, which resulted in providing the military with a strong CA capability. Of recent years, with the passing of proconsuls from the active Army scene, that Civil Affairs capability has been steadily eroding. In May 1977, the Army announced that twelve CA USA-Reserve units would no longer be supported in the overall war plans—an action that could result in deactivation of the units and loss of highly qualified personnel. During the past two years, the two CA general officer mobilization designee positions have been eliminated from the headquarters of the Army in the Pentagon, an action that seriously reduces the CA input at this vital staff level.

Although for years official doctrine specified that CA staff sections should be established at General Staff level (G5) on headquarters down to and including the division, in practice this requirement has been avoided much more than observed. In fact the European theater headquarters has been so devoid of a CA staff and planning capability that CA reserve units in the United States have been requested to undertake this task, thousands of miles from their Allied and United States headquarters counterpart planners.

The basic Army doctrinal manual FM 100-5, *Operations,* which traditionally furnished principles for deployment of Army forces in the entire range of strategic and tactical situations in which the Army could be expected to participate, was revised and redesigned in 1976 to cover only one situation—a plan for a battle on the European plain. For all practical purposes, the manual is devoid of CA doctrine, and United States Army forces are deprived of their own CA capability.

The Civil Affairs School no longer exists as a separate entity. Identifiable Civil Affairs is seldom, if ever, included as part of the curricula in other Army schools. There is no longer an identifiable CA position on the staffs of the Department of the Army or Deputy Chief of Staff for Operations. Unless this trend is reversed, it could ultimately result in loss of the CA capability from our military preparedness posture; a full cycle return to the pre–World War II situation.

The Civil Affairs Association, aware of these developments by continuous contact and through its annual conference, has attempted to reverse this trend. It insists that the CA capability (doctrine, staffs, plans, and organization) must be maintained throughout our entire force structure as the principal means for assuring maximum utilization of local resources in support of our military effort and preventing civilian interference with our military operations. Civil Affairs must be emphasized as a command responsibility, especially of those commanders at the highest levels who have the additional responsibility for gaining Department of State cooperation in defining and overseeing the implementation of our national war objectives.

At least one former Army chief of staff acknowledged the crucial importance of the Civil Affairs capability to military operations. General Fred C. Weyand, addressing the Annual Civil Affairs Conference at Charleston, South Carolina, on May 14, 1977, said:

> One of the unique characteristics of our Army is that it *equips* men whereas the other military services *man* equipment—and for that reason Civil Affairs personnel and units have a special meaning for me—they epitomize the point that the Army is "people." As a matter of fact, a trained Civil Affairs officer is the most potent "force multiplier" the Army has.
>
> We have at worst ignored the decisive potential of Civil Affairs in our defense of the democratic system, and at best we have used our Civil Affairs resources with far less optimum effectiveness. We have never been adequately prepared in the field of Civil Affairs. We have never accepted the fact that people—not equipment—win wars.
>
> The fact is that too much of our effort has been devoted to coping with outside pressures trying to emasculate Civil Af-

fairs. Why? Because too many people don't believe in it. Why don't they believe in it? Because they don't understand it. They don't understand its potential as a decisive force. They don't understand that it is an incredibly effective "force multiplier" and they don't understand that we can't win without it. And, sadly, no one has been able to make the case that would elevate Civil Affairs to the priority position in our overall military program that it merits.

There is no military force in the world as adept as the United States in integrating firepower and bringing it to bear on the enemy, and yet, until we learn how to integrate our economic, political and sociological resources and bring them to bear in support of our military objectives, we can never be certain of victory, no matter how much material, blood and lives we expend.

Chapter 21

The Occupation as
Perceived by the Public,
Scholars, and Policy Makers

Edward N. Peterson

Even papers aspiring to be scientific begin with a human experience of the author and this paper could be traced to my experience in the rear ranks of an infantry division which entered Germany in March 1945. As an "Innocent Abroad," I entered with a clear mind about the German evil which had to be destroyed and about the goodness of American policy about to destroy it, although experience had already made me doubt such capability in the American Army. My mind was not cluttered with facts about German history, but I had learned enough German in three months in Alsace to become an interpreter-interrogator. Replacing the trained people who went home "on points," I commanded, before I was of an age to vote, a military intelligence unit with the assignment to separate for purposes of employment the bad Germans from the not-so-bad Germans, and later to interrogate people leaving the Russian zone.

Immersed in interrogations, I gained an insight at the bottom-line level into the occupation, where matters sometimes contrasted sharply with the simplistic discussion of policy in my only source, *The Stars and Stripes.* It appeared to me that the ideals of freedom did not square with the Army's high-handed dealings with the civilian population, for example, throwing people out of their homes on a two-hour notice. Democracy did not square with the elitism of the occupation, the segregation of victor from defeated, the most mundane example of which being separate toilet facilities for occupational personnel and "the indigenous population." More serious was the obvious failure of economic policies, which left this native population rationed ever closer to the point of near-starvation, kept alive by black-marketing. Nonfraternization appeared to be not only foolish but unenforceable.

Yet on my return to the States in late 1947, any half-realized criticism of occupation policy was half-forgotten in the pressure to start life again in the real world. The nearly three years in Germany meant a latent interest in European history, which led circuitously to the necessary degrees to learn while teaching, but the subsequent occupation was known from the media's reports of policy successes. Memories of failures were obscured by the public and official optimism of victories beginning in 1948. Nearly twenty years later, by the coincidence of two trips to research the Nazi period, occasional interviews and documents struck the lost chords and hinted at unrealized problems of the occupation. For example, I noted that in Eichstätt, people remembered the American military governor, a Captain "Toll," in about the same way as they remembered the Nazi Kreisleiter, who was also "mad."

Researching the occupation began with the flood of material published by scholars and participants, which suggested that the few faults I had seen were but the tip of the iceberg of problems and apparent failures. This research into policy implementation occurred during the deepening debacle in Vietnam which stimulated on my part a more serious reflection on the impact of World War II and postwar occupation on subsequent national policy. It became also clear that the scholarship about this past use of American power had had little impact on the subsequent use of that power. The lessons learned during the occupation were not being applied. This has led me to separate the impact of the occupation of Germany into three elements: its impact on the public, its impact on the scholars, and its impact on the policy makers.

The public, remote from the scene, derived its image of a successful occupation, as I did after 1947, from the media. My research, particularly in the file in the National Archives on the newspaper accounts of the occupation, suggests that whatever the faults of the media now, they were much worse then. Not only did they leave after 1948 the image of a great success, a half-truth, but they left two large images of previous failures, which were less than half-truths. A few newspaper reporters furthered the image of foolish generals, like George Patton, who were unwilling or unable to throw the Nazis out. The alleged survival of Nazis, as a secret conspiracy still in power, has since provided the mass media with sensational stories to sell. Extreme sensationalism, with an impact on the public image, has been reproduced in countless articles on Nazi bestiality. (SS seems to mean sado-sex in mass magazines like *The Police*

Gazette, which incidentally reported recently that Hitler is conspiring to return from his tunnel under Antarctica.) Countless movies, like *Judgment at Nuremberg,* and television thrillers, like "The Ipcress File," occasionally a bestseller like *The Odessa File,* maintain a slightly more reasonable impression that nazism defeated the occupation. The occasional fact, the discovery of a real war criminal brought to a long-delayed justice, gives some substance to a surviving public suspicion that the occupation failed in its basic task to end the Nazi menace.

The other public image created by the media was that the occupation was sabotaged by Communists inside military government. With the Morgenthau Plan these subversives almost cost us, so some conservatives remember, our necessary German allies against our Russian enemies. According to this media-created image, military government, led by General Clay, recognized the danger in time and blew the whistle. This image prevails in the few facts remembered by the anti-Communist public: the Truman Doctrine, the Marshall Plan, the Berlin Airlift, postwar victories in the eternal fight for freedom. NATO has held the line at the Iron Curtain which became visible in the Berlin Wall. In the fantasy media, stories of Americans defeating Communist spies partially replaced stories of Americans defeating Nazi spies.

For either the fantasy media or news media, Berlin remained the cold war center, at least until the Wall of 1961, and the emotional assertion of John F. Kennedy, "Ich bin ein Berliner." General Clay returned as the tangible link to his past victory.

One less obvious element in the public's picture of the occupation would be the hundreds of thousands of men, often with families, who spent years of service in Germany as occupiers and/or defenders. A by-product of this was apparent in a recent sampling of Americans' knowledge of a foreign language. German was second only to Spanish and was the foreign language best known by men of the age group to have served in Germany. Veterans' memories naturally emphasize the scenery and the perceived German cleanliness. Germans, seen as polka dancers or beer drinkers, are better known and liked than many former allies. Army service in Germany has fortified the cold war by creating memories of unsmiling Russians with their tommy guns, their watchtowers, and the Wall.

Perhaps because they have been less impressed by the Alps and German beer, scholars of the occupation have presented a more critical view of the occupation. Most were stimulated by their troubling experience as its officers. Perhaps the most devastating critique appeared already in 1947 by Harold Zink, a former officer in the Political Division, who wrote *American Military Government in Germany,* as a thorough denunciation of how the Army's Standard Operating Procedure ruined the reform intent of the occupation.[1] Lewis Brown's *A Report on Germany,* also 1947, deplored the economic mismanagement of foolish Army controls.[2] B. U. Ratchford's *Berlin Reparations Assignment,* 1947, showed how doing things the Army's way added to the black market mess outside headquarters.[3] Carl Friedrich's *American Experiences in Military Government,* 1948, could have pointed with greater pride to the contribution of émigrés like himself. He noted, however, that the occupation was saved from catastrophe by the common sense of policy implementers.[4] Solomon Lebovitz in his Harvard dissertation of 1949 reported from his experience that American aid in the revival of German political activity had been minor.[5] Reporters like Delbert Clark and Russell Hill described in ominous terms the failure to promote liberal forces, as evident in Clark's title, *Again the Goosestep.*[6] William Griffith in his 1950 Harvard dissertation described his experience in the denazification program in the most scathing terms; Berlin and Washington bungling had made a farce of this vital effort.[7]

The criticisms continued into the 1950s even in official publications like those of J. F. J. Gillen who reported the weakness in effecting state and local government, and in effecting decartelization.[8] John Kormann, also for HICOG, continued the interpretation of denazification as failure.[9] Another dissertation by another participant, Bert Schloss, observed that Americans had been defeated in their efforts to reform by a lack of knowledge of the German reform tradition.[10] A general, Morris Edwards, used the dissertation medium to express his frustration with so many efforts at reeducation, with perhaps only one, the town meeting, catching roots.[11]

Beginning scholarship of a much wider perspective in most difficult comparative history, John Montgomery described the military governments in both Japan and Germany, with the indicative title, *Forced to be Free.*[12] Harold Zink, in his second book concluded in 1957 that despite the well-remembered SNAFUs of the occupation, the end result was oddly not that bad.[13] This moderation in criticism with perspective became more common.

Reflecting already the confusions of the cold war, economic adviser Manuel Gottlieb in his *The German Peace Settlement and the Berlin Crisis,* 1960, retraced the tangled story of how a possible allied cooperation in Berlin was negated by mutual suspicions, and that the Russian suspicion of OMGUS decisions was not without foundation.[14] Criticism went also to the grass roots in John Gimbel's pioneering study of a German community, Marburg, under American occupation. He described the tragedy of a reform elite in this university town being thwarted by a local military government unprepared to help.[15] More of the early bitter criticism came as late as 1967 in Franklin Davis' *Come as Conqueror,* an unpleasant memoir of perceived American arrogance.[16]

In perhaps the third wave of the late sixties and early seventies we have a defense of the intent at least, John Backer's *Priming the German Economy,* 1971, defending the United States from the unjustified charge that the Morgenthau Plan prevented a serious effort to help German recovery.[17] Earl Ziemke's 1975 study of the Army in the occupation dispassionately described how the Army was at least sufficient to its own problems and to German survival.[18] As dispassionately, John Gimbel in his second book, *The American Occupation of Germany,* 1968, traced with thorough documentation the struggle of Clay to make sense of the occupation despite the efforts of the Allies, notably France, to maintain the crippling zonal partitions.[19] A thorough study of his thesis might possibly have dissuaded the large group of historians, usually referred to as cold war revisionists, energetic researchers and passionate writers like Barton Bernstein, Bruce Kuklick, Walter LaFeber, and Gabriel Kolko, who looked at the occupation and concluded that Clay's occupation policy demonstrated the American aggressiveness that set off the cold war.[20]

In the area of civil affairs policy, one should note two official statements coming at the end of the occupation, one by CAD director General John Hilldring. In looking back on his Washington command post, Hilldring lamented the lack of coordination. "There was no organization in Washington capable of hammering out these military government policies and decisions except the War Department. There wasn't even a clear and lasting decision as to what civilian departments and agencies of the government should participate in the making of policy." He recommended in 1951 that there should be immediately a firm policy on who should be responsible, who should administer, and how authority should be administered. Machinery should be in place for policy making. Foreign Service officers should be trained in advance, before they adopted "the bad habits" (unidentified) that Hilldring perceived as prevalent in the State Department. Most capable senior officers of the Army had poor attitudes and were most reluctant to carry out military government responsibilities.[21] Among those unwilling was George Marshall, who explained carefully to Hilldring on his appointment, from the first moment he should plan to get the Army out of governing as quickly as he could.

Despite Hilldring's experience, and thousands of others', the Fahey 1951 study of civil affairs, commissioned by the secretary of the army, concluded that the 1951 organization for military government was back to where it had been in 1941. It would have appeared that nothing that had been created had survived, when Hilldring's Civil Affairs Division and his Office for Occupied Areas had been dissolved in 1949.[22]

Through these and other studies, one might well conclude, as did Zink, that the United States was remarkably ill-suited to control territories outside its own boundaries. Caught up with its own continental problems and opportunities, America could scarcely devote serious attention to the problems of others. When forced to do so, it approached the problems of others with such ignorance that it could do more harm than good. From a 1970 conference on the occupation, the sentence which I best remember was that of the diplomat, Butterfield, who thought it patently foolish to expect good to come from sending hundreds of thousands of young Americans to some other country. This was borne out by the description of the 1945–50 occupation in Bavaria as reported by George Shuster, one of the best of the representatives during the occupation. The problem, he wrote, had been that American officials knew very little about Germany and learned little; they had instead remained in their offices issuing orders; they rarely went outside to come to know the people they were to govern.[23] There was also the saddening observation made by George Kennan in his *Memoirs,* that he had been made heartsick by mindless arrogance of the American conquerors, living in ostentatious luxury amid the degradation and humiliation of the suffering indigenous population.[24] There is also his graphic description of American foreign policy as a great dinosaur sleeping peacefully in its swamp, until aroused, when it thrashed about wildly with its giant tail to destroy its environment and then returned to its slumbers.[25]

The pessimism of such observations, had they been known to the public or the policy-makers, would have seemed before Vietnam unduly myopic about the ability of the United States to conduct a meaningful policy overseas. The leaders of our country, liberal or conservative, apparently shared in more of the public's simplistic view of past American virtue and success than the scholars' skepticism. The occupations "succeeded" and the United States deserved the gratitude of Germans, Japanese, and the world for having brought peace by its military power and prosperity by its economic power. Perhaps born of the politicians' ignorance of the scholars' criticisms, and those of the sobering experience of officers in the field, the official Washington position remained optimistic until Vietnam had come and nearly gone. The truisms were: The Berlin Airlift meant a victory achieved by firmness and American know-how. The Truman Doctrine had worked as military support to allies willing to defend their freedom. The Marshall Plan had worked as economic aid to poor countries, willing and able to work. Truman's toughness plus Kennan's containment had worked. It might not have altered the status quo but it held the line and it was successful with the voters. If one defended a line, as in Germany, one avoided a disastrous political defeat at home and abroad. Crossing that line, as Dulles threatened to do, was extremism, but moderate political fighting to keep what you have had been proven a suitable policy in Germany and Japan.

Thus the public and political image was that of a miracle achieved in those two countries first destroyed by United States bombs and then revived by United States aid. The miracle was also achieved in presumed authoritarian peoples like the Germans and the Japanese who had been led to govern themselves in stable democracies. The miracles seemed to be proof of the correctness of our policy and the evidence of our power. If it could be done 1945–49, it could be done again. The Korean War held the line, after MacArthur unwisely had crossed over the line, and it produced an ally, albeit one yet to copy American institutions, except for the CIA.

The perceived success in Germany and Japan contributed to the persistence of a national security policy which asserted that the United States could and should maintain a military and political presence in the far corners of the world. Yet repeated efforts to defeat communism by giving other countries aid, as was given to Germany and Japan, has not brought forth the same kind of response. An explanation that my research suggests is that the United States has, in its public and policy-maker memories, overestimated the significance of its aid. It has overlooked the fact that aid was given to two countries momentarily on their knees, but each still in possession of an industrial infrastructure, with factories, roads, railroads, skilled workers, skilled management, skilled scientists, all determined to regain what they had lost. The component more important than United States aid was that offered by the recipients, the Germans and Japanese who could make the miracle work.

I would suggest that the popular and official reaction to the victories in the war and the apparent victories in the occupations contributed to an overestimation of American power. The comforting assumption was that United States power had won the war. The fact known to scholars was that the Grand Alliance, carried for years by the long-suffering Russian infantry, had won the war. Even the defeated contributed mightily to the Allied victory, the Japanese by starting a war that they could scarcely win if the Americans were willing to fight, and then bombing Pearl Harbor, which made them willing. Hitler lost the war by creating the Grand Alliance, by starting ever bigger wars that he was not ready to fight.

Allies would also be needed in the postwar world, and in the occupation of Germany at least, one should have learned that the allies can be almost as difficult to deal with as an enemy, surely more than a defeated enemy. The apparent ease with which the NATO alliance was organized by 1949 obscured the four years of conflict evident in Allied occupation policy. The success of NATO in keeping the status quo contributed to the illusion that SEATO and CENTO might serve a comparable purpose, though the assumed allies in Southeast Asia and the Middle East were concerned with other matters than were West Europeans, and lacking the same potential as allies. I would suggest that the undoubted victories in the occupation came in another alliance, with the Germans and Japanese to solve their problems and ours.

If one defines power, as Truman did, as the ability to persuade, what we persuaded the Germans and Japanese to do was what most of them wanted to do: to establish their own governments, much as they had them before, and to assist in a limited way in their own defense. They were rarely, if ever, persuaded to do something which they did not perceive in their own self-interest. One can more easily argue that the United States was persuaded by the defeated enemies to do something less clearly in the United States interest, to defend them all by investing trillions of dollars in the cold war. Presumably American economic power was persuasive, when taxpayers would support foreign aid; America had the most stable currency, and was the world's major source of oil.

I would suggest that our leaders, as we, were persuaded by the superficial history of the great war and the occupations that armies solve problems best. Kennedy and Johnson believed, as we did, partly because they wished to believe, as we did, that American power would suffice to defend freedom anywhere, without paying the price, the sacrificing of big cars and bigger swimming pools. A proper study of the occupation would, I think, have led to an awareness of what was by 1970 described by a senator as *The Limits of Power*. A proper study of the occupation would perhaps have prevented what another senator's book called *The Arrogance of Power*. Those who studied the occupation should not have been surprised by Vietnam or by Watergate; they would have learned that leaders are people, that American presidents and generals share the frailties of us all. The lesson that should have been derived from our experience as conquerors is that the founding fathers were right; there needs to be a check and balance in government, not because of some idea of freedom and democracy, but because freedom and democracy are often, as they were for postwar Germany and Japan, institutions that work best. Like the study of history, the study of the occupation should be a humbling experience to those who regard themselves as a superior race of people. The history of the indigenous populations would be an affirmation of the potential of all humans, even among those regarded as inferior or defective, as were Germans and Japanese in 1945. Or in the more concise words of Lily Tomlin, "Maybe if we listened to it, history would stop repeating itself." The scholars' history of the occupations could still assist the public and the politician to avoid the pitfalls of impossible dreams and the illusions created by an American isolation from the rest of suffering humanity.

Discussion

Laurence Evans: I had nothing whatsoever to do with the occupation of Germany and Japan, so I would like to express my appreciation to the meeting and to the speakers for the information and insights I have received. I know it may sound ungrateful for me to point out what I think is perhaps a missing link, and that is throughout this meeting we have never heard anything about the impact of our foreign policy on our occupation policy. We have heard something about the reverse, but surely our relations with the Soviet Union and the changes in our attitudes and perceptions of the political and military threat of the Soviet Union to American interests must have had a very profound impact on the way we looked at Germany and Germans, and must have had a profound impact on how we treated them. I would like to know if the panel has any brief word to give me of guidance that I might take back to Binghamton to help me to explain some of these problems to my students.

Robert Wolfe: Forrest Pogue stated at the outset, that this was the third leg of a three-legged conference. At the MacArthur Library and at the Marshall Library in the two previous legs, we heard so much about the high-level and international background, that I commented that I wish I had known during the occupation something about all of the thinking on the high level, so that I would have better understood what I was trying to implement at the ground level. The proceedings of the Marshall Conference on the occupation of Germany and Austria, as well as the proceedings at the MacArthur Library on the occupation of Japan have been published.

John D. Montgomery: Thank you, Bob, but I am sure that we do not want our friend to go back to Binghamton with nothing to do but wait for the mail to arrive; so in the meantime my colleague, Professor Peterson, has volunteered to address this question.

Edward N. Peterson: I think very obviously, if you use my terminology, the alliance with the Germans and the Japanese was created in large part by the growing fear of Russia. I think it would have happened presumably in time; we would have seen the need to work more closely with the Germans and to trust them more as we did, relatively soon. Whether without the existence of the Soviet Army across the border, this would have happened in five or ten years, would be speculative. Surely the great change in German policy, the speed with which Clay moved to create a West Germany was very much involved in our foreign policy. Its function, as someone mentioned in discussion, was in many ways simply to deal with the foreign policy of Germany as a representative. As should be emphasized about General Clay, I think he did a marvelous job, particularly by 1947 and 1948, of representing the Germans with the Allies. He became the spokesman for West Germany, and certainly its creator.

Harold C. Deutsch: Colonel Swarm's presentation aroused a swarm of memories in me, and the brilliant presentation that followed it, a few more. It especially brought home to me something which our director of academic affairs put to me before I came to this conference, to suggest perhaps something which could be done at the Army War College in connection with this problem. I have served four years with the National War College faculty and am now in my third year with the Army War College faculty. I think I have lectured at least ten times at the Navy and Air colleges. I do not recall a single lecture which was ever given on the subject of civil affairs, occupation experience, or anything of this kind. At the Army War College I think we offer sixty-two different elective courses of twelve weeks each, and not a single one of them has a single lecture on this subject. There is great danger, it seems to me, to repeat the kind of thing which happened in connection with the last war.

When I was with OSS as director of political research for Europe, North Africa, and the Middle East, we had a situation develop in the late spring and summer of 1943 in connection with the problem of about 100,000 plus prisoners coming to America from North Africa: some of them already were on the high seas. General Donovan naturally was immediately aware, with his great imagination, that there were some possibilities here for intelligence, clearly in the field of interrogation; but especially from the careful perusal and analysis of prisoner mail—the mail they got from Germany and the mail that they would send home. So he sent three of us, from three different branches of the OSS, to Ottawa to find out what the Canadian experience had been. We were horrified at what we saw there, which was that at every single camp the Nazis were in complete control. The anti-Nazis were harrassed to the point where, in many cases, they fled to the gates, begging to be saved from beatings. Finally they were taken systematically out of the camps and then, as there was no other camp available, they were put in an old abandoned prison in Hull, across the river from Ottawa. They had by far the worst place in the world to live in that you could possibly imagine. In every camp, the Nazis were in control and had a precensorship of the mail—no letter went out of the camp before a committee of these people carefully perused it and saw that nothing was in it that might be of use to the enemy.

Now we came home, and I wrote about a twenty-three-page memorandum for General Donovan, suggesting that we take care of this problem by doing exactly the opposite. Make a very careful study as to who were the Nazis as they arrived, put them in a different camp, but leave the common herd of rather colorless individuals to the anti-Nazis to work on, and our problem of reeducation would be well started among these people before they went home. General Donovan was very much in favor of this idea and immediately arranged a conference between me and General Blackshear M. Bryan, who was going to be in charge of the whole prisoner matter. I went over to the Pentagon, after he had read my memorandum, pleaded with all the eloquence I thought I had, and got nowhere at all. His final remark was simply to say, "I am a custodian, and also it is against the rules to propagandize these prisoners." I said "General, there is no question here of propagandizing them, just let nature take its course. There is no rule whatsoever against separating the prisoners in any categories we wish." But he did not listen and the same thing happened. A couple of months later we were drawing in members of our OSS research and analysis staff, Ph.D.s who were handing out uniforms in quartermaster offices and doing other silly jobs. Because many of them knew foreign languages, they were put on as prison guards and at one time or another as interrogators. One of them, a former student of mine, known I am sure to many of you, was Robert Neumann, most recently our ambassador in Morocco and, before that, in Afghanistan and before that head of the international affairs program at U.C.L.A. Bob said: "The Nazis were completely in charge of the camp where I worked. The Colonel in charge of the camp was simply in 'seventh heaven,' the discipline was incredible, they marched with everything but the goose-step to the morning roll call, he walks past the line there and apparently feels that he is reviewing the Prussian Guard and, taking the salute, and thinks this camp is the most wonderful one in the world." What actually was happening was that these German soldiers were being marched every single day to Nazi indoctrination classes. Nothing that could be said to the commandant by any of the more sophisticated people associated with it could help.

I had a good deal of experience with the School for Military Government at Charlottesville—I lectured there four or five times and got to be a crony of Hardy Dillard [deceased 1982—Ed.] who was mentioned here; a marvelous person who, as many of you know, is now a judge of the International Court at The Hague. There was an assemblage of people who did not seem particularly impressive from the standpoint of being highly selected as greatly sophisticated about affairs, German, Italian, or anything else. And, of course, every one of us who was in the occupation (I was there for a matter of about five or six months) can read endless stories about all of the mistakes we made. I think, as was pointed out by our speakers, common sense and basic humanity saved us—in many cases, of course, the corruption of power was only too manifest in those who lived in luxury and in many ways abused their opportunities. But basically, I certainly agree very much with our speakers that we came out fairly well, if you look at the results. Of course, may I say even on this prisoner business, in the last year or so of the war we learned a great deal and we did a good deal to start reeducation here, but this natural process that I have talked about, I think was never taken.

I hope then, Mr. Chairman, that there is more attention in the armed services given to this particular problem, which is a real one. We do not want to have this repeated. First of all, usually shoving off the temperamentally unsuited for that kind of job, like General Bryan. Obviously, of course, your first thought is not to take your most dashing soldier and put him in charge of your military government prisoner control. But the significance of these problems is so great, it is really a fantastic situation—supposedly our military are prepared for war—well, this is obviously, if war comes, a function which, unless we are on the receiving end entirely, is going to be just as vital as it was before and perhaps, in the end, just as vital as the fighting.

John D. Montgomery: Thank you very much, Professor Deutsch. I think this very interesting historical vignette calls for Colonel Swarm to offer us an epilogue, about this reluctance of the military command to accept responsibility. We have talked about the Army's feeling that military government was not its role, partly because of the problem with Congress and getting money, partly because of its sense of inexpertise—but this reluctance had further implications for the people who were thereafter assigned to military government. It affected their careers, and their access to the ears of the decision-makers in the Pentagon. In a larger sense it may even have affected the military's capacity to reach the ear of the policy makers in higher levels of the government. I would like to hear what Colonel Swarm has to say about this.

William R. Swarm: Thank you, Colonel Deutsch, I am glad you brought up the question. I have only one regret—that your nice speech was given to the wrong audience—it should have been given at Carlisle, and then it should have gone out to Leavenworth, and right around the circuit. The last time I appeared at Carlisle at the Army War College, in 1956, I think was the last time they had a civil affairs talk there.

I said if I had time I had a little piece on the present state of the art. I will read it. [There followed the statement now contained in Colonel Swarm's Epilogue to his paper.—Ed.]

John Mendelsohn: I have a question for Professor Peterson. I wonder if you could clarify a statement that you made somewhat earlier; namely, that an occasional war crimes trial suggests the defeat of the occupation. I would like to know what you mean by that, because the way I read it, the proconsuls no longer try war criminals. If it is the children of the occupation, the Germans who try war criminals, that would suggest that the occupation was successful, rather than suggesting defeat of the occupation.

Edward N. Peterson: I think the point you make is quite correct. I suppose you could say, had the proconsuls, when they had the power in 1945 to 1949, done a more effective job they would have prevented these war criminals from escaping. I do not think Mr. Farago is here now, but in his very interesting book about the "Fourth Reich" in Latin America, he was at least able to show that there were a number of escapees—I do not know that they created a Fourth Reich, but were escaping the military government—that they were not all caught (I think that an impossible task) by the emissaries of our proconsulate in West and East Germany. I think it could be perceived as a failure to totally eradicate the Nazi menace. It is fairly evident from what we have been saying that nazism was fairly well dead, if not entirely so, in 1945, and that despite those who escaped, or the war criminals who have to be painfully found and brought back for trial, the essential job was done.

Charles Foster: If there is going to be a fourth leg of this conference, I wonder whether perhaps it should not focus a little bit on the British and the French experiences of occupation. I would just like to ask Mr. Peterson whether he feels that the British and the French left any mark on Germany, or any more of a mark than the Americans, with fewer people or resources?

Edward N. Peterson: As the conference progressed, it has occurred to me as a fascinating topic. It seems to me that German researchers perhaps already are going about the job of trying to decipher what effect each of the occupation forces had. Obviously, the effect of the Russians has been a singular one, but of those who created the elements of what is now West Germany—to what extent can one discern differences in these sections of former French, former British, former American zones? It would be a very long subject and I am really not qualified to comment on it. I think I have read the standard literature. One of the amazing aspects of this is, and I think it goes back to the much-criticized nonfraternization policy, some Germans at least who at the time were comparing the occupation zones said that they did not take exception to the British not talking to us, because the British did not talk to themselves. And they did not take as much exception to the French taking food, because the French would invite them to share the food they had taken, which was not always the case of the Americans. I think perhaps the Europeans more quickly adapted to the subtlety of the situation—the Americans learned it in time. The differences in the long run have not been major, but it would be a fascinating topic to try to find out what survived. There was a comment made, which perhaps the paper reader would take up further, which suggested that the British, with a more thorough approach, had a more lasting effect on local government in their section of Germany. It is probably true—I would argue that we had relatively little lasting effect on local government in our zone.

Robert Wolfe: Some of us have been involved, for copying purposes, with British occupation records interfiled with our own occupation records; after all, we worked with them pretty closely, particularly after we got into Bizonia and earlier when we were working with them in SHAEF. But the British sources will, by 1980 or so, be available when they release the records of their occupation of Germany. [See Archival Sources: PRO—Ed.] I have seen no signs of the Russians letting anybody at their records; if they do, Orwell's "doublethink" will first have been applied. I do not think the French kept any records; perhaps they did not want to keep any records.

John D. Montgomery: They did keep some records because, when I was doing my analysis of the effect of denazification in the different zones, I went to examine some records in France as well as to carry out empirical studies in the various different communities throughout West Germany.

Robert Wolfe: Did they let you look at them?

John D. Montgomery: Yes, they did. In fact, I remember being somewhat shocked that the general in charge of the records walked out of the room, leaving a whole set of French language documents that were marked "SECRET," which I thought meant "secret."

Jacob D. Beam: The British did leave an impression on certain people. They left one on Adenauer because they fired him as mayor of Cologne. He sent an emissary to the political advisors and said he would like to work for the United States, which he did.

I think we left much more of an impact on the Germans than the British for several reasons. We came in with a very active approach, and I suppose we caused more trouble at the beginning, but I think we learned very quickly and we had more impressive people in the end. When you consider General Clay's staff, he himself, and then the people who later contributed to the integration of Europe: General William H. Draper, Jr., who was a man from Dillon Reed; Joseph Dodge, who was undersecretary of the treasury; and George Shuster [former president of Hunter College in New York City]. These people were exposed, and learned, and later contributed, and I think it is understandable that we had the resources and much more vigor and interest than the British did, so I think we deserve credit for a more lasting effect than the British or the French.

Arnold H. Price: I would like to add to Harold Deutsch's remarks on the German prisoners of war in this country. There is a tie-up with the occupation; ultimately PMGO established two schools—one school to train administrators, and a police school at Fort Getty and Fort Wetherill [both in] Rhode Island. I am not entirely sure what the impact on military government itself was, but there were some

very prominent Germans there. The impact on the German development was that Group 47 started in POW camps in this country.

John Gimbel: I would like to ask Ambassador Beam if he would
kindly embellish that last remark he made about Adenauer. I am
sure that my German friends in the audience would be very interested in that, as I am. The remark was that when the British
dismissed Adenauer as mayor of Cologne, he sent an emissary to the
Americans and asked to work for them, which he did. Would you
mind telling us what he did for the Americans after 1946, and
exactly what you meant by that remark?

Jacob D. Beam: I understand he was a little bit too authoritarian for
the British. He had been around a long time in the Resistance and
they did not get along. Two American liaison officers with the
British Military Government came with a message saying that
Konrad Adenauer would like to be in touch with us and exchange
ideas, and he cooperated with us as much as he could.

Kris Mathur: I would like to ask a general question which anyone
may answer. The question is: the major consideration during the
occupation of Germany, as well as Japan, should have been how far
the United States has been successful 1) in short-term, in bringing
forth a spirit of friendship 2) in long-term, to what extent the policies of the United States have been helpful in creating a permanent
source of democracy in Europe as well as in Asia. To what extent,
sirs, do you think we have accomplished these objectives?

John D. Montgomery: Well, I am glad you asked a simple question
because it would be unfair to ask us to deal with a hard one at this
time of the evening. As a matter of fact, I will take the liberty of
talking about that issue myself a little bit later; my strategy will be
to talk about it after the question period has been exhausted so that
you cannot challenge my answer. I cannot really think of any other
way of dealing with a question of that magnitude; on the other hand,
I know there are people in the audience, and people on the platform,
who have thought about this question of attitudes and might wish to
preempt what I was about to say on the subject.

Does any panelist wish to respond to this question of attitudes and
whether we had any effect on them, whether and how these attitudes were a conversion to friendship, whether this had anything to
do with the lasting roots of democracy, and, if it did, whether this
was in any way related to the occupation?

Kurt Glaser: I think perhaps what I want to ask is pertinent. I may be asking out of ignorance, but is there a systematic distinction made between 1) the tactical use of civil affairs in military government, in the sense of keeping order so that our armed forces can do their job and 2) the job as strategic use, using CAMG as a means of producing social change. I could see a great difference between the World War I occupation, where the occupation was there basically as a military thing, and World War II; in the latter case, have we studied enough the limitations on what can be done? Possibly in Vietnam we asked Civil Affairs to do a job it could not do because we did not understand the limitations and the conditions under which it was operating.

William R. Swarm: Nobody asked Civil Affairs or the Army to do any civil affairs job in Vietnam. At one time, General Westmoreland, when he first went out there and saw what the situation was, indicated that the Army would take it, but they did not want any more of these split-up things like we had in Korea, where we had the United Nations and the AID organization, and the Army Civil Affairs, all three working together. He said he would take this thing if they gave us the whole works. As I understand it, it was turned down. My curbstone assumption is that by that time the AID organization operating under the Department of State had been set in concrete, and the hierarchy was not interested in breaking up their organization.

As to your question about limitations: To begin with, the civil affairs organizations can do nothing on their own. They are military organizations just like the infantry, the artillery, and the cavalry, and they are useful only in an operational system. Now, as for the development of the organization, of the doctrine for the employment of the organization, I will take full responsibility for the doctrine that is involved there. It does not matter, under the concept that we developed, whether it is a combat situation or a postcombat situation. It does not matter whether the devastation or disruption of the services is caused by an atomic bomb or by a conventional weapon, or by guerrilla activity. The fundamental thing involved here is that the civil affairs organization puts together and encourages the establishment of governmental services to take care of the needs of the people, which government does and has been doing since day one. What the magnitude of that effort is—and that is where the organization is what we call a flexible, cellular organization—you can make these teams larger or smaller, depending on what the area is that you are going to operate in, what the economic background is, what the condition of the people is, and also the level of their educational development and industrial techniques. It is a very, very adaptable organization.

We do not get into the policy planning, although you have to plan for your specific area, once it is decided where you are going. You have to have a policy, decide what are the national policy objectives, but that is why I threw the words "State Department" in there, because that is their responsibility. But the civil affairs organization is designed to carry out whatever the policy is, in whatever the situation is, and it is designed to do it with people who are functional specialists and have background in what they are doing. The capability is there.

In fact, when General Weyand addressed the Military Government Civil Affairs Convention last Saturday night in Charleston, South Carolina, he said: in retrospect, we failed in that military effort in Southeast Asia because we did not give civil affairs the attention it deserved. If you want to discuss this later on, about when I was at the Senior Seminar at State in 1960, and when we discussed this kind of thing, and how the class was just about evenly divided on whether or not there should be military intervention in Vietnam, and then how it was carried out with a tight control by the Walt Rostow–McGeorge Bundy element in The White House—we could go on forever.

Robert Wolfe: Professor Montgomery, I think we have reached your moment; we want to give you ample time to do your summary for us, so I think we ought to start. We do not want to have the questions go on so long that your major contribution is truncated.

Before you start, however, I will sneak in my last word here, to thank the speakers—not only tonight's panel members, who admittedly ran the greatest risks since I did not give them any elegant paper titles, but also all of the speakers in the other sessions. It is rare and gratifying when execution conforms to plan, as our conference theme has given us ample occasion to note, but I shall not have to alter any of my prefatory remarks. Some of the papers I had seen before, some I had not, but all speakers performed as agreed and beyond, especially as to time. I am very grateful to them for having kept our bargain. We on the program are also thankful to the audience for its close attention and lively, competent questions and comments, which as promised, will be published along with the session papers. Thank you.

Summary
Notes
Biographical Notes
Conference Participants
Archival Sources

Summary

Artificial Revolution Revisited
—From Success to Excess

John D. Montgomery

There are really two questions suggested in this title. The first is: Why did we once consider the occupation a success; how did we reach a conclusion that seems to defy much of the opinion expressed in this conference? The second question is: What misperceptions have Americans had about the occupation that might have led us into further ventures that we do not now regard as successful?

Let me start with this first question. Why did some Americans, at least, consider the occupations a success, especially officials who always had access to the critical documents and records that we have discussed here? It has been suggested here that to judge our occupations of Germany and Japan a success would be a marvel of self-deception. The careful evaluations of the operation presented here do not "confirm" success. My own studies of the two occupations empirically analyzed only one aspect of them: the impact of the denazification and purge on ten or a dozen communities in each country, on their respective bureaucracies, on their political party systems, and on the industrial leadership and organization in each country. The conclusion I reached after this examination was, I am afraid, ambiguous. When my work was completed in 1955, it was not at all clear, although we had displaced the extremists in both countries, that either country was going to turn out to be a democracy or even that either country was going to turn out to be an ally of the United States. Success in small things does not guarantee satisfaction in larger issues.

Comments by Ralph Braibanti and Eleanor Hadley in answer to specific questions from the floor suggested that Japan would probably have been just about the same today without the occupation; how, then, can we claim credit for any lasting consequences of our efforts? Their opinions were presented tentatively, and their answers may be right, so far as they go. But two alternative historical explanations give me pause. First, it is possible that the occupations themselves could have been different and less benign; what we did then made, or contributed to, a difference in the "possible present." After all, it might have been worse! It is also true that whether one regards as marginal the things that we can fairly attribute to our occupations depends on one's judgment of what is important. Whether or not you consider certain occupation-caused effects as essential to democracy, or even as important aspects of the modern polities, there are obviously surviving phenomena that can be traced to that dramatic five years or so in each country. Without deconcentration, decartelization, dismantling of industry, and other interventions in Germany and Japan, as described by Hadley and Backer, it is quite likely that the union movement would have been weaker today, or at least slower off the mark and therefore probably different today. It also seems quite likely, as we were told by John Backer, that industry would probably not have been rebuilt so quickly and with such a modern base without United States assistance. In this case it might not have become competitive internally or internationally to the degree that it did, or as soon as it did. What would have been the consequences of a slower recovery?

Another issue that is still important because of its effects on public attitudes is the public school systems that emerged in the two countries after, and partly because of, the occupations. Greatly improved access to the public schools was achieved under the occupations—as a matter of policy, not of accident. As Harold Hurwitz has reminded us, this policy was stoutly resisted in Germany, where universal education was reversed soon after the occupation, and then later reinstated because of public pressures that would not have existed but for the occupation. To be sure, we cannot satisfactorily measure the difference it makes that we now have in the German universities more students who come from the middle classes and from the laboring classes than had ever been achieved before; the effects are perhaps at the micro rather than the macro level of analysis. The students and alumni who benefited from the opportunities, however, would say that it made a difference. Perhaps future historians will not notice it, but how can this generation ignore it?

I think there also are institutional and structural differences that we would have to attribute to the influence of the occupations. Left to itself, would Japan have outlawed war? Does it make any difference that it did? Would defeat alone have produced the same result? It did not in Germany. What were its consequences for the Japanese governmental budget, for national economy, for Japanese economic relations in Southeast Asia? Would they have been the same without this specific feature of the occupation? Any answer is speculative, but the absence of "as-if" and "if-only" data surely does not justify our ignoring the phenomenon.

What about the land reform in Japan? Is it imaginable that a Japanese government, however reconstructed, could have carried out land reform to the extent that SCAP did? There is a hypothesis (advanced by Samuel Huntington) that land reform can be executed successfully only under conditions of authoritarian rule. My more recent study of thirty land reforms that have taken place in the twentieth century shows exceptions to this rule and explains the success of land reform on quite different grounds. But in the case of Japan, it is quite clear that the two hypotheses merge. The preconditions to successful land reform could not have been generated in Japan without the influence of the occupying forces. Some skeptics argue that the land reform made no difference anyway in the long run because land is being consolidated again, but that argument ignores an interim of decades. Nothing makes any difference in the long run if your perspective is that Olympian.

These perceptions (and one could go on with other hypothetical or unmeasurable differences the occupation made) may explain something of a mystery that has been mentioned several times. That mystery is: Why has there been so little revisionist writing about the occupations? What there is has been associated more with subsequent events than with the occupations themselves. I call your attention to the debates that took place in this room over the last two days concerning the motives of different participants in the decision-making process. Why are their motives, assuming they can be known and codified, so important? The various explanations make it clear that the objectives and goals established by different bureaucratic units and officials involved in the occupations do not lend themselves to simple, coherent explanations. Even the most dedicated revisionists have not been able to apply a consistent theoretical framework in the analysis of these motives. They have had much greater success in reexamining the subsequent actions; their problem is finding which of these actions can be considered a necessary consequence of the occupations. Critics of the occupations have not been more scientific than their defenders.

Most military government officers, like Hans Baerwald and Robert Wolfe, admit disappointment with "their own" handiwork. We are reminded, as Earl Ziemke pointed out, that many of them were bitter because they found they could not "teach democracy." It seems to me that this bitterness reflects a desire which cannot be set aside—the desire to improve conditions for the populations of Germany and Japan. Even if one takes seriously the evidence that there was a "reverse course" after the occupations were over, that desire survived. Harold Hurwitz, in his discussion of the "reverse course," called attention to the fact that it was carried on simultaneously with the continued effort at democratization. These were coexisting thrusts, some of them incompatible and inconsistent. Perhaps the shortage of revisionist history of the occupations is a result of the difficulty of imposing the degree of perverse rationality upon these decision-makers that seems to be necessary to provide really good revisionist writing.

It seems to me that at least part of the reason why Americans considered the occupations a success in spite of their complexities and inconsistencies is simply the exhilaration of the experience. It was the high point in the lives of many government officials who remained in one way or another committed to international adventure, who became Foreign Service officers, who worked in Greece and Turkey in the Marshall Plan, who entered the forerunners of the Agency for International Development. Because of this exhilaration, they carried with them into subsequent operations certain preconceptions and perhaps misconceptions derived from the occupation experience. Unexamined past experience on the part of these officials is a more important explanation for their perception of success than the documents we have examined here or than the evidence which we have produced about their actual, perhaps unmeasured, performance.

What were the misconceptions that led to what could be described as an overestimation of success? I have a feeling that no one in this room will agree with everything I shall say on this subject, though I hope that there will be no one who disagrees with everything. For any discussion of that issue constitutes a brave journey into fantasyland.

The misperceptions that Americans carried with them into other foreign policy fields can be grouped under three headings. The first is the reinforced myth of Washington omnipotence. Much of the discussion in this conference has focused on high-level decision-makers. It has implicitly assumed a kind of rationality in their decision-making process, and a consistency of ideology and thought which none of these leaders would have claimed for himself during the heat of battle. It may be that, to some extent, we historians, economists, and political scientists, with our concern for the big decision-makers, for the big plans, the big thoughts, and the grand schemes, may have missed something by overlooking the cumulative impact of small events. More important, we may have reinforced the misperception that what was going on in the minds of these big planners really mattered very much. One can argue that the military government experience is more like Tolstoy's perception of the War of 1812 than it is of Clausewitz's doctrines of strategy and tactics.

Let me give you some evidence which I have drawn from our conference discussions over the past two days. Earl Ziemke points out "there was no guidance in Germany" (I am quoting his words). General Clay and John H. Hilldring, we are told, preferred to live with wrong concepts in high policy as contrasted with an unending effort of trying to get right concepts, because they were really concerned with doing what was necessary, not fixing up the doctrine. They made their own policy; they did not even worry very much about whether the facts bubbled up to Washington or not. Elmer Plischke mentioned that the widely variant plans that were discussed in Washington "really didn't make much difference in practice." Conflicting laws were on the books; they had to be interpreted in the field. (Any veteran of World War II knows how the field can interpret an instruction "not to do" something as meaning "to do" it if it becomes convenient and the commanding officer can get away with it.)

Truman and Eisenhower both complained that their policies were not being carried out, but that they could do nothing about it. Eli Nobleman reminded us how very few of the military government units went to areas where they were to have been assigned, about which such grand plans were drawn up and communicated to them. John Gimbel noted the extent of field initiative in creating Bizonia, in making policies regarding reparations, and in working out deals and arrangements with other zonal commanders. Hans Baerwald spoke of the unwillingness of General Willoughby's intelligence section to pursue the purgees in spite of instructions to do so; while General Whitney proceeded with his purge and set up his own mechanisms for pursuing them; and both carried out their own programs inconsistently and without very much concern for finding a strategy of coexistence. OMGUS units would cooperate with each other only under extreme pressure, John Gimbel reports. James Riddleberger told us how General Clay created his own political advisory system to avoid having to depend on the State Department's orders and procedures. The MacArthur syndrome of independence is certainly the best example of all, testified to by John J. McCloy and by Eleanor Hadley's account of his dissolution of the trading com-

panies. General MacArthur was an unguided missile of United
States foreign policy long before he crossed the Yalu.

The myth of rational, central control over the details of these
overseas operations persisted in our policies in Greece and Turkey;
our reconstruction of the war-torn areas; in our foreign aid programs, where Washington policies faithfully reflect changing academic doctrine and political whims. We know that when the
Kennedy administration introduced the concept of centralized planning in the Agency for International Development, with its rationality of macroeconomics as a basis for country programming, that
the field responded by reporting that it was doing exactly what
Washington ordered whether it was or not. Field officers in the foreign aid operations overseas soon began to refer to these reports of
mythical compliance (if you will permit the expression) as the
"Jesus factor." To compound the misperception, Washington is capable of deceiving itself by believing in its own rationality (what
else can it do?). It is perfectly sincere in forcing the field to pretend
that its rationalities correspond to what they are doing and observing there. Both sides can misperceive facts in the same way, reinforcing the misperceptions until a Vietnam occurs in which it is impossible for the people operating in the field to report what they
would see if they were willing to look—indeed, after they have been
at it long enough they no longer even see in their minds what they
see with their eyes. Many of us who visited and revisited Vietnam in
the 1960s saw the naked emperor, but we were not a part of the official chain of communications and command. Our perceptions were
too far removed from the perceptions of those who were designing
entirely rational policies to become a useful source of information.

So I see centralized rationality as one of the major misconceptions
of our foreign policy that was reinforced, if not created, by the occupation experience, which, I remind you, was the largest political enterprise ever undertaken by the United States outside of its borders.
Let us not deceive ourselves in our scholarly concentration on the
documents that focus on a very few high level decision-makers. Let
us think rather about how we might capture the actual field experience in implementing high level policies, before we and our memories have shriveled up and we have irretrievably lost valuable
first-hand impressions that thus far have entered so seldom into our
writing and thinking about military government doctrine and history. I am grateful that at this conference we have been able to talk
about some realities of field operations as well as those of planning.

A second source of misperception is the overestimation during the
occupations of the consequences of our social engineering. This

overestimation contributed to the United States government's activism overseas in areas that it would indeed hesitate to touch in dealing with its own state governments. The military government experience afforded an unusual opportunity at social engineering, which we were eager to seize. In retrospect it seems more than possible that we have misinterpreted the universality of the structural changes we introduced, and thought we had identified social and political institutions that could be transplanted anywhere. True, some of the laws and the constitutions we introduced seem to have stood the test of time. Indeed, some of them have been repealed and later reinstated, a process that appears to confirm the wisdom of what we did in the first place. For example, school curricula were reformed, reinstated, and re-reformed; and administrative and structural police reforms were abandoned after the Americans withdrew, but again reinstated in one form or another. Editors, as Harold Hurwitz told us, were taught about a free press; they were later rebuked for learning that lesson, but many of them have survived the rebuke. The media have learned how censorship and guidelines can develop a sense of independent responsibility. But let us examine more carefully how these institutions interacted with their predecessors in creating the present. Let us pause to wonder what difference it made that the Japanese adopted the United States standard 6–3–3 design of school system. To what extent can the occupation's social reforms be attributed to that which was imposed externally, and to what extent can their present form be attributed to reactions and developments from within? It is clear, I believe, that the structural reforms of the occupation created, reinforced, or shaped continuing social reform, but I think we should now try to find out how much they did do. In neglecting the law of actions and reactions, especially in the early postwar years, I think we tended to overestimate the consequences of our social engineering in Germany and Japan and to credit ourselves with too many of their own economic and political achievements.

The misconceptions that I have talked about so far, of which I have been able to give only a few examples, seem to have affected significantly the American presence in the postwar world. We thought we were creating the bureaucratic infrastructure of democracy when we prepared translations of the New York State Civil Service Codes for the benefit of the Japanese and Germans. Our specialists did not know enough at that time to do much more; political and social scientists had not invented the concepts of political development and modernization which they later were able to thrust upon an unprepared world. And the fact that these early fumblings seemed to stand the test of time encouraged the same manipulators to proceed further, and to attach the structural concept to activities that were really not related to an occupation, yet were really not joined to the indigenous experience either. Thus we find in our foreign aid legislation, as early as 1951, injunctions to the State Department and foreign aid agencies to introduce farmers' cooperatives, to promote private enterprise, to encourage local self-government. Ralph Braibanti's paper called attention to the fact that one uniformly accepted proposition among contemporary students of political development is the need for contextual continuity. That concept, as an operating principle, seldom disturbed occupation officials. The absence of such continuities as we have experimented with developmental change abroad is a warning sign to the social engineers which is only now being observed, and which we might have overlooked earlier because of the apparent successes of the occupations. I would like to suggest that we have a very large area for research ahead of us which is the congruence, the fit, if you will, between reform and prestructure. Even in the military government situation, we need to know how what was introduced selectively reinforced the pre-existing traditions. What can one learn from this experience in dealing with countries in such matters as human rights initiatives?

A third misconception we derived from our occupation experiences is that somehow these postwar years reinforced basic American assumptions about world politics and even about the nature of man. Most of us in 1944–48 accepted without much challenge the propositions that a benevolent occupation would take off the shackles that hitherto prevented, or restrained, the emergence of a free people. The natural state of man, we believed, was to be free and even, perhaps, to be entrepreneurial. Such a view was quite openly expressed, for example, by Eugene Dooman, as Marlene Mayo reminded us. It meant that in creating a democracy we could follow Leonardo da Vinci's advice on making a statue—carve off the marble that was not needed. By purging the oppressive classes and laws we could create in each nation a democratic state. A kind of reverse Marxism crept into our thinking during the occupation and has stayed with us still: if we can develop the right economic conditions in downtrodden countries, somehow the "appropriate" political conditions will emerge. For want of time I cannot pursue that argument further here but I think you all recognize it as an old friend.

In closing I want to say that there are true as well as false lessons—things of a somewhat different order that we have learned, or could have learned, from the occupations. We are caught, how-

ever, in one of nature's ironies in trying to apply them. For the
clearer is the knowledge we can derive from the occupation experiences, the less useful it is to us now. What we now know how to do
well, we shall probably never do again. And what we have learned
will have to be applied with such subtlety and wisdom in the future
that it is hard to describe it as a lesson from experience at all.

What are some of the irrelevant techniques that we know better
as a result of the occupation? For one thing, we know how to conduct
a political purge. If we have to do it again, we can call on Hans
Baerwald or Elmer Plischke. We do know how to get rid of undesirable leaders in an occupied enemy country. We know, for example,
that it has to be done soon after the end of the war; we know it has to
be done simultaneously among all groups; we know it has to be an
administrative, not a judicial, activity; we know that there have to
be appeals to take care of the errors. Some of this wisdom we applied
in Japan because of the experiences we had already had in Italy and
Germany. We were learning; it was a conscious learning process.

Secondly, we have learned how to use governmental institutions
in other countries for temporary purposes without necessarily
strengthening them permanently. We created bureaucracies to perform services under a military occupation and then dismantled
them—something we rarely accomplish at home or in a foreign aid
situation. But we will probably never have an intact government
with such bureaucratic perfection as the Japanese presented us with
in the summer of 1945. Again, we probably know how to deconcen-
trate industry if we ever get the opportunity again (which we very
likely will not). Eleanor Hadley and John Backer could do it for us in
the United States, for that matter, but I doubt if they will ever receive such an invitation. And, too, we know how to censor (Marlene
Mayo) or license (Harold Hurwitz) the press, though we do not re-
joice in that knowledge. It is interesting to reflect, in reviewing Colonel Swarm's summaries, that this kind of knowledge has not been
captured in our current military government doctrine. It is the kind
of experience, fascinating as it is to us who lived through it, that we
seem to want to suppress.

In addition to these nonreplicable findings, there are more basic
things that we have learned from the occupations. These less situ-
ation-specific lessons are very much more subtle than the three or
four I just mentioned. Here I can do little more than give you titles of
the topics representing areas where I think our increased understanding lies.

First, I think we have learned something about reform in general.
Reform is an ancient and honorable political custom. It can be traced

historically back for centuries—indeed, for millennia. The occupations reminded us about the necessity for continuity of purpose, for keeping the pressure on, for permitting subtle movements away from structural preconceptions. Much of what we have learned from the processes of changing institutions in Germany and Japan is applicable in other reform situations, though we may never have the power to reform by fiat again. I think we have learned to perform certain technical functions a little better. We know more about the nature of inflation and the consequences of public anticipation of it, about currency reform, about public intervention in the market, and about economic crises in the wake of disaster. We probably know something about the effects of curriculum and other school changes that we have not yet documented but that we could apply if we really wanted. Many of the things we have observed the past two days are familiar in theory; it is our experience that we can now codify and interpret. Most specifically we learned that international inducement to reform can become a continuous, almost routine operation.

To take a still further step in the direction of irresponsible speculation, I think maybe even in issues of world politics we might have learned something. I cannot escape the feeling that the real German miracle was also the Japanese miracle. It was not the *Wirtschaftswunder*. It was the conversion of real enemies into true diplomatic partners. I ask you for the moment to remember the bitterness with which both sides viewed each other in the Second World War, and then compare the attitudes of the current generation. I hope you will also remember, drawing on experience in the First World War, that military occupation does not necessarily produce such friendship. Was there not something about the respect with which we treated these two cultures this time that may tell us something about the processes of diplomacy and world politics? Obviously we do not have to defeat a country in order to become its ally. But what can we learn about the processes of attitude change, or about the reduction of suspicion, that can be applied in the manner of our behavior in relation with other states and peoples? Is there something in our current concern with human rights that can help us reach the aspirations of other peoples directly, transcending the formalities of intergovernmental relations? Is it possible, after all, that the relations among nations can rest first on the affirmation of their common interests, and then on the resolution of their differences?

It seems only reasonable to end on a question, since as a nation we seem most secure when we are dealing with problems, not certainties.

Notes

1. American Wartime Planning for Occupied Japan:
The Role of the Experts / Mayo

1. This paper has been considerably revised since the conference and is based on research for a full-length study of wartime planning for occupied Japan. I wish to thank archivists William Cunliffe and John Taylor for pointing out the importance of the military documents in complementing and expanding upon the diplomatic record and for helping me to find my way through the labyrinthine files of the National Archives. I am also grateful to the Division of Arts and Humanities, University of Maryland, for the award of a semester research assignment, which made possible the completion of this essay.

2. No complete study of policy making for the occupation of Japan has yet been published. There is, for example, no counterpart to Paul Hammond's extensive account, "Directives for the Occupation of Germany," pp. 311–460, in Harold Stein, ed., *American Civil-Military Decisions: A Book of Case Studies* (Birmingham: Univ. of Alabama Press, 1963), or John H. Backer's *The Decision to Divide Germany: American Foreign Policy in Transition* (Durham: Duke Univ. Press, 1978). Also, little has been done on civil affairs planning and the role of the Army comparable to Earl F. Ziemke, *The U.S. Army in the Occupation of Germany, 1944–1946* (Washington, D.C.: Government Printing Office, 1975), or the opening sections of Harold Zink, *The United States in Germany, 1944–1955* (Princeton and New York: D. Van Nostrand, 1957). Among the few works on military government training for Japan are: Arthur D. Bouterse et al., "American Military Government Experience in Japan," in Carl J. Friedrich, ed., *American Experiences in Military Government in World War II* (New York: Rinehart, 1948), pp. 318–54; Justin Williams, Sr., "From Charlottesville to Tokyo: Military Government Training and Democratic Reforms in Occupied Japan," *Pacific Historical Review* 51 (Nov. 1982): 407–22.

Pieces of the planning story, primarily for political foreign policy have been told by one of the participants, Hugh Borton, in two essays, "American Presurrender Planning for Postwar Japan" (*Occasional Papers of the East Asian Institute,* Columbia University, 1967), pp. 3–37; and "Preparation for the Occupation of Japan," *Journal of Asian Studies* 25 (Feb. 1966): 203–12. An interpretive essay has been written by John Maki, who was in the wartime OWI, serving on the Japan desk, "United States Initial Postwar Policy for Japan," in Han-kyo Kim, ed., *Essays on Modern Politics and History* (Athens: Ohio Univ. Press, 1969), pp. 30–56. More recently, Akira Iriye added details and an overview (largely that of neo-Wilsonian integrationism) in his book, *Power and Culture: The Japanese-American War, 1941–1945* (Cambridge: Harvard Univ. Press, 1981); see also his article, "Continuities in U.S.-Japanese Relations, 1941–1949," in Yonosuke Nagai and Akira Iriye, eds., *The Origins of the Cold War in Asia* (New York: Columbia Univ. Press, 1977), pp. 378–405. My account varies considerably from Iriye's in the use of sources, interpretations, approaches, and conclusions. There are also two unpublished doctoral dissertations: Eric H. F. Svensson, "The Military Occupation of Japan: The First Years—Planning, Policy Formation, and Reforms" (Univ. of Denver, 1966); and Michael J. Boyle, "The Planning of the Occupation of Japan and the American Reform Tradition" (Univ. of Wyoming, 1979). Svensson is helpful, as are Boyle's summaries of documents. However, Boyle relies too much on published materials, most of them originating in the State Department, does not deal adequately with the final year of planning, and has neglected conservatism in his treatment of the American political tradition.

3. For the text of the Potsdam declaration, see *Foreign Relations of the United States* (hereafter *FRUS*), *The Conference of Berlin (The Potsdam Conference), 1945*, vol. 2 (Washington, D.C.: Government Printing Office, 1960), p. 1474. A convenient source for SWNCC 150/4/A and JCS 1380/15 is SCAP, Government Section, *Political Reorientation of Japan, September 1945 to September 1948: Report* (Washington, D.C.: Government Printing Office, 1949), vol. 2, app. A, pp. 423–39.

4. SWNCC papers, from the earliest drafts to the final stages, are assembled in National Archives, Microfilm Publication, T-1205, 13 rolls.

5. MacArthur's reminiscences should be used with caution, as those of his chief aides, Generals Courtney Whitney and Charles Willoughby.

6. The basic source for the organization and personnel of the secret planning groups is Harley A. Notter, *Postwar Foreign Policy Preparation, 1939–1945* (Washington, D.C.: Government Printing Office, 1949). It was Notter, a Stanford trained scholar of Wilsonian foreign policy, who alerted the department in September 1939 to the need for planning. Notter joined the department in 1937 as a divisional assistant and was serving in the Division of the American Republics at the time of Hitler's invasion of Poland. For details about Colonel House and his planning group, see Lawrence E. Gelfand, *The Inquiry: American Preparations for Peace, 1917–1919* (New Haven: Yale Univ. Press, 1963).

7. Laurence H. Shoup and William Minter present a conspiratorial analysis of the behind the scenes influence of the Council on Foreign Relations in *Imperial Brain Trust: The Council on Foreign Relations and United States Foreign Policy* (New York and London: Monthly Review Press, 1977). See especially chapter 4, "Shaping a New World Order: The Council's Blueprint for World Hegemony, 1939–1945." Notter's version of the role of the CFR is in *Postwar Foreign Policy Preparation*, pp. 18, 56, and 80–81.

8. Pasvolsky, who was born in Russia, came to the State Department in 1935 as a member of the Division of Trade Agreements. A few years later, Hull appointed him special assistant on economic affairs and in 1939 special assistant on problems of peace. Pasvolsky was to play a substantial role in the research and planning leading to the establishment of the United Nations and in April 1945 led the American technical staff at the United Nations Conference on International Organization, San Francisco. He brought Notter to SR as assistant chief in May 1941. Unless otherwise noted, biographical details in this essay are based on various issues of *Who's Who, Register of the Department of State,* and *Current Biography.*

9. Technically, it is probably incorrect to identify, as does Iriye (*Power and Culture,* p. 59), the Advisory Committee as a State Department committee. It is true that its members were appointed by the president at the request of Secretary of State Hull and that its recommendations were to be channeled through the State Department, but many of its members were private citizens or, as in the case of Norman Davis, had direct access to Roosevelt. The State Department had a substantial but not exclusive role in the preparatory work, 1939–43, and in the establishment of general principles. For other interpretations, see Notter, *Postwar Foreign Policy Preparation,* pp. 58–81, and Shoup and Minter, *Imperial Brain Trust,* pp. 149–50.

10. Several critics have chastised Roosevelt for neglecting political objectives and peace aims during the war and relying too heavily on his military advisers. John J. McCloy, writing after the war, declared that peace planners in the State Department were not "meshed into policy," *The Challenge to American Foreign Policy* (Cambridge: Harvard Univ. Press, 1953), p. 50. Although it was true that strategy for victory was the president's foremost consideration, Roosevelt, as Robert Dallek has pointed out and the extensive Notter File in the National Archives reveals, did give much attention to postwar planning, at first privately and then, beginning in 1943, publicly; *Franklin D. Roosevelt and American Foreign Policy, 1932–1945* (New York: Oxford Univ. Press, 1979), pp. 358–60, 372–73, 422, 440–41. The full story has not yet been told of the president's interaction with the Advisory Committee and the evolution in his thinking about the United States and the postwar world. Hs proclaimed only general principles and resisted being specific about the treatment of defeated enemy states for a variety of political and strategic reasons and to keep his options open.

11. Davis, a banker and financier by profession, was also a former undersecretary of state (at the end of the Wilson administration) and had been the chief American delegate at the World Disarmament Conference, Geneva, 1932–33, the Naval Conference, London, 1935–36, and the Brussels Conference, 1937. His Subcommittee on Security Problems arrived at the unconditional surrender formula in April and May 1942 in the course of discussing terms and methods of surrender (Record Group 59 [hereafter RG], Notter File, Box 76, Diplomatic Branch of the National Archives). The best published account of the influence of Davis, the Advisory Committee, and the JCS in the origins of this doctrine and of the predilections of

Roosevelt dating from World War I is Raymond G. O'Connor, *Diplomacy for Victory: FDR and Unconditional Surrender* (New York: W. W. Norton, 1971), pp. 1–12, 35–39, 50–56.

12. *FRUS, Conference at Washington, 1941–42, and Casablanca, 1943,* pp. 506, 727 (Roosevelt's meeting with the JCS January 7, 1943, and his remarks at the postconference press conference on January 24).

13. The Cairo declaration stated that Japan would be "stripped of all the islands in the Pacific which she had seized or occupied since the beginning of the First World War in 1914," and that it would lose territories it had "stolen from the Chinese" (Formosa, Manchuria, the Pescadores), its Pacific Mandates, and any other territories "taken by violence and greed." Korea "in due course" was to "become free and independent," *FRUS, Conference at Cairo and Tehran, 1943,* pp. 448–49. The Yalta communiqué was released to the press on February 12 and printed in the *Department of State Bulletin* 12 (Feb. 18, 1945), pp. 213–16. Willard Range discusses Roosevelt's conversion to Wilsonian internationalism and his global New Deal in *Franklin D. Roosevelt's World Order* (Athens, Ga.: Univ. of Georgia Press, 1959); and Robert Dallek, in his chapter, "The Idealist as Realist, 1942–45," summarizes the controversy in Washington and at the Quebec Conference (September 1944) over the Morgenthau plan for Germany, in *Franklin D. Roosevelt and American Foreign Policy,* pp. 472–74, 477–79.

14. Notter, *Postwar Foreign Policy Preparation,* pp. 149–53; National Archives, Diplomatic Branch (hereafter NADB), RG 59, Notter File, "Notes, January 1942 to December 1943" (Box 11), and letter from Nelson T. Johnson to George Blakeslee, April 19, 1949 (Box 1); conversation with Hugh Borton, Columbia University Seminar, February 14, 1975. McCloy declares that "the active, energetic new blood which was infused into the Washington scene during the war period largely went into the War Department, Lend Lease, the Armed Forces—everywhere, it seems, except the State Department" (*The Challenge to American Foreign Policy,* p. 50). Charles W. Yost, who was appointed secretary of the Davis Subcommittee on Security Problems and wrote several memoranda on the problems of occupying enemy territories, recalls that "postwar planning, except planning for the military occupation of liberated territories, enjoyed little prestige outside, or even inside, the State Department in 1942," *History and Memory* (New York: W. W. Norton, 1980), p. 112.

15. Although Hornbeck had spent four years in China (mainly in Hangchow and Shanghai) and Manchuria before World War I, he had no significant period of residence in Japan or elsewhere in Asia. Among his early posts was a position on the Inquiry, where he was in charge of Far Eastern research and which earned him a berth as a technical expert at the Versailles Peace Conference, 1919. Hornbeck also served on the expert staff at the Washington Disarmament Conference, 1921–22, and (while on leave of absence from Harvard University) at the Special Tariff Commission in China, 1925–26. He was present at the founding meetings, 1919, of what

was to become the Council on Foreign Relations and, in 1924–25, the American Council of the Institute of Pacific Relations.

16. Ballantine was Hull's interpreter during the Hull-Nomura negotiations in 1941. His Foreign Service assignments in the 1930s included a stint in Manchuria as consul general at Mukden, an experience which gave him a hearty dislike of Japanese army officers (Ballantine manuscript, Hoover Institution Archives, Stanford University). Grew's career after repatriation in 1942 is briefly described in Waldo Heinrichs, *American Ambassador: Joseph C. Grew and the Development of the United States Diplomatic Tradition* (Boston: Little, Brown, 1966), pp. 362–69. The most extensive account of Dooman's career is an unpublished master's thesis, Peter Adams, "Eugene H. Dooman, 'A Penny A Dozen Expert': The Tribulations of a Japan Specialist in the American Foreign Service, 1912–1945" (Univ. of Maryland, 1976).

17. Notter, *Postwar Foreign Policy Preparation,* pp. 518–19. Other Japanese language officers whose advice was later sought or who drafted some of the planning memoranda, 1943–45, were H. Merrell Benninghoff, Beppo Johansen, and Erle R. Dickover. Their primary duties, however, were as desk officers in the Division of Far Eastern Affairs. Younger Japanese language officers, like U. Alexis Johnson and John K. Emmerson, were sent to Latin America, 1942–43, to check on the espionage network and activities of Japanese immigrant groups; John Allison was sent to London. Later, in 1944–45, Emmerson's views on postwar Japan entered the State Department's planning process.

18. "Statement of Major Post-War Problems in the Pacific Area," February 20, 1942 (RG 59, Pasvolsky Office File, Box 2). Jones was head, 1942–43, of the Postwar Trends Unit, SR.

19. Biographical details are from the Blakeslee papers, Clark University. Assessments of his role are based on conversations with Hugh Borton (Feb. 14, 1975; Feb. 11, 1977); Gordon Bowles (Aug. 23, 1980); and Edwin Martin (Oct. 27, 1977; Martin used the phrase, "poor, dear Japan Blakeslee"). The quotation is from *Conflicts of Policy in the Far East,* World Affairs Pamphlet, number 6 (published jointly by the Foreign Policy Association and World Peace Foundation, 1934), p. 11. Blakeslee, too, had been a member of the Inquiry in 1918. In 1940–41, he was president of the board of trustees of the Boston based World Peace Foundation and a member both of the executive committee, American Council, IPR, and the editorial advisory board of the CFR's journal, *Foreign Affairs.*

20. Notter, *Postwar Foreign Policy Preparation,* pp. 518–19. Masland was only peripherally a Japan specialist. His research interests included public opinion and foreign policy, specifically American attitudes toward Japan. Otherwise, he had no language training and little firsthand knowledge of East Asia. Masland returned to his teaching post at Stanford in 1943 and also served there on the staff of the civil affairs training school established at the request of the Army. Subsequently, he became head of the depart-

ment of government and provost at Dartmouth College and an adviser to the federal government on national security affairs (*New York Times,* obituary, Aug. 23, 1968).

21. Based on Borton's oral history, 1956, Special Collections, Columbia University, and taped conversation with Borton (Oct. 1973).

22. Blakeslee was reunited after 1945 with General Frank McCoy, chairman of the Far Eastern Commission, whom he had previously served in 1932 as special assistant when McCoy was the American representative on the Lytton Commission to investigate the Manchurian Incident. During the wartime years, Borton also wrote several papers on Japan's conquests and territories, including Korea. He has been primarily identified, however, with the planning papers which led to SWNCC 228 (Jan. 1946), on the revision of the Japanese constitution. He ended his academic career as president of Haverford College.

23. The five study groups of the War and Peace Studies were apparently the model for the structure of Roosevelt's Advisory Committee and its subcommittees; Davis was chairman of the project and Hamilton Fish Armstrong the vice-chairman (Shoup and Minter, *Imperial Brain Trust,* pp. 118–25). In contrast to Iriye, who stresses throughout his book (*Power and Culture*) the return of the American government to Wilsonian idealism in international affairs and integrationism, Shoup and Minter give a more sinister interpretation to American grand designs. The CFR, dominated by corporate capitalists and their scholars for hire, they argue, wished to solve American domestic economic problems by economic nationalism, world trade, and expansion of the postwar global role of the United States in world affairs—in effect to put the United States at the center of a "single world-spanning political economy" and make the world safe for American capitalism. Specifically, "the War and Peace Studies group, in collaboration with the American government, worked out an imperialistic conception of the national interest and war aims of the United States. This imperialism involved a conscious attempt to organize and control a global empire." The values and goals of the CFR became those of the Advisory Committee and thus influenced "key decisions" for the postwar world, 1942–44 (p. 24 and ch. 4, "Shaping a New World Order: The Council's Blueprint for World Hegemony, 1939–1945," pp. 117–87). There was overlapping between the CFR and the government, but this analysis (as does Iriye's) discounts the institutional identifications of government officials with their own organizations, bureaucratic politics, conflicts of opinion and motivation, and the compromises between realism and idealism at the end of the war. John H. Backer, in questioning revisionist and traditionalist scholarship on the supposed "covering grand design," whether ascribed to Soviet or American imperialism, argues that "long range schemes" in one quarter were often "cancelled out" by other schemes somewhere else. Policy making, instead, was characterized by "a series of small, incremental decisions, sometimes taken at lower levels of government and often prompted by expediency

rather than by long-term considerations" (preface to *The Decision to Divide Germany: American Foreign Policy in Transition* [Durham: Duke Univ. Press, 1978]).

24. Edgar Dean's correspondence with Borton and Blakeslee, October 1941, Study Group Records of the Council on Foreign Relations, New York City. Hornbeck attended at least two of the sessions and as a matter of course received the minutes for all of them. Others present at all or some of the meetings included Roger S. Greene, Tyler Dennett, Nathaniel Peffer, Nicholas J. Spykman, Charles F. Remer, John D. Rockefeller III, Admiral William V. Pratt, General William Crozier, and General Frank McCoy. Together, they represented the academic world, military and naval circles, the media, business and foundations.

25. Study Group Reports, Council on Foreign Relations. Byas was the author of *Government by Assassination* (New York: Knopf, 1942). Blakeslee's questions for discussion (Feb. 1942) asked whether Japan should "be made to suffer the natural results of a military and naval defeat, or should it be maintained as a strong power in order to balance Russia and, possibly, China?" Also, "should exceptional measures be adopted, if necessary, to give Japan a reasonable assurance of economic security and prosperity, in order to remove from the Japanese people any economic incentive to support another imperialist war?" Economic considerations included not only international cooperation and free access to raw materials but also "the establishment of helpful institutions for international finance." Other questions were on the form of international cooperation—global or regional.

26. Borton to Raymond Leslie Buell, May 20, 1942 (file folder, East Asian Institute, Columbia Univ.). Buell had requested Borton's comments on a proposed postwar program for Japan.

27. Notter, *Postwar Foreign Policy Preparation,* pp. 157–59; document P-213, "Generul Problems of the Far East," March 10 and appended document of March 8 (the covering statement briefly listed as questions not only "constitutional and other changes to be required of Japan" but also "possibly the undertaking of social and economic reforms" (Notter File, Box 57).

28. The questions were placed on the agenda for a meeting on March 13. The minutes, unfortunately, are cryptic, but one unidentified speaker, in reference to General Strong's conditions for Japanese surrender, declared that the terms "could not be too drastic." Another participant suggested that instead of Hokkaido, "either the heart of Japan should be occupied or control should be exercised through air power from Korea." The meeting was attended by twenty-four people, including four senators, two representatives, several State Department officials (Berle, Pasvolsky, Hornbeck, Hamilton, and Notter), the librarian of Congress, and a number of influential private citizens (Minutes, Notter File, Box 55).

29. Economic work, as Notter points out, was more advanced than political and territorial work in early 1943 (*Postwar Foreign Policy Preparation,* p. 133). In April 1943, the Advisory Committee on Postwar Foreign Eco-

nomic Policy was set up to replace two economic subcommittees chaired by Assistant Secretaries of State Berle and Acheson and to combine long- and short-range economic planning.

30. Bowman, a distinguished geographer, was still another planner who had been a member of the Inquiry in 1918. His subcommittee began its first full-scale deliberations on Japan and East Asia in June and July 1943 and continued them in the late fall. The papers by the research staff in PS and ES were assigned T numbers (Territorial) or E numbers (Economic). Most of the Japan related papers in this massive series were drafted by Blakeslee, Borton, Fearey, and Williams.

31. Minutes, July 30, 1943 (Notter File, Box 59). Supervision of education was dropped as a topic until reintroduced in 1944 by the Army planners in the War Department. Ballantine had agreed with Blakeslee in July, saying that "he did not believe that it was possible to impose changes in the internal life of Japan."

32. T-315, "Status of the Japanese Emperor," May 25, 1943 (Notter File, Box 63); and "Japan: Postwar Economic Consequences," February 20, 1943 (NADB, Acheson papers, Box 11). Another early paper, one written by Borton at Hornbeck's request, was T-230, "Japan and the Issue of Racial Equality at Paris, 1919," February 3, 1943 (Hornbeck papers, Hoover Institution Archives, Stanford University, Box 350).

33. The conundrum for the Japan planners was how to encourage the Japanese to initiate their own reforms but to do it along recommended lines. By October, Ballantine thought that in addition to moral suasion it might be possible to show the Japanese that it paid to be good. They should tell the Japanese moderates their views and aims. "We should not try to control their conduct of affairs but we should let them know that when their educational system and their political aims had developed in such a way as to approach the objectives which we had considered, we would give them a greater amount of confidence and respect. In this fashion we would be able to win their confidence and make the necessary reforms without direct intervention" (T-Minutes, Oct. 22, 1943, Box 59). The nature and extent of the moderate or liberal group in Japan was a controversial topic among the government planners and in public debate on postwar Japan. See Roman Lavalle, "Have We Any Friends in Japan," *Free World* (Apr. 1944), pp. 347–59, an article which concluded darkly that "The hope for democracy in Japan lies not with the old corrupt leaders but with the people themselves and with our own postwar policy." Lavalle wanted to "erase all vestiges of Japan's feudal and war-breeding institution: the Imperial House, the traditional aristocracy, the industrial trusts, the military and naval hierarchy, and the constitution." Charles Nelson Spinks (in the Office of Naval Intelligence) wrote about "The Liberal Myth in Japan," in *Pacific Affairs* (Dec. 1942), warning that the liberals were above all Japanese nationalists. See also C. Burnell Olds, "Potentialities of Japanese Liberalism," *Foreign Affairs* (Apr. 1944); and "The Dangerous Myth of the 'Moderates,'" a subsection of "A New Far Eastern Policy? Japan versus China" in *Amerasia* (June

9, 1944). The real democratic force, argued the latter, was that of worker and peasant organizations.

34. The original wording of July, before Bowman's group tinkered with it, was closer to Blakeslee's personal views: "Since elements exist in Japan which, after Japan's complete defeat, give some promise of forming" a government which respected the rights of others, "this principle will favor an attempt to create conditions which will strengthen these elements."

35. T-357 (July 28, 1943) and T-357a (Sept. 29, 1943), "Japan: General Principles applicable to the Postwar Settlement with Japan" (Notter File, Box 64). Blakeslee had recommended territorial terms before the Cairo declaration. The Japan hands were not persuaded that China had a strong case for the return of the Liuchius (Ryukyus) nor Russia for Karafuto and the Kuriles. Although, as Borton recalls (in "American Presurrender Planning for Postwar Japan," pp. 12–13), no State Department documents were used at Cairo on Japan's dismemberment, possibly the views of the Advisory Committee were known to Roosevelt, who had already expressed anticolonial sentiments and broached the idea of international trusteeship. For a thorough and careful treatment of the evolution of Roosevelt's views on colonial empires, see Wm. Roger Louis, *Imperialism at Bay: The United States and the Decolonization of The British Empire, 1941–1945* (New York: Oxford Univ. Press, 1978).

36. Based on T-358, "Japan: Recent Political Developments" (July 28, 1943); T-366; "Political and Economic Aspects of the Terms of Surrender" (Sept. 27, 1943); T-381, "Japan's Postwar Political Problems" (Oct. 6, 1943); T-Minutes, Oct. 22, 1943 (all in the Notter File, Boxes 59, 64–65); Borton's oral history, Columbia University. Not only did the Department of State monitor public opinion, it sometimes attempted to shape it. For example, Blakeslee and Borton helped Lawrence Rosinger revise his pamphlet, *What Future for Japan,* issued by the Foreign Policy Association in September 1943 (Blakeslee's notation on letter from Hornbeck, Sept. 22, 1943; Hornbeck papers, Hoover Institution Archives, Box 29). The German experts on the research staff held remarkably similar views to the Japan experts in "The Political Reorganization of Germany," September 23, 1943. "Effective democracy" could survive in Germany only if there were "tolerable" living standards, minimum controls to avoid bitterness, and coordination with the Soviet Union. The United States, the paper urged, should adopt a "program looking to the economic recovery of Germany" (reprinted in Notter, *Postwar Foreign Policy Preparation,* pp. 558–60; the Notter File reveals that it was drafted by David Harris for the Interdivisional Country Committee on Germany; Box 108).

37. Drawn from several papers: "The Economic Effects upon Japan of a Possible Loss of Control Over Its Present Dependencies" (E-131, June 21, 1943); "The Economy of Japan" (E-135, June 25, 1943); "Japanese Postwar Economic Considerations" (E-155, July 21, 1943); "Possible Immediate Postwar Japanese Contributions to the Rehabilitation of the Far East" (E-173, Sept. 6, 1943); "The Postwar Readjustment of Japan's Economy,"

(E-189, Oct. 9, 1943; all in Notter File, Boxes 64–65, 81–82); "Treatment of Japan: Policy with Respect to the Large, Family Concerns in Japanese Industry" (T-470 preliminary, Mar. 25, 1944; Notter File, Box 66); interview with Fearey (May 5, 1978). Fearey also strayed briefly on the emperor issue (T-Minutes, Oct. 22, 1943; Notter File, Box 59).

38. T-Minutes, Dec. 17, 1943 (Notter File, Box 59); Hornbeck memorandum of Sept. 27, 1943; Hornbeck to Grew, June 1, 1943; Hornbeck to Bowman, Dec. 31, 1943, and Jan. 5, 1944 (Hornbeck papers, Hoover Institution Archives, Boxes 350, 467, 468); Ashley Clarke's record of a conversation with Hornbeck, Oct. 13, 1943, in Public Record Office, London, FO 371/F5470/4905/23; Hornbeck's report on his trip to London, as recorded by Borton (Notter File, Box 79); Hornbeck's own memo of his report, written for the secretary of state, Nov. 10, 1943 (Hornbeck papers, Box 468). Hornbeck told Bowman that he was inclined to believe that the Japanese throne would continue but doubted that it was in Japan's best interests. If the institution was to continue, let the responsibility rest with the Japanese, he said, and not with the United States or the United Nations.

39. ST Minutes, May 7, 1943 (Notter File, Box 79). The Security Technical Subcommittee was a working level interdepartmental group under the jurisdiction of the Davis Subcommittee on Security Problems. See also T-Minutes, Dec. 17, 1943 (Armstrong's comments; Notter File, Box 59); Alger Hiss to Hornbeck, Dec. 23, 1943.

40. T-Minutes, Dec. 17, 1943 (Notter File, Box 59).

41. Notter, *Postwar Foreign Policy Preparation,* pp. 176–79, 215–17, 574.

42. Borton, "American Presurrender Planning," p. 11.

43. Military government planning and civil affairs training will be included in the author's full length study. It was understood that civil affairs in Japan would be primarily an American responsibility, but would they be mainly an Army or a Navy responsibility, asked Assistant Secretary of War John McCloy (to General Hilldring, Mar. 28, 1944; in NA, Modern Military Headquarters Branch, hereafter NAMB, RG 107, ASW, 333.9 Cairo). For the initial agreement between the Army and Navy, see Svensson, "The Military Occupation of Japan," pp. 7–12.

44. NAMB, RG 226, 1343, Nov. 19, 1943, "Agenda of Research Requirements for Civil Affairs Administration in Japan." The authorship is uncertain but very likely Remer, then head of the Far Eastern Division, and his assistant and successor, Charles Burton Fahs, had a hand. Fahs, a political scientist with extensive knowledge of the Japanese government, was of missionary background and had taught at Claremont before the war.

45. *FRUS, 1944,* vol. 5 (Washington, D.C.: Government Printing Office, 1965), pp. 1190–92. Another OSS study, "Some Preliminary Political Questions Bearing on Civil Affairs Planning in the Far East" (Feb. 10, 1944), commissioned by CAD, contains some economic questions which were not, for some reason, included in the request of February 18 (R&A 1889).

46. RG 226, R&A 2314 (July 7, 1944), "Salient Problems of Civil Affairs Administration: Japan," a study requested by General Hilldring. R&A 2360, "Questions on Basic Assumptions Concerning Civil Administration in

Japan" (July 19, 1944), asked whether a decision had been made as to whether "the primary purpose of the Military Occupation" of defeated Japan is "(a) punitive, or (b) corrective." And "may it be assumed that the primary purpose of the foreign civil administration will be to: (a) Maintain order and assure stability for a provisional Japanese government so that it may fulfill its peace terms; (b) Supervise or give scope for changes to occur in the political and economic structure of the Japanese nation?" A later version of "Salient Problems" pointed out that civil affairs administration for Japan "is only part of a larger whole and cannot have purposes independent of those of broader United States policy in the Far East." It declared that many of the current planning assumptions were inconsistent or incompatible. "We cannot collect sizable reparations and at the same time prevent competition of cheap Japanese goods in United States industry. It is impossible to allow the Japanese people to choose their own form of government and at the same time to guarantee that the institutions so chosen will be democratic." In speculating about the various types of Japanese leadership which might emerge after defeat, the paper argued that Japan was "less ripe for major social and class upheavals than is Europe." Joining this to the issue of liberals, the authors predicted that the most probable type of postwar government would be "from among the official hierarchy of the last few years but not actively associated with the sponsorship of the war." These men had administrative experience and held "honest doubts" about the war, but would "not be inclined to undertake drastic social or political reforms." A government of liberals, that is men outside the official hierarchy ("Christians, college presidents or professors, business men, opposition or splinter groups in the Diet") could survive only with considerable American support. Such persons, though inexperienced, would be the "most favorable to extensive economic and political reforms." A combination of the two types of leadership, the paper concluded, would be "the most favorable for United States policy."

47. For example, Bradford Smith, head of the Central Pacific Office of the OWI, with headquarters in Honolulu, was on hand in Yokohama and Tokyo in the earliest days of the occupation to set up a system of media control. Joining the Information Division (of the Civil Education and Information Section, SCAP) a few months later was Don Brown, a member of the OWI production staff in New York and a consultant in psychological warfare campaigns in the Pacific. Both knew Japan very well from prewar days when Brown worked for the *Japan Advertiser* and Smith taught English in Japanese higher schools. See my "Psychological Disarmament: American Wartime Planning for the Education and Re-education of Defeated Japan, 1943–1945," in Thomas Burkman, ed., *The Occupation of Japan: Educational and Social Reform* (Norfolk: Gatling Co., 1982), pp. 83–85. At the Japan desk of the OWI in Washington were Arthur Jorgensen, a former YMCA officer in Tokyo; Harold Vinacke, a political science professor and former graduate student of Hornbeck; and John Maki, a Japanese-American whose prewar graduate work had been in English literature. Internal OWI documents, dating from July and August 1944 when a new prop-

aganda line was being discussed, are another revealing source on Washington's internal debate about Japan's liberals and how to approach and use them: "There is a minority in Japan which has had some indoctrination with what may, for convenience, be called Anglo-American economic and political liberalism. These individuals are to be found in those circles which had the pleasantest and most profitable contact with the West as diplomats, naval officers, representatives of business houses concerned with foreign trade, intellectuals in Western countries." Although "militarist pressures made it expedient for them increasingly to suppress their real ideological sympathies," it was "reasonable to conclude that this suppression did not result in a complete elimination of their earlier pattern of thought" (Washington National Records Center, Suitland, Md., RG 208, Box 589, "Draft Suggestions for a Program of Propaganda That Will Divide the Japanese Politically and Encourage Surrender," Aug. 3, 1944). The OWI planned to make its radio appeals to these people; presumably the same kind of individuals would be sought out immediately after the war.

48. *FRUS, Conference of Berlin (Potsdam), 1945,* vol. 1, pp. 487–88.

49. Mayo, "Psychological Disarmament," pp. 46–54, 57–61.

50. See JCS 873/3, "Censorship of Civilian Communications in Pacific-Asiatic Theaters" (Nov. 12, 1944), in NAMB, RG218, CCS 000.73 (2-26-43), Section 2; Mayo, "Psychological Disarmament," pp. 53–54, 72–77. The final documents which went to MacArthur stressed "minimum control and censorship."

51. The final versions of many of these papers are published in *FRUS, 1944,* vol. 5, pp. 1198–1285; notable exceptions are the memoranda on media control, education, and economic policies. Iriye and Boyle rely much too heavily on the final versions of the 1944 State Department papers in arriving at their analyses and conclusions. The full set of papers is in the Notter File, Boxes 109–12.

52. Strictly speaking, the Grew-Dooman approach was moderate and in some cases stern, not soft. For a sampling of the attacks, see the entire issue of *Amerasia* (June 9, 1944), "A New Far Eastern Policy? Japan Versus China;" and *Nation* (Feb. 3, 1945), which singled out Dooman as a "dangerous" expert and a "shortsighted foreign service conservative." Among those presenting a more radical view on the treatment of Japan was Thomas Bisson, as in "The Price of Peace for Japan" (*Pacific Affairs,* Mar. 1944), a call for drastic social and economic change.

53. Sketches based on Heinrichs' study of Grew, *American Ambassador* and Dooman's oral history, Special Collections, Columbia University. The quotation is from Adams, "Eugene H. Dooman," p. 3, citing an interview with Mrs. Dooman, Feb. 25, 1973. Grew once wrote to Secretary Hull that he had "full confidence" in Dooman's "judgment and analytical ability" and that his "view on policy and procedure coincide very closely with mine" (May 18, 1939, RG 59, 894.00/856). Hornbeck's report on Dooman's work in FE in the prewar days, dated June 24, 1933, stated that he "appears to possess less knowledge of the United States and of American foreign relations in general" than of Japan and Japanese foreign relations (Hornbeck

papers, Hoover Institution Archives, Box 146). Dooman's oral history of Columbia, in reflecting on the experience in FE 1933 to 1937, indicates Hornbeck was not objective: "I discovered that he [Hornbeck] had two supreme passions. One was a feeling of affection and sympathy for China. And the second was a pathological hatred of Japan and the Japanese. I can only assume that when Dr. Hornbeck was a young man teaching school in Mukden he had had some unpleasant experiences with the Japanese" (p. 108). Finally, on the problem between Roosevelt's White House and Hull's State Department, Charles Bohlen points to the "feeling in the White House" that the Foreign Service was not in sympathy with New Deal philosophy;" *Witness to History, 1929–1969* (New York: W. W. Norton, 1973). Certainly this was true in Dooman's case.

54. Based on a comparison of CAC 116 (PWC 108), "The Post-War Objectives of the United States in Regard to Japan," Mar. 14, 1944 (Notter File, Box 108), and CAC 116b (PWC 108b), May 4, 1944 (Notter, *Postwar Foreign Policy Preparation*, pp. 591–92). See also IDACFE Minutes, Apr. 15, 1944 (National Archives, Microfilm Publication, T-1197); and PWC Minutes, Apr. 14 and 21 (Notter File, Box 140).

55. CAC 185 preliminary, Apr. 29, 1944 (Notter File, Box 111); and CAC 185b, May 9, 1944 (*FRUS, 1944*, vol. 5, pp. 1257–60); PWC Minutes, Apr. 2 (Notter File, Box 140).

56. CAC 238 preliminary, "Japan: The Education System Under Military Occupation" (Notter File, Box 112), drafted by Hillis Lory and extensively revised by Dooman and others, July 1–15, 1944; IDACFE Minutes, July and August 1944 (Microfilm T-1197); CAC 237 preliminary, "Japan: Occupation: Media of Public Information and Expression," 7 July 1944 (Notter File, Box 112), drafted by Beppo Johansen; Mayo, "Psychological Disarmament," pp. 35–53. Lory, author of *Japan's Military Masters* (New York: Viking Press, 1943), had taught in various Japanese and American schools in the 1920s and 1930s and was brought to FE in 1944 to help handle the heavy work load. Johansen had been appointed a Japanese language officer in 1935.

57. *FRUS, 1944*, vol. 5, pp. 1198–1285; Iriye, *Power and Culture*, pp. 201–13; PWC 283, a summary of recommendations up to that point (Notter File, Box 112); memorandum by Blakeslee, Dec. 2, 1944, summarizing recommendations approved by the PWC and comparing the treatment of Germany and Japan (Notter File, Box 145); Minutes of the Secretary's Staff Committee, Dec. 29, 1944 (Microfilm Publication of the National Archives, M-1054, Roll 3). The decision to retain Japan as one zone was important, as Iriye argues (pp. 203–4), and marked a striking difference between Japan and Germany. These PWC papers, important as they were, did not however, as Iriye believes (p. 110), provide in all cases "the core of final policy recommendations" adopted by SWNCC in 1945.

58. Dooman, oral history, Columbia University, p. 58.

59. CAC-93e (PWC 116d), "Japan: Political Problems, Institution of the Emperor," May 9, 1945, in *FRUS, 1944*, vol. 5, pp. 1250–55; Dooman, Oral History, pp. 141–43. Dooman had previously written Colonel Truman Mar-

tin, chief of the Japan Branch, Military Intelligence Service, stating his belief that the emperor had used what influence he possessed for peace; and "to hold the Emperor responsible for the action of the military would not correspond with reality" but would instead "be a departure from strict justice" (Sept. 11, 1943; Dooman papers, Hoover Institution Archives, Box 1). Dickover was sometimes a maverick in the deliberations of IDACFE: trained as a Japanese linguist and promoted to embassy secretary during Grew's time, his longest period of service was as a consul at Kobe. He was consul general at Melbourne when he rejoined FE in 1944 as head of Japanese affairs. Ballantine stoutly defended in later years IDACFE's recommendation to keep Japan's government centralized. "This was held by the critics to be detrimental to the democratic process. In defending our position we explained that whereas broadening the basis of popular control of the government had been clearly envisaged, decentralization of authority in a country as compact as Japan and with a population homogeneous in culture and closely knit by a community of interests would have no advantage to offset the much higher cost of administration, a vital consideration in a country as poor as Japan" (Ballantine manuscript, Hoover Institution Archives, p. 250).

60. CAC-120, "Japan: Should the Military Administration of Civil Affairs be Punitive, Mild or Primarily to Safeguard Reparations?" (Mar. 22, 1944); CAC-194 preliminary, "Security Policy Vis-a-vis Japan: Economic Aspects" (Apr. 30, 1944); CAC-165 preliminary, "Japan: United States Economic Policies" (Apr. 15, 1944); CAC-160 preliminary, "Japan: United States Economic Policy" (Apr. 12, 1944); CAC-222 preliminary, "Japan: Economic Policies During Military Occupation" (about June 3, 1944); all documents in Notter File, Boxes 109–10. Later, a greater burden was placed on CAC 160 as a statement of long range economic policy, and it was superseded by memoranda drawn up by the economic divisions in the State Department. Borton gives a brief history of CAC-160 and CAC-222 in two memos for Blakeslee, Nov. 18, 1944 (Notter File, Box 118). Moffat, a New York lawyer and politician, was the older brother of Grew's late son-in-law, J. P. Moffat, former chief of the Division of European Affairs, Department of State, and ambassador to Canada.

61. CAC 254 series, "Workers Organizations During the Period of Military Occupation," July and Aug. 1944 (Notter File, Box 113), which stated that employees "should be permitted to form, join or assist labor organizations and to bargain collectively." The drafting officer was Julian R. Friedman, a recent graduate of Harvard and of the Fletcher School. Quotation from CAC-222, July 4, 1944 (Notter File, Box 112). Dooman favored placing some restrictions on Japanese shipping to placate United States public opinion but would not cut back Japan's merchant marine to the point of bringing economic distress upon Japan; Johansen at the same IDACFE meeting argued that the rehabilitation of Japan was in the best interests of the American economy (Minutes, May 23, 1944, T-1197). The zaibatsu question remained very touchy, both in planning for the occupation and for psychological warfare. Williams, at the Bowman subcommittee meetings in De-

cember 1943, had queried whether big industrial concerns, the backbone of Japan's economy and source of power for its ruling classes, could be broken up without destroying the whole economic system (T-Minutes, Dec. 17, 1943, Notter File, Box 59). To Dooman's mind, Japan was so poor in natural resources and so dependent on foreign trade that "it was essential for Japan to have large concentrations of capital to buy raw materials abroad as cheaply as possible and to export finished goods at as good a price as they could get." He agreed that "there were a number of things about the zaibatsu which were undesirable," for example the Mitsui bank made loans only to the Mitsui companies. The remedy was to dissociate the bank from the combine. "There were a number of such undesirable features that had prevailed in Japan, which could have been remedied without any radical change in the need and the essential requirement that there be these large concentrations of capital" (Oral History, pp. 147–48). Grew said almost nothing about the subject in 1944, and the first statement I can find in 1945 was at a Staff Committee meeting, July 7, when once again he expressed his belief that the military and not the emperor were responsible for the war; "what is most important is to eliminate the military machine and the big industrial families of Japan" (*FRUS, Conference at Berlin [Potsdam]*, vol. 1, p. 901). The evidence indicates that strong differences of opinion about the past and future role of the *zaibatsu* muted attacks on big business in official statements and psychological warfare if not in the public media where Bisson led the parade. For example, the head of the San Francisco office, OWI, in a telephone conversation with Fairbank (May 1944) spoke of the "danger of hitting 'Z' because it would alienate large and possibly sympathetic audiences" (RG 208, Box 3105).

62. PWC 287a, Nov. 5, 1944 (Notter File, Box 144). Dooman's original wording was even less sanguine: "No reforms imposed on the Japanese by military government would cause any change in the Japanese mentality or in the attitude of the Japanese with regard to religious, political, and social problems" (Minutes, IDACFE meeting of Nov. 1, 1944, app. A; Microfilm publication T-1197). See also PWC 152b, May 9, 1944, *FRUS, 1944,* vol. 5, p. 1258. In view of the 1944 OSS study of postwar Japanese leadership and the subsequent emergence of career diplomat Yoshida Shigeru (of the so-called Anglo-American school) as the dominant postwar politician and prime minister for much of the occupation period, Dooman's comments in 1935 on Yoshida take on a prescient quality: Yoshida, he reported to Hornbeck, had "shown himself fairly conclusively to be a progressive and enlightened Japanese." Married to the daughter of Count Makino, "the Emperor's principal adviser and confidant and perhaps the most influential of the 'liberal elements,'" Yoshida was "straightforward, frank to the point of indiscretion, and trustworthy" (Hornbeck papers, Hoover Institution Archives, Box 258).

63. Economist Herbert Feis, special assistant to the secretary of war, coined the phrase "Sunday School flavor" in a note of 1945 to Colonel David Marcus, CAD (NAMB, RG 165, CAD 321 CAD [12-21-42] [1], Section 7). For a detailed treatment of the expansion of the State Department's economic

divisions and the clash of opinion on *zaibatsu* dissolution, see my "American Economic Planning for Occupied Japan: The Issue of *Zaibatsu* Dissolution, 1942–45," in Lawrence H. Redford, ed., *The Occupation of Japan: Economic Policy and Reform* (Norfolk: MacArthur Memorial, 1980), pp. 205–28; 252–62.

64. Lockhart to Blakeslee, Aug. 10, 1944 (Notter File, Box 118); Remer and Lockhart to Emilio Collado (chief of FMA), Sept. 11, 1944 (RG 59, 894.50/9-1144); Lockhart to Collado, September 23, 1944 (894.50/9-1144). The Executive Committee on Economic Foreign Policy was set up in April 1944 by order of President Roosevelt to coordinate economic planning. It was interdepartmental with representation from the State Department, Treasury, Agriculture, Commerce, Labor, United States Tariff Commission, and the Foreign Economic Administration—and the OSS (Notter, *Postwar Foreign Policy Preparation*, pp. 218–19). "I attach," wrote Roosevelt to Hull, "the utmost importance to this committee and I trust that you will forthwith call its members together in order that its work may begin without delay." The chairman in 1944 was Assistant Secretary Acheson, and in 1945, Assistant Secretary Clayton. The economists were informed of Roosevelt's letter to Hull in September 1944, restating support for American antitrust statutes in protecting the American consumer against monopoly and also backing liberal principles in international trade. He wanted Hull to work with the United Nations to eliminate such barriers to the free flow of trade as cartels, which, he said, "were utilized by the Nazis . . . as governmental instrumentalities to achieve political ends. . . . The defeat of the Nazi armies will have to be followed by the eradication of these weapons of economic warfare" (800.602/9-644).

65. Walter Rudolph (writing for Terrill) to Lockhart, Dec. 21, 1944 (FW 894.50/9-1144); Terrill to Pearce, November 21, 1944 (894.50/1-2144); Terrill to Gooch, Dec. 6, 1944 (894.60/12-644); Eleanor Hadley, *Antitrust in Japan* (Princeton, N.J.: Princeton Univ. Press, 1970), pp. 3–10; and Hadley's article "Trust-Busting in Japan," *Harvard Business Review* (July 1948). The research on cartels resulted in Cartel Memo 168, "Control of Corporate Organization (Japan)," Nov. 15, 1945 (Notter File, Box 39). The conclusions of an earlier draft were used in writing MacArthur's basic directive and were taken to Japan by Fearey in early October 1945 (Washington National Records Center, Suitland, Md., RG 84, Tokyo Post Files, Box 2275, Vols. 1 and 6). Terrill, a member of the ECEFP's subcommittee on monopolies, held a Stanford Ph.D. and had taught at Reed College. Rudolph had done graduate work at the University of Virginia and Stanford University and had come to the State Department in 1944 after several years in the Department of Agriculture and the Office of Price Administration. Terrill's close friend was antitrust economist Corwin D. Edwards, a wartime consultant to the Justice Department and to the State Department. Edwards was later head of the Mission on Japanese Combines, which arrived in Japan in January 1946, and the principal author of the controversial policy document, SWNCC 302/1 (Jan. 1947)—better known as FEC 230—on deconcentration of economic power in Japan. Hadley was in Japan, 1946–47, as a

member of SCAP's Government Section, where she kept an eye on legislation for *zaibatsu* dissolution and deconcentration of the economy.

66. *Department of State Bulletin* 10 (Jan. 5, 1945), pp. 45–67; *FRUS, 1945,* vol. 6 (Washington, D.C.: Government Printing Office, 1969), pp. 497–515. Bernard Haley, chief of the Commodities Division, had written Remer in November 1944, suggesting that CAC-222 on initial economic policies for occupied Japan be tabled; he thought the president might reject it as "soft" (RG 59, 740.00119 Control [Japan] 11-1144). All of this was taking place at the height of Treasury Secretary Morgenthau's influence on the president.

67. Notter, *Postwar Foreign Policy Preparation,* pp. 347–48, 368–70; Harold W. Moseley et al., "The State-War-Navy Coordinating Committee," *Department of State Bulletin* 13 (Nov. 11, 1945), pp. 745–47. SWNCC was originally to have deliberated on German policy, but the Informal Policy Committee on Germany (IPCOG), created in March 1945, took over this function; it was more broadly interdepartmental than SWNCC and had representatives from the Treasury and FEA (Notter, pp. 369–70).

68. SFE was originally set up in January 1945 as the *ad hoc* Committee to Consider Problems Which Arise in Connection with Control of Pacific and Far Eastern Areas. Notter misleadingly states that the revised SWNCC-SFE papers, "allowing for the adjustments required by developments since the autumn of 1944," did not involve any "radical departure from the policy recommendations" of the PWC (*Postwar Foreign Policy Preparation,* pp. 377–82). Not only were there some changes and new ideas in the State Department but also policy initiatives taken independently of that department. Joining Blakeslee and Borton at the working level of SFE were Lieutenant Colonel Daniel Cox Fahey, Jr., CAD, and Captain Lorenzo Sabin, Military Government Section, United States Navy. In March 1945, TS, the research unit, was dissolved, and the East Asia research staff was joined to the geographical office, FE.

69. SWNCC 16/2, Feb. 19, 1945, in RG 165, ABC 014 Japan (13 Apr. 1944), Section 1-A. The discursive essay style used in the 1943–44 memoranda had been replaced by 1945 with a strict format: the problem, facts bearing on the problem, conclusions, and recommendations. Papers drafted in the State Department were discussed by IDACFE or by the separate subcommittee of economists and then sent to SFE for further comment. From there, papers were submitted to SWNCC and JCS for comment, and after revision or amendment by SFE, were returned to SWNCC for final approval and transmission to the president.

70. *FRUS, 1945,* vol. 6, p. 545; SFE Minutes, Apr. 16, 1945 (National Archives, Microfilm Publication, T-1198).

71. Summary statement in National Archives, Microfilm Publication, T-1205, roll 2; SWNCC 150 in *FRUS, 1945,* vol. 6, pp. 549–54. By then (Apr. 6), General MacArthur was named commander-in-chief, United States Army Forces in the Pacific; in early May he was given responsibility for military government in Japan. MacArthur was late in appointing a military government officer, and his choice, Brigadier General William Crist, did not arrive in Washington for his CAD briefing until mid-July.

72. Interview with Martin (Oct. 27, 1977); private memorandum by Martin, written in June 1945 (copy in my possession); Mayo, "American Economic Planning for Occupied Japan," pp. 219–22. Martin's graduate work in economics was at Northwestern University in the early 1930s. Before joining the OSS, he was with the War Production Board. He remained in the State Department and was appointed head of the Division of Japanese and Korean Economic Affairs in the fall of 1945 as economic policy continued to be handled separately from FE.

73. Draft No. 5 attached to State Department Summary of Apr. 12, 1945, in Microfilm T-1205, roll 2.

74. SFE Minutes, Apr. 14 and 17 (Microfilm T-1198). Dooman, in forwarding SWNCC 150 to the State Department Staff Committee on June 23, was clearly concerned about the new policy line; he stated that the political sections "fall entirely within the framework of PWC papers already approved by the Secretary of State" but the economic part had been approved by Clayton's office (*FRUS, 1945*, vol. 6, p. 555). Lockhart's paper on long-range economic treatment of Japan ("Economic Policy toward Japan: Summary Statement," SC-101, Apr. 23, 1945) was similarly undergoing rough treatment by IDACFE and by the staff Committee, where Acheson dismissed it as full of "meaningless" and "dangerous platitudes." The Treasury and the Army would probably find it too soft (SC Minutes, Apr. 23, 1945; Microfilm M-1054, roll 1 for document; roll 3 for minutes). Land reform for Japan was discussed in late wartime Washington but not extensively at high policy levels. SWNCC 16/3 of March 21, the master list of topics, contained as a new problem for research, "adjustments in system of land tenure"; and SWNCC 100, "Policy with Respect to Rural Land Tenure" (Apr. 7, 1945) called for study of the problem; in RG 165, ABC 014 Japan (13 Apr. 1944), Sections 1 and 28. The assignment went to Fearey, who on May 1 produced two papers: "The Japanese Agrarian Problem" and "Japan: Occupation Period: Agrarian Reform" (PR-12 preliminary and PR-13 preliminary, Notter File, Box 119a). A month later, Fearey wrote Edwin Martin that, after talking to Dickover, Williams, and Johansen in FE, he wished to tone down his recommendations to say "there should be no attempt at comprehensive agrarian reform in the immediate post-hostilities period, i.e. probably for six months or more. Only after a fair measure of economic stability has been achieved, and food production and distribution have been restored to satisfactory working order should the possibility of instituting a reform program be considered." His "personal preference," however, "would be for the military government to assume greater initiative in the matter," rather than leaving it to Japanese leaders (RG 59, 894.52/6-149, misdated 1949). Fearey subsequently was sent to Japan in early October 1945 to join the political adviser's staff, SCAP, and brought his file of papers with him, including those on agriculture. His memorandum on "Japan's Agrarian Reform," which was sent to MacArthur on October 26, was a composite of his earlier PR papers and was given a serious reception in the Natural Resources Section, SCAP; interview with Fearey, May 5, 1978; Fearey's reminiscences in Redford, ed., *Economic Policy and Reform*, pp. 151–52; re-

reprint of Fearey memo of October 1945 in *The Selected Papers of Wolf Ladejinsky: Agrarian Reform as Unfinished Business,* ed. by Louis J. Walinsky (New York: Oxford Univ. Press for the World Bank, 1977), pp. 569–78. Wolf Ladejinsky, of the Office of Foreign Agricultural Relations, Department of Agriculture, had included land reform in the original draft of his civil affairs guide, "Agriculture and Food Program in Japan," but did not win approval for the guide in the summer of 1945 until he deleted the section.

75. PR-24 preliminary, "SWNCC, Politico-Military Problems in the Far East: The Post Surrender Military Government of the Japanese Empire, The Educational System" (July 30, 1945), Notter File, Box 119a; interview with Bowles, Aug. 23, 1980. Bowles did not mention language reform or press for recision of the Imperial Rescript on Education. On the question of reform techniques, Bowles wrote that military government should "initiate reforms through cooperative Japanese to a point where they can be continued without external assistance."

76. SWNCC 162/D, "Positive Policy for Reorientation of the Japanese" (19 July 1945), in RG 165, ABC 014 Japan (13 Apr. 1944), Section 4-A. The policy was approved early in 1946 by SWNCC; *FRUS, 1946,* vol. 8 (Washington, D.C.: Government Printing Office, 1971), pp. 105–9. Though Dooman and other Japan specialists thought that the Gates proposal was grandiose, he too was worried about social unrest and disorder in the early occupation period. And previously, he had written Colonel Martin that the postwar program for Japan should include not only punitive measures of military and economic restriction but also, in order to be successful and permanent, must stimulate "spiritual regeneration" and "a reorientation of their policies." While still in control of Japan, the victors should divest "the Japanese mind of medieval concepts" by helping them realize they are like other human beings and showing them that economic well-being can be attained by peaceful means (letter of Jan. 12, 1944; Dooman papers, Hoover Institution Archives).

77. "Japan: Treatment of Japanese Workers' Organizations," July 12, 1945 (Notter File, Box 119a); comments by Theodore Cohen in Redford, ed., *Economic Policy and Reform,* pp. 162–65, 191–93. Sullivan, who wanted military government to take an active interest in labor reform and thought social unrest might be good for democratic movements, wrote to his chief on August 28, 1945: "'Let the pot brew what it may' so long as it is properly seasoned with popular sentiment and not too highly flavored with the spice of Communism. Under such conditions we may get a real labor movement started" (RG 59, 740.00119 Control [Japan]/8-2845).

78. CAD was ready with a partial draft directive on general and political matters as early as June 11, based on SWNCC 150; see NADB, RG 43, Box 3. It was a little more reformist in declaration of intent than the policy document and called for strengthening of democratic tendencies in government and social institutions (the fuller August 22 draft added economic institutions). In a critical letter of June 20, 1945, General Hilldring asked McCloy whether the Japanese or military government would be responsible

for essential economic controls (in the counterpart German document, the Germans were) and whether unconditional surrender would be by Japan's armed forces or by its government too; in RG 165, CAD 014 Japan (13 Apr. 1944, Section 3). A financial draft directive was ready by July 19, with a revised version by July 31. The working level of Army planners was in close touch with the economic divisions of the State Department and made use of OSS and FEA studies.

79. More research is needed on the Potsdam declaration, particularly its use as a weapon in psychological warfare. Brian Villa supplies some of the answers in "The United States Army, Unconditional Surrender, and the Potsdam Proclamation," *Journal of American History* 63 (June 1976), pp. 66–92, but he is better informed about the military planners than the civilian policy makers.

80. CAC 262 preliminary, "Japan: Terms of Surrender: Underlying Principles," July 26, 1944 (drafted by Borton); and CAC 267 preliminary, "Japan: Unconditional Surrender," August 1, 1944 (drafted by Quincy Wright) raised numerous questions about the legal rights of military occupation, the extent of the rights surrendered, recipients of surrendered rights, who should sign Japan's surrender instrument, and the psychological effect of the Cairo declaration on the Japanese people (Notter File, Box 113). IDACFE voted unanimously (15 present) on August 8, 1944, that Japanese authorities should be given "some idea," before they accepted unconditional surrender, of the treatment to be accorded Japan. They voted 6 to 4 (apparently some abstaining) to put the general policy into a written draft to be read by Japanese authorities rather than using an oral statement by the president or secretary of state (Microfilm T-1197). The CAC-262 version of August 30, 1944, argued that Japan would be more likely to surrender and cooperate with military government if it were assured in a document "that the United Nations do not intend to destroy Japan as a state;" final text of November 13 (PWC 284a) is printed in *FRUS, 1944,* vol. 5, pp. 1275–83. See also: PR-5 (PWC-284b), "Japan: Terms of Surrender: Underlying Principles," Feb. 21, 1945 (RG 59, Hiss papers, Box 26); PR-9 preliminary a, "Japan: Public Statement of Post-Surrender Policy," Apr. 30, 1945 (Notter File, Box 119); Grew, *Turbulent Era, A Diplomatic Record of Fifty Years, 1904–1945,* vol. 2 (Boston: Houghton Mifflin, 1952), pp. 1406–42.

81. Dooman, oral history, pp. 158–68; RG 59, 740.0011EW/5-3145; 740,00119 PW/6-1345 and 6-1645; RG 107, Stimsom Top Secret Safe File, Japan folder, "Draft of a Proposed Statement" (Dooman, May 31, 1945). Grew, as Heinrichs and others have pointed out, mistakenly identified in his book a draft of July 3 as the one prepared by Dooman on May 31 (Heinrichs, *American Ambassador,* p. 379, footnote 57).

82. RG 165, ABC 387 Japan (15 Feb. 1945), Section 1-B and Section 4-A (Historical Drafts); Bonesteel memo for General Lincoln, June 27 and 28, July 1, 1945; Lincoln memo for General Hull, June 28, 29, and 30 (same source); Colonel James McCormack, memo for the record, June 29, 1945, in RG 165, ABC 387 Japan (15 Feb. 1945), Section 4-A; 740.00119 PW/6-2745; Stimson Diary, Yale University, entries for June 20, July 1, and July 2;

Dooman, statement appended to his oral history, Columbia University, in which he claims authorship of the July 3 revision attributed to Grew in *FRUS, Conference of Berlin (Potsdam)*, vol. 1, pp. 897–99. Stimson, in forwarding a draft declaration to President Truman on July 2, alluded in an accompanying statement ("Proposed Program for Japan") to Japan in the 1920s, saying that it "had for ten years lived a reasonably responsible and respectable international life." He added: "I think she has within her population enough liberal leaders (although now submerged by the terrorists) to be depended upon for her reconstruction as a responsible member of the family of nations. I think she is better in this last respect than Germany was" (*FRUS, Conference of Berlin [Potsdam]*, vol. 1, pp. 888–92). Bonesteel and McCormack were working members of an *ad hoc* interdepartmental drafting committee nominated by the Committee of Three on June 26 after the Dooman draft was rejected.

83. *FRUS, Conference of Berlin (Potsdam)*, 1945, vol. 1, pp. 900–902. Hackworth followed through on July 9 with the suggested passage: "The present system of military control in Japan must be uprooted and not allowed again to assert itself. The people of Japan shall be given an opportunity to control their destinies along peaceful lines." Dunn altered Hackworth's second sentence to say: "When the people of Japan have convinced the peace loving nations that they are going to follow peaceful lives, they shall be given an opportunity to control their destinies along peaceful lines."

84. JCS 1275 series for July in RG 165, ABC 387 Japan (15 Feb. 1945), Sections 1-B and F-A (Historical Documents).

85. Stimson's diary for July: Cordell Hull, *The Memoirs of Cordell Hull* (New York: Macmillan, 1948), vol. 2, pp. 1593–95.

86. For changes made by the British in the final text of the proclamation, see Iriye, "Continuities in U.S.-Japanese Relations, 1941–1949," pp. 394–96; and Christopher Thorne, *Allies of a Kind: The United States, Britain, and the War Against Japan, 1941–1945* (New York: Oxford Univ. Press, 1978), p. 532; *FRUS*, Potsdam Conference, vol. 1, p. 1277.

87. IDACFE Minutes, July 27, 1945, and Annex A (Microfilm T-1197); SFE Minutes, Aug. 29, 1945 (Microfilm T-1198); Comparison of Potsdam declaration with the policy of the Department of State, statement inserted after the Staff Committee meeting of July 28, in Microfilm M-1054, roll 4; Willoughby to Wilcox, Aug. 9, 10, in RG 59, 740.00119 Control (Japan)/8.945.

88. NAMB, RG 107, McCloy diaries, Box 4; RG 165, ABC 014 Japan (13 Apr. 1944), Sections 7 and 7-A (SWNCC 150 series and backup papers). McCloy utilized CAD and OPD drafts and advice (he was at the same time working on the surrender documents and general orders).

89. SWNCC Minutes, Aug. 1945 (Microfilm Publications, T-1194).

90. SWNCC 150/3 revised the last sentence to read: "The policies of the United States will govern" (Aug. 30, 1945). See SWNCC 70 series on Allied control machinery for Japan; in RG 165, ABC 014 Japan (13 Apr. 1944), Section 4-A.

91. The drafters apparently had an early version before them of the research study on corporate organization in Japan as well as a copy of the economic documents for Germany. Hadley states that the initial American policies for deconcentration in Germany and Japan were not "undertaken in a spirit of revenge or with the intention to weaken those economies but rather as an outgrowth of thinking first developed toward the American economy." And Washington believed that giant enterprises had supported a policy of foreign aggression (*Antitrust in Japan,* pp. 4–5). McCloy, too, recalling the writing of the basic policy statement and basic directive, stated two years later that "some program for the dissolution of the Zaibatsu was a part of the broad policy which was considered necessary in order to effect the democratization of Japan. It was not primarily intended as a punitive measure in connection with responsibility for war guilt, since there was considerable doubt, at least in the mind of Mr. Stimson, that Zaibatsu elements had actively supported the war party in Japan" (Nov. 21, 1947; RG 59, 894.602/ 11-2147). However, a memo for the record written in early 1948 by Daniel C. Fahey, Jr., who had been chief of the Planning Branch, CAD, in 1945, stresses how the sudden end of the war necessitated the hasty crystallization of American policy "under great duress." He describes SWNCC 150/4/A as " 'tainted' but not 'top-heavy' as a result of the Morgenthau concept for Germany. United States policy for Japan was, however, predicated on the fact that we were mad, and considered Japan's aggression warranted adequate punishment." *Zaibatsu* dissolution in 1945 complied "with the *then existent* philosophy of the U. S. government." By the fall of 1947, the prevailing view had changed, and "there was general Washington agreement (on everything except the language) that there should be a *'shift of emphasis'* towards economic revival in Japan." This shift and "the attainment of a stable Japanese economy was further complicated by the initial and still existent pattern of direction to MacArthur—designed to remove the Japanese war-making capabilities, and only permissive in character, as concerns the revival of her economy." Fahey believed that the recent and heavy cable traffic between Tokyo and Washington on this issue had "thoroughly and properly alerted" MacArthur and his staff "to the dangers that may accrue from an over zealous implementation of economic reform, and that the net result in Japan will be a 'middle of the road program' compatible with U.S. antitrust ideology" (Jan. 16, 1948; RG 165, Entry 468, SWNCC 150 folder, Box 603).

92. In a reversal of procedure, the economic section of the basic directive seems to have been written before the adoption of the final policy paper. On July 31, Mason's successor in Clayton's office, Willard Thorpe, gave his approval to an advanced economic draft; RG 165, CAD 014 Japan (7-8-42) (1), Section 4. It borrowed heavily from the phraseology and wording of the directive for Germany, JCS 1067.

93. Microfilm M-1205, roll 2; and RG 165, OPD 336 TS, Case 124. There is some question as to whether or not MacArthur actually received the latest revised text of the general initial policy statement by cable on August 29, as

most collections of printed or published documents state. I have yet to find such a cable among the numbered messages from the War Department to AFPAC either at the National Archives or at the MacArthur Memorial. Moreover, the text which is invariably given of the alleged August 29 cable is, in fact, the version officially released by President Truman on September 22 (SWNCC 150/4/A). MacArthur, of course, was kept informed of important changes, but in this case the means employed seems to have been the War Department's courier service. In addition, his chief of staff, General Sutherland, had been in Washington in early August on emergency duty and had seen President Truman "off the record" on August 13 just before returning to Manila (Harry S Truman Presidential Library, Truman Papers, Official File, Box 1397, memorandum for Mr. Connelly, Aug. 13, 1945). Undoubtedly, Sutherland brought back a raft of documents, including SWNCC 150 (at that stage, SWNCC 150/2) and backup papers. The version, therefore, of the general policy document which MacArthur possessed as he was preparing to leave the Philippines for Japan was probably SWNCC 150/3 (the next document in the series, SWNCC 150/3 revised, containing a few changes requested by SWNCC, SFE, and JCS, was approved on August 30, Washington time). MacArthur's public announcement on September 9 of policy for Japan was a deft but only partial restatement of the basic aims dictated by Washington and a clarification of his superior status relative to the Japanese emperor and government. It was accompanied by a call for good behavior by the occupying troops (*New York Times,* Sept. 10, 1945). As indicated, the full policy text was disclosed on September 22.

94. A separate directive on war criminals followed in September, again warning MacArthur not to move as yet against the emperor. The language of the basic directive directing him to conduct a purge was changed between August and November. He was to remove not "flagrant" but "active exponents of militant nationalism and aggression." Moreover, "in the absence of evidence, satisfactory to you, to the contrary, you will assume that any persons who have held key positions of high responsibility since 1937, in industry, finance, commerce or agriculture have been active exponents of militant nationalism and aggression." For the debate on this wording, see SWNCC Minutes of October 1945 (Microfilm T-1194). On the issue of combines, the drafters were assisted in their work by such FEA studies as "A Preliminary Survey of the Holdings of the Japanese Economic Oligarchy," June 18, 1945 (copy in OSS files, RG 226, 140182C), and "The Importance of Zaibatsu Investments in the Economic Life of Japan," July 10, 1945; copy in RG 165, CAD 014 Japan (7-8-42) (1), Section 4.

95. The language pertaining to Shinto was clarified, apparently at Dooman's initiative. The final text of November 3 read: "The dissemination of Japanese militaristic and ultra-nationalistic ideology and propaganda in any form will be prohibited and completely suppressed. You will require the Japanese Government to cease financial and other support of National Shinto establishments."

96. The adjective "large" had been added to the November 3 text in de-

scribing the combines which would be the targets for dissolution. John Backer summarizes the controversy over similar "contradictory elements" in JCS 1067 for Germany. The economic section, for example, stated that "the commander in chief should take no steps which would lead toward the economic rehabilitation of Germany or which were designed to maintain or strengthen the German economy" (Morgenthau's influence). These and other negative provisions prompted General Clay's financial adviser, Lewis Douglas, to charge that JCS 1067 "had been designed by economic idiots." Backer points out that the disease and unrest formula was a "War Department escape clause," giving flexibility to military government in the light of existing chaotic conditions. He also argues that the "directive's negative economic provisions" were rendered "inoperative" by the Potsdam agreement, or at least were, as Clay stated in December, made "workable" by Potsdam (*The Decision to Divide Germany*, pp. 104–5). The controversy becomes even more fascinating when it is remembered that Douglas was McCloy's brother-in-law. The same controversy arose over the contradictory elements in the directive for Japan, and MacArthur had an escape clause similar to Clay's.

97. The Military Government Section, AFPAC, was activated in Manila on August 5 under an acting head (by then, MacArthur had been secretly briefed about the atomic bomb and knew that he should greatly accelerate preparations for military government in the event of sudden capitulation) and dissolved in Tokyo on October 2, when SCAP was created. Its head as of August 20 was Brigadier General William Crist, previously deputy commander for military government in Okinawa. As MacArthur's newly designated chief military government officer for Japan, Crist was assigned to Washington on temporary duty in late July and early August for consultation with planners in the Civil Affairs Division, War Department. The "Basic Plan for Institution of Military Government, Blacklist Operations (tentative), Military Government Annex," dated August 6, 1945, seems to have been written in Washington and taken to Manila either by Sutherland or by Crist where it formed the basis of various annexes to operations instructions, subject to further changes in high policy; MacArthur Memorial, RG 4, USAFPAC, Series 4, Operations, Beleaguer-Blacklist documents, Box 4; NA, RG 165, CAD decimal top secret file, 1946–47, CAD 014 Japan; Justin Williams papers, Prange Collection, McKeldin Library, University of Maryland, "Report of the Military Government Section, GHQ, USAFPAC, Covering the Period 5 August to 2 October Inclusive." Everything had to be scrapped or rewritten when word came from Washington in late August that the occupation would be indirect. On August 27, Brigadier General Charles A. Willoughby, chief military officer for AFPAC, pointed out, presumably after the arrival of the draft policy statement and draft directive, that "a punitive strain, based on erroneous premises" ran through the annexes to the operations instructions of August 15. "The initial drafts of this literature," he declared, "were obviously inspired" by corresponding docu-

ments for Germany, "which represent a totally different background; the German occupation involved the complete dissolution of a hostile Government and its ideology; Japanese occupation involves its complete maintenance and the use of a specific ideology, the Shinto basis of secular Government." He argued that, given the limited numbers of occupation forces available, "punitive or disciplinary features are impracticable now and may become fatal, if initiated prematurely." Willoughby recommended an immediate revision of the annexes. Subsequently, "Military Government," annex 8, dated August 28 (to operations instructions no. 4, Aug. 15), stated that MacArthur would issue orders through the Japanese emperor and the imperial Japanese government. Also on August 28, MacArthur informed his subordinate commanding generals by cable that there had been "a major change in the concept of conditions under which the occupation of Japan will take place." He explained that it was "now contemplated that the occupation will take place without violence and the Japanese government will continue to function. It is intended that the Japanese government and all available public agencies will be utilized to a maximum extent to carry into effect the terms of the surrender." His commanders, therefore, were not "to take over any governmental or other civilian institutions" (MacArthur Memorial, RG 5, SCAP, Correspondence, "Japanese Surrender File No. 2," Box 1; NA, RG 200, Sutherland papers, General Correspondence, Box 8, Willoughby to Chief of Staff, Aug. 27, 1945, "Punitive Features of Annexes to Operations Instructions"). Obviously, MacArthur had less opportunity and time for military government planning than Eisenhower and Clay in Europe, though the JCS had ordered him in June for the possibility of Japan's sudden surrender or collapse, the genesis of Blacklist Operations. He appears to have acquired, however, a number of planning documents through his own channels before he was supposedly authorized to have them and was well informed of the controversy in Washington over the final phraseology of the policy statement and military directive. He also obviously had some preconceived ideas about the treatment of Japan after surrender, as expressed for example on February 28, 1945, when Secretary of the Navy Forrestal visited Luzon. "So far as our relations with Japan after the war were concerned," the secretary noted in his diary, MacArthur "said we had to realize that this Japanese control of their population was based on (a) feudalism and (b) a mystical religious conception which fitted into a pattern of feudalism. He said he saw no hope of being able to deal with Japan until this feudalism concept was destroyed. He mentioned two forms of this feudalism, one being the military and the other being business, but business, he said, always having been subordinate to the military" (Forrestal Diary, unpublished portion, Princeton University Library). And in response to a cable sent by Marshall from Potsdam, July 25, soliciting MacArthur's views on such matters as the size of occupation forces for Japan, the nature of participation by the Allies, and "the extent to which existing Japanese governmental ministries and organizations should and can be utilized," he replied on July 27 that fourteen centers should be occupied (with first priority to Tokyo) and a single coordinating authority under United States command and control should be set up. He estimated that twenty-two and two-thirds reinforced divisions and twenty air groups would be required for the job and recommended "a maximum utilization of existing Japanese governmental agencies and organizations" (MacArthur Memorial, RG 4, USAFPAC, Correspondence Series, War Department cables).

98. SCAP, Government Section, *Political Reorientation of Japan,* vol. 2, app. F, 741.

99. Dooman was present throughout August at the SFE meetings and informal deliberations on changes in the wording of the policy statement and draft directive. He was therefore still in government service when the basic paper, SWNCC 150, was rewritten as SWNCC 150/3 and SWNCC 150/3 revised. Some additional revisions were made in early September after he left, but the basic policies, it bears repeating, were set in August and forwarded to MacArthur while Dooman was in office (though he may not have known about the secret courier service). In his oral history, Dooman paid tribute to Grew for making it possible for him to resist critics in the State Department and the Treasury in drawing up principles for the treatment of Japan. "What we tried to do was to formulate principles and policies in the broadest possible way, so that we would not be tied down during the occupation to any specific planning; that these policies would be broad enough so that within that compass it would be possible for General MacArthur to do the things that he considered wise and necessary in the interests of the United States" (p. 138). Dooman glosses over his failure in defining economic principles and the bureaucratic process by which that took place, and makes no mention of McCloy's role.

100. Ballantine manuscript, Hoover Institution Archives, p. 267; Dooman, oral history, pp. 143–44 (and assorted accusations by Dooman in his papers at the Hoover Archives); Howard Schonberger, "The Japan Lobby in American Diplomacy, 1947–1952, *Pacific Historical Review* 46 (Aug. 1977), pp. 327–59. In a similar fashion, Grew in 1946 criticized the Washington directives as "harmful and ill-conceived. Considering the fact that the so-called 'Japan Crowd' in the State Department was completely dispersed after I left office last August, thus depriving our Government of the expert knowledge and mature judgment of men who had spent the better part of their lives in Japan and thoroughly understood the problems there, it is perhaps not surprising that some of the directives from the State Department were short-sighted and ill-conceived" (letter to Kenneth C. Colegrove, July 5, 1946; MacArthur Memorial, RG 9, Official Correspondence of General MacArthur). There were still a few Japan hands around, at least at the working level of SWNCC and in the State Department, such as Hugh Borton and E. O. Reischauer. Grew's remarks ignore the growing differences of opinion among Japan hands; they were not necessarily a monolithic group.

101. See Joan Hoff Wilson, "Herbert Hoover's Plan for Ending the Second World War," *International History Review* 1 (Jan. 1979), pp. 84–102.

2. Improvising Stability and Change in
Postwar Germany / Ziemke

1. Memo, President for the Secretary of War, Oct. 29, 1942, in PMG, MG Div, classified decimal file 333.

2. Draft, Final Report of the Present Director, MG Div, PMGO, Mar. 1945, in PMG, MG Div, decimal file 314.7.

3. Hist Rpt, Hqs, CAC, ASC, to Chief Hist Subsec, SHAEF, sub: Activities of CAC, Jan. 18–Feb. 1, 1944, in SHAEF G-5, 17.12.

4. Hqs, ECAD, Classification Sec, AG, to SHAEF G-5, sub: Classification of Enlisted Personnel for ECAD, Aug. 10, 1944, in SHAEF G-5, 17.12, Jacket 4.

5. SHAEF, Standard Policy and Procedure for Combined Civil Affairs Operations in Northwest Europe, Dec. 13, 1943, in SHAEF SGS, 014.1.

6. John Morton Blum, *From the Morgenthau Diaries,* vol. 3 (Boston: Houghton Mifflin, 1967), p. 334.

7. Cable, PWD, SHAEF, to SHAEF Forward, Sept. 17, 1944, in USFET SGS 388.5/1.

8. SHAEF, PWD, Mr. R. H. S. Crossman, Impressions of a brief Tour of Occupied Germany, Nov. 7, 1944, in SHAEF SGS, 091.4/1.

9. Ibid.

10. Office, Allied Naval CinC, to SHAEF G-5, sub: German Civilians and Military Government Control, Apr. 1, 1945, in SHAEF G-5, 803, Jacket 3.

11. OMGUS, Control Office, Quadripartite Access to and Control of Berlin, vol. 2 [no date], in OMGUS 23-2/5, Folder V205-3/2A.

12. Hist Rpt, Third Army, ACofS G-5, Mar. 1–31, 1945, in SHAEF G-5, 17.10, Jacket 4.

13. Hist Rpt, 12th AGp, ACofS G-5, Apr. 1945, in SHAEF G-5, 17.16, Jacket 10. USFET, General Board, Study No. 34, p. 38.

14. JCS 1067, Directive to Commander in Chief of U.S. Forces of Occupation Regarding the Military Government of Germany in the Period Immediately Following the Cessation of Organized Resistance (Post Defeat, Sept. 24, 1944, in OPD, ABC 387.

15. SHAEF G-5 Forward to DACOS G-5, sub: Field Survey, Apr. 4, 1945, in SHAEF G-5, 204.

16. Ltr, Clay to Hilldring, May 7, 1945, in OMGUS 177-1/3.

17. Ltr, Hilldring to Clay, May 21, 1945, in OMGUS 177-1/3.

18. Report by Potter-Hyndley Mission, June 7, 1945, in USFET SGS 463.3, vol. 1.

19. Memo, President for the Secretary of War, Oct. 29, 1942, in PMG, MG Div, classified decimal file 333.

20. Memo by Acting Secretary of State Joseph C. Grew, May 10, 1945, in Department of State, *Foreign Relations, 1945,* vol. 3, p. 509.

21. Min, US Gp CC, Staff Meeting of Division Directors, June 22, 1945, in OMGUS 12-1/5, V60-12/1.

22. OMGUS, History, Office of Military Government for Germany, ch. 3, pp. 2–4.

23. Department of State, *Foreign Relations,* 1945, vol. 3, pp. 132–34.

24. SHAEF, ACofS G-5, Weekly Journal of Information, No. 15, June 16, 1945, in SHAEF G-5, 131.11.

25. Hqs, Com Zone, ETO, Command and General Staff Conference, May 4, 1945, in ETOUSA, Admin Hist Collection, No. 146.

26. Hqs, US GP CC, Analytical Section, sub: Notes on Differences Between Agreed Report of Tripartite Conference of Berlin and JCS 1067/6/8, Aug. 14, 1945, in OMGUS 358-2/5.

27. Summary Sheet, ACofS OPD to CofS, sub: German Interim Financing, Aug. 5, 1945, in OPD, 336, sec. 5, Case 104.

28. Msg from General Eisenhower to the German People in the U.S. Zone, Aug. 6, 1945, in Admin Hist Collection, ETOUSA, No. 155.

29. Hqs, ETOUSA, to CG, 12th A Gp, sub: Removal of Nazis and Militarists, Jun. 29, 1945, in OMGUS 411/2/3.

30. Hist Rpt, Det B 262, Jun. 30, 1946, in OMGUS 10-1/5.

31. JCS 1517/2, Summary of Sep 45 Report of the Military Governor, Nov. 13, 1945, in CCS 383.21.

32. Memo for Record, USFET, ACofS G-5, Advisor (Dr. Walter L. Dorn), sub: Min. Pres. Friedrich Schäffer and the Tardy Denazification of the Bavarian Govt., Oct. 2, 1945, in USFET SGS 000.1.

33. *New York Times,* Sept. 23, 1945.

34. Min, US Gp CC, Staff Meeting of Div. Directors, Sept. 24, 1945, in OMGUS 411-2/3.

35. Hqs, USFET, to CG's, Eastern and Western Military Districts, sub: Administration of Military Government in the U.S. Zone, Law No. 8, Sept. 26, 1945, in OMGUS 411-2/3.

36. Hist Rpt, OMG, Bavaria, 1945, vol. 3, p. 433.

37. Ltr, Clay to McCloy, Sept. 16, 1945, in OMGUS 410-2/3.

38. History of Military Government in Land Wuerttemberg-Baden, pt. 1, p. 254.

39. Wk Rpt, Det 205, Nov. 22, 1945, in OMGUS 1-2/5.

40. Memo, Hqs, USFET, ACofS G-5, for CofS, sub: Program for Introduction of Classified Civil Service, Sept. 6, 1945, in USFET SGS 200.3.

41. Department of State, *Bulletin,* Sept. 30, 1945, pp. 456–61.

42. Cable, Eisenhower to Marshall, Oct. 13, 1945, in USFET SGS 000.7.

43. Memo, W.B. Smith for Byron Price, Oct. 14, 1945, in USFET SGS 014.113.

44. Memo, Dep Military Governor for CG, USFET, sub: Organization of Military Government, Sept. 15, 1945, in OMGUS 177-2/3.

45. Ltr, Clay to McCloy, Sept. 16, 1945, in OMGUS 410-2/3.

46. Diary, Seventh Army, ACofS G-3, June 45–Mar. 46, Oct. 1, 1945, in Seventh Army 107-0.3.0.

47. Memo, Clay for Price, Oct. 14, 1945, in OMGUS 177-3/3.

48. Memo, USFET, Civil Admin Br, for CofS, sub: Proposed Directives, Oct. 4, 1945, in USFET SGS 014.1.

49. Hqs, USFET, to CG's, Eastern and Western Military Districts, sub:

Reorganization of Military Government Control Channels, Oct. 5, 1945, in USFET SGS 014.1.

50. Hqs, USFET, Director of Military Government (U.S. Zone), to Directors of Military Government, sub: Action to Strengthen German Civil Administration in the U.S. Zone, Nov. 21, 1945 in USFET SGS 014.114.

51. Memo, Hqs, USFET, ACofS G-2, for ACofS G-5, sub: German Responsibility for Civil Order, Oct. 31, 1945, in USFET SGS 014.113.

52. Hist Rpt, Det G-34, Dec. 45, in OMGUS 8-2/5.

53. OMGUS, German Governmental Organization and Civil Administration, Monthly Report No. 8, Mar. 20, 1946.

4. Governing the American Zone of Germany / Gimbel

1. For a discussion of the issue see Jerome Slater and Terry Nardin, "The 'Military-Industrial Complex' Muddle," *Yale Review,* vol. 65 (Autumn 1975), pp. 1–23; and *The Annals of the American Academy of Political and Social Science,* vol. 406 (Mar. 1973).

2. See, for example, Clay to McCloy, June 29, 1945, OMGUS Papers, Box 410/3, National Archives (hereafter NA) and Lucius D. Clay, *Decision in Germany* (Garden City, N.Y.: Doubleday, 1950), p. 54 et passim. For further discussion and documentation see John Gimbel, *The Origins of the Marshall Plan* (Stanford, Calif.: Stanford Univ. Press, 1976), esp. chapter 3.

3. Matthews to McCloy, June 15, 1945, RG 59, H. Freeman Matthews files, Box 1, folder M, NA; Clayton to McCloy, June 18, 1945, *Foreign Relations of the United States* (hereafter *FRUS*), 1945, Potsdam 1, p. 470; McCloy to Clayton, June 21, 1945, Potsdam 1, pp. 470–71; Clayton to McCloy, June 30, 1945, Potsdam 1, pp. 477–78.

4. Stimson to SecState, June 4, 1945, *FRUS,* 1945, Potsdam 1, pp. 479–81.

5. Apparently the State Department had no formal record of Truman's approval of its memorandum of July 16. Byrnes submitted it to him again on August 30, 1945, indicated that Truman had approved it at Potsdam, and asked him for "a formal indication of your approval," which Truman gave. See Byrnes to Truman, August 30, 1945, *FRUS,* 1945, vol. 3, p. 958.

6. Truman to Stimson, July 29, 1945, *FRUS,* 1945, Potsdam 2, pp. 821–23.

7. Murphy to SecState, Aug. 10, 1945, *FRUS,* 1945, vol. 3, pp. 830–32; SecState to USPOLAD, Berlin, Aug. 22, 1945, RG 59, Box C-124, Control (Germany), NA.

8. Clay, *Decision in Germany,* pp. 41–42; John H. Backer, *Priming the German Economy: American Occupational Policies, 1945–1948* (Durham, N.C.: Duke Univ. Press, 1971), pp. 74–76; John Gimbel, *The American Occupation of Germany: Politics and the Military, 1945–1949* (Stanford, Calif.: Stanford Univ. Press, 1968), pp. 20–21. Ross Berkes, an American member of the Allied Secretariat in Berlin, wrote later that "Potsdam seemed to

make good sense to the Americans at the time," and that they sent more proposals into the committees and directorates of the ACC than the other three powers combined. Ross Berkes, "Germany: Test Tube of Peace," *The American Scholar,* vol. 16 (Winter 1946-47), pp. 46-55.

9. OMGUS, Monthly Report of the Military Governor, N. 2, Sept. 20, 1945, p. 1; Civil Administration, p. 1.

10. Murphy to SecState, Sept. 8, 1945, *FRUS,* 1945, vol. 3, p. 960; Oct. 1, 1945, vol. 3, 969-71.

11. USFET, Subj: Organization of Military Government, Sept. 26, 1945, OMGUS Papers, Box 367-2/5, NA.

12. Clay to McCloy, Sept. 16, 1945, RG 165, file ASW 370.8, Germany— Control Group, NA. The letter is partially quoted in J. F. J. Gillen, *State and Local Government in West Germany, 1945-1953* (Mehlem: HICOG, 1953), p. 8.

13. For discussion and documentation see Gimbel, *The American Occupation of Germany,* esp. pp. 48-51 and 92-100.

14. Clay, *Decision in Germany,* p. 88; Murphy to SecState, Aug. 20, 1945, *FRUS,* 1945, vol. 3, pp. 957-58; Sept. 8, 1945, vol. 3, p. 960; Gimbel, *The American Occupation of Germany,* pp. 36-44, 47-51, 92-100 et passim.

15. Eisenhower to Marshall, Oct. 13, 1945, RG 165, file WDSCA CAD 321, Sec. 1, Box 202, NA.

16. Eisenhower to Truman, October 26, 1945, in State Department *Bulletin,* vol. 13 (Nov. 4, 1945), p. 711.

17. SecWar to SecState, Nov. 2, 1945, *FRUS,* 1945, vol. 3, pp. 996-97; Minutes of Meeting of SecState, War, Navy, Washington, Oct. 23, 1945, ibid., p. 989.

18. See State Department *Bulletin,* vol. 13 (Dec. 16, 1945), pp. 960-63.

19. Donald Russell to Murphy, Oct. 15, 1945; Russell to SecState, Dec. 29, 1945, Byrnes Papers, folder 611(1), Clemson University Library.

20. Patterson to Eisenhower and Hilldring, Dec. 21, 1945, RG 165, file WDSCA CAD 321, Sec. 1, Box 202, NA; Russell to SecState, Subj: Administrative Responsibility for German Control, Jan. 2, 1946, RG 59 file 740.00119 Control (Germany) Box 3729, NA; SecWar to ActgSecState, Dec. 22, 1945, *FRUS,* 1945, vol. 3, pp. 1019-21; SecWar to SecState, Dec. 29, 1945, RG 165, file OSW 091 Germany, NA; Eisenhower to Patterson (copy), n.d., filed Jan. 2, 1946, RG 59, file 740.00119 Control (Germany), Box C-131, NA.

21. Russell to SecState, Jan. 2, 1946, RG 59, file 740.00119 Control (Germany), Box 3729, NA. In April, 1946, only a portion of a much longer draft memorandum on "Principles and Procedures Regarding Policy-Making and Administration of Occupied Areas" was submitted to Truman for final approval. The shorter, approved version omitted plans for a transfer and merely outlined what had become practice since the Potsdam conference. See *FRUS,* 1946, vol. 5, pp. 674-77.

22. See Gimbel, *The American Occupation of Germany,* esp. pp. 35-51, 61-70, 87-91, 131-40; and Gimbel, "Die Konferenzen der deutschen Ministerpräsidenten 1945-1949," *Aus Politik und Zeitgeschichte: Beilage*

zur Wochenzeitung Das Parlament, vol. 31 (July 1971), pp. 3–28. See also, Wilhard Gruenewald, *Die Münchener Ministerpräsidenten Konferenz 1947: Anlass und Scheitern eines gesamtdeutschen Unternehmens* (Meisenheim am Glan: Verlag Anton Hain, 1971).

23. John Gimbel, "The American Reparations Stop in Germany: An Essay on the Political Uses of History," *The Historian,* vol. 37 (Feb. 1975), pp. 276–96.

24. John Gimbel, "Die Vereinigten Staaten, Frankreich und der amerikanische Vertragsentwurf zur Entmilitarisierung Deutschlands," *Vierteljahrshefte für Zeitgeschichte,* vol. 22, no. 3 (July 1974), pp. 258–86.

25. John Gimbel, "Byrnes und die Bizone—Eine amerikanische Entscheidung zur Teilung Deutschlands?" in *Aspekte deutscher Aussenpolitik im 20. Jahrhundert: Aufsätze Hans Rothfels zum Gedächtnis,* Wolfgang Benz and Hermann Graml, eds. (Stuttgart: Deutsche Verlags-Anstalt, 1976), pp. 193–210.

26. U.S. Delegation Record, CFM, July 11, 1946, *FRUS,* 1946, vol. 2, pp. 896–98; Proposal by the U.K. Delegation, July 11, 1946, ibid., p. 900.

27. Murphy to SecState, Aug. 3, 1946, *FRUS,* 1946, vol. 5, pp. 587–88; Aug. 11, 1946, ibid., pp. 590–92; Aug. 17, 1946, ibid., pp. 592–93; Aug. 29, 1946, ibid., pp. 595–96.

28. Gimbel, *The American Occupation of Germany,* pp. 106–10.

29. For discussion and documentation see Gimbel, *The American Occupation of Germany,* esp. pp. 82–85, 94–101, 113–17, and *The Origins of the Marshall Plan,* pp. 162–63.

30. OMGUS to War Department, Jan. 3, 1947, RG 165, file CAD 100, Sec. 7, Box 286, NA; Murphy to SecState, Jan. 14, 1947, RG 165, file WDSCA 091.31, Sec. 15, Box 267, NA; OMGUS to AGWAR, Jan. 28, 1947, CC 7826, RG 316, Clay Papers, Box 3, NA.

31. See U.S. Congress, Senate, Special Committee Investigating the National Defense Program. Confidential Report to the Special Committee Investigating the National Defense Program on the Preliminary Investigation of Military Government in Occupied Areas of Europe, Nov. 22, 1946. By George Meader, Chief Counsel. Released to the press on Dec. 4, 1946.

32. Tracy S. Voorhees, Memorandum for the Secretary, Dec. 21, 1946, RG 107, file ASW 430, Book 1, Box 76, NA; The President's Economic Mission to Germany and Austria, "Report No. 3—The Necessary Steps for Promotion of German Exports, so as to Relieve American Taxpayers of the Burdens of Relief and for Economic Recovery of Europe," Mar. 18, 1947, OF 950-B (Economic Mission as to Food and Its Collateral Problems), Truman Library. See also *New York Times,* Mar. 24, 1947, p. 4.

33. Acheson to Marshall, Mar. 20, 1947, *FRUS,* 1947, vol. 2, pp. 394–95; Teleconference, Washington-Berlin (Noce, CAD, and Clay and Draper, OMGUS) Mar. 5, 1947, RG 107, file ASW 430, Book 2, Box 76, NA.

34. Clay, *Decision in Germany,* p. 174; *Die Neue Zeitung,* Apr. 28, 1947, p. 1. See OMGUS, from Clay, to Marshall, May 2, 1947, *FRUS,* 1947, vol. 2, pp. 915–18, for a summary of the discussions in Berlin.

35. See George F. Kennan, *Memoirs, 1925–1950* (Boston: Atlantic–Lit-

tle, Brown, 1967), pp. 325–26; Joseph M. Jones, *The Fifteen Weeks* (*February 21–June 5, 1947*) (1955; rpt. New York: Harcourt, Brace & World, 1964), pp. 223–24; Harry B. Price, Notes of an Interview with George F. Kennan, Feb. 19, 1953, Truman Library. See also Gimbel, *The Origins of the Marshall Plan,* pp. 194–99.

36. Kennan to Acheson, May 23, 1947, *FRUS, 1947,* vol. 3, pp. 223–30.

37. Gimbel, *The Origins of the Marshall Plan,* pp. 220–26.

38. Matthews to Hilldring, May 15, 1947, RG, H. Freeman Matthews files, folder: Memoranda, 1947, Box 10, NA; Minutes, Committee on European Recovery Program, June 25, 1947, RG 59, file 840.50 Recovery/8-2547, NA; Memorandum, H. R. Labouisse to Kindleberger, Subj: European Recovery Proposals, July 11, 1947, RG 59, file 840.50 Recovery/7-447, NA.

39. James A. Stillwell to Saltzman, Subj: Basic Directive to General Clay, Aug. 25, 1947, RG 59, file 740.00119 Control (Germany)/8-2547, NA.

40. Teleconference, Clay and Petersen, TT-8382, July 24, 1947, RG 316, Clay Papers, Box 2, NA.

41. Clay to AGWAR, for Royall, July 28, 1947, CC-1047, RG 316, Clay Papers, Box 4, NA; Royall to Clay, W-84501, August 19, 1947, ibid.

42. Saltzman to Lovett, Aug. 25, 1947, RG 59, file 740.00119 Control (Germany)/8-2547, NA.

43. Royall to Lovett, Sept. 3, 1947, with attached "Outline Plan for Transfer from War Department to State Department . . . ," War Department Papers, file SAOUS 014.1 German/State, NA; Royall to Lovett, Sept. 9, 1947, RG 59, file 110.721/9-947, NA, and other materials in the same file.

44. T. N. Dupuy, Memorandum for the Record, Subj: Meeting Between Secretary Marshall and Secretary Royall, Jan. 19, 1948, War Department Papers, file SAOUS 014.1 Germany/State, NA; Clay to Draper, Jan. 8, 1948, ibid.; War Department, CSCAD, to Clay, Subj: State Takeover of Occupied Areas, Jan. 15, 1948, ibid.; Draper to Clay, Jan. 27, 1948, ibid.; OMGUS, Public Information Office Release, Jan. 28, 1948, OMGUS Papers, Box 1-2/4, NA; Noce to Draper, repeating White House Release, Mar. 23, 1948, War Department Papers, file, SAOUS 014.1 Germany, NA.

45. See Gimbel, *The American Occupation of Germany,* chapters 11–14.

7. From Deconcentration to Reverse Course in Japan / Hadley

1. Eleanor M. Hadley, "Concentrated Business Power in Japan" (Ph.D. diss., Radcliffe College, 1949), app. 1, pp. 373–79a.

2. In the chapter by Richard Caves and Uekusa, "Industrial Organization" in the Hugh Patrick–Henry Rosovsky edited volume, *Asia's New Giant* (Washington, D.C.: Brookings Institution, 1977), it is observed, pp. 494–95:

The competitive significance of a firm's extra-market assets and activities is a controversial question in industrial organization—and nowhere more so than in Japan where *zaibatsu* and other affiliations link industrial, commercial and financial firms in a thick and complex skein of relations matched in no other industrial country.

The late John M. Blair opened his chapter on "Conglomerate Concentration" in his study *Economic Concentration* (New York: Harcourt Brace Jovanovich, 1972) in this way, (p. 41):

In discussing the state of economic thinking concerning conglomerate expansion, Corwin D. Edwards has observed that the subject "falls outside the limits of our customary analyses of competition and monopoly or of vertical integration. Like those parts of medieval maps of the world that were labeled 'Terra Incognita' the area covered is one in which our awareness and curiosity have outrun our knowledge." Two theoretical articles on conglomerate activity begin respectively: "The problem of the multiple-product firm has lain in virtual neglect on the threshold of the theory of monopolistic (or imperfect) competition since the pioneering efforts of Chamberlin and Joan Robinson" [Eli Clemens]; and "It appears that very little has been written about the multiple-product firms, [J. C. Weldon]."

3. *State-War Mission On Japanese Combines, Report,* Part 1, Mar. 1946, p. vii. (Department of State Publication 2628, Far Eastern Series 14.)

4. G. C. Allen in E. B. Schumpeter, ed., *The Industrialization of Japan and Manchukuo* (New York: Macmillan, 1940), p. 682.

5. Reproduced among other places in Edwin M. Martin, *The Allied Occupation of Japan* (Stanford, Calif.: Stanford University Press, 1948), pp. 138–40.

6. For discussion of the program, cf. Eleanor M. Hadley, *Antitrust in Japan* (Princeton, N.J.: Princeton Univ. Press, 1970); T. A. Bisson, *Zaibatsu Dissolution in Japan* (Berkeley: Univ. of California Press, 1954); also, Kazuo Kawai, *Japan's American Interlude* (Chicago: Univ. of Chicago Press, 1960). For articles written in the time of "battle", cf. Hadley, "Trust Busting in Japan," *Harvard Business Review* (July 1948), pp. 425–40, and "Japan: Competition or Private Collectivism?" *Far Eastern Survey* (Dec. 14, 1949), pp. 289–94.

7. Cf. Hadley, *Antitrust,* n. 60.

8. Ibid., pp. 77–106. For a colorful account of dissension within the Headquarters, cf. Charles A. Willoughby, *Shirarezaru Nihon Senryō: Uirobii Kaikoroku* [Unknown history of the Japanese occupation: Willoughby's memoirs] (Tokyo: Banmachi Shobo, 1973), 318 pp., esp. "GS to G2 no Tairitsu" and "GHQ no Naisen," pp. 135–203. This book was published posthumously and only in Japanese.

9. Actually 453 were removed; 186 were "barred." To be "barred" under the economic purge meant that one could stay in the position presently occupied but could not move to "designated" positions in "designated" companies.

10. Hadley, *Antitrust,* p. 110.

11. Ibid., p. 112.

12. Ibid., p. 113.

13. The text of FEC 230 will be found, ibid., app. 9. SWNCC 302 was the designation of what, upon submission to the Far Eastern Commission, became FEC 230.

14. Hadley, *Antitrust,* pp. 137–38.

15. Ibid., p. 138.

16. Ibid., p. 134.

17. Ibid., pp. 133–34. In 1948 American aid amounted to $461 million, in 1949 to $534 million, and in 1950 to $361 million.

18. Ibid., pp. 115–18.

19. Ibid., p. 140.

20. Ibid., p. 141.

21. Ibid.

22. Ibid., pp. 141–42.

23. Ibid., pp. 166–67.

24. Ibid., p. 167.

25. Ibid., pp. 168–72.

26. Ibid., pp. 173–74.

27. Ibid., pp. 178–80.

28. Ibid., pp. 147–48.

29. Ibid., p. 147.

30. Cf. Willoughby, *Shirarezaru Nihon Senryō* [Unknown history of the Japanese occupation]. Note, among other places, p. 136, where after bestowing compliments on Whitney, Willoughby adds, "but in my eyes I cannot but consider him procommunist (a fellow traveler)." The Japanese term is *yokyoshugisha.*

31. George F. Kennan, *Memoirs, 1925–1950* (Boston: Atlantic–Little, Brown, 1967), p. 393.

32. Shigeru Yoshida, *The Yoshida Memoirs* (London: Heinemann, 1961), p. 150.

33. Mitsubishi Economic Research Institute, *Mitsui-Mitsubishi-Sumitomo* (Tokyo, 1955), p. 30.

34. Misstatement. No securities were taken over in consequence of initial designation under this law.

35. True, but "uncertainty" from a multitude of causes including shattering military defeat.

36. Mr. Kennan was clearly unaware, that while he, Senator Knowland, and General Willoughby might so argue, that the Japanese Communist party branded the legislation an expression of "monopoly capitalism," cf. Hadley *Antitrust,* pp. 140–41.

37. An extraordinary statement for so careful an observer.

38. The contrast between Kennan's assessment and that of Kazuo Kawai, editor of the *Japan Times* during the occupation and subsequently faculty member of Washington University, in his University of Chicago publication, *Japan's American Interlude,* is striking. Of the purge, Kawai wrote in his *American Interlude* (p. 95):

Despite some injustice and irregularities, however, in relation to the tremendous scope and complexity of the operation, the purge was conducted with about as little abuse as could predictably be expected. It seems to have worked out better than the "de-Nazification" procedure in Germany, where the semiautomatic purge gave way to judicial judgments that carried sentences of stiff fines and other punishments. Whereas the court trials in Germany apparently afforded opportunity for much inconclusive wrangling over questionable testimony inspired by the political bias or personal spite, the virtually automatic administrative character of the Japanese purge allowed the intrusion of a minimum of petty politics or subjective influences. Unlike the war crimes trials, it carried practically no punitive connotations; it was primarily a constructive political measure to facilitate the emergence of fresh national leadership.

8. From Morgenthau Plan to Marshall Plan / Backer

1. Memorandum Secretary of War to Harry Hopkins, 5 Sept. 1944, on Policy Recommendations for the Treatment of Germany. National Archives Record Group 107. Office of the Secretary of War.

2. Henry Morgenthau, *Germany Is our Problem* (New York: Harper, 1945), photographic copy of memorandum to the President.

3. Herbert Feis, *Churchill, Roosevelt, Stalin* (Princeton, N.J.: Princeton Univ. Press, 1957), pp. 369–70.

4. Henry L. Stimson, *On Active Service in Peace and War* (New York: Harper, 1947), p. 582.

5. Paul V. Hammond, "Directives for the Occupation of Germany: The Washington Controversy," in *Civil-Military Decisions,* edited by Harold Stein (University: Univ. of Alabama Press, 1963), passim.

6. Lucius D. Clay, *Decision in Germany* (Garden City, N.Y.: Doubleday, 1950), pp. 10–19.

7. Robert Murphy, *Diplomat among Warriors* (Garden City, N.Y.: Doubleday, 1964), p. 250.

8. Clay, *Decision in Germany,* pp. 41–42.

9. Memorandum Charles Fahy, Legal Advisor, Headquarters U. S. Group Control Council (Germany) to Assistant Deputy of Public Service, 9 August 1945, OMGUS Records 4-35/10.

10. Hammond, "Directives for the Occupation of Germany: The Washington Controversy," p. 372.

11. John H. Backer, *Priming the German Economy* (Durham, N.C.: Duke Univ. Press, 1971), chapter 2.

12. Memorandum Milburn to all Divisions. OMGUS Records. Shipment 16. 367-2/5.N.A.

13. 80th Congress, First Session. House Hearings on First Deficiency Appropriations Bill 1947, p. 693.

14. Richard McKinzie interview with General Lucius D. Clay, New York, New York, 16 July 1974, Truman Library.

15. John H. Backer interview with Mr. Jackson Bennett, Chapel Hill, North Carolina, 1981.

16. William Griffith, "The Denazification Program in the United States Zone of Germany" (Ph.D. diss., Harvard Univ., 1950).

17. Alvin Johnson,"Denazification," *Social Research,* vol. 14 (1947), pp. 59–74. Richard Schmid, "Denazification," *American Perspective,* vol. 2, no. 5 (Oct. 1948), pp. 231–42. Louis P. Lochner, "The Idiocy of Our Denazification Policy," *Readers Digest* (June 1948), pp. 130–36. John H. Herz, "The Fiasco of Denazification in Germany," *Political Science Quarterly,* vol. 63 (Dec. 1948), pp. 569–94. Max Reinstein, "Renazifying Germany," *University of Chicago Magazine* (Apr. 1947), pp. 5–8.

18. John H. Backer, *The Decision to Divide Germany* (Durham, N.C.: Duke Univ. Press, 1978), chapter 3.

19. Ibid.

20. *U.S. Strategic Bombing Survey,* "The Effects of Strategic Bombing on the German War Production," 1945, Rare Book Collection, Library of Congress.

21. Gustav Stolper, *German Realities* (New York: Reynal and Hitchcock, 1948), pp. 84–87, 96–98.

22. Manuel Gottlieb, *The German Peace Settlement and the Berlin Crisis* (New York: Paine-Whitman, 1960), p. 58; J. P. Nettl, *The Eastern Zone and Soviet Policy in Germany, 1945–1950* (New York: Farrar, Straus and Giroux, Octagon Books, 1977), p. 162.

23. Ratchford and Ross, *Berlin Reparations Assignment* (Chapel Hill: Univ. of North Carolina Press, 1947), passim.

24. Backer, *The Decision to Divide Germany,* app. 4.

25. Ibid., chapter 10.

26. Ibid., annex 5.

27. Ibid., chapter 11.

28. Maurice Dobb, *Soviet Economic Development since 1917* (New York: International Publishers, 1948), pp. 98–160.

29. E. C. Harmssen, *Am Abend der Demontage* (Bremen: F. Trueje Verlag, 1951), p. 176.

30. As quoted in Jen Hacker, *Soviet Union & DDR zum Potsdamer Abkommen* (Cologne: Wissenschaft und Politik, 1968), p. 118.

31. *Foreign Relations of the United States: Potsdam 1,* (Washington, D.C.: Government Printing Office, 1945), pp. 614–21.

32. John Gimbel, *The Origins of the Marshall Plan* (Stanford, Calif.: Stanford Univ. Press, 1976), chapter 12.

33. Clay, *Decision in Germany,* p. 196.

34. Backer, *Priming the German Economy,* pp. 106–14.

35. E. A. Tennenbaum, "Why do we Trade for Dollars?" Office of the Financial Advisor, 15 Feb. 1948 (OMGUS records 84-2/1, RG 260, National Archives.

36. Gimbel, *The Origins of the Marshall Plan,* chapter 13.

11. Denazification in Germany: A Policy Analysis / Plischke

1. Together with disarmament, reparations and the restitution of looted property, and the extirpation of nationalism and militarism.

2. Together with reeducation, rehabilitation, and reorientation.

3. See John Herz, "The Fiasco of Denazification in Germany," *Political Science Quarterly,* vol. 63 (Dec. 1948), p. 570.

4. See Karl H. Knappstein, "Die Versäumte Revolution," *Die Wandlung,* vol. 2 (1947), p. 664, quoted in Constantine FitzGibbon, *Denazification* (London: Michael Joseph, 1969), p. 177. Knappstein argues that it was imposed rather than inherent, and that the intrinsic aim of every revolution is a genuine transformation to deprive the former elite of its power and to elevate a new elite into the key position by natural means, which was lacking in postsurrender Germany.

5. In the Atlantic Charter, President Roosevelt and Prime Minister Churchill subscribed to self-determination (pars. 2 to 4), peace and freedom from fear (related to security, par. 6), and the disarmament of aggressors (par. 8), and specific allusion was made to "the final destruction of the Nazi tyranny." The texts of this and the following documents are readily available in U.S., Department of State, *The Axis in Defeat: A Collection of Documents on American Policy Toward Germany and Japan* (Washington, D.C.: Government Printing Office, n.d.). Basic United States and joint policy statements concerning World War II are also conveniently available in U.S., Senate, Committee on Foreign Relations, *A Decade of American Foreign Policy: Basic Documents, 1941–49,* Document No. 123 (Washington, D.C.: Government Printing Office, 1950), Part 1.

The Atlantic Charter was reconfirmed by the preface to the United Nations Declaration of January 1, 1942, which eventually was subscribed to by nearly fifty of the United Nations at war with the Axis, and it became their basic war aims. At Yalta in February 1945 it was determined by the Big Three that in order to participate in the San Francisco Conference to negotiate the United Nations Charter, a state had to subscribe to the United Nations Declaration (and, therefore, indirectly to the Atlantic Charter) and to declare war on at least one of the Axis powers before March 1, 1945. This arrangement rendered the principles of the Atlantic Charter basic to planning for the postwar period. For commentary on these developments, see U.S., Department of State, *Postwar Foreign Policy Preparation, 1939–1945* (Washington, D.C.: Government Printing Office, 1949), pp. 377, 385, 392–93, 396, 410.

6. The Moscow declaration referred to the "maintenance of peace and security," liberation from "the menace of aggression," and the disarmament of the enemy.

7. The Tehran declaration of December 1, 1943, alluded to the "destruction of the German forces," the winning of an "enduring peace," the banishment of the "scourge and terror of war," the "elimination of tyranny," and the creation of "a world family of democratic nations."

8. For a handy compilation of pertinent documents, for example, see U.S.,

Department of State, *Peace and War: United States Foreign Policy, 1931–1941* (Washington, D.C.: Government Printing Office, 1943), pp. 179–82, 315–17, 486–88, 767–72, 784–87; and *A Decade of American Foreign Policy,* pp. 8–9.

9. At this early stage, denazification was posed in terms of the dissolution of the Nazi party and its affiliated organizations, arrest and detention of Nazis, dismissal from office of various Nazi groups, and the prohibition of Nazi insignia, uniforms, and parades. For pre-Quebec Conference proposals and consideration respecting the postsurrender treatment of Germany, see U.S., Department of State, *Foreign Relations of the United States: The Conference at Quebec, 1944* (Washington, D.C.: Government Printing Office, 1972), pp. 48–158; hereinafter referred to as *Quebec.* For the Treasury Department plan, see pp. 86–91; for the Department of State plan, see pp. 95–97; for War Department views, see pp. 123–28; and for a more complete War Department statement, see pp. 482–85. The Treasury Department also prepared a separate briefing for the president; see pp. 101–8. According to Robert Murphy, at this time the president also discussed with him such matters as the elimination of German militarism, the treatment of war criminals (to be "dealt with summarily"), and reparations (although the United States was not interested in acquiring them for herself); see pp. 144–45.

10. The principal pre-Quebec Conference version of the Morgenthau Plan appeared in the Treasury Department "Briefing Book" for the Quebec meeting; see *Quebec,* pp. 128–44.

11. For comment on the president's delegation, see *Quebec,* p. 279, n. 1. No member of the Department of State was included. Secretary of the Treasury Henry Morgenthau, not a regularly scheduled member of the delegation, accompanied President Roosevelt from Washington to Hyde Park, and he was later summoned to Quebec by the president; see *Quebec,* p. 43. Secretary of State Hull declined the president's request to accompany him to Quebec, because he was not well and because he was busy with the Dumbarton Oaks meeting; see *The Memoirs of Cordell Hull* (New York: Macmillan, 1948), vol. 2, p. 1602.

12. For text, see *Quebec,* pp. 466–67, with a note respecting how the document was initialed. For Secretary Morgenthau's diary record of what transpired at the meeting at which the agreement was reached, see *Quebec,* pp. 360–62.

13. The Treasury Department was able to manage this, in part, by virtue of its participation in the Cabinet Committee.

14. One might wonder how the process would have differed had the president utilized the State-War-Navy-Coordinating Committee (SWNCC) functioning at the cabinet, rather than the subcabinet, level for this purpose instead of the special Cabinet Committee on Germany, or had the president restricted or omitted the Treasury Department from its deliberations. For subsequent use of SWNCC, see later comment in this section and n. 33.

15. James F. Byrnes, who later became secretary of state, reports that, not only was the Morgenthau Plan widely discussed in the American press,

but it also was used propagandistically against the United States by the Russians and it was "greatly exaggerated to inspire the Germans to fight and die rather than surrender." See *Speaking Frankly* (New York: Harper, 1947), p. 181, and *All in One Lifetime* (New York: Harper, 1958), pp. 366–67.

16. See Richard N. Current, *Secretary Stimson: A Study in Statecraft* (New Brunswick, N.J.: Rutgers Univ. Press, 1954), p. 217. Secretary Hull branded it "a plan of blind vengeance"; for his comments on his and Secretary Stimson's reactions, see Hull, *Memoirs,* vol. 2, pp. 1606, 1614–15.

17. See *Quebec,* p. 362; also Hull, *Memoirs,* vol. 2, p. 1615.

18. Editorial: "How Does Denazification Work in Germany?" *Saturday Evening Post,* vol. 220 (July 12, 1947), p. 148.

19. Edward R. Stettinius, *Roosevelt and the Russians: The Yalta Conference* (Garden City, N.Y.: Doubleday, 1949), pp. 40–41. He based his judgment on Roosevelt's memorandum to Secretary Hull of October 20, 1944, quoting the president's comment on economic policy. But for a different, official version of the memorandum, not containing this comment, see U.S., Department of State, *Foreign Relations of the United States: The Conferences at Malta and Yalta, 1945* (Washington, D.C.: Government Printing Office, 1955), pp. 158–59; hereinafter referred to as *Yalta.*

20. Robert Murphy, *Diplomat Among Warriors* (Garden City, N.Y.: Doubleday, 1964), p. 227; also Robert E. Sherwood, *Roosevelt and Hopkins: An Intimate History,* rev. ed. (New York: Harper, 1950), p. 818.

21. As a matter of fact, President Truman says that he opposed the Morgenthau policy of pastoralizing Germany and he adds that he did not favor it even when he was in the Senate. As noted later (see note 35), he excluded Morgenthau from his Potsdam Conference delegation. *Memoirs by Harry S Truman: Year of Decisions* (Garden City, N.Y.: Doubleday, 1955), vol. 1, p. 235.

22. Although Robert Murphy claims that the president approved—"O.K. FDR"—a preliminary draft of the Treasury Department plan (see Murphy, *Diplomat,* p. 227), this is not confirmed in *Quebec,* pp. 86–91, 98, 101–8.

23. This document was included in the conference communiqué, for which, see *Quebec,* p. 477.

24. For documentary citations, see note 9 above. Most of the functional aspects of denazification listed below (see Table 1), except for those concerned with the seizure of premises, assets, and archives, and the changing of street names and the removal of statues and memorials, were included in these early proposals. In addition, both departments recommended the breaking up of Junker estates. It is interesting to note that Secretary Hull scarcely mentions denazification, and certainly not by that designation, in his memoirs.

25. Dated September 29, 1944. See *Yalta,* pp. 156–58. The secretary of war generally agreed with the Department of State proposals, not only on denazification, but also on the recommendations to eliminate Germany as a dominant economic power in Europe and to provide a subsistence living standard, whereas the Morgenthau Plan demanded the deindustrialization

of Germany and an extremely limited subsistence level. See Current, *Stimson,* p. 217. For additional comment on the subsistence matter, see Stettinius, *Roosevelt and the Russians,* p. 39.

26. Among the president's comments to Secretary Hull were such statements as "I dislike making detailed plans for a country which we do not yet occupy," and "I agree except for going into too much detail and directives at the present moment." See *Yalta,* pp. 158–59; also Sherwood, *Roosevelt and Hopkins,* pp. 818–19. For proposals and commentary on economic policy, see *Yalta,* pp. 172–76.

27. Byrnes, *Speaking Frankly,* p. 181.

28. For a State Department summary of the activity of the Cabinet Committee, and its consideration of the State and Treasury Department plans, see *Yalta,* pp. 160–63. For the secretary of state's interpretation, see Hull, *Memoirs,* vol. 2, pp. 1604–11.

29. The text of the Briefing Book Paper is given in *Yalta,* pp. 178–90; the portion concerned with denazification is given on pp. 181–82. Separate papers on economic policies are given on pp. 190–93 and on reparations and restitution on pp. 193–97.

30. The conference agenda included discussion on the establishment of the United Nations as well as the war with Germany and Japan. For a list of United States delegation members, see *Yalta,* pp. 968–69. Unlike the situation at Quebec, in addition to two White House advisers, the president's delegation included Secretary of State Edward R. Stettinius and three other members of the State Department as well as Ambassador W. Averell Harriman, the military chiefs of staff and several other military officers, and the director of the Office of War Mobilization (James F. Byrnes), but not the secretaries of war, navy, or treasury.

31. *Yalta,* pp. 970–71; the entire conference communiqué appears on pp. 968–75, and the Protocol of Proceedings is given on pp. 975–83. The pastoralization of Germany, as reflected in the Morgenthau Plan, was not explicitly reaffirmed by these commitments.

32. It appears from the record that the Cabinet Committee on Germany was not employed by President Truman.

33. SWNCC grew out of conversations of the secretaries of state, war, and navy respecting the need for a continuing coordinating mechanism to integrate and recommend proposals concerning politico-military problems. Initially it was intended primarily to deal with issues relating to the Far East, but it was broadened to concern itself also with German affairs. Eventually it was supported by nine subcommittees, two of which pertained to military government and civil affairs. For background and commentary, see Edwin J. Hayward, "Co-ordination of Military and Civilian Civil Affairs Planning," *Annals of the American Academy of Political and Social Science,* vol. 267 (Jan. 1950), pp. 19–27. Also see Harold Zink, *American Military Government in Germany* (New York: Macmillan, 1947), pp. 209–10; Harold Zink, *The United States in Germany, 1944–1955* (Princeton, N.J.: Van Nostrand, 1957), pp. 90–91. For plans to focus policy direction for Germany in SWNCC, see U.S., Department of State, *Foreign Relations of the United*

States, 1946, vol. 5 (Washington, D.C.: Government Printing Office, 1969), pp. 659–60. In 1947 this agency was changed to the State-Army-Navy-Air Coordinating Committee (SANACC).

34. Such as the disarmament and demobilization of Germany, and the elimination of German industry amenable to military production (or industrial disarmament).

35. U.S., Department of State, *Foreign Relations of the United States: Conference of Berlin (Potsdam), 1945* (Washington, D.C.: Government Printing Office, 1960), pp. 1477–98 for the entire protocol, and pp. 1481–82 for section on denazification; hereinafter referred to as *Potsdam.* The stipulations concerning denazification also were reiterated in the conference tripartite communiqué; see pp. 1499–1514. Approximately two-thirds of the members of the president's delegation to the conference represented the Department of State, whereas only five were military officers, one of whom was concerned with war shipping rather than the military forces; see p. 512. Apparently Secretary of the Treasury Morgenthau was anxious to be included in President Truman's delegation, and threatened to resign if he was not invited; in any case, he did resign the day before the president departed for Europe. See Murphy, *Diplomat,* p. 270.

36. The bizonal arrangement continued until it was superseded by the Anglo-American-French Trizonal Fusion Agreement in 1949, which played an important role in paving the way for the establishment of the West German Federal Government, under the Occupation Statute for Germany and the Allied High Commission. For commentary, see Elmer Plischke, *History of the Allied High Commission for Germany* (Mehlem/Bad Godesberg: Historical Division, Office of the U.S. High Commissioner for Germany, 1951), chapter 1; and Elmer Plischke, *The Allied High Commission for Germany* (Mehlem/Bad Godesberg: Historical Division, Office of the U.S. High Commissioner for Germany, 1953), chapters 1–3. Both contain texts of pertinent documents in appendices.

37. When in his memorandum to the president of September 1944, Secretary Hull referred to the work of the commission on these three draft agreements, President Roosevelt responded: "we must emphasize the fact that the European Advisory Commission is 'advisory' and that you and I are not bound by this advice" and he worried that "they may go ahead and execute some of the advice, which, when the time comes, we may not like at all." See *Yalta,* p. 158. Also see comment in Murphy, *Diplomat,* pp. 227–28. For commentary on the origin and purpose of the European Advisory Commission see Hayward, "Military and Civil Affairs," p. 25.

38. This draft surrender instrument, approved in advance by the three governments, was not signed at Reims on May 7, 1945. Instead, an instrument prepared by General Eisenhower's headquarters was used. The Soviet government objected, so that this surrender was declared to be preliminary, and an "official surrender" was held two days later in Berlin, using the European Advisory Commission negotiated draft, which explains the reason for the double surrender. See Murphy, *Diplomat,* pp. 240–41. General Eisenhower refers to the second surrender simply as "a ratification" of the

surrender, without explaining the differing documents; see Dwight D. Eisenhower, *Crusade in Europe* (Garden City, N.Y.: Doubleday, 1948), pp. 424–27.

39. For the texts of these draft agreements, see *Yalta,* "Unconditional Surrender of Germany," pp. 113–18; "Protocol" on the zones of occupation, pp. 118–23; and "Agreement on Control Machinery in Germany," pp. 124–27. Also see *Yalta,* pp. 511–12, for British views at the Malta Conference on broadening the European Advisory Commission's area of concern.

40. See Current, *Stimson,* pp. 216–17.

41. Ibid., p. 216. This attitude was substantiated by Roosevelt's determination to exact an unconditional surrender rather than produce a negotiated armistice, as well as a delayed normalization of conditions, including procrastination in evolving a peace settlement. See Sherwood, *Roosevelt and Hopkins,* p. 715. For additional commentary on Roosevelt's attitude toward the Germans and the *Handbook,* see Hull, *Memoirs,* vol. 2, pp. 1602–3.

42. The *Handbook* was supplemented with a number of functional manuals. For an account of these early developments by a participant in the German Country Unit, see Zink, *American Military Government in Germany,* pp. 17–20, 42–43, 130–33, 139–41; and Zink, *United States in Germany,* pp. 18–21, 105, 111, and for the agency's concern with denazification, pp. 151–53.

43. An early version of this draft is given in *Yalta,* pp. 143–54; appendix A, "Political Directive," pp. 145–49, is particularly relevant.

44. The directive, issued on May 14, 1945, was the sixth version, technically designated JCS 1067/6; see Zink, *United States in Germany,* p. 93.

45. Especially paragraphs 6, 8, and 9. For the text of JCS 1067, see U.S., Department of State, *Germany, 1947–1949: The Story in Documents* (Washington, D.C.: Government Printing Office, 1950), pp. 21–33, hereinafter referred to as *Germany, 1947–1949.*

46. When it was replaced by the Allied High Commission for Germany, as the Federal Republic of Germany was created.

47. Robert Murphy, a career diplomat, served as POLAD. For his experiences in this capacity, see his memoir, *Diplomat,* cited above.

48. It is important to note that by this time much of Germany was already in the hands of the occupying powers, and the surrender was to take place early in the next month. For an account of early developments and difficulties in executing the denazification program in the field, see Zink, *American Military Government in Germany,* pp. 132–41; and Zink, *United States in Germany,* pp. 157–59.

49. For comment on the preparation of this coordinating annex to the Basic Preliminary Plan, see Elmer Plischke, "Denazifying the Reich," *Review of Politics,* vol. 9 (Apr. 1947), p. 155; and Elmer Plischke, "Denazification Law and Procedure," *American Journal of International Law,* vol. 41 (Oct. 1947), p. 808.

50. *Potsdam,* pp. 1447–49, 1478–81, 1500–1501.

51. U.S., Department of State, *Foreign Relations of the United States,*

1947, vol. 2, *Council of Foreign Ministers: Germany and Austria* (Washington, D.C.: Government Printing Office, 1972), pp. 427–28, 462; also *Germany, 1947–1949,* p. 109.

52. For the text of JCS 1779, see U.S., Department of State, *Directive Regarding the Military Government of Germany, July 11, 1947* (Washington, D.C.: Government Printing Office, 1947); and *Germany, 1947–1949,* pp. 34–41. By this time, far more attention was paid to such positive actions as developing German self-government, political parties, economic revival, agricultural production, and education.

53. For a survey of United States policy development, see J. G. Kormann, "U.S. Denazification Policy in Germany, 1944–1950," originally prepared as a Ph.D. dissertation at Columbia University and subsequently issued in multilithed form by the Historical Division of the Office of the U.S. High Commissioner for Germany in 1952. It is interesting to conjecture as to what might have occurred respecting denazification policy planning had the Department of State been assigned responsibility for the program when the transition was made from military government to civil affairs at the conclusion of the hostilities, especially when Major General John H. Hilldring, head of G-5 (Civil Affairs Department) of the War Department transferred and was appointed as assistant secretary of state, early in 1946. As noted earlier, responsibility was turned over to SWNCC. For comment on civil-military relations immediately following the war, see Zink, *United States in Germany,* pp. 121–22.

54. Thus, John Herz prescribed the following six stages in his analysis: direct military government control, Law of Liberation, amnesties, amended Liberation Law, further amendment, and liquidation of the program. See Herz, "Fiasco," pp. 570–77. A similar treatment is provided by William E. Griffith, who defines the following stages; initial, intensification, German takeover, changes in the law, and final fiasco; see "Denazification in the United States Zone of Germany," *Annals of the American Academy of Political and Social Science,* vol. 267 (Jan. 1950), pp. 68–76.

55. This approach is employed by those who treat denazification in its broader context. For example, see Plischke, "Denazification Law and Procedure," pp. 807–27, and Plischke, "Denazifying the Reich," pp. 153–72.

56. Military Government Law No. 5—"Dissolution of the Nazi Party"— applied to the party and some fifty specified affiliated Nazi organizations as well as eight Nazi paramilitary groups, including the SS (*Schutzstaffel*), SA (*Sturmabteilung*), and HJ (*Hitler Jugend*). Unless otherwise indicated, the texts of military government laws and directives are provided in the *Military Government Gazette—Germany.* Also Control Council Law No. 2— "Providing for the Termination and Liquidation of the Nazi Organization," which applied to some sixty enumerated organizations. Additional action was taken to dissolve the *Wehrmacht,* certain police units, racial organizations, and the like. For commentary with additional documentation, see Plischke, "Denazification Law and Procedure," pp. 808–10. Some of the Nazi affiliates were identified in selected early policy statements discussed above. Several of the military government and Control Council laws and

orders referred to in this and the following notes are conveniently reproduced in U.S., Department of State, *Occupation of Germany: Policy and Progress, 1945-1946* (Washington, D.C.: Government Printing Office, 1947), appendix.

57. Control Council Law No. 1—"Repealing of Nazi Laws"—required the repeal of twenty-five fundamental laws enacted under the Nazis, together with subsidiary explanatory laws, ordinances, and decrees. This was founded on the somewhat less detailed American Military Government Law No. 1—"Abrogation of Nazi Law." In the United States zone, a Committee on Reform of German Law was created to refine and purge the German legal system, which was assisted by German legal experts under American supervision. In January 1946, Control Council Law No. 11—"Repealing Certain Provisions of the German General Code"—was issued, which eliminated those sections of the code and other criminal laws that contributed to nazism and militarism. For commentary, see Plischke, "Denazification Law and Procedure," pp. 810-11.

58. Military Government Law No. 52—"Blocking and Control of Property"—and Control Council Law No. 2, referred to above. Disposition of some of the accumulated organization funds, running into billions of marks, and the assets of some 400,000 families in the American zone, created difficulties that took some time to resolve. For commentary, see Plischke, "Denazification Law and Procedure," pp. 818-19.

59. The matter of German and Nazi archives created a number of problems, because it involved efforts to preserve governmental and other archives from intentional and unintentional destruction and loss. Special teams functioning as "Operation Goldcup" were used to penetrate German territory, sometimes immediately behind assault tanks, to secure such archives. One such team captured the German Foreign Office records in the Harz Mountains, which were later processed and published by the United States and the United Kingdom for historical purposes. Early in 1946 a central archival depot was established at Offenbach, near Frankfurt, where nearly two million items were collected, including looted archives, which were returned to their original owners. See Zink, *American Military Government in Germany,* p. 128. In addition, Allied forces were interested in securing Nazi party records, and early in the occupation a set of card files of members of the Nazi party and its affiliates was located in Bavaria and transferred to Berlin. It proved to be invaluable in administering the vetting program referred to later. See Lucius D. Clay, *Decision in Germany* (Garden City, N.Y.: Doubleday, 1950), p. 68; and Murphy, *Diplomat,* p. 284.

60. To a large extent these aspects of denazification were achieved by the dissolution of the Nazi organization and the seizure and disposition of its funds and property.

61. Military parades, Nazi anthems, and the public display of Nazi flags and other paraphernalia were prohibited by Military Government Law No. 154—"Elimination and Prohibition of Military Training"—which was reconfirmed by a Control Council policy statement approved on September 20, 1945. Earlier the Control Council also adopted a separate proposal for "Pro-

hibiting the Wearing of Uniforms by Disbanded Personnel of the Former German Army," supplemented by Ordinance No. 4 issued in the United States zone. In addition, Military Government Law No. 7—"Removal from Official Seals of National Socialist Emblems"—contributed to applying this aspect of the program. For commentary, see Plischke, "Denazification Law and Procedure," pp. 822–23.

62. Although occupation forces had already begun to carry such measures into effect, in July 1945 the United States issued a directive for the "Denazification and Demilitarization of German Street Names and Memorials." Quadripartite action, though more limited, followed under Control Council Directive No. 30—"Legislation Dealing with the Liquidation of German Military and Nazi War Memorials and Museums." For commentary, see Plischke, "Denazification Law and Procedure," p. 823.

63. Elimination of Nazi ideology and influence from public information media was a difficult and important assignment for those responsible for denazification. This program came under Military Government Law No. 191—"Control of Publications, Radio Broadcasting, News Services, Films, Theaters, and Music and Prohibition of Activities of the *Reichsministerium für Volksaufklärung und Propaganda.*" The objective was to eliminate information media that propagated antidemocratic ideas or Nazi policies including racism and race hatred, constituted an incitement to riot or disorder, or interfered in any way with the process of occupation control, and to contribute to reeducation and democratization. For additional commentary, see Plischke, "Denazification Law and Procedure," pp. 819–22.

64. Related to the concept of denazification but more reflective of the Morgenthau philosophy and JCS 1067, nonfraternization with Germans was ordered by American military government headquarters. It has been adjudged a failure that "foundered on the indestructable reefs of human nature." For commentary, see FitzGibbon, *Denazification,* pp. 83–87, and Zink, *United States in Germany,* pp. 133–36.

65. Control Council Directive No. 38—"The Arrest and Punishment of War Criminals, Nazis, and Militarists and the Internment, Control, and Surveillance of Potentially Dangerous Germans," October 12, 1946. For text, see *Occupation of Germany: Policy and Progress,* pp. 122–33.

66. This was approved by the Joint Chiefs of Staff in Washington and was concurred in by the United States Chief of Counsel for the war crimes trials at Nuremberg. The seven categories included: 1) Gestapo (Secret Police) and SD (*Sicherheitsdienst* or Security Service of the SS); 2) officers and noncommissioned officers of the *Waffen* (Armed) SS and *Allgemeine* (General) SS, and officers of the SA holding the rank of major or higher; 3) the leadership corps of the Nazi party, including Nazi officials down to the rank of *Ortsgruppenleiter* (Local Party Leader); 4) members of the Reich Cabinet after January 30, 1933; 5) members of the General Staff and High Command of the German armed forces; 6) war criminals; and 7) security suspects.

67. For commentary, with reference to documentation, see Plischke, "Denazification Law and Procedure," pp. 811–14, 823–27.

68. The estimate was expected to be halved by deaths and duplication. Associated Press report, February 28, 1946, cited in Plischke, "Denazification Law and Procedure," p. 813.

69. For comment, see Plischke, "Denazification Law and Procedure," p. 813.

70. Later, also Control Council Directive No. 24—"Removal from Office and from Positions of Responsibility of Nazis and of Persons Hostile to Allied Purposes," January 12, 1946. For text, see *Occupation of Germany: Policy and Progress,* pp. 113-18.

71. Comparison of the language of these basic statements reveals that the American removal directive of July 7, 1945, which quoted directly from JCS 1067, was more encompassing than that contained in the Potsdam summit agreement. For comment on this comparison, see Plischke, "Denazification Law and Procedure," p. 814.

72. For example, the directive on "Removal of Nazis and Militarists," Part 1, par. 3a (also quoted from JCS 1067, Part 1, par. 6c) defined active Nazis as those who had: "(a) held office or otherwise been active at any level from local to national in the Party and its subordinate organizations, or in organizations which further militaristic doctrines; (b) authorized or participated affirmatively in any Nazi crimes, racial persecutions or discriminations; (c) been avowed believers in Nazism or racial and militaristic creeds; or (d) voluntarily given substantial moral or material support or political assistance of any kind to the Nazi Party or Nazi officials and leaders." See Plischke, "Denazification Law and Procedure," p. 815. Even this specification left considerable room for interpretation and disagreement.

73. For commentary and enforcement documentation, see Plischke, "Denazification Law and Procedure," pp. 814-16, 823-27. For a satirical analysis from the German perspective, see E. von Salomon, *Fragebogen,* English translation (New York: Putnam, 1955).

74. This categorization was established in connection with the "Law for Liberation from National Socialism." For excerpts of the text of the law for the United States zone, see *Occupation of Germany: Policy and Progress,* pp. 119-20.

75. For comments, see *Occupation of Germany: Policy and Progress,* pp. 16-18; Clay, *Decision,* pp. 68-69; and Plischke, "Denazifying the Reich," pp. 158-59. In part, the criticism of both Germans and American military government personnel was leveled at its arbitrary nature, in that nominal as well as active Nazis were affected, and the nominal could redeem themselves only after removal or exclusion, and through a complicated and delaying review procedure. See Plischke, "Denazifying the Reich," pp. 165-66.

76. According to General Clay, the main reasons for this transfer of responsibility were to implement the program more systematically and comprehensively, to relieve Americans of this massive function at a time when trained personnel were being redeployed, and to enable Germans to pass judgment on their own fellowmen because they "were far better able than we to determine the real Nazi." See Clay, *Decision,* pp. 69-70. For addi-

tional commentary, see Plischke, "Denazification Law and Procedure," pp. 823–25; and Herz, "Fiasco," pp. 571–73.

77. Including the young, born after January 1, 1919, except for fanatics occupying positions of leadership, the disabled, and those whose income during the Hitler regime was so low as to indicate that they did not profit financially from Nazi party affiliation.

78. In September 1944 the military government detachment responsible for recruiting a German administration to govern Aachen, advised by the local German bishop, chose a Bürgermeister who, though not a Nazi party member, was not anti-Nazi, and he set up a rightist regime. Press reaction in the United States roused indignation even in high-level circles. The incident occurred early in the military government experience, and official reaction affected both policy-making in Washington and implementation in the field. For comment, see FitzGibbon, *Denazification,* pp. 88–91; and Zink, *American Military Government in Germany,* pp. 134–35. To make allowances for military necessity during the early phases of military action, a "Cologne Compromise" formula was developed under which a Nazi Bürgermeister would be dismissed although lesser officials could be retained temporarily while metropolitan communities remained within military division or corps areas of control; see Donald B. Robinson, "Why Denazification is Lagging," *American Mercury,* vol. 62 (May 1946), p. 567.

79. General George S. Patton, military governor of Bavaria after the surrender, revealed in press interviews that the administration of German territory would be improved if more former Nazi party members were used, and later, responding to a journalist's question, he gave the impression that in his view Nazis joined their party much as Americans became Republicans and Democrats. Though distorted by the press, the incidents left General Eisenhower little alternative but to transfer Patton. For comment see Murphy, *Diplomat,* pp. 294–95; FitzGibbon, *Denazification,* pp. 91–94. For Patton's comment, see the final paragraphs of George S. Patton, Jr., *War As I Knew It* (Boston: Houghton Mifflin, 1947), pp. 389–90.

80. Murphy, *Diplomat,* p. 285; also see Plischke, "Denazifying the Reich," p. 167.

81. For a summary of the early difficulties, see Plischke, "Denazifying the Reich," pp. 166–71.

82. Murphy, *Diplomat,* p. 287.

83. FitzGibbon, *Denazification,* p. 119.

84. For general comments on the implementation of denazification in the British, French, and Russian zones, see Zink, *United States in Germany,* pp. 165–67, and for some early comparative statistics, see W. Friedman, *The Allied Military Government of Germany* (London: Stevens, 1947), p. 332.

85. According to Harold Zink, this resulted in French cynicism; see *United States in Germany,* p. 166.

86. Allied Control Council Directive No. 38, referred to earlier. For commentary on the French program, see FitzGibbon, *Denazification,* pp. 102–3, 107–9, and for statistical results, see p. 114.

87. FitzGibbon, *Denazification,* pp. 100–101. Although FitzGibbon pro-

vides some statistics, he adds that official figures are not available, and that they would be almost worthless if they were.

88. Such as Herz, "Fiasco," pp. 569–94; Robinson, "Denazification," pp. 563–70; Artur Straeter, "Denazification," *Annals of the American Academy of Political and Social Science,* vol. 260 (Nov. 1948), pp. 43–52.

89. Such as Louis P. Lochner, "The Idiocy of Our Denazification Policy," *Reader's Digest,* vol. 52 (June 1948), pp. 130–36; Griffith, "Denazification," pp. 73–76.

90. Straeter, "Denazification," p. 49.

91. "Denazification—Decommunization," *Commonweal,* vol. 48 (Oct. 1, 1948), p. 585.

92. Lochner, "Idiocy," p. 130.

93. Straeter, "Denazification," p. 43.

94. Lochner, "Idiocy," p. 131.

95. FitzGibbon, *Denazification,* p. 133, quoting General Lucius D. Clay.

96. For commentary, see Max Rheinstein, "The Ghost of the Morgenthau Plan," *Christian Century,* vol. 64 (Apr. 2, 1947), pp. 428–30.

97. FitzGibbon, *Denazification,* p. 184.

98. Lucius D. Clay, *Quarterly Report on Germany,* December 31, 1950, quoted in FitzGibbon, *Denazification,* pp. 137–38.

12. War Crimes Trials and Clemency in Germany and Japan / Mendelsohn

1. Because of poor health, former Foreign Minister Konstantin von Neurath was released in 1954, Grand Admiral Raeder left in 1955, while former Economics Minister Walter Funk was released in 1957, although von Neurath had been sentenced to fifteen years and his two companions to life imprisonment.

2. These cases consisted of:

Case No.	*United States* v.	Popular Name	No. of Defendants
1.	*Karl Brandt et al.*	Medical Case	23
2.	*Erhard Milch*	Milch Case (Luftwaffe)	1
3.	*Josef Alstoetter et al.*	Justice Case	16
4.	*Oswald Pohl et al.*	Pohl Case (SS)	18
5.	*Friedrich Flick et al.*	Flick Case	6
6.	*Carl Krauch et al.*	I. G. Farben Case (Industrialist)	24
7.	*Wilhelm List et al.*	Hostage Case	12
8.	*Ulrich Greifelt et al.*	RuSHA Case (SS)	14
9.	*Otto Ohlendorf et al.*	*Einsatzgruppen* Case (SS)	24

Case No.	*United States* v.	Popular Name	No. of Defendants
10.	*Alfried Krupp*	Krupp Case	12
11.	*Ernst von Weizsaecker et al.*	Ministries Case	21
12.	*Wilhelm von Leeb et al.*	High Command Case	14

Four of the 185 defendants committed suicide (Carl Westphal, Altstoetter Case; Lieutenant General Franz Boehme, List Case; SS Major Emil Haussmann, Ohlendorf Case; and General Johannes Blaskowitz, Leeb Case); four other defendants were physically unable to stand trial (Karl Engert, Altstoetter Case; Max Brueggemann, Krauch Case; Field Marshall Maximilian von Weichs, List Case; and SS Brigadier General Otto Rasch, Ohlendorf Case).

3. *Complete list of War Crimes Case Trials,* HQ EUCOM, Office of the Judge Advocate, National Archives and Records Service (hereafter NARS), Record Group (hereafter RG) 153, Records of the Judge Advocate Army. Hereafter cited as *Complete List.* See also National Archives Microfilm Publication Pamphlet M 1106, hereafter NAMP.

4. Trials of Class "B" and Class "C" War Criminals, *SCAP Monograph No. 5,* Supreme Commander Allied Powers, History of the Nonmilitary Activities of the Occupation of Japan, 1945–51. NARS, RG 331, Records of Allied Occupational and Operational Headquarters, World War II. Hereafter cited as *SCAP Monograph No. 5.*

5. John Mendelsohn, "Trial by Document: The Problem of Due Process for War Criminals at Nuernberg," *Prologue* 7, no. 4 (Winter 1975): 230.

6. Ibid.

7. *United States of America* v. *Martin Gottfried Weiss et al.,* Case 000-50-2, *Complete List,* pp. 29–30. See also NAMP M 1174.

8. *United States of America* v. *Arthur Kurt Andrae et al.,* Case 000-50-37, *Complete List,* p. 54. See also NAMP M 1079.

9. *SCAP Monograph No. 5,* p. 89.

10. A. Frank Reel, *The Case of General Yamashita* (Chicago: Univ. of Chicago Press, 1949), pp. 210–31, 251–324.

11. Ibid.

12. Douglas MacArthur, *Reminiscences* (New York: McGraw-Hill Book Company, 1964), p. 269.

13. Telford Taylor, *Nuremberg and Vietnam: An American Tragedy* (New York: Bantam Books, 1971), p. 53.

14. *United States of America* v. *Josias Prince Zu Waldeck et al.,* Case 000-50-9 in *Complete List,* p. 53.

15. Cable by Clay to Department of the Army, Sept. 27, 1948, in *The Papers of Lucius D. Clay: Germany 1945–1949,* ed. Jean Edward Smith, 2 vols. (Bloomington, Indiana: Indiana Univ. Press, 1974) vol. 2, p. 881. Hereafter cited as *Clay Papers.*

16. Cable by Clay to Royall, Oct. 2, 1948, *Clay Papers,* pp. 888–89.

17. Interim Report of the Investigations Subcommittee of the Committee on Expenditures in the Executive Departments pursuant to Senate Resolution 189, Dec. 27, 1948, Report No. 1775, Part 3, Eightieth Congress, Second Session, *Senate Reports,* vol. 4 (Washington, D.C.: GPO, 1948).

18. Ibid., p. 22.

19. Telephone interview with Judge Robert L. Kunzig in Washington, D.C., Jan. 22, 1979. Hereafter cited as Kunzig Interview.

20. *Washington Post,* Jan. 16, 1957.

21. Kunzig Interview.

22. *United States of America* vs. *Valentin Bersin et al.,* Case 6-24, *Complete List,* pp. 2–3.

23. *Malmedy Massacre Investigation Hearings before a Subcommittee of the Committee on Armed Services, United States Senate, Eighty-First Congress, First Session, pursuant to S. Res. 42,* p. 3. Hereafter cited as *Malmedy Hearings.*

24. *Complete List,* pp. 2–3.

25. *Malmedy Massacre Hearings, Report of the Subcommittee of the Committee on Armed Services, United States Senate, Eighty-First Congress, First Session, pursuant to S. Res. 42,* pp. 4–20. Hereafter cited as *Malmedy Report.*

26. *Malmedy Hearings,* p. 98.

27. *Malmedy Report,* pp. 34–35.

28. Message by Commander in Chief, U.S. Army in Europe, to Commander in Chief, Europe, Paris, June 11, 1958, Administrative Files Mixed Board, NARS, RG 338, Records of the United States Army Commands, 1942–, Boxes 148–50.

29. Report of the Simpson Commission including tabs, September 14, 1948, NARS, RG 335, Records of the Office of the Secretary of the Army, OSA File .0005.

30. Staff Announcement No. 117, 7-18-50, HICOG Clemency Board Files, National Archives Collection of War Crimes Records, NARS, RG 238, Box 2.

31. Ibid.

32. Introduction to Report and Report of HICOG Clemency Board to the High Commissioner. 8-28-50. HICOG Clemency Board Files, NARS, RG 238, Box 2.

33. *Trials of War Criminals under Control Council Law No. 10 Nuernberg 1946–1949,* 15 vols. (Washington, D.C.: GPO, 1949–53), vol. 15, pp. 1176–91. Hereafter cited as *TWC.*

34. According to the recently discovered report of the High Commissioner's Clemency Board, McCloy was very generous, to the *Einsatzgruppen* in particular, in extending commutations of at least three death sentences to them, where his board had recommended no clemency. See also note 33.

35. *United States of America* v. *Oswald Pohl et al.* Case 4. See also NAMP M 890.

36. *TWC,* vol. 15, p. 1184.

37. *United States of America* v. *Wilhelm von Leeb et al.* Case 12. See also NAMP M 898.

38. *TWC,* vol. 15, p. 1184.

39. Parolee Files of Nuernberg Prisoners at Landsberg, EUCOM War Crimes Files, NARS, RG 338.

40. "Current West German views on the War Criminals Issue," Report No. 153, Series 2, 9-8-52, Issued by HICOG Office of Public Affairs Reaction Staff and Administrative Files, Interim Board, NARS, RG 338, Boxes 148–50.

41. Especially the Ilse Koch and the Malmedy Massacre Trial Investigations resulted in an unusually critical attitude toward Army conduct of the war crimes trials, fueled by McCarthy's attacks on the Army.

42. Report of the Deputy Judge Advocate for War Crimes European Command, June 1944 to July 1948, NARS, RG 153.

43. The EUCOM Modification Board was composed of five senior officers in the Command: the director of personnel and administration (chairman), the adjutant general (JAG), the inspector general, the provost marshal and the director of intelligence.

44. Memo by Major Joseph L. Haefele of the War Crimes Section of the Judge Advocate General, EUCOM, to the Acting Judge Advocate General on a conference with HICOG (High Commissioner for Germany) on War Crimes, Aug. 5, 1950, Administrative Files HQ USAREUR, Judge Advocate Division, Internal Affairs Branch, NARS, RG 338, Boxes 148–50. Hereafter cited as Haefele Memo.

45. Memorandum of the Judge Advocate General to the Secretary of the Army on the functions of the Modification Board, 7-18-49, Administrative Records, Modification Board, NARS, RG 338, Boxes 148–50.

46. Haefele Memo.

47. Ibid.

48. History of the Army War Crime Program in Europe, Administrative Records, Modification Board, NARS, RG 338, Boxes 148–50. Hereafter cited as History.

49. Haefele Memo.

50. Ibid.

51. Summary of War Crimes, Clemency and Parole Program during operation of IMPAC Board, Administrative Files, IMPAC Board, NARS, RG 338, Boxes 148–50.

52. *War Crimes Trials Records of Case 9, United States of America* v. *Otto Ohlendorf et al. Nuernberg, Special List No. 42,* comp. John Mendelsohn (Washington, D.C.: National Archives and Records Service, 1978), p. 3.

53. History.

54. History.

55. *Selected Data on the Occupation of Japan prepared by General Headquarters SCAP and the Far East Command* (No place: FEC Printing Plant, 1950), p. 83.

56. *New York Times,* Dec. 31, 1958.

57. Letter by War Crimes Branch (JAGO) to EUCOM, May 17, 1954, Administrative Records USAREUR, NARS, RG 338, Boxes 148–50.

58. SCAP Circular No. 5, "Clemency for War Criminals," Mar. 7, 1950, NARS, RG 331, Box 1394.

59. Ibid.

60. Minutes of the first meeting of Parole Board, Mar. 17, 1950, NARS, RG 331, Box 1394.

61. Ibid.

62. Sugamo Prison Files, NARS, RG 338, Box 80.

63. Instructions for Parole Supervisors, Records of the NOPAR Commission, NARS, RG 331, Box 1394.

64. Ibid.

65. "Executive Order establishing a Clemency and Parole Board for War Criminals," published in *Department of State Bulletin,* Mar. 15, 1952, pp. 408–9.

66. "Executive Order 19747 Designating the Secretary of State to Act for the United States in Certain Matters Pertaining to Japanese War Criminals," published in *Department of State Bulletin,* Jan. 20, 1958, p. 94.

67. *Christian Science Monitor,* Dec. 14, 1957.

68. *New York Times,* Dec. 31, 1958.

69. *Time,* Sept. 26, 1955, p. 31.

70. Ibid.

71. *Sentences in Trials of the Major War Criminals before the International Military Tribunal, Nuremberg, 14 November 1945–1 October 1946,* 42 vols. (Nuremberg: old Streicher Press, 1947–49), vol. 23, pp. 588–89 and *TWC,* vol. 14, pp. 1003–4.

13. Civil Censorship and Media Control in Early Occupied Japan: From Minimum to Stringent Surveillance / Mayo

1. No one has done more to draw attention to the question of civil censorship in occupied Japan, especially press and literary censorship, than Eto Jun, essayist, literary and social critic, and professor of comparative literature and culture at the Tokyo Institute of Technology. In numerous papers given in the United States, 1979–80, while he was a fellow of the East Asia Program at the Wilson Center, Washington, D.C., he discussed the impact of censorship on the Japanese collectively and on individual Japanese. A full-scale study of American civil censorship operations in Japan has been undertaken by Professor Furukawa Atsushi of the Tokyo College of Economics, using the files of the Press, Publications, and Pictorial Branch, Civil Censorship Detachment (PPB, CCD) in the Prange Collection, McKeldin Library, University of Maryland; CCD records at the National Records Center, Suitland, Maryland; and the Joint Chiefs of Staff materials at the National Archives. I wish to thank both professors Eto and Furukawa for

sharing materials, insights, and copies of papers and articles. Thus far, very little work has been done on the counterpart problem of media guidance and propaganda controls in occupied Japan. For the larger and necessary historical context of prewar and wartime domestic censorship and dissemination of propaganda in Japan, see Ben-Ami Shilloney, *Politics and Culture in Wartime Japan* (Oxford: Clarendon Press, 1981), parts 4 and 5; Gordon Daniels, "Japanese Domestic Radio and Cinema Propaganda, 1937–1945: An Overview," *Historical Journal of Film, Radio and Television*, 2, no. 2 (1982): 115–32; and the recent monograph by Richard H. Mitchell, *Censorship in Imperial Japan* (Princeton: Princeton Univ. Press, 1983). On the American side, there is the pioneering study by Allan W. Winkler, *The Politics of Propaganda: The Office of War Information, 1942–1945* (New Haven: Yale Univ. Press, 1978) and Robert William Pirsein's *The Voice of America: An History of the International Broadcasting Activities of the United States Government, 1940–1962* (New York: Arno Press reprint, 1979).

2. National Archives, Record Group (hereafter NA, RG) 59, "Conditions for Japanese Surrender to the United Nations" (Document 18a, May 27, 1942; revised Oct. 2, 1942), Notter File, Box 76; NA, RG 165, CAD 091.1, Pence to Hilldring, Sept. 24, 1943, forwarding "Directive on Military Government for the Japanese Island of Hokkaido" (1-1-47) (1). The basic reference for the work of the Advisory Committee on Post-War Foreign Policy, 1942–43, is Harley A. Notter, *Postwar Foreign Policy Preparation, 1939–1945* (Washington, D.C.: Government Printing Office, 1950).

3. FM 27-5, Dec. 22, 1943 (copy in NA, RG 407, Modern Military Headquarters Branch). The 1940 edition had also made clear provision for censorship. "It is forbidden to send, transmit, or knowingly to receive by any means of communication whatever any information concerning the American forces, their location, numbers, morale, arms, equipment, or movements, or the identity of units of such forces" or "any message containing anything hostile, detrimental, or disrespectful to the United States, its armed forces, their personnel, or the military government" (p. 37). On the media specifically, the earlier manual stated: "*Publication* is forbidden in any newspaper, magazine, book, leaflet, poster, or otherwise of any printed, typed, or written matter . . . which is hostile, detrimental, or disrespectful to the United States, its armed forces, or their personnel, or tends to promote dissatisfaction or bad feelings with them."

4. NA, RG 218, CCS 000.73 (6-26-43), Section 1, containing CCS 271 series, "Definition of United States and British Responsibility for Censorship of Civilian Communications in Eur-African Areas"; and Memorandum to Commanding Generals (26 Aug. 1943), especially attachment 2 (no date), "Censorship of Civilian Communications in Territory Occupied or Controlled by the Armed Forces." Military censorship as distinct from civilian censorship covered communications to or from military personnel. The United States Office of Censorship had been set up by Executive Order 8985 on December 19, 1941, under the First War Powers Act. Its director, Byron Price, was an experienced newsman and had been executive director of As-

sociated Press prior to the war. He was to receive a Pulitzer Prize in 1944 for his development of voluntary newspaper and radio censorship codes. Censorship ended in the United States on August 15, 1945, and the office was abolished the following November 15. For a record of American wartime censorship, see NA, RG 216, "A History of the Office of Censorship," seven manuscript volumes.

5. NA, RG 218, CCS 000.73 (6-26-43), Sections 1 and 2, JCS 873 series, "Censorship of Civilian Communications in Pacific-Asiatic Theaters." Leahy's letter to Price had been drafted by CAD, which coordinated its recommendations with military and naval intelligence officers. Within the military, the operational responsibility for civil censorship was assigned to intelligence—and subsequently to counterintelligence.

6. Price to Leahy, Sept. 11, 1944, enclosure in JCS 873/2, Sept. 25, 1944, in CCS 000.73 (6-26-43). The Army-Navy planning assumptions for 1944 recognized that the governance of land masses was primarily the Army's military government responsibility. In the Japanese-language and area civil affairs training courses which went into operation, 1944–45, 75 percent of the officers were Army and 25 percent Navy.

7. NA, RG 165, OPD 000.73, Section II-A, Case 47, memorandum of Aug. 24, 1944, on "Civil Censorship in Japan."

8. JCS 873/3, Nov. 12, 1944, in CCS 000.73 (6-26-43), Section 2; JCS Policy Memorandum, No. 4, Nov. 28, 1944, in OPD 000.73, II-A, Case 47.

9. NA, RG 165, CAD 353 (8-8-43), Section 5, "Plan for Civil Censorship in Japan," Dec. 27, 1945, and attached documents (especially "General Plan for Civil Censorship in Japan," Nov. 24, 1944); and OPD 000.73, II-A, Case 47. The approved plan was sent to the director of military training in early January 1945.

10. The failure to make explicit provision for press and radio censorship in the first detailed plan for Japan is puzzling, unless as previously suggested the original intention was to assign the operational responsibility to public relations rather than to intelligence. Another document drawn up at about this time, "General Order No. 2" (Subannex 3 of "Surrender Terms for Japan," Dec. 27, 1944), called for the censorship of the press and cessation of all electrical means of communications under Japanese control. This was the work of the Joint Post-War Committee, JCS, chaired by General Strong; see United States, Department of State, *Foreign Relations of the United States, 1945,* vol. 5 (Washington, D.C.: Government Printing Office, 1969), pp. 512–13 (hereafter *FRUS*).

11. Notter File, Box 57, Document P-213, "Agenda for the Meeting of March 13, 1943," and attachment, "General Problems of the Far East," Mar. 8, 1943. The Subcommittee on Political Problems was chaired by Undersecretary of State Sumner Welles; the research secretary was Harley Notter.

12. Blakeslee statement in Minutes, Subcommittee on Territorial Studies (chaired by Isaiah Bowman, president of Johns Hopkins University), July 30, 1943 (Notter File, Box 59). See also Blakeslee's "Japan: General Principles Applicable to the Post-War Settlement with Japan," T-357, July 28,

1943 (and revised version of Sept. 29, 1943), Notter File, Box 64. Borton's opinions and recommendations are in "Political and Economic Aspects of the Surrender of Japan," T-366, Sept. 27, 1943; and "Japan: Postwar Political Problems," T-381, Oct. 6, 1943 (both in Notter File, Box 64).

13. PWC Minutes of Apr. 27, 1944 (Secretary of State Hull presiding), Notter File, Box 140.

14. CAC 167 preliminary a, "Germany: Occupation Period: Re-education," May 4, 1944, views of the Interdivisional Committee on Germany (Notter File, Box 110).

15. Document CAC 185b, May 9, *FRUS, 1944,* vol. 5 (Washington, D.C.: Government Printing Office, 1965), pp. 1257-60 (for preliminary drafts, see Notter File, Box 111); CAC 116b, May 4, 1944 (Notter, *Postwar Foreign Policy Preparation,* pp. 591-92.

16. CAC 237 preliminary a, "Japan: Occupation: Media of Public Information and Expression," July 7, 1944 (Notter File, Box 112). Johansen had been appointed a Japanese-language officer in 1935 and subsequently served in consular posts at Yokohama, Harbin, and Tientsin. IDACFE accepted the paper with little comment; Minutes, July 8, 1944 (National Archives, Microfilm Publication T-1197).

17. Assistant Secretary of War John J. McCloy to General John Hilldring, director, CAD, Oct. 26, 1944, in NA, RG 107, ASW 370.8, file on "Germany—Long Term Policy."

18. Buss to Owen Lattimore, July 31, 1944, in National Records Center (hereafter NRC), Suitland, Maryland, RG 208, Box 3104; MacLeish to Byrnes, July 4, 1945 (RG 59, 862.42/7-445); Davis, draft statement to Hull, Dec. 26, 1942 (NRC, RG 208, Entry 1, Box 5); Davis to Truman, July 4, 1945, in *FRUS, Conference of Berlin (Potsdam), 1945,* vol. 1 (Washington, D.C.: Government Printing Office, 1960), 487-88. MacLeish had written earlier, July 1, in an emotion-laden note to a friend in the State Department that the crucial job ahead was "to change the German people somehow—to undo the satanic work of Nazism by some means." He believed fervently that Americans had "a duty now not only to occupy and police and feed and punish, but to convert and to persuade. If we believe in the forces which have created us as a nation, it should not shock us to face that fact and act upon it"; NA, RG 59, 740.00119 Control (Germany)/7/145. For MacLeish's views and OWI career, see Winkler, *Politics of Propaganda,* pp. 9-13, 15-16, 24, 32-38.

19. Jane Alden to C. Martin Wilbur, Oct. 21, 1944; and undated memorandum, "Civil Affairs Guide: Japan: Public Relations Problems" (both in NA, RG 226, R&A 2362 folder).

20. IDACFE, Minutes of Nov. 14, 1944, together with Annex A and Annex B; and Minutes of Nov. 15, 1944, and Annex A (in microfilm T-1197). Maxwell Hamilton, former chief of the Division of Far Eastern Affairs, State Department, 1937-43, took the leading role in stiffening the policy. He was then special assistant to the secretary of state and would shortly be appointed minister to Helsinki. The revised final paper, PWC 288b, Nov. 1,

1944, is in the Notter File, Box 144. A convenient source on the origins and organization of SWNCC is "The State-War-Navy Coordinating Committee," *Department of State Bulletin,* vol. 13 (Nov. 11, 1945), 745–47.

21. SWNCC 91, "Control of Media of Public Information and Expression in Japan," Apr. 7, 1945 (National Archives, Microfilm Publication, T-1205, Roll 4); RG 59, 740.00119 Control (Japan)/5-1745, summary of meeting on May 17, 1945, to discuss postwar control of information in Japan; RG 208, Box 66, memorandum, John K. Fairbank to George Taylor, May 1945, on postcombat information program in Japan. Prior to joining the State Department in 1941, Begg had worked in radio and educational film production and in motion picture advertising. In his review of Johansen's IDACFE paper the preceding November, Begg had voiced opposition to restoring broadcasting facilities in Japan to a government monopoly and recommended instead the breakup of the Japanese system into separately owned stations; RG 59, 740.00119 Control (Japan)/11-344.

22. War Department cables to MacArthur, notifying him of his new command designation and of his responsibilities for military government and civil censorship in Japan, April–May, are conveniently located at the MacArthur Memorial (Norfolk, Virginia), RG 4, USAFPAC, Correspondence Series, War Department, Box 17. For CCD and the Philippines, see MacArthur Memorial, RG 23, Willoughby papers, Intelligence Series, vol. 10, *Operations of Military and Civil Censorship, USAFFE/SWPA/AFPAC/ FEC* (GHQ, Far East Command, Military Intelligence Section, General Staff, 1950), pp. 36–54. As a captain, Hoover had briefly headed the Press and Pictorial Section under the chief postal censor, United States Office of Censorship, 1942 ("A History of the Office of Censorship," vol. 4, p. 147).

23. MacArthur Memorial, RG 23, Intelligence Series, vol. 10, Documentary Appendices, no. 41, "Basic Plan for Civil Censorship in Japan," Apr. 20, 1945. At that point, CCD was under the operational and policy control of the assistant chief of staff, G-2, AFPAC. The only passages relevant to media control in this plan stated: "Civil Censorship will have censorship jurisdiction over all civilian communications. This jurisdiction does not include censorship of communications to or from Allied military personnel or civilians who are part of, or directly attached to, [the] military establishment of the United Nations, nor does it include the censorship of press communications or radio broadcast scripts which in this theatre are the responsibility of the Public Relations Office, GHQ. It is, however, the function of the Civil Relations, to insure that electrical communications of the latter type have been censored by the appropriate authority before passage through civilian channels." CCD, USAFFE (United States, Army Forces Far East), special report on Japanese censorship in the Philippines, Jan. 14, 1945, is in RG 208, Box 446.

24. NRC, RG 331, Box 8568, "Basic Plan for Civil Censorship in Japan," July 10, 1945, approved by Deputy Chief of Staff, AFPAC, July 27, 1945 (in this plan, CCD was placed under the operational and policy control of the chief of counterintelligence, AFPAC, GHQ); MacArthur Memorial, RG 23, Intelligence Series, 9, *Operations of the Civil Intelligence Section, GHQ,*

FEC and SCAP, Appendix no. 42, "Plan for Japan in Event of Capitulation (Blacklist Operations)," July 9, 1945; and attached "Plan for Civil Censorship—Kyushu," drafted by Hoover.

25. SWNCC 150, in *FRUS, 1945,* vol. 6, pp. 545–54; SWNCC 150/4/A, reprinted in *Department of State Bulletin,* vol. 13 (Sept. 23, 1945), 423–27.

26. CAD draft directive, June 11, 1945, in NA, RG 43, Box 3; Basic Directive, drafts of Aug. 22 and Aug. 25, 1945, in Microfilm, T-1205, roll 2.

27. FRUS, *Conference of Berlin (The Potsdam Conference), 1945,* vol. 2, p. 1474.

28. SWNCC 162/D, July 19, 1945, "Positive Policy for Reorientation of the Japanese," in RG 165, ABC 014 Japan (April 13, 1944), Section 4-2. Gates, a longtime personal friend of Secretary Forrestal, was a banker and a former vice-president and president of Time, Inc., before joining the Navy Department in September 1941. Just who drafted this statement for Gates is for the present a mystery. For the follow-up work by Borton and Bowles, see Notter File, Box 119, Minutes of the Subcommittee on the Far East, SWNCC, Microfilm Publication, T-1198; SWNCC Minutes, Microfilm Publication, T-1194; SFE 116 series and SWNCC 162 series, Microfilm, T-1205, roll 4; and SWNCC 162/2, January 8, 1945, *FRUS, 1946,* vol. 8 (Washington: Government Printing Office, 1971), 105–9. Eisenhower's directive (JCS 1067) is in *Department of State Bulletin,* vol. 13 (Oct. 7, 1945), 538–45.

29. RG 165, CAD 014 Japan (7-8-42) (1), Section 3.

30. Fellers' activities and recommendations to MacArthur, 1943–45, are documented in the Fellers Collection, Hoover Institution Archives, Stanford University.

31. MacArthur Memorial, RG 4, USAFPAC, War Department, Box 17, Cable from CINCAFPAC to Crist, July 25, 1945; RG 4, Operations, Beleaguer-Blacklist, Box 38, "Basic Plan for Institution of Military Government, Blacklist Operations (tentative), Military Government Annex," Aug. 6, 1945; GHQ, USAFPAC, Military Government Section, "Report of Military Government in Japan and Korea," Oct. 10, 1945, and GHQ, SCAP, "Report of the Military Government Section, General Headquarters, United States Army Forces, Pacific," covering the period 5 August to 2 October 1945 inclusive, both in the Justin Williams papers, Prange Collection, McKeldin Library, University of Maryland. The model military government annex (drafted by CAD the War Department, Washington, with the help of Lieutenant Colonel Edgar G. Crossman, confidant of Stimson and a member of MacArthur's civil affairs staff in the Philippines) did not contain details on civil censorship since that was a function of military intelligence. For intelligence planning in Manila, see MacArthur Memorial, RG 23, Intelligence Series, 9, Documentary Appendices II, "Basic Intelligence Plan," Annex 5d, Aug. 14, 1945, Blacklist Operations. An earlier document, "Counter Intelligence Operations," USAFPAC, July 24, 1945, repeated that the jurisdiction of the civil censorship detachments did not "include the censorship of press communications or radio broadcast scripts which are the responsibility of the Public Relations agencies" (Hoover Institution Archives, Fellers papers, Box 14).

32. RG 208, Item 392, Box 599; Sidney Hyman, *The Many Lives of William Benton* (Chicago: Univ. of Chicago Press, 1964); Pirsein, *Voice of America,* pp. 100–114.

33. Fellers papers, Box 13, "Plan for an Information Control Service in Japan"; RG 208, Box 598, Bradford Smith's report of Nov. 8, 1945. A Columbia graduate, Smith had taught English, 1931–36, at Tokyo Imperial University and at Rikkyo University. This Manila outpost plan seems to have had some influence on Fellers and Greene, although Smith did not think so. The five objectives of information control were: "to promote cooperation with Military Government, to assist in the orderly transition from war to peace, to assist in destroying the influence of militarism in Japanese life, to assist in strengthening democratic tendencies in Japan, to create the conditions under which Japan can ultimately choose her own form of government according to the terms of the Potsdam Declaration." The contemplated information controls were "to assure that nothing shall appear in the press or on the radio to prevent the orderly occupation of Japan" and to help channel proclamations and military orders. They should "stimulate the output of accurate information" and "prohibit the publication of irresponsible material." Dōmei, the plan recommended, should carry over its national wire service only news cleared by a press control officer; one central radio station should originate all broadcasts, with all programs approved in advance by a radio control officer. The press should adhere to a set of principles proclaimed by the supreme commander; violations would be punishable by suspension. Since "the Japanese press of the past with its servility, corruption and lack of standards played a prominent part in leading Japan into war," it would be necessary to raise the quality of Japanese journalism. Finally, "publication of worthwhile democratic materials such as the lives of democratic leaders, methods of representative government and the development of western civilization should be encouraged." This would require a file of approved world news, an information library, and the importation of certain foreign publications. There would be "freer expression of opinion than has hitherto existed" if not total freedom. The aim was to allow press and radio discussion of issues by all interested parties, not a few groups. Avoidance of statements which might agitate the people or stir up resentment should "not prevent responsible discussion of problems relating to Military Government, Japanese politics, or persons in public or private life whose actions have a bearing on the welfare of the Japanese people." This OWI outpost plan, however, tended to confuse censorship and guidance and would require some rethinking.

34. Aug. 15 and Aug. 22 studies in Fellers papers, Box 13; Annex to Operations Instructions No. 4, Information Dissemination Section, Aug. 27, 1945, Fellers papers, Box 3. Crist had arrived in Manila August 20, presumably with a raft of draft policy planning documents. This may have included a July 27 study by G2 propaganda branch on the personnel and organizational requirements for information control in Japan. NRC RG 319, MID 385 Psychological, Entry 47, Box 598.

35. MacArthur Memorial, RG 9, Messages, War Department, Blue Binder

Series, cables of Aug. 18, 1945 (another copy in NA, RG 200, Sutherland papers, War Department, Box 3, carries Diller's initials) and of Aug. 22. Intelligence Series, 10, states: "It had been planned that censorship of the media of mass communications would be undertaken in Japan by Public Relations personnel and the Office of War Information," Radio Tokyo, for example, and the press. "Further reflection, however, determined that a considerable monitoring job might be necessary and that CCD assistance probably would be requested. . . . If CCD was to be expected to provide personnel to aid in censoring radio and the press, it was logical that the CCO [Civil Censorship Officer] assume responsibility for the entire operation" (p. 58). This explanation, however, obfuscates as much as it explains since the OWI was a propaganda and psychological warfare outfit and not trained for censorship. Diller was known to war correspondents as "Killer Diller," and the MacArthur public relations staff in general, according to William Coughlin, was thought of as "bigoted, insolent, uncooperative, and dictatorial," *Conquered Press: The MacArthur Era in Japanese Journalism* (Palo Alto: Pacific Books, 1952), p. 111. In his diary entry for June 17, 1945, President Truman refers to "Mr. Prima Donna, Brass Hat, Five Star MacArthur. He's worse than the Cabots and the Lodges—they at least talked with one another before they told God what to do. MacArthur tells God right off." If Roosevelt had let MacArthur be captured by the Japanese and ordered Wainright home, then "we'd have had a real General and a fighting man" and "not a play actor and a bunco man such as we have now"; see *Off the Record: The Private Papers of Harry S Truman,* ed. by Robert H. Ferrell (New York: Harper & Row, 1980), p. 47.

36. RG 226, R&A 2362, "Public Information in Japan," Aug. 10, 1945, and document 133722, "Relaxation of Censorship under Suzuki," June 1945 (the source was a Thai traveler from Tokyo considered to be highly reliable); and "Outline Notes on Japanese Public Information Facilities," in RG 208, Entry 370, Box 403.

37. SFE 118 series, "Control of Media of Public Information and Expression in Japan," in Microfilm T-1205, Roll 4.

38. Draft directive, together with covering letter, Taylor to MacLeish, Aug. 15, 1945 (Microfilm T-1205, Roll 4); War Department cable to MacArthur (MacArthur Memorial, RG 9, Messages, Blue Binder Series). MacLeish, then on the eve of leaving office, was involved in facilitating the incorporation of the OWI into the State Department and in work preparatory to persuading Congress to fund a peacetime information service; see SC-161, "United States Government International Information Service after the War," Aug. 13, 1945, and covering letter from MacLeish to Secretary Byrnes of the same day (Library of Congress, MacLeish papers, Box 31). In a press release which accompanied Truman's executive order, transferring the OWI to the State Department, Aug. 31, 1945, the president stated that "the nature of present-day foreign relations makes it essential for the United States to maintain informational activities abroad as an integral part of the conduct of our foreign affairs." The role of the government would be to "supplement" private information agencies in seeing to it that

"other peoples receive a full and fair picture of American life and of the aims of the United States Government"; *Department of State Bulletin,* vol. 323 (Sept. 2, 1945), p. 306.

39. Exchange of cables, MacArthur Memorial, RG 9, Messages, Blue Binder Series; Intelligence Series, 10, p. 58.

40. MacArthur Memorial, RG 9, Messages, Blue Binder Series (Aug. 28 is the incoming date).

41. MacArthur Memorial, RG 5, SCAP, Correspondence, Box 1 (Japanese Surrender File No. 2, folder 7).

42. SCAP monographs, unpublished, History of the Non-Military Activities of the Occupation of Japan, "Radio Broadcasting," p. 2, and "Freedom of the Press," pp. 5–8, which effusively credits MacArthur with the "unprecedented" decision of permitting the press to function without cessation and calling it a "unique sociological experiment" (NRC, microfilm); Intelligence Series, 10, p. 55 and documentary appendix no. 23 (Check sheet, Thorpe to Deputy Chief of Staff, Sept. 3, 1945); Elliot Thorpe, *East Wind, Rain: The Intimate Account of an Intelligence Officer in the Pacific, 1939–1949* (Boston: Gambit, 1969), pp. 191–92, in which Thorpe takes credit for persuading MacArthur to keep Dōmei in continuous operation.

43. Coughlin, *Conquered Press,* pp. 4–5, 7–8, 16, 18, 113; "Radio Broadcasting," pp. 7–8; *New York Times,* Sept. 9, 1945; Shilloney, *Politics and Culture in Wartime Japan,* p. 109. Japanese journalist Iwanaga Shinkichi (whose father was Iwanaga Yukichi, first president of Dōmei) argues that these statements by the Cabinet Board of Information and the prime minister were simply "gestures on the part of the government in view of the imminent arrival of the Allied forces and nothing more meaningful than that," in *Story of Japanese News Agencies* (Tokyo: Shimbun Tsūshin Chōsa-kai, 1980), p. 78.

44. Coughlin, *Conquered Press,* pp. 18, 20–21, and appendix A, p. 147; "Radio Broadcasting," p. 9; History Compilation Room, Radio & TV Culture Research Institute, Nippon Hōsō Kyōkai, *The History of Broadcasting in Japan* (Tokyo: Nippon Hōsō Kyōkai, 1967), pp. 147–48; Intelligence Series, 10, p. 133 and documentary appendix no. 22. The latter source argues in retrospect that the code was too much of "a catch-all designed to cover, and forbid, any news item whose suppression was desired, for whatever reasons." It did not give adequate and realistic guidance either to the Japanese media or to the SCAP censors as to what was forbidden. Point two in particular, "Nothing shall be printed which might, directly or by inference, disturb the public tranquility," was "at the least, badly phrased. All news items are designed to prick and disturb 'public tranquility.' Any news item that did not do so would not be read. Perhaps the addition of the word 'inflammatory,' in some connotation, would have clarified this point" (p. 216).

45. "Freedom of the Press," pp. 9–10, 22–23; Intelligence Series, 10, pp. 55, 66, 73–74, 108, 133–34. The SCAP intelligence volume on censorship operations (prepared under the direction of General Charles Willoughby

and reflecting his biases and differences of opinion with other staff officers) makes numerous references to Japanese unreliability, amounting almost to a diatribe. It asserts, "The initial hostility of nationalistic Japanese editors, producers, and broadcasters necessitated pre-censorship, and the immaturity and inability of their associates and successors to accept public responsibility caused its continuance, for nearly three years" (p. 116); "It had been planned that the Japanese media would undergo a mild and non-restrictive surveillance and rehabilitation, but die-hard editors grew increasingly bold in their efforts to discredit the Occupation" (pp. 120–21). PPB was organized into several divisions: Press and Publications, to deal with newspapers, magazines, books, and pamphlets; Pictorial, handling motion pictures, theatrical productions, lantern slides, and *kamishibai* (picture-story shows); Broadcast, for radio; and Research, a unit set up for propaganda confiscation, including presurrender books, magazines, and films (Intelligence Series, 10, p. 73). At first, the radio censors apparently examined only English translations of scripts and did not check live broadcasts (see letter of Bradford Smith, Nov. 8, 1945, in NRC, RG 208, Item 392, Box 598).

46. NA, RG 457, MAGIC diplomatic Summaries, No. 1255, Sept. 1, 1945, No. 1269, Sept. 15, 1945, and No. 1271, Sept. 17, 1945; Coughlin, pp. 20, 111–17. NHK's request, Sept. 14, to resume overseas Japanese language broadcasts was denied by SCAP; see "Radio Broadcasting," p. 9 and appendix 6.

47. Lafe F. Allen, "Effect of Allied Occupation on the Press of Japan," *Journalism Quarterly* (Dec. 1947), pp. 323–31, citing skeptical accounts in the *New York Times*; William Coughlin, *Conquered Press,* pp. 15–17, 48, who adds that Radio Tokyo, even before September 2, had broadcast reports that American sailors had raped Japanese women; "Press Freedom in Japan," pp. 9–10, 23, which also states that Dōmei on September 4, after reporting several cases of American brutality and looting, advised Japanese women "as a last resort" in self-defense to "bite, scratch, and tear off insignia to be used as evidence" and in general warned the public not to display watches or fountain pens; Intelligence Series, 10, p. 107. Once again, the intelligence volume is at pains to justify the censorship, referring to a "torrent of open slander" (p. 108), "slanderous press accounts" (p. 122), and an old guard which "bent every effort to incite among the Japanese people fear and hatred of the Occupation" (p. 107). "One must remember," it declares, "that the Japanese had been carefully bent and twisted by years of thought control," reaching "into all phases of Japanese life" (p. 106, footnote 12), making it inevitable that CCD's work would be "educative" as well as "preventive" (p. 108). Frank L. Kluckhohn, reporting from Yokohama, wrote in the *New York Times Sunday Magazine,* Sept. 9, 1945, that "so far our army has conducted itself with amazing decorum and lack of display of any strong antagonism" ("First Impressions of Conquered Japan"); and the MAGIC diplomatic summary for Sept. 10, 1945, quotes Foreign Minister Shigemitsu as reassuring Japan's representatives in Europe: "Up to the present (4 September) the occupation of the Japanese mainland by the Allied Armies has

gone along smoothly. Although there have been a number of unfortunate acts on the part of individual American soldiers, nothing inauspicious on a large scale has occurred." Whatever the facts, MacArthur took notice of the existing and potential problem, ordering the commanding general of the 8th Army, Sept. 6, to take steps to prevent the recurrence of incidents involving occupation troops, such as annoying women and children, insulting the civil police, or entering civilian dwellings (NRC, RG 331, Box 763). In a memorandum to the Japanese, Oct. 3, 1945, SCAP promised to apprehend and punish violators and asked for assistance in gathering evidence against alleged offenders (RG 165, CAD 014 Japan [Oct. 3–Dec. 10, 1945]). Even if the first troops were disciplined and well-behaved, MacArthur's military police would need to remain alert. As Robert Jay Lifton reminds his readers, "Exemplary conduct on the part of American troops could last just so long, and there soon appeared the inevitable collusion between groups of occupiers and occupied in prostitution, narcotics, and petty crime"; he alludes to a "wide gamut of GI abuse of Japanese, from humiliating shows of prejudice or contempt to physical violence and murder" (*Death in Life: Survivors of Hiroshima* [New York: Random House, 1967], p. 329). Presumably, none of this seamy news eluded the censors.

48. Hoover's speech is reprinted (with slight variations) in Coughlin, *Conquered Press,* appendix B, pp. 148–49. His comments were released to the press and published in the *New York Times,* Sept. 16, where they were read by none other than Elmer Davis, who was distressed to learn in addition that day that the *Chicago Tribune* had started publication in Tokyo. "Colonel Donald Hoover," he wrote to the secretary of war, "speaking for General MacArthur, yesterday warned the directors of the Japanese press and radio that no coloring or slanting of news would be permitted, no destructive criticism of the allied powers, and nothing disturbing to public tranquility. Whether these restrictions apply also to the Tokyo edition of the *Chicago Tribune* does not appear" (it was once again accusing President Roosevelt of starting the Japanese-American war). Would Japanese newspapers, Davis wondered, be held to higher standards than the *Tribune* (Sept. 16, 1945; Library of Congress, Davis papers, Box 1)?

49. Intelligence Series, 10, pp. 107–8, 120–21; Coughlin, *Conquered Press,* pp. 21–22; *New York Times,* Sept. 19, 20, 1945; "Freedom of the Press," pp. 10–11.

50. Coughlin, *Conquered Press,* pp. 25–26, 149–50, appendix C; "Radio Broadcasting," p. 9 and appendix 7; Intelligence Series, 10, documentary appendices nos. 22 and 48 ("Slanderous press comments," repeats this source, "led to a rapid expansion of precensorship," p. 122.); "Freedom of the Press," pp. 25, 182–83. SCAP crossed wires in this instance, for on October 1, Colonel Raymond C. Kramer, head of the Economic and Scientific Section, told the Central Liaison Office of the Japanese government that headquarters wanted the *Oriental Economist* to resume publication "at once" and be given proper facilities; see SCAP monograph, History of the Non-Military Activities of the Occupation of Japan, "The Purge," p. 49. A possible explanation is that Kramer, as *Newsweek* divined, needed the journal

and its files for economic information (May 26, 1947). Ishibashi was purged in 1947 on charges that the *Oriental Economist* had supported aggressive and militarist policies, 1937–41, but the real reasons were political and economic as his file in the Government Section of the SCAP records reveals; ESS, under General William F. Marquat charged him in May 1947 with a record "of continuous obstructionism toward occupation economic objectives" (examples in NRC, RG 331, Box 2275E). Magazine surveillance by PPB apparently began in Tokyo on September 19, 1945, leading to the mishap over the *Oriental Economist,* a monthly published in English, and the *Tōyō Keizai Shimpō,* the parent magazine published weekly in Japanese ("Freedom of the Press," p. 25, for censorship date).

51. Revised plan and PPB manual are in RG 331, Box 8568; see also Intelligence Series, 10, pp. 70, 113. Both CCD and CI&E would claim an educative function to democratize the Japanese media; the rivalries and duplication are discussed from G-2's point of view in Intelligence Series, 10, p. 211. The two sections had completely different operational plans "and no functional connection," points stressed by Robert H.Berkov, "The Press in Postwar Japan," *Far Eastern Survey,* vol. 16 (July 23, 1947), pp. 162–66 (Berkov, an OWI employee, was an early head of CI&E's Press and Publications Branch but was eased out of SCAP after running into trouble with Willoughby for speaking too candidly with Japanese about the real authorship of the constitution).

52. Intelligence Series, 10, pp. 118, 121–22, 123–24, 128–29, and 132; Coughlin, *Conquered Press,* pp. 48–49; "Freedom of the Press," pp. 23–26; SCAP, History of the Non-Military Activities of the Occupation of Japan, "Theater and Motion Pictures," p. 6.

53. Iwanaga, *Story of Japanese News Agencies,* pp. 81–93; Coughlin, *Conquered Press,* pp. 23–24, 59–63, 111–17; "Freedom of the Press," pp. 50–51.

54. Intelligence Series, 10, pp. 104–6. Toshio Nishi says that the Sept. 27 SCAPIN, "Further Steps toward Freedom of Speech and Press," was in fact issued on Sept. 29 but backdated to the day of the emperor's call on MacArthur. This is plausible, but Nishi gives no source; see his *Unconditional Democracy: Education and Politics in Occupied Japan, 1945–1952* (Stanford: Hoover Institution Press, 1982), p. 91.

55. "How to Treat the Japanese: A Complex Issue"; Memo for the Record, "Press Censorship Policy in Japan," Nov. 10, 1945 (approved by Thorpe, Nov. 13), RG 331, Box 8569.

56. Interview with Costello, Mar. 5, 1980; Paul Vincent Miller, "Censorship in Japan," *Commonweal* (Apr. 25, 1947), p. 35 (for citation of *haiku*). Decisions about deletions in the case of books and magazines were made at "relatively low supervisory echelons," states Intelligence Series, 10, but precensored daily newspapers were "the most sensitive field of CCD operations, and many news items each day were referred up the chain of command for decision at some higher echelon." As a result, "final action was taken on many stories by the Chief, PPB," or went on up the chain to the civil censorship officer, the deputy chief of CIS, or even to General Wil-

loughby or General MacArthur, but the formalities did not prevent the system from working "extremely well in actual practice" (pp. 124–25). Russell Brines, head of the AP news agency in Japan, is less complimentary, declaring that "in time censorship became erratic, slow and frequently incompetent. Stories often were held up for days while being sent upstairs to some busy staff officer for a final decision," *MacArthur's Japan* (Philadelphia and New York: J. B. Lippincott Co., 1948), p. 247. And Kazuo Kawai, then editor of the *Nippon Times,* recalls that at the beginning of the occupation, censors held up about two items a month but in the second year this jumped to fifteen or sixteen a day, "although the majority were approved after several days' delay," *Japan's American Interlude* (Chicago: University of Chicago Press, 1960), p. 214, footnote 8.

57. "Psychological Warfare News Coverage in the Philippines," no date, Fellers papers, PWB File No. 3, Box 3; Fellers to Greene, Sept. 9, 1945, Fellers papers, Box 3. John Gunther declares that "news" in the Pacific theater under MacArthur "was either controlled at the source, or built up to the personal aggrandizement of the commander"; *Procession* (New York: Harper & Row, 1965), p. 315.

58. Fellers' memorandum on information dissemination (RG 165, CAD 014 Japan, July–Sept. 1945, Section 1); War Department cable of Sept. 13 (Fellers papers, Box 3); Harold Henderson, Oral History, Columbia University, Special Collections.

59. General Orders, Oct. 2, 1945 (RG 208, Box 598); mission of CI&E ("Education in Japan," Feb. 15, 1946, unpublished SCAP monograph, pp. 56–57).

60. *Who's Who in America,* 1954–55, Entry for Dyke.

61. Smith, report of Nov. 8, 1945, covering IIIS activities Sept. 6 to Nov. 1 (RG 208, Item 392, Box 598).

62. Dyke's testimony, confidential minutes of 5th meeting in Japan, Far Eastern Advisory Commission, Jan. 14, 1946 (RG 43, Box 3). In 1946, on Dyke's return to NBC, he was replaced by Lt. Col. Donald Nugent. Coughlin portrays Dyke and CI&E sympathetically but cannot resist saying that the "occupation was going at the job of selling democracy as though it were an advertising campaign for a new soap," *Conquered Press,* p. 45.

63. "Non-operational Review of Developments in Japan," Sept. 24, 1945, Office of Naval Intelligence, in CINCPAC-CINCPOA, Strategic Plans Division, Operational Archives, Navy History Divison (Navy Yard), Washington, D.C. (it gives a figure of twenty-three Japanese); Iwasaki Akira, "The Occupied Screen," *Japan Quarterly,* vol. 25 (July–Sept. 1978), pp. 304–5; "Theater and Motion Pictures," pp. 4–6, 12–14, 18–19. According to the latter source, SCAP disapproved of 322 of 518 classic and neoclassic plays by December and had them withdrawn from the repertories; titles of the banned films included "Symphony of Revenge," "Swords Flash in Cherryblossom Time," and "Human Bullet Volunteer Corps."

64. *The History of Broadcasting in Japan,* pp. 149–51, 173–74 (which identifies a Captain Ross [Roth] as the chief of the Radio Branch), and

176–79; "Radio Broadcasting," pp. 10–11, 13, 15 (For "Man on the Street," people at first—"passersby on the Ginza"—were "suspicious and reluctant to speak" when asked the question, "how do you find life today"), 19, and 27; Smith report of Nov. 9, 1945.

65. Smith to George Taylor, Oct. 5, 1945 (Microfilm T-1205, roll 4); Smith to Taylor, Oct. 27, 1945, and report of Nov. 9 (RG 208, Item 392, Box 598); and Coughlin, *Conquered Press,* p. 27.

66. "Radio Broadcasting," p. 11; Smith reports, Oct. 27 and Nov. 9. Smith wrote on October 27 that even after the Civil Rights Directive,"we are still being led around by the nose." The Japanese "ruling clique" had "by passive resistance negated the spirit of our directives." One of the friendly liberals who went on the air for SCAP was Katō Shidzue; see Helen M. Hopper's paper, "Katō Shidzue, Socialist Party M.P., and Occupation Reforms Affecting Women, 1945–1948," in Burkman (ed.), *The Occupation of Japan, Educational and Social Reform,* pp. 380–83.

67. Press release, CI&E, Oct. 24, 1945 (RG 331, Box 5379); Coughlin, *Conquered Press,* pp. 32–35, citing the release.

68. Lattimore Diary, entry for Nov. 11, 1945 (RG 59, Pauley Reparations Mission, Box 24). Lattimore added that Dyke "complains of slow and inefficient policy directives from Washington; also of the fact that too many directives are vague in wording and of an 'Atlantic Charter' character rather than good guides to operations. He thinks that we ourselves do not know where we are going, and that is a fundamental hindrance to knowing where we want to make the Japanese go."

69. Linebarger memorandum on information control in Japan, Nov. 6, 1945, in RG 165, CAD 319.1 (July 31—Dec. 31), Section 1; Buttles and Schuler memorandum, "United States Information Activities in Japan and Korea," Dec. 7, 1945; "Radio Broadcasting," pp. 16 (Japanese studio audiences were at first reluctant to ask questions of round table participants), 22; NHK, *History of Broadcasting in Japan,* pp. 174, 177–78; "Freedom of the Press," appendix 6; Coughlin, *Conquered Press,* pp. 69, 79.

70. "Radio Broadcasting," p. 12; Iwasaki, "Occupied Screen," pp. 312–13; Coughlin, *Conquered Press,* pp. 20, 44–45; "Theater and Motion Pictures," pp. 30–31. Coughlin refers to the radio series as "True History of the War," Iwasaki as "Here is How Things Really Are," and "Radio Broadcasting" as "Now it Can be Told." From the descriptions, it is clear they are all referring to the same program.

71. McCloy's discussions with MacArthur on the relationship between SCAP and IIIS (Microfilm T-1205, roll 9). The solution to the jurisdictional problem was to transmit the weekly IIIS (later OIC) central directives, containing approved national information themes, to CI&E via the Propaganda Branch, G-2, War Department. For Brown, see cable, Nov. 24, 1945, RG 331, Box 2055. CI&E's Information Division as Brown arrived contained a Policy and Programs Branch, Press and Publications Branch, Radio Branch, Motion Picture and Theatrical Branch, and an Information Centers Branch. Fellers' executive assistant, J. Woodall Greene, stayed on as chief of the

Analysis and Research Division (later called Public Opinion and Sociological Research Division).

72. *History of Broadcasting in Japan,* p. 147. Ironically, CCD's operations in Japan are perhaps one of the best documented cases in the history of censorship. There is a rich lode of materials at NRC, RG 331, covering all aspects of civil censorship, and at McKeldin Library, University of Maryland, which houses the Gordon W. Prange Collection, containing monographs, periodicals, newspapers, and portions of PPB files, including galley and page proofs and working papers of censors. Yūshōdō Booksellers is completing part 1 of a new microfilming project, "Microfilms of Censored Japanese Periodicals, 1945–1949," containing about 3,500 periodical titles, over 11,000 censored articles, and a total of 150,000 pages of print. The materials illustrate precensorship and postcensorship. To assist the researcher, Eizaburō Okuizumi has compiled and edited a 550 page guide, *Senryōgun Ken'etsu Zasshi Mokuroku, 1945–1949 (User's Guide to the Microfilm Edition of Censored Periodicals, 1945–1949)* (Tokyo: Yūshōdō Booksellers Ltd., 1982). The official summary of CCD's activities presented in Intelligence Series, 10, is supplemented by details in another SCAP-inspired volume, *Reports of General MacArthur,* vol. 1 Supplement, *MacArthur in Japan. The Occupation: Military Phase* (Washington, D.C.: Government Printing Office, 1966), pp. 236–41.

73. Eto Jun, "The Civil Censorship in Occupied Japan" (in English), *Hikaku Bunka Zasshi* [The annual of comparative culture], vol. 1 (1981), pp. 5–7; Intelligence Series, 10, pp. 68–69, 77, 207, 210; "Freedom of the Press," p. 26; RG 331, Key Log of Apr. 24, 1946, in Box 8568.

74. MacArthur Memorial, RG 23, Willoughby papers, Introduction to the Intelligence Series, *A Brief History of the G-2 Section, GHQ, SWPA and Affiliated Units* (GHQ, Far East Command, Military Intelligence Section, General Staff, 1950), p. 119; Coughlin, *Conquered Press,* p. 50; Reports of General MacArthur, vol. 1 Supplement, p. 240; RG 59, 740.00119 Control (Japan)/1-748, forwarding CCD report of Nov. 1947; RG 331, memorandum for the record, Feb. 28, 1949 (stating that 40,368 copies of propaganda materials had been confiscated), Box 8568; Paul Vincent Miller, "Censorship in Japan," pp. 36–37.

75. "Theater and Motion Pictures," pp. 6, 14–15 (in May 1946, 2,488 prints of banned films were destroyed); Intelligence Series, 10, pp. 132–33 (copies of certain suppressed films were saved and used by the United States Army for intelligence purposes); RG 331, study, undated (probably 1945), entitled "Background, Activities, and Aims of the Pictorial Section, PPB Division," pp. 5–7, Box 8569; Eto, "The Civil Censorship in Occupied Japan," case of Yoshida Mitsuru's *Battleship Yamato,* pp. 8–11; Erik Barnouw, "How a University's Film Branch Released Long-Secret A-Bomb Pic," *Variety* (Jan. 5, 1972), pp. 24, 26; Lifton, *Death in Life,* pp. 453, 456, 327–28. Lifton cites a Japanese leftist woman writer reacting to strict censorship of discussion about the atomic bomb: "Talking about the meaning of

the A-bomb disaster was supposed to be against Occupation policy and was not permitted. We felt that this was not very democratic, and that although Americans claimed to be democratic, they were taking away our freedom" (p. 328).

76. Eto, "The Civil Censorship in Occupied Japan," pp. 13–16; Iwasaki, "Occupied Screen," pp. 312–22; Prange Collection, McKeldin Library, University of Maryland, in CCD files, under title of *Jimmin Hyōron* [Popular review], Sept. 1948 (roundtable discussion of "History of Cultural Oppression and Resistance in Wartime Japan"). I would like to thank Eizaburō Okuizumi for bringing the item in the Prange Collection to my attention. Iwasaki (production manager at Nichiei) does not reveal in the article that one copy of *The Tragedy of Japan* was sold to the Soviet Union (according to PPB central files, RG 331, Box 8579). He characterizes the early CI&E Motion Picture Branch as made up of "conscientious and progressive New Dealers and Marxist leaning leftists," eager to root out militarists and democratize Japan (p. 303). David Conde left CI&E in mid-1946 to work for INS and Reuter's news services and was accredited as a correspondent in Japan but was forced out after incurring the wrath of SCAP for an article in the *St. Louis Post-Dispatch,* July 1947, critical of censors who cut John Hersey, Tolstoy, James Bryce, and a speech by Secretary of Agriculture Henry Wallace; see Coughlin, *Conquered Press,* pp. 125–26, and Jim Hopewell, "Press Censorship: A Case Study," *Argus,* vol. 6 (May 1971), p. 63. Kamei went on to direct films after the occupation, including the *World is in Dread* (1957), described by Lifton as sensationalist (*Death in Life,* pp. 457–58).

77. Miller, Apr. 27, 1947, pp. 35–38 (Miller alludes to a trip to Kumamoto where he saw a proscribed dance and cites what appear to be internal working documents of CCD); Baldwin, *New Leader,* Aug. 16, 1947; Baldwin, letter of May 1, 1947 (Tokyo) to friends (Roger Baldwin papers, Princeton University Library); RG 165, CAD 014 Japan, Section 15, Draper to MacArthur, Oct. 30, 1947. For the rules against mentioning censorship or indicating deletions, see Intelligence Series, 10, p. 113.

78. *Reports of General MacArthur,* vol. 1 Supplement, pp. 239–40; Intelligence Series, 10, 117–18; *A Brief History of the G-2 Section,* pp. 119–20; RG 331, "Chronological Index of PPB History" (Kabuki had to be performed in complete plays and by actors of "highest merit"; censors were relatively unconcerned about Bunraku and Nō because the audiences were limited), Box 8569; same location, Check Sheet, G-2 (Willoughby) to Chief of Staff, Sept. 10, 1947, Box 8569.

79. OIR (Office of Intelligence Research, Division of Research for Far East), Report No. 4246, "The Development of Media of Information in Japan Since the Surrender," Oct. 1, 1947, pp. iv, 23–24.

80. *FRUS, 1948,* vol. 6 (Washington, D.C.: Government Printing Office, 1974), p. 781, quoting PPS 28/2, May 26, 1948; same source, Sebald letter, Feb. 7, 1948, p. 675.

81. Costello interview, Mar. 5, 1980; Intelligence Series, 10, p. 110;

Coughlin, *Conquered Press,* pp. 106-7; *Reports of General MacArthur,* vol. 1 Supplement, p. 210; *A Brief History of the G-2 Section,* p. 120; RG 331, "Chronological Index to PPB History (on Apr. 30, 1948, PPB was ordered to conduct 100 percent surveillance of the Communist media to obtain intelligence). The intelligence leads helped SCAP catch five enlisted men who had beaten five Japanese civilians to death in Jan. 1947 (Intelligence Series, 10, p. 210).

82. Costello interview, Mar. 5, 1980 (Costello had a six months course in Japanese language and area studies at the University of Michigan civil affairs training school); Coughlin, *Conquered Press,* pp. 56-57, 144-47; Intelligence Series, 10, pp. 126-27, 142-43; Eto, "The Civil Censorship in Occupied Japan," pp. 3-4, 11-12, 16-17. The official report (Intelligence Series, 10) agrees that the Japanese nationals at "the base of the personnel pyramid" were crucial to the operations of CCD. It adds that many "were well-educated and highly competent individuals" and also that many "professed a genuine feeling that in working for the Occupation they were contributing to the rehabilitation and democratization of their own nation. Attitudes of recalcitrance, hostility, or fear of being labeled collaborationist, were conspicuously absent, or if extant, were well hidden." However, their utilization presented several problems because of "their inability to follow or even approximate Western thought patterns." They thus followed instructions but often without real understanding of the underlying policy and assumptions, making "censorship operations highly mechanical" and resulting in errors. One of the biggest problems was getting the Japanese examiners to understand the necessity in a democracy of "free and frank discussion" of the imperial institution. "Many of them, unable to cast off the mental shackles of their reverence for the concept of a divine Emperor, considered any criticism of or levity with the Imperial institution to be a gross sacrilege . . . and, furthermore, a violation of censorship policy. American supervisors found it necessary to remain alert to prevent abuse of censorship by examiners such as these" (pp. 119-20, and footnote 26, p. 120). In 1946, two movie producers were given suspended sentences for illegal distribution, a *kamishibai* producer was sentenced to prison for forging a censorship stamp, and a Taiwanese was fined and deported for press violation (all in July and August); see "Chronological Index of PPB History," RG 331, Box 8569. Severe sentences were given to two Koreans and a Japanese in 1949 for press violations (Intelligence Series, 10, pp. 125-26).

83. There is a glimpse of reorientation activities in the SCAP monographs "Radio Broadcasting," "Freedom of the Press," and "Theater and Motion Pictures," but little insight into the daily operations and issues. In published accounts, Coughlin gives some sense of CI&E's positive program in guiding the Japanese press into democratic ways in his chapter "Lessons in Democracy" (*Conquered Press,* pp. 31-45; also pp. 243-46). Russell Brines provides a short, tantalizing review of radio programs and reforms in *MacArthur's Japan,* pp. 243-46; Kawai gives less information, *Japan's*

American Interlude, pp. 219–21. For an insider's overview, see John W. Gaddis, *Public Information in Japan under American Occupation* (Geneva: Imprimerie Populaires, 1950).

84. OIR report, Oct. 1, 1947, pp. 9–10, 13 (and footnote 4), 18, 21; Allen Raymond, "Literary Censorship in Japan," *New York Herald Tribune,* Apr. 27, 1948; "Theater and Motion Pictures," pp. 15–16; "Chronological Index of PPB History"; Baldwin, letter of May 1, 1947; Colonel W. P. Putnam, memo for the record, "SCAP Youth Programs in Japanese Occupation," no date (probably Oct. 1949), in NA, RG 335, SAOUS, Draper-Voorhees Project Decimal File.

85. "Radio Broadcasting" pp. 12–19; "Theater and Motion Pictures," p. 26; Brines, *MacArthur's Japan,* pp. 244–45; Intelligence Series, 10, p. 130; Lifton, *Death in Life,* p. 329. Kawai stresses the large number of radio sets in Japan, second only to the United States, making it SCAP's most important medium of communication; he credits CI&E's radio experts with benefiting from mistakes and giving freer rein to Japanese writers to create scripts (*Japan's American Interlude,* p. 221).

86. NHK, *History of Broadcasting in Japan,* pp. 151–67; Coughlin, *Conquered Press,* pp. 69–97; "Freedom of the Press," pp. 144–45; RG 335, SAOUS, 350 J, Cable of Jan. 7, 1949.

87. Stratemeyer letter, Sept. 26, 1949, in RG 335, SAOUS, Draper-Voorhees Project Decimal File (and accompanying memos and draft replies). See Nishi, *Unconditional Democracy,* for what appear direct follow-up actions, pp. 247–67.

88. OIR report, Oct. 1, 1947, pp. 34–37; Coughlin, *Conquered Press,* pp. 104–6; "Freedom of the Press," pp. 149–82; "The Purge," pp. 87–103; Hans H. Baerwald, *The Purge of Japanese Leaders Under the Occupation* (Berkeley and Los Angeles: University of California Press, 1959), pp. 36–40, 94–96. Figures for media people, 1948–49, are based on Baerwald's findings; those for Communists in the media come from the SCAP monograph, "The Purge," which covers only the year 1950 and may be a low estimate (*Akahata,* the Communist party newspaper and 1,387 other Communist or leftist newspapers were suspended; 582 Communist or leftist newspapermen were discharged or resigned; and 119 leftist broadcasters were dismissed).

89. Byron Price, Aug. 24, 1945, transmitting his memorandum, "A Basis for Censorship Planning," in the event of a future war, RG 216, Entry 4, vol. 1, "A History of the Office of Censorship" (reproduced under the date of Nov. 15, 1945, as the introduction to *A Report on the Office of Censorship* [Washington, D.C.: Government Printing Office, 1945], pp. 1–2); and 016A folder, night lead of June 1, 1945. The *New York Times* reported on Sept. 9, 1945, that American delegates to the Third Inter-American Communications Conference, Rio De Janeiro, had presented a freedom of information resolution, calling for free access to domestic sources of information and unrestricted interchange of news between peoples.

14. Comparing American Reform Efforts in Germany:
Mass Media and the School System / Hurwitz

1. A German version of this paper was published under the title "Anti-kommunismus und Amerikanische Demokratisierungsvorhaben in Nach-kriegsdeutschland," in *Aus Politik und Zeitgeschichte*, Beilage zur Wochen-zeitung *Das Parlament* 28 (July 22, 1978): 29–46.

2. John Gimbel, *The American Occupation of Germany: Politics and the Military, 1945–1949* (Stanford, Calif.: Stanford University Press, 1968). John Gimbel, *The Origins of the Marshall Plan* (Stanford, Calif.: Stanford University Press, 1976).

3. Gimbel, *American Occupation*.

4. *Conference of Scholars on the Administration of Occupied Areas, 1945–1955, April 10–11, 1970*, transcript, edited by Donald R. McCoy and Benedict K. Zobrist (Independence, Mo.: Harry S Truman Library Institute for National and International Affairs, 1970), p. 50.

5. Gimbel, *Origins of the Marshall Plan*.

6. For a comprehensive and balanced treatment, see Lutz Niethammer, Ulrich Borsdorf, and Peter Brandt, eds., *Arbeiterinitiative 1945, anti-faschistische Ausschüsse und Reorganisation der Arbeiterbewegung in Deutschland* (Wuppertal: Peter Hammer Verlag, 1976), passim; Leonard Krieger, "The Interregnum in Germany, March–August 1945," *Political Science Quarterly* 64 (1949): 507 ff.

7. Eberhard Schmidt, *Die verhinderte Neuordnung 1945–1952* (Frankfurt: Europäische Verlagsanstalt, 1970), passim; Ernst-Ulrich Huster, Gerhard Kraiker, Burkhard Scherer, Friedrich-Karl Schlotmann, Marianne Welteke, *Determinanten der Westdeutschen Restauration, 1945–1949* (Frankfurt: Suhrkamp Verlag, 1970), passim; Rolf Badstübner and Siegfried Thomas, *Restauration und Spaltung: Entstehung und Entwicklung der BRD, 1945–1955* (Cologne: Pahl-Rugenstein Verlag, 1975), passim. Badstübner and Thomas are East German historians.

8. Gimbel, *Origins of the Marshall Plan*.

9. Ann J. Merritt and Richard L. Merritt, *Public Opinion in Occupied Germany: The OMGUS Surveys, 1945–1949* (Urbana: University of Illinois Press, 1970), pp. 56–57.

At the outset MG reeducators and reformers were often quite sensitive to the problem. It may explain some of the caution Clay called for when he finally proceeded, in October 1947, to counteract long-standing propaganda attacks by Soviet controlled East German media by launching the American anti-Communist campaign "operation backtalk." The problem remained a cause for contention between members of ICD for some time to come, and it explains part of the reluctance of German anti-Nazis in West Germany to support the new campaign. See Harold Hurwitz, *Die Stunde Null der Deutschen Presse: die amerikanische Pressepolitik in Deutschland, 1945–1949* (Cologne: Verlag Wissenschaft und Politik, 1972), pp. 325–39.

In Berlin the roles were somewhat different; Americans were finally committing themselves fully to support a popular struggle against Communist domination that Social Democrats and trade unionists had been organizing since early 1946.

10. Barbara Mettler, *Demokratisierung und Kalter Krieg: zur amerikanischen Informations- und Rundfunkpolitik in Westdeutschland, 1945–1949, Rundfunkforschung* 2 (Berlin: Verlag Volker Spiess, 1975).

11. For the following see Henry P. Pilgert, *Press, Radio and Film in West Germany, 1945–1953* (Historical Division of the Executive Secretary, Office of the U.S. High Commissioner For Germany, 1953), pp. 14–31, 43–55; Hurwitz, *Stunde Null,* pp. 117–299.

12. Hurwitz, *Stunde Null.*

13. Richard Straub, "Postwar Developments of the German Press", *Department of State Bulletin* 28, no. 1713, p. 298.

14. Oron Hale, *The Captive Press in the Third Reich* (Princeton, N.J.: Princeton University Press, 1964), passim.

15. Hurwitz, *Stunde Null,* pp. 153–160.

16. These were businesses that produced boiler-plate front and feature pages, including editorials, for small local newspapers.

17. Hurwitz, *Stunde Null,* p. 193.

18. Initially the licensee-panel of the *Frankfurter Rundschau* agreed that this paper be transformed into a *gemeinnützige Stiftung* after the end of the occupation. The Communist and Social Democratic licensees claimed they had approval from DISCC (District Information Services Control Command) 6871 to commit themselves in this sense (*FR,* Sept. 22, 1945, p. 1). Although the major spokesman for the idea was Wilhelm Karl Gerst, a former Center party activist who was supporting the Communist line, the idea was supported in Hesse by licensees with quite different party orientations. A majority of the licensees rejected the idea in Bavaria in March 1946 and in Hesse in August 1946. At that time the licensees in Hesse were told categorically by the press officer Anderson that *Stiftung* experiments were not called for. There are no indications of renewed German initiatives having been taken in this direction once military government controls were lifted and the profit motive really took over.

19. Hans Ulrich Reichert, *Der Kampf um die Autonomie des deutschen Rundfunks* (Heidelberg & Stuttgart, 1955), pp. 348–76; Heinz Wilkens, *Die Aufsicht über den Rundfunk* (Dissertation, Faculty of Law, Johann Wolfgang Goethe-University, Frankfurt, 1965), pp. 41 ff.

20. Liselotte von Reinken, *Rundfunk in Bremen, 1914–1974: Eine Dokumentation* (Bremen: Radio Bremen, 1975), pp. 51–52.

21. Considerations of military security may have excluded consideration of licensing German radio stations in 1945–46.

22. Reichert, *Kampf,* p. 24; Mettler, *Demokratisierung,* p. 106. OMGUS did obtain the *Länderrat's* formal agreement to private ownership of radio, but discovered that the privatization that the German state governments intended was actually a revival of the Weimar system of having corporations that could attract private capital but were actually controlled by government. Relevant in this connection is that when OMGUS considered turning over licensing and control of the information media to the Germans

by instructing the *Länderrat* to prepare legislation in December 1945, the ICD-approved law that this body finally passed, after nearly a year of negotiations, provided for independent semipublic representative bodies — *Land* licensing committees and self-governing press control councils — along lines of the BBC model, but with strong representation by publishers and journalists. This design was rejected, however, by OMGUS because the Legal Division held that any regulation of the press was a prerogative of government. The idea to turn over licensing to the Germans had been in keeping with General Clay's intention to get out of direct control responsibility as soon as possible. ICD opposed that principle but had no choice but to seek the best solution within that policy, until it became clear that controls could not be forfeited in 1946–47. Only because the *Länderrat* press law was rejected did it become possible for ICD to continue providing the licensed press with its protective patronage under conditions that were free from capitalistic competition for another two-and-a-half years. See Hurwitz, *Stunde Null,* pp. 179–83.

23. Pilgert, *Press, Radio and Film,* p. 30. Nothing came of the intention to turn over the radio stations to the Germans at a much earlier time. This threat influenced the December 1946 resignation, in protest, of Field Horine, chief radio control officer in Bavaria. Barbara Mettler makes much of this episode to argue that anticommunism was already influencing Americans to forsake earnest anti-Nazi reorientation at that time, but she does not heed Clay's quite different motivation in this connection or point out that the early turnover did not take place. Mettler's thesis throughout rests — perhaps unwittingly — on the assumption that direct controls by military government were a precondition for an active anti-Nazi reorientation program in early postwar Germany (Mettler, *Demokratisierung,* passim, esp. pp. 199–201).

24. Gimbel, *American Occupation,* passim; Gimbel, *Origins of the Marshall Plan,* pp. 201–20, 235, 277. A dissertation being prepared by Georg Schnelzer is likely to throw further light on this subject.

25. James Stewart Martin, *All Honorable Men* (Boston: Little, Brown, 1950), pp. 186, 197 ff., 226 ff., 235 ff.

26. Lutz Niethammer, *Entnazifizierung in Bayern: Säuberung und Rehabilitierung unter amerikanischer Besatzung* (Frankfurt: S. Fischer, 1972), pp. 483–515.

27. For treatments of the American experience in trying to reform German education, see in more general studies: Harold Zink, *The United States in Germany, 1944–1955* (Princeton, N.J.: D. Van Nostrand, 1957), pp. 193–214; John Gimbel, *American Occupation,* pp. 240–43; comparing educational reform in the four zones, Helen Liddell, ed., *Education in Occupied Germany* (Paris: Librairie Marcel Riviere, 1949); Henry P. Pilgert, *The West German Educational System, with Special Reference to the Policies and Programs of the Office of the U.S. High Commissioner for Germany* (Historical Division, Office of the Executive Secretary, HICOG, 1953); a comparative analysis by a British scholar of education reform developments in Germany

from 1945 to 1970 is Arthur Hearnden, *Bildungspolitik in der BRD und DDR* (Düsseldorf: Pädagogischer Verlag Schwann, 1973).

German dissertations that have been written after consulting the OMGUS records are Hans-Joachim Thron, *Schulreform im besiegten Deutschland: Die Bildungspolitik der amerikanischen Militärregierung nach dem Zweiten Weltkrieg* (Dissertation, Philosophische Facultät, Ludwig-Maximilian University, Munich, 1972, offset print); Karl-Ernst Bungenstab, *Umerziehung zur Demokratie? Reeducation-Politik im Bildungswesen der US-Zone, 1945–49* (Düsseldorf: Bertelsmann Universitätsverlag, 1970). Other studies describing the interaction between military government and German parties, interest groups, and state governments have also been written, as dissertations, with regard to Bavaria and Berlin: Isa Huelz, *Schulpolitik in Bayern zwischen Demokratisierung und Restauration in den Jahren 1945–1950,* Series: Geistes- und sozialwissenschaftliche Dissertation, no. 1 (Hamburg: Hartmut Lüdke Verlag, 1970); Marion Klewitz, *Berliner Einheitsschule 1945–1951: Entstehung, Durchführung und Revision des Reformgesetzes von 1947/48,* Series: Historische und Pädagogische Studien, vol. 1 (Berlin: Colloquium Verlag, 1973).

28. Thron, *Schulreform,* p. 63. Indeed, when in March 1949, under the influence of the Swiss, British, and American experiences, the former Minister President Wilhelm Högner (SPD) proposed making local communities responsible for schools in Bavaria, United States Military Government indicated that this was going too far. Huelz, *Schulpolitik,* pp. 166–67.

29. Evidence that supports my thesis may be found in Lutz Niethammer's fundamental study, *Entnazifizierung in Bayern,* pp. 172–74. Such social tensions were, of course, greatly aggravated by the necessity to accommodate millions of expellees.

30. Regarding decartelization, land reform, and *Gewerbefreiheit,* see Hans-Hermann Hartwich, *Sozialstaatspostulat und gesellschaftlicher status-quo* (Cologne: Westdeutscher Verlag, 1970), pp. 75–90.

31. Thron, *Schulreform,* pp. 74–77; Liddell, *Education,* pp. 107–8.

32. Thron, *Schulreform,* pp. 77–78; Liddell, *Education,* pp. 106, 120.

33. Harold Zink, *American Military Government in Germany* (New York: Macmillan, 1947), pp. 151–52.

34. Zink, *The United States in Germany,* pp. 195, 199–200.

35. Liddell, *Education,* pp. 107–17.

36. Zink, *The United States in Germany,* pp. 198–99.

37. The relationship, and perhaps rivalry, between Clay and McClure remains an unexplored theme in military government history. Robert McClure's diary has not been published or consulted by researchers, as far as I know. It is in the possession of his son, also a professional Army officer.

38. Jean Edward Smith, ed., *The Papers of General Lucius D. Clay: Germany, 1945–1949,* vol. 1 (Bloomington: Indiana University Press, 1975), Clay personal communication to Noce, director, CAD, War Department, Jan. 31, 1947, pp. 308–9.

39. Smith, ed., *Papers of General Lucius D. Clay,* vol. 1, passim.

40. Mettler, *Demokratisierung,* pp. 69–70, documents Clay's resistance in the fall of 1947 to State Department pressure to ask for a higher budget to buy newsprint in support of the anti-communist program "operation backtalk" that he had recently launched. In the transcript of the *Conference of Scholars on the Administration of Occupied Areas* (cited in note 4), p. 50, John Gimbel described Clay's opposition to the retention of Liaison and Security Detachments, which Edward Litchfield, deputy chief of CAD, and the State Department advocated. They survived until 1952 as a costly grassroots reorientation program that was quite inappropriate to the German scene after 1949 but had some home-directed public relations value for the High Commission.

41. Smith, ed., *Papers of General Lucius D. Clay,* vol. 2, Clay personal communication to Draper, Oct. 9, 1948, p. 896.

42. John Taylor, chief of the ERA Section, went to the States on two occasions with help of the War and State Departments to look for qualified personnel, including an "outstanding American educator" to replace himself. This occurred in December 1945 (Thron, *Schulreform,* p. 36). At the time the Zook Commission was sent to Germany in the summer of 1964, ERA had 71 slots, only 55 of which were occupied (ibid., p. 64). Although Clay gave the Zook Commission's Report which recommended a radical increase in staff, his immediate attention, ERA was about the same size in April 1947: 54 officers in comparison to 150 ERA officers in the British zone (ibid., p. 131).

43. Ibid., pp. 84–85.

44. Ibid., pp. 64–65.

45. Indiana University President Herman B. Wells joined OMGUS as General Clay's education and cultural advisor in September 1947 and became head of the Education and Cultural Affairs Division when it was finally created on March 1, 1948 (see Clay's request for him in Smith, ed., *Papers of General Lucius D. Clay,* vol. 1, personal communication to Noce, Aug. 7, 1947, p. 394; Thron, *Schulreform,* p. 133; Zink, *The United States in Germany,* pp. 200–201). Wells stayed less than a year in Germany. He knew little about German society and the Weimar reform tradition, but he was an energetic exponent of intervention during the school reform legislation controversy. His successor, former commissioner of education in Connecticut Alonzo G. Grace, did not have a better knowledge of German matters, but he opposed intervention, holding that moral renewal alone, not planned institutional change, would bring reform. Grace did not press hard for making educational reform explicitly an area in which the High Commission should reserve authority. Without this, there was no further possibility of influencing legislation in the direction of reform by Americans after 1949. (Zink, *The United States in Germany,* pp. 204–7; Thron, *Schulreform,* pp. 159–63). Grace's approach alienated experienced education officers on his staff. A month after his departure, in December 1949, the staff made a last attempt to revive the reform program as a directive binding activity in this field under the High Commission (Thron, *Schulreform,* pp. 162–63).

46. *Decision in Germany* (Garden City, N.Y.: Doubleday, 1950), p. 287.

47. "The Potential for Democratization in Germany," in John D. Montgomery and Albert Hirschmann, eds., *Public Policy* 17 (Cambridge: Harvard University Press, 1970), p. 58.

48. Ibid., p. 35.

49. Thron, *Schulreform*, pp. 107, 167.

50. Hurwitz, *Stunde Null*, pp. 166 ff.

51. An outstanding study of this process is that by Wolfgang Rudzio, *Die Neuordnung des Kommunalwesens in der britischen Zone, Zur Demokratisierung und Dezentralisierung der politischen Struktur: eine britische Reform und ihr Ausgang,* vol. 17, *Quellen und Darstellungen zur Zeitgeschichte* (Stuttgart: Deutsche Verlagsanstalt, 1968).

52. Thron, *Schulreform*, pp. 92, 100.

53. Ibid., pp. 104, 107–8.

54. Ibid., pp. 108, 110–11.

55. Even Bavaria's third draft law had accepted in principle a six year grammar school and obligatory education for nine years.

56. Thron, *Schulreform*.

57. Ibid., pp. 123, 128.

58. Ibid., pp. 155–57.

59. Ibid., pp. 147–48.

60. Ibid., p. 151.

61. Ibid., pp. 153–55.

62. Hearnden, *Bildungspolitik*, p. 40. Although the SPD was committed to school reform ideas that were consistent with the democratization concepts of the occupying powers, the party had always tended to treat its education reformers with deprecatory nonchalance, without, however, depriving them of influence altogether.

63. Clay's change was probably a reaction to the fact that the new orientation had finally compelled him to give up his mismanaged denazification effort (see Niethammer, *Entnazifizierung in Bayern*) and, possibly also, that he had backed down altogether where decartelization was concerned (of interest in this connection are recollections of Clay's gradually changing attitude in Martin, *All Honorable Men*, passim).

64. Regarding the autocratic strain, see Smith, ed., *Papers of General Lucius D. Clay,* vol. 1, p. xxv. During the very days when General Clay was issuing orders to West German minister presidents on the school reform question (Thron, *Schulreform*, pp. 150–52), he was similarly belaboring them for having decided to emphasize, in various ways, the provisional character of a future West German state, its constitution, and parliament. (See Willy Brandt and Richard Loewenthal, *Ernst Reuter: ein Leben für die Freiheit* [Munich: Kindler Verlag, 1957], pp. 472–74.)

65. Huelz, *Schulpolitik*, p. 125.

66. Frederic Spotts, *The Churches and Politics in Germany* (Middletown, Conn.: Wesleyan University Press, 1973) pp. 82–87. Spotts consulted Muench's papers for his study. Muench later became papal nuncio in Germany.

67. Ibid., pp. 86–87.

68. Ibid., pp. 83 ff. Muench's anti-Semitism is also well documented. He did everything possible to effect a purge of Jews and émigrées in the military government.

69. Ibid., p. 86.

70. Ibid., p. 87. The French government had asked the pope to remove Muench in February 1947 before it turned to Clay, who flew him to the States but could not convince Cardinal Spellman of the wisdom of keeping him there.

71. Thron, *Schulreform,* passim; Huelz, *Schulpolitik,* passim.

72. Hearnden, *Bildungspolitik,* pp. 53–54.

73. Pilgert, *Press, Radio and Film,* p. 30.

74. Mettler, *Demokratisierung,* p. 109. Resistance lasted until April 1949 in Württemberg-Baden, six months later than in Bavaria.

75. Reinken, *Rundfunk in Bremen,* p. 114.

76. Reichert, *Kampf,* pp. 39–44.

77. Rolf Steininger, "Rundfunk zwischen Bund und Ländern, 1953–1961." Ein Beitrag zur Innenpolitik Adenauers, *Politische Vierteljahresschrift* 17, no. 4 (Dec. 1976): 474–519; Steininger, "Rundfunkpolitik im ersten Kabinett Adenauers," *Vierteljahreshefte für Zeitgeschichte (VfZ),* 21, no. 4 (Oct. 1973); 389–454.

78. Advantage was not taken of the compromise that OMGUS had made: inclusion of some *Landtag* representatives in the *Rundfunkräte* and creation of the *Verwaltungsräte.*

79. Wolfgang Jacobmeyer, "Politischer Kommentar und Rundfunk, Zur Geschichte des Nordwestdeutschen Rundfunks, 1945–1951." *VfZ* 21, no. 4 (Oct. 1973): 386–87.

80. RIAS's reputation in this respect is, among journalists, still associated with "the American influence."

81. Steininger, "Rundfunkpolitik im ersten Kabinett Adenauers," pp. 409–10.

82. Shown in a comparative content analysis of front-page treatments in the *Neues Deutschland* and *Der Tagesspiegel* from 1945 to 1949, conducted in connection with the "Berlin-Project" which the author directs in the Zentralinstitut für Sozialwissenschaftliche Forschung of the Freie Universität Berlin.

83. Mettler evasively concedes this point. She ignored, however, the development of PIB activities between 1947 and 1949 outlined here. *Demokratisierung,* p. 54.

84. The transfer of PIB from Berlin to Frankfurt (later Bad Nauheim) was accompanied by a change of branch chiefs. The influence of PIB in the field operations of ISD in the *Länder* was hampered by bitter rivalry between ISD's two deputy directors, Alfred Boerner, who was responsible for policy, and Thomas Haeden, the deputy chief for operations. The feature service *Amerika Dienst* became PIB's major activity under the new chief of branch, Charles Arno.

85. Other changes of this nature in American overt media that did continue had a specific Berlin character: a local edition of the *Neue Zeitung* and RIAS's programs for the Soviet zone.

86. See above, note 22.

87. Hurwitz, *Stunde Null,* pp. 210–43.

88. Ibid., pp. 183–85.

89. Ibid., pp. 186–88.

90. Ibid., pp. 188–89; Pilgert, *Press, Radio and Film,* p. 25.

91. Pilgert, *Press, Radio and Film,* pp. 189 ff. The authoritarian gains of the Württemberg-Baden government were not in all cases repeated in Hesse and Bavaria. The Hesse law protected editors against false rebuttal statements (p. 190) and the Bavarian law explicitly forbade taxation of newspapers (p. 189).

16. United States Military Records in the National Archives Relating to the Occupations of Germany and Japan / Hastings

1. The OMGUS project, in progress since 1977, was completed early in 1982. Of approximately 8,000 cubic feet of OMGUS records, around 25 percent of the folders were selected and described by some thirty archivists and historians from the participating German institutions, and reproduced on about 133,000 microfiche containing over seven million images. Summary descriptions of those folders not deemed worthy of reproduction are also available. Microfiche copies are available from the National Archives, the Bundesarchiv, the Institut für Zeitgeschichte, and participating German state archives. For interim reports on progress on the project, see Wolfgang Benz, "Das OMGUS Project," *German Studies Review* (1979), pp. 89–94; John Mendelsohn, "The OMGUS Record Project, *Prologue* 10, no. 4 (1978): 259–60. For a German appreciation on completion of the project, see Josef Henke, "Das amerikanisch-deutsche OMGUS Projekt," *Der Archivar* 35, no. 2 (1982): 149–58. For a listing of OMGUS records, see Archival Sources: OMGUS, pp. 551–53, below.

2. Inspired by the OMGUS project, a similar program for the 10,000 feet of SCAP records began in 1977. Responding to insistent requests of Japanese researchers for access to American records of the occupation of the Japanese homeland, the National Diet Library in Tokyo requested that the National Archives microfilm selected SCAP records. As of mid-1982, about 80 percent of the records were being selected by Japanese researchers for reproduction on 16 mm. roll microfilm; at that rate, by the time the SCAP project closes in 1989 it may produce as many as 30 million frames. The National Archives retains a copy of each microfilm roll, and of each data sheet to serve as a finding aid. For a listing of SCAP records, see Archival Sources: SCAP, p. 550, below.

17. Resources of Presidential Libraries for the History of Post–World War II American Military Government in Germany and Japan / Zobrist

1. The author gratefully acknowledges staff members of all of the presidential libraries who assisted him in compiling the information presented in this paper. A version of this paper has appeared in *Military Affairs* 42, no. 1 (Feb. 1978): 17–19.

2. See "Notes on Resources" in Earl F. Ziemke, *The U.S. Army in the Occupation of Germany* (Washington, D.C.: Center of Military History, United States Army, 1975), pp. 450–56.

3. This paper is a sequel to the author's article, "Resources of Presidential Libraries for the History of the Second World War," *Military Affairs,* vol. 39 (Apr. 1975), pp. 82–85. An earlier version of the paper appears in James E. O'Neill and Robert W. Krauskopf, eds., *World War II: An Account of its Documents* (Washington, D.C.: Howard University Press, 1976), pp. 113–23.

20. Impact of the Proconsular Experience on Civil Affairs Organization and Doctrine / Swarm

1. Until 1947 the generic term Military Government (MG) was used by the military to denote all-inclusive civil affairs and military government activities. From 1947 (FM 27-5, Oct. 1947) to about 1960, the all-inclusive term Civil Affairs/Military Government (CAMG) was used. About 1960, the generic term Civil Affairs (CA) was adopted in order to emphasize the non-coercive aspects of the activity.

In this paper the term "CAMG" is used because 1) the paper deals primarily with experiences of the proconsuls derived mainly while conducting military government operations in occupied territory, and 2) the official title of the activity was "CAMG" during the period of the major developments recounted herein.

CAMG may be generally defined as a grouping of terms employed for convenience to refer to either Civil Affairs or Military Government, depending upon the context, in which Civil Affairs pertains to operations in a friendly country, whereas Military Government pertains to operations in an occupied area.

2. Harry L. Coles and Albert K. Weinberg, *Civil Affairs: Soldiers Become Governors,* United States Army in World War II: Special Studies (Washington, D.C.: Office of the Chief of Military History, Department of the Army, 1964), p. 7.

3. Ibid.

4. The following MG functions were recognized and implemented during WWII; all appeared in the 1947 FM 27-5, except "Religious Affairs" which was made official in 1962.

Governmental	Economic
Civil Government	Economics
Legal	Commerce and Industry
Public Safety	Food and Agriculture
Public Health	Price Control and Rationing
Public Welfare	Property Control
Public Finance	Civilian Supply
Public Education	
Labor	

Public Facilities	Special
Public Works & Utilities	Civil Information
Public Communications	Displaced Persons
Public Transportation	Arts, Monuments and Archives
	Religious Affairs

5. "A Bicentennial of Civil Military Operations" (Silver Spring, Md.: The Civil Affairs Association, 1976).

6. Ibid.

7. Colonel J. Strom Thurmond, USAR, a native of Aiken, S.C., and a European theater proconsul who had served on the First United States Army G5 staff throughout World War II, was then commander of the 360th CAMG Area A Headquarters unit. His collection of official CAMG documents, developed and promulgated during combat operations from the invasion of Normandy on D-day until VE-day, were an invaluable addition to those of the MG Department. Together they provided the basis for the concept of the G3/G5 relationship: that is, G3 assists the chief of staff in planning and coordinating operations "to defeat the enemy's armed forces" while G5 does the same "to utilize local resources in support of our military forces and control the land and the people."

8. The Scientific and Professional Personnel (SPP) program was originally restricted to enlisted personnel who had PhDs or MAs in the "hard" scientific disciplines: math, physics, engineering, and so forth. At the instigation of the chief, MG Department, OPMG took action which resulted in opening the program to enlisted personnel with the same levels of education in political science disciplines. The MG Department was a "first customer" to use them.

9. Popularly known as "The Fahey Study" by Daniel Cox Fahey, Jr., entitled "Findings, Conclusions, Recommendations, and Analysis, Concerning U.S. Civil Affairs/Military Government Organization, February 1951." Available in the Pollock Papers (Michigan Historical Society, Ann Arbor).

10. FM 41-10 describes some of these measures as follows:

22. CAMG Career Pattern and Reserve Branch of Service

a. General. The CAMG career pattern for officers in the Active Army and the CAMG Branch in the Army Reserve provide effective measures for the selection, procurement, and control of qualified CAMG officers in the Active Army and insure that the CAMG Reserve organization can attract, train, and furnish effective CAMG units to meet operational requirements.

b. CAMG Career Pattern. In accordance with the provisions of AR 616-170, a CAMG area of specification is established within the framework of career management for selected officers in the Active Army to include provisions for their utilization in controlled duty assignments, the conduct of advanced training in specialized subjects for such officers in civilian colleges and universities, and their attendance at military schools operated by other services or allied governments. For details on the career pattern in the CAMG field, see DA Pam 600-3.

c. CAMG Branch of Army Reserve. AR 140-108 establishes the CAMG Branch of the Army Reserve, provides selection and assignment criteria for Reserve officers and enlisted reservists, provides appropriate peacetime assignments of personnel to Reserve CAMG units, insures the development of the military and educational qualifications of such individuals, and develops an adequate source and continuity of training for such personnel.

11. Author of Special Text 41-20-50.
12. FM 41-10, pars. 1 and 51, a.

1. Purpose and Scope

This manual is published for the use of all personnel concerned with civil affairs/military government (CAMG) operations. It is intended for use in conjunction with FM 27-5 and FM 41-15. It is generally applicable to situations of combat or anticipated combat and contains techniques and procedures employed by CAMG staff sections and units, as integral parts of the Army in the field, in planning, conducting, and supervising CAMG activities; in controlling populations; providing maximum support to military operations; fulfilling international obligations; and furthering the national policies of the United States. The material presented herein is applicable without modification to both atomic and nonatomic warfare.

51. General

a. The CAMG organization, which consists of staff sections and units, is an integral component of the military force. It supports army forces in the conduct of tactical military operations. It assists in fulfilling the military commander's legal obligations with respect to the inhabitants, government, and economy of the area. It serves as the military agency with primary concern for the attainment of ultimate national objectives and provides for the future transfer of CAMG responsibilities to a designated civil agency of government.

13. FM 100-5, pars. 2 and 8. (1954)

2. Army Forces

Army forces, as land forces, are the decisive component of the military structure by virtue of their unique ability to close with and destroy the organized and irregular forces of an enemy power or coalition of powers; to seize and control critical land areas and . . .

. . . In addition, Army forces have the unique capability to accomplish any or all of the following tasks under all conditions of terrain and weather:

a. Insure a positive defense against enemy land forces. . . .

f. Provide positive and continuous control of the enemy's land areas and the populations therein, and enforce surrender terms, once victory has been achieved.

8. Limitations

Military forces are justifiable only as instruments of national policy in the attainment of national objectives. Since war is a political act, its broad and final objectives are political; therefore, its conduct must conform to policy and its outcome realize the objectives of policy. . . .

FM 100-5, Sect. IV, par 15. (1962)

Section IV. The Nature and Role of Land Forces
15. General

Land forces are those military forces organized, trained, and equipped for sustained combat incident to operations in the *land environment*. The land environment consists of the earth's land surfaces and the contiguous boundary layers of air and water. Land forces, therefore, include not only ground units, but certain ground/air systems and waterborne elements as well.

a. The United States Department of Defense is organized on the premise that the day of separate land, sea, and air warfare is gone forever. No single element of the nation's overall military power will suffice. Nor can the nation dispense with any element of its strength. Land, sea, and airpower are interdependent elements to be applied under unified direction and command toward the attainment of United States' objectives.

b. Landpower is the power to exercise direct, continuous and comprehensive control over the land, over its resources, *and over its peoples*. In peace, landpower is the basis of the stability, law, and order essential to a free society. In war the ultimate and decisive act is the exercise of landpower. War is won only when one nation imposes its will upon another, a process in which landpower is the matrix of national power. The ultimate aim of both sea and airpower is to influence the situation and operations on land; landpower makes permanent the otherwise transient advantages which air and naval forces can gain.

14. FM 41-10, par 51, c.

c. The CAMG organization must be flexible and adaptable to local political, economic, and sociological conditions. It must be prepared to implement policies transmitted by proper authority. . . .

15. FM 41-10, par 44.

. . . When a subordinate unit deviates from policy guidance, it promptly transmits notice of such departure to higher authority furnishing justification for such action and information on the probable duration of the period of deviation.

Par 51, c.

. . . It is responsible for recommending changes or modifications to policies and providing substantiation for such recommendations through the observation of results in the field.

16. FM 41-10, par 51, b.

b. The CAMG organization serves as an agency at the disposal of the military commander to assist in the accomplishment of his assigned mission and to combat enemy action which may be either planned or unplanned. Planned enemy action may consist of driving refugees into friendly lines to disrupt military operations; sending infiltrators into friendly lines to gather information and attack vulnerable lines of communication and administrative installations; and disrupting the political, economic, and sociological structures of countries under enemy occupation in order to weaken the will of population to resist. Unplanned enemy action may include the damage to civilian economies and centers of population which normally accompanies full scale military operations. Resulting chaos and confusion must be reduced in the shortest possible time in order to reduce interference with the conduct of military operations.

17. FM 41-10, par 51, d.

d. The CAMG organization is concerned with the regulation of those social processes which represent the changing ways in which human beings relate themselves to others. Social processes constitute a complex and unpredictable medium. Detailed prior planning enables the commander to employ the CAMG organization in the regulation of social processes and in the control, supervision, or influence of the local population, government, and economy.

18. FM 41-10, par 124.

Section III. Administrative and Judicial Controls

124. Forms of Administrative and Judicial Control

a. Administrative and judicial controls are utilized to control or supervise the people, government, and economy of areas in which CAMG operations are conducted. Administrative controls include coercive measures which can be enforced and noncoercive measures which offer an incentive for compliance. All judicial controls are coercive in nature.

b. Whenever possible noncoercive controls are employed; resort is made to coercive measures only when necessary. In many instances, both coercive and noncoercive measures can be combined to accomplish a desired result, or one can be applied with the other held in reserve.

c. In the conduct of civil affairs activities, reliance must be placed entirely on noncoercive measures to secure the cooperation of the local population. The strongest measure available may be the withholding of assistance which is desired by the local government.

d. A sanction is the legal application of a penalty as a result of a specific violation of law. A sanction may be imposed by force, if necessary. . . .

19. FM 41-10, pars. 36 and 37.

36. Duties of the CAMG Officer (G5)

a. In general, the assistant chief of staff, G5, assists the chief of staff in the planning for and coordination of those functions pertaining to the civil population, government, and economy of areas in which armed forces are employed, and the conduct of CAMG operations.

b. G5 is assigned primary general staff responsibility in the planning for, preparation, and execution of CAMG policies, plans, orders, and directives, and is charged with keeping the commander and members of the staff informed on all matters pertaining to CAMG operations or activities. The other general staff sections of the headquarters assist G5, as appropriate, in the planning for and performance of those functions of personnel, intelligence, planning coverage, and logistics, which are related to CAMG operations and in which they have a primary interest.

c. G5 assists the commander in providing positive and continuous control over the land areas and populations therein for which the commander has responsibility. He advises the commander on those vital installations and local resources which should be spared from destruction in order to provide a basis for building a peace when the conflict is over. When a friendly nation is liberated from enemy occupation, G5, in conjunction with the political adviser (if present), advises the commander on the implementation of those directives pertaining to the restoration of the political and territorial integrity of the nation.

d. For information on the specific duties of G5, see FM 101-5.

37. Staff Supervision

a. The G5 insures that CAMG plans, operation orders, letters of instruction, and other documents are received by subordinate units or agencies. He makes certain that the documents are correctly understood and, when necessary, assists in their implementation. Close supervision is necessary to assure that the intent of orders and instructions is carried out as desired by the commander. Supervision is effected by visits and by study and analysis of special and routine reports of subordinate CAMG units. . . .

20. FM 101-5, par. 21, a, b, c.

21. Civil Affairs/Military Government Officer (G5)

a. The assistant chief of staff, G5, assists the chief of staff in the planning and coordination of those functions pertaining to—the civil population, government, and economy of areas in which armed forces are employed; and the conduct of civil affairs/military government operations.

b. He is responsible for the planning and supervision of civil affairs/military government training of his own section and, in coordination with G3, exercises general staff responsibility for such training within the command.

c. His specific duties normally include primary general staff responsibility of activities pertaining to—

(1) *Internal affairs and government.* This includes public safety, public health and sanitation, public welfare and relief, . . .

21. FM 41-10, par. 42, a, b.

42. Planning

a. General. The successful accomplishment of national objectives in military operations in which United States armed forces participate depends in large part on the recognition of the necessity for prior planning at the theater level for the conduct of CAMG operations. Since detailed prior planning is also essential at all echelons of command within the theater, the theater or senior United States commander must provide an overall CAMG plan for the guidance of his subordinate commanders in order to prescribe the objectives of CAMG operations and insure continuity of policies and uniformity of their application. Although responsibility for the conduct of CAMG activities should be transferred to a designated United States or allied civil agency of government as expeditiously as the military situation permits, the theater plan should insure that authority and responsibility for CAMG activities during military operations are vested in military commanders and not divided between military and civil agencies.

   b. Development of Theater Plan. The military force serves primarily as an instrument of national policy in the attainment of political objectives. . . .

22. FM 41-10, par 41, a.

Section II. Estimates, Plans, Orders, and Reports
41. Estimates of the Situation

   a. The commander's decision is influenced not only by the relative combat power of opposing forces but also by characteristics of the area of operations. The CAMG estimate accordingly assists the commander in reaching a decision by weighing the effects which the lines of action open to him may produce with respect to his mission, evaluating for him those political, economic, and sociological conditions in the area of operations, and determining the degree of assistance or interference such conditions may present to the proposed operation (FM 100-5).

23. FM 101-5, par 21, c, (5).

   (5) *Plans and directives.* The preparation of civil affairs/military government estimates, directives, and civil affairs/military government annexes to operational and administrative orders.

24. FM 41-5, par 31, c, (1) and (2).

   . . . and uniformity of CAMG operations, limit the number of tactical or administrative commanders to whom area authority for CAMG should be delegated. In general, such delegation should be to those subordinate commanders whose military operations require that they have responsibility within their assigned areas.

   (1) A mobile or unsettled situation favors the delegation of authority for the conduct of CAMG operations to subordinate commanders. In such situations the operational chain of command is employed.

   (2) A static or settled situation favors the retention of military government authority in a higher commander in preparation to the transfer of responsibility to a civil agency of government. When this occurs the CAMG chain of command is employed.

25. FM 41-10, par. 56, a, b.

56. Chains of Command

   The operations of CAMG units may be directed through an *operational chain of command or a CAMG chain of command.* Either or both may be utilized within a theater, together with technical channels for the exchange of information.

a. Operational Chain of Command. This chain of command is employed primarily in the combat zone when tactical considerations are of paramount concern and when the situation is fluid or unsettled. In this situation, CAMG activities are directed by the commanders of those major tactical commands to whom CAMG area authority is delegated. Instructions of a higher commander pertaining to the conduct of CAMG operations in the area of a subordinate major unit are transmitted through normal command channels. The commander of a CAMG command or area support unit receives his directives from the commander of the major unit to which his CAMG unit is assigned or attached. Although this chain of command facilitates the discharge by major unit commanders of their CAMG obligations, it generally requires detailed direction to insure continuity and uniformity of operations.

b. CAMG Chain of Command. This chain of command is used in areas where the situation is static or stabilized and the commanders of subordinate major tactical and administrative units are not delegated CAMG area authority. It is particularly desirable to use the CAMG chain of command after hostilities have ceased in order to focalize the direction of CAMG operations in the higher levels of command, to insure uniformity and continuity of effort, and to prepare for the transfer of CAMG responsibilities to a civil agency of government. Under the CAMG chain of command, the commander of the major unit delegated CAMG area authority transmits instructions through his CAMG command direct to all CAMG units within his area of responsibility.

21. The Occupation as Perceived by the Public, Scholars, and Policy Makers / Peterson

1. Harold Zink, *American Military Government in Germany* (New York: Macmillan, 1947), pp. 24–25, 27, 48–52, 91, 140, 238–40.

2. Lewis Brown, *A Report on Germany* (New York: Farrar, 1947), pp. 48, 119, 122.

3. B. U. Ratchford and W. D. Ross, *Berlin Reparations Assignment* (Chapel Hill: Univ. of North Carolina Press, 1947), pp. 10, 15, 23.

4. Carl J. Friedrich, *American Experiences in Military Government in World War II* (New York: Rinehart, 1948), p. 16.

5. Solomon Lebovitz, "Military Government and the Revival of German Political Activity" (Ph.D. diss., Harvard Univ., 1949), pp. 26, 50, 165. This position would be borne out by the later scholarly studies of John Golay, *The Founding of the Federal Republic of Germany* (Chicago: Univ. of Chicago Press, 1958), pp. 22, 23, 108; and Peter Merkl, *The Origins of the West German Republic* (New York: Oxford Univ. Press, 1963), pp. xvi, 21, 88, 97.

6. Russell Hill, *Struggle for Germany* (New York: Harper, 1947), pp. 121,

143–45; Delbert Clark, *Again the Goosestep* (Indianapolis: Bobbs, Merrill, 1949), pp. 47–50, 80.

7. William Griffith, "The Denazification Program in the U.S. Zone of Germany" (Ph.D. diss., Harvard Univ., 1950), pp. 6, 7, 34, 37, 39, 82–83, 90, 96, 105, 107–8, 173–74, 177–80, 310–12, 324, 331–37.

8. J. F. J. Gillen, *American Influence on the Development of Political Institutions* (Karlsruhe: HICOG, 1951), p. 2; *Deconcentration and Decartelization* (Bonn: HICOG, 1953), pp. 73, 88; *State and Local Government in West Germany, 1945–1953* (Mehlem: HICOG, 1953), pp. 5, 50, 74–75.

9. John Kormann, *United States Denazification* (Bad Godesberg: HICOG, 1952), pp. 22, 31, 92, 124.

10. Bert Schloss, "The American Occupation of Germany, 1945–1952. An Appraisal," (Ph.D. diss., Univ. of Chicago, 1955), pp. 311, 326, 329.

11. Morris Edwards, "A Case Study of Military Government in Germany During and After World War II" (Ph.D. diss., Georgetown Univ., 1957), pp. 93–94, 258, 303.

12. John Montgomery, *Forced to Be Free* (Chicago: Univ. of Chicago Press, 1957), pp. 77–83.

13. Harold Zink, *The United States in Germany, 1944–1951* (NewYork: Van Nostrand, 1957), pp. 77–79, 93.

14. Manuel Gottlieb, *The German Peace Settlement and the Berlin Crisis* (New York: Paine-Whiteman, 1960), pp. 81–82, 107, 110, 115, 121, 186.

15. John Gimbel, *A German Community under American Occupation: Marburg, 1945–1952* (Stanford, Calif.: Stanford Univ. Press, 1962), chs. 11–13.

16. Franklin Davis, *Come as a Conqueror* (New York: Macmillan, 1967), pp. 142–45.

17. John Backer, *Priming the German Economy* (Durham: Duke Univ. Press, 1971), pp. 77, 86, 104.

18. Earl Ziemke, *The U.S. Army in the Occupation of Germany* (Washington: Office of Military History, 1975), pp. 14, 65, 114, 222, 313.

19. John Gimbel, *The American Occupation of Germany* (Stanford, Calif.: Stanford Univ. Press, 1968), pp. 1–31.

20. Barton Bernstein, ed., *Politics and Policies of the Truman Administration* (Chicago: Quadrangle, 1970); Gabriel Kolko, *The Politics of War* (New York: Random House, 1968); Gabriel Kolko, *The Roots of American Foreign Policy* (Boston: Beacon Press, 1969); Bruce Kuklick, "American foreign Economic Policy and Germany, 1939–1946" (Ph.D. diss., Univ. of Pennsylvania, 1968); Walter LaFeber, *America, Russia and the Cold War 1945–1946* (New York: Wiley, 1967).

21. Hilldring to Greenfield, OCMH, Aug. 1950, CA, File 70, Drawer 3. Edwards, "A Case Study," pp. 47–50, lists Hilldring's suggestions for planning "firm policies."

22. Daniel Cox Fahey, Jr., "Findings, Conclusions, Recommendations and Analysis, Concerning U.S. Civil Affairs/MG Organization, February 1951," available in Pollock Papers (Michigan Historical Society, Ann Arbor).

23. George Shuster, *The Ground I Walked On* (New York: Farrar, 1961), pp. 191–94, 208.

24. George Kennan, *Memoirs, 1925–1950* (Boston: Little, Brown, 1967), p. 452.

25. George Kennan, *American Diplomacy, 1900–1950* (Chicago: Univ. of Chicago Press, 1951).

Biographical Notes

Carl G. Anthon, who retired as professor of history in 1976 from American University in Washington, D.C., was at the time of this 1977 conference on the staff of the National Endowment for the Humanities. Between 1949 and 1953 he was higher education advisor to the United States High Commission in Germany, and in 1958–60 executive secretary of the United States Education Commission in Bonn. Among his published works are several articles on postwar Germany in *Current History*.

John H. Backer at the time of this 1977 conference was legislative assistant to Senator S. I. Hayakawa. During the Second World War, he was an intelligence officer with the 82nd Airborne Division in Europe. He served the United States Military Government for Germany as deputy chief, Zonal Operations, in 1946, and as chief, Export Promotion Branch, Joint Export-Import Agency, 1947–48. He subsequently served with the State Department in Germany as a research officer in the United States Mission, Berlin, 1956–59; as director of the United States Information Center in Hannover, 1960–61; and as consul and public affairs officer in Frankfurt am Main, 1962–64. He is the author of: *Priming the German Economy: American Occupational Policies, 1945–1948* (Durham, N.C.: Duke Univ. Press, 1971); *The Decision to Divide Germany: American Foreign Policy in Transition* (Durham, N.C.: Duke Univ. Press, 1978); and *Winds of History: The German Years of Lucius DuB. Clay* (New York: Van Nostrand Reinhold Co., 1983).

Hans H. Baerwald, professor of political science at the University of California at Berkeley, served as a language officer, Allied Translator and Interpreter Section, and Government Section, GHQ-SCAP, in Tokyo from 1946 to 1949. Among his published works are: *The Purge of Japanese Leaders under the Occupation* (Berkeley and Los Angeles: Univ. of California Press, 1959); and (with Tsurumi Shunsuke and Matsuura Sozo) "Tsuiho wa Nihon no Seiji wo do kaheta ka?" [What changes did the purge bring about in Japanese politics?] in *Shiso No Kagaku* [Science of thought], August 1966, pp. 2–12.

Jacob D. Beam, United States ambassador to Poland, 1957–61, to Czechoslovakia, 1966–69, and to the Soviet Union, 1969–72, served before the Second World War as secretary, United States Embassy in Berlin from 1934 to 1940. During the war, he was secretary, United States Embassy in London, 1941–45, and during the occupation was political advisor, United States Forces in Germany from 1945 to 1947, and chief, Central European Division, State Department, 1947–49.

Hugh Borton at the time of this 1977 conference was a senior research associate of the East Asian Institute of Columbia University, where he had taught Japanese language and history from 1937 to 1942 and from 1946 to 1957, attaining the post of professor of Japanese and director of the institute, before becoming president of Haverford College from 1957 to 1967. From 1942 to 1946, he taught at the Charlottesville School for Military Government; then served in the Department of State as a research associate, and later as chief of the Division of Japanese Affairs; he was also a member of the SWNCC subcommittee for the Far East and of the American delegation to the Far Eastern Commission in Washington. Among his published works are: *Japan's Modern Century: From Perry to 1970,* 2nd ed. (New York: Ronald Press, 1970); "The Allied Occupation of Japan, 1945–1947," in F. C. Jones, Hugh Borton, and B. R. Pearn, eds., *The Far East, 1942–1946* (London: Oxford University Press, 1955), pp. 307–430; "Preparation for the Occupation of Japan," *Journal of Asian Studies* 25 (Feb. 1966): 203–12; and "American Presurrender Planning for Postwar Japan" (New York: Occasional Papers of the East Asian Institute, Columbia Univ., 1967), pp. 3–37.

Ralph Braibanti is James B. Duke Professor of Political Science and Director of Islamic and Arabian Development Studies at Duke University. He served in the United States Army during the Second World War and for two years was military government officer in the prefecture of Yamanashi, Japan. He received the Army Commendation Medal for his work there. As a civilian in 1952, he was political advisor to the civil administrator for the Ryukyu Islands. His published works include: *Administration of Occupied Japan: A Study Guide* (with Philip H. Taylor) (1950); *Research on the Bureaucracy of Pakistan* (1966); *Political and Administrative Development* (1969); and *Tradition, Values and Socio-Economic Development* (with J. J. Spengler) (1961).

Lucius D. Clay was successively United States deputy military governor and military governor of Germany from April 1945 to May 1949. During the Second World War he was director of materiel for the War Department, and simultaneously a member of the Munitions Assignment Board and the War Production Board. Detailed to Europe in the autumn of 1944 where he untangled the snarl at the then key port of Cherbourg, he returned to Washington to serve as deputy to James F. Byrnes, director of War Mobilization and Reconversion, until his designation as deputy military governor in April 1945. After retirement from active duty in June 1949, he was chief executive officer of Continental Can Company and then a director of the Wall Street firm of Lehman Brothers until his death in April 1978.

Mabel E. Deutrich retired as assistant archivist for the National Archives in 1979. A historian and records manager for the Department of the Army, she transferred to the National Archives in 1950 where she served as director of the Military Archives Division from 1970 to 1975. She is the author of *Struggle for Supremacy: The Career of General Fred C. Ainsworth* (Washington: Public Affairs Press, 1962), and a number of articles published in professional journals.

Willard A. Fletcher, professor of history at the University of Delaware, following his release from German internment, 1942–44, enlisted in the 14th Armored Division, was assigned to temporary duty with the Counter Intelligence Corps in Germany, and then to G2 Fourth Army. He served as director of the American Historical Association microfilm project for captured German records in 1960–61, and edited a number of that project's *Guides to German Records Microfilmed in Alexandria, Va.* He has published in the field of modern German history, and is currently working on German occupation policies during the Second World War.

John Gimbel, professor of history at Humboldt State University in California, served with Detachment G-34, 2nd Military Government Regiment, which administered Landkreis Friedberg in Germany at the close of the Second World War. He is the author of: *A German Community under American Occupation: Marburg, 1945–1952* (Stanford, Calif.: Stanford Univ. Press, 1961); *The American Occupation of Germany: Politics and the Military, 1945–1949* (Stanford Univ. Press, 1968); and *The Origins of the Marshall Plan* (Stanford Univ. Press, 1976).

Milton O. Gustafson has been chief of the Diplomatic Branch of the National Archives since 1971. He directed a 1969 conference and edited the proceedings thereof entitled *The National Archives and Foreign Relations Research* (Athens: Ohio Univ. Press, 1974), and has published a number of articles on the sources for United States diplomatic history.

Eleanor M. Hadley is adjunct professor of economics, George Washington University. From 1974 to 1981 she was a group director, International Division, United States General Accounting Office. During the Second World War, she served as a research analyst with the Far Eastern Division, Research and Analysis Branch, Office of Strategic Services, and in 1946–47 she was an economist, Government Section, GHQ-SCAP, in Tokyo. She is the author of: *Antitrust in Japan* (Princeton, N.J.: Princeton Univ. Press, 1970); "Japan: Competition or Private Collectivism?" *Far Eastern Survey,* December 14, 1949, pp. 289–94; and "Trust Busting in Japan," *Harvard Business Review,* July 1948, pp. 425–40.

James J. Hastings, now deputy director of the Nixon Presidential Materials Staff at the National Archives, had at the time of this conference spent several years as an archivist working with the records of United States military government from the Second World War. He is the author of: "MacArthur's Revenge: A Guide to the Operational Files of GHQ, SCAP," a paper presented to the Association of Asian Studies in March 1976; "Sources in the National Archives Pertaining to Legal Reform in Japan," at the MacArthur Memorial Symposium, April 15, 1977; and "Die Akten der amerikanischen Besatzungsverwaltung in Deutschland" ("Die Akten des Office of Military Government for Germany [US]"), in *Vierteljahrshefte für Zeitgeschichte,* January 1976, pp. 75–101.

Harold Hurwitz has been a professor of political sociology at the Free University of Berlin since 1967. He came to Germany as an American civilian employee of OMGUS, Information Services Division, Political Information Branch, where he served from 1946 to 1950. From 1960 to 1967, he supervised the opinion research program of the Berlin city government. He is the author of: *Der heimliche Leser: Beiträge zur Soziologie des geistigen Widerstandes* (Cologne: Verlag Wissenschaft und Politik, 1966); *Die Stunde Null der deutschen Presse: Die amerikanische Pressepolitik in Deutschland, 1945–1949* (Cologne: Verlag Wissenschaft und Politik, 1972); "Antikommunismus und amerikanische Demokratisierungvorhaben in Nachkriegsdeutschland," *Parlament* 28, no. 29 (1978): 29–46; and *Die politische Kultur der Bevölkerung und der Neubeginn konservativer Politik,* first volume in a forthcoming series *Demokratie und Antikommunismus in Berlin nach 1945* (Cologne: Verlag Wissenschaft und Politik, 1983).

John J. McCloy during the Second World War served as assistant secretary of war under Henry L. Stimson, including among his responsibilities the coordination of Army planning for civil affairs and military government in liberated and occupied territories. President of the World Bank from 1947 to 1949, he was United States military governor and high commissioner for Germany from 1949 to 1952. During the First World War, he was an officer in the American Expeditionary Forces, and also saw duty afterward in the United States-occupied Coblenz bridgehead. He distilled some of this experience in two wars and their aftermath in *The Challenge to American Foreign Policy* (Cambridge: Harvard Univ. Press, 1953).

Marlene J. Mayo, associate professor of history at the University of Maryland, was a student in 1954–55 at the London School of Economics, and in 1958–59 at the University of Tokyo, to which she returned as a Fulbright research scholar in 1967–68. She has published many articles on Japan, among them: "American Economic Planning for Occupied Japan: The Issue of *Zaibatsu* Dissolution, 1942–1945," in *The Occupation of Japan: Economic Policy and Reform,* ed. Lawrence H. Redford (Norfolk: MacArthur Memorial, 1980), pp. 205–28 and 252–62; and "Psychological Disarmament: American Wartime Planning for the Education and Re-Education of Defeated Japan, 1943–1945," in *The Occupation of Japan: Educational and Social Reform,* ed. Thomas Burkman (Norfolk: Gatling Printing and Publishing Co., 1982), pp. 21–128. She has in progress in 1984 a book bearing the working title "Redesigning Japan: American Wartime Planning for the Occupation and Control of the Defeated Enemy, 1942–1945."

John Mendelsohn is projects chief of the Modern Military Headquarters Branch of the National Archives and Records Service, and a specialist in war crimes trial records of the Second World War and its aftermath. He experienced the United States occupation as a young resident of Berlin, before emigrating to the United States and serving in the United States Air Force. His 1974 doctoral dissertation, "Trial by Document: The Use of Seized Records in United States Proceedings at Nuernberg," is scheduled for publication by the Federal German Archives in 1984. Besides compiling or supervising the compilation of numerous National Archives finding aids on war crimes trial records and military government records, he is the editor of *The Holocaust: Selected Documents,* in 18 volumes (New York: Garland Press, 1982); and author of "Trial by Document: The Problem of Due Process for War Criminals at Nuernberg," *Prologue,* Winter 1975, pp. 226–34; "The OMGUS Records Project, *Prologue,* Winter 1978, pp. 259–60; and "The Holocaust: Rescue and Relief Documentation in the National Archives," in *Reflections on the Holocaust* (Philadelphia: Annals of the American Academy of Political and Social Science, July 1980), pp. 237–49.

John D. Montgomery, professor of public administration and chairman of the Department of Government, Harvard University, was an Army officer in the Pacific theater and with the 76th Military Government Company in Japan from 1942 to 1946. He is the author of: *The Purge in Occupied Japan* (Chevy Chase, Md.: Johns Hopkins University Operations Research Office, 1953); *Forced to Be Free: The Artificial Revolution in Germany and Japan* (Chicago: Univ. of Chicago Press, 1957); *The Politics of Foreign Aid* (New York: Praeger, 1962); *Foreign Aid in International Politics* (Englewood Cliffs, N.J.: Prentice-Hall, 1967); and *Technology and Civic Life* (Cambridge: MIT Press, 1974).

Eli E. Nobleman, at the time of this 1977 conference in his thirtieth year as counsel to the United States Senate Committee on Governmental Affairs, during the Second World War served in Europe with G5 of the First Army as public safety and legal officer with various military government units trying over one thousand military government court cases in one year. In 1945, he was named chief of the German Courts Section, and in 1946 of the Military Government Courts Section, Legal Division, OMG Bavaria. He has remained a member of civil affairs reserve units through the years, and was recalled to active duty during the Berlin crisis of 1961, serving as director of instruction at the United States Army Civil Affairs School, Fort Gordon, Ga. Dr. Nobleman is the author of numerous military-legal studies and a contributor to civil affairs doctrine and manuals, among them: "The Administration of Justice in the United States Zone of Germany," *Federal Bar Journal,* 8: 70–97, Washington, D.C., Oct. 1946; "American Military Government Courts in Germany," *American Journal of International Law,* 40:

803–12, Washington, D.C., Oct. 1946; "American Military Government Courts in Germany," *Annals of the American Academy of Political and Social Science,* 267: 87–97, Philadelphia, Jan. 1950; "Military Government Courts: Law and Justice in the American Zone of Germany," *American Bar Association Journal* 33: 777–80, 851–52, Chicago, Ill., Aug. 1947; and "Procedure and Evidence in American Military Government Courts in the United States Zone of Germany," *Federal Bar Journal,* 8: 212–48, Washington, D.C., Jan. 1947.

Edward N. Peterson, chairman, Department of History, University of Wisconsin at River Falls, served as an infantryman and intelligence sergeant in Germany from 1945 to 1947. He is author of: *The Limits of Hitler's Powers* (Princeton, N.J.: Princeton Univ. Press, 1969); and *The American Occupation of Germany: Retreat to Victory* (Detroit: Wayne State Univ. Press, 1978).

Elmer Plischke, professor emeritus of government and politics at the University of Maryland, and adjunct professor, Gettysburg College, after training at the Columbia University Naval School of Military Government and Administration, 1943–44, served in the Civil Affairs Division, Commander United States Naval Forces for Europe, London, 1944–45, and in the Office of the Director of Political Affairs, OMGUS, during 1945, where he coordinated denazification policy. From 1950 to 1952, he was special historian with the Historical Division, HICOG. Among his published works are: *History of the Allied High Commission for Germany* (1951); *Revision of the Occupation Statute for Germany* (1952); *Allied High Commission Relations with the West German Government* (1952); *The West German Federal Government* (1952); *Berlin: Development of its Government and Administration* (1952); *The Allied High Commission for Germany* (1953); and (with Henry Pilgert) *U.S. Information Programs in Berlin* (1953)—all published by the Office of the U.S. High Commissioner for Germany, Bad Godesberg/ Mehlem. Other pertinent publications are "Denazifying the Reich," *Review of Politics,* vol. 9 (Apr. 1947), pp. 153–72; and "Denazification Law and Procedure," *American Journal of International Law,* vol. 41 (Oct. 1947), pp. 807–27.

Forrest C. Pogue is the director of the Smithsonian Institution's Dwight D. Eisenhower Institute for Historical Research. He was a historian with the First Army, attached to V Corps, from the Normandy invasion to VE day, and a civilian historian with the Office of the Chief of Military History from 1945 to 1952, during which time he wrote *The Supreme Command* volume for the series *United States Army in World War II: The European Theater of Operations* (Washington, D.C.: OCMH, 1954). A former director of the George C. Marshall Library and Research Center, he is the author of a four-volume definitive biography of General Marshall, three volumes of which have already appeared: *George C. Marshall: Education of a General, 1880–1939* (New York: Viking, 1963); *Ordeal and Hope, 1939–1942* (New

York: Viking, 1966); and *Organizer of Victory, 1943–1945* (New York: Viking, 1973).

Jacques J. Reinstein, a member of the Atlantic Council of the United States, served during the Second World War as financial advisor, Liberated Areas Division, and in the Financial Division, Department of State, 1943–45. In postwar service with that department, he was director, Office of German Economic Affairs in 1949–50, special assistant to the United States High Commissioner for Germany, 1950–51, special assistant to the director, Bureau of German Affairs, 1952–54, and director in 1955–58. During this State Department service, he was also a member of several delegations negotiating on German and European affairs; Economic Advisor to the United States Delegation, Council of Foreign Ministers, 1945–46, 1947, 1949, 1954, and the Paris Peace Conference, 1946; alternate delegate, Intergovernmental Study Group on Germany, London, 1950–51; delegate, Conference on German Debts, London, 1952–53.

James W. Riddleberger, most recently associated with the Population Crisis Committee, during his long career in the Foreign Service was assigned to key positions dealing with German affairs almost continuously from 1935 to 1953: second secretary of the Berlin Embassy from 1936 to 1941; the German desk in the State Department in Washington in 1941–42; the Blockade Section of the Economic Warfare Division in London, 1942–44; chief, Division of Central European Affairs in Washington (simultaneously serving during 1946 as chairman of the Secretary's Policy Committee on Germany functioning under the cover name "Working Security Committee," a forerunner of SWNCC), 1944–47; counselor, Office of the United States Political Advisor for Germany, 1947–49; political advisor to the United States high commissioner for Germany, and concurrently director of political affairs for the Office of Political Affairs, Frankfurt, 1949–50; ECA (Economic Cooperation Administration), Paris, 1950–52; director, Bureau of German Affairs, Washington, 1952–53. During these assignments, he also served as a member of the United States delegations to the meetings of the Council of Foreign Ministers at Potsdam in July–August 1945; Paris, April–May 1946; New York, December 1946; Moscow, March–April 1947; and to the London Tripartite Talks on Germany, February–April 1948. He died on October 16, 1982.

William R. Swarm, recently retired from the Emergency Preparedness staff of the General Services Administration, entered on active duty in 1940 as a captain of field artillery, graduated from the Command and General Staff College in 1942, and served successively as a battery commander and battalion commander of artillery until 1943. Assigned in that year to military government duty, he attended the Western Reserve University Civil Affairs Training School. In 1944, as deputy assistant chief of staff, G5 of VIII Corps, he planned, deployed, and supervised civil affairs and military government detachments in Normandy, Brittany, Belgium, Luxembourg, and Germany, which included control of refugees and search for infiltrators during VIII Corps' withdrawal from Bastogne, and the establishment of provincial government in the Russian zone of Germany temporarily occupied by that American corps. From war's end until March 1948, he commanded military government detachments in Büdingen, Darmstadt, and Kassel, Germany, his last assignment being deputy director, Internal Affairs Division, OMG Bavaria. In 1949–50 he was on temporary duty with the State Department, Bureau of German Affairs, assisting in transfer of occupation responsibilities from Army to State. As chief of the military government department of the Provost Marshal General's School, Camp Gordon, Georgia, he developed and published the school text, *Fundamentals of the Military Government Activity,* from which were derived many of the basic doctrines and organizations incorporated into civil affairs and military government manuals produced during his tour of duty as chief, Military Plans and Policy Division, Office of Chief, CAMG, at the Pentagon in 1954–57. During assignments in Korea in 1953–54, and in Hawaii from 1957 to 1960, as chief CAMG officer for Commander-in-Chief of the Pacific (CINCPAC), he was able to apply this doctrine in the field, and to assist in the training of civil affairs officers of our Pacific area allies. From 1961 to 1964, he was commandant of the United States Army Civil Affairs School, Fort Gordon, Georgia.

Robert Wolfe, chief of the Modern Military Headquarters Branch at the National Archives, has also served that agency since 1961 as specialist for captured German records. An infantry officer in the South Pacific and Europe from 1942 to 1945, he was in the Information Control Division of the Office of Military Government, Württemberg-Baden, from 1945 through October 1948. He taught history at Brooklyn College from 1954 to 1960, and was an assistant professorial lecturer for George Washington University from 1961 to 1965. He has directed conferences at the National Archives on captured German records and on the Nuremberg war crimes trials, respectively, and edited the published proceedings of the conference on *Captured German and Related Records* (Athens: Ohio Univ. Press, 1975). Among his published articles and scholarly papers are: "Putative Threat to National Security as a Nürnberg Defense for Genocide," in *Reflections on the Holocaust, Annals of the American Academy of Political and Social Science* (Philadelphia, July 1980), pp. 46–67; and "From Information Control to Media Freedom," a paper presented at the annual meeting of the American Historical Association at San Francisco in December 1978.

Earl F. Ziemke, professor of history at the University of Georgia, served in World War II with the United States Marines in the Pacific theater. He was a member of the staff of the Bureau of Applied Social Research at Columbia University from 1951 until 1955, when he joined the staff of the Center of Military History, United States Army, where he had achieved the position of deputy chief of the General History Branch when he left for the University of Georgia in 1967. He is the author of: *The German Northern Theater* *of Operations, 1940–1945* (Washington, D.C.: Department of the Army Pamphlet No. 20-271, 1959); *Stalingrad to Berlin: The German Defeat in the East,* Army Historical Series (Washington, D.C.: Office of the Chief of Military History, United States Army, 1968); and *The U.S. Army in the Occupation of Germany, 1944–1946* (Washington, D.C.: Center of Military History, United States Army, 1975).

Benedict K. Zobrist, director of the Harry S Truman Library, has been with that institution since 1969. He was a manuscript specialist at the Library of Congress, 1952–53, at the Newberry Library, 1953–54, a historian for the Ordnance Weapon Command at Rock Island Arsenal, 1954–60, and assistant dean of faculty at Augustana College, 1960–69. He co-edited with Donald R. McCoy the transcript of a *Conference of Scholars on the Administration of Occupied Areas, 1943–1955,* held at the Truman Library on April 10–11, 1970 (Independence, Missouri: Harry S Truman Library Institute for National and International Affairs, 1970).

Conference Participants

Frederick Aandahl
Department of State

Robert H. Alexander
MacArthur
Memorial Library

Laszlo M. Alfoldi
United States Army
Military History
Research Center

Dean C. Allard
Naval History
Division

Morris Amchan
Arlington, VA
(Nuremberg trials,
1945–48)

Carl G. Anthon
American
University

John H. Backer
United States Senate
staff

Hans H. Baerwald
University of
California, Los
Angeles

Helen Bailey
Joint Chiefs of Staff,
Historical Division

Richard A. Baker
Historical Office,
The Capitol

M. Edward Bander
Silver Spring, MD

Jacob D. Beam
Department of State
(ret.)

Gail Becker
Washington, DC

Peter W. Becker
University of South
Carolina

Silvio A. Bedini
Smithsonian
Institution

Tristan E. Beplat
Princeton, NJ
(SCAP, Financial
Division, 1945–48)

Dale Birdsell
United States Army
Materiel
Development &
Readiness Center

Porter Blakemore
Madison College

Martin Blumenson
Army Center of
Military History

Hugh Borton
Columbia University
(ret.)

Carl Boyd
Old Dominion
University

John H. Boyle
California State
University

Ralph Braibanti
Duke University

William R. Braisted
United States Naval
Academy

Kent C. Brandt
Oxon Hill, MD

Rennie W. Brantz
Appalachian State
University

Richard D. Breitman
American
University

Pierce B. Browne
Concord, MA

Dr. & Mrs. Roy Bullock
North Arlington, VA

Thomas W. Burkman
Old Dominion
University

George Chalou
National Archives

Brewster S.
Chamberlain
Institute for
Contemporary
History, Munich

Moreau B. Chambers
Army Center of
Military History

Sung Yoon Cho
Library of Congress

Barbara Chotiner
University of
Maryland

Jeffrey J. Clarke
Army Center of
Military History

Robert W. Coakley
Army Center of
Military History

Wayne Cole
University of
Maryland
James L. Collins, Jr.
Army Center of
Military History
Doris Condit
Office of the
Secretary of Defense
Kenneth W. Condit
Joint Chiefs of Staff,
Historical Division
Stanley R. Connor
Army Center of
Military History
Yayoi Cooke
University of
Maryland
Robin E. Cookson
National Archives
Robert B. Coords
Prince George's
Community College
Alfred E. Cornebise
University of
Northern Colorado
Edwin S. Costrell
Department of State
C. L. Cox
Miami-Dade
Community College
Jules Davids
Georgetown
University
Roderic Davison
George Washington
University
Sebastian deGrazia
Rutgers University
Charles E. Delzell
Vanderbilt
University
Marion Deshmukh
George Mason
University

Donald S. Detwiler
Southern Illinois
University
Mabel E. Deutrich
National Archives
Harold C. Deutsch
Army War College
(OSS, 1944–45;
State Dept., Special
Interrogation
Mission to Germany,
1945)
Rolf Dodd
Blue Springs, MD
Elsie C. Dolling
Falls Church, VA
(OMGUS, 1946–49;
HICOG, 1949–53)
Robert M. Donihi
Washington, DC
(IMTFE, 1945–46;
European War
Crimes Commission,
1946–48; legal
adviser, OMGUS,
1948–49; HICOG,
1949–52)
G. M. Richardson
Dougall
Department of State
Sherrod E. East
National Archives
(ret.)
Corwin D. Edwards
Lewes, DE
(Chief, U.S. Mission
on Japanese
Combines [so-called
Zaibatsu mission],
Jan.–Mar. 1946)
Frank T. Edwards
California State
College
Daun van Ee
The Johns Hopkins
University

Carol Ehlers
Trenton State
College
Howard M. Ehrmann
University of
Michigan (ret.)
Carolyn Eisenberg
State University of
New York, Stony
Brook
James M. Erdmann
University of Denver
Rudolf Erlemann
Embassy of the
Federal Republic of
Germany
Laurence Evans
State University
New York at
Binghamton
Daniel Cox Fahey, Jr.
Chevy Chase, MD
(War Department
General Staff, Civil
Affairs Division,
1945)
Stanley L. Falk
Army Center of
Military History
Ladislas Farago
Bridgewater, CT
Michael Fichter
Free University of
Berlin
Detmar Finke
Army Center of
Military History
Richard & Dallas Finn
Washington, DC
(Far East
Commission,
1946–47; Foreign
Service, Japan,
1947–54)
Ernest F. Fisher
Army Center of
Military History

Willard A. Fletcher
  University of
  Delaware
Charles Foster
  Department of
  Health, Education &
  Welfare
Benis Frank
  Marine Corps
  Historical Office
Selma G. Freedman
  Department of State
  (ret.)
Naomi Fukuda
  University of
  Michigan
Arthur L. Funk
  University of Florida
John Gimbel
  Humboldt State
  University
Kurt Glaser
  Southern Illinois
  University
Craddock R. Goins, Jr.
  Smithsonian
  Institution
Norman Graebner
  University of
  Virginia
Rebecca Greene
  Washington, DC
Gerold Guensberg
  McLean, VA
Dagmar Gunther-Stirn
  University of
  Hartford
Milton O. Gustafson
  National Archives
Eleanor M. Hadley
  General Accounting
  Office
Fred L. Hadsel
  George C. Marshall
  Library

Russel W. Hale
  Arlington, VA
  (SCAP, Economic
  and Scientific
  Section, 1947–52)
June Haley
  Atlantic Council
Niels Hansen
  Embassy of the
  Federal Republic of
  Germany
J. M. Harper
  Arlington, VA
James J. Hastings
  National Archives
John H. Hatcher
  Office of the
  Adjutant General
Petronilla Hawes
  National Archives
Siegfried Heimann
  Free University of
  Berlin
Thomas T. Helde
  Georgetown
  University
Dale Hellegers
  Columbia University
Charles J. Herber
  George Washington
  University
Walter G. Hermes
  Army Center of
  Military History
Robin Higham
  Kansas State
  University
Brooke Hindle
  Smithsonian
  Institution
Joseph Hobbs
  The Johns Hopkins
  University
Nina D. Howland
  University of
  Maryland

Gene T. Hsaio
  Southern Illinois
  University
Alfred F. Hurley
  North Texas
  University
Harold Hurwitz
  Free University of
  Berlin
John W. Huston
  Air Force History
James S. Hutchins
  Smithsonian
  Institution
Vincent C. Jones
  Army Center of
  Military History
Jürgen Kalkbrenner
  Embassy of the
  Federal Republic of
  Germany
Henry J. Kellerman
  Georgetown
  University
  (OSS, 1944–45;
  Nuremberg trials,
  1945; State
  Department,
  German Cultural
  and Public Affairs,
  1949–54)
Thomas Kelly
  Army Center of
  Military History
George O. Kent
  University of
  Maryland
Key K. Kobayashi
  Library of Congress
Arthur G. Kogan
  Department of State
Judith A. Koucky
  National Archives
Max W. Kraus
  Washington, DC
  (OMGUS, 1945–49;
  HICOG, 1950–54)

Joseph Langbart
Alexandria, VA
Harold D. Langley
Smithsonian
Institution
Karl G. Larew
Towson State
University
Loyd E. Lee
State University of
New York, New
Paltz
Franklin Littell
Temple University
(OMGUS, 1949;
HICOG, 1949–52)
Wallace W. Littell
Bethesda, MD
(Foreign Service,
Germany, 1949–54)
Sidney W. Lowery
George C. Marshall
Research
Foundation
David W. Mabon
Department of State
John J. McCloy
Millbank, Tweed,
Hadley & McCloy
Orville J. McDiarmid
Falls Church, VA
(SCAP, Finance
Division, 1945–46;
State Department,
Young and Joseph
Dodge missions,
1948–49)
Theodore McNelly
University of
Maryland
Wayne C. McWilliams
Towson State
College
Philip E. Mancha
Montgomery College

Louis Mark, Jr.
Foreign Service (ret.)
(OMGUS, 1947–49;
HICOG, 1949–54)
Myles Marken
United States Army
Materiel
Development &
Readiness Center
Edwin M. Martin
Washington, DC
(OSS, 1944–45;
State Department,
Japanese and
Korean Economic
Affairs, 1945–47;
Liquidation of Enemy
Assets, 1947–54)
James V. Martin, Jr.
Washington, DC
(Foreign Service,
Tokyo, 1949–54)
Vojtech Mastny
University of Illinois
Kris Mathur
University of the
District of Columbia
John A. Maxwell
West Virginia
University
Martin Mayes
Arlington, VA
(OMGUS, 1945–49;
HICOG, 1949–52)
Marlene J. Mayo
University of
Maryland
Heinz K. Meier
Old Dominion
University
Elizabeth Mendelsohn
Washington, DC
John Mendelsohn
National Archives
James E. Miller
National Archives

Martha Mills
Accokeek, MD
Sybil Milton
Leo Baeck Institute
Chanley M. Mohney
Alexandria, VA
John D. Montgomery
Harvard University
Col. & Mrs. Robert L.
Moore
Reserve Officers
Association
Ronald A. Morse
Department of State
Jon Moulton
Xavier University
James Nanney
George C. Marshall
Research
Foundation
Kenneth R. Nelson
Eisenhower College
Eli E. Nobleman
United States Senate
staff
Albert Norman
Norwich University
(OMGUS, ICD,
1945–46)
Sister Thomas
Aquinas O'Connor
Saint Mary's College
Edward J. O'Day, Jr.
Southern Illinois
University
Elizaburo Okuizumi
University of
Maryland
Mark T. Orr
University of
Southern Florida
John Curtis Perry
Harvard University
Agnes F. Peterson
Hoover Institution

Edward N. Peterson
University of
Wisconsin, River
Falls
Lucille Petterson
Falls Church, VA
(Nuremberg trials,
1946–48; OMGUS,
1948–49; HICOG,
1949–54)
Elmer Plischke
University of
Maryland
Forrest C. Pogue
Smithsonian
Institution
Gordon M. Prange
University of
Maryland
(SCAP, Historical
Division, 1946–51)
Arnold H. Price
Library of Congress
(OSS, 1942–46;
State Department,
foreign affairs
specialist, 1946–55)
Mr. & Mrs. Karl Price
Washington, DC
Raymond L. Proctor
University of Idaho
Diethelm Prowe
Carleton College
Carl N. Raether
Department of State
Steven Rearden
Office of the
Secretary of Defense
Jacques J. Reinstein
Atlantic Council
Jürgen Rohwer
Bibliothek für
Zeitgeschichte,
Stuttgart
George K. Romoser
University of New
Hampshire

Andreas Röpke
Staatsarchiv
Bremen
Kurt Rosenbaum
West Virginia
University
Albert Rosenblatt
McLean, VA
Beate Ruhm von
Oppen
St. John's College
Walter Rundell
University of
Maryland
Tsukas Sato
Georgetown
University
John J. Sbrega
Richmond, VA
Edward A. Schaefer
United States Air
Force
Edmund Schechter
Washington, DC
(OMGUS, Radio
Branch, 1945–49;
HICOG, Radio
Branch, 1949–51)
Ute Schmidt
Free University of
Berlin
Damaris A. Schmitt
Washington, DC
Hans Schmitt
University of
Virginia
Ephraim Jack
Schulman
Fairfax, VA
Nicholas Schweitzer
George Washington
University
Fred Seiler
Garland Press

Robert Sherrod
Washington, DC
(Far East
correspondent, *Time*
and *Life,* 1945–52)
Wesley M. Shoemaker
Washington, DC
Frank Joseph Shulman
University of
Maryland
Irwin H. Shwe
Prince George's
Community College
Jack A. Siggins
University of
Maryland
Sherman E. Silverman
Silver Spring, MD
Donald L. Singer
University of
Maryland
William Z. Slany
Department of State
Robert P. Smith
Office of the
Adjutant General
William L. Spalding,
Jr.
Great Falls, VA
Donald Spencer
Alexandria, VA
(Nuremberg trials,
1946–50)
Rogers D. Spotswood
Alexandria, VA
James M. Stefan
United States
Military Academy
Craig Stein
Swarthmore College
William F. Strobridge
Army Center of
Military History
John M. Stuart, Jr.
New York, NY
(OMGUS, 1946–49;
HICOG, 1949–50)

Kristi Suelzle
American
University
Lawrence Howard Suid
Washington, DC
William R. Swarm
General Services
Administration
John E. Taylor
National Archives
Philip H. Taylor
Alexandria, VA
(Editor in chief,
SCAP monthly
Summation,
1945–46; School of
Government for
Occupied Areas,
1946–48)
James F. Tent
University of
Alabama
James R. Thomason
Wheaton, MD
Wayne C. Thompson
Lynchburg College
Vance Tiede
Arlington, VA

William J. Tobin
Office of Joint Chiefs
of Staff
David F. Trask
Department of State
Charles M. Traynham,
Jr.
Wingate, NC
R. Fred Wacker
University of
Michigan
Johanna M. Wagner
National Archives
Judith A. Walters
Joint Chiefs of Staff,
Historical Division
Eckhard Wandel
Tübingen University
Wilcomb E. Washburn
Smithsonian
Institution
Peter Weileman
Arlington, VA
Hermann Weiss
Institute for
Contemporary
History, Munich

Christoph Weisz
Institute for
Contemporary
History, Munich
Justin Williams, Sr.
Washington, DC
(SCAP, Government
Section, 1946–52;
diplomatic and legal
adviser, U.S. Army,
1952–54)
Wallace R. Winkler
Crofton, MD
Ingeborg E. Wolfe
Alexandria, VA
Robert Wolfe
National Archives
John K. Zeender
Catholic University
Earl F. Ziemke
University of
Georgia
Benedict K. Zobrist
Harry S Truman
Library

Archival Sources

SCAP

Records of the Supreme Commander Allied Powers (SCAP) in National Archives Record Group 331, Records of Allied Operational and Occupation Records, World War II. The original records of SCAP are arranged according to administrative units in records center boxes as follows:

Administrative Unit	Record Center Box Nos.
General Headquarters	1–2
Deputy Chief of Staff	3–17
Public Information Section	18–28, 34
Diplomatic Section	29–33
Office, Chief of Staff	35–39
Office of the Comptroller	40–205
Assistant Chief of Staff, G-1	206–30
Assistant Chief of Staff, G-2	231–379ZZ(27)
Assistant Chief of Staff, G-3	380–84C(3)
Assistant Chief of Staff, G-4	385–407
Adjutant General's Section	408–785(46)
Legal Section	786–2029F(6)
Government Section	2030–2275JJ(36)
Civil Affairs Section	2276–3155
Civil Communications Section	3156–3246
Civil Historical Section	3247–3649
Civil Property Custodian	3650–5058
Civil Information and Education Section	5059–5975
Economic and Scientific Section	5976–8516
Civil Intelligence Section	8517–8708
Civil Transportation Section	8709–72
Natural Resources Section	8773–9303
Public Health and Welfare Section	9304–9493
Judge Advocate Section	9494–9893
Provost Marshal Section	9894–9900
Miscellaneous File	9901–10130

OMGUS

*Records of the United States Military Government in Germany,
World War II, National Archives Title Inventory.
RG 260: Records of U.S. Occupation Commands, World War II.*

A-1: Records of the Office of Military Government U.S. Zone (OMGUS)

B-1: Records of the Executive Office
    C-1: Records of the Chief of Staff
    C-2: Records of the Adjutant General
    C-3: Records of the Control Office
    C-4: Records of the United States Group Control Council
        D-2: Records Assembled by the Historical Branch ("Historical
            Division")

B-2: Records of Functional Offices and Divisions
    C-1: Records of the Intelligence Office
    C-2: Records of the Office of the Chief Counsel for War Crimes
    C-3: Records of the Regional Government Control Office
    C-4: Records of the Economics Division
    C-5: Records of the Information Control Division
    C-6: Records of the Civil Administration Division
    C-7: Records of the Legal Division
    C-8: Records of the Manpower Division
    C-9: Records of the Transportation Division
    C-10: Records of the Property Division
    C-11: Records of the Finance Division
    C-12: Finance Records, OMGUS Liquidation Group
    C-13: Records of the Education and Cultural Relations Division

B-3: Records of Inter-Allied Organizations
    C-1: Records of the U.S. Element, Allied Control Authority
    C-2: Records of the U.S. Element, Bipartite Control Office
        D-1: Records of the Office of the U.S. Chairman
        D-2: Records of the ERP Secretariat
        D-3: Records of the U.S. Secretariat
        D-4: Records of the Joint Secretariat
        D-5: Records of Advisory Bodies
            E-1: Records of the Management & Budget Branch
            E-2: Records of the Trade and Agreements Branch
            E-3: Records of the Food & Agriculture Committee
            E-4: Records of the Plans and Allocations Branch
            E-5: Records of the Directorate of Internal Affairs and
                Communications
            E-6: Records of the Civil Service Group

     E-7: Records of the Reports & Statistics Branch
     E-8: Records of the Control Office
   D-6: Records of the Commerce & Industry Group
   D-7: Records of the Food & Agriculture Group
   D-8: Records of the Finance Group
   D-9: Records of the Joint Export-Import Agency
   D-10: Records of the Library Branch
   D-11: Records of the Communications Group
  C-3: Records of Other Allied Organizations
   D-1: Records of the Allied Banking Commission

B-4: Records of the Land and Sector Military Governments
  C-1: Records of OMG, Bavaria
   D-1: Records of the Land Director
   D-2: Records of the Field Operations Division
     E-1: Records of the Historical Section
     E-2: Records of District I (Munich)
     E-3: Records of District II (Regensburg)
     E-4: Records of District III (Nürnberg)
     E-5: Records of District IV (Würzburg)
     E-6: Records of District V (Augsburg)
   D-3: Records of the Intelligence Division
   D-4: Records of the Economics Division
   D-5: Records of the Manpower Division
   D-6: Records of the Finance Division
   D-7: Records of the Transportation Advisor
   D-8: Records of the Public Affairs Division
   D-9: Records of the Education and Cultural Relations Division
   D-10: Records of the Food and Agriculture Division
   D-11: Records of the Property Division
   D-12: Records of the Civil Administration Division
   D-13: Records of the Information Control Division
  C-2: Records of OMG, Berlin Sector
   D-1: Records of the Director
   D-2: Records of the Political Affairs Division
   D-3: Records of the Public Affairs Division
   D-4: Records of the Labor Affairs Division
   D-5: Records of the Legal Affairs Division
   D-6: Records of the Economic Affairs Division
  C-3: Records of OMG, Bremen
   D-1: Records of the Executive Office
   D-2: Records of the Administration and Personnel Division
   D-3: Records of the Public Information Division
   D-4: Records of the Information Control Division
   D-5: Records of the Finance Division
   D-6: Records of the Legal Division

D-7: Records of the Public Health and Welfare Division
D-8: Records of the Denazification Division
D-9: Records of the Manpower Division
D-10: Records of the Education Division
D-11: Records of the Youth Activities Office
D-12: Records of the Civil Administration Division
D-13: Records of the Economics Division
D-14: Records of the Transport Division
D-15: Records of the Waterfront Division
D-16: Records of the BICO Agencies furnished support by OMG, Bremen
D-17: Records of the Bremerhaven Liaison and Security Detachment
C-4: Records of OMG, Hesse
    D-1: Records of the Residence Office
    D-2: Records of the Administration Division
    D-3: Records of the Historical Division
    D-4: Records of the Office of the Land Commissioner
    D-5: Records of the Joint Export Import Agency
    D-6: Records of STEG
    D-7: Records of the Education and Cultural Relations Division
    D-8: Records of the Civil Affairs Division
    D-9: Records of the Information Service Division
    D-10: Records of the Public Relations Division
    D-11: Records of the Legal Division
    D-12: Records of the Intelligence Division
    D-13: Records of the Economics Division
    D-14: Records of the Property Division
C-5: Records of OMG, Wuerttemberg-Baden
    D-1: Administration Division
    D-2: Governmental Affairs Division
    D-3: Information Service Division
    D-4: Control Office Division
    D-5: Field Operations Division
    D-6: Education and Cultural Relations Division
    D-7: Legal Division
    D-8: Economic Affairs Division
    D-9: Property Division

HICOG

*Records of the U.S. High Commissioner for Germany (HICOG)
and related records to be accessioned by the National Archives
into Record Group 84, Records of the Foreign Service Posts of
the Department of State.*

Classified and Unclassified Records from the U.S. Embassy in Bonn, part of Accession No. 61-A53

	Box Nos.
Office of General Counsel, Chief Attorney's Files, 1949–55	1–6
Office of General Counsel, Law Committee Files, 1951–55	7–28
Office of General Counsel, Extradition Board Files, 1947–53	29–116
Office of General Counsel, Extradition Case Files, 1951–54	117–23
Office of General Counsel, Prisons Division Files, 1944–57	124–98
Land Commissioner Files, Württemberg-Baden, 1951–52	325
Land Commissioner Files, Hesse-Intelligence Files, 1946–51	326–52
Judge William Clark's Files, Chief Justice, Court of Appeals, 1950–56	353
High Commissioner John J. McCloy's Files, 1949–52	354–65

The McCloy files consist primarily of correspondence memoranda with some reports, but also include a journal, diaries, minutes of meetings, and HICOG regulations. Most of the records are carbon copies, indicating that these files were not actually McCloy's "personal" files, but rather were collected for him as information copies. This conjecture is substantiated by third person annotations on some of the documents. (See Robert Donihi's statement, above, in the Discussion of the Session on "Realities of Implementation.") The arrangement is chronological by year and month; within the folder for each month, the documents are numbered sequentially, and appear to have been grouped by subject within the monthly folder.

Records of U.S. *Land* (State) Commissioners in Germany, part of Accession No. 56-A684

	Box Nos.
Bonn Land Commissioner—Legal Advisor's Office, OMGUS, HICOG, SCDL, 1946–51, 29 cu. ft.	1–29
Württemberg-Baden Land Commissioner Central Files, 1948–52, 11 cu. ft.	30–40
Hesse Land Commissioner, Legal Affairs Division, 1948–52, 9 cu. ft.	41–49
Bavaria Land Commissioner, Legal Affairs Division, 1949–51, 24 cu. ft.	84–107
Hesse Land Commissioner, Central Files, 1947–51, 12 cu. ft.	108–19
Munich Land Commissioner, Civil and Criminal Cases from Legal Division, 1947–50, 24 cu. ft.	120–43

Bavaria Land Commissioner, Central Files, 1948–52, 13 cu. ft.   144–56
Office of Land Commissioner Regensburg District II, Central
    Files, 1947–51, 4 cu. ft.   157–60
Alsfeld-Bergstrasse Office of Land Commissioner Field
    Operations Division, 1949–51, 26 cu. ft.   161–86
Bremen Land Commissioner, Central Files, 1949–52, 37 cu. ft.   187–223
Bonn Land Commissioner, Real Estate Division, 1946–52,
    9 cu. ft.   230–38
Hesse Land Commissioner, Resident Office, Kassel, 1949–51,
    10 cu. ft.   239–48
Bavaria Land Commissioner, Political Affairs, Child Welfare
    and Intelligence Branch files, 1950–51, 12 cu. ft.   249–60
Hesse Land Commissioner, Economic Affairs Files, 1952–53,
    2 cu. ft.   261–62
Württemberg-Baden OLC, German Justice Files, 1949–52,
    83 cu. ft.   263–345

Records of Military Government Court Cases, 1945–51

> Accession No. 64-A598, 1561 cu. ft.
> Accession No. 66-A1161, 20 cu. ft.
> Accession No. 73-003 and 004, 121 cu. ft.

Accession No. 62-A26 consists of HICOG Economic and Financial files pertaining to various industries, including the decartelization of the motion picture and other combines.

N.B.: In those numerous cases above where the beginning dates of HICOG series antedate the mid-1949 transition from OMGUS to HICOG, many such records were OMGUS files continued in use and incorporated into HICOG series.

PRO

Public Record Office (PRO), London, Holdings Pertaining to the British Military Government in Germany

Reference FO 1010	Date	Description	File Series
		Military Government	229/MG
1	1945	2nd Army weekly summary	X/11P
		Conferences	
2	1945–47	Command	3/2/SEC
3	1946–48	General	3/2/SEC
4	1945–47	Economic Division	3/6/SEC
5	1945–46	Organisation of the Reich administrations	3/9/SEC
6	1945	Liaison with Russians	3/10/SEC
7	1946	Meetings between chiefs of Provinces and Länder	3/12/SEC
8	1946	Commission on overcrowding in the British zone	3/15/SEC
9	1946–47	Conferences involving the Regional Commissioner	3/18/SEC
10	1946	Monthly report of HQ Manpower Branch	7/10/SEC
11	1947–49	Bizonal Military Governors' conference with Minister Presidents	10/8/SEC
12	1949	Special Conference of Chief of Staff and Regional Commissioners	10/21/SEC
13	1948	Prisoners of war from Russia	15/1/SEC
14	1947–48	Münster Lager: POW camp	16/SEC
15	1945–46	Bremen enclave: part I	19/1/SEC
16	1946–47	Ditto: part II	19/1/SEC
17*	1945–46		
18	1945–49	Economic matters	22/SEC
19	1945	Conference of Land/Regierungsbezirk detachment commanders	24/SEC
20	1945–49	Reparations: deliveries and restitutions	25/SEC
21	1948	Financial reform	27/1/SEC

22	1948–49	Detention without trial and extradition	28/1/SEC
23	1947–48	Transport movements: fortnightly progress reports	29/4/SEC
24†	1946–49		
25	1946–48	Subversive literature	37/1/SEC
26	1945–46	Refugees	40/SEC
27	1945–47	Denazification: part I	41/SEC
28	1947–49	Ditto: part II	41/SEC
29	1946	Appointment of Inspector General of Denazification	41/4/SEC
30	1947–48	Demonstrations in the British zone	42/SEC
31	1945	Assumption of control by Control Commission	43/D/SEC
32	1945	Re-organisation of HQ Military Government, Hannover Region	43/E/SEC
33	1947	Correspondence of Deputy Regional Commissioner: part I	44/SEC
34	1947	Ditto: part II	44/SEC
35	1946	Financial technical report	50/SEC
36	1945–46	Local Government Instructions: part I	51/SEC
37	1946–48	Ditto: part II	51/SEC
38	1948–49	Prohibition of movement of goods to Soviet zone	51/SEC
39	1949	Re-opening of allied communications between western zones and Berlin	51/1/SEC
40	1945–47	Internees	52/SEC
41	1949	Dutch frontier rectifications	52/1/SEC
42	1947	Control Commission broadcasts	53/SEC
43	1947	Press conference: Regional Governmental Officer	55/SEC
44	1946–48	Information services control: surveys	55/SEC
45	1946	Ditto: newspapers	55/SEC
46	1945–46	Ditto: press and miscellaneous	55/SEC
47	1946–47	Public relations: general surveys	55/1/SEC
48	1947	Public opinion survey: social and political questions	55/1/SEC

*Retained by department under Sec. 3(4).
†Retained by department.

Reference FO 1010	Date	Description	File Series
		Military Government (cont.)	
49	1947	Public relations: round-up of media activities	55/4/SEC
50	1946–49	BAOR Liaison Officers	60/SEC
51	1945–47	Soviet displaced persons	61/9/SEC
52	1946	Take-over by 1 Corps of part of 30 Corps District	71/SEC
53	1948–49	Establishments	71/6/SEC
54	1946–48	Boards of investigation: loss of goods, arrests	71/7/SEC
55	1946	Background information for German officials	75/SEC
56	1946–47	Internal affairs and communications	78/SEC
57	1945–47	Education subjects	80/SEC
58	1948	Zonal Fine Arts Repository: Schloss Celle	80/SEC
59	1947–48	Old people's home: Lehre	82/SEC
60	1946–49	German scientists: amenities for dependants	86/SEC
61	1947–49	Ditto: body of consultants Operation "Matchbox"	86/1/SEC
62	1948	Associations, clubs and organisations for Germans	86/5/SEC
63	1948–49	Combined airlift task force	89/SEC
64	1946–47	Miscellaneous industrial and building subjects	101/2/SEC
65	1945–48	Coal and oil industries and public utilities	101/3/SEC
66	1946	Food and agriculture: part I	101/4/SEC
67	1947–48	Ditto: part II	101/4/SEC
68	1946–48	Reorganisation of the Trade and Industries division of the Economic Sub-Commission	101/6/SEC
69	1947–48	British zone trade fair	101/11/SEC
70	1946	CCG liaison with military	106/6/SEC
71	1946–47	Wilhelmshafen: redeployment plan	114/SEC
72	1946–48	Industrial relations: trade unions	119/SEC
73	1947	Ditto: minutes of meeting between the Regional Economic Office and trade unionists, 2 June	119/SEC

74	1945–47	North German timber control: part I	134/SEC
75	1947–48	Ditto: part II	134/SEC
76	1946	East Frisian islands: illegal issue of residence permits	135/SEC
77	1946–49	Police matters: British and German	137/SEC
78	1946	De-centralisation of powers to Land government and delegation of powers to Germans: part I	
79	1946–47	Ditto: part II	144/SEC
80	1948–49	Parliamentary structure for Western Germany	188/SEC
		Education reports for the Hannover Region	
81	1945–46	Administration and general	2001/ED
82	1945	Ditto: text books, part I	2001/2/ED
83	1945–46	Ditto: text books, part II	2001/2/ED
84	1945–46	Administration and general: buildings	2001/3/ED
85	1945–46	General reports	2002/ED
86	1945	Education and religious affairs	2002/9/ED
87	1945–46	Teaching equipment: films	2005/1/ED
88	1945–46	Re-opening of vocational schools	2006/6/ED
89	1945–46	Conferences of education control officers	2012/3/ED
90	1945–46	Internal security and organisation	2015/1/ED
91	1945–46	Teacher training colleges	2020/ED
92	1945–46	Higher education	2021/ED
93	1945–46	University of Göttingen	2022/ED
94	1945–46	Vetting of teachers: correspondence	2025/1/ED
95	1945–46	Adult education	2027/ED
96	1945–46	Operation "Stork": evacuation of children from Berlin to Hannover Region	2036/ED
97	1945–46	Military Government policy	5401 C
98	1946–47	Military Government ordinances	5402 E
99	1946	Rail policy	5403 A/1
100	1946	Functional arrangements	5403 B

Reference FO 1010	Date	Description	File Series
		Military Government (cont.)	
101	1946	Refugees	5405 D
102	1946–47	Bipartite Transport Panel	5406 D
		Regional Transport Board Meetings	
103	1946–47	Hannover: minutes	5407 G
104	1946–47	Münster: minutes	5407 G/2
105	1946	Ruhr: minutes	5407 G/3
106	1946–47	General conferences concerning Hannover Region	5410 A
107	1947	Münster progress reports	5411 G
108	1945–47	Railway construction and maintenance	5416 A/TD
		Monthly Manpower Reports to HQ Military Government, Hannover Region	
109	1945–46	Hildesheim	6501/117/Man
110	1946	Brunswick	6501/120/Man
111	1945–46	Hannover, Oldenburg, Lüneburg and Hildesheim	6501/504/Man
112	1945–46	Osnabrück	6501/604/Man
113	1945–46	Stade	6501/611/Man
114	1945–46	Aurich	6501/613/Man
115	1946–47	Aurich	108
116	1945–46	Oldenburg	6501/821/Man
117	1947	Oldenburg	6501/214/8
118	1945	Lüneburg	6501/914/Man
119	1945–46	Lüneburg	6501/914/Man/335
120	1945–46	Headquarters	6502/Man
121	1946	Bremen	6519/BPC/Man
122	1946	Copies of correspondence for Landesarbeitsamt	6612/Man

123	1945	Hildesheim area	LA/1/1
124	1945	Osnabrück area	LA/1/4
125	1945	Stade area	LA/1/5
126	1945	Oldenburg area	LA/1/7
127	1945	Reports on Labour Offices: appendices A and B	21/AGP/32017/1/CA
128	1945	Legal affairs	800/MG
129	1945	Military Government Courts: procedure	808/MG
130	1945	Ditto: Control Commission instructions and directives	861/MG
131	1945–46	Ditto: statistics	862/MG
132	1945–46	Legal practice: notes	864/MG
133	1949–50	British Relations Board	

Internal Affairs and Communications

		Control of University Research	
134	1946	Bonn University: part I	INTR/63096/11/ED
135	1946	Ditto: part II	INTR/63096/11/ED
136	1946	Ditto: part III	INTR/63096/11/ED
137	1946	Cologne University	INTR/63096/12/ED
138	1945–46	Hamburg University	INTR/63096/14/ED
139	1946	Kiel University	INTR/63096/15/ED
140	1945–46	Brunswick University	INTR/63096/18/ED
141	1945–46	Hannover University	INTR/63096/19/ED
142	1946	Düsseldorf Medical Academy	INTR/63096/20/ED
143*	1949		
144*	1947–50		
145*	1951–54		
146*	1948–49		

*Retained by department under Sec. 3(4).
†Retained by department.

Reference FO 1010	Date	Description	File Series
		Internal Affairs and Communications (cont.)	
147*	1951		
148*	1949–51		
		Public Safety	
149	1946–47	Operation "Sparkler": recovery of precious metals and stones	
150*	1947–52		
151*	1947–52		
152*	1948–49		
153*	1948–51		
154	1949–50	Illegal importation of cigarettes: Bergen to Belsen	
155	1950	Unreliability of German police	
156	1950–51	Friedrich Buhning: alleged murder of allied airmen	
		Political	
		Situation Reports: British Residents	
157	1950–52	Dannenberg	2/85/72
158	1950–52	Gifhorn	2/85/75
159	1950–52	Wesermünde	2/85/78
160	1950–52	Leer	2/85/84
161	1950–52	Cloppenburg	2/85/87

162	1951–52	Bückeburg	2/85/90
163	1950–52	Holzminden	2/85/92
164	1950–52	Osterode	2/85/94
165	1950–52	Wolfenbüttel	2/85/96
166	1950–52	Helmstedt	2/85/97
167	1950–52	Delmenhorst	2/85/99

Belsen War Memorial

168	1945–47	Part I	229/MG/9578
169	1949–52	Part II	229/MG/9578
170	1945–47	National contributions to commemorative plaques on Belsen Memorial	229/MG/9578 DP

Services Liaison Section

171	1950–52	Zonal Executive Instruction 99, claims for compensation in respect of training and manoeuvre damage: part 1	2/29/95
172	1953	Ditto: part 2	2/29/95

Land Oldenburg

173*	1945–50		

* Retained by department under Sec. 3(4).
† Retained by department.